VINCENZO BELLINI
QUI NACQUE
ADDI III NOVEMBRE
MDCCCI

G...
·Die ...
"Die Zaubergeige
von WERNER FGK
1901 – 1983
taglich 11⁰⁰ und 16⁰⁰

Geburtshaus
Komponist
z X. Grub
denktafel am Schulh

Der Dichter
omponist und Maler
Ɔ. Amadäus Hoffman
inte in diesem Hause
1809 – 1813.

STAND DAS HAUS IN DE
ANN SEBASTIAN BAC
ON 1708-1717 WOHNTE
IER WURDE GEBOREN
RIEDEMANN BACH
M 17. NOVEMBER 1710
LIPP EMANUEL BAC
AM 8. MÄRZ 1714

Sur les marches de cette maiso
naquit le 19 Décembre 1915
dans le plus grand dénuemen
EDITH PIAF
dont la voix, plus tard,
devait bouleverser le monde

ТУТ, У ФАЛЬВАРКУ УбЕЛЬ,
5 МАЯ 1819 ГОДА НАРАДЗІЎСЯ
ВЯЛІКІ ПОЛЬСКІ КАМПАЗІТАР
СТАНІСЛАЎ МАНЮШКА

Tu, w folwarku Ubel,
5 maja 1819 roku urodził się
wielki polski kompozytor
Stanisław Moniuszko

Zde se narodil
BEDR. SMETANA
hudební mistr

ОМ ДОМЕ С 1906 ГОДА
л и 19 июня 1915 года ско
ющийся русский композ
ЕРГЕЙ ИВАНОВИ
ТАНЕЕВ

W TYM DOMU
URODZIŁ SIĘ
12·VI·1897 R.
I SPĘDZIŁ TU
PIERWSZYCH
17 LAT ŻYCIA
Aleksander
TANSMAN
światowej sławy
kompozytor polski
1897-1986

CASA DI RIPOSO
per
MUSICISTI
FONDAZIONE VERDI

AN DIESER STELLE
STAND DAS HAUS.
WELCHES DER TONDICHTE
ICHAEL HAYD
BIS ZU SEINEM TODE 1806
BEWOHNTE

CALLING ON THE COMPOSER

CALLING ON THE COMPOSER

A GUIDE TO EUROPEAN COMPOSER HOUSES AND MUSEUMS

Julie Anne Sadie and Stanley Sadie

YALE UNIVERSITY PRESS
NEW HAVEN AND LONDON

For information about this and other Yale University Press publications, please contact:
U.S. Office: sales.press@yale.edu yalebooks.com
Europe Office: sales@yaleup.co.uk www.yalebooks.co.uk

Set in Minion by J&L Composition, Filey, North Yorkshire
Printed in Great Britain by T.J. International Ltd, Padstow

ISBN 0–300–10750–1

Library of Congress Control Number: 2005926050

A catalogue record for this book is available from the British Library

10 9 8 7 6 5 4 3 2 1

CONTENTS

To our friends, the composers, pictured within, and those who guard their memory.

ILLUSTRATION ACKNOWLEDGMENTS

The ownership of illustrations is noted below, by page number. Where a photographer is separately identified he/she is listed with the letter p.

6, Ediz. G.V. Organizzazione, Parma (p. A. Ceresa); 8, 26, 260, 260, 261, Internationale Stiftung Mozarteum, Salzburg (260 p. Ritschel and Anrather); 11, 134, Museet Lysøen; 24, Réunion des musées nationaux, Paris; 33, Jeff Driggers (p. Mrs Henry L. Richmond); 34, Emily Wentworth; 37, Bank Austria, Vienna; 43, Fondazione Puccini Lucca; 44, Arnold Schoenberg Centre, Vienna; 46, Centre international d'études pédagogiques, Sèvres; 52, Aline Bessand-Massenet, Egreville; 63, 206, Cheltenham Art Gallery and Museums; 64, Aune-Forlag, Bergen (p. Thor Melhuus); 65, 104, Beethoven-Haus Bonn (104 p. Petersen); 65, 222, 223, Kodály Zoltán Emlékmúzeum, Budapest (222, 223 p. Féner Tamás); 66, 407, Studio Eugène Ysaÿe Musée d'art religieux et d'art Mosan, Liège (p. José Mascart); 94, Thomas-Verlag Leipzig; 105, 199, 264, 328, 329, 356, Museen der Stadt Wien; 118, Musée Hector Berlioz, Conservation du Patrimoine de l'Isère, La Côte-Saint-André; 122, Brahmsgesellschaft Baden-Baden; 123, Kammerhofmuseum der Stadt Gmunden; 130, Geburtshaus Anton Bruckners, Ansfelden; 131, Kunstverlag Hofstetter, Ried im Innkreis; 137, Vil·la Casals, Sant Salvador; 144, Krajowa Agencja Wydawnicza, Warsaw (p. Z. Kapuścik); 158, D'Indy family, Boffres (p. Philippe Fournier); 161, Museo Donizettiano, Bergamo; 164, Památník Antonína Dvořáka, Nelahozeves (p. Miroslav Krob); 168, Gene Adams, Hampstead (also on jacket); 184, 186, Willy Haraldsen (184 also on jacket); 192, Händelhaus, Halle; 193, 194, Handel House Museum, London; 227, 228, Lehár Villa, Bad Ischl (p. Hofer); 233, Liszt Ferenc Memorial Museum, Budapest; 234, Stiftung Weimarer Klassik (p. E. Schäfer); 255, Internationale Mendelssohn-Stiftung, Leipzig; 268, Foto und Verlag Stadt Augsburg; 271, T. Ermakova, Naumovo; 275, Carl Nielsen Museet, Odense; 291, 292, Peterson-Berger Stiftung, Frösön (p. Bengt Weilert); 300, 301, Memoryal'nïy Muzey S.S. Prokof'yeva selo Krasnoye; 307, Abteilung Musikgeschichte der Meininger Museen, Schloß

Elisabethenburg (p. Manfred Koch); 314, Casa Rossini, Pesaro; 321, Maisons Satie, Honfleur; 337, Sibelius Birthplace Museum, Hämeenlinna; 341, Silchermuseum, Schnait; 349, Smetana Museum, Prague (also on jacket); 359, Stephen Walsh; 381, Istituto nazionale tostiano, Ortona; 394, Richard Wagner Museum, Graupa; 395, Richard Wagner Museum, Lucerne (p. Urs Bütler); 397, Richard-Wagner-Museum, Bayreuth.

Photographs on pages not listed above are (with the exception of a small number of early photographs) by Julie Anne Sadie. We are grateful to copyright holders who have given their kind permission for reproduction and apologize to the very few whom, despite repeated efforts, we have been unable to contact; we invite them to write to us through our publishers.

INTRODUCTION

The origins of this book lie in a journey we undertook in 1993. At the time we were engaged in trying to save Handel's London house, threatened with development as a shop with offices above, and to establish a museum there. The trip was intended partly as a holiday, partly to see what we could learn from how other museums commemorated their subjects, and partly to assemble material for JAS's MA dissertation in museum and gallery management. We drew up an itinerary taking in some 30 museums we knew of and could visit in the time available.

As we were arriving in Bonn, our first port of call, we noticed by chance a signpost: 'Schumann-Museum'. This – stumbling upon a museum whose existence had been unknown to us – was an experience to be repeated, in one form or another, many times over in ten years of museum travels. It could still happen. It was soon afterwards that we decided it would be useful, worth while and interesting to try to write a guide to European composer museums. Here was an obvious lacuna in musical reference material and travel information for the music lover, indicative of the neglect that this particular part of our musical heritage has suffered.

We supposed there might be some hundred or so museums to visit and we set about methodical investigation, writing to national museum authorities, cultural attachés and tourist boards, many of whom replied helpfully. But often their information was incomplete, out of date and misleading. We perused a good deal of literature, including travel and city guides, but found them largely uninformative, apart from Helmut Kretschmer's invaluable survey of the Viennese musical memorials and three or four other specialized volumes. We drew on our professional acquaintance and talked to museologists, musicologists and music librarians; later we used the internet, although that often proved undependable. We found that published lists of musical museums usually omitted some categories, such as privately owned memorial houses, small independent museums, local museums that celebrate a composer's connection with a town or a region, and standing memorial displays within larger institutions; of these we often learnt by word of mouth from the many friendly and helpful museum staff members whom we met, and in casual conversation with friends and colleagues. We heard of many by sheer serendipity. It will be evident that the difficulty of achieving some degree of comprehensiveness underlines the need for such a book as the present one.

We recognize, however, that this book is unlikely to be as complete as we would have wished. So we would invite readers who know of any composer museums or memorial houses, or significant standing displays to a composer in a local, regional or national museum, that have slipped through our net to write to us, directly or through the publisher, and tell us about them, so that we can repair the omission in any future edition.

What is 'our net' intended to catch? It may be useful to give an indication of what we mean by composer museums and memorials.

First, we include any museum or house or other kind of living or working accommodation (a flat, even a hut) that is dedicated to the commemoration of a composer and, generally speaking, open to the public. Most of these are (at least supposedly) birthplaces or sometime residences. Secondly, we include any dedicated museum, or any permanent commemorative display to a composer, within a more general museum or other building open to the public. Some of the institutions included are not 'museums' in the full sense; many of the establishments we list display only derivative material (photographs, photocopies, reproductions etc., copies of furniture, pianos of the period and so on). The purist and pedant must forgive us if sometimes we gloss over the distinction between museum and memorial, of which we are keenly aware, for the sake of avoiding clumsy and finicky prose. Here and there we have included borderline cases, among them some houses not regularly open to the public but to be seen by appointment and perhaps likely to be open in the future. We do not include research institutions, archives and the like that are closed to the public, although we may refer to these. A difficult borderline category is the small composer display in a local history museum. It would be impossible to include or even to find all of these, but we note those we have found with permanent displays that seem worth drawing to readers' notice. We have also included composers informatively commemorated in a larger collective or general museum, such as the Halle Händel-Haus (also a museum of local musical history), the Lugoj Casa Musicii and the Terezín museum.

When planning this book, we considered very carefully whether the basic arrangement should be by place or by composer: whether, for example, our discussion of the Beethoven museum at Bonn should be found under 'Bonn', 'Germany: Bonn' or 'Beethoven'. It was not simply a matter of reverting to old lexicographical ways (of which we have some experience) that led us to decide on the last of those. This is a book about the commemoration of composers, and it would not be appropriate to have its discussion of the commemoration of Beethoven divided into 12 sections, one per museum, or of Brahms into seven. The individual commemorations of 'multi-museum' composers can thus be placed in the wider context of the composer's life and works, allowing some perspective on the variety of ways of commemorating a composer. For those who want to use the book as a travel guide, we include a series of country maps (pages 73–88) indicating the whereabouts of composer museums, and some information is included where necessary in individual entries.

We have tried to indicate, for each museum, something of its background and history, its relation to the composer's life, the facilities it offers and what the visitor can expect to see. We refer to other memorial sites where appropriate, particularly plaques and sculpted memorials. We offer no rating system and hope that our texts will tell readers which museums are worth a special journey, worth a detour, and so on. At the end of each composer entry, we give the name and address of each museum in the order in which they are discussed in the text (which will normally reflect the chronology of the composer's life), with a telephone number (with codes from abroad / within the country), any fax number and an e-mail address, and often a website (the museum's own, where it has one, or otherwise another informative site, generally of a municipality or a tourist office). We also give opening days and times, which are correct at the time of going to press; we urge prospective visitors to check individually, as they are not infrequently subject to instant and radical change, as we often discovered. (Checking on the internet may not be sufficient: different sites give different days and times and even wrong addresses.) We append to many entries a short bibliography, of publications relevant to the actual museums or memorial sites (a range of literature not usually found in bibliographies); unless there is some special reason, we do not cite biographies or other writings on the composers themselves. We hope that, by pulling this information together for the first time, however incompletely and imperfectly, we may encourage the formation of some official body that could serve to draw greater attention to the museums' activities, increase their support and institute a stronger framework for their future management and their long-term benefit. And we hope too to make it easier for people to visit them.

As this is a reference book, there will inevitably be some overlaps of information. A particular museum or memorial may illustrate several different points in the introductory chapters; so we ask readers to bear with us if they find the same museum discussed in different contexts. The composer entry will always contain the basic information about each museum.

We aimed to visit every museum considered in the book, to lend immediacy and authority to our observations and enable the text to reflect our personal reactions. We very nearly managed that, but not quite. We were however able to obtain, often from the museums themselves and sometimes from other sources, information about the few that eluded us. These are marked with an asterisk in the entries concerned. Generally speaking, we visited museums as ordinary paying members of the public, but we tried to see an official if there were questions to which we needed answers.

We made more than 40 forays to the European mainland. Most we relished: what better holiday pursuit than visiting composer museums for musicologist-lexicographers who still love music and travel? The number however is far greater than it would have been had we known in advance more about the museums' disposition. New ones have been founded since we began our journeys, and several existing ones have changed to an extent that has made a further visit obligatory. Almost all our journeys were necessarily made by road, in our own car or in rented cars, because of the often remote rural regions we needed to visit. We learnt a good deal about places: if you are looking for Mahler's birthplace, try the Kaliště near Humpolec, not the one near his childhood home in Jihlava; if you want to see if there is any Chopin commemoration at the George Sand museum, go to the Nohant close to La Châtre, not the one further north; and there isn't a Glinka museum at Glinka or a Saint-Saëns one at Saint-Saëns, nor is Guido d'Arezzo celebrated at Arezzo. We found out all these, and more, the hard way.

Acknowledgments

There are numerous people to whom we are indebted for help during our journeys. First, we would like to record our thanks to the (former) Museums and Galleries Commission for a grant towards the cost of the first of our three journeys to Russia (1995) and to *Music & Letters* for a substantial one to cover our second to Romania (1999). The Austrian National Tourist Board provided generous help for the flights on two of our many journeys to Austria, as well as some hotel bookings and car hire, and their office in Linz was particularly helpful. The Finnish Tourist Board gave help for a hotel and a car in Helsinki; the Spanish Tourist Board provided hotel accommodation and a car on one journey; the Bulgarian Tourist Board gave us a guide-interpreter; and Hungarian Airlines, Finnair and SAS made concessions over flights. Six trips were adjuncts to lecturing journeys undertaken for Martin Randall Travel. The editor of *Gramophone*, James Jolly, let us try out our ideas by providing a forum over a period of three years for a column by JAS, 'At home with the composer'.

We are also greatly indebted to the many friends, here and abroad, who drew particular museums to our notice, or helped us to visit them, or both. Some travelled with us in countries where we were linguistically handicapped: Larisa Chepurnaya in Ukraine, Tanya Arkatova in Russia, Adeodatas Tauragis in Lithuania, Jan Spacek in the Czech Republic (he also carried out extensive telephone investigations for us with Czech museums, and visited Trnava on our behalf; Jana Slimáčková also helped us there in the early stages). Boris Nikitin – Geoffrey Norris kindly made this contact for us – helped organize our journeys in the Moscow area and to Udmurtia and accompanied us on parts of them; Larissa Chirkova (formerly of the Rimsky-Korsakov museum) helped us in and around St Petersburg, as did Aleksandr Bazikov in Tambov and Ivanovka and Natasha Naida in Belarus. We had the pleasure of the company of Marketa Hallová, of the Czech Music Museum, on a Dvořák pilgrimage, and of meeting Olga Mojžíšová, of the same museum, on a Smetana one. Ilinca Dumitrescu gave us invaluable guidance in Bucharest and over Romanian museums generally. Metoda Kokole kindly organized and for the most part accompanied us in Slovenia, as did Vjera Katalinić and her husband Stanislav Tuskar in Croatia. For our Serbian coverage we had the help, and again mostly the company, of Tatjana Marković. Halina Goldberg gave much help with our Polish coverage. George Leotsakos provided us with information on museums in Greece. José Vázquez and Nikolaus Turner kindly made possible JAS's visits to museums in the Munich area. In Vienna, Dorothea Link was generously helpful in preparing the ground and in treading much of it with us. We are particularly indebted to Federica Riva for her enthusiastic assistance towards making our Italian coverage comprehensive. Eivor Cormac drew several Swedish museums to our notice. Stephen Walsh generously gave us access to his material on the Stravinsky museum. Maurice Neal helped us with our late updating of the Tosti entry. Emily Wentworth kindly assisted our work in France. We are grateful to the schoolchildren and their teacher near Kąsna Dolna, Poland, who returned our car to the road after a skid in a blizzard, and to the doctors at Velikiye Luki who cared for us after our 1999 car accident before, thanks to the American Medical Center in St Petersburg, we were flown to the Royal Free Hospital in Hampstead (close to our then home) for comprehensive repairs.

Almost everywhere museum directors, custodians and other staff gave generously of their time and expertise and patiently answered our queries. The sheer numbers make it impossible for us to name and thank them individually, but a few particular visits need individual acknowledgment. Several kind people, all anonymous, helped us one bitter snowy day in the Czech Republic: the schoolteacher in Nová Říše who answered an appeal over the address system for someone who understood English, French or German, and might guide us to the Wranitzky museum, the German speaker in Kamenice nad Lipou who found us lost and spent the evening finding us an interpreter and guiding us to the Novák museum, and to the delightful interpreter there, an elderly professor of French, who (after a medicinal schnapps all round) came out in the snow to help us. Another time, in Dorohoi, Romania, we were dismayed on arrival one Tuesday morning to find 'and Tuesday' freshly added to the list of closure days in the window of Enescu's father's house, but a kind lady from the town museum came with an English speaker to open it and accompanied us to Enescu's birthplace nearby. Near Moscow, at Dyut'kovo, the custodians of the Taneyev cottage undertook an arduous and tiresome journey to open it for us and were generous with their time and help. Many other museum custodians went way beyond the call of duty to help us. Among the museums opened out of hours were the Hoffmann one at Bamberg, the Brand one at Langenzersdorf, the Enescu one at Sinaia, the Slavenski one at Čakovec (Croatia), the Glinka house at Novospasskoye and the museum to Leontovych at Tul'chyn (Ukraine). In Estonia, we were grateful to the local librarian at Suure-Jaani, when we found the Kapp museum closed, for telling us of another composer museum close by, devoted to Mart Saar, and for assuring us that the Kapp one was bound to be open about five o'clock as the custodian would have to be back from the shops in time to milk the cows (and she was). Several custodians, especially in Italy, gave us splendid pictorial books about their composers, and we acquired a substantial library of CDs of music by composers whose houses we visited. We were several times unexpectedly entertained. At Horodyshche, Ukraine, we were given a formal municipal luncheon, with many vodka toasts, after seeing the Gulak-Artemovsky museum. At Lyubensk, we were deeply grateful to Tat'yana Rimsky-Korsakova for showing us her grandfather's dachas and for the surprisingly happy combination of tea and vodka that made the visit even more enjoyable. We were presented with the Pleyel vintages in Ruppersthal, those from the Smetana country near Obříství and the best Slovenian ones in Ljubljana. At Les Faugs, near Boffres in the Ardèche, we were given a delightful luncheon by the late Comte and Comtesse d'Indy after we had seen his grandfather's house. We had musical treats too, for example from the organist of Ryba's church at Rožmitál pod Třemšínem, who played and sang to us music from the famous Czech Christmas mass on Ryba's own instrument, and at Staburags, where we were most touched when six ladies, local teachers, took time off to come in Latvian folk dress to the Barisons museum and sing us folksongs.

The writing of this book has been extraordinarily stimulating. We have travelled more than 60,000 km / 37,500 miles by road and tens of thousands more by air, and met many people who share our curiosities and passions. We have been treated with great kindness and forbearance by many people, not least our own children. We hope the book will be as much a pleasure to read and to use as it has been to write.

Cossington, Somerset, January 2005   JULIE ANNE SADIE
                                                      STANLEY SADIE

We should 'declare an interest'. We worked on the Handel House Trust up to 1998, JAS as director of the incipient museum, SS initially as chairman and later as president. JAS served as a trustee of the Holst Birthplace Museum, 1999-2003, and SS has been its president since 2003.

I HERITAGE AND THE COMPOSER MUSEUM

Cultural memory and custodianship

The cultural memory of a literate and sophisticated society is bound to be determined by what has survived and has in some way been recorded for future generations. In the arts, the earliest collectors were the wealthy and the literate; accordingly, more often than not, we have inherited the objects – or such of them as have survived – that princes and bishops valued and wanted around them. In Europe, their castles and their cathedrals dominate our oldest architecture; and the art and imagery, the literature and the record keeping, the music and music-making that best served their ends still colour our collective cultural identity.

The early history of music is largely informed by what those two groups chose to safeguard for themselves and for future generations. Because of the particular nature of music and the social and professional position of musicians, up to early modern times, only a small proportion of what was produced has survived, much of it anonymously. Not until the 18th century do we have relatively complete artistic legacies of individual composers, some of the material printed but much of it in manuscript. The earliest printed music dates from the end of the 15th century, but even as late as the 18th a great deal of music, especially when written for the church or the theatre, existed only in manuscript. Little is known of the daily lives and circumstances of early musicians except insofar as it pertained to the life of a church or a court; archival documents provide only the barest details.

Not until the late 18th century did heirs and admirers begin to preserve the personal possessions of composers, or other objects associated with them. Some such collections have been passed down to the present day. They include the musical sources themselves, the manuscripts and printed editions; the means, which is to say the musical instruments and other tools of their trade; and affirmation of their musical activities, for example in reminiscences, diaries, correspondence, reports and reviews as well as various forms of iconography and, from the 20th century, recordings. In the 19th century came a more acute awareness of and interest in the personalities and lives of great composers. Succeeding generations collected and preserved not only what was of direct musical import but also quite mundane objects, such as furniture, collections of books, clothes and other personal artefacts. This curiosity, even reverence, about the way of life of great creative artists led inevitably to an interest in the actual buildings in which they lived. The acquisition of such buildings offered an opportunity to experiment with re-creating the composer's world, using such artefacts as might have survived, but in any case using the hallowed space they inhabited. This increasing enthusiasm for the past, and in the doings of great men, was not of course exclusive to the world of music: the Shakespeare birthplace in Stratford-upon-Avon was acquired for a museum in 1847, and the Goethe birthplace museum in Frankfurt am Main was opened in 1859. The first composer museum opened in 1880. Today, the number and variety of surviving collections and sites within Europe associated with specific composers are likely to astonish even the best-informed music lover.

Nature, conflict and commerce – the ravages of the elements, war and property development – have not always served these sites benevolently. Many have simply not survived (as we shall see in Chapter III). And often some, especially those from remoter times, are lost to us: we have no idea where Monteverdi or Purcell, for example, actually lived. A number of greatly loved composers have yet to be commemorated by a museum or significant memorial. Sometimes that is because there is no specific site that invites it (or, as with Delius, the obvious site is in a country foreign to the composer) but also because of the effort and energy and finance needed for the establishment of any kind of

Plaque on Delius's house, Grez-sur-Loing

museum. The list of such composers is formidable – to name a few of them, active since 1600: Monteverdi, Sweelinck, Lully, Corelli, Purcell, the Scarlattis father and son, Vivaldi, Rameau, Telemann, Gluck, C.P.E. and J.C. Bach, Boccherini, Meyerbeer, Gounod, Offenbach, Franck, Borodin, Balakirev, Bizet, Sullivan, Fauré, Hindemith, Poulenc, Webern. . . . Some of these made their careers in countries other than those of their birth, which creates a special difficulty: no-one is particularly eager to commemorate either a foreigner or a fellow countryman who settled abroad. But one might reasonably have expected Mantua or Venice to celebrate Monteverdi, Paris Lully, Venice Vivaldi, Dijon Rameau, Lisbon Domenico Scarlatti, Berlin or Hamburg C.P.E. Bach, Madrid Boccherini, perhaps London Sullivan (Gilbert is remembered at the Grim's Dyke Hotel, formerly his villa, at Stanmore, north-west of London).

Those sites we do have vary enormously in scale and scope, from the professionally managed and fully staffed institution to a room or two within a house still occupied by members of the composer's family. Among the former, prime examples include the Händel-Haus in Halle, the Mozart Geburtshaus in Salzburg, the Beethoven-Haus in Bonn, the Grieg house at Troldhaugen near Bergen and the Tchaikovsky house at Klin. Several others are family homes, among them the Verdi villa at Sant'Agata and the d'Indy country house at Boffres; these, like the Puccini villa at Torre del Lago Puccini, which is still in the ownership of the family but not lived in by them, were built under the direction of the composers themselves. A few composers have actually lived in their own museums: in Moscow, Aleksandr Goldenweiser willed his entire estate to the State in 1955 and opened his flat to the public while continuing to live in it until his death six years later; and his widow remained there for many years. There are other examples: we were shown Rimsky-Korsakov's dachas by his granddaughter, Revuts'ky's flat in Kiev by his son, Lyudkevych's study in L'viv and Walton's island paradise in Ischia by their respective widows, Wildgans's house outside Vienna by his sister-in-law, Saar's cottage deep in the Estonian countryside by his niece, Parry's refuge in the Sussex downs by his great-granddaughters.

Composers may often have been able to choose where they lived, and though some preferred isolation most, perforce, lived in urban centres near their places of work. But they could not choose where they were born. Many memorial houses, by virtue of being birthplaces, are in isolated positions, difficult of access, far from the centres of tourism and without the benefit of promotional resources. Numerous 18th- and 19th-century composers of central Europe were the sons of village schoolmasters, born in a cottage or the school itself next to a church. Some, especially in the former Russian Empire, were born in very humble village houses, although others – for example Glinka and Musorgsky – came from the opposite end of the social scale and spent their early years on large estates (Rakhmaninov was not born into an estate, but married into one and spent some of his middle years there).

Musical heritage

It may be appropriate at this point to consider, in broader terms, just what the term 'musical heritage' may be said to constitute, as far as museums and memorials are concerned, and to itemize its categories. Clearly, primacy among them belongs to actual musical works, that is, the musical sources: autograph manuscripts, sketches and drafts, secondary copies, early printed editions. Then there is performance, for the actual act of music-making is a continuing and constantly developing part of the heritage, preserved in sound recordings (and sound combined with a visual record), and also in the existence of historic instruments. Performance history has its own records: concert tickets, programmes, handbills, posters, promotional literature (musicians, musical organizations, publishers) and other sources of reportage (contemporary descriptions, criticism). More broadly, there is the literature of music: books, periodicals, journal and newspaper articles. The iconography of music is a large category, comprising drawings, paintings and other representations, photographs, statues, busts and masks, and portrayals of scenes of music-making and other relevant events. Then there are documentary records relating to musicians: birth, marriage and death certificates, school reports, passports, certificates of diplomas, degrees, memberships or awards, correspondence and diaries; related to these are commemorative objects, such as medals, wreaths, presentation items and various kinds of memorial such as plaques and tombstones. Lastly, there are artefacts connected, usually through ownership, with musicians and music-making: furniture, writing equipment, reading glasses, utensils and ornaments, clothing, and the actual premises in which composers lived. It is these last, in particular, that form the subject of this essay.

The standard repositories of musical heritage are of course national, regional, ecclesiastical and academic libraries, archives and museums. For most composers of the past, the bulk of manuscripts and important early printed editions have generally found their way into such institutions, although a significant number remain in private collections. Other source material, such as letters, documents and personal artefacts, has not been so methodically collected. Some composer museums have collections that enable them to vary their displays from time to time, but only a relatively modest number hold significant quantities of primary source material. A few, in particular those attached to research institutes or libraries, or the recipients of important private collections, have developed, or in some cases inherited through familial links, important archival collections of their own. While acquiring and preserving material for posterity, as libraries and archives do, museums seek in addition to interpret their collections for a range of audiences, young and old, the novice and the informed visitor.

Birthplaces, deathplaces, workplaces

Composer museums and memorial rooms occupy buildings of all sorts. A large majority are, of course, in the actual houses where the composers were born, where they lived – for anything from a few months to 30 years or more – or where they died. Most of the truly great composers from Schütz to the end of the 19th century who are commemorated at all are commemorated at the houses of their birth, where those houses survive: among them are Handel, Bach (the actual birthplace is unknown, but the commemorative house is at least close by), Haydn, Mozart, Beethoven, Schubert, Rossini, Donizetti, Bellini, Berlioz, Chopin, Schumann, Liszt, Verdi (possibly the wrong house), Smetana, Bruckner, Musorgsky, Tchaikovsky, Dvořák, Puccini, Mahler, Debussy, Elgar, Sibelius and Rimsky-Korsakov. For most of the notable absentees from that list there is at least a plaque to indicate the site, if it is known. Many of the rather lesser composers represented in this volume, of that era and beyond, are also remembered at their birthplaces, with plaques and sometimes busts or statues. Broadly speaking, birthplace museums tend to be general rather than specialist, and to include some account of the composer's entire life, not merely the years spent in the house.

For all the sentimental connotations of a birthplace, a place of death offers greater scope for evocation, and a museum that commemorates long residence may tell us more about the composer's way of life than one at which he happens to have been born. The way of life of early composers – most were fairly mobile, and they often lived in staff quarters of some sort – makes them difficult to commemorate. Handel's period of 36 years at his chosen London house is a striking exception, and in itself predictive of a new relationship between the composer and society. Of the houses or flats commemorating the Classical Viennese composers only Haydn's, at Eisenstadt and Vienna, represent reasonably long-term spells of residence. Handel and Haydn both died in their town houses, Bach, Mozart and Beethoven in buildings that no longer stand. But the circumstances of Beethoven's death are presented in the museum displays at Heiligenstadt, in north Vienna, and in the centre of the city the pathetic circumstances of Schubert's are even more movingly brought home in the actual flat where he died, asking to hear Beethoven's C sharp minor quartet played in the room next to the tiny one in which he lay.

Many other images of composers' deaths are evoked in these museums, not exclusively in the actual places of death. In this, perhaps unsurprisingly, the Italian opera composers' museums excel. A room at Rossini's birthplace relates the circumstances of his death, with the famous Doré engraving, his burial and reburial. The room in which Donizetti spent his last days is evoked by the presentation of his deathbed and his invalid chair; nearby, his last portrait, in which he is seated in the chair, provides graphic corroboration as much by the tactful omission of the chair's tray and headrest as by its faithful reproduction of its other salient features. The museum also displays the black tailcoat in which he was first buried, recovered 'almost intact' at his exhumation. The Bellini birthplace museum goes further, displaying the coffin in which he was interred in Paris before the exhumation and return of his remains to Sicily. In the Verdi museum at his villa, Sant'Agata, the room in which he died in the Hotel Grand et de Milan is re-created, with the original furniture; there is also an account of his death in one of the Busseto museums, and it is possible to visit both the hotel

The room of Verdi's death, as re-created at Sant'Agata

room where he died and his grave in the Casa di Riposo for musicians that he established in Milan. Spontini too was buried in a retirement home of his own creating in Maiolati (his kindliness and munificence towards his native village compares interestingly with his reputation for mean behaviour in the wider world). For Puccini no extra excursion is needed: he and other family members are interred within the museum itself at Torre del Lago, in the chapel of his villa.

Wagner, of course, met his death in Venice, and that is duly commemorated in the Ca' Vendramin Calergi, where he had been living: the staircase can be seen down which he was borne to the *lugubre gondola* to start his journey back to Bayreuth, where he is buried in the garden of what is now the Wagner museum. Close by, the house in which Liszt died, rebuilt after wartime destruction, is also a museum. At Bonn, the asylum in which Schumann died, now a public music library, has two rooms to commemorate him. The St Florian monastery in Austria, with which Bruckner was closely associated all his life, displays his deathbed in one of the rooms open to the public and his actual coffin in the crypt of the Stiftkirche. Several other Austrian composers' deaths are particularly commemorated – Lehár's, Koschat's and Einem's – by the re-creation of the rooms in which they died (or simply their maintenance as they were), and in the Franz Schmidt memorial rooms the visitor may find himself sitting on the sofa on which the composer's body was rested when he died. Other strong death images include the jacket worn by the Latvian Emils Dārziņš when he was struck and killed in a railway accident, the desk on to which the Romanian Tudor Ciortea fell as he died and the sofa on which the Ukrainian Mykola Leontovych was shot (the bullet hole is clearly to be seen).

The reconstruction – or sometimes the retention – of a composer's working environment may often be revealing. The earliest example must be the hut to which Mozart was consigned to concentrate on finishing *Die Zauberflöte*, originally in Vienna, now rebuilt in Salzburg. The most famous composing huts, hidden away in woods or by lakesides or both, are the three of Mahler's, all now mini-memorials. Grieg had two, one by a lake in the beautiful Hardanger country, at Lofthus, and later the one at Troldhaugen, and Wilhelm Kienzl had one by the Aussee; a similar need for quiet and seclusion led Dora Pejačević to build a pavilion in the grounds of her palace in Našice, in Croatia.

Several composers who needed to spend the concert season, or the academic year, in a city relished the opportunity to escape to rural peace in the summers. Many of Beethoven's summer excursions, to Heiligenstadt or the Döbling area north of Vienna, or Mödling or Baden to the south, are commemorated by museums. So is Weber's summer residence at Hosterwitz, then in a wine-growing area outside Dresden, and so too are some of

The 'Magic Flute' hut at the Mozarteum in Salzburg

Brahms's, to spas (Baden-Baden), lakeside resorts (Gmunden, Pörtschach) or walking country (Mürzzuschlag), although not all of his holiday homes survive. Tchaikovsky's favourite summer haunt was Kamenka, his sister and brother-in-law's estate in Ukraine, now a museum jointly to Tchaikovsky and Pushkin; there is a large cave in a nearby hillside – it has since engaged the attention of architects and builders – to which he is said to have resorted for the quiet he needed to compose. His pupil Taneyev kept closer to home for his summer escapes; he is commemorated in his friend's cottage close by the one he rented in Dyut'kovo, not far west of Moscow, in 1908–15.

Summer homes in attractive areas lend themselves happily to adaptation as memorial houses. The earliest of these must be Ole Bull's architectural frolic on the island of Lysøen, built in the 1870s. In 1914 Peterson-Berger built his own country house, at Frösön, in north central Sweden, with a fine view across the water from his study, for his summer breaks up to 1930, when he retired there. Jāzeps Vītols was given his country estate by a grateful Latvia for his services to music, but had no pretensions and was content to spend his summers in the brewer's house there from 1922. It was also in the 1920s that Janáček bought a cottage in his native Hukvaldy, in north Moravia, as a retreat: the study in which the flowering of his late years took place is preserved, as too are the contents of his study in Brno. About the same time Szymanowski began to visit Zakopane, in the Tatra mountains of southern Poland, for the sake of his health; the villa he rented there from 1930 is now his striking memorial. The last of the summer villas is the one George Enescu built at Sinaia, in the hilly country north of Bucharest, in the 1920s, and used until he left Romania in 1946.

The rooms in which composers worked, the sites of their creative inspiration, are naturally a constant source of interest to the visitor, and many museums have taken pains to keep them or even to re-create them. They are often suggestive of sources of inspiration – d'Indy's lofty perch at the top of his château, with its views across to the Alps, for example, or the second of Mahler's composing huts in the woodland above the Wörthersee at Maiernigg, or Klemetti's, in a former sauna, with its outlook through a Finnish pinewood to a lake – or of working methods, as in Rimsky-Korsakov's, where his wife was assigned a smaller desk nearby at which she, a trained composer, could perform some of the more menial tasks. The Mahler huts, and the similar ones used by Mozart, Grieg and Pejačević, speak of the composer's need for peace and seclusion, as too does Peterson-Berger's island lair and, in a different way, the upholstered door that Bartók installed on his veranda.

Lysenko's study, in which he died in his Kiev flat, had to be painstakingly reconstructed from photographs after nearly 70 years. Others, such as both of Alban Berg's, in his Wörthersee Waldhaus and his Vienna drawing-room, or Kodály's in Budapest, or Vītols's in the Riga Academy of Music, could be left

Yuliya Rimsky-Korsakova's desk

as they were. Orff's at Diessen, with its extensive library and instrument collection, is precisely what one might expect to find. When the property in which a composer lived is no longer available, because of demolition or alternative use, the study has sometimes been transplanted and re-created. The most distant must be Schoenberg's, from Los Angeles to his Vienna museum. Some have been re-created in conservatories – in Parma, for example, which houses Boito's and Pizzetti's. Nielsen's is carefully assembled in his museum at Odense. Josip Slavenski's is in the Serbian Music Information Centre in Belgrade, in the actual building where he lived, although there is a larger museum to him in his native Croatia. Part of the leading Croatian composer Ivan Zajc's study is reconstructed in the Zagreb City Museum, as is Reger's from Jena in the Schloß in Meiningen; others include Elgar's, near Worcester, Ysaÿe's in Liège, Ciortea's in Braşov, Schneider-Trnavský's in Trnava and Gustave Charpentier's in the Musée de Montmartre, the totality of his commemoration there.

Most of these are quite sparsely furnished, with a well-worn desk and chair and a piano (often an upright). There are piles of manuscript paper, pencils and pens or an inkstand (sometimes a decorative one, a gift from a music society), the ubiquitous five-nibbed rastrum for drawing stave-lines, a pair of glasses and usually an ashtray and lighter. The walls are lined with pictures and photographs of people and landscapes as well as shelves of books, often revealing hitherto unsuspected interests and linguistic capacities, and scores. It is perhaps ironic that almost all composers' studies are presented in silence, without a background of recorded music. The visitor is free to think about the music composed here and to imagine the sound, if not to hear it.

The buildings

Very few composer museums are purpose-built. One such is the Čiurlionis National Art Museum in Kaunas, designed to accommodate his paintings rather than any musical relics; another is the museum to Revuts'ky, at the Ukrainian village of Irzhavets'. Sometimes new buildings have been put up alongside old ones where the needs of a museum have outgrown the possibilities within the existing house, as at the Grieg museum at Troldhaugen, the Tchaikovsky one at Klin or the Elgar cottage outside Worcester. A wing of the city concert hall in Odense was adapted to form the Nielsen museum.

Several museums are in houses that the composers themselves planned or designed. Ole Bull's timber extravaganza at Lysøen, already mentioned, is perhaps the most arresting of these; it is in fact foreshadowed by his earlier

The music room at Bull's 'Little Alhambra', Villa Lysø

house at Valestrand, just north of Bergen, and still in the family. Then there are the villas, Sant'Agata and Wahnfried, of Verdi and Wagner, and Puccini's Italian Gothic revival villa at Torre del Lago. Scandinavians have favoured a more rustic style, as witnessed by Grieg's Troldhaugen, Peterson-Berger's Sommarhagen on Fröson, and indeed Sibelius's Ainola in the woods of Järvenpää; the more recent granite and pine mansion built by Harald Sæverud represents a reinterpretation of that tradition. Stravinsky himself made the initial designs for his house, now his museum, at Ustyluh, on the Ukrainian-Polish border, influenced by Swiss chalet design, but after wartime depredations and rebuilding it now has a more Stalinist appearance. The design of d'Indy's tall, neo-Gothic château in the Ardèche seems very much of a piece with his music. Two composers built Mediterranean villas, Casals a beachside one at Sant Salvador, Walton his island refuge on Ischia. As to interiors, the Ysaÿe studio in Liège designed for him by Serrurier-Bovy is a fine example of *Art Nouveau*, as too is the Nottara house in Bucharest; another remarkable interior, though highly eclectic with its Greek Revival, Art Deco, *japonaiserie* and much else, is Ravel's house at Montfort-l'Amaury.

Numerous museums have been set up within historic buildings, generally but not always buildings with some connection with the composer. Two women composers, Pejačević and Zuylen, are commemorated in the castles in

Našice and Utrecht that once belonged to their families. But not many composers came from the castle-owning classes. The Benda brothers and Smetana are commemorated at one where they worked, at Benátky nad Jizerou, as is Bach at Köthen (also in one at Ohrdruf, close to where he briefly lived). There is a memorial room to Haydn at the Esterházy family Versailles in Hungary, Eszterháza, near Fertőd, and there are Beethoven commemorations at the castles of his patrons – the Lichnowsky family at what is now Hradec nad Moravicí in North Moravia, and the Brunsvik family at what is now Dolná Krupá in Slovakia and Martonvásár near Budapest (the latter more country house than castle). Schubert is remembered at an Esterházy estate at Želiezovce, now in Slovakia, where he gave music lessons, as well as at the castle at Atzenbrugg, west of Vienna, where he attended house parties. Brahms is commemorated along with Reger at the castle that was once the seat of the Saxe-Meiningen court. As a young man Chopin occasionally played in country houses not far from Warsaw (Antonín, Sanniki and Szafarnia), and a visit from the greatest Polish composer is something that warrants continuing celebration, in festivals and summer courses as well as memorial rooms. One of the Verdi museums at Busseto is in a palace that once belonged to the local noble family, the Pallavicino, and is now owned by the municipality, and one belonged to Verdi's first father-in-law and patron Antonio Barezzi, whom to some extent it commemorates. One of the several Tchaikovsky museums spread across Russia and Ukraine is in the country house that belonged to his patron Nadezhda von Meck (the main part of which is an agricultural college, as too is Eszterháza). Paderewski's country house at Kąsna Dolna, near Tarnów in southern Poland, is part museum, part hotel, part site of piano competitions and like events. In Croatia Prejac and in Poland Kurpiński are remembered at castles, not because of any historical connection with them but simply through the social and political circumstances in those countries that led to the use of grand houses for the honouring of local worthies.

Some museums are accommodated in ecclesiastical buildings. Besides the memorial rooms to Bruckner at St Florian, there are rooms dedicated to Michael Haydn at St Peter's Abbey in Salzburg, for which he composed and where he is buried, and rooms for the Wranitzky brothers at the Premonstratensian monastery in Nová Říše, South Moravia, where they had their schooling. Chopin's chilly winter with George Sand at Valldemossa, in Majorca, is commemorated in the monastery where they stayed. There is a necessarily rather small memorial to Martinů on the elevated site of his birth, up 200 stairs, at the top of the church tower in Polička, Eastern Bohemia. Until recently there was a museum to Peter Singer, a leading figure in Salzburg musical life in the 19th century and inventor of the Pansymphonikon, in the

Franciscan monastery there, but little now remains. Some museums reach church premises almost by accident. There is no discernible logic to the assignment of an outbuilding of the basilica of St Nicolas in Braşov to a commemoration of Ciortea, whose interests lay in instrumental and Transylvanian folk music. The birthplace of Tomášek, in Skuteč in Eastern Bohemia, happens to have been taken over by a Czech evangelical sect which happily could spare a room for the composer. Through the bequest by his mistress of Mascagni materials to the parish of Bagnara di Romagna, the museum to him is housed in church property. In England there is a modest celebration in Down Ampney church of Vaughan Williams, a non-believer, whose father had been vicar there when he was born. The commemoration of Parry is in the remains of a medieval priory.

Other historic buildings with composer memorials include a former customs house on a Stockholm island, where the poet-composer Bellman is commemorated. At a neo-Renaissance villa at the foot of the Wartburg, outside Eisenach, there is, aptly, a museum to Wagner. In King Ludwig II of Bavaria's castle of Neuschwanstein, huge murals depict scenes from his music dramas. One of the oddest sitings of a museum is in a building adjoining the Hellerhof monastery in Paudorf, Lower Austria, where Kienzl, whose opera *Der Evangelimann* has as its climax the destruction of the Hellerhof, is celebrated.

Anyone who visits 300 or so composer museums is bound to notice recurring patterns among them and to note ways in which they fall into groups. Reference has already been made to the large number of museums made out of former schoolrooms and reflecting the relative likelihood of the son of a village schoolmaster, who generally also served as village organist, becoming a composer, especially in central and eastern Europe. Familiar examples are Schubert and Bruckner, both of whose birthplaces are now museums; others include four Czechs (Dussek, Janáček, Jindřich, Ryba), two Latvians (Dārziņš, Melngailis) and two more from Austro-Hungary (Pleyel, Erkel). There are further examples from Germany (Silcher) and Belgium (Tinel). Several of the original school buildings are now museums. Schools are also sometimes used for memorial displays for want of any better place: as in Novi Bečej, Serbia, where a substantial Marinković collection can be seen in a headmaster's study in a school in the street where he was born, or in Kirovohrad, in Ukraine, where a collection of the theatre composer Meytus is exhibited, or in Azernï, in Belarus, where Moniuszko is commemorated close to the site of his birth.

The transplanted studies in music colleges, conservatories and universities have been noted above. There are also other types of museum in such institutions: to Rossini in Pesaro, where there is a dedicated 'little temple' or *tempietto*, filled with his manuscripts; to Donizetti in the conservatory in Bergamo; to Piccinni in Bari (where the university music department is directly above the humble *basso* where he was born); to Schumann in Leipzig (where first-floor rooms, probably the site of his original flat, commemorate him and Clara within a primary music school); to Franz Schmidt in Perchtoldsdorf, just south of Vienna (two memorial rooms within the eponymous municipal music school); to Dittersdorf in the North Moravian town of Javorník (where his original house is a junior music school); to Janáček in Brno (in the house built for him in the conservatory grounds); to Matecić Ronjgov, just outside Rijeka (in the institution he established in his native village, mainly for the study of Istrian folk music); and to Liszt in Budapest (where he was assigned a flat in the then music school, with doors leading directly into the concert room). This last, like the grace-and-favour Vītols estate, is one of the few bestowed on a composer: other examples are the house in Tibble, near Leksand in central Sweden, bought for Alfvén by his admirers to mark his 70th birthday; and Haus Wahnfried in Bayreuth, presented to Wagner by Ludwig II. Liszt in reality had two such gifts, for his flat at the Hofgärtnerei in Weimar was set aside by the Grand Duke on his death and made into a museum the following year at his command.

Not many composers enjoyed such lofty patronage. Many, posthumously of course, have had to be content with municipal pride. Small communities in various parts of Europe have assigned space within even quite modest public buildings to the honouring of distinguished local composers. There is a room dedicated to Reger, who was born in a house just across the road, in the tiny mayoral offices of Brand, in the Oberpfalz, north Bavaria. A rather grand one honours Sarasate in the local archive offices at Pamplona.

The tradition of the Heimatmuseum, or local history museum, favoured in Austria particularly invites this type of commemoration and there are many examples of it there: to Brahms at Gmunden, on the Traunsee, which he often visited; to Bruckner at Vöcklabruck in Lower Austria, where his sister lived; to Suppè at Gars am Kamp, north-west of Vienna, although he was a visitor rather than a native; and to Gruber, composer of *Stille Nacht*, who is extensively fêted in the Salzburg area, with displays not only in municipal premises at Arnsdorf and Oberndorf but at two other sites nearby. A comparable example is the assignment of a room to Max Brand in the museum to the sculptor Anton Hanak in Langenzersdorf, on the northern outskirts of Vienna.

In Germany, Weber is commemorated at the regional museum in Eutin, where he was born, and the celebrations of Bach in Wechmar, Eisenach, Ohrdruf and Arnstadt are within town museums. The Czech equivalent of the

Heimatmuseum is the Městské Muzeum, of which there are many examples featuring composers, among them the Dussek gallery at Čáslav, the display for Jindřich in the museum at Klenčí pod Čerchovem, the Martinů commemoration in the town museum (as opposed to the one in the church tower) in Polička and the Ryba celebration at Rožmitál pod Třemšínem as well as the Smetana/Benda and Dittersdorf memorials noted above. Of the same kind, in Poland, is the display to Tansman in the palatial local history museum in Łódź.

There are several examples in the former Yugoslavia. Osterc is the subject of a display in the north Slovenian village of Veržej; space is assigned to Kogoj in the municipal library of the west Slovenian town of Kanal, and Žalec in central Slovenia devotes a floor in the local art gallery to Savin. In Croatia Livadić is commemorated in his own house in Samobor, along with local art and archaeology, and the Medjimurian Museum at Čakovec has a room honouring Slavenski. In Serbia, there is a display to Nastasijević in the local museum at Gornji Milanovac.

In Italy, Cilea is remembered in the civic museum at Palmi; in Belgium, two composers who worked for the Flemish cause are commemorated in local museums, Benoit in Harelbeke and Veremans in Lier, and a re-creation of Ysaÿe's studio is accommodated in space adjoining the Liège museum of religious and local art; in France Saint-Saëns in honoured in the city from which his family came, Dieppe. The presence of a Debussy museum in the tourist office at Saint-Germain-en-Laye belongs in a slightly different category, since it was Debussy who came first: it is in the house of his birth. At Prades, in the Pyrenean region of France, a back room in the tourist office is at present given over to Casals, long a resident of the town. In England, the local authority at Dorking, where Vaughan Williams lived, allows a corner of its music library to be used for a display.

It is to be expected that some museums would be associated with the performance of music. Besides the Nielsen museum at the Odense concert hall, the museum to Pergolesi is in the building of the Jesi city theatre, the Teatro Pergolesi, which also accommodates a smaller memorial to Spontini, another local composer. There is a museum attached to La Scala, Milan, rich in composer materials for 19th- and 20th-century Italian opera, and behind the Staatsoper in Vienna is the Österreichisches Theatermuseum, which celebrates the city's operetta traditions with individual rooms devoted to some of its main practitioners. There is one commemoration in a former cinema, in Horodyshche in Ukraine, to the baritone and composer Gulak-Artemovsky. In a slightly different category is the Chopin commemoration in the instrument museum at Poznań, where a room is devoted to the composer.

Then there are museums associated with industry. The most striking is the Tchaikovsky museum at his birthplace, Votkinsk, in Udmurtia, on the estate where his father had been manager of an ironworks that built cannons and anchors, more recently the site of the Votkinsk Intercontinental Ballistic Missile factory. Part of a 12th-century convent founded by Hildegard of Bingen is preserved in her memory within the premises of a firm in Bingerbrück. The Novák memorial rooms in Skuteč were at one time part of a shoe factory, owned by his wife's family. The museum to Dima and Mureşianu in Braşov had been a printing works. The Albéniz museum at Camprodón, on the Catalonian side of the Pyrenees, is in a former police station, down the street from where he was born.

A handful of composer museums are on islands. The Bellman customs house in Stockholm, the Chopin museum at Valldemossa, the Tobias museum on Hiiuma and Peterson-Berger's house on Frösön have already been mentioned. The two Greek museums, to Carrer and Vamvakaris, are on the islands, respectively, of Zakynthos and Syros. There are two others worth visiting merely for the beauty of their sites – the retreat that Ole Bull created for himself at Lysøen, 30 km south of Bergen, and the home and tropical garden on Ischia lovingly tended by Lady Walton in her husband's memory.

Garden at La Mortella, Ischia

There are also several museums in or attached to hotels and taverns, now or historically. The Brahms commemoration at Pörtschach is at Schloß Leonstain, a hotel with a view across the Wörthersee. The Kienzl museum at Waizenkirchen, near Linz, is in the inn where he was born. Ángel Barrios was born in a tavern in Granada and his museum stands on its rebuilt site in the Alhambra. One of Grieg's composing huts lies in the grounds of a hotel in the Hardanger region. Similarly, two of Mahler's composing huts were built for him in the grounds of the hotels where he spent his summers, and the hotels, in Steinbach am Attersee and Dobbiaco (formerly Toblach), are still there, nurturing in their way his association. He had been born in a coaching inn, in Kaliště, and his childhood was spent in the family inn in Jihlava; the building on the latter site, much restored, contains a museum to his youth in the town. From inn to vineyard: Beethoven's last journey from Vienna, in 1826, was to his brother Johann's house at Gneixendorf, now a Beethoven memorial and still centre of a vineyard, where you can buy wines from the vines, or rather their progeny, that supplied the wine he drank.

Lastly, there are memorials in more sombre circumstances. Four of the Jewish Czech composers who passed through Terezín *en route* to their deaths at Auschwitz are the subject of commemorative displays in the section devoted to music in the Magdeburg Barracks at the Terezín memorial: Haas, Klein, Krása and Ullmann.

Composers and others

Many museums commemorate a family rather than, or in conjunction with, a famous composer – two, even without commemoration of the composers themselves: the little museum attached to the local court at St Gilgen commemorates Mozart's mother in the house where she was born as well as his sister, who lived there later, while the museum at Ehrenbreitstein, on the Rhine near Koblenz, commemorates Beethoven's mother, not in her own right but because of her son. From the other end of Beethoven's life, the Gneixendorf house touches on his relationship with his nephew and, in the event crucially, or fatally, with his brother Johann. Several museums, where there is no other musician or other kind of artistic collaborator in the family, cast light on family relationships and help supply context for the composer's life. Berlioz's family background, for example, is sharply illuminated at his birthplace at La Côte-Saint-André, near Grenoble, as too is Rimsky-Korsakov's to his at Tikhvin; so is Tchaikovsky's relation to his sister at Kamenka and Dvořák's to his sister-in-law Josefina at her mansion in Vysoká

u Příbrami. In some museums music rubs shoulders with the other arts: the
Nottara house in Bucharest commemorates the actor father as much as the
composer and violinist son, and in the Wildgans house in Mödling it is the poet
father, Anton, who is primarily remembered rather than Friedrich.

But many more commemorate musical families, which of course includes
the Bachs, for the cottage bakery in the village of Wechmar where the family is
first recorded is the 'Bach-Stammhaus', the root of the fruitful family tree –
although, surprisingly, there is no museum that sets a context for J.S. Bach and
his sons. Often it is brothers who are conjointly remembered: the two Haydns
at their birthplace at Rohrau, between Vienna and Bratislava, the Bendas at
Benátky nad Jizerou, the Wranitzkys at Nová Říše, the Schuberts (it was in
Ferdinand's flat that Franz died) in Vienna, the Petrauskas brothers (composer
and tenor) in Kaunas, the three Budriunas brothers in Pabirże, northern
Lithuania, and the Tchaikovskys at Klin – for Modest, though not a musician,
was his brother's librettist and biographer, and creator of the museum. One
museum celebrates four brothers, the Latvian family Jurjāns, at Ērgļi. A loose
fit into this category of family museums is the one at Tescani-Bacău, in
Romania, where in the mansion that belonged to the family of Enescu's wife
there are displays dedicated to both Enescu and her cousin Mihail Jora.

Several of these family museums are given over to father and son. Mozart's
father is commemorated on his own at his birthplace in Augsburg, and then at
Salzburg, in particular at the Wohnhaus which devotes rooms specifically to
him and to Mozart's sister Nannerl (also remembered with her mother at St
Gilgen). There are several father-son museums: to the Mureşianus, in Braşov,
celebrating the contributions of several family members other than the musicians, both called Jacob Mureşianu, to Romanian culture; to the Ipavec family
in Šentjur, central Slovenia, where two brothers and the son of one of them are
commemorated; and in south-east Hungary the displays in the museum to
Ferenc Erkel also reflect the music of three of his four sons (the fourth was
among Bartók's teachers). The Kapp family, at Suure-Jaani in Estonia, does
better still, with a father, his two sons, and their two sons.

There are several man-and-wife museums. All three of the Schumann
museums embody some commemoration of Robert's wife, Clara, most of all
(curiously) his birthplace at Zwickau, where two of the rooms are devoted to
her exclusively. In the Verdi museum in the Barezzi house in Busseto both his
marriages – to Margherita Barezzi and to Giuseppina Strepponi – are
commemorated, and at Sant'Agata Strepponi's original room is lovingly
preserved. The Wagner museum at Lucerne, Haus Tribschen, reflects Cosima's
centrality in his life – this is where she was serenaded with the *Siegfried Idyll* –
and her presence is felt too in Bayreuth, where she is buried alongside her

husband. But perhaps the most remarkable of husband-wife museums is the Nielsen one at Odense: Marie Anne Nielsen was a sculptor, and here her work is presented alongside that of her husband.

The museums Tchaikovsky shares with Madame von Meck and Pushkin have already been mentioned. Chopin shares several of his museums with women. Three of his amorous attachments are recorded: in the house in Skierniewice of his supposed first love, Konstancja Gładowska; in the Důrm Chopin at Mariánské Lázně in the Czech Republic, where he spent time with Maria Wodzińska; and at Valldemossa, where he stayed with George Sand (in reciprocation, Chopin is cursorily noted both in her house museum in Nohant and in the municipal museum to her at La Châtre, in the Indre *département*). A number of women composers associated with men commemorated by museums are – with the honourable exception of Clara Schumann – only fleetingly mentioned as composers themselves: there is little to indicate the creative capacities of the Dussek ladies, Fanny Mendelssohn, Nadezhda Nikolayevna Purgold, Alma Mahler or Imogen Holst.

A number of museums commemorate not only a composer but someone or something else too: it may be another composer or group of composers, or a musical genre, or a local person of eminence, or even something quite apart from music. Among the two-composer museums are two in Vienna: the Haydn museum, in which one room is assigned to Brahms, and the house which once belonged to Emanuel Schikaneder (Mozart's *Zauberflöte* librettist and first Papageno, and himself a composer in a small way) and later to Lehár, fitted out as a Lehár museum but with some Schikaneder items. The Mureşianus share their accommodation in Braşov with Dima, the Bendas with Smetana at Benátky. At Meiningen, along with Reger and Brahms – for this is a museum celebrating the traditions of the once-famous Meiningen orchestra – the clarinettist Richard Mühlfeld and the conductor Hans von Bülow are commemorated. In several museums there is a modest gesture towards a second composer: Georg Benda is noted in the Schütz museum at Bad Köstritz, near Dresden, where he had retired and died; Manfroce, another local composer, who died young, is commemorated in the Cilea museum at Palmi; Muzio, Verdi's sole pupil, is accorded a corner of the Verdi museum in the Casa Barezzi in Busseto. In the museum to Donizetti generous space is accorded to his mentor, Simon Mayr, who was also an important figure in Bergamo. Some such secondary displays are, at least by intention, temporary: the Lithuanian composer Šimkus moved in with the Petrauskas brothers in Kaunas, pending the reconstruction of his own memorial house, and in an outbuilding of the Tchaikovsky museum at Klin there is a substantial Taneyev display, to move in due course to the Taneyev family house nearby.

Among the museums with larger musical counterthemes is the Wagner house at Bayreuth, which also celebrates the history of the Bayreuth Festival, and the Spohr display in Kassel, which broadens into a museum of the history of violin playing; and there are two museums that celebrate male-voice ensembles – in Klagenfurt, to Koschat and the Carinthian partsong, and in Schnait, near Stuttgart, to Silcher, which is also the central commemoration of the 19th-century Sängerbund movement in Germany. Singing traditions underlie the Casa Muzicii at Lugoj, in Romania, which houses memorial displays to three composers (Barbu, Brediceanu and Vidu), and the commemoration of Gerbič at Cerknica in Slovenia. Another multiple museum is the Händel-Haus at Halle, which, uniquely, is also a museum to the musical history of the region, with displays on eminent local composers (Scheidt, W.F. Bach, Reichardt, Türk, Franz and Loewe). Equally, the Melngailis museum near Vidriži serves the revival of Latvian folksong.

Several museums, predominantly those run in association with local authorities anxious to foster education, celebrate a composer in parallel with a quite different theme. The cottage of Joseph Parry in Merthyr Tydfil is a museum equally to his musical career and to the living conditions of ironworkers in Victorian times. At Cheltenham, the Holst birthplace museum serves too as a museum to Victorian middle-class domestic life. In the Latvian town of Ērgļi the museum to the Jurjāns brothers is partly a museum to the rural way of life in the middle and late 19th century, and in Vidriži, nearby, the museum to Melangailis serves to illuminate life in the farming community. So does the museum to Tobias, at Käina on the Estonian island of Hiiumaa. The Jindřich museum at Domažlice, in the south-west corner of the Czech Republic, with his formidable collection, is almost primarily a museum of local folk art, and the Weill commemoration at Dessau, in one of the Meisterhäuser of the Bauhaus, is devoted equally to music and architecture. The Paderewski museum in Warsaw commemorates Polish emigration to the United States. Sometimes two museums are adjacent but unrelated in subject matter, as with the slightly incongruous conjunction of a doll museum with the Werner Egk museum at Donauwörth.

A number of museums scarcely touch on the actual music composed by their subjects, usually with good reason. The museum in Bath to William Herschel is understandably more concerned with his attainments as an astronomer (he discovered Uranus) than as a composer, and in the same city there is no reference whatever in the William Beckford museum to his compositions, admittedly unimportant compared with his achievements as writer and art collector. Outstanding practical musicians who were only secondarily composers are honoured primarily for their success as performers –

Toscanini, at his house and his study in Parma, the violinists Ysaÿe in Liège and Sarasate in Pamplona, the singer Prejac at Veliki Tabor (Croatia), and in some degree the cellist Casals, although the museum that was his house at Sant Salvador, near Barcelona, lays some stress on his compositions designed to promote world peace. Paderewski is celebrated more as pianist and statesman than as composer, Bellman more as poet and actor, Noël Coward more as actor and playwright and Edith Piaf more as *chanteuse*. Some museums even to great composers favour 'life' to the exclusion of 'works'; if that could be said of the Verdi 'birthplace' at Roncole, at least there are several other Verdi museums close by.

II CELEBRATING COMPOSERS

Valuing the past

In the times when music was thought of as a progressive art – that is, when it was taken for granted that the music of any generation represented an improvement on that of the one preceding – the idea of glorifying composers of the past would have seemed strange. A composer's reputation was unlikely to survive long, in a wider world, when styles and fashions were changing rapidly and change was regarded as progress. Only in the hermetic world of the musicians themselves did reputations persist, and there only briefly. As early as the 14th century, the fact that Guillaume de Machaut took the trouble to collect his works, literary as well as musical, following a tradition initiated by poets in the previous century, implies some sense of history or posterity. But in the 15th and the early 16th century, the music of even the most widely acknowledged and admired composers rarely outlived them in any repertory for more than a few years, although they were sometimes remembered through the citation and praise of their work by theorists and the quotation and reworking of elements from it by composers of the next generation. A few were mourned in music by their pupils, friends or contemporaries, for example Jean de Ockeghem, in a lament by Josquin des Prez.

The perpetuation of a composer's memory took on more serious dimensions during the time of Josquin himself. When he died numerous laments were composed by his colleagues, anecdotes about him circulated, and theorists drew on his music for exemplary quotations. The process accelerated in the late 16th century, when the printing of music could ensure a far wider distribution. Palestrina, reverently remembered not only for his music itself but also for its supposed role in ecclesiastical musical history, achieved an unprecedented reputation, and his music enjoyed a currency that easily eclipsed Josquin's. At this time too, the notion developed of a 'classical' repertory of church music – works by Palestrina and others in Italy, for example, or

Byrd and others in England – that was to continue in regular liturgical use, as it still does.

Pre-eminent musicians, like their counterparts among painters and poets, were accorded a status beyond the expectations of their social group, and a few of them won places in some of the collective biographical surveys of the time. Dictionaries of music that include biographical accounts of composers began to appear at the end of the 17th century and the beginning of the 18th, and it was then too that the idea of giving physical embodiment to the subjects of reverence seems to have originated. Evrard Titon du Tillet drew up plans, never realized, for a vast monument, 'Parnasse François', intended to be built on the site in Paris where the Arc de Triomphe now stands, made up of statues of poets and musicians of the Louis XIV era: his first version was to have included a statue of Lully and portrait medallions of Lalande, Marais and La Guerre.

The first statue actually erected to a composer was Roubiliac's of Handel, in Vauxhall Pleasure Gardens in London in 1738. Handel too was the subject of the first published monograph on a composer, the first to be commemorated in a massive 'centenary' festival, in 1784, the first to have a collected edition published of his works and the first to be interred and commemorated with a monument in a national shrine (even if at his own request and own expense).

Statue of Lully: detail from Loüis Garnier's model, 'Parnasse François', commissioned by Titon du Tillet

Almost a century before, a splendid monument had been placed over Lully's grave, but in a local church and at the request and expense of his widow. Purcell had been buried in Westminster Abbey, though without a monument, and Corelli in the Pantheon at Rome. In the 19th century ceremonial burial was more widely practised. Many composers rest in the Zentralfriedhof in Vienna, most of them in a dedicated area for musicians, often with elaborate memorial stones, and the great figures of the French musical scene are to be found at Père Lachaise. Most of the distinguished Russian composers were buried in a corner of the Tikhvin cemetery in St Petersburg, the great Czechs in the Vyšehrad cemetery in Prague. Lesser men, eminent figures in their own towns, were often granted places of honour in their local cemeteries.

Until the middle of the 18th century, virtually all music heard in public or private, in all European countries, was new music, composed during the preceding ten or 20 years. The only exceptions were (as we have seen) in liturgical contexts, in performances by groups specifically dedicated to the investigation and revival of older music (such as the Academy of Ancient Music in London) and in the preservation of certain privileged repertories. In France, the operas of Lully and later the motets of Lalande were kept alive, under royal patronage, well beyond their composers' life-spans. In England, the music of Handel and Corelli remained in currency well after the middle of the century, and a clear dichotomy came to be perceived between 'ancient' and 'modern' styles, respectively those of Corelli and Handel on the one hand, Haydn, J.C. Bach and other living composers on the other.

It was this solidifying of a repertory of 'old music', to which that of J.S. Bach was soon to be added, coupled with the social and economic developments of the early 19th century and their aesthetic consequences – the growth of the musical public, the beginning of cheap music publishing, the rise of music journalism, the building of larger concert halls and opera houses, the development of transport, making international interchange swifter and easier – that led to the establishment of a 'musical canon', a central repertory that could claim international celebrity. It varied in some degree from country to country, as it still does, and it renewed itself in each generation as fresh repertory accrued and some of the old and some of the new fell away. But a solid core of 'classics' remained, and it still remains. The link between the formation of a canon and the construction of national identities is plain, and its centrality in the two great European countries that found national unity only during the 19th century speaks for itself: in the German-speaking countries the symphonic tradition, beginning with Haydn and Beethoven and culminating in Brahms and indeed Wagner, in Italy the operatic tradition from Rossini to Verdi and Puccini.

The composer as hero

It is in this context of national and local pride and the assertion of identity that the celebration of composers at this period has to be understood. Statues of composers, just like those of kings and generals, began to be put up in the middle of the century. In the 1830s a bust was added to the Haydn memorial in Rohrau. Then there was Beethoven in Bonn in 1840, Mozart in

Salzburg in 1842 and Vienna in 1859, Bach in Leipzig in 1843, Gluck in
Munich in 1848, Handel in Halle in 1859, Weber in Dresden in 1860. An
early statue outside the German-speaking areas is the one to Grétry, in Liège,
with his heart buried in it; it dates from 1842, shortly after Belgium acquired
statehood. In Italy, Verdi's birthplace was claimed in 1872, and statues to
Bellini were erected in Catania and Naples in 1882 and 1884.

The affixing of a plaque represents another form of commemoration. It is
intended to increase the awareness, of passers-by, visitors and residents alike,
of local historical events and associations with famous or locally prominent
people. Plaques reflect the pride felt in the connection and enhance civic
consciousness and a sense that the locale was important to a great man or
woman. Probably the earliest for a composer was the one affixed to Grétry's
house in Liège in 1811, two years before his death; in 1840 one was placed on
Haydn's house in Vienna, and in 1853 one on Weber's birthplace (now a café)
in Eutin. In 1859 the Mozart house in the Makartplatz in Salzburg was labelled
'Mozarts Wohnhaus' (as he lived there for only six years it was thought proper,
50 years later, to add an 'L' in front, as Leopold lived there much longer). A
plaque was affixed to the Raiding birthplace of the 'deutscher Meister' Liszt in
1881. Since the late years of the 19th century numerous plaques have been
affixed to buildings, often to mark centenaries or other notable anniversaries.
In several large cities, most of all Vienna, London and Paris, a veritable plaque
industry flourishes, noting passing visitors as well as residents, and supported
and to some extent controlled by national heritage institutions.

There are other, more recent traditions of paying tribute to a great man, in
music as in other spheres. One is through the naming of streets, squares and

The Mozart Wohnhaus in the early 20th century (oil painting by Karl Hayd)

institutions after them. Germany is bespattered with Bachstraßen and Austria with Mozartstraßen, and no self-respecting town in Italy today lacks a Via Verdi or a Piazza Verdi. Every Italian music conservatory bears the name of a composer, usually a local one. In France, the town of Chaumes (Brie) has a Rue Couperin and an Ecole Couperin named after its most famous native family of musicians, and Paris has recently named a street in the 8th *arrondissement* Rue de Chevalier de Saint-Georges after the 18th-century native of Guadeloupe who had a successful French career as violinist and composer. Britain has been less ready to pay tribute to musicians, or indeed to other famous people, although there was once an ELGar telephone exchange.

In the 20th century some countries, Italy and Romania in particular, went better still and applied the name to entire communities. Verdi's native Roncole is now 'Roncole Verdi'; the town where Puccini built his villa is 'Torre del Lago Puccini'; the village of Maiolati is 'Maiolati Spontini' after the composer who donated his fortune to good works there; and Paderno Fasolaro, near Cremona, has become 'Paderno Ponchielli'. The birthplace of Enescu, then Liveni-Vîrnav, is now simply George Enescu, and the village of Stupca where the composer of the Romanian national anthem lived is Ciprian Porumbescu (although the old name tends to drift back, if only because two syllables are preferable to seven).

The age of 'the composer as hero', however, is rightly regarded as beginning with Beethoven, whose life, attitudes and indeed his music represent a change in the social position of the composer, no longer content to be even a superior kind of servant. Handel had lived an independent existence, as a freelance, unlike virtually all others of his time, but his freelance work was safely under-pinned by the royal pension he received for most of his life. Mozart had a spell as a freelance but with little success. Up to the time of Haydn and Mozart the composer expected to be an employee and to write music to order, as directed and needed by his employer. There are ample indications that Mozart was restless in that situation – witness his famous remark about being made to dine with the cooks and the footmen – but he nevertheless sought new posts when he lost his old one. Beethoven saw his social position differently: he never sought an appointment but he felt entitled to ask his patrons for a subsidy (and they complied), and he courted as an equal some of his pupils from noble families; several famous remarks are recorded that show his attitude to his social position, of which the one about there being 'many princes but only one Beethoven' is the most telling.

Society came to share that view. E.T.A. Hoffmann, applying Romantic theory to music, talked of Beethoven's standing at the gates of 'the infinite realm of the spirit'. A generation on, Franz Liszt mixed easily in aristocratic circles and lived with princesses and countesses. The public perception of the role of the creative artist – the musician along with the poet and the painter – underwent a change in the early decades of the 19th century. His study was no longer a mere workshop but a place of creative visitation. His home life was not that of a craftsman but of a genius, and accordingly of interest to the larger world, a shrine, to be treated with due reverence. His birthplace – well, one need only cite the plaque on the house at Roncole: 'In this dwelling on 10 October 1813 the musical genius of Verdi took its first breath'.

Early composer museums

Of the composers commemorated by memorials considered in this book, the earliest are Guido d'Arezzo and Hildegard of Bingen (although there is no true museum to either). The only Renaissance composer is Palestrina, and just two, Scheidt and Schütz, flourished as long ago as the 17th century. A (necessarily approximate) count shows that five were born in that century, 12 in the first half of the 18th century and 26 in the second, 44 in the first half of the 19th and 94 in the second, and 26 in the 20th. There is a sharp peak for dates of birth in the 1870s and a rapid tailing-off after 1910.

Entrance of Suppè's Sophienheim, Gars am Kamp

Most but not all of the early composer museums are dedicated to composers universally regarded as great. The first was Mozart's Geburtshaus in Salzburg. A centenary exhibition had been held there in 1856, and in 1880 part of the house was opened as a museum. More surprisingly, a Musée Grétry was set up at the Liège Conservatoire in 1882, by a keen collector and enthusiast; in 1913 it moved to his birthplace. The Liszt flat in Weimar was set up as a museum in 1887, at the command of the Grand Duke. Three years later the Beethoven-Haus at Bonn opened as a museum. Also in 1890 a Saint-Saëns display was opened in Dieppe, based on objects that the composer himself had given to the museum in the town where his family had originated, and this became a Musée Saint-Saëns in 1897 (attached to the Hôtel de Ville, for the time being). In 1895, when Suppè died, his wife turned their house at Gars am Kamp into a museum to him (it remained so until her death; later the contents passed to the municipality); the same year, a private collector donated his Wagner collection, previously exhibited privately in Austria, to the city of Eisenach, where it served as the basis of a museum.

The years before World War I saw the establishment of several further museums, mostly in Germany and Austria: to Brahms in Gmunden (on the estate of a family who had been his friends and hosts there), Bach in Eisenach, Wagner in Graupa near Dresden, Haydn and Schubert in Vienna, Schumann in Zwickau, Liszt in Raiding, Spohr in Kassel and Silcher in Schnait, near Stuttgart (Silcher himself is a slight figure, but central to the German Sängerbund movement, which his museum also commemorates). In Italy the Rossini and Donizetti houses opened, and in Belgium the house where Peter Benoit, a champion of the Flemish-speaking population, spent his early months was opened as a museum within a year of his death. Several of these museums came into existence through public interest and municipal enterprise, some through private benefactions and some through families.

The museums opened before 1914 – it is impossible to be certain that there were no others, not now known to us – are then as follows: to Bach, Haydn, Grétry, Mozart, Beethoven, Spohr, Silcher, Rossini, Schubert, Donizetti, Schumann, Liszt (two), Wagner (two), Suppè, Brahms, Benoit and Saint-Saëns. The fact that 14 are to German, two each to Italian and French and one to Flemish speakers is a commentary on the German musical hegemony of the time. But the oddity of the assortment is worthy of comment too because it emphasizes the chance factors that determine whether or not a particular composer shall be commemorated. The central figures here present no problems, but the inclusion of Silcher, Suppè, Benoit and Saint-Saëns is less a commentary on the importance of their music than on chance factors: respectively, an association with a powerful lobby, the existence of a devoted widow, a representative role in a politically oppressed group, and a readiness to give away one's possessions.

The establishment of a museum to a composer is not, then, a simple measure of his generally acknowledged importance or recognized greatness. There are numerous other reasons why a museum may or may not be founded, then, later or now. It may be in a house that he occupied and where his actual working environment can be evoked only if the original house (or possibly a replica) stands; if it does, the project will depend on where it is, on whether it has remained in the composer's family or has been sold, and whether it is still lived in; on whether there exist any artefacts connected with the composer that can suitably be shown, and on whether portraits, drawings, documents and music (or reproductions) can be displayed; and whether the necessary funding can be found. In some cases a widow, child or sibling of the composer has partly underwritten a museum. Otherwise the availability of funding will depend on the readiness of national, regional or local authorities, business firms, foundations or private individuals to provide it, and on the readiness of a group of enthusiasts to seek it and organize the enterprise. If sufficient local pride and prestige are involved, this may happen quite readily – in Italy, for example, where banks and local businesses, as well as local government, are usually eager to provide support. In such cities as Paris and London the situation is different. There the cost of property is almost prohibitive for a small museum, and cultural activity exists at such a level that civic pride in the existence of a museum is a small factor. Combined with the long traditions of centralization in France and England, with their single court and single state structure, which have drawn most significant composers to the capitals, it is easy to see one reason why there are so few composer museums in those countries. Rather different factors apply, of course, to the establishment of a composer commemoration within an existing museum. But it will be clear that, where there is a substantial element of national, regional or local pride, and especially where the composer represents something rather more than simply a body of music, for example a political aspiration, the establishment of a museum is likely to be far easier.

National patterns

The way these factors relate in different regions of Europe, and their relation to the social and political history and the commercial organization of the various countries, has contributed to the diversity of the picture of European composer museums. In the large countries with long and well-established musical traditions, central to European music, most of the widely recognized composers are commemorated, some of them many times over. In Austria, for example, the major figures of Viennese music (including operetta) and the composer of *Stille Nacht* account between them for more than three-quarters of the museums or memorial houses; the remainder are men with a special local reputation or beloved by an enthusiast. Very much the same applies in

Germany and Italy. France, Spain and England, with fewer great figures, have relatively small numbers of sites, and the want of strong local traditions and rivalries in most parts of those countries, which have longer histories of national unity, has meant that there has never been so much spur to claim prestige through a famous local composer: Gloucestershire and the Isère feel no need to assert themselves through a Holst or a Berlioz. In none of these countries will you find many museums to composers who are not nationals, nearly always native but just occasionally adoptive (such as Beethoven in Austria, Handel in England).

The situation is different, however, in the countries that attained nationhood comparatively recently, or with particular groups within them. In Belgium, there are three museums in which composers, little known elsewhere, who pioneered the setting of Flemish texts during Walloon domination are commemorated. But this applies more forcefully in central and eastern Europe, especially in lands that were long part of an empire, Russian, Austrian or Ottoman. Many of the composers celebrated in the Baltic countries, for example, were among the earliest to set words in their own national tongue, sometimes when it was prohibited, and were often involved in collecting and setting their countries' folksong; in several cases, there is an open-air auditorium close to the museum where choirs sing their music at an annual festival. In Romania, long divided between empires, there are museums commemorating composers who have written national songs or anthems and another collective museum to a group of composers who particularly nurtured the local choral traditions, while five are devoted to Enescu, the first Romanian composer to become an international figure.

The southern Slavonic countries too primarily commemorate composers who pointed towards a national identity in music, often by being among the earliest from their region to achieve an international reputation or the earliest to set their own language. Some composers even adopted Slav names in preference to their existing Germanic ones. In Bulgaria a museum commemorates the first conductor of the leading Bulgarian choir, who composed settings of national choral songs. Although Ukraine's situation within the Russian Empire is symbolized by its museums to Tchaikovsky, Prokofiev and Stravinsky – all on holiday or country estates that belonged to Russians – most of its remaining museums are to composers concerned with national identity. The countries that belonged to, or were closer to, the Habsburg lands present a more complex picture. In Poland, more than half of all the composer museums are dedicated to Chopin. In Hungary, Haydn and Beethoven are commemorated along with national figures (Liszt, Erkel, Kodály and Bartók). In the Czech Republic – which stands third to Austria and Germany for the number of its museums, and second to none in its national organization of them through an enlightened central museum – visiting composers are remembered (Mozart, Beethoven, Chopin) as well as the country's own most distinguished sons (five sites for Smetana, four for Dvořák) and a host of further Czech composers, commemorated at the houses of their birth or domicile – be it, sometimes, very simply – or in larger institutions. Other countries too are happy to claim the connection with a great composer from abroad: Beethoven is remembered in Hungary and both he and Schubert in Slovakia.

The dates at which museums came to be established, seen in relation to current political developments, speak for themselves. The inter-war years saw the setting up of the first Baltic museum and the house celebrating choral traditions in Romania, and the creation of no fewer than seven museums in what was Czechoslovakia and the first Chopin museum in Poland. During World War II such developments came to a halt, although the foundation of museums to Rimsky-Korsakov and Tchaikovsky in Tikhvin and Votkinsk may perhaps be seen as an assertion of national culture. After the war many were rebuilt and reopened, but there have been some notable flurries of activity here and there, for example in the creation of six museums in Romania and five in Czechoslovakia, signalling the availability of public funding for the fanning of national pride and prestige in the socialist countries, where the State ownership of property made it easier. In the West, the increasing prosperity of the 1970s and 80s is reflected in the foundation of numerous new museums, particularly in Austria and Germany.

The political changes that swept through central eastern Europe at the end of the 1980s do not seem to have affected the patterns. During the socialist years there was always some funding for cultural pursuits, especially where they favoured composers who could be seen to be 'of the people', which was officially interpreted as meaning those who drew on national folksong in their music, as so many were obliged to do. But a fresh spur was provided by newly established independence and often nationhood. In the West, while the base of support for 'classical' music seems to have been shrinking in the closing decades of the 20th century and the early years of the 21st, several new museums have come to be founded and old ones refurbished, celebrating composers of all periods since the 18th century. The more immediate past, as usual, will need to wait. Perhaps, with the establishment by the National Trust of house museums in Liverpool to McCartney and Lennon, others to popular musicians may follow; and certainly Andrew Lloyd Webber's art collection already has a museum potential. But there remains ample scope for museums to the most distinguished composers of recent times, such as Messiaen, Berio and Tippett, and there is no shortage of candidates for the future. The process will surely continue.

There are, of course, composer museums outside Europe. But essentially the tradition is a European one. In the great cultures of Asia the idea of honouring an individual as a creative artist, generally speaking, carries less weight, and the lack of an individually composed historical repertory militates against the idea of celebrating composers in museums. Nearly all the composer museums known to us outside Europe are in the Americas, Australia and the Caucasus. They lie beyond the scope of this book but it may be useful to add a note about them here.

Beyond Europe

Several Europeans who sought fortunes or refuge in the United States are remembered there. Dvořák's time at the Czech colony at Spillville, Iowa, is commemorated in an exhibit in the Bily Clocks Museum there. The plantation house in which Delius lived near Jacksonville, Florida, is now preserved on the campus of the university, with his own piano, and a monument marks its original site at Solano Grove. There is also a monument to Ernest Bloch near his former home at Agate Beach, Oregon. A number of sites are named after Ole Bull in Pennsylvania and there is a small Bull archive in Sudbury, Massachusetts. In Puerto Rico, there is a Casals museum in San Juan, established by his widow, and in Jamaica Noël Coward is commemorated in his two houses (one now a hotel). There is also a museum to Bob Marley in Jamaica.

Delius's Solano Grove house in Florida (1939)

Ives's birthplace at Danbury, Connecticut

In Argentina, a museum was established in 1970 to Falla, in the house in which he died in Alta Gracia, near Cordóba. John Lennon is commemorated in a museum set up in Tokyo by his widow. (The Tchaikovsky museum in Alapayevsk, narrowly in Asian Russia and so strictly outside our area of coverage, is noted in the entry on him for the sake of completeness.)

Some non-Europeans too are commemorated. In Brazil, there is a museum to Carlos Gomes at his birthplace in Campinas and one to Villa-Lobos in Rio de Janeiro. In the United States, the Charles Ives birthplace at Danbury, Connecticut, is a museum, and Edward MacDowell is commemorated at the MacDowell Colony at Peterborough, New Hampshire. There is a museum to J.P. Sousa in West Lafayette, Indiana, and two to Stephen Foster, a memorial one at the University of Pennsylvania and another at White Springs in Florida. There is a Scott Joplin museum at his house in St Louis, Missouri, and one to W.C. Handy at his birthplace in Memphis, Tennessee. In 2003 a museum to Louis Armstrong was set up in his house at Corona, Queens, New York. There are museums to Liberace in Las Vegas, Nevada, and to Jimi Hendrix in Seattle, Washington.

The only Australian museum is the fine one to Percy Grainger at Melbourne University, notable for its collection of his specially designed instruments and for his extensive correspondence. In the Caucasian countries, there are two museums to Uzeir Hajibeyov in the Azerbaijani cities of Baku and Kutaisi; Paliashvili is commemorated in Tbilisi, Georgia, and Khachaturyan and Spendiaryan in the Armenian capital, Yerevan.

III   A FRAGILE LEGACY

Collecting the musical past

It is often pointed out that, unlike a painting, the object that serves to perpetuate a piece of music is not itself a work of art. It is simply a series of instructions for producing one. So the collecting of composers' manuscripts has never been a preoccupation among the rich and the connoisseurs in the way that collecting pictures has been. People have collected music in order to perform it, not to look at it. Accordingly, music collections and libraries initially developed as necessary adjuncts to performing institutions, mostly in ecclesiastical and princely establishments. Other objects associated with composers have not been valued or collected at all until relatively modern times.

Once the age had dawned when composers came to be highly regarded, however, collectors showed increasing interest in their manuscripts. Many extensive collections were built up during the late 18th century and over the 19th. Most substantial music collections have by now found their way into national, regional, academic or ecclesiastical libraries, some bequeathed or sold by their owners (or in some famous cases exchanged for a pension), but some have been sold off at auction after their owner's death and dispersed. Many private music collections still exist, but their number diminished greatly during the 20th century, and the process continues.

Interest in composers' personal possessions and objects associated with them developed more slowly. Very few such artefacts survive even from the early 18th century. Seen as worthless at the time of the composer's or his widow's death, they were simply destroyed or, if of residual use, dispersed. Now, however, objects such as those itemized on p.4 are valued by collectors, especially documents, likenesses of all sorts and personal items, including, for example, locks of hair, writing implements and reading glasses, cigarette holders, pipes and walking-sticks, and of course the actual musical instruments that composers played. All such objects acquire a special aura through their proximity to the composer, and are invaluable to museums where any attempt is made towards a re-creation of his world. Much more survives from the 19th and 20th centuries than from earlier periods, partly because less time has elapsed but mainly because of the increasing importance ascribed to the wider legacy of composers. The precedents established in museums commemorating writers and artists have encouraged the families and friends of composers to retain and preserve as much as possible.

Echoing the traditional formula used in musical biographies, many composer museums relate their subject's life story on illustrated display boards on the walls, with glass cases below them in which relevant objects together with manuscript and printed music from the relevant time are displayed. If the museum is in a house in which the composer lived, space is allocated to his life and times, with special attention to the works written there and his connections with the area. Birthplaces usually tell the whole life story: the family background (often showing a family tree), with detailed chronological surveys of the composer's life (birth, schooling, musical training, personal and professional career) and works (often broken down by genre). Places of death more often summarize the life and then focus on the final years and the late works, tributes to the composer, his musical legacy and its posthumous reception. These sites are of particular interest where the composer is relatively little known outside the region. Displays concentrating on the period the composer spent in the house or the area may, however, be of even greater interest: with these a museum can contribute what are often entirely new perspectives to our appreciation of the music he wrote there. The best displays are usually the result of a successful collaboration between curators and scholars, and most depend to some degree on loans and reproductions from libraries, archives and private collections. They are further supported by images of key events in the composer's life and the places where he lived and worked, usually shown as they were in his own day through prints or old photographs. The presence of art in musical museums encourages us to forge visual associations with sound.

Images of the composer and his times

Images of the composer 'at home' enhance the relevance and credibility of houses and rooms, as both composing and performing venues, and provide evidence of the composer's world and his place in it. Many composer museums display unparalleled collections of graphic and plastic art. Some images on display may be by famous contemporaries, artists who were personal friends and occasionally collaborators on projects such as the sets and costumes for opera productions. But the art in composer museums is rarely in itself of very high quality. Not many of the greatest artists painted composers and their friends. The art is there and it is valuable because it shows us the composer (or his family or friends), not – like a picture in an art gallery – because of its inherent beauty or artistic worth.

Inevitably, images of the composer himself generally constitute the central element, and the largest, in these collections of art. Among the best served are Liszt in Bayreuth and Rossini in Pesaro. The Mozart, Beethoven and Schumann birthplaces have rich collections. The most important portraits are those from life – drawings, watercolours and oils, reliefs, busts and statues, plaster casts of hands and life masks – and also death masks. They may illuminate unexpected corners, personal, social and historical. The succession of Dussek portraits at Čáslav, for example, shows his startling personal inflation over the years. Kupelwieser's watercolours capture the exuberance of Schubert and his friends during their summer idylls (1820–22) at Atzenbrugg, much as does the 1894 Bayros group portrait of the Strauss-Abenden in the composer's flat in the Vienna Praterstraße. Exhibitions at Bad Köstritz of the 'Weltbild', focussing on the achievements of distinguished contemporaries of Schütz, cast fresh light on his creative context.

The power and value of the evidence of portraits, many of them directly connected with a particular time and the place in which they now hang, is

'Ein Abend bei J. Strauss' (oil painting by Franz von Bayros)

difficult to overstate. The well-known formal portraits of the four Mozart family members in the Salzburg Geburtshaus date from the 1760s, when the family still lived in Getreidegasse, just as the later Della Croce group portrait on display at the Wohnhaus across the river reflects their changed situation in the 1770s and 80s. Uniquely among composer memorials, the museum in the reconstructed house where Liszt died in Bayreuth celebrates his life through portraits, masks and sculpture. Chronologically arranged and supported by excerpts from his correspondence, they provide a personal context for his music; recorded examples are transmitted through speakers embedded in the walls. Puccini's last portrait, completed just a month before his death, hangs in the Torre del Lago villa; although ravaged by his terminal illness, he is portrayed with great dignity. The transition from life to death is under-lined by the presence of the composer's remains in the chapel a few steps away. Schoenberg's expressionist self-portraits in the Vienna museum challenge the viewer to suspend time and space to meet his gaze.

Other likenesses faithfully reproduce or take inspiration from a few surviving portraits held in diverse collections, many of them private; still others are posthumous portrayals, sometimes imaginative, sometimes inter-pretative. Caricatures may often be revealing, cruelly or benevolently, of quirks otherwise unrecorded. For composers who flourished after the mid-19th century (including Liszt, Wagner, Verdi and Brahms), there are often rich photographic resources. Nowhere but in a few specialist books devoted to the iconography of a handful of individual composers and the occasional signifi-cant anniversary exhibition – such as those mounted by the National Portrait Gallery in London for the tercentenary of Handel's birth or for the Mozart bicentenary by the Historisches Museum der Stadt Wien – are the surviving images so systematically assembled for public view. Composer museums often own or borrow the originals of portraits we normally know only from repro-ductions; many have their own high-quality reproductions of well-known portraits. The smaller, underfunded museums necessarily place great reliance on photographic reproductions for their displays, but these too may yield some surprising images: photographs at Braşov show Dima riding a camel in the Egyptian desert, and at Ērgļi in Latvia the four Jurjāns brothers in their boat, serenading the villagers from the lake with their quartet of french horns.

It has been popular since the 19th century to make plaster and metal casts of pianists' hands. Reproductions of the right hands of Chopin and Liszt can be seen at every shrine to them and sometimes at those commemorating their admirers. Most moving of all is the pair cast from moulds of the hands of the violinist George Enescu, taken late in life and exposing extensive gnarling caused by arthritis.

Sculptures from life and death masks may also effectively reduce the distance between the vertices of the triangle formed by viewer, effigy and subject. The terracotta bust by Roubiliac in the Gerald Coke Handel Collection at the Foundling Museum records the very pores and texture of Handel's face; the approaching visitor becomes aware that he would never dare venture so close were it the man himself. As with Roubiliac's more intimate Vauxhall Gardens statue, 'Handel as Orpheus', one half-expects, half-fears, that the composer will utter one of his pungent remarks at any moment. Death masks, at the time considered an important record of the end of life, may now poignantly convey an image of age and illness, as in the cases of Haydn, Beethoven, Chopin, Liszt, Wagner and many others, and may strike some viewers as a gratuitous invasion of privacy. The juxtaposition of Beethoven's life and death masks in the Bonn museum is arresting. To many visitors the two death masks of Bellini, taken 41 years apart, may seem slightly macabre, exhibited along with documents associated with his final illness, his death, his burial and his exhumation and the purple velvet coffin in which he was initially interred, open for all to see.

Composer museums also collect and display unparalleled collections of images of their subject's families (especially parents), patrons and pupils, friends and colleagues. When arranged chronologically or in relation to the composer's time in the particular house or the locale and the music he was composing, museum displays can offer fresh impressions of the composer and the nature of his life and his circle, until then perhaps only dimly perceived. That is certainly the case for Tansman at Łódź, for example, but also for many other 20th-century figures for whom large photographic archives exist.

The impact of artefacts

Objects once directly associated with composers, even if themselves devoid of musical import, may bring to life the composers' domestic and working environments and shed light on the times in which they lived and their position in them. That is the case with examples of their own artistic endeavours. The proclivities of composers towards the visual arts, an unfamiliar topic, is one that museums are well fitted to serve. The Mendelssohn apartment in Leipzig has offered exhibitions of his watercolours, and the Schoenberg museum in Vienna possesses several of his oils. Čiurlionis was of course a distinguished artist; his work, much of it musically inspired, is fully represented at Kaunas and there are further examples at his family home in Druskininkai. The museums to Alfvén, d'Indy, Egk, Elgar, Enescu, Glinka, Novák, Schmidt,

Schumann and Smetana hold examples of their subjects' paintings or draw-ings; the visitor can also see Martinů's and Donizetti's witty caricatures, the detailed instrument drawings of Melngailis and the doodles of John Lennon.

Handel's interest in art, as a collector (he is said to have owned two Rembrandts), is hinted at in his London house. The collections of objects and fine art amassed by a few composers (notably Ravel, Golovanov, Lehár and Nottara) are as striking as the carefully preserved trivia of others or the apparent lack of feeling for such things evidenced by most. The presence of an original Picasso painting in Falla's modest little house in Granada reminds us of their friendship and their collaboration on *El sombrero de tres picos*. Possessions can be uniquely revealing of acquired tastes and outward values as well as deeply held enthusiasms, although to some extent it is inevitable that the collections as we see them now simply represent what others have chosen, or have been able, to retain. Some personal effects may have passed through the hands of private collectors; others will have remained within the composer's family before finding their way into museum collections.

It is for those charged with their display to rediscover their significance so that visitors to the collections may encounter or experience them much as the composer might have done. At their best, displays have the power to inform our appreciation of music. As visitors, we are free to take away any insights, mental images and associations and apply them to our future experience of a composer's music. In a museum context even copies of relics (or even, where nothing survives or is known, others of the right period and provenance) can be highly educative; in terms of impact, they succeed or fail as much according to their relevance to the displays as by the quality of their reproduction.

While music manuscripts and correspondence are of obvious interest, visitors may be surprised by the power of quite mundane objects to bring the composer to life for them. The display of a composer's clothes offers a particularly evocative illustration of their impact. As music lovers, we are accustomed to seeing the image of a composer as portrayed by a particular artist. The small size of a great man may often take us by surprise: we forget that people in the past were in general considerably smaller than today. When a composer's clothes are shown on mannequins, preconceptions fade. Often an overcoat is hung in an entry hall, with hats, walking-sticks and umbrellas arranged nearby, as if he were at home, perhaps at work in his study. The well-worn slippers at the bedside – as in the museums to Brahms (at Mürzzuschlag), Saar and Einem – remind us they are no longer needed.

We scrutinize his clothes for evidence of a composer's feeling for style, his taste and his degree of prosperity and his vision of himself as well as to acquire a feeling for past events. Liszt's rabbit-fur abbot's hat, Brahms's colourful bow ties and Mozart's decorative buttons hint at sartorial vanity, while the academic robes, uniforms and court clothes of Donizetti, Ziehrer, Hubert Parry, Elgar, Dvořák and Enescu betoken professional achievement. Brand's white laboratory coat and Coward's leisure clothes – smoking jacket and cravat, silk dressing gown and monogrammed slippers – reflect their lifestyle. The macabre sartorial legacies of Donizetti and Dārziņš are difficult to banish from memory. Visitors to Lucerne are invited to revise their impressions of Wagner through an enlarged copy of an 1866 photograph of him sitting in the Tribschen garden, placed apparently alongside the green velvet chair on which he was sitting and the clothes he was wearing. Together, they provide a sharp reminder that Wagner had actually lived here, just as the autograph manuscript of the *Siegfried Idyll* underlines its genesis in the house as a loving gift to Cosima.

While music and its literature are deposited in libraries, and images in a range of media normally reside in galleries, where – except in a dedicated memorial room or building – might one reasonably expect to find assemblages of personal artefacts and other evidence of private pleasures? Where – except in carefully researched biographies – might the tangents with time and place, and the implications for music, be explored? In the grounds at

One of Verdi's carriages at Sant'Agata   *Wagner at Tribschen (photo, 1866)*

Tribschen the visitor discovers the hexagonal stone enclosure built for Wagner's peacocks Wotan and Fricka, and at Wahnfried realizes that Wagner loved his dog enough to be buried with him. Along with the thousands of letters Mascagni wrote to his beloved is the huge picnic basket that accompanied them on their *al fresco* trysts, a testament to their appetites. Even composers have earthly appetites: you can see at Eisenstadt Haydn's recipe for punch, brought from England, Melngailis's fish scaler at Vidriži, Tomášek's nutmeg grater at Skuteč.

Travelling was undertaken more often for business than pleasure, but in its pursuit composers acquired an array of luggage; Mendelssohn had a painted trunk, the gift of his English admirers, and Liszt's cases are decorated with his coat of arms, Tchaikovsky's with his personal monogram. Beethoven's secretaire, a travelling miniature desk, is in Vienna, Donizetti's travelling toilet kit is at Bergamo, Paderewski's portable travelling loo is displayed at Kąśna Dolna and Verdi's fleet of carriages is garaged at Sant'Agata (see p.41). More prosaic are Elgar's cycling maps and Tinel's cycle clips. Travelling virtuosos, including Liszt and even Mozart, took with them dummy practice keyboards, or *Stummerli*, and many had walking sticks, of which perhaps the most notable is the one presented to Liszt by the Pope. Both Mozart museums in Salzburg take due note of his youthful travels: one with a room demonstrating the rigours of the family journeys, the other with an interactive display of his routes. The Brahms memorial at Mürzzuschlag focusses on the composer's love of third-class rail travel and his apparent need to escape Vienna to seek inspiration in nature and to enjoy access to friends.

Evidence of keenness for certain sports and even personal fitness also finds places in composer museums. In the *Tanzmeistersaal* of the Mozart Wohnhaus in Salzburg there is a display of rude shooting targets of the sort the young Mozarts enjoyed aiming at. At Torre del Lago Puccini's hunting gear and some of his taxidermal trophies are displayed. Mascagni, to judge by the photographs, was keen on tambourello, a ball game in which tambourines serve as the racquets. Elgar's golf clubs can be seen in the birthplace. Peterson-Berger's tennis court at the back of his house is still in good order. Taneyev appears to have lifted weights for his health, as too did Falla, whose hypochondriac tendencies are clear from the still amply fortified medicine chest on the wall of his bedroom. Alfvén suspended rings in his study to prepare himself physically for conducting engagements.

The proclivity of composers for rural walks has led to another form of tribute, one that offers the opportunity to follow in a great man's footsteps. Brahms was a keen walker, and there are several country walks marked 'Brahms Weg' near some of his favourite retreats – the Aussee, Meiningen,

Puccini's hunting gear and trophies at Torre del Lago

Mürzzuschlag and by the Rhine at Rüdesheim. There is a 'Beethoven Weg' near Mödling and a 'Gottfried von Einem Wanderweg' close to his retirement cottage at Oberdürnbach, north-west of Vienna. There are similar country walks connected with Dvořák near Vysoká and Smetana at Jabkenice, where he spent his last years. In England, the 'Elgar Route' around Worcester and Malvern is longer and intended for driving (or cycling, his own preferred mode of transport) between Elgar-related sites rather than taking an Elgarian stroll.

   Only in a specialist museum can one discover at first hand that Schoenberg invented an ingenious chess-like game for four players, that Goldenweiser regularly played chess with his friend Leo Tolstoy, or that Elgar loved cross-word puzzles, owned a microscope and became interested in chemistry. Herschel is best known as an astronomer, but few will know that d'Indy had a telescope or that Slavenski, like Herschel, built them. The occult – in the form of tarot cards, astrology and other forms of mysticism – attracted Skryabin, Wolf and Taneyev, and Taneyev both spoke and set texts in Esperanto. Holst took a keen interest in astrology and also in Sanskrit. Many of those who eagerly tapped folk-music traditions in their compositions also collected decorative folk art, notably among them Jindřich (whose extensive collection of art and artefacts of his native Chodsko region is displayed at Domažlice), Bartók, Kodály and Orff. Ravel and Puccini took a connoisseur's approach to contemporary interior design.

Schoenberg's 'Coalition chess'

Occasionally a single object or a group of objects catches the visitor unawares. Beethoven's ear trumpets, graduated in size as his affliction worsened, seem to us pitifully unequal to the task for which they were intended; they are heart-breaking to behold. Similarly, Schubert's shattered spectacles somehow reflect the frailty of his brief life. Not all are so painfully moving. The existence of surviving scent in the mysterious Madame von Meck's vial at her country house in Braïliv stirs the imagination; would Tchaikovsky have been aware of that same scent on his visits? Rimsky-Korsakov's childhood coverlet, made by his mother, at his birthplace in Tikhvin, hints at a vulnerability in someone we always think of as a figure of authority. The presence of ashtrays, pipes, cigar cutters and even the charred ends of cigars alongside the usual desktop para-phernalia remind us that many late 19th- and 20th-century composers habit-ually smoked while they worked. Artefacts that reveal personal foibles offer visitors brief moments of empathy. The objects themselves may be vulnerable: the *chaise* on which Wagner died has threadbare patches after suffering the depredations of generations of souvenir-seekers.

Most music lovers would agree that a major composer's personal posses-sions are worthy of preservation, but few are aware of what survives or where and how they are preserved. Aside from manuscripts, correspondence and images, the earliest example would seem to be Handel's pocket watch, in the British Museum. Mozart's birthplace displays snuff-boxes. His tiny child's

Haydn's octet table at Eisenstadt

violin, his fortepiano and his travelling keyboard are among the earliest known surviving instruments, other than church organs, directly associated with a composer (none of the claimed 'Handel harpsichords' can be shown to be authentic). The dining table that incorporates a series of music stands for octet playing owned by Haydn and displayed at his house in Eisenstadt represents the earliest piece of furniture.

Issues of authenticity

Lovers of classical music will be familiar with the concept of 'authenticity' and will associate it with the movement to perform music, especially from before 1800, using texts that reflect most closely the composers' intentions and the period instruments and performance styles of their day. Extending this pursuit, a few performers have also sought out contemporary venues and donned period costumes to re-create a sense of the original context for the music. The desire to reveal the past, whether through the informed presentation of surviving buildings and artefacts or through faithful representations of them, applies equally to museological sites of historic interest.

The remoter the time, the harder it is to establish associations between buildings and the people who once lived in them. The medieval buildings and architectural fragments connected today with Guido d'Arezzo and Hildegard von Bingen are difficult to authenticate. Neither they nor Palestrina would recognize the renovated buildings and the ruins mentioned

Pavilion Lulli at Sèvres

in the entries for them in this book. Sometimes the association itself is hazy: the pavilion in the rear courtyard of the former porcelain factory at Sèvres, west of Paris, is sometimes claimed as a remnant of a château once occupied by Lully, but there is no record to confirm the legend.

It is rare to find an old building that has not been altered and modernized by successive generations without what we would consider due regard to the building's historical importance. Such work continues at many sites today, sometimes taking note of the hopes of preservation societies in conflict with commercial interests. Sometimes a careful photographic record is kept of renovation work, and great care is taken to investigate the history of the building; this was done with the Handel House Museum in London, to ascertain the probable paint colour when Handel lived there (similar operations were performed, often enabling the visitor to see the successive paint colours on a patch of wall, in the Haydn house in Eisenstadt, the Haydn and Mozart houses in Vienna, and the Berlioz birthplace at La Côte-Saint-André), and panelling of the right period was acquired, from a demolished building, so that the walls could be restored in authentic style. A photographic record similarly documents the restoration of the Dom hudby in Trnava which contains the Schneider-Trnavský museum. The heavy remodelling of the house in which Bartók had a flat has turned it into what is primarily a showcase for 20th-century Hungarian design, folk arts and crafts, with a room for recitals – perhaps more arts centre than composer memorial. The appropriately named Kleinmuseum to Bruckner in Kronstorf appears from the outside to be an 'end of terrace' house, the one in which he lived. But in reality it is more of a bookend than a dwelling, all corridor and staircase: apparently much of his living space has been taken into the neighbouring property.

The location (particularly when the composer has chosen the site), the character of the building, the proportions of the rooms and the original surviving décor can tell us much about the composer. When the exact location of a composer's birthplace or residence is no longer known with certainty, an appropriate local site may serve to represent it, as with Bach's birthplace at Eisenach. Almost half the Beethoven museums rest on insecure foundations of authenticity: no-one really knows whether three of the Viennese museums (the house at Heiligenstadt, the Eroicahaus and the Pasqualatihaus) are on the actual sites where he lived, and the museums to him at Dolná Krupá in Slovakia and Martonvásár in Hungary commemorate visits that may never have taken place. Elsewhere, when the location has proved intractable, different solutions have been found. The tourism-wise residents of Hochburg neatly solved their problem by simply dismantling the Gruber birthplace and putting together a replica near the crossroads in the centre of the town. The Pann birthplace, which celebrates the Romanian national anthem, was also moved to a more convenient position in Râmnicu Vâlcea. In several cases just a composer's study has been preserved or reproduced and re-created in another building (see pp.9–10).

Many houses have fallen victim to the need for modernization and development, not least those in which Bach, Mozart and Beethoven died. Fire, war and revolution have also caused the loss of historic houses. Some have been reconstructed, including Chopin sites in Warsaw (the Krasiński Palace) and Sanniki, the Mozart Wohnhaus, the Glinka mansion, the main house on the Rakhmaninov estate, the Rimsky-Korsakov dachas and the house in Ukraine that Stravinsky built in the early years of the 20th century. Others have been replicated as faithfully as possible, at least externally; still more have been substantially altered to meet immediate needs unconnected with the house's historical significance. Just occasionally a house survives occupying the same role as it did centuries ago: the one at Gneixendorf, north-west of Vienna, where Beethoven visited his brother – departing, in a rage, to his final illness – is still an adjunct to a working vineyard (with, it is believed, the murals that Beethoven saw still gracing the walls of his room). Another house with a remarkable air of authenticity, though not, alas!, a museum, is Paganini's mansion at Gaione, near Parma, now a convent, where his lavish musical décor is not unappreciated by the nuns.

When a building does survive – unless it is quickly established as a memorial site – it will often no longer retain the contents or even the layout that the composer knew. This may offer an invitation to ignore period considerations and create a fresh modern environment for a collection or series of displays (as in the Liszt house in Bayreuth), or to leave the house virtually empty (as in the Verdi house at Roncole). Others may see it as a challenge to re-create plausible period interiors. There may be testimonial, documentary or icono-graphical sources to inform them, or it may be a matter for guesswork, conjec-ture and the tasteful and informed selection of period furniture and artefacts. A historical reconstruction can be an expensive and time-consuming project requiring the assistance of specialist architectural historians. Not many prospective museums can call on the resources of the National Trust in England, which has achieved remarkable results through careful research and planning, with almost no primary artefacts to display, in the Liverpool childhood houses of the Beatles John Lennon and Paul McCartney.

There as elsewhere, the provenance and the status of individual objects on display are not always made clear. Facsimiles are not always identified as such, leaving the visitor to deduce the fact from what they can see. Sometimes, for example at the Chopin birthplace, the unspoken rationale for everything on display is notional. Visitors may not always be alert to the subtle caveats about the authenticity of furnishings and artefacts that are in fact merely 'of the period'. Most of the original furnishings at Troldhaugen were sold after Grieg's death. There are many museums where a hesitant query as to whether the furniture is original is met with the answer that it is of the right period and provenance. There are even some where the original usage of the rooms is uncertain: in the Schubert birthplace in Vienna, one room is claimed as the site of his birth, but if you ask for the evidence, it is simply that, as the warmest room, it is the one his mother is likely to have used for her confinement. Photographs and plaster casts can be assumed to be copies, or copies of copies, as usually are extracts from archival docu-ments; this does not of course affect the significance of their content. However, it strains credulity to accept assurances that every piano said to be in some way associated with Chopin and Liszt was indeed an instrument they owned or even played. Often it is impossible to confirm or refute these claims: items of a personal nature handed down over generations inevitably acquire attributions and anecdotage.

Questions of attribution and authenticity inevitably remain. Surely the primary reason why there is no birthplace museum to Gluck is that no one is certain in which of two neighbouring villages, in 1714, he was actually born: Erasbach or Weidenwang, near Berching in the Oberpfalz, not far from the Czech–German border. A monument was erected in Weidenwang in 1871. More recently a 'Gluck trail' through the village was established, signalled by nine information boards reinforcing Weidenwang's claim. A building in

'Straße B' designated as the birthplace bears a plaque to that effect, though the house appears relatively modern. In 1967 the villagers of Erasbach erected a Gluck memorial obelisk in Beethovenstraße, claiming that as Gluck's father had built a house in the village in 1713, which he sold four years later, the composer would have been born there. Perhaps it is surprising that we don't yet have two birthplace museums. Gluck is honoured elsewhere with plaques and monuments: in the Promenade-Platz in Munich, King Ludwig I unveiled a statue of the composer in 1848; on the front of the house at Wienergasse 22 in Perchtoldsdorf, just south of Vienna, where he lived between 1781 and 1787; and with busts that grace numerous opera houses.

Composers' houses as artefacts

Buildings link us directly with the past. The way a person lives, his or her everyday surroundings and living environment, helps make him what he is. If we are interested in composers' lives, their background and their homes are an essential part of it. To see them, to contemplate *in situ* the daily circumstances of a person's life, is to gain insight into who and what they are. If birth and death places have always enjoyed a certain cachet, the most interesting places, with the greatest power to spark new perspectives, are the houses in which composers elected to live during their mature years and where they were inspired to compose great works. Practical and economic factors weigh on composers as on everyone else; yet, making due allowances, a composer's house or flat will give some indication of his place in the world and how he himself saw it, as well as providing an actual, physical setting for his creativity. Here the visitor may contemplate the circumstances of his life, his status and his opportunities as well as his domestic context. Peterson-Berger's summer retreat on the Swedish island of Frösön is a case in point: to protect his privacy he had secret exits and peepholes incorporated into the plans so that he could see and evade unwanted callers. The limitations of Ježek's near-blindness are starkly exemplified by the blue room in his parents' Prague flat. The miniature scale of Ravel's house at Montfort-l'Amaury, and the shortened legs of Grieg's piano at Troldhaugen, remind us that great composers may be small men who have had to adapt the world to their needs.

It may not be too fanciful to seek reflections of a composer's musical style and philosophy in the houses they commissioned themselves. A number of these were referred to earlier (see pp.10–11), but examples are apposite here too. Some are iconic: Wagner's Wahnfried, Grieg's Troldhaugen and Sæverud's Siljustøl nearby, Nottara's Bucharest flat, Sibelius's Ainola at Järvenpää, d'Indy's 'Les Faugs', Ravel's distinctive interiors at Montfort-l'Amaury, Puccini's villa at Torre del Lago. Still other buildings leave lasting impressions on the visitor that merge with the experience of hearing associated music. That is the case with Gruber and the chapel at Oberndorf, Mahler and his composing huts and even Martinů and the cramped, inhospitable watchtower in Polička where he spent his formative years. Whether they are given special status depends ultimately on the priority accorded to heritage by the owners, the community and the government. A few buildings have sufficient architectural import – the octagonal Radziwiłł hunting lodge at Antonín visited by Chopin, the Bauhaus Meisterhaus in Dessau where the Weill memorial rooms are situated – and/or craftsmanship – Bull's Norwegian island retreat or Ysaÿe's study in Liège – to warrant protection and preservation, not least because of our interest in understanding how they served the creative processes of their most famous residents.

Some of the issues surrounding the establishment of a composer house museum were touched on in the preceding chapter. Houses are oversize architectural artefacts, expensive to acquire and to maintain. Individuals, members of the public, musicians and musicologists alike, may understandably be reluctant to become involved in property management and the legalities associated with collections and public access. In the past, this task has often fallen to widows, descendants, enthusiasts, and dedicated societies and trusts. Clara Schumann's loving custodianship of her husband's legacy and the documentation of the intimacy of their collaboration, sustained by their daughters Marie and Eugenie, ensured the survival of the fine collection now at Zwickau. The Kodály flat in Budapest was set up through the generosity of his widow; Casals's widow ensured that her husband's early home was opened to the public, and Gottfried von Einem's established a museum in his final home at Oberdürnbach. The Stolz and Orff museums were also set up with their widows' help.

There are however a number of composers' houses that for one reason or another survive almost exactly as they were when the composer lived there. The faithfully preserved Kodály flat and the Orff and Einem houses are among them. So are the Sibelius house, lived in by his widow and daughters long after his death, and Lehár's villa at Bad Ischl, bequeathed to the municipality as long as it was preserved intact as a museum to him. Other examples are Skryabin's Moscow flat and Ravel's house at Montfort-l'Amaury, which both look as if the composer had just slipped out; the same might be said of Falla's cottage in Granada, diligently maintained after his departure for Argentina (where there is a museum to him). These time-capsule museums include too Enescu's house behind the Cantacuzino palace in Bucharest, the Golovanov

Verdi's lakeside grotto at Sant'Agata

and Goldenweiser flats in Moscow, the Revuts'ky flat in Kiev, the Nottara house in Bucharest, Ioduţă's flat in Cluj-Napoca, Saar's Estonian cottage and Klemetti's house in Kuortane, mostly dating from around the middle of the last century, often maintained by family members or local enthusiasts. The Holst museum in Cheltenham was founded by his daughter, Imogen. The precise replication of Nielsen's study was effected through the efforts of his daughters, and of the Rimsky-Korsakov dacha at Lyubensk through those of several family members, his granddaughter Tat'yana in particular.

Their importance as architectural specimens is often secondary to their status as artefacts pertaining to the life of a creative musical genius. The visitor is likely to take particular interest in the composer's workplace and the spaces he most valued or developed. Many composers took country walks but others expressed their love of nature through its nurture. All the natural settings of the Scandinavian composer museums are extremely beautiful, and there are also the more cultivated gardens of Verdi's Sant'Agata, with its grotto, lake and avenues of exotic trees, Rakhmaninov's Red Alley, Gruodis's apple orchard and Walton's near-tropical paradise.

Preserving the legacy

The fate of any historic building depends on a variety of factors, but ultimately it turns on the importance attached to it by succeeding generations and the balance between that and commercial pressures, for its use in other ways, its development or its demolition. In the case of a composer's house, such factors as whether it remains in the family, whether there is any record of how the composer lived in it and the extent to which it has been altered will all affect its fate. Most buildings have undergone periods of neglect and then renovation that have destroyed what, from the perspective of a museum that values authenticity, is historically relevant fabric. In practice, the preservation of a composer house often turns on the momentum generated in the run-up to an important anniversary, such as a centenary, for the impetus to renovate and establish a memorial. If long-term financing, management and maintenance are not taken into account the future of the memorial is likely to be jeopardized.

It may then be salutary at this point to consider those composer museums that have not successfully weathered difficult times, or are having trouble in doing so. Several have simply closed. One is the museum to Niels Gade, at Humlebæk, just north of Copenhagen (close to the admired Louisiana art gallery), which was open from 1973 to 1983. Another is the Château d'Egreville, just south-east of Fontainebleau, originally part of an ancient Gallo-Roman villa, which was Massenet's summer home and where in 1912 he chose to be buried; his widow remained there up to her death in 1938, and after World War II it was used by other family members and open to visitors, with some of Massenet's rooms left in their original state. But it was clearly difficult to maintain and in the late 1990s it closed. The last home of Gian Francesco Malipiero, an attractive early 18th-century hillside cottage in the beautiful Alpine town of Asolo, served after his death in 1973 as a Casa Museo Malipiero and as an archive and research centre, but early in the 21st century the archival material was moved to the Fondazione Cini in Venice and the museum was closed, although memorabilia remain in the house and he was buried in the garden. There was at one time a permanent display reproducing the study of the opera composer Riccardo Zandonai in the

Massenet's château at Egreville

Museo Civico in Rovereto, but it was abandoned around the year 2000 and the artefacts were put into storage at the local opera house, the Teatro Zandonai. A museum at the birthplace in Cēsis of the Latvian composer Alfrēds Kalniņš (1879–1951) closed in the 1990s. Some Czech sources list museums in their native towns to Zdeněk Fibich and František Ondříček, but these are pious hopes rather than realities; the town of Soběslav is planning to honour the composer and conductor Otakar Ostrčil (1879–1935), who had a summer home there, with a permanent display including a reproduction of his study in the municipal museum (in the Náměstí Republiky). In Romania, at Leordeni, a museum to Dinu Lipatti, who was a composer as well as a pianist, opened in his former country home in 1985, but in 1999 it was raided by gypsies and largely emptied. The small Salzburg museum to Peter Singer in the Franciscan monastery still exists, but only skeletally: the main musical exhibits were sent to a monastery in the Tyrol for storage. In France, the house of Déodat de Sévérac (1872–1921) at Saint-Félix-Lauragais, in the Haute-Garonne between Carcassonne and Toulouse, was for a time maintained as a museum but the family members living there recently decided to admit no more visitors.

There are a few museums that are closed for the time being, with hopes of reopening. In Grodków, in southern Poland, the birthplace of Chopin's teacher Józef Elsner at 8 ulica J. Elsnera, in the old part of the town, became a museum in 1996 but closed in 2001 for renovation. The house where Szymanowski spent much of his youth, in Kirovohrad in Ukraine, is in poor condition but may in time be used to commemorate him. There was a Mascagni museum in his native Livorno, at via Calzabigi 54, but the space it occupied, the gatehouse of the Biblioteca La Bronica, was needed for the offices of an aquarium and it closed in 2002 pending the allocation of new premises. The Smetana museum at Obříství was severely damaged by the floods of summer 2002 and awaits extensive repair and renovation.

There have long been plans for a Prokofiev museum at his flat in Moscow and its opening, long delayed, is likely in 2005. The cellist Mstislav Rostropovich has worked hard and given generously towards the planning of new museums in St Petersburg to Musorgsky and Shostakovich; others have hopes for a Tchaikovsky museum there, in the flat where he died, and memorial rooms will soon open in his Moscow flat. There are also plans for a Taneyev museum on the former family estate near Klin, which was largely demolished; it would take the materials that at present are exhibited in an outbuilding of the Tchaikovsky museum nearby. In Bulgaria, there are hopes for a house museum to Pancho Vladigerov in the southern suburb of Sofia, where he lived; and in Serbia, at Novi Bečej, a new museum to Josef

Marinković is contemplated close to the site of his birthplace to take the collection at present exhibited in a school. In Zagreb, the flat at 15 Mesnička in the upper town that was once the home of the cellist and composer Rudolf Matz (1919–88), little touched since his widow's death in 1998, may become a museum in due course (he is featured in the city museum, but as a distinguished sprinter; one photograph shows him with his cello but there is no reference to him as a composer). In Switzerland, the marital home of Belle van Zuylen at Colombier, near Neuchâtel, is privately owned but is used for events relating to her and the possibility has been raised of a museum there; and there could at some point be a commemoration of Paul Hindemith at his former chalet in Blonay, now the Hindemith-Musikzentrum. In Germany, there will at some point be a Henselt room in the local museum at his birthplace, Schwabach, near Nuremberg. In France, parts of Poulenc's 16th-century house at Noizay, above the Loire near Tours, are still very much as they were at his death in 1963 and there is at least the potential for a museum at some date. Puccini's last home, a villa he built in Viareggio, is now owned by a foundation which plans to create a museum in it, the fourth to him in the region. Richard Strauss's villa at Garmisch-Partenkirchen is still used by his grandsons but is expected to become a museum after their time, and Dvořák's Villa Rusalka at Vysoká u Příbram, also still in the family, may do so too. So might Ralph Lundsten's lush 'pink castle' overlooking the Stockholm archipelago.

Museums lovingly maintained by a composer's family may not survive their passing unless safeguards have been put in place. Some, such as the Wildgans house at Mödling, are protected by a government edict on properties lived in by national figures: the family and future owners are obliged to maintain it in perpetuity. Part of the flat in Moscow that was once the home of Reyngol'd Glier is maintained in his memory, with his piano, his awards and a massive collection of photographs, but it is also lived in by his granddaughter and her family. How long such memorials as the Lyudkevych flat at L'viv, the Revuts'ky flat in Kiev or Saar's house in Hüpassaare will outlive their present occupants must be uncertain. There are, then, new possibilities, but also new threats.

Taking a longer view

Composer museums present a number of challenges, to their owners and their visitors alike. Most are sited arbitrarily, determined by accidents of birth. Many are in remote country areas, difficult or impossible of access by public transport. Some of their buildings are primitive and ill-suited to public display, and (ironically) renovation would damage or destroy the contact with its celebrated inhabitant that gives the site its value. Often the structure, design and fabric are already changed beyond recognition; only the location will have meaning, and that may have changed radically too. Many rural places of birth, residence or death, however, have often changed little, especially in the parts of central and eastern Europe where many composer museums lie and economic 'progress' has been slow – although that may also mean that the depredations of time will have been worse. Urban sites can be no less problematic because of opportunistic developers: the buildings in which Mozart and Beethoven died, for example, have long since disappeared altogether.

Even where composers' houses are adequately preserved, and are accessible to visitors, it is not often that private houses are fitted to become museums. They are generally too small to accommodate, along with historically significant rooms and display space, the necessary service facilities: offices, stores, shop, cloakrooms and the like, not to mention rooms large enough for musical performances. Several have managed to expand by acquiring neighbouring premises (as with the Handel museums in both Halle and London, the Mozart and Beethoven birthplaces and the Berlioz and Kodály museums), and where land space was available some have built into it, as at Troldhaugen and Klin, but these are the exceptions that prove the rule.

Their ability to expand, and indeed to remain open over many years, depends of course on their financial resources. Many composer museums receive support from local, regional or national governments, and some from established foundations, but many, created by small groups of enthusiasts, are dependent on revenue and private help, and in no small measure on volunteer staffing and assistance. With limited publicity and promotion, they attract only modest numbers of visitors and therefore a very limited income. Many struggle to cover their running costs and essential maintenance. Municipal and regional funding is rarely available to enable improvements. As tourism expands, so do expectations: visitors to composer museums bring with them the experience of a wider, more international spectrum of historic house museums, many of them on a grander scale, better funded and more professionally run.

It is a source of surprise that so few who think of themselves as lovers of music have taken time to visit composer museums; but then, composer museums, or rather composers' homes and the collections they house, are poorly served in the traditional literature of music. Few composer biographies are informative about their subject's place of birth or residence, and any photographs are rarely accompanied by commentary. The importance of place has only lately come to be considered by writers and scholars, perhaps partly through the sense of the visual fostered by television. In the scholarly literature the treatment of commemoration has been little addressed until recently. Isolated examples elsewhere apart, it is the Viennese who have led the way, from Otto Erich Deutsch to Rudolf Klein, H.C. Robbins Landon, Otto Biba and Walter Brauneis, and one may also cite articles on Lully and Paris by Marcelle Benoit and Harrison J. Wignall's *In Mozart's Footsteps*. There are also useful books on musical commemorations in particular cities, especially Vienna, Paris and London, as cited in the bibliographies to the composer entries.

In the circumstances, it is not surprising that the majority of composer museums lack professional curators, let alone ones with the desirable musicological background. Any professionally trained musicians in museums tend to work on collections of instruments, where their technical expertise is essential. There exists an International Committee of Musical Instrument Museums, under the aegis of the International Council of Museums (ICOM), which promotes debate on issues of concern, sharing expertise and raising their institutions' profile. For curators of house museums and 'personality' museums there are further ICOM committees, one devoted to historic house museums and another to literary museums, but none at present for composer museums.

Few European countries have a museum service that offers complete, up-to-date information on musical historical sites. The Czech Republic has an organization in Prague which administers several museums and provides professional expertise to others, and in Russia there is a supervising body in the Glinka State Central Museum in Moscow. If the musical public is poorly informed about these sites, it is partly because curators and owners have yet to establish effective lines of communication with their colleagues. From time to time museums become vulnerable to proposals for other uses for their sites and the resources required to maintain them. And yet, as reflections of national, regional and local cultural identity, they are often the focus of enormous pride. Beyond surveying what has survived to the beginning of the 21st century and encouraging musical tourism, we hope that this book will initiate a more informed debate on how best to safeguard this part of our European musical heritage.

IV   MUSIC ON DISPLAY

Seeing and hearing

Musical museums attract the music lover whose main experience of music is as a listener. If visitors are lucky, they will discover something to give added meaning to their pleasure in music. It may be that the museum is connected with familiar or favourite works, or perhaps that the room in which the composer chose to work, the view from his study window, the singing of birds or the rustling of leaves, may offer some lingering resonance with the music.

Anyone who sings or plays an instrument is accustomed to reading from clearly printed modern editions. It may come as a surprise to see an autograph manuscript, betraying as so many do the signs of the struggle that accompanied the written manifestation of a composition; another may seem to have been set down with evident ease. To judge by their manuscripts, the creative process for Beethoven was an agonizing effort, for Mozart seemingly routine. Whether a manuscript on display is in fact an autograph or a reproduction, the essential connection can still be made between the 'object' and its creative context.

For those lucky enough or sufficiently trained to be able to hear music as they read it, that connection can be immediate. A visitor knowing a work on display may note differences between what can be seen and what is familiar from other copies, and that may increase the awareness of how music is transmitted, adjusted and reinterpreted. For others, the state of the manuscript, the paper on which the composer wrote, the annotations he and perhaps others made later, will in themselves command attention. Signatures on scores may reveal clues to the history and sometime ownership of a particular copy, as too may the bindings or annotations on the title-page or the first page of the music. For other visitors, the composer's calligraphy – often a very personal shorthand – will be interesting as art representing sound, and indicative of the composer's age, his state of mind and even his health, not to say his creative processes. Notated music, of course, is only a visual analogue of the imagined sound, so recordings (especially those involving the composer himself) represent a significant part of the experience of connecting the composition to a specific environment. Facsimiles of manuscripts, modern editions and CDs of music associated with the composer's residence in a house or a region are often available in museum shops.

The sound of music, whether as a background to a personal tour or emanating from listening stations, is an obvious adjunct to a composer museum. Some of the most modern museums incorporate visual projections and video presentations, often including historical film footage, into the visitor's experience. Audio-visual interpretation can be central to the success of these commemorations as visitor attractions, especially when the house or room site lacks a significant collection to display. The birthplace of Handel in Halle provides a recorded tour in any one of several languages. The birthplace of Satie in Honfleur explores the eccentricities of the composer's personality through a series of *tableaux* that rely on portable sound systems to convey music and commentary, spoken as if by Satie himself, and enhanced by lighting and projections, theatrical props and video installations. An increasing number of the larger composer museums make available personal sound systems, usually hand-held, which interact with individual displays; among them are the Mozart Wohnhaus in Salzburg, the Berlioz birthplace in La Côte-Saint-André, and the museums to Smetana in Prague, to Wagner in Bayreuth and to Nielsen in Odense. Video presentations can serve efficiently to summarize the life of a composer as well as to introduce visitors to the museum and to particular artefacts on display; these are usually shown at regular intervals or at pre-arranged times, and sometimes in a choice of languages. The exceptional use of live performers and costumed interpreters to represent the composer and his circle, especially when the performances are of a high standard, may be extremely effective: this is done at the Tchaikovsky birthplace at Votkinsk, with readings (in Russian, but the visitor is handed a summary in other languages) based on family letters of the time.

The impact of context

In the 1990s the Historisches Museum der Stadt Wien renovated all eight of their *Musikergedenkstätten*. In appointing the Viennese-born architect Elsa Prochazka to redesign the exhibitions, they stepped away from individualized period re-creation in favour of a corporate modern design image. The museums – one each to Haydn, Mozart and Johann Strauss, two to Schubert and three to Beethoven – all have the same distinctive museum furniture, with tall stands and much polished wood, though with different colours of wood stain (if it is kiwi green, for example, you know you are in a Beethoven museum): the sense of a dwelling place belonging to a particular era and a particular person is eliminated. This would seem to represent a design philosophy that favours an uncluttered, objective uniformity even if at the expense of atmosphere, individuality and re-creation; the cynical visitor may wonder why such a museum needs to be in the composer's living-space at all. Perhaps the displays devoted to the *genius loci* are planned as a gesture of compensation. Such an approach might well focus attention on the items displayed were it not that the cabinet mechanisms, in the interest of having the visitor 'interact' with the displays, require the lifting of spring-loaded wooden covers to reveal the captions. This is surely tiresome and discouraging; there is no way of taking in display and caption at a glance. It is difficult to see in what sense the memory of the composer is served or the connection with his music enhanced by this gratuitous additional degree of separation between visitor and object.

The interpretation of its collection is part of any museum's present-day *raison d'être*. The most exciting collections carry within them evidence of past contexts. The legacy of Robert and Clara Schumann in Zwickau illustrates this most movingly. Just as their marriage and household diaries offer unparalleled glimpses of a loving, collaborative and fruitful union, so too does their copy of the Beethoven piano sonatas, bearing annotations in both their hands – and the annotations by Robert and by Mendelssohn in a copy of Bach's chorale preludes speak to the two men's collegial friendship (and perhaps their different thoughts on Bach interpretation). In the Donizetti and Bellini museums, the rich collections of musical manuscripts on display include tantalizing glimpses of operas and sketches for uncompleted works. In Prague, the comprehensive survey of Smetana's music includes drafts, versions and music omitted from the final scores as well as evidence of the composer's involvement in the early productions of his operas, limned out in extracts from his diaries.

Many museum displays focus on the music of a particular period of a composer's life, coinciding with his period of residence in the building. That is the case with most of the Viennese museums. It is a policy often pursued when a composer is commemorated in two or more museums, which can represent different phases of his creative life. The museums at Graupa and Lucerne, for example, largely limit their displays to the periods in which Wagner lived in each place.

Presenting music

An assumption underlying most museum displays is that visitors should not be expected to have much practical knowledge of music. Displays installed during the past two decades suggest that people are rather more interested in (and better informed about) history, social history in particular, to the extent that the presentation of the 'house' as 'home' takes precedence over the coverage of music. This is in part a reflection of the interest that musicologists have taken since the 1970s in the wider context for music. It is also indicative of how difficult the display of music as such actually is, calling for specialist musical knowledge as well as the normal skills of museum professionals.

Faute de mieux, the objects of music, especially manuscripts and editions, are apt to be treated as if they were minor works of art. Few would dispute that written or printed music is not usually in itself a thing of great beauty, except perhaps in a calligraphic or typographical sense. There are of course exceptions, such as illuminated manuscripts of the Middle Ages or the Renaissance, or in a minor way the elegant Rococo title-pages of the 18th century and the *Art Nouveau* ones of the late 19th. The external, 'artistic' quality of an object is one issue; its internal or inherent value, in the case of music, quite another. The presentation *vis-à-vis* music represents yet a third. Visitors are usually provided with only minimal clues towards the interpretation of music on display, through labelling and the sequence and groupings in which exhibits are arranged. It is rare for attention to be drawn to particular passages that might be of special interest, or to be encouraged to observe evidence of the compositional process, as for example when making comparisons between versions of a work.

Virtually all museum displays include examples of the composer's manuscripts, elucidated in captions, sometimes in more than one language. Occasionally originals are shown, but usually only for limited periods because of the effect of light on paper and ink and the damage to bindings from leaving volumes open too long at the same place. Facsimiles are increasingly being substituted; the techniques for their production and the replication of period paper are now so refined that it is often almost impossible for the visitor to differentiate them from the original, especially when looking through glass.

Editions, their number and kind, provide insight into the transmission of the music and ultimately its popularity. Hidden between its covers, printed music cannot easily be appreciated when displayed in a glass case. Title-pages may embody interesting information that can be easily read and related to other objects on display, but they are not themselves 'the work of art'. Inside, the printed music represents a stage between the act of composition and its performance and can be viewed only a page at a time or on two facing pages. It is hardly surprising, then, that the display of music can in some senses be disappointing. But alongside musical scores many museums display relevant excerpts from diaries and correspondence, posters, programmes and published reviews of early performances which provide useful, sometimes unique, contextual clues to its interpretation.

There are museums that focus on single compositions, most obviously the Gruber sites. There are two sites for Kienzl's once-famous opera *Der Evangelimann*, the chalet by the hotel at Aussee where he composed it and the museum at Paudorf overlooking the church at the centre of the drama. The displays in the museums devoted to the Romanians Pann and Porumbescu make much of their patriotic compositions, and the Lysenko museum in Kiev emphasizes his nationalist opera *Taras Bul'ba*. The Handel House in London, where *Messiah* was composed in 1741, displays a portrait of the librettist Charles Jennens and a letter he received from Handel referring to *Messiah* that contribute unique details to our impressions of the circumstances of its composition. Other museums that celebrate their association with particular works include Haydn's house in Vienna (*The Creation*), the Bertramka house in Prague (Mozart's *Don Giovanni*), Beethoven's former lodging in Baden (the Ninth Symphony), E.T.A. Hoffmann's house in Bamberg (*Undine*), two Wagner residences, at Graupa (*Lohengrin*) and Lucerne (*Siegfried Idyll*), and the Enescu memorial at Tescani (his opera *Oedipe*). The link between d'Indy's château in the Ardèche and his *Symphonie sur un chant montagnard français* is less explicit, though apparent enough in the light of its setting, and that between Dvořák's lodging at Zlonice and his First Symphony is no more than nominal. Understandably, at the memorial house at Heiligenstadt more emphasis is placed on the famous testament that Beethoven wrote than on the music he composed there, which includes the Second Symphony. A few houses are known by musical sobriquets, but it is worth noting that the displays at the Figarohaus and the Eroicahaus in Vienna are not confined to their eponymous works.

Certain houses come to be associated with a wider creative legacy by virtue of a composer's long residence there. The Handel House in London is again one of these; his 36 years in the same place may constitute some sort of record. Others include Brahms's summer lodging at Lichtental, on the edge of Baden-Baden, and Puccini's hunting lodge at Torre del Lago. Brahms spent ten summers at Lichtental while Clara Schumann resided nearby and many of the works he composed there have links with her circle. At Torre del Lago Puccini worked on *Tosca*, *Madama Butterfly* and *La fanciulla del West*, and

Rakhmaninov wrote his first two symphonies, his second and third piano concertos and his greatest choral works at Ivanovka.

Few composer museums are equipped to mount temporary exhibitions that would enable them to focus on different musical topics. Among the institutions that do so are the Bach and Mendelssohn museums in Leipzig, the Wagner one at Bayreuth, the Grieg at Troldhaugen, the Archivo Manuel de Falla in Granada, the Richard-Strauss-Institut in Garmisch-Partenkirchen and the Schoenberg museum in Vienna. They are able to draw on their own substantial collections and have sufficient visitors, display facilities and resources to develop and promote their exhibitions. The varied approach to each of the exhibitions at the Richard-Strauss-Institut sets a particularly high standard.

Instruments and music-making

The instruments the composer owned and played are usually on display, though very few can be kept in playing condition. (For a fine collection of 'authentic' keyboard instruments with direct links to composers and mostly in playing order, the visitor should go to the Cobbe Collection, at Hatchlands, Surrey; or, for a series of rooms with instruments from different composers' times, to the Kunsthistorisches Museum in Vienna.) Although the 'Neue Haydn-Orgel' on display at Eisenstadt can no longer be played, it remains an object of fascination because Beethoven is known to have played it in the first performance of his Mass in C.

The accepted practice in museums is to differentiate between instruments that have always been maintained in playing condition and those that haven't. Instruments that have remained unrestored are of study value to scholars, instrument makers and 'period' performers, as radical maintenance work or refurbishing would involve the loss of historical evidence. As a compromise, some museums owning historic or generally unusable instruments have commissioned recordings on the original instruments as well as replica instruments, which can of course be played in concerts. But live performances and demonstrations in museums are at best occasional. Most museums lack the necessary facilities and resources. Nevertheless, composers' instruments, like their manuscripts, are closely associated with the creative process and the opportunity to examine and experience in some way these primary artefacts (for example, the piano Holst used when composing *The Planets*) can be one of the lasting thrills of a visit. Several museums preserve recordings, from piano rolls to CDs, of performances by the composer himself.

Holst's piano at the Birthplace Museum, Cheltenham

The experience of hearing works composed on instruments directly connected with the composer and the site is unique. But to the curator, concerts and demonstrations are necessarily secondary to the care and display of the instruments, in the light of environmental factors and the risk of wear and tear. In many instances the size and disposition of the site itself may prove unsuitable for public events.

Musicians have always gathered in their homes to play informally and in particular to read new music. Some museums try to preserve that tradition. Rimsky-Korsakov and his wife held regular Wednesday concerts in their St Petersburg flat and the Goldenweisers inaugurated 'Musical Thursdays' in theirs in Moscow; both continue today. Visitors to the Handel House in London often come across groups of young musicians rehearsing in the room the composer used for the same purpose. When composers had their own houses built they often incorporated large music rooms: there are examples in the houses of three Scandinavians, Bull, Peterson-Berger and Sæverud, and at Wagner's house in Bayreuth. Liszt's studio at the Budapest Academy of Music opened directly into the public concert hall, and his drawing-room in the garden house of the electoral palace at Weimar provided the setting for his summer master classes. (The Budapest Academy flat today houses a variety of instruments, representing the then state-of-the-art keyboard technology: who else would need his dummy keyboard to be a Bösendorfer?) Enescu had access to the more formal surroundings of the Cantacuzino palace in Bucharest and today the stately building in Warsaw housing the Paderewski museum enjoys the facilities of the ballroom for concerts.

For the museum, the most satisfactory solution is an attached, purpose-built recital room. This has been especially skilfully achieved on a large scale at the Beethoven birthplace in Bonn and at Troldhaugen, but many others have smaller-scale recital spaces, most often rooms within the house adapted as recital venues and generally seating about 60. They include those to Bartók, Brahms (Mürzzuschlag), Chopin (the birthplace and several others), Čiurlionis (Druskininkai), Debussy, Dvořák (Prague and Zlonice), Enescu (Bucharest and Tescani), Handel (the birthplace), Kodály, Mendelssohn, Paderewski (Kąśna Dolna), Perlea, Rakhmaninov (Ivanovka), Schoenberg, Schubert (Atzenbrugg), Schumann (Zwickau and Leipzig), Smetana (Jabkenice), Tartini (Piran), Tchaikovsky (birthplace), Verdi (Busseto, the Barezzi house) and Wagner (Graupa). The open air provides another possibility, appropriate to choral folksinging and opera; the Estonians hold choral events near the house of Mart Saar, the Latvians at the country homes of the Jurjāns brothers and Vītols. In Russia, outdoor performances take place in the gardens of the Rimsky-Korsakov dachas and at Rakhmaninov's summer home. In the Czech Republic there are recitals in the garden of the Bertramka house in Prague and in Germany in the garden of Weber's summer home at Hosterwitz. In Italy, at Torre del Lago, close to the Villa Puccini, there is an open-air auditorium for opera. Purpose-built concert facilities flourish near the houses of Falla at Granada, Casals at Sant Salvador and Britten at Snape. It is hardly surprising that so many communities

Interior of the Troldsalen at Troldhaugen, with Grieg's composing hut and the fjord in the background

around museums and memorials often establish annual music festivals and competitions, drawing on the composer's local connections and those to the sites associated with him.

Other resonant artefacts

Many visitors to composer museums will find themselves deeply touched by the implications for music-making of some of the artefacts on display. At Beethoven's birthplace in Bonn it might be the ear trumpets. At Ježek's flat in Prague it might be the large-format manuscript paper and oversized pencils the half-blind composer had to use to see what he was doing. The practicalities are distressing to contemplate and may prompt visitors to reconsider assumptions they have never before questioned. The cryptic messages in Beethoven's and Puccini's conversation books can be seen as further testimony to determined spirits in the face of adversity.

The tools of a composer's trade, the objects usually found on a study desk, help the visitor to visualize the composer at work. Sometimes there will be something quite out of the ordinary, like Janáček's chronoscope or Kodály's field recording equipment. Where composers who collected folksongs are commemorated, the museums usually display their notebooks, wax cylinders and the paraphernalia associated with their collecting forays. Klemetti went on long cycling trips to collect Finnish folksong: his bicycle is still propped up in the porch of his house at Kuortane. Pretty enough as an *objet d'art*, Ysaÿe's Emile Gallé vase is so made that it can also serve as a tuning device (though one imagines that the violinist himself had perfect pitch). Sometimes reality disappoints. We have all read with fascination about Skryabin's use of the

Beethoven's ear trumpets, by J.N. Mälzel   *Kodály's field recording equipment*

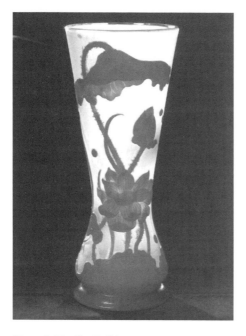

Ysaÿe's Emile Gallé vase

correspondences he perceived between colour and pitches and in particular his use of coloured lamps in performance, but the set on display in his Moscow study could not be described as either quaint or lurid, whatever allowances one might make for the passage of time. There are other charming examples of developing music technology. Two spring to mind, Slavenski's trautonium at Čakovec and Brand's Heath Robinsonian synthesizer at Langenzersdorf.

Occasionally it is something unconnected with music that may prompt us to understand something new, or at least not otherwise widely known, and send us home thinking differently about particular compositions. An autograph manuscript of George Sand's *Un*

Mahler's composing hut at Maiernigg

hiver à Majorque on display at the monastery at Valldemossa lends authority to the legends surrounding Chopin's time there, encouraging the visitor's awareness of the historical context for the composition of such works as the 'Raindrop' Prelude. Mahler's inscriptions 'What the animals tell me' and 'What the flowers tell me' gather meaning around his composing huts, especially the one in the woods above the Wörthersee at Maiernigg, in face of the audible presence of nature.

THE COMPOSER HOUSES
AND MUSEUMS

MAPS

This volume is designed to serve as a guide book. It is intended not only to describe each museum or memorial but also to help the reader to find it. Accordingly, we include a series of maps on the following pages to give an indication of where the museums are. These are not, of course, touring maps, but they should serve to help the traveller, first, in locating the towns to visit (some are too small to be included on all but the most detailed touring maps) and, secondly, in planning a tour or a succession of visits. We have tried to make the maps clear and easy to use by including only capital and a few other principal cities besides the places with museums; on each map page the places are listed alphabetically by country, showing which composers are commemorated at each. A scale is given for each map.

There are no composer museums, as far as we have been able to discover, in Albania, Cyprus, Iceland, Ireland, Luxembourg, the Former Yugoslav Republic of Macedonia, Malta, Moldova, Portugal or Scotland nor in any of the independent European cities. No map of Greece is included: one museum there is on the Ionian island of Zakynthos, to the west of the Peloponnese, and the other is on Syros, an Aegean island south-east of Athens. For reasons of space, areas where there are no composer museums are excluded on certain of the maps.

List of Maps	*Map*
Austria	1
Belarus	16
Belgium	3
Bosnia and Herzegovina	14
Bulgaria	11
Croatia	14
Czech Republic	4
Denmark	13
England	5
Estonia	2
Finland	13
France	6
Germany	7
Hungary	8
Italy	9
Latvia	2
Lithuania	2
Netherlands	3
Norway	13
Poland	10
Romania	11
Russia (European, central)	12
Serbia and Montenegro	14
Slovakia	8
Slovenia	14
Spain	15
Sweden	13
Switzerland	6
Ukraine	16
Wales	5

Map 1 – *Austria*

Ansfelden	- Bruckner	Oberndürnbach	- Einem
Arnsdorf	- Gruber	Paudorf	- Kienzl
Atzenbrugg	- Schubert	Perchtoldsdorf	- Schmidt, Wolf
Baden	- Beethoven	Pörtschach	- Brahms
Bad Ischl	- Lehár	Raiding	- Liszt
Deutschkreutz	- Goldmark	Rohrau	- Haydn
Eisenstadt	- Haydn	Ruppersthal	- Pleyel
Gars am Kamp	- Suppè	St Florian	- Bruckner
Gmunden	- Brahms	St Gilgen	- Mozart family
Graz	- Stolz	Salzburg	- Gruber, M. Haydn,
Hallein	- Gruber		Mozart(2), Singer
Hochburg-Ach	- Gruber		
Klagenfurt	- Koschat	Steinbach am Attersee	- Mahler
Krems-Gneixendorf	- Beethoven	Velden	- Berg
Kronstorf	- Bruckner	VIENNA	- Beethoven (4), Berg,
Langenzersdorf	- Brand		Brahms, Haydn, Kálmán,
Maiernigg	- Mahler		Lehár, Mozart,
Mödling	- Beethoven,		Schikaneder, Schoenberg,
	Schoenberg, Wildgans		Schubert (2),
			J. Strauss, Ziehrer
Mürzzuschlag	- Brahms	Vöcklabruck	- Bruckner
Oberndorf	- Gruber	Waizenkirchen	- Kienzl

Map 2 – *Estonia, Latvia and Lithuania*

| 0 | 100 km |

ESTONIA

☐ TALLINN

Tartu

RUSSIAN FEDERATION

Kaïna ●
(Hiiumaa)

Suure-Jaani
●●
Hüpassaare

● Gaujīena

● Vidriži   ● Jaunpiebalga

● Ērgļi

■ RIGA   ● Staburags

LATVIA

●
Pabiržė

LITHUANIA

Kaunas ●   VILNIUS ■

RUSSIAN
FEDERATION

● Druskininkai

POLAND   BELARUS

ESTONIA	
Hüpassaare	- Saar
Käina (Hiiumaa)	- Tobias
Suure-Jaani	- Kapp family

LATVIA	
Ērgļi	- Jurjāns
Gaujīena	- Vītols
Jaunpiebalga	- Dārziņš
RIGA	- Vītols
Staburags	- Barisons
Vidriži	- Melngailis

LITHUANIA	
Druskininkai	- Čiurlionis
Kaunas	- Čiurlionis, Gruodis, Petrauskas, Šimkus
Pabiržė	- Budriunas
VILNIUS	- Budriunas, Čiurlionis, Vainūnas

Map 3 – *Belgium and Netherlands*

0   100 km

NETHERLANDS

AMSTERDAM ▣

○ The Hague   ● Utrecht

○
Rotterdam

Antwerp
○
○   ● Lier
Bruges   ●
Sinaai

GERMANY

● Harelbeke   ▣ BRUSSELS

BELGIUM   ●
Liège

FRANCE

LUX.

BELGIUM		NETHERLANDS	
Harelbeke	- Benoit	Utrecht	- Zuylen
Liège	- Grétry, Ysaÿe		
Lier	- Veremans		
Sinaai	- Tinel		

Map 4 – *Czech Republic*

Benátky nad Jizerou	- Benda family, Smetana	Litomyšl	- Smetana
Brno	- Janáček	Mariánské Lázně	- Chopin
Čáslav	- Dussek	Nelahozeves	- Dvořák
Domažlice	- Jindřich	Nová Říše	- Wranitzky family
Hradec nad Moravicí	- Beethoven	Obříství	- Smetana
Hukvaldy	- Janáček	Policka	- Martinů
Humpolec	- Mahler	PRAGUE	- Dvořák, Ježek,
Jabkenice	- Smetana		Mozart, Smetana
Javorník	- Dittersdorf	Rožmitál pod Třemšínem	- Ryba
Jihlava	- Mahler	Skuteč	- Novák, Tomášek
Kaliště	- Mahler	Terezín	- Haas, Klein,
Kamenice nad Lipou	- Novák		Krása, Ullmann
Klenčí pod Čerchovem	- Jindřich	Vysoká u Přibrami	- Dvořák
Křečovice	- Suk	Zlonice	- Dvořák

Map 5 – *England and Wales*

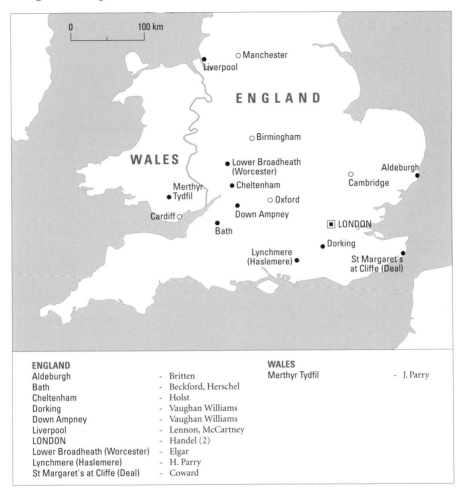

ENGLAND		WALES	
Aldeburgh	- Britten	Merthyr Tydfil	- J. Parry
Bath	- Beckford, Herschel		
Cheltenham	- Holst		
Dorking	- Vaughan Williams		
Down Ampney	- Vaughan Williams		
Liverpool	- Lennon, McCartney		
LONDON	- Handel (2)		
Lower Broadheath (Worcester)	- Elgar		
Lynchmere (Haslemere)	- H. Parry		
St Margaret's at Cliffe (Deal)	- Coward		

Map 6 – *France and Switzerland*

FRANCE
Alboussière	- D'Indy
Dieppe	- Saint-Saëns
Honfleur	- Satie
La Châtre	- Chopin
La Côte-Saint-André	- Berlioz
Montfort-l'Amaury	- Ravel
Nohant	- Chopin

PARIS
	- Charpentier, Piaf
Prades	- Casals
St Germain-en-Laye	- Debussy

SWITZERLAND
Brissago	- Leoncavallo
Lucerne	- Wagner
Morges	- Paderewski

Map 7 – *Germany*

Arnstadt	- Bach	Halle	- Handel (with W.F. Bach, Franz,
Augsburg	- L. Mozart		Loewe, Reichardt, Scheidt, Türk)
Baden-Baden	- Brahms	Hamburg	- Brahms
Bad Köstritz	- Benda, Schütz	Hosterwitz (Dresden)	- Weber
Bamberg	- Hoffmann	Kassel	- Spohr
Bayreuth	- Liszt, Wagner	Koblenz-Ehrenbreitstein	- Beethoven
Bergedorf	- Hasse	Köthen	- Bach
Bingen	- Hildegard	Leipzig	- Bach, Mendelssohn, Schumann
Bonn	- Beethoven	Meiningen	- Brahms, Reger
Brand	- Reger	Munich	- Orff
Dessau	- Weill	Ohrdruf	- Bach
Diessen am Ammersee	- Orff	Teuchern	- Keiser
Donauwörth	- Egk	Wechmar	- Bach family
Eisenach	- Bach, Wagner	Weiden	- Reger
Endenich	- Schumann	Weimar	- Liszt
Eutin	- Weber	Weinstadt-Schnait	- Silcher
Garmisch-Partenkirchen	- R.Strauss	Weissenfels	- Schütz
Graupa	- Wagner	Zwickau	- Schumann

Map 8 – *Hungary and Slovakia*

HUNGARY		SLOVAKIA	
BUDAPEST	- Bartók, Kodály, Liszt	BRATISLAVA	- Hummel
Fertőd	- Haydn	Dolná Krupá	- Beethoven
Gyula	- Erkel	Trnava	- Schneider-Trnavský
Martonvásár	- Beethoven	Żeliezovce	- Schubert
Siófok	- Kálmán		
Szekszárd	- Liszt		

Map 9 – *Italy*

Bagnara di Romagna	- Mascagni	Milan	- Verdi
Bari	- Piccinni	Ortona	- Tosti
Bergamo	- Donizetti (2)	Paderno Ponchielli	- Ponchielli
Busseto	- Verdi (3)	Palestrina	- Palestrina
Catania	- Bellini	Palmi	- Cilea
Celle dei Puccini	- Puccini	Parma	- Boito, Pizzetti, Toscanini, Verdi
Dobbiaco	- Mahler	Pesaro	- Rossini (2)
Empoli	- Busoni	Roncole Verdi	- Verdi
Ischia	- Walton	Sant'Agata	- Verdi
Jesi	- Pergolesi, Spontini	Talla	- Guido d'Arezzo
Lucca	- Puccini	Torre del Lago Puccini	- Puccini
Maiolati Spontini	- Spontini	Venice	- Wagner

Map 10 – *Poland*

Antonín	- Chopin	Skierniewice	- Chopin
Barczewo	- Nowowiejski	Szafarnia	- Chopin
Kąśna Dolna	- Paderewski	WARSAW	- Chopin (2), Paderewski
Łódź	- Tansman	Włoszakowice	- Kurpiński
Poznań	- Chopin	Zakopane	- Szymanowski
Sanniki	- Chopin	Żelazowa Wola	- Chopin

Map 11 – *Bulgaria and Romania*

ROMANIA		BULGARIA	
Braşov	- Ciortea, Dima, Mureşianu	Provadiya	- Obretenov
BUCHAREST	- Enescu, Nottara	Razgrad	- Nenov
Cluj-Napoca	- Toduţa	Shumen	- Vladigerov
Dorohoi	- Enescu		
Liveni/George Enescu	- Enescu		
Lugoj	- Barbu, Brediceanu, Vidu		
Ograda	- Perlea		
Ploieşti	- Constantinescu		
Râmnicu Vâlcea	- Pann		
Sinaia	- Enescu		
Sânnicolau Mare	- Bartók		
Stupca/Ciprian Porumbescu	- Porumbescu		
Tescani-Bacău	- Enescu, Jora		

Map 12 – *Russia (European, central)*

Alapayevsk	- Tchaikovsky
Dyut'kovo	- Taneyev
Ivanovka	- Rakhmaninov
Klin	- Taneyev, Tchaikovsky
Lyubensk	- Rimsky-Korsakov
MOSCOW	- Goldenweiser, Golovanov, (Prokofiev), Skryabin
Naumovo	- Musorgsky
Novospasskoye	- Glinka
St Petersburg	- Rimsky-Korsakov
Tikhvin	- Rimsky-Korsakov
Vechasha	- Rimsky-Korsakov
Votkinsk	- Tchaikovsky
Yoshkar-Ola	- Klyuchnikov-Palantay

Map 13 – *Denmark, Finland, Norway and Sweden*

DENMARK		NORWAY	
Nørre Lyndelse	- Nielsen	Lysøen	- Bull
Odense	- Nielsen	Rådal (Siljustøl)	- Sæverud
		Paradis (Troldhaugen)	- Grieg
FINLAND			
Hämeenlinna	- Sibelius	**SWEDEN**	
Järvenpää	- Sibelius	Leksand	- Alfvén
Kuortane	- Klemetti	Luleå (Ersnäs)	- Lundsten
Loviisa	- Sibelius	Östersund	- Peterson-Berger
Turku	- Sibelius	Saltsjö-Boo	- Lundsten
		STOCKHOLM	- Bellman

Map 14 – *Bosnia and Herzegovina, Croatia, Serbia and Montenegro and Slovenia*

SLOVENIA		CROATIA	
Cerknica	- Gerbič	Čakovec	- Slavenski
Kanal	- Kogoj	Desinić	- Prejac
Piran	- Tartini	Našice	- Pejačević
Šentjur	- Ipavec family	Rongji	- Matetic-Ronjgov
Slovenj Gradec	- Wolf	Samobor	- Livadić
Veržej	- Osterc	ZAGREB	- Zajc
Žalec	- Savin		

BOSNIA & HERZEGOVINA		SERBIA & MONTENEGRO	
Banja Luka	- Milošević	BELGRADE	- Slavenski
		Gornji Milanovac	- Nastasijević
		Negotin	- Mokranjac
		Novi Bečej	- Marinković

Map 15 – *Spain*

Camprodón	- Albéniz
El Vendrell	- Casals
Granada	- Barrios, Falla
Pamplona	- Sarasate
Sant Salvador	- Casals
Valldemossa	- Chopin

Map 16 – *Belarus and Ukraine*

BELARUS		Kirovohrad	- Meytus
Azernï	- Moniuszko	Krasnoye	- Prokofiev
		Kvitky	- Stetsenko
UKRAINE		L'viv	- Lyudkevych
Braïliv	- Tchaikovsky	Tul'chyn	- Leontovych
Horodyshche	- Gulak-Artemovsky	Ustyluh	- Stravinsky
Irzhavets'	- Revuts'ky	Vepryk	- Stetsenko
Kam'yanka	- Tchaikovsky		
KIEV	- Lysenko, Revuts'ky		

ALBÉNIZ

Isaac Albéniz spent only his first two years in the small Pyrenean town of Camprodón, where in 1860 he was born: Barcelona, Madrid, Paris and Nice were his home cities during most of his brief life. But he retained his feeling for his native town, and asked to be buried there; in the event, after his death at Cambo-les-Bains in 1909, he was buried in Barcelona. Camprodón, some 120 km from Barcelona, hilly, attractive, with many old buildings and a large single-span 12th-century bridge over the river Ter, remembers him with an annual festival (inaugurated by Alicia de Larrocha on his 125th anniversary in 1985), a plaque on the building on the site in the central Plaça de l'Ajuntament of the house in which he was born, and with a museum, established in 1999 in a 16th-century building (formerly a police station) overlooking the Ter, close by the bridge.

Most of the contents of the museum came from the family, in particular Albéniz's grandson in Barcelona. The main ground-floor room has a comprehensive display. The piano, the property of his sister Clementina, on which he learnt to play – he made his début at the age of four, and entered the Paris Conservatoire at six – is there, as too is the Bechstein grand given to his daughter Enriqueta as a wedding present by Albéniz's English patron and collaborator, the banker Francis Money-Coutts. Two cases show his baptism and first communion clothing, a bonnet, an embroidered velvet hat, a velvet cloak and his mother's white gloves; another, the Quintet Albéniz and photocopies of his manuscripts; and several have sheet music and letters, some written by Albéniz but also one to him from Granados. On the walls are a portrait by Marqués and a copy of one by Ramón Casas, along with many photos, some of them from his childhood, some with his own family, some with his patrons and pupils. His reading half-glasses, his pince-nez and his ivory letter opener are in a central case, with a collection of commemorative stamps.

There are two rooms upstairs. The larger front one is a bedroom, where his bed, part of a white and gold painted suite, has his monogrammed sheets; over the chairs are draped a black feather boa, a black lace scarf and a white lace jacket. The walls are lined with photos, and above the dressing-table is a portrait of Enriqueta by his other daughter Laura, a painter. In the rear room are several display cases, with more photos, recordings and sheet music, Albéniz's own copies of the piano repertory and newspaper cuttings. It is all clearly labelled, in Catalan (Albéniz was half-Catalan, half-Basque), Spanish, French and English.

Museu Isaac Albéniz
Sant Roc 22
17867 Camprodón
Spain

phone +34/0 973 741166
e-mail ajcamprodon@retemail.es
websites www.ajcamprodon.com,
www.elripolles.com/isaacalbeniz

open Wednesday–Monday 11.00–19.00

Map 15

ALFVÉN

The Swedish composer Hugo Emil Alfvén's house at Tibble, a tiny riverside hamlet just outside Leksand in central Sweden, was specially built for him by public subscription in 1942, to mark his 70th birthday. He moved there with his second wife, Karin, in August 1945; she died in 1956 and he in 1960. Thanks to postwar copyright laws, the royalties from his published works, spanning six decades, have enabled it to be preserved.

Trained as a violinist and then a composer and choral conductor, Alfvén had served for nearly 30 years as *Director Musices* of Uppsala University. His music, mainly choral and orchestral, is post-Romantic in style and was popular in his day. His other creative passion was painting, which he took up in 1887, then dropped for 30 years before resuming in 1922. He enjoyed the good life and he lived beyond his means, travelled extensively, loved many women and married three times. At the age of 74 he began compiling four volumes of memoirs, which he published in the late 1940s and early 50s.

Although born in Stockholm in 1872 and obliged by his post to live for many years in Uppsala, Alfvén regularly spent his summers in the Dalarna region of central Sweden. With his first wife, Maria, he built a home at Tällberg, which she kept when they divorced in 1936; she died only four years later. When their daughter Margita, a film actress, died in 1962, the Tällberg house and its contents passed to Maria's elder daughter from her own first marriage, Wibeke Kröyer, who promptly sold both the house and its contents.

Meanwhile, Alfvén married again in 1938 – though not happily – and in 1939 he retired to the Leksand area. Retirement and the added privations of the time led Alfvén into depression, which was alleviated only in his last years. Shortly after his second wife died, two sisters moved into the house at Tibble to look after the elderly composer. One of them, Anna Lund, had been his lover 50 years earlier and nine months before his death they were married. During those last years, Alfvén lived on advances from his royalties, which after his death his widow channelled into the Hugo Alfvén Foundation. Anna Alfvén died in 1990.

It had been Alfvén's specific wish that the house should become a museum and so, two years after his death, Anna opened it to the public, incorporating items of furniture that she had acquired when Wibeke liquidated the Tällberg property. Open to the public only in summer, the house is used in winter as a retreat for student workshops and rehearsals. Annually, on the first Friday in July, in conjunction with the Lake Siljan Music Festival, a Hugo Alfvén Prize is awarded on the lawn, following a ceremony at his grave in the main cemetery in Leksand and a boat trip downstream on the Österdalälven to Tibble.

Alfvén's two-storey house, built by a local craftsman, is now surrounded by an enclave of similar reddish-brown houses. The back of the house looks down on the riverbank, partly obscured in the summer by leafy birch trees. The entrance hall is lined with pen-and-ink portraits of the composer; in the cloakroom his cape hangs and his extraordinary collection of hats is displayed. To the right is the dining room, with its scrubbed wooden furniture, Swedish linens and Italian pottery; to the left the rustically elegant, stencilled drawing room with some of the items reclaimed from his first wife's estate sale, including an early 19th-century spinet and the 1828 Malmsjö grand piano – which belonged to Maria's first husband and was never played by Alfvén. There are Danish rococo chairs and an antique sofa, Empire armchairs and a glass case of silver, orders and other ceremonial awards. Among the works of art are a large oil painting by Alfvén, two portraits of the composer and his daughter by Kjell Löwenadler, a plaster outline of Mille's sculpture *The Wings* and Mille's portrait bust of Alfvén.

At the far end of the ground floor, through an italianate garden room, is the composer's study, dominated by his own Steinway grand. The walls are lined with bookcases of music (his own manuscripts are in the Uppsala University Library), desiccated laurel wreaths, his self-portraits and watercolours of Lake Siljan and Capri, and photographs of his choirs and his wives. His paints and brushes are neatly stored and editions of his songs are carefully displayed under glass on his desk. Dangling from a beam near the fireplace are two rings that he used to maintain his fitness for conducting. Up the circular staircase are bedrooms and bathroom, and a terrace with a view over the river.

Hugo Alfvén Museum

Alfvéngården
Tibble
79391 Leksand
Sweden

phone +46/0 247 15109, 37165
fax +46/0 245 37115
e-mail info@alfvengarden.nu
website www.alfvengarden.nu

open 18 June–18 August,
Tuesday–Sunday 12.00–16.00; tours
on the hour

Map 13

BACH family

'Bach' means Johann Sebastian Bach to music lovers the world over, and the sites associated with the places in Thuringia and Saxony where he lived and worked form a well-trodden path of pilgrimage. A number of travel guides, in the form of monographs and brochures, containing a mine of useful information such as itineraries and maps, are available from local tourist information bureaux; several are listed below. In addition to museums and memorials, they include places he merely visited, the churches with which he had connections and the organs he tuned. Most however are available only in German.

Many earlier members of the Bach family pursued musical careers, and they too are particularly remembered in Wechmar, Eisenach and Arnstadt. It comes then as a surprise that, apart from a single room devoted to Wilhelm Friedemann Bach in Halle, where he worked for a time, there is no museum or memorial place dedicated to any of Bach's sons. Carl Philipp Emanuel lived in Frankfurt an der Oder in the mid-1730s, and in the concert hall that bears his name there is a small display devoted to him; he might aptly have been honoured by Berlin or Hamburg. Johann Christian could appropriately have been remembered in London.

Wechmar, a small Thuringian town south-east of Gotha, boasts the only surviving original 'Bach house' (called the 'Stammhaus', 'ancestral house'). As early as 1892 a memorial plaque was erected on the building, but it was taken down in 1927 and lost until 1994 when the building was restored and opened to the public. Most of the Wechmar displays focus on Bach family genealogy, incorporating facsimiles of early archival documents, but the little house enjoys a wider remit as a local history museum. The remnants of a bakery on the ground floor, including a working oven and tables and chairs for serving coffee and cake, compete for space with the displays

*The ancestral
Bach house
at Wechmar*

and occasional concerts. The upper floor houses a museum to Thuringian musicians and instrument makers, with a violin workshop and a historic organ among the exhibits.

Members of the Bach family lived in Wechmar between the mid-16th century and the 19th: the earliest verifiable Bach was documented in 1561. The first to live in the house was Johann Sebastian's great-great-grandfather, Veit Bach (c1555–1619), a baker who played the 'cythringen' (the cithrinchen is a bell-shaped cittern, used in north Germany) and who had emigrated from Pressburg (Bratislava) during the Counter-Reformation; the ruins of his mill (the Niedermühle, or Bachmühle), a few minutes' walk away at Mühlenstraße 24, still exist. His son Hans (c1580–1626), a 'Spielmann', and apparently a travelling musician and carpet-maker, settled in Wechmar and died there. Johann Sebastian's elder brother Johann Christoph lived in Wechmar and so, still later, did his grandson Ernst Christian, a Kantor (1747–1822).

More than one strand of the family lived in Eisenach, where Johann Sebastian himself was born on 21 March 1685, the youngest son of Johann Ambrosius Bach, a 'Stadtpfeifer'. The house where his family lived at Fleischgasse 35 (now Lutherstraße) no longer exists. In the 19th century it was mistakenly thought that they lived at Frauenplan 21 and in 1868 that house was designated the Bachhaus; it was bought by the Neue Bachgesellschaft in 1906 and opened as a Bach family memorial museum the following year.

In 1973 a larger museum – incorporating displays of Thuringian social history (furniture arranged in room settings together with typical musical instruments), together with educational, research and performance facilities – was created by connecting it with two adjoining houses. Instruments from the museum's collection of more than 300, from the 17th and 18th centuries, many of them kept in playing condition, are displayed in the room used for concerts and lectures. A statue of Johann

Sebastian by Adolf von Donndorf has presided over the Frauenplan, a large square, since 1884. Eisenach was the home of several other Baroque composers – Johann Pachelbel, Daniel Eberlin, Pantaleon Hebenstreit and Georg Philipp Telemann (he lived at Markt 16) – who held posts at the ducal court at various times. In addition to the annual Thüringer Bach-Wochen and Eisenacher Bach-Tage in March there are biennial Telemann-Tage in June.

In 1695, after their father's death (their mother had died the previous year), Johann Sebastian and his brother Johann Jacob were sent to Ohrdruf to live with their eldest brother, Johann Christoph, organist at the Michaeliskirche; he was there for five years and is said to have had his first music lessons there. A memorial plaque claiming Bach's residency marks the long supposed Bach house, in what was formerly the Schulgasse and is now the Johann-Sebastian-Bach-Straße. But contemporary maps show no street corresponding to the part of it in which the house now stands – it is in an extension, added only after a fire had consumed much of the town in 1753 – and local scholars believe that the Bachs in fact lived in a house in the adjoining Lappengasse, now no.5, which clearly has been somewhat rebuilt over three centuries. The tower of St Michael's, restored in 1999 and all that remains of the church after wartime destruction, is visible down Johann-Sebastian-Bach-Straße. At Schloß Ehrenstein there is a small Heimatmuseum, a museum of local history, which (besides an exhibition of rocking-horses, a local industry) devotes one room and parts of two adjoining areas to Bach. There are original school registers, showing his position in the class, and the matriculation book in which his departure to Lüneburg (when his brother no longer had room for him) is noted, as well as a letter of 1690 from his brother and a report of 1693, by Pachelbel, on the Michaeliskirche organ along with the book recording organ repairs. An original 17th-century pigeonhole rack for rolled-up documents shows how Bach as a child could have purloined his brother's music manuscripts, as related in the famous anecdote. There are also records of later Bachs in Ohrdruf, where members of the family survived up to 1933.

Bach got around a good deal, and in various parts of northern, eastern and central Germany there are plaques recording his one-time presence: on the St Michael's church at Lüneburg where as a young man he was a chorister, on St Bartholomew's church in Dornheim (just east of Arnstadt) where in 1707 he and his cousin Maria Barbara Bach were married, and on St Blasius's church in Mühlhausen where he was briefly organist in that year, as well as on the site in Weimar (Markt 16) of his house, next to the Elephant Hotel, where Wilhelm Friedemann was born in 1710 and Carl Philipp in 1714 (had it survived, like the Goethe and Liszt houses nearby, it too would surely have become a museum).

Several other members of the Bach family – including the family of the organist Johann Michael, who became Johann Sebastian's father-in-law – lived and worked in Arnstadt throughout the 17th and 18th centuries; 25 of them are buried there. The Neue Kirche – in the corner of the marketplace, near the Rathaus – where Johann Sebastian was organist between 1703 and 1707 has been known since 1937 as the Bach-Kirche; just in case there was any doubt, his portrait nestles among the pipes of the early 20th-century organ now in use. Houses with a Bach connection still survive at Kohlgasse 7 and Ledermarkt 7; Johann Sebastian probably lived at the latter, possibly both.

Most of the ground floor of the local history museum, the 'Haus zum Palmbaum', is devoted to the Bach family. Two rooms chronicle the lives of several earlier members of the family who worked in Arnstadt, with reproduced documents, family trees, and a series of large books in which facsimiles of documents are shown, with transcriptions and explanations opposite – they cover not only the Bachs but also their contemporaries among other Arnstadt musicians and local musical activities more generally. In the room devoted to J.S. Bach himself stands the original organ console installed in the Neue Kirche in 1703 and used in Bach's time there. There are various documents relating to his life, including his appointment, his marriage, his notorious journey to Lübeck and his letter of resignation, and also an account of the local court and the hierarchy of the musical establishment in Arnstadt during Bach's years there. The tercentenary of his birth in 1985 was celebrated with the erection in the marketplace of a statue of the young Bach by Bernd Gröbel.

In 1717 Johann Sebastian left his court post at Weimar for one in Köthen (then spelt 'Cöthen'). It is not known where he and his family lived, only that his first wife died there in 1720, but the castle where he worked survives. The throne room, its wall lined with mirrors, must have been where the court orchestra performed and where early versions of the Brandenburg Concertos Bach composed in Köthen might have been heard. Until 1996 there was a Bach exhibition in the local Historisches Museum, but that gave way to a larger one in the castle museum. In the collection are original letters from Carl Philipp Emanuel to his publisher and a copy of a vocal partbook for one of their father's cantatas in Wilhelm Friedemann's hand. The state rooms – in which presumably Bach sometimes performed with

The castle at Köthen

Thomaskirchhof and former Thomasschule in Leipzig

Prince Leopold and his musicians – are large and splendid, although there is not a great deal in them now that is strictly relevant to Bach. Since 1983 concerts have been given in the castle in the Bachsaal, a highly decorated room (seating 270) above the 1730 chapel, itself reconstructed and restored in 1991 with its fine late Baroque gallery together with its 1754 Zuberbier organ. In 1885, on the bicentenary of Bach's birth, a bust by Heinrich Pohlmann was erected in the Bachplatz in the town.

Bach spent his last 27 years in Leipzig, moving there in 1723 on his appointment as Thomaskantor, in charge of music at the Thomasschule, and director of music at both the Thomaskirche and the Nikolaikirche, where many of his cantatas and the Passions were first performed. He, his second wife Anna Magdalena Wilcke and their family took up residence in the school, adjacent to the Thomaskirche; the Thomasschule, alas, disappeared in 1902, but the church itself still stands, thanks to restoration and rebuilding. Bach's tenure there is commemorated by a large statue near the entrance, by Carl Seffner, erected in the Thomaskirchhof in 1908 (nearby there is an earlier Bach memorial bust, by Eduard Bendemann, in the public gardens of the Dittrichring, whose erection in 1843 was organized by Mendelssohn); inside, beneath the floor of the choir, is the grave containing what are supposed to be his remains, moved from the Johanniskirche cemetery after their 'authentication' in 1894.

Directly across the street, the 400-year-old Bosehaus at Thomaskirchhof 16 has served since 1985 – it was opened on the tercentenary of his birth – as the Johann-Sebastian-Bach-Museum. In Bach's day it belonged to the Bose family, who were merchants dealing in precious metals. The café a few doors away serves to remind pilgrims of Zimmermann's café (the site is marked by a plaque in Katherinenstraße), where Bach's *collegium musicum* used to perform and for which much of his chamber music and many of his concertos were composed.

The Leipzig Bach Museum is one of a group of museums administered by the city and it benefits from their combined resources, which include the Thomasschule collection of Bach autographs and other important Bachiana (including further manuscripts and early printed editions), as well as the famous 1746 portrait by Elias Gottlob Haussmann – the only certainly authentic representation of the great man. The museum displays, in five rooms on the first floor (one of them devoted to changing exhibitions), are neatly and logically organized. The entry room is concerned chiefly with the Thomasschule and Bach's role there, portrayed on glass panels, with some characteristically German touches of wit. A second room pictures his contemporaries, pupils and successors. Another room charts the lives of Bach's sons and some of his other relatives, and the next explains Bach's responsibilities as *Director Musices* and the history of the position of Thomaskantor (a map shows how Bach's pupils, and his influence, travelled after his death). There are early editions of his music. At the rear there is an attractive chamber music salon, which together with the adjoining rooms displays the city's fine collection of period keyboard instruments.

In 1950, on the bicentenary of Bach's death (28 July 1750) – long before the museum was founded – the Bach-Archiv Leipzig was established in the Bosehaus.

Now the leading centre of Bach scholarship and research, it curates the collection (which in addition to primary sources includes extensive collections of microfilms and Bach bibliography) and is responsible for mounting the regularly changing exhibitions in the museum; it publishes the *Bach-Jahrbuch* and is involved with the Bach-Institut in Göttingen in producing the new critical edition of Bach's music, the Neue Bach-Ausgabe.

It should be noted that Bach's coffee-house music-making in Leipzig is commemorated, not on the original Zimmerman site, destroyed in World War II, but in the Coffee-Baum opposite the Rathaus (said to have been Schumann's favourite coffee-house), where there is a small display on the top floor, chiefly concerned with the Coffee Cantata.

Ironically, it is in the Händel-Haus in Halle, which also serves as a museum of local musical history, that Wilhelm Friedemann Bach is commemorated. Born when his father was in Weimar, in 1710, he had lived in Köthen and Leipzig with his family and in 1733 took the position of organist at the Sophienkirche in Dresden. In 1746 he moved to Halle as organist of the principal church, the Liebfrauenkirche or Marktkirche, and *Director Musices* of the city, regarded as one of the most important organist's posts in Germany (and one his father had earlier coveted). But Pietist Halle did not suit him and he relinquished the post in 1764, though he remained in the city until 1770, living at Grosse Klausstraße 18, just off the Marktplatz; he died in Berlin in 1784. In a room on the second floor of the Händel-Haus, his Halle years are commemorated with a number of facsimile manuscripts and printed items and with the characterful portrait of him by Friedrich Georg Weitsch, in his fur-lined coat and black hat, where his sardonic smile and gleaming eyes make it all too clear that Halle was not the place for him. The naming of the square in front of the Moritzburg after W.F. Bach

perhaps shows that Halle has forgiven this gifted son of the great man.

Bach-Stammhaus Wechmar

Bachstraße 4
99869 Günthersleben-Wechmar
Germany

phone, fax +49/0 3625 622680
e-mail gv-guenthersleben-wechmar@t-online.de

open Wednesday–Sunday 13.00–17.00
or by appointment

Bachhaus

Frauenplan 21
99817 Eisenach
Germany

phone +49/0 3691 79340
fax +49/0 3691 793424

open April–September,
Monday 13.00–18.00,
Tuesday–Sunday 09.00–18.00;
October–March, Monday 13.00–17.00,
Tuesday–Sunday 09.00–17.00

Museum im Schloß Ehrenstein

Schloßplatz 1
99885 Ohrdruf
Germany

phone +49/0 3624 402329
fax +49/0 3624 313634
e-mail schloss.ehrenstein@ohrdruf.de

open Tuesday–Thursday 12.00–16.00,
Friday and Saturday 09.00–12.00,
13.00–16.00,
Sunday 10.00–12.00, 13.00–16.00

Bachgedenkstätte:
Stadtgeschichtsmuseum Arnstadt
'Haus zum Palmbaum'

Markt 3
99310 Arnstadt
Germany

phone, fax +49/0 3628 2978
e-mail haus.zum.palmbaum@t-online.de

open Monday–Friday 08.30–16.30,
Saturday, Sunday and holidays
09.30–16.30

Bach-Gedenkstätte Schloß Köthen und Historisches Museum für Mittelanhalt

Schloß Köthen
Schloßplatz 4
06366 Köthen/Anhalt
Germany

phone +49/0 3496 212546
fax +49/0 3496 214068
e-mail koethenerherbst@t-online.de
websites www.kulturstatten.koethen.de,
www.koethenerherbst.de

open Tuesday–Friday 10.00–17.00,
Saturday and Sunday 10.00–13.00,
14.00–17.00

Johann-Sebastian-Bach-Museum Leipzig

Die Bosehaus
Thomaskirchhof 16
04109 Leipzig
Germany
(postal address PF 101349, D–04013 Leipzig)

phone +49/0 341 964 4135
fax +49/0 341 964 4122
e-mail museum@bach-leipzig.de
website www.bach-leipzig.de

open daily 10.00–17.00; tours, weekdays at 11.00 and 15.00 or by arrangement

(W.F. Bach)

Händel-Haus
Grosse Nikolaistraße 5
06108 Halle (Saale)
Germany

phone +49/0 345 500900
fax +49/0 345 50090 411
e-mail haendelhaus@halle.de
website www.haendelhaus.de

open daily 09.30–17.30 (Thursday to 19.00)

Map 7

I. Domizlaff: *Das Bachhaus Eisenach* (Eisenach, 1984)
W. Felix and others: *Johann-Sebastian-Bach-Museum Leipzig im Bosehaus: Bach in Leipzig: Leben – Wirken – Nachwirken* (Leipzig: Nationale Forschungs- und Gedenkstätten Johann Sebastian Bach der DDR, 1985)

C. Oefner, I. Lehmann, W. Wenke: *Bachhaus Eisenach* (Munich, 1991)
M. Gretzschel and G. Jung: *Auf Johann Sebastian Bachs Spuren* (Hamburg, 1993)
K. Kreuch: *Die Urväterheimat der Musikerfamilie Bach* (Wechmar, 1994)
Thüringer Landesfremdenverkehrsverband e. V.: *Johann Sebastian Bach aus Thüringen* (Erfurt, 1995)
M. Boyd, ed.: *J.S. Bach: Oxford Composer Companions* (Oxford: Oxford University Press, 1999) [NB the entries for cities associated with J.S. Bach]
M. Petzoldt: *Bachstätten: ein Reiseführer zu Johann Sebastian Bach* (Frankfurt am Main and Leipzig: Insel, 2000)

The Allgemeine Deutsche Automobil-Club publish a map with a Bach chronology and descriptions of all relevant Bach sites: 'Unterwegs mit J.S. Bach in Thüringen, Sachsen-Anhalt und Sachsen'.

BARBU

The Casa Muzicii in Lugoj, a town in western Romania with a particularly vital tradition of choral music-making, has a number of memorial rooms dedicated to the different composers associated with the town. Filaret Barbu, a native of Lugoj (he was born there in 1903), has perhaps the strongest claim of all, since the actual house was his. He died in Timișoara, where had he spent his last years, in 1984; the next year the Casa Muzicii moved to the house, owned then by the state.

The house is just across the river from the main part of Lugoj. There is a display for Barbu, a choral conductor and operetta composer and a pupil of Ion Vidu, in the main room on the ground floor, with posters, pictures and programmes of the Corul Ion Vidu, of which he was conductor for many years (*see* VIDU). He also shares a room on the upper floor with the tenor Traian Grozăvescu (1895–1927), another eminent Lugojan whose international operatic career was cut short when he was murdered by his wife in a *crime passionel*; the local theatre bears his name. The Barbu exhibits include an oil portrait and a death mask, his small harmonium, a table with such personal items as his glasses, his tuning-fork, his cloth cap and his writing implements, as well as pictures of the Corul Ion Vidu under his direction.

Casa Muzicii
Str. Magnoliei 10
1800 Lugoj
Timiş
Romania

phone +40/02 56 354903
website
www.infotim.ro/patrimcb/tm/lugj/muzieap/casamuz

open 15 May–14 October, daily 09.00–17.00; 15 October–14 May, daily 08.00–16.00

Map 11

BARISONS

Pēteris Barisons came from a farmstead at Staburags, in rural Latvia, and the museum in his memory is not easy to find. You need to start from Aizkraukle, a small town on the river Daugava in the south of the country (the site of Aizkraukles Mūzikas Skola Pētera Barisona), cross the river and drive east some 19 km, along a dirt-track road; then, to the right, four kilometres along another rudimentary road and then a right fork for just over a kilometre. There are fingerposts to the farmhouse, Skudras, which Barisons himself built in the 1920s (the original house, in which he was born in 1904, was destroyed in World War I). The farmyard serves as a car park.

The museum was established on the upper floor in 1974, on the 70th anniversary of Barisons's birth. Barisons spent most of his professional life in Riga, where he was a professor at the conservatory and a choral conductor, but he returned to Staburags for the summers, and his son Gunras (himself a composer, working in Riga) was born there in 1946. Pēteris however died the next year, still in

his early 40s. He wrote orchestral music, including three symphonies, but his chief contribution was choral – as a local group, of six ladies in Latvian folk costume, charmingly illustrated by singing some of his folksong settings for our benefit.

Barisons is commemorated in two rooms. In one are posters, programmes, photographs and music facsimiles, and his own square piano, from Germany; the other, rather larger, is fitted out as a simple bedroom, with a dummy keyboard he made, photographs evoking his life in Riga, his baton and his autograph book, a portrait of Beethoven and a photograph of his teacher Vītols, and a piano. It is a modest display, but touching, and clearly important to the locals, proud of Staburags' son who helped raise the musical flag of Latvia.

Pētera Barisona Muzejs
Skudras
Staburags
5128 Aizkraukles rajons
Latvia

phone +371/0 825 144357

open by appointment

Map 2

BARRIOS

Within the complex of buildings, ancient and modern, that constitute the Alhambra in Granada lies an old Arab bathhouse, dating from the beginning of the 14th century; and within that lies the site of the former tavern El Polinario, which during the late 19th and early 20th centuries was a meeting-point for people in the city's artistic circles. There Antonio Barrios, himself known as 'El Polinario', played his flamenco guitar, and his son, Ángel Barrios Fernández, was born in 1882. Ángel Barrios went on to a musical career, studying in Paris, where he was a friend of Albéniz, Granados, Falla and Ravel, later establishing a Trío Iberia (guitar, lute and bandurria, for which he adapted a large Spanish repertory) and touring Europe with it. He divided his time between Granada – where in the late 1920s he was professor at the university and musical head of the Centro Artistíco, and during the Civil War director of the Banda Municipal and the Falange symphony orchestra – and Madrid, and after his father's death in 1939 he settled in the capital, enjoying modest success as a theatre composer. He died there in 1964.

When Barrios left Granada, he gave the house to the Patronato del Alhambra, and when in 1939 the Arab baths were restored it was demolished. But the tavern site was adapted to take a house museum, and in 1977 the Casa Museo Barrios opened there. Barrios's daughter Ángela, goddaughter of Falla and his sister, had presented the city with the entire art collection from the former tavern as well as much documentary and photographic material, an archive and several musical instruments. There are three display rooms with objects pertaining to Barrios and his family, including his own piano and guitar, various items of furniture and many photographs and documents. But what makes this composer museum unlike any other is the presence of an art collection of high quality, much of it contributed originally to El Polinario by the artists themselves, including Santiago Rusiñol and Manuel Ángeles Ortiz.

Casa Museo Ángel Barrios*
Calle Real de la Alhambra
18009 Granada
Spain

phone +34/0 958 027900 (Patronato de la Alhambra; tourist office, 221022, 225990)
fax +34/0 958 226363
e-mail otgranada@andalucia.org (tourist office)
website www.alhambra-patronato.es

open only when featured on the Alhambra 'Espaces del mes' schedule; enquire in advance

Map 15

M. Orozco Días: 'El Museo de Ángel Barrios en la Alhambra', *Revista de Museología*, no.14 (1998), 65

BARTÓK

Béla Bartók was born on 25 March 1881 in a far corner of the Austro-Hungarian Empire: today Sânnicolau Mare (in Hungarian Nagyszentmiklós, in German Gross Saint Nikolaus) is part of Romania, a few kilometres from the Hungarian border. His father was head of the local school for peasant children. A bilingual plaque, in Romanian and Hungarian, marks the house that now occupies the site of his birthplace, on the western edge of the town, at Strada Cerbului 3. Sânnicolau Mare further commemorates Bartók with a bust and, since 1981, an exhibition emphasizing his Romanian connections, which in 1998 was moved to a bright, spacious room in the local history museum (formerly the town's manor house). The displays include pictures of his family and of the town where he lived until he was eight; examples of his folksong collecting, along with his correspondence with the Romanian ethnomusicologist Constantin Brăiloiu; copies of the Romanian folk music he edited as well as the music it inspired him to compose; a summary of his connections with other Romanian musicians (notably George Enescu) and cities (Arad, Braşov, Bucharest, Cluj, Lugoj, Oradea and Timişoara); and publications about Bartók in Romanian and Hungarian.

In 1907 Bartók took up a piano professorship at the Budapest Academy of Music. From 1932 to 1940 he and his family lived in the hillside suburban villa in Buda, at Csalán út 29, now open to the public in his memory. They occupied the first-floor flat, with one Bechstein and two Bösendorfer pianos. Bartók gave private lessons and rehearsed at home for his concerts, all the while composing: he produced the Fifth String Quartet in 1934, Music for Strings, Percussion and Celesta in 1937, the Violin Concerto and *Contrasts* (for Joseph Szigeti and Benny

Bartók's house in Buda

Goodman) in 1938 and Divertimento for Strings (for Paul Sacher) in 1939.

To visit the Bartók house, take the No.5 bus from the city centre to the end of the line (Pasaréti tér), and walk onwards up Csévi utca to where it meets Csalán út: No.29 will be immediately in front of you. Here, in a relatively rural setting, Bartók sought refuge from the bustle of the city. Shortly afterwards, in 1934, he retired from the Academy; at the same time he undertook to edit the Hungarian folksong collection of the Hungarian Academy of Sciences.

In spite of the beauty of the Buda neighbourhood where Bartók lived, it did not turn out to be entirely tranquil. The hill was used by motorcycle racers for training sessions (there was a strategic hairpin turn just in front of the house) and in 1936 the plot on which the villa stands was divided and permission was granted for houses to be built on either side. In a vain attempt to combat the noise of it all, Bartók had the veranda door upholstered.

At the same time, Hungary was becoming politically inhospitable to him. He was under attack from the Hungarian and Romanian press for his anti-fascist views, and he refused to have his works performed in Germany and eventually even in Budapest; from 1937 he forbade the broadcasting of his music in Germany and Italy. He abandoned his publishers Universal Edition, now taken over by the Nazis, for Boosey & Hawkes. After his mother's death in December 1939, he left Hungary.

In 1981, just over 40 years after Bartók's departure for New York (where he died in 1945), and on the centenary of his birth, the City of Budapest opened his former home as a museum and cultural centre. For this purpose the villa, built in 1924, was substantially altered by the architect György Fazakas. A stairwell was added to the side and an administrative wing to the back. A small amphitheatre for open-air concerts was sculpted in the front garden, presided over by a characterful life-size statue of the composer by Imre Vagra. The main entrance was decorated with an organ-pipe motif by the goldsmith József Pölöskei. The ground floor, once the concierge's flat, now serves as the reception area; a portrait was commissioned from István Fillenz for the foyer and, to adorn the admissions kiosk, a map of the planet Mercury featuring the crater named after Bartók from Sándor Mester. With the exception of an 18th-century painted wooden ceiling panel installed in the large first-floor recital room, the house is intended to serve as much as a showcase for modern Hungarian design as a memorial to the country's greatest 20th-century composer. It plays host to conferences and concerts, attracting large numbers of performers and visitors from abroad.

The composer's elder son, Béla, remained in Budapest in 1940 and took responsibility for maintaining his father's personal effects, which now belong to the city; he helped to fund the reconstruction of the villa to create the museum. The two second-floor rooms used by the composer and his family are today once again furnished with carved and decorated folk pieces made for Bartók as early as 1907 by the Transylvanian craftsman György Gyugyi Péntek, who also made pieces for Kodály. Like Kodály, Bartók collected pottery and textiles as well as folksongs and these too are on display. In an adjoining room there are more traditional museum displays, addressing his life and work, showing not only of Bartók as a composer but equally his achievement as a scholar and performer.

However, it would be an exaggeration to suggest that Bartók's own world was in any way re-created in the museum. The villa has no formal link with the distinguished Bartók Archivum (housed with the Museum of the History of Music in the Erdődy Palace on Castle Hill, overlooking the Danube) where much of Bartók's manuscript legacy is preserved (there are also Bartók archives in New York and in Brussels, the Fonds Denijs Dille at the Bibliothèque Royale de Belgique).

Expoziţia Béla Bartók

Castel Nako
Strada Republicii 15
1976 Sânnicolau Mare
Romania

phone +40/02 5623 0042

open Monday–Friday 08.00–21.00, Saturday 08.00–15.00

Bartók Béla Emlékház

Csalán út 29
1025 Budapest II
Hungary

phone +36/0 394 2100
fax +36/0 394 4472
e-mail bartok-1981@axelro.hu
website www.bartokmuseum.hu

open Tuesday–Sunday 10.00–18.00

Maps 11, 8

M.M. Strack and L. Somfai, eds.: Béla Bartók Memorial House (Budapest: Budapest History Museum, 1981)

H. Kretschmer: *Wiener Musikergedenkstätten* (Vienna: J & V Edition, 3/1992)

J. Vadas: 'Béla Bartók: Shrine to a Great Composer', *Courier Diplomatique*, no.5 (July 1993), 20–21

BECKFORD

The inclusion of William Beckford here may raise eyebrows. Music was one of the ruling passions of his privileged life and composition one of his leisure pursuits. He is best known as author of the 'oriental' novel *Vathek*, although he also published diaries of his European tours with numerous references to the musicians he met and heard. Born in London in 1760, he was the son of Alderman Beckford, who left him a vast legacy of sugar plantations in Jamaica as well as Fonthill Splendens, the family estate in Wiltshire. Beckford claimed to have had music lessons from Mozart in Frith Street, during the Mozarts' visit in 1764–5; the family townhouse was in nearby Soho Square. According to Beckford, his father invited the Mozarts to Fonthill.

Beckford was a high tenor, said to have sung castrato arias in their original keys, and an accomplished harpsichordist, pianist and organist. He was passionate about Haydn and Mozart and opera and counted many famous singers among his acquaintances. His own compositions, mainly from the 1780s, include only one published work (an overture to the ballet *Phaeton*, which appeared in Paris in 1781–2); only a handful survive, including an 'Arcadian Pastoral' given privately in London in 1782.

Architecture was another of his preoccupations. Unencumbered by financial restraints, he commissioned James Wyatt to design a Gothick ruin for Fonthill in 1790; the result was Fonthill Abbey. Beckford filled it with art treasures, mainly French, opportunely acquired in Paris in 1789. He eventually tired of his grandiose folly and in 1822 sold it; three years later the central tower collapsed, for the second and last time.

In 1822 Beckford moved to Bath, buying two intercommunicating houses, nos.19 and 20 Lansdown Crescent. He also bought land behind the Crescent, extending uphill for a mile. He rode up to the top each day and from the beginning intended to build a tower from which to contemplate the surrounding countryside. He commissioned Henry Goodridge to produce plans for a 120-foot tower, inspired by Italian and Greek models, with a belvedere and lantern at the top and a two-storey building at its base; by 1827 the exterior was completed. The 'Belvidere', with its 12 plate glass windows, is reached by a circular stone staircase of 154 steps, from which 53 wooden steps ascend through an octagonal lantern to the cast-iron cupola. Beckford thought it gave 'the best prospect in Europe'.

The building at the bottom was always more museum than dwelling. He filled the rooms with art including paintings by Titian, Raphael and Canaletto, drawings by Rubens and engravings by Rembrandt and Dürer, and portions of his extensive library. The Scarlet Drawing Room on the ground floor provided a setting for his finest china. Beckford's love of music continued undimmed: his collection of instruments in Lansdown Crescent included an upright grand piano (possibly a Broadwood) and several string instruments, including a 1647 Stradivarius violin.

After Beckford's death at the age of 83 in 1844, his daughter, the Duchess of Hamilton, sold the Tower to a publican for a beer garden, then bought it back. Beckford had intended to be buried there, but as it was unconsecrated he was buried in the Bath Abbey cemetery. After the Duchess gave the Tower and grounds to the local parish her father's body was re-interred there and the stone piers and ornate iron railings surrounding his pink granite sarcophagus designed by Goodridge were installed. The Tower and grounds were consecrated in 1848 and the Scarlet Drawing Room became a funeral chapel. A fire in 1931 destroyed much of the original interiors and during World War II the Tower was requisitioned by the Home Guard as an observation post. In 1972 the ground and first floors were converted into a residence known as Beckford House. Today the Tower is owned by a trust and open to the public. The first floor and the Tower are now a museum. The former libraries are devoted to a display of Beckford's early life at Fonthill, while the former Crimson Drawing Room contains displays of items associated with his time in Bath.

Beckford's admirable collections have been dispersed, his writings and music largely forgotten (if preserved in the Bodleian Library, Oxford). While nothing remains of the house in Soho Square or of Fonthill Abbey, a small plaque on 19 Lansdown Crescent recalls his residence there and the Tower and cemetery still celebrate his memory. There are no known musical associations with the Tower, and nothing in the current museum displays refers to Beckford as a composer. But the view from the Tower make a pilgrimage to this unlikely memorial to a forgotten musical amateur worth while.

Beckford's Tower & Museum

Lansdown Road
Bath BA1 9BH
Great Britain

phone +44/0 1225 422212

open Easter–31 October, Saturday and Sunday 10.30–19.00

Map 5

J. Millington: *Souvenirs of Fonthill Abbey: an Exhibition to Commemorate the 150th Anniversary of the Death of William Beckford* (Bath: Bath Preservation Trust, 1994)
J. Millington: *Beckford's Tower, Bath, an Illustrated Guide* (Bath: Bath Preservation Trust, 6/1996)

BEETHOVEN

No composer is better served by museums than Beethoven. That is not surprising: almost universally seen as the greatest of the great during most of the 19th century and the first half of the

20th, and having slept in almost as many houses in central Europe as Queen Elizabeth did in England, he is clearly a strong candidate for widespread commemoration. There are in fact no fewer than 12 museums or memorial sites to Beethoven, in five countries.

One of them is not exactly a museum to Beethoven: it is a museum to his mother. Maria Magdalena van Beethoven (as she was to be) was born, in 1746, as Maria Magdalena Keverich, in the small town of Ehrenbreitstein, just across the Rhine from Koblenz. Daughter of the kitchen overseer at the castle of the Elector of Trier, which towers over Ehrenbreitstein, she was married in 1763 to a valet to the elector, and widowed two years later, having lost her only child. In 1767 she was married again, to Johann van Beethoven, a musician at the electoral court at Bonn; three of their children survived infancy, Ludwig (born in 1770), Caspar (1774) and Johann (1776). She died in 1787. Her brother was prior at the nearby Carmelite monastery.

The house is by no means exactly as it was in her time. It dates from the early 17th century and was rebuilt after the 30 Years' War. Maria's father took it in 1730 and her mother sold it after Maria's marriage. Various changes were made in the 18th century. It was acquired by the City of Koblenz at the end of the 1960s and restored, with help from the Land Rheinland-Pfalz and the Deinhard Foundation, and opened in 1975. In 1984 it was severely damaged during a fire in a neighbouring house and was largely rebuilt, incorporating however the original 18th-century newel and spiral staircases at the front and the rear respectively. It reopened in 1989.

Beethoven's links with Ehrenbreitstein were not confined to his mother. By a curious coincidence, the family of his friend Franz Wegeler is now involved with the Deinhard wine firm, and through this connection the museum has some of their correspondence and music and also some illustrative material. A Keverich room is devoted primarily to Maria's family, a Beethoven room to materials linked with the composer, including a square piano of the period and the Wegeler family's treasure box for their Beethoven items. There is a further room, furnished in Biedermeier style, with a variety of portraits and showcases with letters and music. Further Beethoven connections with Ehrenbreitstein, through acquaintances (among them Clemens Brentano and the singer Henriette Sontag) who were born or lived there, are also commemorated. The displays are chiefly in the rooms on the first floor (the ground floor is kept only lightly furnished as the Rhine is apt to flood); on the top floor there is a recital hall which can seat 100.

It is symptomatic of the centrality of Beethoven that when in 1889 a dozen Bonn worthies, determining to save the house of his birth from demolition, set up the Verein Beethoven-Haus, they took only a year to raise the funds to buy the property, rehouse the 60 people then living in it, restore it and open it as a museum. Some 50 years before, Franz Liszt had abandoned his retirement from the concert platform to help support the committee planning to erect a Beethoven statue in Bonn (in the central square, by Ernst Hähnel); this time, to meet the running costs, Joseph Joachim initiated a series of five-day chamber music festivals, held eight times over the ensuing years.

The house into which Johann van Beethoven and Maria Magdalena moved, in 1767, was at the rear of the present Beethoven-Haus, which is in fact a combination of two houses. The buildings date back to the beginning of the 18th century, when Bonn was substantially reconstructed after a siege in 1689, although the foundations are much older. The Beethovens occupied four rooms in the smaller house, on the first and second floors; they moved out in 1774, as the family grew. None of their other homes in Bonn survives.

In the original planning of the museum, the rear house was left almost as it was, but the larger front one, Bonngasse 20, was adapted to its new use

Beethoven's birthplace in Bonn

distinguish from originals) are normally used. Entry is at the museum shop: on the ground floor are three rooms, one with its walls lined with pictures of performers who have played in the house, the next with a display of programmes and publications, the third with a Beethoven genealogy and maps of the city. The main display, upstairs, is probably the richest and most comprehensive of all those described in this book.

The first room, the 'Bonn Room', has portraits of Beethoven's grandfather, the court Kapellmeister (Beethoven had the original of this with him in Vienna), his teacher C.G. Neefe, the tenor Anton Raaff and the violinist J.P. Salomon, and a display case shows Beethoven's earliest music publication, of 1782. There are also prints of views in Bonn. The next room is concerned with the family background, of his paternal grandfather in Mechelen and his mother, and contains Beethoven's baptismal entry; the third deals with Beethoven's youth and his friends, among them the Wegelers, the Breunings and the Ries family, all of whom played significant roles in his later life. The other, larger rooms and the hallway that separates them belong to the Bonngasse house. Of these the first is dominated by the console of the organ from the Minorite church, on which Beethoven played as a boy, and his own viola, which he played in the court orchestra; there are also portraits of two electors, as well as music and letters. The earliest representation of Beethoven in this room, a silhouette drawn when he was 16, can be contrasted with the powerful bronze bust by Franz Klein, made from a life-mask when he was 42, in the hallway. There are more images in the front room, a copy of the Mähler painting of 1815 and the Schimon of 1818–19. The five showcases here are used for changing exhibitions, largely of music autographs, including sketchbooks, and letters (or facsimiles of those), complemented by a cabinet with the writing tools from Beethoven's desk. The busts include one of his pupil

and some of the walls between the houses were removed. The buildings underwent structural repairs in the 1930s, with further renovations in 1968–9 and the mid-1990s. The Beethoven archive established at the time of the centenary in 1927 was moved from the neighbouring house to Bonngasse 24–6, which is now the leading institute for research, documentation and publishing on Beethoven. A foyer links the buildings at the rear. There is an impressive semicircular chamber-music hall, seating 199, of wood, leather and marble. Immediately below the platform is the vault in which some two-thirds of Beethoven's autograph manuscripts are carefully and securely stored.

The Beethoven-Haus has the enormous advantage of being able to draw on its archives for its displays and its short-term exhibitions, as well as the support of ample scholarly resources – although, in tune with modern conservation policies, originals are only occasionally displayed and high-quality facsimiles (often hard to

Giulietta Guicciardi, dedicatee of the 'Moonlight' Sonata.

On the upper floor the two large rooms are devoted to Beethoven's life in Vienna. The 1823 Graf piano, Beethoven's last, is the only one of the several early pianos in the museum that actually belonged to him. A string quartet of instruments, given to him by Prince Lichnowsky, is preserved in a glass case. There are oil portraits of the Brentano and Brunsvik families, along with miniatures that once belonged to Beethoven of family members; there is also an oil of Archduke Rudolph, in his archiepiscopal finery, and the Stieler and Waldmüller Beethoven portraits. Poignantly, four of his ear-trumpets (for illustration see p.65) are shown, with a facsimile of the famous 'testament' about his deafness written at Heiligenstadt (see below). There are other personal objects, his glasses, some seals, bookends and an inkwell, a clock, a razor, a walking stick, locks of hair; some of these are from the Bodmer collection, which also includes numerous letters and autograph music, bequeathed to the Beethoven-Haus in 1959 and not regularly on display. One corner is devoted to Beethoven's death, his will and his funeral and interment. The juxtaposition of the 1812 life mask with his death mask speaks eloquently of his suffering in those late years. It is perhaps symbolic that after that one can walk through a passage into the room of his birth – still with its original floor-

Objects on Beethoven's desk

boards – to see just a simple marble bust of the great man, on a pillar, at his own actual height (5 ft 4 ins /1.63m.).

In 1792 Beethoven moved to Vienna. During his early years in the city he sometimes stayed in a patron's house as a guest. Later he took apartments of his own, but he rarely stayed in one for long: one authority (Smolle) lists 87 moves, including his sallies out of Vienna ('Sommerfrische') to escape the heat and the noise of the city – and there are periods on which we have no information. Some degree of mobility was usual, particularly for a man living alone, but Beethoven was a restless spirit and a difficult and demanding tenant and his record must be exceptional. There were times when he held leases on two, even three or four, flats simultaneously. Accordingly, Vienna and the surrounding districts are bespattered with houses lived in or visited by Beethoven, and many of those that survive bear plaques recalling the connection. Within the present city itself, four of his former residences (or supposed ones, for there is often at least a degree of doubt about which is the actual house or apartment) are designated as memorial sites or museums.

Of these the first, in the chronology of Beethoven's life, is the house in Heiligenstadt, where he stayed during the summer of 1802, probably from about May until October, the time of the composition of the Second Symphony. Heiligenstadt, four kilometres north of the centre of the city, and even now a pleasantly leafy suburb, was wholly rural, a wine-making village and a spa whose waters, Beethoven's doctor vainly hoped, might improve his hearing. This was the time when Beethoven came to terms with his encroaching deafness, as is shown by the Heiligenstadt Testament – the remarkable, anguished document in which he described the effect on him of his affliction, and whose writing (it was addressed to his brothers but apparently never sent) seems to have been a conscious and in the event successful attempt to face and exorcise his despair and rally his determination to fight back.

The memorial house at Probusgasse 6 – there can be no certainty that this is the actual house in which Beethoven stayed: the only 'evidence' is anecdotal, and based on a presumption made in 1902 – dates back to the 16th century. In 1970 the house, with its attractive inner courtyard, was restored to something close to its condition in 1800, although the wooden balcony at the rear is an addition of the 1930s. The Vienna Beethoven Society, founded in 1954, has its offices in the front wing, with a separate exhibition devoted to Beethoven's relationship with the Heiligenstadt and Unterdöbling areas: there are several contemporary views and facsimiles of letters and works written there or referring to his time there.

Two spacious rooms are given over to displays. As one of the official City of Vienna museums, it follows in its general design a standardized pattern, with much use of polished, stained wood (here it is kiwi green), vertical stands for exhibits, hinged covers and pull-down captions. In one room part of the display is concerned with the Heiligenstadt area itself and its appearance in Beethoven's time there, and part with his acquaintances of the time (Giulietta Guicciardi, Carl Czerny, Prince Lichnowsky); and there is of course a reproduction of the Testament itself. The other, pursuing the theme of his illness, deals with his late years and his death in the Schwarzspanierhaus – there is a death mask, a lock of hair, reproductions from his diaries, his will, the people around him (his brother, his nephew, his doctor) and the actual locks and key-plates from his last apartment (the house itself, Schwarzspanierstraße 15, in the Alsergrund district just north of the centre, was demolished at the beginning of the 20th century; its site is marked by a plaque).

Beethoven returned several times to Heiligenstadt, in 1807, 1808 and 1817: the houses in which he is believed to have stayed on the last two visits, Grinzingerstraße 64 (where much of the Pastoral Symphony was composed, and known as the Beethoven-Grillparzer house as composer and poet met there) and Pfarrplatz 2 (at the top of Eroicagasse), are both marked by plaques. There is also a statue to him, erected in 1910, on the east side of the park off Grinzingerstraße, and a bust, the earliest to him in Vienna, dating from 1863, in the Beethovengang in Kahlenberger Straße. The finest Beethoven statue in the city, however, is the 1880 one by Caspar Zumbusch in the Beethovenplatz, near the Konzerthaus.

The area north of Vienna was one that Beethoven favoured for his summer homes. Just south of Heiligenstadt lies Unterdöbling, and south of that is Oberdöbling. On one of the main roads (and the tram route) from Heiligenstadt to central Vienna lies the Eroica-Haus, Döblinger Hauptstraße 92. Now a busy suburban thoroughfare, the Döblinger Hauptstraße was a country lane through a wine-growing area when Beethoven stayed there, probably in the summer of 1803, when he was at work on the 'Eroica' Symphony, and possibly for a brief spell late in the following summer. Most Beethoven scholars believe that the actual house he lived in no longer stands, but at least this one lies close by. Since Beethoven's day it has been extended and a second storey was added to part of it in about 1840. It is entered through a courtyard. There are three display rooms, rather austerely set out. Two ('Genius loci') show contemporary watercolours and prints of Döbling. One has a portrait of Gellert and reproductions of music from the time, among them the recent Gellert settings, the Waldstein Sonata, the

Courtyard of Probusgasse 6, Heiligenstadt

Triple Concerto and *Christus am Ölberge*; the other is the Eroica Room, with Napoleon and Prince Lobkowitz (at whose palace the symphony was first performed), and a print of the Theater an der Wien, where Beethoven currently had use of an apartment. The third room has a single display case with three prints. Another of Beethoven's residences in Döbling, at Silbergasse 4, is commemorated with a plaque, but the actual building in which Beethoven stayed in 1815 no longer stands.

The third of the City of Vienna museums is in the Pasqualati-Haus, Mölkerbastei 8, on the north-west edge of the central first district. This is a large block of flats, built at the end of the 18th century by the family of a friend and admirer of Beethoven, a nobleman, property developer and composer, Baron Johann Baptist von Pasqualati, who owned a part of it. Beethoven moved there, probably from Döbling, in September 1804, and it was his main residence until the middle of 1808 (at times he had use of other flats, and he travelled out of Vienna in the summers); he returned briefly the following spring, then again in 1810, where it served as his main home until early in 1814. He then briefly occupied an apartment in the neighbouring house, Mölkerbastei 10, but was back again at the end of 1814, leaving finally in spring 1815. Most of his great middle-period works were composed here.

Once again, it is impossible to be certain which flat he lived in; he may have had different ones at different times. Some callers talk of visiting him on the third floor, some on the fourth (which, counting the ground floor, may mean what we call the third), but the consensus today is that it was truly the fourth, and descriptions of his situation and his view suggest that it was at the east end of the building.

The memorial rooms are probably not in Beethoven's actual apartment but as the Viennese museums do not seek to recreate his living environment that is of less consequence. The display, then, is focussed on his middle period. An ante-room is devoted to 'Genius loci', with the architectural plan of Mölkerbastei 8. The first room has various personal relics: a small cabinet, a clock, and Beethoven's sugar-bowl and salt and pepper holders, as well as a Streicher piano (a Viennese make that Beethoven favoured) and the stern bust of him by Franz Klein. In the next is a large display focussing on the city of Vienna and on Beethoven's middle-period works: *Fidelio*, with the music itself, the librettists, the singers, the performances; Count Razumovsky and his quartets; and the symphonies from no.4 to no.8 and the *Battle of Vittoria*. A third has the original oil portraits of Beethoven's grandfather and Beethoven himself by Mähler, as well as the Klein life mask; and in the last are portraits of many of Beethoven's acquaintances – the Breunings, the violinist Ignaz Schuppanzigh, the publisher Artaria, members of the Brunsvik, Lobkowitz and Lichnowsky families and Bettina von Brentano. As in several museums of this group, there is a listening console.

Most of the Viennese Beethoven museums, like this one, have pianos of the kinds he used. But the enthusiast in this direction would do best to visit the Kunsthistorisches Museum, whose Sammlung alter Musikinstrumente (collection of ancient instruments) is arranged chronologically, with reference to Viennese composers; Room XIV, the Beethoven Room, ranges from a Walter piano of 1790 to a Graf of about 1820, with several in between, and busts or portraits of some of the leading Viennese makers.

The common management of the Viennese municipal composer museums, and the unity of style imposed upon them by the decision to redesign them all in the 1990s, precludes any attempt to create atmosphere specific to any of the composers or indeed any particular period. One might have wished for more expenditure of historical imagination. Perhaps Beethoven suffers from this more than most of the others as his reported way of life relates uncertainly to the crisp tidiness of the Viennese museum livery. The city possesses a great deal of

Beethoven material, which is divided between the several houses; but it is nowhere made clear to the visitor that there is at best a considerable degree of uncertainty as to whether the master actually lived at any of the three Gedenkstätte.

Still within Vienna today, in the Floridsdorf district across the Danube to the north-east of the city, is the modest country seat of the Erdődy family, built in a large park in 1795 in the village of Jedlesee by Count Peter and Countess Anna Maria Erdődy. The Countess (she and her husband quite soon separated) was a patron, admirer and friend of Beethoven's; he dedicated his two piano trios op.70 and two cello sonatas op.102 to her. There is no firm evidence as to when he visited her country house; it was reasonably close to Heiligenstadt and Döbling and he may well have done so from there. We do know that he was her guest at her house in Krugerstraße, in central Vienna, for several months in 1808–9. He may have been to Jedlesee as early as 1802, or around the time he was in Krugerstraße; they quarrelled in 1809 and were reconciled in 1815.

A small display in the house, inaugurated in 1973, celebrates the connection. A pair of rooms, with appropriate portraits looking down on proceedings, also serves as a recital hall, seating about 70. There is further pictorial matter, and Biedermeier furniture, in the meetings room. A bust of Countess Erdődy surveys the reception area. The collection is modest, but it includes a Beethoven autograph, letters of the Countess, a lock of hair thought to be Beethoven's and other documents and notebooks. A stable wing, burnt down in 1863, has been reconstructed to serve as a small museum of the house's history.

This is not the only instance of a shortage of precise information about Beethoven's visits to his friends. A family with which he was deeply entangled over many years was the Brunsviks, whose daughters Therese and Josephine were his pupils; at one time he nurtured hopes of marriage with Josephine, who some scholars believe is the 'Eternally Beloved' of the famous letter (although the weight of evidence favours Antonie Brentano). Their mother had bought Beethoven's op.1 piano trios by subscription in 1795, but probably Beethoven did not meet them until 1799. The family had country homes in Hungary, at Martonvásár, 20 km south-west of Budapest, on the main road between the capital and Lake Balaton, and at Korompa (now Dolná Krupá, in Slovakia; in Beethoven's day it would have been known by its Hungarian name).

Beethoven is known to have visited Hungary several times, first in 1796, then in 1800, when he spent some time in Budapest, and possibly in 1806 and 1809.

The Brunsvik home at Martonvásár

The only documentary proof that he ever visited the family there comes from remarks by Therese Brunsvik ('er kam nach Martonvásár') and a reminiscence of his pupil Carl Czerny. The Brunsviks' country house, standing in a large park with fine rows of chestnuts, was built in the 1780s and added to in the 19th century. It became a Beethoven museum in 1958. Four rooms, one of them used for a video installation, are assigned to Beethoven. The displays, attractive and spacious, focus on the Brunsvik family and Beethoven's Hungarian connections (among them the Esterházy and Erdődy families), with portraits and drawings, copies or facsimiles of music and letters and other Brunsvik family papers, collections of books from the family library and early editions of Beethoven works.

The Brunsviks' other country house is at Dolná Krupá, a small town about 50 km north-east of Bratislava (Pressburg, in Beethoven's time) and about 15 km north of Trnava: a large palace, in imperial yellow, in extensive grounds with a lake and woods. Again, there is no certainty about Beethoven's visits, but again it seems probable that he would have been there at some point. At any rate, the charming little lodge to the left of the main building is kept as a memorial to him. In the ground-floor room facing the park is a bust, a square piano, a writing

Beethoven memorial rooms at Dolná Krupá

desk and various facsimiles, with a Brunsvik family tree, and in the small dining-room is an inlaid table and chairs along with reproduced portraits of Beethoven and the Brunsviks. Up a spiral staircase are two more rooms, one for listening, the other, rather sparse, but with a display of relevant facsimile material.

We do know rather more about Beethoven's visits to another patron's castle – that of Prince Lichnowsky at Hradec nad Moravicí, eight kilometres south of Opava in northern Moravia, on the edge of Silesia (known in Beethoven's time as Grätz, south of Troppau). He was Lichnowsky's guest in the autumn of 1806 and, briefly, in the late summer of 1811. It was on the first visit that one of the more colourful anecdotes about Beethoven was generated, the tale of his walking out and, in a thunderstorm, returning to Vienna in a rage, when asked to perform for visitors (in one version, the visitors were officers in Napoleon's army); the tale is borne out by the smudged autograph score of the 'Appassionata' Sonata, which he was composing and carrying at the time.

The castle itself was built in 1797, when an older one had burnt down, in a neo-classical Empire style, and underwent various modifications in the 19th century. It had belonged to the Lichnowskys since 1778. It is now open to the public as a general historical museum with, on the first floor, a Beethoven memorial room. In it is the Erard piano of 1803, built for Lichnowsky, on which presumably Beethoven played (and refused to play), a music desk that he is said to have used, a set of string quartet instruments, and early Viennese furniture; on display are facsimiles of various Beethoven works with Lichnowsky connections (the op.1 trios, the *Sonate pathétique*, the op.35 'Eroica' Variations), and a plaque put up in 1909 to commemorate his visits. A vaulted side room, off the main exhibition, has photos of recent Lichnowskys and paintings by some of them, letters on musical topics (visits from Liszt and Cosima Wagner) and the local countryside.

In his later years, Beethoven often favoured the country areas south of Vienna, rather more distant from the centre, for his 'Sommerfrische' journeys. He paid his first, brief visit to Mödling, about 17 km to the south-west, in 1799, then went there for longer spells – generally May or June to September or October – for three years, 1818, 1819 and 1820. He liked the countryside there, with its romantic landscapes – in a letter of the time he refers to 'roaming the mountains, the ravines and the valleys with music-paper in my hand' – but for much of the time he was in the grip of anxieties about his nephew who was in his care, and sometimes so foul-tempered that his servants walked out. Nevertheless, in the Mödling months he worked on such music as the Hammerklavier Sonata, the *Missa Solemnis* and the Diabelli Variations. In some of these summers, he actually moved in, bringing his furniture from Vienna; and it was in Mödling that he received the gift of a six-octave Broadwood piano from London (it is now in the Hungarian National Museum, Budapest).

In 1819, and probably also the preceding year, he lived in the 'Hafnerhaus', a former pottery workshop; he had a suite on the first floor, an ante-room and a pair of rooms linked by an archway (the building had originally been a convent). The acoustical properties afforded by the vaulted ceilings would, alas!, have been lost on him by this date. The building now belongs to the municipality and in 1970 the rooms he occupied were dedicated as a memorial. Their austerity is relieved by a few items of furniture of the period, among them a Viennese grand piano of 1794 (by Carl Stein), some reproductions of prints of Mödling and three display cases, with facsimiles of relevant material (sketches, prints, letters, pictures). There is also a bust and a death mask. The house where Beethoven stayed in 1820, the Christhof (Achsenaugasse 6), is nearby.

A further 15 km in the same direction from Vienna lies the larger, more fashion-

Beethoven's rooms in the Hafnerhaus at Mödling

able spa of Baden, another of Beethoven's (and formerly Mozart's) favourite watering-places. He had paid brief visits to friends there as early as 1803–4, then had visited the town almost every summer from 1807 to 1816, for anything between a few days and three or four months. After his flirtation with Mödling, he reverted to Baden and spent time there, sometimes going on after a spell in Döbling, each year from 1821 to 1825. Two of his favourite lodgings were the Johanneshof, in Johannesgasse, and the Alter Sauerhof, in Weilburgstraße, neither of which still stands. But in 1821 and 1823 he stayed in the Rathausgasse, at the present no.10, on the corner of what is now Beethovengasse. He may have been there briefly in 1822, but he also stayed at two other addresses, and there is a plaque outside the former Zur goldenen Schwan (now Antonsgasse 4) stating that he composed the *Consecration of the House* overture there.

The building in Rathausgasse, on two storeys, was acquired by the municipality in 1962 and a museum was established in the first-floor rooms that Beethoven occupied. The building is called the 'Haus der Neunten', as he worked on the Ninth Symphony there in 1823 (though the same name is applied to the Vienna house, Ungargasse 5, in the Landstraße district, to which he returned in October, now marked with a bronze relief). On his first visit he worked on the *Missa Solemnis*. There is a small anteroom and a spacious principal room, with display cases showing relevant facsimiles (notably of the Ninth) and pictorial items, as well as a survey of Beethoven's sojourns in Baden and his various homes in the town. There is a particularly interesting account book from a Baden inn. In Beethoven's bedroom there is period furniture as well as display material, with elegantly presented portraits of his contemporaries. A large alcove off this room is used for temporary exhibitions on musical topics unrelated to Beethoven but germane to Baden's musical history.

Beethoven visited Baden twice more in the following years, staying at the Schloß Gutenbrunn (now a sanatorium in Peregrinistraße). In 1826 he remained in Vienna until September, when he at last accepted his brother Johann's invitation to visit the summer estate and vineyards, covering about 1.5 sq. km (nearly 400 acres), that he had acquired in 1819 at Gneixendorf, a village just north of Krems (80 km west of Vienna, at the confluence of the Krems and the Danube). Beethoven and his nephew Karl arrived there, to stay two weeks, but remained until the beginning of December, when they left in a hurry after the brothers quarrelled about Karl. The rest of the story is well known: Beethoven and Karl, hurrying to get back to Vienna, travelled in an open milk-wagon; cold and wet, Beethoven contracted pneumonia and died the following March.

The Gneixendorf properties have been owned since 1867 by the Gettinger family, who continue the tradition of wine-making on the estate, which had originally been owned by a monastery and was secularized in 1806. Beethoven and Karl stayed not in the main house, the Wasserhof, but

Beethoven's brother's house at Gneixendorf

in another close by, the Trautingerhof, where they occupied the first floor; here Beethoven completed the op.135 string quartet, wrote the new finale for the op.130 one, and began work on a string quintet op.137. The Gettingers have set these rooms aside as a memorial to Beethoven. There is a small anteroom off the landing, where there are facsimiles of some letters and a sketchbook, then a large central room, notable for its striking murals, a series of slightly faded, delicately romantic, early 19th-century landscapes, presented as if seen from a loggia, and signed Friedrich Wilhelm Reinhold. Frau Gettinger believes these have stood unchanged since Beethoven's time.

This central room certainly has its original floors and doors; there is a bust of the great man, a grand piano, and some furniture, made by earlier Gettingers, dating back to the 19th century. One side is a dining-room, furnished with family pieces, and there is a bedroom, with a large bed between two pillars. The property has undergone various vicissitudes: it was a Nazi prisoner-of-war camp for a time after 1939, then a typhus hospital, and from 1945 the Russians occupied the estate for two years. But enough seems to have survived to make it a moving memorial to Beethoven's last months.

Mutter-Beethoven-Haus
Wambachstraße 204
56077 Koblenz-Ehrenbreitstein
Germany

phone +49/0 2611 292531, 292502
(Mittelrhein-Museum)
website www.koblenz.de/touristik_kultur

open 15 April–15 October,
Tuesday–Saturday 10.30–17.00,
Sunday 11.00–18.00 (other times of
year by appointment)

Beethoven-Haus Bonn
Bonngasse 20
53111 Bonn
Germany

phone +49/0 228 981 7525
fax +49/0 228 981 7526
e-mail museum@beethoven-haus-bonn.de
website www.beethoven-haus-bonn.de

open April–September,
Monday– Saturday 10.00–17.00,
Sunday 10.00–13.00; October–March,
Monday– Saturday 10.00–14.00,
Sunday 10.00–13.00

**Beethoven-Gedenkstätte
Heiligenstädter Testament**
Probusgasse 6
1019 Wien
Austria

phone +43/0 1370 5408
e-mail post@magwien.gv.at
website www.museum.at

open Tuesday–Sunday 10.00–12.15,
13.00–16.30

Beethoven-Gedenkstätte Eroicahaus
Döblinger Hauptstraße 92
1019 Wien
Austria

phone +43/0 1369 1424
e-mail post@magwien.gv.at
website www.museum.at

open Tuesday–Sunday 10.00–12.15,
13.00–16.30

**Beethoven-Gedenkstätte
Pasqualatihaus**
Mölkerbastei 8
1010 Wien
Austria

phone +43/0 1535 8905
e-mail post@magwien.gv.at
website www.museum.at

open Tuesday–Sunday 10.00–12.15,
13.00–16.30

**Die Beethoven-Gedenkstätte in
Floridsdorf**
Jeneweingasse 17
Jedlesee
1212 Wien
Austria

phone +43/0 1278 5267

open Monday, Wednesday 09.00–11.00

Beethoven Emlékmúzeuma
Brunszvik-kastély
Brunszvik utca 2
2462 Martonvásár (Fejér)
Hungary

phone +36/0 22 569500
fax +36/0 22 460213
website www.museum.hu/martonvasar

open Tuesday–Friday 14.00–16.00;
Saturday and Sunday, 10.00–18.00
(closes 16.00, November–April)

Pamätník Ludwiga van Beethoven
Kaštiel'
91965 Dolná Krupá
Slovakia

phone +421/0 33 557 7260
e-mail info@muzeum.sk

open Tuesday, Thursday 10.00–14.00

Státni Zámek Hradec nad Moravicí
74741 Hradec nad Moravicí
Czech Republic

phone +420/0 553 783485
(reservations, 783444)
fax +420/0 553 783915
e-mail sekretariat@muhradec.cz

open May – September, Tuesday–Sunday
09.00–17.00; April, October, December,
Saturday and Sunday 10.00–16.00

Beethoven-Gedenkstätte
'Hafnerhaus'
Haus Mödling
Hauptstraße 79
2340 Mödling
Austria

phone +43/0 2236 24159 (Mödling Bezirks-Museum-Verein) or +43/0 2236 26727 (Tourist Office, Elisabethstraße 2)

open Monday–Wednesday 09.00–12.00, or by arrangement

Haus der Neunten
Rathausgasse 10
2500 Baden
Austria

phone +43/0 2252 86800, 230233

open Tuesday–Sunday 16.00–18.00, Saturday and Sunday also 09.00–11.00

Beethoven-Erinnerungsräume
Schloßstraße 19
3500 Krems-Gneixendorf
Austria

phone +43/0 273 286876

open by appointment

Maps 7, 1, 8, 4

K. Smolle: *Wohnstätten Ludwig van Beethovens von 1792 bis zu seinem Tod* (Munich and Duisburg: Beethoven-Haus Bonn and Henle, 1970)
Beethovens Beziehungen zu Koblenz und Ehrenbreitstein (Koblenz: Deinhard-Stiftung, 1975)
Anna Maria Erdödy geborene Niczky (Vienna: Verein der Beethoven-Gedenkstätte in Floridsdorf, 1987)
Beethoven's Birthplace in Bonn (Bonn: Beethoven-Haus, 1989)
S. Brandenburg, ed.: *1889–1989: Verein Beethoven-Haus* (Bonn: Beethoven-Haus, 1989)
R. Klein and others: *The Beethoven Memorial Sites Administered by the Vienna Municipal Museums* (Vienna: Vienna Municipal Museums, 1992)
K. Kramert, ed.: *Beethoven in Heiligenstadt* (Vienna: Wiener Beethoven-Gesellschaft, 1992)
H. Kretschmer: *Wiener Musikgedenkstätten* (Vienna: J & V Edition, 3/1992)
W. Brauneis, O. Biba and others: *Beethoven Musikergedenkstätten: Beethoven-Gedenkstätte "Heiligenstädter Testament" . . . "Eroicahaus"* (Vienna: Historisches Museum der Stadt Wien, n.d. [c1996])

R. Klein, H.C. Robbins Landon and others: *Beethoven Musikergedenkstätten: Ludwig van Beethoven "Pasqualatihaus"* (Vienna: Historisches Museum der Stadt Wien, n.d. [c1996])
G. Gefen: *Composers' Houses* (London: Cassell and Vendome, 1998), 18–23
R. Kallenbach, D. Kerber and M. Schwickerath: *Sanierung Ehrenbreitstein: eine Dokumentation der Stadt Koblenz* (Koblenz: Stadtverwaltung, 1999), 145–8

BELLINI

The son and grandson of musicians, Vincenzo Bellini was born in 1801 in Catania, on the island of Sicily, in the shadow of Etna. The three-room flat in which his parents lived, on the first floor of the Palazzo Gravina Cruylias in the Piazza San Francesco d'Assisi, is now the Museo Belliniano.

To judge from a manuscript account of his childhood, in the archive of the Museo, Vincenzo, nurtured by his father and grandfather, demonstrated remarkable musical precocity. When he was 18 he was granted a four-year stipend by the city council to study at the Real Collegio in Naples, on condition that he submitted compositions and verification of his regular attendance and that afterwards he would return to live in Catania.

But opportunities to compose for Europe's greatest opera houses – in Milan, Vienna, Parma, Venice, Bergamo, London, Paris and Naples – soon beckoned, and he returned only on occasional family visits (1825, 1827 and 1832). The city council nevertheless showed their approval and indeed their pride in his spectacular success abroad by striking a medal in his honour in 1830. Later, in 1876, the city fathers succeeded in arranging for his remains to be exhumed from the Père Lachaise cemetery in Paris (he had died unexpectedly at his home in Puteaux on 23 September 1835 and had a very grand funeral at the Hôtel des Invalides) and re-interred, with pomp and ceremony, in the 11th-century cathedral close to his birthplace in the centre of the city. In 1882 a monument to him was put up in the Piazza Stesicoro. Taking their cue from Catania, the City of Naples, which already had a theatre named after him, erected a monument in 1884.

The Museo Belliniano, opened by King Vittorio Emanuele III in 1930, has changed very little over the years and exudes a slightly eerie atmosphere that visitors will not readily forget. It occupies the equivalent of what must have been two flats in the palazzo, of which five rooms are used for display and one is a library. The first room is hung with 19th-century prints of Catania as Bellini would have known it. The second, the room where he is thought to have been born, displays some of his personal possessions – the piano at which he is said to have composed *Norma* in 1831, his pocket watches, a silk handkerchief, stick pins, medals and various presents that he received – as well as a portrait, the original death mask, autograph letters and documents relating to his final days (five manuscript medical bulletins from 20–23 September 1835 and photographs of his death certificate and the autopsy report). The third room, lined with collages of hundreds of reproductions of portraits and scenes (mostly unlabelled) from the Catania, Milan, Naples, London and Paris periods, also exhibits his grandfather's harpsichord.

The fourth room is a treasure trove of Bellini autographs – the operas (including *Adelson e Salvini* and *Bianca e Gernando*) as well as sketches of incomplete works, together with editions, librettos, playbills and facsimiles of set designs and portraits of Bellini singers; there is also his square piano, built in Milan by Carl Fuchs. The fifth is voyeuristic and representative of attitudes to death, equally in 19th-century France and 20th-century Sicily: the visitor is invited to peer at Bellini's original coffin (its top ajar) and other funerary relics, examine photographs of the exhumation and compare death masks of the composer made 41 years apart. Finally, there is the Sala Biblioteca, a dedicated research library, whose archive contains further Belliniana and autograph manuscript music by Bellini's grandfather.

Museo Civico Belliniano

Piazza San Francesco d'Assisi 3
95100 Catania
Sicily

phone +390/0 95 715 0535

open 09.00–13.30 (Sunday, to 12.30)

Map 9

B. Condorelli: *Il Museo Belliniano: Catalogo storico, iconografico* (Catania, 2/1939)

S.E. Failla: *Bellini Vincenzo in Catania* (Catania: Giuseppe Maimone, 1985)

N. Simeone: *Paris: a Musical Gazetteer* (New Haven and London: Yale University Press, 2000)

The Bellini birthplace museum at Catania

BELLMAN

Carl Michael Bellman (1740–95) was more Swedish troubadour than composer, and is affectionately remembered by his Swedish countrymen as a poet. In his heyday he entertained at the court of Gustavus III, having made his reputation as a performer of satirical drinking songs. A keen observer of lowlife, he attached his verses to popular melodies, some of them Swedish airs and dances and *ariettes* from French *opéra comique*, others purloined from works by Handel and Haydn; probably he composed a handful himself. By the time his royal patron was murdered in 1792, Bellman had published two major collections of verse, *Fredmans epistlar* (1790) and *Fredmans sånger* (1791), but while they ensured his place in Swedish letters, they could not save him from the scourges of illness and poverty in his last years.

In Stockholm, on the fabled island of Långholmen in Lake Mälar, a permanent exhibition to the life and works of Bellman was installed in what was originally a 17th-century customs house and now doubles during the tourist season as a theatre and outdoor café. The displays were formerly housed on another Stockholm island, Skansen, where one of the entrances to the Open-Air Museum there is named after Bellman ('Bellmansro'), and in 1990 they were briefly exhibited at Haga Park, north of the city centre, where Gustavus III had a pavilion built for the entertainment of his intimates.

Although Bellman never lived in the charming diamond-paned, wood-built customs house, he was familiar with it, judging from his 48th epistle, which mentions passing the building during an all-night drinking spree on the island, which was then dominated by a prison (now revamped as a hotel). Once inside the customs house the visitor is obliged to resist the tempting array of freshly baked food and turn sharply right into the exhibition, to be engaged instead by the colourful and theatrical nature of the displays, which, alas, are labelled exclusively in Swedish. Five small rooms are devoted to Bellman, the fifth doubling as a backstage store for the balcony stage on which a musical drama about Bellman's life is presented by the caretaker (who lives upstairs) during the summer.

The first room charts the tenuous connection between Bellman and Långholmen with a map of 1747 and a picture of the customs house from 1783, with 18th-century clothing and furniture as props. The second confronts the conflicting images of Bellman as alcoholic and polished courtier, illustrated by portraits from the 1780s by Per Krafft (in which Bellman is playing a lute) and Per Hilleström, caricatures and a death mask. Through a false window is a view of the Stockholm neighbourhood where Bellman was born. There are also silhouettes of his parents and facsimiles of his correspondence from 1749. The third room is set up as a seaside inn. Amid barrels and playing cards, pride of place is given to copies of Bellman's two collections of verse, supported by 21 framed engraved and coloured Hogarthian caricatures of the 'Fredmans Gestalter', produced in 1805 for the promotion of the epistles (fictional letters describing imaginary episodes in the lives of real contemporaries). Further underlying the two sides of his character, also displayed here is a small copy of a three-metre statue of Bellman dressed in formal clothes, seated, playing the lute. The fourth room evokes the royal theatres of Drottningholm, Gripsholm and Ulriksdal during the reign of Gustavus III. Bellman is depicted as an actor. On display are a copy of Bellman's cantata libretto, *Fiskarena* (1792), a 1787 medallion portrait relief by Johan Tobias Sergel in which Bellman is depicted as Bacchus, his hair festooned with grapes, and behind a series of cupboard doors are illustrated facsimiles of his printed letters. The final room is decorated with reproductions of 18th-century Stockholm and on display is a lute with its case by the court luthier and maker of Bellman's lute, Matthias Petter Kraft. At this point the visitor once again finds himself in the café, this time free to take refreshment.

Bellmanmuséet

Stora Henriksvik

Långholmen

11733 Stockholm

Sweden

phone +46/0 8669 6969

open June–August, daily 12.00–1800; May and September, Saturday and Sunday 12.00–16.00

Map 13

O. Byström: *Bellman i Haga parkmuseum* (Stockholm, 1990) [exhibition catalogue]

BENDA brothers

The Bendas were, indeed still are, one of the great dynasties of Czech music. The founding father was Jan Jiří Benda, a linen weaver and village musician who married a member of another such dynasty, the Brixi family. This union produced, among their ten offspring, František in 1709 and Jiří Antonín in 1722. These two are better known to musical history as Franz, a composer and violinist at the court in Potsdam of Frederick the Great, and Georg Anton, who worked chiefly as a Kapellmeister at Gotha and was a pioneer of the melodrama (Mozart wrote of him: 'of all the Lutheran Kapellmeisters, Benda has always been my favourite'). Their descendants are still active in German musical life.

These two were born in what was then Staré Benátky, now Benátky nad Jizerou, some 40 km north-west of Prague. The house of their birth, close to the church, was demolished in the 1930s, but the plaque put up in 1926 is now on the house that replaces it. Their place of work while they remained in Benátky was the castle, up on the hill, which is now the local museum.

Since 1998 a room on the second floor has been devoted to a display dedicated to the two brothers (a neighbouring room is given over to Smetana, who worked there too: *see* SMETANA). Inevitably, most of the material is loaned from Prague collections. The nine showcases give some picture of the two men and their lives, with early editions, engravings, photographs (among them one of Georg's house in Gotha), modern editions, documents and maps. Something of the activities of other family members, including recent and living ones, is included. There are also various instruments, of no specific relevance to the Bendas but perhaps a useful garnish for educational purposes.

Franz Benda died in Potsdam in 1786, and Georg in Bad Köstritz, near Dresden, in 1795; there is a small commemoration of him in the Schütz museum there (*see* SCHÜTZ).

Městské Muzeum Benátky nad Jizerou

Zámek 49

29471 Benátky nad Jizerou

Czech Republic

phone +420/0 326 316682

e-mail muzeum.benátky@seznam.cz

open April–October, Tuesday–Sunday 09.00–12.00, 13.00–17.00

Map 4

J. Antoš, P. Štifter and others: *Bendové a Benátky nad Jizerou* (Benátky nad Jizerou: Osvětová beseda Benátky nad Jizerou and Okresní Muzeum, 1986)

BENOIT

Peter Benoit, champion of the Dutch language and the music of the Flemish-speaking people of Belgium, was born on 17 August 1834 in a modest cottage at Markstraat 57 in Harelbeke, a West Flanders town, close to Kortrijk (Courtrai), between Bruges and Gent. He came from a family of musicians: his father Petrus and his uncle Jan Baptist were active in local musical life (Petrus left a set of memoirs and Jan had an extensive music library), and his father and his brothers Edmond and Constant were also composers. Although Peter lived in the house only a year, it has been preserved and opened to the public, together with an adjoining museum dedicated to his life and works.

Benoit's nationalist commitment to Dutch/Flemish has meant that much of his vocal music – dramas, operas, oratorios, cantatas and sacred works – is less known outside Belgium than it might otherwise have been: he specified in his will that all performances of his music should be in Flemish. But it is precisely that commitment that has ensured his place in the history and the hearts of the Belgians of Flanders.

Within a year of his death (8 March 1901) in Antwerp, where he had served as director of the Vlaamse Muziekschool (a royal conservatory from 1879) and as the driving force behind the development of a national music curriculum, Peter Benoit societies were established in Harelbeke, Antwerp and Brussels. A plaque was erected on his birthplace and an archive established. The archive forms the basis of the collection of documents, manuscripts, editions, programmes, portraits, photographs, posters, correspondence and memorabilia (including a lock of hair and a death mask) on display at Markstraat 55.

During 1902–3 the birthplace was restored, and in 1929 it was given to the town of Harelbeke. In the year of Benoit's centenary (1934) a dispute arose over whether the house had actually been his birthplace, but it was resolved by 1937 when it was classified a national monument. Storing and exhibiting the collection in the birthplace would not have been possible without destroying its character, and so the adjoining house, Markstraat 55, was acquired for the purpose. In 1978 the museum and birthplace officially opened to the public. The cottage is decorated very simply with period furnishings, presented much as it would have been in the 1830s.

On the 50th anniversary of his death (1951) a statue was erected to Benoit in Harelbeke municipal park, very close to the museum.

Stedelijke Museum en Geboortehuisje Peter Benoit
Markstraat 55–7
8730 Harelbeke
Belgium

phone +32/0 56 713901

open March–November, first and third Saturday of the month 14.00–17.00; December–February by appointment

Map 3

Peter Benoit op de voet gevolgd [In the Footsteps of Peter Benoit] (Antwerp: Vlaamse Volkskunstbeweging, 1976)
Inventaris van het Peter Benoit Museum Harelbeke (Harelbeke: Stadsbestuur Harelbeke-Diest Kultuur, 1981)

BERG

There is no museum devoted to Alban Berg. But his flat in a Viennese suburb and his Carinthian summer retreat, Waldhaus, on the south side of the Wörthersee near the resort of Velden, belong to the Alban-Berg-Stiftung, established in 1969 by his widow, Helene, and are by and large maintained as he left them. Although not open to the public, the flat and villa may be seen by appointment if a strong enough case can be made.

For the determined Berg pilgrim there are yet more places to visit. Born in Vienna in 1885, Berg spent his childhood holidays at the family's alpine estate, Berghof, on the Ossiachersee. Vienna remained his base, in particular the 13th district, just west of Schönbrunn. Alban and Helene Berg were married on 3 May 1911 in the parish church of Hietzing and went to live in an upper-ground-floor flat at Trautmannsdorffgasse 27. After Berghof was sold at the beginning of the 1920s, the Bergs took their walking holidays in the Styrian Alps, where Helene's family had a home at Trahütten, near Deutschlandsberg, 30 km south-west of Graz; that house is now a *pension*.

If you are lucky enough to gain entrance to the small Hietzing flat, you will first enter the living-room, which doubled as Berg's study. It is dominated by his Bösendorfer grand piano (with two chairs for playing duets) and his desk, on which stand a bust and a death mask. Unusually, he had opaque glass installed in the windows facing the street and dark brown and black hessian-type wallpaper. A comfortable sofa and several armchairs with cushions, photographs (including one of Mahler and one of the original *Wozzeck* stage set), paintings and a bookcase stocked with literature and music relieve the prevailing austerity and isolation. The adjoining dining-room is also secluded by opaque glass and is furnished with a small round table and four chairs.

Berg composed *Wozzeck* while serving in the army and living at Trautmannsdorffgasse and at Trahütten. *Lulu* was inspired by summers at Berghof, when at family play-readings he had first come across Wedekind's two Lulu plays, but he composed the opera mainly at the Waldhaus in 1934–5, along with the violin concerto. In 1935 the Bergs stayed on at the Waldhaus until mid-November while he continued to work on *Lulu*. In late summer he developed the infection that eventually caused his death from blood poisoning on Christmas Eve. His grave in the Hietzing parish cemetery, at Maxingstraße 15, is marked by a simple cross of larchwood from the forest adjoining the Waldhaus.

The Bergs had bought the Waldhaus at auction in 1932. The two-storey house, on a knoll in the village of Auen, affords a view of the Wörthersee through the forest from the wooden balcony extending from the study. Both study and bedroom are maintained as the Bergs left them; the main rooms are used by the Alban-Berg-Stiftung as a summer venue for composition courses. Berg's much-loved Ford convertible is still parked in the garage and is said to be kept in running order. In the nearby village of Schiefling am See a roadside memorial to Berg, a bust and a plaque, gives details of his connection with the area.

Alban-Berg-Stiftung
Trautmannsdorffgasse 27
1130 Wien
Austria

phone +43/0 1 8777 716410
fax +43/0 1 8777 716427
e-mail praesidium@albanbergstiftung.at
website www.albanbergstiftung.at

open by appointment only, office hours

Villa Waldhaus
Bergweg
Auen
9220 Velden
Austria

phone +43/0 4274 4305

open by appointment only, May–August

Map 1

A. Fuchs: *Auf ihren Spuren in Kärnten: Alban Berg, Gustav Mahler, Johannes Brahms, Hugo Wolf, Anton Webern* (Klagenfurt: Kärntner Druck- und Verlagsgesellschaft, 3/1997), 5–19
H. Kretschmer: *Wiener Musikergedenkstätten* (Vienna: J & V Edition, 3/1992)

BERLIOZ

Until he was 18, Hector Berlioz lived in the house where, on 11 December 1803, he was born: 69 rue de la République, La Côte-Saint-André, in the Bas-Dauphiné region. He was the eldest of the five children of a respected doctor in this small town, now of around 5000 people, about halfway between Grenoble and Lyons, close to the A48 motorway. His father taught him the flageolet and then sent him to a teacher imported from Lyons by the better-off *côtoise* families for lessons on the flute and guitar; Hector taught himself harmony from the treatises of Rameau and Charles-Simon Catel.

Berlioz was a precocious child: he was 12 when he conceived the passion for the 18-year-old Estelle Duboeuf that was to draw him repeatedly to the region in his late years. He had left it in 1821, with a bachelor's degree in medicine from Grenoble, to study in Paris. Three years later he abandoned medicine and committed himself to music, in defiance of his father, who was affectionate but domineering (and who never heard a performance of any work of his son's). He struggled through his Conservatoire studies without adequate support. In 1823 and 1825 he visited La Côte, but the reunions were acrimonious, and it was not until 1830, when he won the Prix de Rome, that his parents recognized that his passion for music was based on a true gift and there was a reconciliation. The next year he spent a month at home, and the following year five months; he returned only in 1847, the year before his father's death, bringing with him Louis, the son of his first marriage, to Harriet Smithson. In 1848 the house was closed; his sister Adèle owned it until her death in 1860 when it passed to her two daughters, who sold it in 1874.

Built in the 1680s and acquired in 1732 by Berlioz's great-grandfather, the house is spacious, on four floors with an attic. The façade to the rue de la République, the main street of the town, is rather austere, but the rear is charming, with a U-shaped balcony at first-floor level, overlooking a garden with ivy-covered walls. It was purchased by the Société des Amis de Berlioz in 1932 and opened as a museum in 1935. Little was done, however, to maintain the building, and just before the Berlioz centenary year, 1969, it was taken over by the *département*

The Berlioz family home, seen from the garden

of Isère, classified as a national monument, restored and put under the direction of the Association Nationale Hector Berlioz with an honorary curator. It was further restored in 1984 and again in time for the bicentenary year of 2003.

It manages to be both a well-organized survey of Berlioz's life and times and at the same time a museum of 19th-century family life, with its display of middle-class French furniture of the time. On the ground floor are a foyer and a shop and two display rooms: one with a diorama surveying 'L'Europe romantique' and the people who most influenced Berlioz, the other '1803–69: Episodes de la vie d'un artiste', with the 1840 portrait by Paul de Pommayra and a series of display boards highlighting a number of phases of his life (he died in 1869). The visitor has use of a handset, with a choice of languages, in which the captions (exclusively in French) are translated.

On the mezzanine floor, at the rear of the house, are a family kitchen, restored as it might have been in Berlioz's childhood, and Dr Berlioz's room, where a set of contemporary medical instruments is to be seen along with his umbrella, a surgical book that he wrote and his wife's gold watch, all overseen by his portrait. Berlioz's grandparents watch over the small, family dining-room, in tasteful décor of the time, with a cupboard of china and silver. Across the landing is Hector's own bedroom (it is made clear that there can be no certainty about the original role of each room, but the putative arrangement is plausible and sensible). Here, with the walls restored to their probable original blue, are reproductions of his birth registration, his diplomas and letters, books that represent his early enthusiasms, a flute and a guitar of the time and early portraits.

On the first floor, at the front of the house, is the 'Petit salon-bibliothèque', restored in Louis XVI style with a display devoted to Berlioz's love life, in pictures and correspondence. The 'Grand salon' is more formal, in a Louis XV style; in it is the Erard upright piano that Berlioz chose for his nieces, as well as family portraits and a letter to his sister Adèle. The exhibit in the small anteroom is concerned with his musical education. There is a smaller Erard, a table piano, in the room taken to be that of his birth, where there are china and glass, a pen and inkstand, a tie-pin and a wax seal from his Paris house of the mid-1830s, along with trophies from further afield – china from Grand Duchess Yelena of Russia, a laurel wreath from Vienna, an eagle from Prussia, a silver baton from Brunswick and a variety of diplomas.

The rooms thought to have been his sisters' are on the second mezzanine: Adèle's contains letters and portraits, Nanci's some more personal objects: his Légion d'honneur, a lock of his hair (snow white), a death mask, a facsimile of the last lines of his memoirs, a silver laurel from Hungary, a ruby crown from Grenoble and other busts and memorials. On the second floor proper, where material is available through an interactive computer terminal, one room is devoted to his work as a writer – his escritoire, his books, his letters, his concert notes, his memoirs – and the other to his work as a musician, conductor as well as composer, organized by genre and enhanced by display boards on the Conservatoire and open-air music and an expense account for a performance of the *Symphonie fantastique* (note the 'Sapeurs pompiers [firemen], 5 fr. 50').

There is a basement too in this capacious museum: two rooms deal with performance history, up to modern times, and there is a video room seating 25 and exhibition space. The museum's meticulous labelling and audio commentary are exemplary.

Le Musée Hector Berlioz

69 rue de la République
38260 La Côte-Saint-André
France

phone +33/0 4 7420 2488
fax +33/0 4 7420 8333
website www.musee-hector-berlioz.com

open March–December,
Wednesday–Monday 09.00–12.00,
15.00–18.00; February, 14.00–17.00; closed January

Map 6

Le Musée Hector Berlioz (La Côte-Saint-André: SAEP, 1991)
G. Gefen: *Composers' Houses* (London: Cassell and Vendome, 1998), 30–39

BOITO

The Parma conservatory, one of the premier institutions of its kind in Italy, is called the Conservatorio di Musica 'Arrigo Boito', and it is there that the eponymous composer and librettist is commemorated. Boito was not from Parma himself, but in 1889 he went there to take over the directorship of the conservatory from his ailing friend, Franco Faccio. Born in Padua in 1842, he studied in Milan; he enjoyed only one substantial success as an opera composer, with the 1875 revision of his *Mefistofele*. His *Nerone*, left incomplete after almost 60 years of intermittent struggle, was given only in 1924, six years after his death in 1918. But he is remembered for his librettos, especially those for the *Otello* and *Falstaff* of his friend Verdi and that of Ponchielli's *La Gioconda*.

His study, based on the one in his brother's house in Milan, is one of three studies preserved at the conservatory in Parma, whose structure around open, arcaded courtyards attests to its monastic origins. This and the Toscanini study are in a special museum area on the second floor, housed behind glass; the Pizzetti study is linked with the library. Installed in 1984, Boito's sharply reflects his preoccupations. There are orderly bookcases, well stocked with a wide range of contemporary and classical literature, French, English (including four Shakespeare editions) and of course Italian (among them a dedication copy from D'Annunzio). His notebooks are preserved, among them the jottings he took after visits to Verdi with a view to writing a biography. There are his librettist's tools – two volumes of glossary and two of words arranged alphabetically by numbers of syllables. His ten boxes of notes on the composition of *Nerone* witness all too clearly the agonies he underwent. Much of his furniture is there: his desk (with crystal paperweights, a clock, a tiny globe), his working chair, his upright piano, leather easy chairs. A tuning-fork, a set of Helmholtz resonators and a set of piano-tuning implements bespeak his membership of a commission to determine pitch standards. There is a statuette of Verdi and photos of Verdi and others.

Museo Storico 'Ricardo Barilla'

Conservatorio di Musica 'Arrigo Boito'
Via Conservatorio 27
43100 Parma
Italy

phone +390/0 521 381958
fax +390/0 521 200398
e-mail ssboito@provincia.parma.it

open Tuesday 09.00–14.00,
15.00–19.30, Wednesday 09.00–14.00,
15.00–17.30, also by appointment

Map 9

G. Piamonte and G.N. Vetro, eds.: *Parma Conservatorio di Musica* (Parma: Luigi Battei, 1973) [incl. M. Conati, 'Arrigo Boito direttore onorario del Conservatorio di Musica di Parma con oltre 70 documenti inediti)', 109–69]

G.N. Vetro: 'Lo studio Boito', *Premi, lasciti, donazioni dalla fondazione ad oggi* [Musica a Parma, 8] (Parma: Conservatorio di Musica 'Arrigo Boito', 1987), 48–9

BRAHMS

A whistle-stop tour is very much in the spirit of Johannes Brahms's life. He was a great traveller, mainly in Germany, Switzerland and Austria, but also to Italy and eastern Europe, nearly always in the cause of music or, if not, in the persuit of friendship. Travelling forms the main theme of the imaginatively conceived Brahms museum at Mürzzuschlag, in Styria, where he spent two apparently idyllic summers (1884 and 1885). Some of the places with which he is associated, like Pörtschach in Carinthia and Altaussee in north Styria, he discovered while on tour

or on holiday. Others, like Baden-Baden in the Black Forest, Rüdesheim on the Rhine and Gmunden on the Traunsee (where the first Brahms Museum opened in 1900), he visited at the invitation of friends and then happily returned to. From the evidence of the surviving buildings and furnishings, contemporary accounts and photographs we know that, wherever he was, Brahms lived simply and without personal vanity.

He harboured mixed feelings about his native Hamburg. The family was not (as some biographers have said) impoverished, but was never very well off. They lived first in the Schluterhof at Specksgang 24, where he was born on 7 May 1833, and moved to larger flats in 1835 and 1851. His parents provided their son with an excellent education, even if in his teens he played the piano in bars and dance halls to earn money. From 1853 he was often away from Hamburg, although it remained his base until 1862 when he decided Vienna would better suit his purpose. While several times invited to conduct and perform with the Hamburg Philharmonic, his hopes of a permanent post with the orchestra were never realized.

Any lingering disappointment was finally put aside when, in 1889, the title of Honorary Citizen of Hamburg was conferred on him. Further marks of favour followed. But perhaps it was too late when all the ships in the Hamburg harbour flew black flags and lowered their ensigns to half-mast at the hour of his funeral in Vienna on 6 April 1897. In 1906 a plaque was erected on his birthplace; when the building was destroyed by bombing in 1943 the plaque was salvaged and later attached to a freestanding memorial stone placed nearby in 1958. Another plaque (see p.121) commemorates the building close to its original site. A marble memorial sculpture by Max Klinger was unveiled in the first-floor foyer of the Grosse Musikhalle on the anniversary of his birthday in 1909; other commemorative sculptures by Maria Pirwitz and Thomas Darboven ('Brahms-Kubus') appeared in 1981 in

Plaque near the site of the Brahms birthplace

front of the hall, in Karl-Muck-Platz. Nearby, in the entrance of the Kleine Musikhalle, is a 'Relief-Büste' by Walter Zehle. In 1983 a plaque in memory of his baptism was erected in the St Michaelis-Kirche.

In 1969, a Johannes Brahms-Gesellschaft Internationale Vereinigung was founded to establish a Brahms memorial room and archive in Hamburg at Peterstraße 39, where the society now has its offices and two first-floor rooms are open to the public. The displays are drawn from the distinguished Hofmann Collection, the largest privately held Brahms archive (formerly in Hamburg but now attached to the Musikhochschule, at Jerusalemsberg 4, D–23568 Lübeck, *phone* +49/0 451 1505 401; it is available primarily to scholars). These include surviving items from Brahms's childhood: his baptism spoon, silver tumbler and confirmation cup; a photograph of his first music teacher; a copy of his C major

Piano Sonata op.1 (1853); a copy of the 14 November 1855 concert programme in which Brahms appeared with Clara Schumann and Joseph Joachim; and facsimiles of other works associated with his time in Hamburg such as the op.24 Variations and Fugue on a Theme by Handel, dedicated to Clara in 1861. The document relating to his honorary citizenship is reproduced along with a death mask.

Brahms's meeting with Robert and Clara Schumann in 1853, when he was 20, altered the course of his life: where he lived, how he lived, what he composed. Schumann's mentorship was sadly brief as only months later he suffered a nervous breakdown, followed by confinement and in 1856 death (*see* SCHUMANN). But from the time of Schumann's incapacitation Brahms seems to have dedicated himself to Clara, 14 years his senior, and her children. Their friendship, which was lifelong, involved their spending several summers in close proximity in Lichtental, on the edge of Baden-Baden, a spa town that attracted other musicians, including Johann Strauss, Hermann Levi and Pauline Viardot-García.

During the summers between 1862 and 1873 Clara moved her family and two grand pianos to a house in Lichtental that backed on to the River Oos and the oak-tree promenade known as the Lichtentaler Allee; the house, at Hauptstraße 8, still stands and is marked by a commemorative plaque. Brahms first went to Baden-Baden in 1863, staying with a surgeon, Dr Hammer. He returned in 1864, this time staying briefly with Anton Rubinstein and then at the Hotel zum Bären, where he completed the Piano Quintet in F minor op.34.

The following summer he rented two rooms in a hilltop house, built in 1790, overlooking the Kloster Lichtental not far from Clara's house. The address was Lichtental 136, later Hauptstraße 138 and today Maximilianstraße 85. His 'hübsche Haus auf dem Hügel' was – and still is – reached by steep steps. His regime involved rising early and taking a long walk in the woods, then working until

5 p.m., visiting Clara, returning to work and then rejoining Clara for dinner and piano duets. Brahms returned every summer until 1873, when he stayed only a few days; he visited there again in 1876 and 1877. In 1883 he gave a birthday party for Clara at the Hotel zum Bären on 13 September and in 1887 joined her and their friends, the cellist Robert Hausmann and the violinist Joseph Joachim, to play through the Double Concerto op.102, which they performed for an invited audience at the Kurzhaus in Baden-Baden on 23 September. Shortly before Clara's death, in 1896, Brahms wrote to her about meeting again in Lichtental.

Lichtental proved to be a place where Brahms was able to compose: here he completed the *Deutsches Requiem* and the first two symphonies. Besides the Piano Quintet he produced the String Sextet op.36, the Horn Trio op.40 and the E minor Cello Sonata op.38. Closely associated with Clara and her family are his four-hand piano arrangement of Schubert's Mass in E flat (D950) and the *Alto Rhapsody* op.53, which he wrote in 1869 as a wedding present for Julie Schumann. The *Liebeslieder-Walzer* op.52 and the *Lieder und Gesänge* op.58 also date from his time at Lichtental.

The top-floor rooms in which he lived and worked have been open to the public since 1968, after being saved from demolition. The restored Blue Parlour once had a piano but now is decorated with period furniture, portraits and a

Brahms's summer retreat at Lichtental

bust. The small dormer bedroom is also furnished, with a bust of Clara Schumann by Friedrich Christoph Haussmann and photographs. A third room is incorporated as a display room, with a chronology of Brahms's time in Baden-Baden and a photo collage relating to his life in Vienna, Clara Schumann, his death and memorials. Among the items on display are a statuette (1892) by Carl Kundmann and a death mask, a ring made from Mendelssohn's hair, poetry and an album of Brahms's music owned by Julie Schumann, and an autograph letter from Clara. Downstairs, once a coffee house, is a studio fitted out as a flat which the Brahmsgesellschaft Baden-Baden (founded in 1966) makes available to visiting musicians, composers and musicologists. Baden-Baden honours the composer every other year with a series of *Brahmstage*, and two town squares are named after Brahms and Clara Schumann.

Brahms first visited Altaussee, the Styrian resort that still serves as an embarkation point for walking tours of the Austrian Alps, when he was on holiday with his father in 1862. They stayed two days so that Brahms might have his shoes repaired. He is said by locals to have returned 13 years later, to join Clara Schumann when she was renting a lakeside house. He certainly returned in 1882 for a performance of his Piano Trio in C op.87 and the String Quintet in F op.88. The concert is commemorated with a plaque on the side of the Hotel Seevilla, which also remembers him with a Brahms Café.

Brahms discovered the delights of Pörtschach, a luxurious spa perched on a peninsula on the northern side of the Wörthersee, when performing at the casino in Klagenfurt in 1867. He returned ten years later and spent three summers in a row there, the first (1877) in two tiny rooms in the household wing of the Schloß Leonstain, south-west of the town, as the guest of Baron von Pausinger and his wife Fanny. Brahms played duets with the baroness, who in 1882 presented him with a map with 37 watercolour and pen-and-ink drawings of the area as a souvenir. For the next two summers he rented the first floor of a private house not far away, the Krainer-Häuschen (today the Haus Rapatz), from where he could take hour-long walks in the forest surrounding the local Benedictine monastery of St Paul. In his final summer there he gave a concert with the Viennese soprano Louise Dustmann and the 15-year-old violinist Marie Soldat: the programme included newly composed piano music (op.76), the Violin Concerto op.77, the Violin Sonata op.78 and lieder. A marble bust of Brahms (1907) by his friend Berta Kuppelwieser stands in the courtyard of the Schloß Leonstain, which is today a hotel. There is a Brahms room on a corner on the first floor, room no.6, overlooking the lake, dedicated to his memory: in it are facsimiles of letters, a portrait and facsimiles of pages from the Violin Concerto and the *Triumphlied*, with a photograph of the room as it was in Brahms's day. Another memorial room contains ten pianos dating from 1840 to 1930. During the last week of August a Brahms competition and in the first week of September a Brahms festival are held in Pörtschach.

After Lichtental, fashionable Bad Ischl in the densely wooded heart of the Salzkammergut became Brahms's favourite retreat. When he began going there in 1880, it was the summer home of Emperor Franz Josef and his court; later, from 1910, it was the home of Franz Lehár (*see* LEHÁR). Unlike the Emperor and Lehár, Brahms was content to rent two upstairs rooms (with views of the mountains and the confluence of the Traun and Ischl) in the 'Gruberhaus' at Mastaliergasse 5, belonging to a city official, on the edge of town near the road to Salzburg. In his first summer there he composed the Tragic and Academic Festival overtures. He returned in 1882, when he completed the C major Piano Trio, the F major String Quintet and the *Gesang der Parzen* op.89, and then every summer between 1889 and 1896. The

house remains in private hands, but its wooden porch railings are now displayed in the Brahms museum in Mürzzuschlag and the bust that stood in the garden, almost obscured by the hedge, was moved to the garden of the municipal museum in Bad Ischl in 1997.

During this period Brahms often travelled from Bad Ischl to Gmunden to visit his Viennese friends, Viktor and Olga von Miller zu Aichholz, who in 1885 acquired a villa there, at Traunleiten 30 (today the Brahmsschule, Lindenstraße 11). Viktor von Miller zu Aichholz was a wealthy industrialist and a passionate lover and collector of Brahms's music. He was the founding president of the Wien Brahms-Gesellschaft. In 1900 he opened the first Brahms Museum in the garden house where Brahms had stayed on his Gmunden estate, and in 1905 published photographs of Brahms at the Miller-Aichholz homes in Vienna and Gmunden (*Ein Brahms Bilderbuch*).

The museum, at Brahmsstöcklweg 12, occupied seven rooms and displayed personal items including Brahms's

The former museum in the Brahms Villa at Gmunden

baptism shawl, his father's trumpet and his toy soldier collection; the Bösendorfer grand piano, music and furniture from his Bad Ischl home; his batons and opera glasses; coffee and tea machines and services; and his slippers and original death mask. In 1939 the Miller-Aichholzes gave the museum to the city and in 1965 the contents were moved to the local history museum, the Kammerhofmuseum der Stadt Gmunden, where in 1989 a room was dedicated to Brahms. Items from the Miller-Aichholz collection were again displayed, along with photographs of the interior of the Bad Ischl house corroborating the displays. Also shown is a red velvet wallet with Brahms's name in gold leaf, his Viennese calling card and statuettes of Brahms and Joachim as well as letters and Olga's diaries. In 1997, on the centenary of his death, the museum mounted an exhibition, 'Johannes Brahms und die Familie Miller-Aichholz in Gmunden: Dokumente einer grossen Freundschaft'.

Brahms spent the summers of 1884 and 1885 in the village of Mürzzuschlag, in the Styrian Alps. It is here that he composed the Fourth Symphony between walks in the forest, today commemorated by a 'Brahms-Weg'. Mürzzuschlag is the home of the Österreichische Brahms-Gesellschaft and of a museum in the complex of buildings at Wiener Straße 2 where he rented rooms. The entrance, marked 'Overture', uses imaginatively conceived theatre maquettes with audio accompaniment in a darkened room to illustrate the outlines of Brahms's life, setting the stage for a more personal view of him. The main part of the museum is devoted to his summer holidays and trips abroad. The building's sun porch is transformed into that of an Italian villa, with quotations from his correspondence with Clara on the walls. There is a copy of a 19th-century Baedeker guide to Italy, a map with flags and period postcards; in the background is the sound of a cricket. His summer in Pörtschach is represented by scenes with quotations from his letters,

excerpts from Marie Soldat's diary, a violin with broken strings (she evidently broke strings while playing Herr Brahms's new sonata and concerto) and a recording of the violin sonata in the background. A chair with a coat and hat slung over it and muddy shoes below complete the scene. To illustrate his summers at Bad Ischl, a place next to Brahms is cut out and a mirror inserted in a life-size photo of the composer and a group of friends, enabling the visitor to join the picture. Also on display is an oil painting, which once belonged to Brahms, of the house, a medal similar to the one he received from the Emperor in 1889 and Brahms's calling card.

A bridge made from the railings of the Bad Ischl house and the sound of rain create a transition to Pressbaum, a suburb of Vienna where Brahms spent the summer of 1881, illustrated with a train set (Brahms loved trains and evidently always travelled third class). A partly open door invites the visitor to peek in: inside is a trunk with Brahms's travelling clothes (including shirt fronts and cuffs and his well-worn slippers), surrounded by bookcases with scores and a desk, a portable coffeemaker and other travelling paraphernalia. The final display room is devoted to his summer in Mürzzuschlag: in the centre is a 'Wissen Turm' (Tower of Knowledge), with glass-topped drawers to pull out and examine on each of its four sides; one contains Brahms's own silk bow ties. The walls are decorated with quotations from letters written from Mürzzuschlag. At the end of the tour is a concert room seating 70 with a Bachmann grand piano that belonged to friends and on which he played.

During the winters Brahms toured extensively, playing and conducting. In the 1880s and into the 90s he was a regular visitor at the court of Meiningen in Thuringia, where his champion Hans von Bülow was Hofmusikdirektor (1880–85); the second, third and fourth symphonies were all tried over at Meiningen before their official premières. Brahms developed a warm friendship with the Duke and Duchess, with whom

*Brahms and his friends, displayed at
Mürzzuschlag*

he corresponded and who accommodated him in the Schloß on his visits.
Today the palace is a museum – or rather
a series of museums, one of which is
musical and incorporates memorial
rooms to von Bülow and Max Reger (*see*
REGER), who was also a great admirer of
Brahms, as well as to Brahms himself. In
addition, the Brahms Room celebrates
his connection with the court clarinettist
Richard Mühlfeld (1856–1907), for
whom he composed the Clarinet Trio
op.114 and the Clarinet Quintet op.115
in 1891 and the two clarinet sonatas
op.120 in 1894, and with whom Brahms
toured in 1895. Mühlfeld's A clarinet is
on display along with programmes
from the Meiningen Herzogliches
Hoftheater, copies of music owned by
Reger and a copy of the *Gesang der Parzen*
which Brahms dedicated to the Duke in
1886. Portraits of Joachim, Hausmann,
Mühlfeld and Brahms (by Fedor Enke)
line the walls. The chapel, in a separate
wing of the palace, is now converted into
a Konzertsaal Johannes Brahms, seating
200; installed there are a piano Brahms
once played and an organ given in
memory of Reger. In the palace park is a
Brahms-Weg and there is a bust of him
(the first German Brahms memorial) in
the English Garden created by Adolf von
Hildebrand in 1899. Mühlfeld is buried
in the park.
     Bearing in mind his long residence in
Vienna and close association with the

Gesellschaft der Musikfreunde (which
now owns his library and named the small
hall of the Musikverein the Brahms-Saal),
one might have expected to find an
important Brahms museum in the city.
He lived at a number of addresses when he
first arrived: Novaragasse 39 and 55 in
1862–3 and, in 1863–5, in the fourth-floor
flat of the house in which Mozart lived
during 1781, Singerstraße 7, near the
Stephansdom; in 1866–7 he lived at
Postgasse 6 and in 1869–71 at Ungargasse
2 ('Zur goldenen Spinne'). In 1872,
when he was appointed Director of the
Gesellschaft der Musikfreunde, he moved
to permanent quarters on the third
floor of Karlsgasse 4, a block of flats near
the Karlskirche and within sight of the
Musikverein. At first he rented two rooms
from the Vogl family, later adding a third
for his library; soon after the last member
of the family died in 1886 he bought a
lease on their apartment and installed a
housekeeper.
     Brahms died at home on 3 April 1897
and was buried near Beethoven and
Schubert in the Zentralfriedhof; the
memorial sculpture is by Ilse Conrat.
Karlsgasse 4 would have been the most
appropriate for a *Gedenkstätte* had it
not been demolished to make way for
the Technische Universität in 1907 –
though not before Brahms's friend
Maria Fellinger photographed the
rooms as Brahms had known them.
Towards the end of his life Brahms was
close to the Fellinger family, who lived
at the Arenbergschlößl at Landstraßer
Hauptstraße 96, where there is a bronze
relief plaque commemorating the friendship. Not until 1922 was a plaque attached
to the new building at Karlsgasse 4, but as
early as 1908 a Brahms statue, by Rudolf
Weyr, was erected in the green space (the
Resselpark) between his home and the
Musikverein.
     A memorial room was finally opened
in 1980 on the first floor of the Haydn
Museum at Haydngasse 19, in part to
commemorate Brahms's admiration for
Haydn. On display is a facsimile of his so-
called Haydn variations for two pianos
op.56b and the Ferdinand Hofmann

clavichord (c1800) that belonged first to Haydn and later to Brahms. There is also furniture from the Karlsgasse flat, including a piano stool given to him by Maria Fellinger as a Christmas present. On the walls are watercolours of the exterior of Karlsgasse 4 by Rudolf Schmidt and of the rooms of the flat by Wilhelm Nowak (1904) as well as a portrait (c1892) by Fritz Luckhardt and photographs by Maria Fellinger.

There are still more sites marked by plaques: where he held posts (the Hotel Stadt Hamburg at Detmold, where he was choirmaster in 1856), stayed with friends (the Wiesbaden house at Adolfsallee 23, home of the Bererath family), spent summers (on houses where he stayed at Rüschlikon near Zürich in 1874 and at Pressbaum in 1881) and sought in vain to restore his health (the house in Karlsbad where he stayed in the autumn of 1896).

Johannes-Brahms-Museum
Peterstraße 39
20355 Hamburg
Germany

phone +49/0 40 452158
e-mail info@brahms-hamburg.de
website www.brahms-hamburg.de

open Tuesday, Thursday 10.00–13.00, first Sunday of each month (and third, May–September) 11.00–14.00

Brahmsmuseum im Brahmshaus Baden-Baden
Maximilianstraße 85
76534 Baden-Baden-Lichtental
Germany

phone +49/0 7221 71172, 99872
fax +49/0 7221 71104
e-mail brahms.baden-baden@t-online.de
website www.brahms.baden-baden.de

open Monday, Wednesday and Friday 15.00–17.00; Sunday and holidays 10.00–13.00; during Brahmstage, daily 10.00–16.00

Brahms-Museum
Schloß Leonstain
Hauptstraße 205

9210 Pörtschach am Wörthersee
Austria

phone +43/0 4272 4072
fax +43/0 4272 377

open May–September by appointment

Brahms-Museum
Kammerhofmuseum der Stadt Gmunden
Kammerhofgasse 8
4810 Gmunden
Austria

phone +43/0 7612 794244
e-mail museum@gmunden.ooe.gv.at

open Tuesday–Saturday 10.00–12.00, 14.00–17.00, Sunday and holidays 10.00–12.00

Brahms-Museum
Wiener Straße 2
8680 Mürzzuschlag/Semmering
Austria

phone, fax +43/0 3852 3434
e-mail info@brahmsmuseum.at
website www.brahmsmuseum.at

open May–September, daily 10.00–12.00, 14.00–17.00; November–April, Thursday–Sunday 10.00–12.00, 14.00–16.00

Abteilung Musikgeschichte
Meininger Museen
Schloß Elisabethenburg
98617 Meiningen
Germany

phone +49/0 3693 881023
fax +49/0 3693 503644
e-mail service@meiningermuseen.de
website www.meiningermuseen.de

open Tuesday–Sunday 10.00–18.00

Brahms-Gedenkraum
Haydn Museum
Haydngasse 19
1060 Vienna
Austria

phone +43/0 1596 1307
e-mail post@mus.magwien.gv.at
website www.museum.vienna.at

open Tuesday–Sunday 09.00–12.15, 13.00–17.30

Maps 7, 1

O. Biba: *Johannes Brahms in Wien: Ausstellung Archiv der Gesellschaft der Musikfreunde in Wien 19 April bis 30 Juni 1983* (Vienna: Gesellschaft der Musikfreunde, 1983)

O. Biba: 'Brahms-Gedenkstätten in Wien', *Österreichische Musikzeitschrift*, xxxviii (1983), 4

E. Prillinger: 'Brahms und Gmunden', *Brahms-Studien*, v (1983), 181–204

O. Biba: 'Brahms in Wien', *Hamburger Jahrbuch für Musikwissenschaft*, vii (1984), 259–71

U. Tobisch-Kohlbecker, G. Abel and J. Heinen: *Johannes Brahms* (Baden-Baden, n.d. [c1985])

K. Hofmann: *Johannes Brahms und Hamburg* (Hamburg: Dialog, 2/1986)

H. Kretschmer: *Wiener Musikergedenkstätten* (Vienna: J & V Edition, 3/1992)

H. Müller: *Schloss Elisabethenburg Meiningen* (Munich and Regensburg: Schnell & Steiner, 1993)

H. Müller: *Auf den Spuren von Johannes Brahms in Meiningen* (Stadt Meiningen, n.d.)

I. Zinnow: '25 Jahre Brahms-Gesellschaft Hamburg', *Brahms-Studien*, x (1994), 57–9

R. and K. Hofmann: *Johannes Brahms in Baden-Baden* (Baden-Baden, 1996)

O. Biba, R. Hofmann, K. Hofmann, J. Neubacher: '. . . in meinen Tönen spreche ich . . .' für Johannes Brahms, 1833–1897 (Hamburg: Braus, 1997) [exhibition catalogue, Museum für Kunst und Gewerbe, Hamburg, 1997]

W. Ebert: *Brahms in Aussee* (Altaussee: Hotel Seevilla, 1997)

A. Fuchs: *Auf ihren Spuren in Kärnten: Alban Berg, Gustav Mahler, Johannes Brahms, Hugo Wolf, Anton Webern* (Klagenfurt: Kärntner Druck- und Verlagsgesellschaft, 3/1997), 37–53

A. Schusser, ed.: *Joseph Haydn-Gedenkstätte mit Brahms-Gedenkraum, Wien 6, Haydngasse 19* (Vienna: Historisches Museum der Stadt Wien, n.d. [c1997]), 64–9

I. Spitzbart: *Johannes Brahms und die Familie Miller-Aichholz in Gmunden und Wien* (Gmunden: Kammerhofmuseum der Stadt Gmunden, 1997)

G. Gefen: *Composers' Houses* (London: Cassell and Vendome, 1998)

W. Herrmann: *Musik ist eine heilige Kunst: Komponisten, Dirigenten, Sänger im Ausseerland* (Liezen: Jost Druck & Medientechnik, 1999), 15–18

BRAND

The Austrian composer Max Brand is remembered almost entirely for a single composition: his opera *Maschinist Hopkins* (1929), a kind of industrial, working-class counterpart to *Lulu*, which reached 41 theatres in four years and then – with the rise of Fascism and Brand's flight to the USA – went into total eclipse until the 1980s. Brand, born in Lemberg (now L'viv) in 1896, lived in Vienna from 1924, left for America in the 1930s and returned to Austria in 1975, spending his last years in the small town of Langenzersdorf (he lived at Chiamanistraße 10), an outer suburb of Vienna to the north of the city, on the main road to Prague. He died nearby in 1980.

During his American years Brand had been active as a stage composer and especially in the development of electronic music. A Max Brand prize is awarded annually in New York to young electronic music composers. He had a studio in his cellar in Langenzersdorf; his original synthesizer is preserved in a Brand memorial room set up in 1989 within the museum, in Langenzersdorf, to the well-known Austrian sculptor Anton Hanak (1875–1934). Built and designed in New York in the late 1950s by Brand himself, in collaboration with Robert A. Moog, it is something of a period piece with its two manuals (fitted with special glissando devices), its four pedals, its tape decks, generators and oscilloscope.

This prototype synthesizer is its centrepiece, but the Brand room also contains a number of photos from his life, photocopies of letters (from Berg, Krenek, Villa-Lobos, Antheil, Eimert and others), his brown overcoat and beret and his pipe, and reproductions of posters and handbills of performances of his works (among them a 1944 performance of his scenic oratorio *The Gate* at the Met in New York). Little survives of his own electronic output as in his last years he inadvertently destroyed many of the tapes.

Max Brand Archiv und Museum

Anton Hanak Museum
Oberer Kirchengasse 23
2103 Langenzersdorf
Austria

phone +43/0 1 2244 2308

e-mail langenzersdorfer-museen@aon.at,
helmuth.schwarzjirg@siemens.at
website
www.members.aon.at/langenzersdorfer-
museen/brand

open 15 April–15 November, Tuesday
09.00–12.00, Saturday and Sunday
09.00–12.00, 13.30–18.00 or by
appointment

Map 1

BREDICEANU

The town of Lugoj, in western Romania,
is generally recognized as the country's
leading centre of choral music. It takes
great pride in its musical heritage and has
a Casa Muzicii, a museum in what was
formerly the house of a leading composer
and conductor, in which there are rooms
and areas within rooms dedicated to the
memory of the town's eminent musicians
(*see* VIDU *and* BARBU).

Among these, Tiberiu Brediceanu has
a strong claim to pre-eminence, for his
activities stretched far beyond the
confines of his native town. Born in
Lugoj in 1877, he was involved in the
foundation of conservatories in Cluj and
Braşov and the national opera and
theatre in Bucharest, and he also held the
directorships of the opera houses in Cluj
and Bucharest during part of the inter-
war period. He was an avid collector of
folk music and his compositions show its
influence. He died in 1968, in Bucharest.

Two of the rooms in the Casa Muzicii
have displays devoted to him. He is represented, by a portrait and other material, in
the upper-floor room mainly dedicated to
Vidu, and some of his furniture is shown
in the room assigned to the choir. Other
members of his family too were prominent in Lugoj cultural life and are represented at the Casa Personalităţilor, a
commemoration of the town's eminent
people, at Splaiul Coriolan Brediceanu 11.

Casa Muzicii
Str. Magnoliei 10
1800 Lugoj

Timiş
Romania

phone +40/02 56 354903
website
www.infotim.ro/patrimcb/tm/lugj/muzieap/
casamuz

open 15 May–14 October, 9.00–17.00;
15 October–14 May, 08.00–16.00

Map 11

BRITTEN

Both Benjamin Britten and Peter Pears
made it clear in their wills that they did
not want the Red House, their Aldeburgh
home from 1957, to become a museum:
they were more interested in the future
than in commemorating the past. The
trustees of the Britten–Pears Foundation
have of course respected their wishes. But
the fact remains that admirers of their art
are eager to see where and how the great
men lived, and from time to time small
groups and individuals are allowed to visit
the house (as too are people associated
with music-making in the Aldeburgh
Festival, who often stay there) – which is
so redolent of the two men, their values
and their way of life, that it cannot fail to
illuminate the music by providing a
context for its creation.

Both Britten (*b* 1913) and Pears (*b*
1910) died in the house, in 1976 and
1986 respectively. They had lived elsewhere in the area since before World War
II – at the Old Mill, in Snape, which
Britten bought in 1937, and then at Crag
House (4 Crabbe Street), close to the
Aldeburgh Jubilee Hall – before they
moved to the Red House, exchanging
houses with the artist Mary Potter. The
house, parts of which date from the 17th
century, is part of an estate that also
comprises a large library, made from
what was originally stable buildings
(and which in Britten's time included a
swimming pool), and three cottages,
Red Studio (built for Mary Potter in
1962), Cosy Nook (built for their housekeeper in 1972) and Red Cottage, which
until the early 1970s contained Britten's

own composing study but is now altered and used for archive storage. In later years, when noise from a nearby airbase troubled him, they bought another house, at Horham (some 40 km inland), where Britten wrote his last works. That house was sold after his death, but the composing studio is marked by a blue plaque. So too are the Old Mill and Crag House, his birthplace in Lowestoft (21 Kirkley Cliff Road) and two of his London residences (45 St John's Wood High Street, NW8, and 8 Halliford Street, N1). Concurrently with each Aldeburgh Festival, exhibitions are held in the library, in which nearly all Britten's manuscripts are deposited.

The reception rooms on the Red House ground floor are still very much as they were in Britten and Pears's time. The furniture is an assortment, some of it from Britten's family, some from Pears, some bought (chiefly from Heal's in London), some given to them. Many ornaments and other such items are gifts, mostly acquired abroad, often from distinguished musicians such as Rostropovich and Shostakovich. There is some William Morris wallpaper and some cork wall covering, and Meissen and Crown Derby china. Pears was an eager and discriminating art collector, and the house accommodates many fine pictures, particularly by their friends and colleagues such as Mary Potter, John Piper, Duncan Grant, Sidney Nolan, Keith Grant and Milein Cosman, as well

as several that he commissioned from their protégés; and there are bronzes by Georg Ehrlich, mostly in the extensive gardens. The admirer of Britten's music – and come to that of Pears's singing too – will find a great deal in the house that in some curious way resonates with it.

The Red House
Golf Road
Aldeburgh
Suffolk IP15 5PZ
Great Britain

phone +44/0 1728 452615
fax +44/0 1728 453076
e-mail bpl@britten-pears.co.uk
website www.britten-pears.co.uk

not normally open to the public (see above)

Map 5

BRUCKNER

In Bruckner's time and for several centuries before, the monastery of St Florian, near Linz in Upper Austria, huge, grand and powerful, dominated the region. It also dominated Bruckner's life and his psyche, and it still possesses him today.

Anton Bruckner was born on 4 September 1824, eight kilometres away, in what was even then the quaintly provincial Upper Austrian village of Ansfelden, the eldest son of the village

The Red House at Aldeburgh

schoolmaster and church organist. As a child he lived in the 17th-century schoolhouse, nestled on a hillock just below the parish church, where, from the age of ten, he deputized at the organ.

The Ansfelden schoolhouse became a Bruckner museum in 1971. The birth room and the schoolroom itself are commemorated on the ground floor; a further room vividly illustrates Bruckner's life in a picture collage – the years in and around Linz, at Ansfelden, Hörsching (a plaque marks the schoolhouse where he studied with his cousin Johann Baptist Weiss), St Florian and in Vienna, as well as his travels to London, Paris, Switzerland and within Austria. At the top of the stairs Bruckner's death mask is displayed behind a wrought iron gate. On the first floor there are two exhibition rooms, one primarily dedicated to his ecclesiastical connections (among them church relics and a Last Supper picture with Bruckner's face superimposed on one of the disciples) and a second, larger one with a quite dramatic display of facsimiles, accompanied by brief recorded excerpts.

On the death of his father in 1837, the 13-year-old Anton was sent to St Florian, where he was taken in as a chorister; when his voice broke he continued to play a part in musical activities as a violinist and deputy organist. St Florian remains a working Augustinian monastery, with an important choir school. The present complex

Bruckner's birthplace at Ansfelden

of buildings, a splendid example of Austrian Baroque architecture, includes a vast and beautifully kept library, a characteristically elaborate chapel and a seemingly endless succession of imperial rooms, of which the last two open on the public tour are now devoted to the commemoration of Bruckner: in the first, his deathbed is displayed, along with photographs of his last days and wreaths from his funeral service, while the second contains furniture from the schoolhouse in Ansfelden. Concerts are given in the imposing Baroque marble hall and there are daily organ recitals in the chapel.

Bruckner decided to follow in his father's footsteps; he was trained as a schoolteacher in Linz and had spells of teaching in small villages. He was briefly at Windhaag bei Freistadt, some 60 km to the north, close to the Czech border (the school where he taught, now the Alte Anton Bruckner-Schule, bears a plaque commemorating his time there). Then in 1843 he moved to Kronstorf, about 12 km south-west of St Florian, as assistant schoolmaster (*Schulgehilfe*). As such, he had a room on the upper floor of the schoolhouse, in front of the church. A plaque was put up in 1913 to mark the house in which he lived, and on his centenary in 1924 it was decided that the rooms associated with him should be dedicated to his memory. That was not possible until 1974. The Kleinmuseum, or Bruckner-Zimmer, was opened in its present form in 1989. It is clear that the little terrace of houses has been somewhat reorganized since Bruckner's day, for the space in no.4 Brucknerplatz – it is tucked back off the road, behind the Marktgemeindamt (the local administrative office), close to the church – consists of little beyond a corridor and a staircase, and upstairs a landing. The walls bear a modest display about Bruckner's Kronstorf years, with information about the works he wrote there (all sacred, but not without echoes in his symphonic music), the school and other musicians linked with the village. The prize item is the schoolmaster's violin, in a display case upstairs, by Joseph Pauli of Linz (1805), on which Bruckner is likely to have played when in Kronstorf.

In 1845 he returned to St Florian, first to instruct the choirboys, before he obtained his first music post three years later, as a 'provisional organist'. A performance in 1847 of Mendelssohn's *St Paul* at Linz was the catalyst for his gradual move towards composition, signalled by performances at St Florian of his Requiem Mass (1849) and his *Magnificat* and *Missa solemnis* in B flat minor (both 1854). Bruckner might not recognize the heavily restored instrument known now as the chapel's 'Bruckner-Orgel'; the keyboards and pedals of the four-manual instrument that he did know are now on display at his birthplace.

Bruckner left St Florian in 1856 to take up the post of cathedral organist (which also included duties at the Pfarrkirche) at Linz; the organ Bruckner played is still in use. Although he was granted the freedom of the city on his 70th birthday and his name graces the main concert hall in Linz, there is no Bruckner museum there. But on the strength of his eight visits between 1869 and 1892 to the small town of Vöcklabruck, 60 km to the south-west, where his married sister Rosalie lived, the local history museum there devotes a room to him, displaying his black hat, an oil portrait of his biographer and resident of Vöcklabruck, Max Auer, a letter of 1883 from Bruckner and photographs of the plaque erected in 1884 in his honour, near the clock tower in the town square.

Bruckner finally settled in Vienna in 1868, when he was appointed to succeed his teacher, Simon Sechter, at the Konservatorium der Gesellschaft der Musikfreunde. In spite of the many great symphonies he wrote in Vienna, he lived largely in the shadow of Brahms and in fear of the anti-Wagnerians. He is not among the many musicians currently commemorated in a Viennese museum. But he is not entirely neglected in the city. Memorial plaques grace the house at Währinger Straße 41, where he lived on the second floor (flat no.10) between 1868 and 1876, when he composed symphonies nos.2–5, and the building at Heßgasse 7 (now Schottenring 5) where, between 1877 and 1895, he lived gratis in a fourth-floor flat thanks to the generosity of an admirer, Dr Anton Özelt-Newin. He died on 11 October 1896 in an imperial grace-and-favour apartment in the Belvedere where he had lived during his last year; the memorial plaque can be seen at Prinz-Eugen-Straße 27. Since 1899 a bust, with the muse of music in attendance, has adorned the central Stadtpark, and there is another, dating from 1912, at Vienna University.

Bruckner bequeathed his music manuscripts to the Hofbibliothek (now the Österreichisches Nationalbibliothek), but at his request he was not buried at the Zentralfriedhof among the musical giants of Vienna: instead, after his funeral at the Karlskirche, his coffin was taken to St Florian and installed in the crypt of the Stiftkirche, beneath the Bruckner-Orgel and surrounded by an elaborate, faintly macabre arrangement of the skulls and bones from some of the earliest burials on the site.

Bruckner's sarcophagus at St Florian

Bruckner Geburtshaus
Augustinerstraße 3
4052 Ansfelden
Austria

phone +43/0 7229 82376

open April–October, Sunday 0.00–12.00,
14.00–17.00, Wednesday 14.00–17.00

Anton Bruckner-Gedenkräume
Stift St Florian
Stiftstraße 1
4490 St Florian
Austria

phone +43/0 7224 8903
fax +43/0 7224 890260

open daily; guided tours at 10.00,
11.00, 14.00, 15.00 and 16.00
(recitals on the Bruckner organ 16
May–15 October except Saturdays,
14.30)

Museum Kronstorfer Brucknerzimmer
Brucknerplatz 4
4484 Kronstorf
Austria

phone +43/0 7225 82560
(Marktgemeindeamt)

open Monday–Friday 08.00–12.00,
Saturday and Sunday 16.00–18.00 (or
by arrangement; key available from
Cafehaus Arbeithuber, opposite, +43/0
7225 8824, in working hours, daily
09.00–18.30)

Anton Bruckner-Gedächtnisraum
Heimathaus Vöcklabruck
Hinterstadt 19
4840 Vöcklabruck
Austria

phone +43/0 7672 25249

open May–September, Monday–Friday
09.00–12.00, 13.00–15.00;
October–April, Wednesday 09.00–12.00

Map 1

H. Kretschmer: *Wiener Musikergedenkstätten*
(Vienna: J & V Edition, 3/1992)

[L. Nowak, L. Schultes and others:] *Das
Geburtshaus Anton Bruckners, Ansfelden:
Führer* (Linz: Ober-Österreichisches
Landesmuseum, n.d.)

BUDRIUNAS brothers

The three Budriunas brothers played a
central role in the Lithuanian choral
tradition in the middle years of the last
century. They were born in the small
town of Pabiržė, near Birzai in northern
Lithuania, across the turn of the previous
century, Motiejus in 1898, Antanas in
1902 and Bronius in 1909; all three were
conductors and composers, but only
Antanas remained in his native country,
where he taught in Kaunas and Vilnius
and died in 1966. Motiejus worked
chiefly as an editor and teacher, and in
1944 settled in Germany, where he
worked among Lithuanian immigrants
and died in 1969; Bronius, primarily a
choral director, also went to Germany
and then in 1949 to the USA, where he
taught and conducted Lithuanian choirs,
nurturing traditional music, and died in
Los Angeles in 1994.

Their sister Elena Budrainitė lived in
the house in which they were born until
1979 and after her death half the house
was set aside as a museum to the three
men. A 19th-century building, it is
furnished in the style of the beginning of
the century; the exhibits include family
photographs and published works by all
three composers.

Antanas Budriunas spent his working
life in Vilnius, as a choral conductor and
teacher at the Lithuanian State Conservatory. His study in the house he built
for his family, who still live there, is
preserved in his memory, exactly as he left
it: his own piano is there, his working desk,
his armchairs, his records and his library,
of both books and music, including much
of his own manuscript material.

Birthplace of the Budriunas brothers*
Ramioji gatvė 2
5288 Pabiržė
Lithuania

phone +370/0 4505 9227

open by appointment only

Antanas Budriunas Memorial Room*
8–1 Kuosu gatvė
2055 Vilnius
Lithuania

phone +370/0 5234 1686

open by appointment only

Map 2

BULL

The violinist Ole Bull (1810–80) was a lovable and gifted if quirky character, largely forgotten today despite international fame in his lifetime as a virtuoso and a champion of Norwegian nationalism. He is amply commemorated, both in Norway and in the USA, as well as by diverse writers – Hans Christian Andersen ('An Episode of Ole Bull's Life'), George Sand (*Malgré tout*), Ibsen (*Peer Gynt*) and Longfellow (*Tales of a Wayside Inn*). His idiosyncratic playing gained few followers and his naive violin music has not stood the test of time.

While pursuing his own career, Bull championed Norwegian writers and composers, notably Grieg, 33 years his junior. At the age of 40 he established the first Norwegian theatre in his native Bergen, where he is commemorated by a statue and fountain by the sculptor Ambrosia Tønnesen. His hopes of establishing a Norwegian music conservatory in Oslo were realized only in 1883, three years after his death. In his 50s, he built the first of two important houses: the first – still in the family – at Valestrand, north of Bergen, the second a Moorish fantasy on the tiny island of Lysøen, 30 km to the south, which in 1974 was donated to the Norwegian Society for the Preservation of Ancient Monuments and ten years later became a memorial museum.

In the 1850s, Ole Bull contemplated American citizenship. Flushed with the success of his concert tours in the USA,

he purchased, sight unseen, 17 square miles (44 sq. km) of forestland near the Allegheny Mountains of Pennsylvania, to found a colony of Norwegian settlers, 'Oleana'. But his settlers began arriving before sensible provision could be made for them and they soon became disenchanted. As many as 300 were attracted to New Norway, the first of three planned villages, founded in September 1852, but after a harsh winter most went wearily on their way, either west to Wisconsin and Minnesota (where, strangely enough, a statue of Ole Bull was erected in a Minneapolis park in 1897) or back to the old Norway. The remaining two villages were never realized, though an 'Ole Bull Run' and a two-storey 'Ole Bull Castle' evidently were. Bull became involved in another unrealistic scheme in 1855, this time to found an opera company in New York City. But he survived the financial chaos and continued lucrative concert tours during the winters, returning to Norway each summer. Today, in the Kettle Creek Valley of Pennsylvania, all that remains of Oleana is a crossroads in an open field within Ole Bull State Park and a monument erected in 2002. Elsewhere in America, Bull's portrait hangs at Vesterheim, the Norwegian-American Museum in Decorah, Iowa, and, at the Wayside Inn (of Longfellow fame) in Sudbury, Massachusetts, a small Ole Bull archive (pictures, a signed piece of music and a few mementoes) is faithfully maintained. Ole Bull's 1687 Stradivarius violin is now in the Herbert R. Axelrod Quartet at the Smithsonian Institution in Washington, DC.

From a child prodigy Ole Bull grew into an immensely charismatic and attractive man who never lacked for admirers. In 1836 he married Félicie Villeminot, the granddaughter of his Parisian landlady. Their son, Alexander, inherited the summer estate at Valestrand, which passed through his sister's children to the present heirs. Although not formally open to the public, it can be visited by appointment. From a distance 'Bullahuset', atop a hillock, appears relatively conventional, but on closer inspection the pink-painted building turns out to be embellished with green dragons with bright red tongues. Inside, the house offers a clear foretaste of the flamboyance of Lysøen. Passing through the three reception rooms on the ground floor and up the curved pine staircase, the caller comes to two extraordinary rooms. The first, inspired by Italian church architecture, is dominated by a marble fireplace and barley-sugar wood columns supporting scalloped arches. On the bed in the corner is an apparently infamous tiger-skin rug. There are busts of Bull and Grieg and on the desk opposite the bed a statue of Beethoven. Across the hall and through the peaked doors, the second, larger room, with its vaulted wooden ceiling, is dominated by the polar bear rug on the floor and a saddle resting on a stand. Around the walls are photos, lithographs and a large oil portrait of Bull, a portrait of a folk violinist and a map of the USA.

Bull married his second wife in 1870, two years before acquiring the island of Lysøen (Island of Light) and ten years before his death there. Wealthy and American, Sara Chapman Thorp, from Madison, Wisconsin, was 40 years younger than her husband; their only child, Olea, was born in 1871. When Bull

Villa Lysø

took possession of the 170-acre (70-hectare) fjord island, there were only a few farm buildings on it. The island had once belonged to the Bernadine monks of the medieval abbey Lysekloster. Instead of refurbishing the existing buildings, Bull engaged an architect, Conrad Frederik von der Lippe, and a local carpenter to build a new house of pinewood on the east of the island as a summer retreat. The design incorporated an exotic onion-shaped dome, supported by barley-sugar columns, and intricate trelliswork inside and out. Bull called his exotic villa his 'little Alhambra'. He financed the project with earnings from his concerts in America but in 1873 sold it to his father-in-law Senator Joseph Thorp who in his will secured Lysøen for his granddaughter Olea, who passed it on to her adopted daughter Sylvea Bull Curtis (born in 1907). Sylvea spent most of her summers on the island before she donated it in 1973.

Based in New England in the winters (at 'Elmwood', in Cambridge, Massachusetts, and in West Lebanon, Maine), Ole Bull and his young family returned each year to Norway to spend their summers on the island. Bull mapped it out, planned paths to the two island lakes, bathing houses and gazebos as well as orchards and lily ponds. He acquired boats to ferry his family and friends on visits. His music room today seats more than 100 and is decorated with souvenirs of his concert career. He died in the villa on 17 August 1880 and was accorded a state funeral (then the largest ever), at which Grieg delivered the oration. His grave in Bergen, in the Assistenkirkegården near the old city gate, is surmounted by a large urn.

Bullahuset
Valestrandfossen
5281 Valestrand
Osterøy
Norway

phone +47/0 5639 4264

open by appointment

Ole Bulls Villa

Museet Lysøen
5215 Lysekloster
Lysøen
Norway

phone +47/0 5630 9077
fax +47/0 5630 9372
e-mail lysoen@online.no
website www.lysoen.no

open mid-May–end August,
Monday–Saturday 12.00–16.00,
Sunday 11.00–17.00; September,
Sunday 12.00–16.00; ferries from
Buena Kai at Sørestraumen on the hour
during opening hours, guided tours,
concerts

Map 13

C.O. Gram Gjesdal: *Lysøen: an Introduction*
    (Bergen: Norwegian Society for the
    Protection of Ancient Monuments, 1980)
E. Haugen and C. Cai: *Ole Bull: Norway's
    Romantic Musician and Cosmopolitan Patriot*
    (Madison: University of Wisconsin Press,
    1993)
G. Gefen: *Composers' Houses* (London: Cassell
    and Vendome, 1998), 40–48

BUSONI

To most travellers, Empoli is simply the first place on the way from Florence to Pisa or Livorno. This town, of some 45,000 people, was the birthplace of Ferruccio Busoni, on 1 April 1866; and it does due honour to its son, the composer, pianist and musical thinker who occupies so personal and so critical a role in early 20th-century music.

Busoni in fact spent only his first months in Empoli; his family moved to Trieste, and he led a fairly peripatetic life, primarily in Germany and Austria and from 1894 mainly centred on Berlin, where he died in 1924. The house of his birth, in the central square of Empoli, is now the headquarters of the Centro Studi Musicali Ferruccio Busoni. The ground floor is a shop; the Centro Studi, a lively institute that fosters not only documentation and research but also performances and editions of his music, has its offices on the first floor.

The second floor of the Casa Busoni, a small museum, opened in 1976. In the front room, where he is believed to have been born, stands a piano, of Viennese origin, that was his. On display are photographs of his parents and his Swedish-born wife, a Busoni autograph manuscript (his *Finnländische Volksweisen*, for piano duet) and facsimiles of others (including the *Fantasia contrappuntistica*), an original libretto of *Doktor Faust*, photographs of his studio and library, various letters and a bust. In the rear rooms is a library, including the collection, acquired in 1992, assembled by the musician and Busoni scholar Felice Boghen, with 20 unpublished letters between Busoni and his contemporaries and more than 200 from leading figures in early 20th-century musical life. There are more photographs here too, including one of Busoni at the harpsichord.

Museo Casa Busoni

Piazza della Vittoria 17
50053 Empoli (Firenze)
Italy

phone +390/0 571 711122
fax +390/0 571 78236
website www.comune.empoli.fi.it

open Monday–Friday 10.00–13.00,
15.30–18.00

Map 9

CARRER

The Ionian islands, west of the Peloponnese, were an important musical centre during much of the 19th century. In the 18th they had been under Venetian rule, then from 1797 under the French. From 1814 they were ruled by the British until their reunion with Greece in 1864. Italian traditions died hard, and it is chiefly as a centre of Italian opera and vocal music that the islands were musically significant during most of the century. The leading native composer was Pavlos Carrer (1829–96), born on Zakynthos island, who was trained locally and in Milan and wrote a dozen operas (of which four had their premières in Zakynthos) as well as many songs and much piano music.

The Museum to Solomos and Eminent Zakynthians, originally opened in 1966, then substantially rebuilt in the 1990s and reopened in 1999, partly serves as a memorial to the civilization of the Ionian islands after the damage wrought by the 1953 earthquake. It is chiefly devoted to the poet Dionysios Solomos but prominent among the others commemorated there are Carrer, to whom a room is dedicated. In that room are Carrer's own piano, a bronze bust and a portrait of the composer, a showcase with several of his personal objects, manuscripts and printed librettos, a silver wreath and other awards.

Mouseio Solomou kai Epiphanon Zakynthion*

Plateia Aghiou [St Mark's Square] 6
29100 Zakynthos
Greece

phone +30/0 6950 48982

open daily 09.00–13.00

Y. Demetis: *Odigos tou Mouseiou Solomou kai Epiphanon Zakynthion* [Guide to the Museum of Solomos and Eminent Zakynthians] (Athens, 1987)
P. Zora: *To kainourghio prosops tou Mouseiou Solomou kai Epiphanon Zakynthion* [The New Character of the Museum of Solomos and Eminent Zakynthians] (Athens: EELM, 2000)

CASALS

Casals, the great cellist, a composer? Yes, though mainly in the service of his faith and of his mentorship of younger cellists. For Pablo – or Pau, as he was known in his native Catalonia – was above all a man of conscience and humanity. He was fortunate both that his genius was recognized early and admired by the Queen-Regent Maria Cristina of Spain, by Queen Victoria and later by Queen Elisabeth of Belgium and the American First Lady Jacqueline Kennedy; and that his early career coincided with the advent

of recorded sound. A champion of Bach's solo suites, Casals at once popularized the cello and, through his work in Barcelona during the 1930s and in France during the Franco years, associated the instrument with the greatest crusade of the century: freedom from oppression. In 1958 he made a speech and played for the delegates of the United Nations; in 1971 they awarded him the Peace Medal; in 1977 they commemorated his courage by erecting a bust by Robert Berks at the UN in New York. In the meantime, Casals undertook to conduct his oratorio *El pessebre* ('The Manger') all over the world and, in recognition of his efforts on behalf of democracy and world peace, President Kennedy presented him in 1962 with the highest American honour, the Medal of Freedom.

Casals rose from humble but musical beginnings in the small town of El Vendrell, on the north-eastern coast of Spain. The evidence is plain to see, for his birthplace and spartan childhood home, not far from the Eglésia de Sant Salvador where his father served as organist, is open to the public. A man of principle, Casals forsook the comforts and luxury that artistic success had brought him – evidenced by the seaside villa he built in 1909 at Sant Salvador (close to El Vendrell) and enjoyed as a summer retreat until 1936, now a museum – in response to the Spanish Civil War and later the atrocities of Nazi Germany. He chose retirement from the world stage and indigent exile rather than tacit condonation. The quiet French Pyrenean-Catalan border town of Prades was his home and the base of his efforts on behalf of refugees between 1939 and 1956. In 1950 he came out of retirement to celebrate the bicentenary of Bach's birth and founded an annual music festival at Prades that brought together some of the finest musicians from all over the world (and still continues). His departure from Prades six years later was prompted by his desire, at the age of 80, to retire and marry again (over the years he had many mistresses, including the glamorous cellist Guilhermina Suggia, and as many as three wives). He chose as his final home Puerto Rico, where both his mother and his last wife, Marta Montañez (60 years his junior), had been born. He is commemorated in San Juan by a music festival and a museum.

El Vendrell is the central port of call for Casals pilgrims. He claimed never to have forgotten 'the child of El Vendrell that I was'. The simple stucco townhouse where he was born on 29 December 1876 and lived until he was 12 was opened to the public by the town fathers in 1998, on the 25th anniversary of his death. Serving parties of schoolchildren and cellists, it displays no original artefacts. Instead, it tells on the ground floor the story of Casals's life, with quotations from his thoughts writ large on the walls, and on the upper floors presents the Casals family's way of life in the house during the last quarter of the 19th century. Just south-east of the railway lines is the cemetery of El Vendrell where in 1979 his remains were brought from Puerto Rico and re interred.

A short distance due south from the town centre lies the Mediterranean resort of Sant Salvador, situated between Barcelona to the north-east and Tarragona to the south-west. Casals had known Sant Salvador from his childhood and in particular was familiar with the

hermitage there, and it was here that he returned. Today the Vil·la Casals houses the Museu Pau Casals, which opened in 2001 and is owned and operated by the Fundació Pau Casals. The walled complex includes a series of courtyards and formal gardens, esplanade and beach frontage, and a gift shop. The ten ground-floor rooms of the villa that surround an inner courtyard tell the story of his life. On display are a wealth of original instruments, furniture, documents, music manuscripts, editions and recordings, portraits and sculpture, photographs and film footage, awards great and small (among them the UN Peace Medal) and other personal possessions. In the music room facing the beach and the sea beyond, a video runs in which Casals plays the Allemande from Bach's G major suite. In the final room there is an opportunity to watch a video of him conducting at the UN. Among the manuscripts of his compositions on display are his Sonata for piano and violin in D minor (Prades, 1940), his *Hymn to the United Nations* (Puerto Rico, 1971) and *El cant des ocells* ('Song of the Birds', 1972, known in both its choral and cello orchestra versions). Across the Avenida Palfuriana, which runs parallel to the coastline, is the Auditori Pau Casals, inaugurated in 1981 and seating 400, and

Vil·la Casals at Sant Salvador

next to it the Placa J.S. Bach, with its compelling statue of a robed cellist ('Bach es un miracle') by Subirachs.

When in 1939 Casals, under threat from the Franco regime, sought refuge on the French side of the Spanish border, Prades was barely more than a village. He stayed first at the Hôtel Hostalrich in what is now the Avenue du Général de Gaulle and then in a succession of loaned houses. To the residents he was something of a recluse, although visited by other famous musicians and even royalty. Local people and visitors to Prades would stop on the pavement outside his house to listen to him practise the cello (it is said that he habitually smoked his pipe while practising), and occasionally observe him walking his dog, swimming or playing tennis. By 1942 he was living at Villa Colette (today 34 route de Ria) with one of his students, Frasquita Capdevilla (whom he may have married on her deathbed in 1955), a niece and four members of the Alavedra family. They existed on a meagre diet, mainly the produce they were able to grow in the garden. Seen from the outside today (still called Villa Colette, it remains a private residence), the detached two-storey house with obligatory tiled roof, shutters and balcony retains its air of modesty.

Casals is commemorated in Prades with a 'promenade' taking in seven places within the town. They include a view of the bust by Marcel Homs erected in 1975 at the corner of the rue du docteur Laviall and a stop at the Musée Pau Casals, currently housed in the Office de Tourisme. The museum collection was assembled by a local enthusiast, Jacques Anglade, who willed it to the festival. It includes some of the cellist's clothes, photographic montages of Casals with other famous musicians (including the violinists Grumiaux, the Oistrakhs, Menuhin, Schneider and Stern, the cellist Tortelier and the pianists Serkin and Istomin) and friends (including Albert Schweitzer), an original score of *El pessebre*, an upright piano said to come from the Sant Salvador villa and a cello he evidently played in a private concert

for the Queen of Belgium, as well as newspaper and magazine cuttings, festival programmes and recordings, portraits, plaster casts of his hands and various personal possessions (including his 1940 identity card and souvenirs from his travels). There is even a poster from his 75th birthday concert in Zürich, signed by the musicians (123 cellists!) who took part. Two kilometres south of Prades, along the avenue Pau Casals, is the Abbaye St Michel de Cuxà, where the Prades Festival events take place in late July and early August.

Casals had barely touched ground in San Juan before he began planning a new Festival Casals. What began in 1957 as a series of chamber concerts in his own house (his music room seated 200) in the hills above the capital are today glittering events in the Luis A. Ferré Performing Arts Centre, and among the most important in Latin America. In 1958 he helped found the Puerto Rico Symphony and the national conservatory. He was 96 when he died of a heart attack on 22 October 1973. He is commemorated in a small museum in a two-storey 18th-century building next to the cathedral in the main square of historic Old San Juan (101 Calle San Sebastián), a World Heritage site.

Casa Nadiua de Pau Casals
Santa Anna 2
43700 El Vendrell
Spain

phone +34/0 977 665684
fax +34/0 977 665685
e-mail cultura@elvendrell.net

open 15 September–30 June, Monday–Friday 10.00–14.00, 17.00–19.00; 1 July–15 September, Monday–Friday 10.00–14.00, 18.00–20.00; all year Saturday 11.00–14.00, 17.00–20.00, Sunday 11.00–14.00; guided visits by appointment

Vil·la Casals
Museu Pau Casals
Avenida Palfuriana 59

Sant Salvador
43880 El Vendrell
Spain

phone +34/0 977 684276
fax +34/0 977 684783
e-mail museu@paucasals.org
website www.paucasals.org

open Tuesday–Saturday,
16 September–14 June, 10.00–14.00,
16.00–18.00 (Saturday to 19.00); 15
June–15 September, 10.00–14.00,
17.00–21.00; all year, Sunday
10.00–15.00

Musée Pablo Casals
Office de tourisme de Prades
4 Rue Victor Hugo
66599 Prades
France

phone +33/0 4 6805 4102
fax +33/0 4 6805 2179

open October–May, Monday–Friday
09.00–12.00, 14.00–17.30, Saturday
by appointment; June, September,
Saturday 09.00–12.00; July–August,
Saturday 09.00–12.00, 14.00–17.30,
Sunday 10.00–12.00

Maps 15, 6

CHARPENTIER

In a room of the Musée de Montmartre
in Paris the study of the composer
Gustave Charpentier has been reconstructed. Charpentier, born in 1860,
spent most of his life in Montmartre,
although he was a recluse in his flat at
66 Boulevard Rochechouart for nearly
half a century from the end of World War
I until his death on 18 February 1956. By
the time Charpentier had moved there he
had already achieved his greatest success:
the performance of his scandalously
bohemian opera, *Louise*, at the Opéra-
Comique (1889). Through glass door-
ways, visitors can peer at the small study
from no.66 – with its pink-striped wallpaper, fireplace, oil stove, furniture, velvet
cushions and curtains – at Charpentier's

Charpentier room, Musée de Montmartre

four-octave miniature piano and a pile of
sheet music, musical statuettes, telephone, typewriter, gramophone with
microphone and writing implements.
His coat and scarf are draped over a chair,
his shoes and cane close by.

Auguste Renoir was among the residents of the building that is now the
museum at 12 Rue Cortot, where the
focus of the displays and audio-visual
presentation is the colourful cabaret era
of Le Chat Noir. The composer and
cabaret pianist Erik Satie lived only a few
doors away, in no.6, for many years (his
lover, Suzanne Valadon, was later also a
resident of no.12), but he is not represented in the musical displays which,
besides Charpentier's study, include
portraits of some of the other composers
with Montmartre associations (Berlioz,
Henri and Robert Casadesus, Honegger
and Milhaud).

Musée de Montmartre
12 Rue Cortot
75018 Paris
France

phone +33/0 1 4606 6111
fax +33/0 1 4606 3075
website
www.paris.org/musees/montmartre

open Tuesday–Sunday, 11.00–18.00

Map 6

CHARRIÈRE

See ZUYLEN.

CHOPIN

As one of the most Romantic and most appealing of composers, Fryderyk Chopin is widely commemorated – most of all, of course, in his native Poland, but also in the Czech Republic and Spain and to a modest extent elsewhere. The most important collection of Chopiniana is, appropriately enough, in Warsaw, at the museum of the Frederic Chopin Society. But for lovers of his music there are other shrines: his birthplace at Żelazowa Wola, the Holy Cross Church in Warsaw where his heart is interred in a pillar, the Carthusian monastery at Valldemossa on the Mediterranean island of Majorca where he spent the winter of 1838–9 with George Sand, and his tomb – perpetually flower-strewn – in the Paris cemetery of Père Lachaise.

Chopin left Poland when he was 20, and he never returned. His compatriots understandably make the most of his few Polish years. It seems that his memory is nurtured at almost every place he visited: at Brochów (where he was christened), Duszniki Zdrój, Poznań, Sanniki, Sulechów, Szafarnia and Antonín, and the Krasiński Palace in Warsaw, at all of which he spent a holiday period or played or both. Chopin memorial rooms, societies, centres, concert halls, festivals and piano competitions commemorate the connections.

Abroad too: in the Bohemian spa Mariánské Lázně (Marienbad), which he visited, in the Carthusian monastery at Valledemossa where he passed several chilly weeks with George Sand, and in France at La Châtre (seven kilometres from Sand's house at Nohant) where he spent seven summers. Elsewhere plaques mark some of the places – for example in Paris, London and Vienna – where he once stayed. But Paris lacks the museum that his long residence (from 1831, in effect) and his death there (in 1849) would surely justify, and the Nohant commemoration too is modest.

In the Mazovian countryside, some 45 km west of the capital, close to the main road that leads to Łódź and to Poznań, is Żelazowa Wola, then the estate of Count Fryderyk Skarbek, Chopin's godfather. There, on 22 February or 1 March 1810 (sources differ), Chopin was born. His father, a Frenchman, was tutor to the count's children, and his mother had a family connection with the Skarbeks. Most of the estate, which was sold in the 1850s, was destroyed in a fire later in the century, but the cottage (or *dwór*) survived, the only building to do so. The earliest thoughts of turning it into a Chopin memorial came from the Towiańskis, the family who bought the estate from the Skarbeks, but nothing was done under successive owners until 1891, with an initiative by the Russian composer Mily Balakirev with the Warsaw Music Society. An obelisk commemorating Chopin was erected there and dedicated, with an appropriate musical ceremony, in 1894. It was only in 1931 that a committee, including Ignacy Paderewski, arranged to take over the ownership of the cottage and to have it restored as a museum with a recital room. The surrounding land was attractively landscaped as a park and in 1939 the house was opened to the public. During World War II it suffered damage but it was restored and reopened in 1949, the centenary of Chopin's death, under state ownership but from 1953 in the care of the Frederic Chopin Society. That restoration was limited in scope but efforts were made in the ensuing years to

Chopin's birthplace, Żelazowa Wola

enlarge the displays and improve the decor, culminating in a more historical restoration in 1968; at that time, too, the 1894 monument, which had been moved to a side of the park, was replaced by a stone bust by Stanislaw Sikora and a bronze monument by Józef Goslawski.

The cottage opens to a courtyard, surrounded by chestnut trees; to the south are vines in a trellis arbour which had originally linked the cottage with the estate house. The cottage itself has a high sloped roof with mansard windows, which like the wooden entrance porch were a later addition. The interior however still follows the original layout. There is a brick-floored hallway through the centre, with three rooms on each side. To the right is a room with a fireplace, presumed to have been the kitchen, now equipped with suitable Polish furniture and kitchenware of Chopin's time, including a tiled stove. Next is the drawing-room, with furniture believed to have adorned the Skarbek house, as well as several portraits, including copies of those of Chopin by Maria Wodzińska and Eliza Radziwiłł, and a modern concert grand piano: this room is used for recitals, which are relayed to the audience on the terrace outside and in the park beyond. The third room on the right is the dining-room, with Biedermeier-style furniture, china and porcelain and engravings after Canaletto of 18th-century Warsaw. To the left of the central corridor are what were presumably the family's private rooms: first, the mother's, the largest, with a 19th-century piano, a fine wall clock in ivory and bronze (thought to have belonged to the Skarbeks), an 18th-century desk with musical decorations, more Biedermeier furniture, portraits including copies of lost originals of Chopin, his sisters and his parents, and facsimiles of marriage and birth certificates – and there is an alcove supposed to be the actual spot where Chopin was born; second, a children's room, re-created; and third, his father's room, soberly furnished but with historical etchings and a facsimile of Chopin's own drawing of a village land-scape. On the upper floor are rooms for visiting recitalists.

In the summers of 1824 and 1825, when he was 14 and 15, Chopin was invited by a fellow pupil at the Lyceum in Warsaw, Dominik Dziewanowski, to spend some time with him and his family at their country house in Szafarnia, about 150 km north-west of Warsaw, not far from Toruń. His memory is preserved in this attractive lakeside mansion, now a Chopin Centre, in a Chopin competition held each May and in a small Chopin museum. There is a pleasant, light recital room, seating about 80, with a bust of Chopin (there is another by the front entrance) and a fairly comprehensive set of Chopin portraits, in good reproductions, around the walls, along with posters. Probably this is the room where Chopin played at the Dziewanowski family soirées. Next to it is a spacious and elegant octagonal exhibition room, which one may survey to a background of piano music and Polish commentary (chiefly about current events at Szafarnia). A prize exhibit is a group of copies from the *Kurier Szafarski*, a home-made newspaper edited by Chopin and produced by him and his friends when he was there. There is a plaster cast of Chopin's left hand and many reproductions of pictures connected with his life and his death, the women in his life, his teachers, his family and some letters, and also a copy of a landscape drawn by Chopin himself. Much of the material is concerned with the musical events held at Szafarnia, which include, along with the competition, regular recitals and occasional symposia.

Of the Chopin sites outside Warsaw, none is more remarkable than Prince Antoni Radziwiłł's former hunting lodge at Antonín, some 275 km west and slightly south of Warsaw (about 20 km south of Ostrów Wielkopolski). A three-storey, wooden folly set in parkland, it is now a youth hostel, café and memorial rooms, with accommodation in the four wings extending out from the central octagonal body of the building. Built early in the 19th century to a design believed to be by

*The former
Radziwiłł
hunting lodge at
Antonín*

Karl Friedrich Schinkel (as centre of a complex including a shepherd's house with a milk-drinking salon, a forester's lodge, stables and a small chapel, where family members are buried), it was presumably just as astonishing in its day as it is now, with its galleries overlooking the octagon, its huge central column of fireplaces and its dramatic wood ceiling. It provided a unique setting for Chopin's performances on his visits in 1827 and 1829. For the prince, an amateur cellist, he composed the op.3 Polonaise for piano and cello and the Piano Trio op.8, in which they were joined in performance by the prince's violinist daughter. Off the octagon, on the ground floor, are two rooms devoted to Chopin, containing two pianos, furniture and reproductions of portraits and music. A modern concert grand resides in the octagon room, where chamber recitals are held: each September there is a Chopin festival and every other year since 1988 there have been seminars for young Chopin scholars, 'Vacations with Chopin'.

About 25 km west of Żelazowa Wola, not far from Płock, lies Sanniki, where the family of another of Chopin's school friends, Konstanty Pruszak, had an estate. Chopin accepted an invitation to spend a holiday there in the summer of 1828; while he was there he wrote the Rondo

for two pianos op.73. The country house in which he stayed later burnt down and was replaced in 1910 by a much more palatial building, opposite the village church. This is now largely given over to local government offices, a public library and a nursery school, but since 1981 one wing has housed a Frederic Chopin Centre. In the concert room, which holds 120 people, there are monthly Sunday afternoon recitals, with recitations of Polish poetry, between February and October. On the upper floor is the library that once belonged to the Chopin scholar Mateusz Gliński (1892–1976), supplemented since his time, and a reading room. In the foyer of the hall and the hall itself Chopin materials, from the Frederic Chopin Society in Warsaw, are displayed, among them reproductions of Chopin portraits and manuscripts, contemporary illustrations of Warsaw and porcelain of the period. In front of the building is a bronze statue by Ludwika Kraskowska-Nitschowa, unveiled in 1985 on the 175th anniversary of the composer's birth, and there is a plaque commemorating Chopin's connection with Sanniki, dating from 1925.

Later in 1828 Chopin visited Berlin, and on the way home paused in Poznań where he played at receptions given by the Archbishop and Prince Antoni

Radziwiłł. His visit is commemorated in a Chopin Room in the Poznań Museum of Musical Instruments, with a small but fine collection. It includes a piano from Antonín, a late 18th-century instrument, which Chopin might have played; a bust, a model for the monument in Warsaw; several portraits, including a drawing by Teofil Kwiatowski of Chopin at the time of his death and a pastel by him of a ball, showing Chopin with various people who played roles in his life, as well as a lithograph by Henryk Siemiradzki of Chopin playing at a concert at Antonín; and a death mask and a cast of Chopin's hand.

During his years at the conservatory in Warsaw, Chopin was evidently in love with a fellow pupil, Konstancja Gładkowska, a singing student, and his feelings seem to have been reciprocated to some extent, although Konstancja later expressed surprise at the strength of feeling for her that he showed in letters to others. He went away, and she married a nobleman. Blind from the age of 36, she was widowed in 1879 and moved to the town of Skierniewice, near her husband's estates, about 75 km south-west of Warsaw. In 1987 her house, behind St Jakub's Church just off the town square, was turned into a museum to Chopin and Konstancja. There are copies of their letters – hers to him, his to others – that record their love, but no original material; the rooms however are fitted out with furniture of the mid-19th century. There is a recital room, seating 40, where concerts are held regularly, with special events on the birth and death anniversaries of Chopin and Konstancja.

Warsaw itself retains many associations with the composer. The Saski Palace, where the Chopin family lived in quarters provided for the Lyceum faculty for the first six years, no longer exists, though the Saski Gardens do. When in 1817 the Lyceum moved to new quarters, the Chopins were allotted rooms in the right annexe of the Kazimierzowski Palace (now part of the Warsaw University campus); a profile relief of Chopin and a memorial plaque mark the

building. The Krasiński Palace, where the family occupied a spacious third-floor flat from mid-1827, was rebuilt after its destruction in 1944 and the drawing-room was faithfully re-created from drawings (by Antoni Kolber). In the original flat the young Chopin had a study upstairs in the garret, where he had a piano and a desk. The drawing-room was the scene of his parents' frequent soirées and it was there, on 7 February 1830, that Chopin first performed his F minor Concerto. And it was from there that he set off for Paris on 2 November of that year, never to return to Poland. Today the palace, at Krakowskie Przedmieście 5, is occupied by the Fine Arts Academy, through which one must thread one's way to reach the drawing-room at the front of the building. The drawing-room was opened to the public in 1960, on the 150th anniversary of the composer's birth, and, in addition to period furniture, it displays three pianos (an Erard that once belonged to Liszt, a Buchholtz grand and a Pleyel upright; Chopin's own piano was destroyed, apparently, when Russian soldiers threw it out of the window), two caricatures drawn by Chopin and a clock set at 18.03, said to be the time of his birth.

In 1927 – the year in which the Chopin International Piano Competition was founded – the City of Warsaw erected a monument, sculpted by Wacław Szymanowski, just inside the main gate of the Łazienki Park (the wooden model is in the collection at Poznań). In 1949 plans were set in motion to restore the 16th-century Ostrogski Castle, which between the wars had housed the Warsaw Conservatory, and establish a museum. Five years later the Frederic Chopin Society Museum opened, with Chopin displays on the ground floor, dedicated to his youth in Poland, and the second floor, covering his mature period abroad; the second floor also houses a recital hall, a library and, since 1984, an evocation of the study of the prominent pianist and teacher Jerzy Żurawlew (*d* 1980). The collection includes a large number of Chopin's autographs, including the early

Display at the Ostrogski Castle, Warsaw

F minor Polonaise, op.71, several of the op.10 Etudes, the op.65 Cello Sonata and the last F minor Mazurka, op.68. The many original portraits include pencil drawings by Princess Eliza Radziwiłł and an oil by Ambroży Mieroszewski, both from 1829, and a watercolour painted in 1836 at Mariánské Lázně by Maria Wodzińska, as well as a copy of the joint portrait of Chopin and George Sand by Eugène Delacroix – the separated likenesses here reunited – which was originally painted in Paris in 1838, an 1848 oil by Antoni Kolberg, and a series of final portraits by Teofil Kwiatkowski. There is Chopin's last Pleyel piano; unique memorabilia including his childhood drawings; letters; early editions and programmes; and other personal documents, among them his birth and baptismal certificates and his passport.

There are three other Polish towns where Chopin is commemorated. About seven kilometres north-west of Żelazowa Wola is Brochów; his parents were married there at the church of St Roch, in 1806, and four years later he was baptized there. Brochów honours his memory with a Frederic Chopin Music Didactic Centre. In 1826 Chopin visited the spa of Duszniki Zdrój, not far from Wrocław in south-west Poland, and gave two recitals; an International Chopin Festival is now held there each August, in the building (the Spa Park or Manor) in which he played. Nearby is an obelisk bearing a portrait and a bas-relief of Chopin, put up in 1897, and a more recent monument. On his way home from Berlin in 1828, according to one of his early biographers, Chopin stopped briefly at Sulechów, a village near Zielona Góra: stretching his legs, he came across a piano in an inn, and began playing – and the villagers gathered to hear what became a full-scale recital. Sulechów commemorates this event with an annual competition for young pianists, held each May. One of Chopin's early and most important teachers, Józef Elsner, has been commemorated in the house of his birth in Grodków, south of Wrocław in Silesia, but the museum is closed pending refurbishment.

Chopin's first stopping place when he left home in 1830 was Vienna, where he lived in the centre of the city until July 1831 before continuing his journey. The building at Kohlmarkt 9 where he stayed was demolished at the beginning of the 20th century but the present building commemorates his stay with a portrait relief and plaque. He also passed through Salzburg, where he visited the Mozart house.

In Paris Chopin lived at eight different addresses between 1831 and 1849, many of which are marked by memorial plaques. The longest period was in the Square d'Orléans (1842–9), in the ninth *arrondissement*, but he died on 12 October 1849 at 12 Place Vendôme, in the first, where he had moved scarcely a month before; the house no longer stands, but a plaque marks the site. Chopin's funeral, at which the Mozart *Requiem* was performed, was in the nearby Madeleine, with burial at Père Lachaise.

Although Chopin never returned to Poland, he spent a month with his parents in Karlovy Vary (Karlsbad), in Bohemia, in 1835. On the return journey he visited Dresden, where he met the Wodziński family, whose sons had lodged with the Chopins in Warsaw, and was greatly taken with the sister, Maria, who played the piano, sang and composed. The following summer he took up an invitation from the Wodzińskis to join them on holiday in Mariánské Lázně. They took rooms in an 18th-century inn, the White Swan (the Wodzińskis stayed on the first floor, Chopin was on the second); Chopin composed and Maria painted him in watercolours. After three weeks Chopin accompanied Maria and her mother to Dresden and, on his last night there, he proposed marriage: she consented but her parents' permission proved impossible to secure. Her letters, found among his possessions after his death, now belong to the Frederic Chopin Society in Warsaw. The White Swan, known now as the Chopin House, still stands on the main street of Mariánské Lázně; the building is municipally owned but on permanent loan to the Czech Chopin Society. The room in which Chopin is thought to have stayed is filled with displays prepared by the society, documenting his Czech connections and including Czech porcelain and glassware as well as a little-known oil portrait by an unknown painter. Since 1960 an International Chopin Festival has been held there every August, and there are also piano competitions.

Two months later, in November 1836, Chopin met the writer George Sand (Amantine Aurore Lucile Dupin Dudevant, who from 1832 published under the male *nom de plume*) in Paris at the salon of Franz Liszt and Marie d'Agoult at the Hôtel de France. Their friendship, which by June 1838 had turned to love, lasted nine years. (Delacroix painted them that summer, at the height of their mutual passion; it is sadly appropriate that he left the portrait unfinished and that it was subsequently cut in two, Chopin going to the Louvre, Sand to the Ordrupgaard Samlingen in Copenhagen.) She gave up her *penchant* for dressing as a man for his sake. Legally separated from her husband, Baron Casimir Dudevant, with children and another lover living at her country residence in Nohant, she had ample reason to wish to go abroad, though Chopin's deteriorating health provided in itself ample pretext for persuading him to go south with her for the winter of 1838–9.

Palma, on the Spanish island of Majorca, was their destination. When they arrived on 11 November they had to seek accommodation and the villa they eventually found, 'So'n Vent' in the suburb of Establiments, which by local custom was rented without doors and windows, proved uninhabitable. In truth, this unconventional menagerie of foreigners was unwelcome and, when Chopin's health took a further downward turn and news got out that he might have an infectious disease, they were compelled to decamp to a more isolated spot. The disused and relatively inaccessible Carthusian monastery on the slope of a mountain at Valldemossa, 18 km north of Palma, with views of the Mediterranean, seemed to offer the best option.

On 15 December Chopin and George Sand – with her children, Maurice (15) and Solange (10), and a maid in tow – travelled there by coach as far as they could, then clambered up the stony track to the town. They settled in three south-facing monks' cells, with gardens overlooking the hillside orchards of oranges, olives and almonds, and the valley below. They had to provide doors and windows, their own furniture and a stove to heat the rooms during what was an exceptionally harsh winter. They had to do their own shopping and cooking, even acquiring a goat and a sheep for milk, as well as the basic housework. The Pleyel piano they had arranged to be sent was delayed in customs and arrived only in mid-January. In defiance of his illness, Chopin composed a ballade, a polonaise, a scherzo and the 'Palma Mazurka', and worked on the op.37 Nocturnes and the B flat minor Sonata. And although George Sand, now more nurse than lover, tutored and amused her children by day, she wrote by night, completing a novel, *Spiridion*, and compiling materials for a memoir of their stay, *Un hiver à Majorque* (1841), in which she referred to Chopin as 'our invalid' and 'one of us'. But they paid dearly for their would-be idyll in Spain: when they left, on 13 February 1839, Chopin was almost too ill to make the return journey, their funds were seriously depleted and their relationship had changed for ever.

The monastery at Valldemossa, today one of the major tourist attractions of Majorca, is at the end of the main street, which is lined with souvenir shops. Within the monastery one can visit the church, the municipal museum, a re-creation of an 18th-century pharmacy and a prioral cell as well as Cells 2 and 4, each of three rooms, which commemo-rate the two months Chopin and Sand stayed there. The whitewashed rooms still retain their elegantly arched ceilings if not their fretted rose-windows. To some extent their memories are merged in the displays. Cell 2 is partly furnished; there are reproductions of the Delacroix portraits, with watercolours by Sand here and photographs of modern Chopin interpreters there; wall niches where a death mask, a cast of his left hand and copies of letters and pen-and-ink draw-ings by Kwiatkowski are displayed; a manuscript copy of *Un hiver à Majorque* and letters in Sand's hand; the small Majorcan piano with which Chopin made do until his Pleyel arrived, and a concert grand occasionally used for recitals. The main room of Cell 4 – 'Celda Chopin' – is more formal and very much a memorial. The Pleyel piano he left behind takes pride of place, its certificate of authenticity on view. There is a bust of the composer on a plinth, photocopies framed with dried roses; in an alcove to the side is a bed. In a second room there are displays of original documents (in desperate need of conservation) – among them letters, accounts and floor-plans – as well as facsimiles, including Chopin's letter (dated Palma, 3 December 1838) to his Paris publisher, Julien Fontana, in which he admitted to being 'malade comme un chien'.

Chopin and Sand were away from Paris for nearly a year, returning only in October 1839, after spending the summer recuperating at her country house at Nohant in Berry. In Paris they rented separate flats in the ninth *arrondissement* (his at 5 Rue Tronchet, hers at 16 Rue Pigalle, in fact straddling two houses), though in the autumn of 1841 he abandoned his for quarters at

The monastery cells at Valldemossa

hers. In 1842 they moved to the same building but different flats in the Square d'Orléans: Sand took a suite on the second floor, he took bachelor quarters (a salon and a bedroom) on the ground floor. Although Sand may have envisaged regular seasonal migrations between Paris and Nohant, it never quite worked that way. He loved the city while she preferred the countryside: during the summers they spent at Nohant he was often in Paris and he missed out summer 1840 altogether. Nevertheless, Nohant provided much-needed stability and contentment even for Chopin, who – between picnics, country walks, alfresco meals and amateur theatricals – composed many of his finest works there. If no longer lovers, Sand and her 'petit Chop' remained deeply dependent on one another. She drew his portrait and he entertained her guests. He was one of her family and yet he wasn't; the tensions of their life together served as a continuing source of inspiration for her novels. When in 1847 the tensions could no longer be borne, they parted, meeting briefly by chance only once, on 4 March 1848.

Six weeks later Chopin was in London, at the invitation of his pupil, Jane Stirling, who hoped to take Sand's place in his life. Plaques commemorate the sites of his first performance – on 23 June at the elegant home of the singer Mrs Adelaide Sartoris, at 99 Eaton Place, SW1 – and the house at 4 St James's Place, SW1, from where he went to the Guildhall in the City of London to give his last public performance seven months later, on 16 November.

Nohant, now a national heritage site open to the public, is a tiny village just north of La Châtre with a church, an auberge and a three-storey manor house. At the age of 18, Sand had married Casimir Dudevant and they lived at Nohant, which belonged to her family; she retained the manor when they separated. It was her paradise: she died there in 1876 and was buried in the family cemetery in the grounds. The house, restored in 1996 and still retaining much of the original ambience and domestic detail, commemorates Sand's life, not Chopin's. The kitchen, where she is said to have made strawberry jam, has an indoor barbecue; the dining-room, with its Venetian chandelier, is set for a hypothetical dinner party; in the adjoining blue salon, lined with family portraits (pre-eminently a ravishing one of Sand herself by Charpentier) and furnished with furniture that she designed, there is a Pleyel piano, now paying tacit tribute to the exquisite private performances

Chopin gave there. At the other end of the house is the theatre she built in his honour in 1847, in vain anticipation of his arrival for the summer; in addition to a raised stage there is a tiny orchestra pit and a marionette theatre at the side which Maurice and Solange built for themselves. Upstairs, with garden views, are what were Sand's and Chopin's bedrooms, separated only by a sitting-room, now a library; after their break-up she used his bedroom as a workroom and for storage. Chopin's presence in the house is hardly alluded to and can only be inferred by those who visit Nohant with him in mind. Outside there is the cemetery, a rose garden and a summer house to explore; in a corner of the stables – which otherwise display carriages, saddles and harnesses – there is a video presentation and, upstairs, an exhibition of marionettes and sound-effects machinery related to the theatre.

Since 1968 an annual Fêtes Romantiques de Nohant has been held in June and, only seven kilometres south in La Châtre, an annual piano competition, 'Chopin chez G. Sand', takes place in July. La Châtre's municipal museum, the Musée George Sand et de la Vallée Noire, occupies a 15th-century fortress and former prison: the George Sand Salle, installed in 1966, displays manuscripts, editions, letters, portraits, watercolours, caricatures, photographs and a plaster cast of her right hand; the single case devoted to Chopin contains reproductions of the usual portraits and correspondence between composer and writer. Somewhere along the journey from Poland Chopin slips quietly away from public gaze.

Fryderyk Chopin Birthplace
96503 Żelazowa Wola
Poland

phone +48/0 468 633300
fax +48/0 468 634076
e-mail info@chopin.pl
website www.chopin.pl

George Sand's château at Nohant

open May–September, daily

09.30–17.30; October–April,
daily 10.00–16.00 (concerts:
spring and summer, Sunday 11.00
and 15.00)

Ośrodek i Muzeum im. Fryderyka Chopina
Ośrodek Chopinowski w Szafarni
Szafarnia
87404 Radomin
Poland

phone +48/0 566 831322
fax +48/0 566 832280

open Tuesday–Friday 08.00–15.00,
Saturday and Sunday 10.00–15.00

Salon Muzyczny
Pałac Myśliwski Radziwiłłów
63422 Antonín
Poland

phone +48/0 64 348114
fax +48/0 64 366545

open daily 08.00–21.00

Zespol Płacowo-Parkowy imiena Fryderyka Chopina w Sannikach
Pałac w Sannikach
09540 Sanniki
Poland

phone +48/0 242 776058, 776170
e-mail sanniki@zgwrp.org.pl

open by appointment

Chopin Room
Muzeum Instrumentów Muzycznych
Stary Rynek 45–7
61772 Poznań
Poland

phone +48/0 618 520857
fax +48/0 618 515882
e-mail muzinstr@man.poznan.pl

open Tuesday 10.00–17.00, Wednesday,
Friday, Saturday 09.00–17.00, Thursday
10.00–16.00, Sunday 11.00–16.00

Izba Historii Skierniewice
Znajduje sie tu stala ekspozycja
poswiecona Fryderykowi Chopinowi i
Konstancji Gładkowskiej
ulica Floriana 4
96100 Skierniewice
Poland

phone +48/0 468 334471
e-mail izbahistorii@wp.pl

open Tuesday, Friday 10.00–17.00,
Wednesday, Thursday 09.00–16.00,
Saturday and Sunday 10.00–13.00

Salonik Chopinów
Pałac Krasińskich
Krakowskie Przedmieście 5
Warszawa
Poland

phone +48/0 223 200275, 228
266251
e-mail info@chopin.pl
website www.chopin.pl

open Monday–Friday 10.00–14.00

Muzeum Fryderyka Chopina
Zamek Ostrogskich
ulica Okólnik 1
00368 Warszawa
Poland

phone +48/0 228 265935
fax +48/0 228 279599
e-mail info@chopin.pl
website www.chopin.pl

open May–September, Monday,
Wednesday, Friday 10.00–17.00,
Thursday 12.00–18.00, Saturday and
Sunday 10.00–14.00; October–April,
Monday–Wednesday, Friday, Saturday
10.00–14.00, Thursday 12.00–18.00
(concerts September–June, Wednesday
19.00)

Památník Fryderyka Chopina
Dům Chopin
Hlavní 47
35301 Mariánské Lázně
Czech Republic

phone, fax +420/0 354 622617

open May–September, Tuesday, Thursday,
Sunday 14.00–17.00

Cartuja
Valldemossa
07170 Majorca
Spain

phone +34/0 971 612106

open Monday–Saturday 09.30–16.30,
Sunday 10.00–13.00

Maison de George Sand
36400 Nohant-Vic
France

phone +33/0 2 9954 3527
fax +33/0 2 5449 2292

open daily, guided tours only: April–June,
9.30–11.15, 14.30–17.30; July–August,
09.30–18.30; September–15 October,
9.30–11.15, 14.30–17.30; 16
October–March, 10.30–11.15,
14.30–15.30

Musée George Sand et de la Vallée Noire
71 rue Venose
36400 La Châtre
France

phone +33/0 2 5448 0247

open daily, February–March,
October–December, 09.00–12.00,
14.00–17.00; April–June,
September, 09.00–12.00, 14.00–19.00;
July–August, 09.00–19.00;
closed January

Maps 10, 4, 15, 6

Chopin Museums in Poland: Tourist Guidebook
   (Warsaw: Frederic Chopin Society, n.d.)
J. Iwaszkiewicz: *Żelazowa Wola* (Warsaw, 1976)
J. Szczpanski: *Sanniki i okolice* (Warsaw:
   Wydawnictwo PTTK Kraj, 1987)
H. Kretschmer: *Wiener Musikergedenkstätten*
   (Vienna: J & V Edition, 3/1992)
S. Delaigue-Moins: *Chopin chez George Sand à
   Nohant: Chronique de sept étés* (Argenton-
   sur-Creuse: Les Amis de Nohant, 3/1992)
E. Lee: *Musical London* (London: Omnibus,
   1995)
F. Małkus: *Konstancja w Raduczu* (Skierniewice:
   Towarzystwo Przyjaciół Skierniewic, 1996)
Chopin na Mazowszu (Warsaw: Mazowieckie
   Towarzystwo Kultury, 1999)
N. Simeone: *Paris: a Musical Gazetteer* (New
   Haven and London: Yale University Press,
   2000)

CILEA

Palmi is a middle-sized town on the Calabrian coast, on the toe of the boot of Italy; it is about 450 km south of Naples, about 50 north of Reggio Calabria. It is the native town of Francesco Cilea, born on 23 July 1866, one of the leading composers of the *giovane scuola*, the 'young school' of opera composers that included Puccini. Like most of them, excepting of course Puccini himself, he is now remembered by just one or two operas – his *L'arlesiana* (1897) is still occasionally heard, his *Adriana Lecouvreur* (1902), beloved of aging prima donnas, rather more often.

His native town still takes pride in him. He spent most of his working life in Naples, and he died in the north, in Varazze, not far from Genoa, in 1950; his villa was for a time used for arts conferences. But Palmi held a Celebrazione Maestro Francesco Cilea on the 25th anniversary of his death, holds a music competition in his name, has a monument to him in the Piazza Pentimalli (with a frieze depicting the story of Orpheus), and also maintains a room to him in the Casa di Cultura of the Museo Civico. The house of his birth was destroyed in the 1940s.

A wide range of Cilea exhibits are housed in a single room. There are photographs of his family, his teachers, his colleagues (Puccini and Toscanini among them) and his early interpreters, many in particular associated with *Adriana Lecouvreur*, including Caruso (whose career *L'arlesiana* helped launch). Busts show an affable face; there is also a death mask. Certificates, diplomas, medallions and ribbons testify to his reputation. The collection also holds his very comprehensive cuttings books, more than 2000 of his letters (and those of his widow), and his own music library, which includes many of his music manuscripts.

Palmi was also the native town of Nicola Antonio Manfroce (1791–1813), a composer of great talent and unfulfilled promise: his first opera was given in Rome when he was 19, his second and last in Naples two years later. One showcase in the museum is devoted to his memory.

Museo Civico F. Cilea e N.A. Manfroce
via San Giorgio
89015 Palmi (Reggio Calabria)
Italy
(administered by Casa della Cultura, via
F. Battaglia, Palmi)

phone +390/0 966 26250, 411080

open Monday–Thursday 08.30–13.30,
15.30–17.30, Friday 08.30–13.30

Map 9

CIORTEA

Among the buildings nestled in the grounds of the basilica of St Nicolas in Braşov is one designated the 'Tudor Ciortea Memorial House'. Ciortea (1903–78), a composer of music inspired by Transylvanian folksong, was born in Braşov and studied music there with Gheorghe Dima at the Romanian Gymnasium. He never in fact occupied the building, but in 1987 some of his personal effects were deposited there by his widow. Ciortea spent most of his life in Bucharest, where he taught for 30 years at the Conservatory; but his manuscripts and other papers are kept separately in Braşov, at the Archive of the Casa Memorială Gheorghe Dima (Piaţa Sfatului 25).

In what was once two small rooms and a central hall the furniture and personal effects from Ciortea's study and, perhaps, a sitting-room in his home are arranged, providing a brief glimpse of this relatively little-known composer. Particularly poignant is the desk, at which he was sitting when he died; on it are his glasses – broken when he fell on them – and the unfinished score of a sextet on which he was working. There are two keyboard instruments, an American harmonium and a small upright piano, an Edison Home Phonograph, Transylvanian pottery, a bust of Beethoven, bookcases full of musical scores and books about French and Romanian composers (he studied with Paul Dukas and Nadia Boulanger in Paris) as well as monu-

ments of German and Romanian literature. On the walls are portraits of his mother (in Romanian costume), his wife, his daughter (the dancer Vera Proca-Ciortea) and himself; there is also an engraved portrait of Mozart.

Braşov also honours Ciortea with a chamber music festival named after him.

Casa Memorială Tudor Ciortea
Muzeul Primer Scoli Românesti din
Scheii Braşovului
Piaţa Unirii
2200 Braşov
Romania

phone +40/02 68 143879

open by appointment

Map 11

ĈIURLIONIS

Mikolajus Konstantinas Ĉiurlionis is held in the same kind of regard by Lithuanians as Sibelius is by Finns, and he is similarly commemorated in his country. Ĉiurlionis was the first serious Lithuanian composer and is regarded, like Sibelius, as having laid the foundation for a national musical style. Today his piano pieces, folksong arrangements and symphonic poems are performed in Lithuania, but the nearly 300 works he composed between 1896 and 1911 also include organ preludes and fugues, movements for string quartet, a choral *De profundis*, a Polonaise for wind and a fragment of a symphony, all largely unknown.

What is unique about Ĉiurlionis is that he has equal standing as artist and composer. Yes, Glinka, Mendelssohn, Satie and Schoenberg drew and painted, as a pastime; but for Ĉiurlionis art competed seriously with music for his creative energies. And although music was his first vocation and painting his second, Ĉiurlionis – whose life was cut tragically short at the age of 35 – is today more widely known as an artist than as a composer. In 1921 the M.K. Ĉiurlionis National Art Museum was established in Kaunas; the present gallery was built in

1936. It holds the largest collection of his works, maintaining a permanent exhibition of his drawings and paintings and holding occasional concerts in its recital room, and it is the centre for research on both his art and his music. Soft music provides a background as you move through the gallery.

Čiurlionis was born in 1875 in Varėna, 100 km east of Vilnius, on the Merkys River, but the family left when he was three years old. Varėna was destroyed during World War II. From 1877 the family lived at Druskininkai, an attractive spa town (*druska* means 'salt') in a forest along the Nemunas River, near the Polish border, 124 km south of Kaunas and 150 km from Vilnius. On the centenary of Čiurlionis's birth, the 50-km route between Varėna and Druskininkai was dubbed the 'Čiurlionis Way' and lined with 20 traditional wooden sculptures by local craftsmen.

The family spoke Russian as well as Polish (their preferred tongue), but not Lithuanian, regarded as a peasant language by the father, Konstantinas, who was organist of the local parish church. Čiurlionis was the eldest of ten children, all of whom learnt music: they followed a rigorous domestic schedule of piano practice – one child after another every two hours – with choral singing at the end of the day.

The growing family lived in a compound with two small, single-storey, timbered houses at Druskininkai, along the main road, not far from the parish church. One building served as the family gathering place, where they ate, played and sang and where the parents and youngest children slept; the other served as a dormitory for the elder children. Since 1963 these houses have been furnished in period style as part of what is now a larger complex of wooden buildings, open to the public, incorporating a newly built chamber music hall seating 35, with photographic collages of the composer's life and a memorial garden; a barn devoted to an exhibition of reproductions of his paintings and drawings, and displays of his music, with a gallery at the rear where exhibitions by living artists are held.

As in Čiurlionis's own time, a grand piano is the central feature of the main room of the grey house, which was destroyed in World War II and rebuilt on a slightly smaller scale. There is also the family harmonium and a second, upright piano given to them by his patron, Prince Ogiński. Today the grand piano is next to the rear-facing window so that in the summer, with the window open, recitals can be given with the audience on benches in the garden.

In the nearby yellow house, the smaller of the two rooms belonged to Čiurlionis; it is decorated with an easel, sketches and music and pictures of his mother and wife. The larger room recalls the family's religious life and displays another piano, from Poland, where Čiurlionis spent his last months. Wherever he was living – Warsaw, Leipzig, St Petersburg or Vilnius – he returned each summer to the family home at Druskininkai.

Beyond the picket fence surrounding the houses is the red exhibition hall. Although most of its space is devoted to displays of Čiurlionis's original drawings (among them musical graphics), reproductions of his paintings and editions and recordings of his music, this is intended as a Čiurlionis family museum. So there are also cases devoted to family portraits, including those of his wife, Sofija Kymantaitė (1886–1958), and his

The Čiurlionis family home, Druskininkai

only child, Danutė (1910–95); to the work of his sister Valerija (1896–1982), the first art historian to survey her brother's output; and to that of another sister, Jadvyga (1899–1992), a distinguished musicologist. In the background is the recorded sound of one of his tone poems, *In the Forest* (1900) or *The Sea* (1907). The main street of Druskininkai bears Čiurlionis's name, as does the local music school, and in the woodland park near the parish church there is a striking centenary memorial to him.

Čiurlionis first left home at the age of 14 to study at an orchestral school on Prince Ogiński's estate at Plungė in western Lithuania. The prince made it possible for Čiurlionis to study the piano and composition at the Warsaw and then the Leipzig conservatory. He had hardly completed his musical training in Leipzig when, after a summer of reflection at Druskininkai in 1902, he returned to Warsaw to study art. Among his subsequent, often mystical drawings – some of which he called 'compositions' – and paintings are several cycles with musical titles: 'Fantasies' (ten), 'Funeral Symphony' (seven), 'Hymn' (three), Prelude and Fugue (a diptych), and 'Sonata' (seven sonatas, each consisting of three or four paintings, with 'movement' titles such as 'Allegro' or 'Andante'). His creative gifts were henceforth divided between the two arts, and through them he was drawn into the Lithuanian national movement: he gave piano recitals and conducted choirs, published folksongs, exhibited his work in Warsaw and St Petersburg and wrote articles on Lithuanian art and culture.

In the autumn of 1907 he moved to Vilnius, where he took a room at the rear of the house at Savičiaus gatvė 11, in the oldest part of the city. Today it is known as the M.K. Čiurlionis House and is open to the public for small exhibitions, recitals and other gatherings. The entrance is through an archway alongside the house. A portrait and a floral arrangement decorate the room in which he lodged; reproductions of his paintings line the walls of the middle room; and a grand piano (in playing condition) that once belonged to a friend of his dominates the front room, which seats 60.

In Vilnius he met Sofija, who was also involved in the Lithuanian national movement; the following summer he introduced her to his family, who asked her to teach them to speak Lithuanian. The couple were married at the beginning of 1909. In 1910 they collaborated on a book, *In Lithuania*, and by the end of the year, when Sofija was expecting their child, Čiurlionis, in St Petersburg, suffered severe depression. He spent his last months at the Czerwony Dwor Sanatorium in Pustelnik, near Warsaw, where he died on 10 April 1911. A plaque marks the building, now known as the 'Red Estate'. He was buried in Lithuania, in the Rasos Cemetery on the outskirts of Vilnius.

M.K. Čiurlionis National Art Museum
Vlado Putvinskio 55
3000 Kaunas
Lithuania

phone +370/0 37 229475
fax +370/0 37 222606
e-mail mkc@takas.lt
*website*s www.travel-lithuania.com/ciurlionismuseum,
www.vdu.lt/ciurlionis.index.lt

open Tuesday–Sunday 11.00–17.00

Mikolajus Konstantinas Čiurlionis Memorial Museum
M.K. Čiurliono gatvė 35
4690 Druskininkai
Lithuania

phone +370/0 313 52755 (with *fax*),
51131
e-mail mkcmemorialm@takas.lt
website
www.muziejai.mch.mii/lt/druskininkai/ciurlionis_mem_muziejus

open Tuesday–Sunday 11.00–17.00

M.K. Čiurlionis Namai
Savičaus gatvė 11
2600 Vilnius
Lithuania

phone +370/0 262 2451
fax +370/0 212 6414
website www.vilnius.lt/new/gidas

open Monday–Friday 10.00–16.00

Map 2

M.K. Čiurlionio memorialinis muziejus Druskininkuose ([Kaunas: M.K. Čiurlionis State Museum of Art], 1988) [leaflet]
A. Nedzelskis, ed.: *M.K. Čiurlionis and Druskininkai* (Kaunas: M.K. Čiurlionis State Museum of Art, 1994) [with Eng. trans.]
M. Kulikauskienė and others: *Mikolajus Konstantinas Čiurlionis: Days and Years* (Kaunas: M.K. Čiurlionis State Museum of Art, 1996) [with Eng. trans.]
B. Verkelytė-Fedaravičienė, ed.: *Mikolajus Konstantinas Čiurlionis: Paintings, Sketches, Thoughts* (Kaunas: M.K. Čiurlionis State Museum of Art, 1997) [with Eng. trans.]

Constantinescu's house at Ploieşti

CONSTANTINESCU

Were it not for the lure of the Carpathian mountains, few tourists in Romania would be likely to venture the 62 km north of Bucharest to the industrial city of Ploieşti – best known for its oil refineries and its clock museum – where on 30 June 1909 Paul Constantinescu was born. In the Romanian pantheon of composers, Constantinescu stands second only to Enescu himself, and he was more a national figure, Enescu an international one. Trained at Bucharest Conservatory, where he studied composition with Jora and Castaldi, and later in Vienna with Schmidt and Marx, Constantinescu pursued his career in the capital from 1937, teaching harmony and composition at the Academy of Religious Music and, from 1941, at the Conservatory. His opera *O noapte furtunoasă* ('A Stormy Night', 1934) was given at the Opera Română, and he produced several film scores; his ballet music (inspired by his Romanian folk-music studies), concertos, choral music (informed by Byzantine chant) and chamber music were widely performed in Romania and stoutly championed by his students. But Constantinescu, who died on 20 December 1963, remained close to his roots and spent whatever time he could in Ploieşti. His works include a *Simfonia Ploieşteană* A local choir proudly bears his name and there is a dedicated society, the Cenaclului Muzical 'Paul Constantinescu'.

His importance as a local figure can be gauged by the size and the prominence of the museum dedicated to his memory. It is in the centre of Ploieşti, on a main road. This elegant if now slightly shabby mansion, surrounded by protective iron railings, is where he lived with his wife Maria between 1937 and 1939. Inside the house, the central room, its walls lined with instruments and a portrait by Nicolae Yasilescu, is used for lectures and chamber music concerts (it seats about 35). Three adjoining rooms display photographs of his family and his child-hood, editions and LP recordings of his music, as well as a manuscript of his opera, posters and concert programmes. There is a pen-and-ink caricature by Arturo Silvan, and press cuttings, awards and a commemorative stamp issued to mark his 75th birthday. In addition to a concert grand piano, there is a gilded bust of the composer, a brass Turkish coffee set, a zither and a harmonium, his gramophone and items of furniture from his study. These are the relics of a composer generally credited with forging a truly Romanian national style.

Muzeul Memorial 'Paul Constantinescu' Ploieşti
Stradă Nicolae Bălescu 15
2000 Ploieşti
Prahova County
Romania

phone +40/02 44 122914

open Tuesday–Sunday 09.00–17.00

Map 11

COWARD

Composer, actor, playwright, librettist, singer, pianist, painter: Noël Coward was the complete man of the theatre, with a style of his own that in many ways epitomizes the lighter side of English society in the second quarter of the 20th century. It is symbolic that *Bitter-Sweet* (1929), an 'operette', was his first unqualified success. 'The Master' had little formal musical training and relied on others to notate most of his music, but from the late 1920s until the early 60s he produced a stream of songs, distinctive in flavour, mostly for revues, musicals of various kinds and films.

Coward had several homes at different times, and often several at the same time. London was mostly his base; three of the houses he lived in, in Teddington (131 Waldegrave Road, where in 1899 he was born), Sutton (56 Lenham Road) and Belgravia (15 Gerald Road), bear blue plaques, and 111 Ebury Street, Victoria, was for a time the Noël Coward Hotel. There is a plaque in the 'Actors' Church', St Paul's, Covent Garden, and a floor-stone to him in Westminster Abbey, as well as a statue at the Theatre Royal, Drury Lane. There are identical ones in the Gershwin Theatre, New York, and in the garden of his last house in Jamaica: all were unveiled by members of the royal family. It is in Jamaica that he is buried. He chiefly lived there in his later years, first at a villa 'Blue Harbour', which is now a seedy hotel but retains the connection with a display of photographs, and finally in the small, white, modernist house, 'Firefly', that he built there and in which he died in 1973. This is now a museum to Coward: among the exhibits are his own wall paintings (described as of purple flowers, emerald sea and muscular black men in a state of undress), his typewriter, some shirts and a song half written when he died.

He had a European retreat, too, in Switzerland, at Les Avants, near Montreux, and another in Kent, a house, 'Goldenhurst', just south of the village of Aldington, near Lympne. This was commandeered by the Army and not available to him in the years immediately after World War II, so in 1945 he bought a lease on a house on the beach at St Margaret's Bay, between Deal and Dover. He was there until 1951. It is one of a group of five; preferring a degree of privacy, he acquired them all, using them for his employees, friends and relatives including his mother. His own was the end one, 'White Cliffs', a gentle stone's throw from the sea even at low tide. And there are plenty of stones on this coarse, pebbly beach.

St Margaret's celebrates his connection with the village by assigning a room to a Noël Coward display at the local museum, which is primarily given over to maritime matters and the crucial role played by the area in the war years. The Coward collection is extensive and the display is regularly changed. Typical items shown include some of his clothes (slippers, a velvet jacket with silk braiding and a cravat), theatre programmes, publicity photographs, copies of his sheet music and one of the flasks disguised as leather-bound books that Coward gave to the original *Bitter-Sweet* cast. There is also one of his paintings, 'The Cliffs above St Margaret's Bay'.

Items relating to Noël Coward are on display in the Theatre Museum in Covent Garden, London, including production photos, designs, a silk dressing-gown of Coward's (there is another in a display at New York Public Library) and another of the leather-bound flasks as well as general biographical and photographic files. Apart from his diaries, which are in an American university, his papers will in due course be held at the University of Birmingham.

St Margaret's Museum
South Sands Lodge
Beach Road
St Margaret's Bay

Dover
Kent CT15 6DZ

phone +44/0 1304 852764
fax +44/0 1304 853626

open end May–beginning September,
Wednesday–Sunday 14.00–17.00

Map 5

J. Melhuish and C. Jewell, eds.: *Noel Coward and St. Margaret's Bay* (St Margaret's Bay: The Bay Museum, n.d.)

J. Gerard: 'Mad about the Bay', *The Times* (11 December 1999), 30

DĀRZIŅŠ

A life that was to end tragically began quietly in an isolated parish school, perched on a hill, at the end of a lime-tree alley, off the dirt track road between Old and New Piebalga, some 135 km east and slightly north of Riga. The Latvian composer Emils Dārziņš was born to the schoolmaster and his wife on 3 November 1875. The two-storey building that served as the Jāņskola for nearly a century is now the local museum, established in 1925, incorporating a function room for musical events and commemorating not only the composer Dārziņš but also, more recently, a local poet, Jānis Sudrabkalņš (1894–1975).

Two exhibition rooms on the first floor are devoted to Dārziņš. They display items collected long after the composer's death by his mother and donated in 1930 – family pictures, his christening certificate and school reports, his pens and an alarm clock, and the clothes he was wearing when on 31 August 1910 he was found dead on the railway line between Riga and the seaside resort, Jūrmala, where he was living. Arresting portraits of this exceedingly handsome man, his mother and his son Wolfgang (also a pianist, composer and critic) dominate the larger room, which also contains an upright piano that he played and seating for visiting schoolchildren.

The Jāņskola is more memorial place than museum. Although an important Latvian composer of solo and choral songs, Dārziņš destroyed much of his music after criticism that he had 'borrowed'. None of it is on display, but the keeper is pleased to play a recording of his popular and appealing 'Melancholy Waltz' for orchestra in the adjacent hall. Dārziņš was also an admired writer on music and the first Latvian critic, though none of his writings is on display.

Emila Dārziņa un Jāņa Sudrabkanal Muzeis 'Jāņskola'
Jaunpiebalga
4125 Cēsu rajons
Latvia

open 15 May – 1 November,
Tuesday–Sunday 10.00–17.00

phone +371/0 416 2354

Map 2

DEBUSSY

Claude Debussy was born in Saint-Germain-en-Laye, the well-heeled outer suburb west of Paris, on 22 August 1862. On the ground floor of the tall 17th-century building where he and his parents lived, in the narrow, winding Rue au Pain, was a porcelain shop, which his father attempted without much success to run. Behind the shop was a small courtyard with an attractive open-timbered staircase leading to three upper storeys. The family remained there until Claude was two years old.

The schoolhouse museum at Piebalga

Debussy's birthplace, Saint-Germain-en-Laye

Today the ground floor of the Maison Claude Debussy houses the Saint-Germain-en-Laye *office de tourisme*. If you venture in – as you must! – and ask for Debussy, the staff of the bureau will greet you warmly and usher you through the courtyard and up the stairs to the first-floor rooms. There you will be amazed to discover a *bijou* museum in which a cleverly crafted microcosm of Debussy's life, works and artefacts – including his formal concert clothes (now adorning a mannequin) and his desk collection of antiquities – is presented in two small rooms. Only the French could do it with such elegance and style. The first room is a magical maze of partitions supported from the ceiling by plumb-lines, while the second evokes a domestic ambience without any pretence of re-creation.

While the first floor is dedicated to displays, the second is given over to a beautifully appointed auditorium, with a period Bechstein piano and seating for 50 people, and serves regularly for recitals, masterclasses, lectures, themed *salons de musique* and educational events for children. In 1992, bound by the terms of the will of Madame de Tinan, Debussy's step-daughter, the city set up its own research and documentation centre on the third floor, superbly fitted out with library furniture and listening booths.

The significance of the house was first acknowledged in 1921, three years after Debussy's death, when a plaque was put up by his English admirers, but it was opened to the public only in 1990. The impetus had originally come in 1986 from the Tinan bequest: she left a sum of money to Saint-Germain-en-Laye subject to the foundation of a museum and documentation centre in the house within a short time after her death. With support from the Ministry of Culture it was duly established and her collection of Debussy's personal possessions was put on display there, including the famous oriental lacquered *poisson d'or* which inspired the eponymous piece in the second set of *Images* (1907). Political disputes, however, prevented the removal there, as had been hoped, of the Centre de Documentation Claude Debussy, founded a dozen years earlier by the leading Debussy scholar, the late François Lesure, and now housed in the music department of the Bibliothèque Nationale.

Maison Claude Debussy

38 rue au Pain
78100 Saint-Germain-en-Laye
France

phone +33/0 1 3451 0512
fax +33/0 1 3973 1015
website www.saint-germain-en-laye.fr

open Tuesday–Friday 14.00–18.00
(closing 17.30, November–February),
Saturday 10.00–12.30, 14.00–18.00

Map 6

N. Simeone: *Paris: a Musical Gazetteer* (New Haven and London: Yale University Press, 2000), 51–6

DIMA

Despite the name of the museum in his native Braşov, on the southern edge of the Carpathian mountains, Gheorghe Dima is no longer commemorated in the house in which he was born. That house still stands, at Sirul Gheorghe Dima 4, just outside the old city walls; the first Dima museum opened there in 1957, but in 1990 the displays and the Dima Archive were temporarily moved to another Braşov museum in the medieval main square of the city (*see* MUREŞIANU).

Gheorghe Dima was born on 10 October 1847, into an old and well-known Braşov merchant family. He went abroad to study music, to Vienna and finally to Leipzig, returning to Romania first as a baritone recitalist and then a teacher at the Romanian Gymnasium in Braşov, and later in Cluj (the conservatory where he served as director from 1919 until his death in 1925 bears his name), as a choral conductor in Braşov and Sibiu, and as a composer of folksong-based vocal music.

Today Dima's legacy shares its quarters, in the former print room of the Mureşianu publishing firm, with recital facilities – a boudoir grand piano and seating for 35. On display around the periphery of the room are a bust, a plaster death mask and a cast of his right hand, Dima's desk and other furniture, as well as programmes and music. There are also wall panels with reproductions of documents and photographs, among them one showing this rather dignified and serious man riding a camel on holiday in Egypt.

Muzeul Memorial Casa Mureşenilor
Piaţa Sfatului 25
2200 Braşov
Romania

phone +40/02 68 147 7864
website www.muzeulmuresenilor.ro

open Monday–Saturday 09.00–15.00

D'INDY

A panoramic view of the Alps inspired Vincent d'Indy not only to compose his *Symphonie sur un chant montagnard français* (1886) but also to build a neo-Gothic château about 25 km west of Valence in the Ardèche. To reach Les Faugs, you leave the A6 autoroute at Valence and take the D533 to Alboussière, then bear left, passing through the village of Boffres and going a little beyond. Today the château is owned by d'Indy's descendants, who first opened it to the public on its centenary in 1990 and continue to reside there during the summer months. To be received at Les Faugs by the d'Indy family offers something out of the ordinary for music lovers and composer museum connoisseurs alike. With luck, your visit may coincide with a concert of his music in the subterranean chapel or on the terrace.

Although d'Indy was born in Paris (in 1851), his roots were in the Ardèche. Chabret was the family estate in the commune of Boffres where he stayed during the summer holidays until he was 18. His paternal grandmother put a stop to these idylls in 1869, when he fell in love with his cousin, Isabelle de Pampelonne. The two met again in 1872, at their grandmother's funeral, and three years later they were married. By then d'Indy had undertaken military service (the family had strong military traditions) and studied law before deciding to pursue musical studies as a pupil and disciple of César Franck; henceforth he would always divide his time between Paris and the south. Following the birth of their son in 1879, Vincent and Isabelle decided to build a home of their own on family land. Work began in 1885 and Les Faugs was completed five years later.

D'Indy's enduring passion for the Ardèche region had always extended to its music. In 1892 he published transcriptions of *Chansons populaires du Vivarais*, following it with a larger collection in 1900, to which he eventually added a companion volume in 1930. His

Château des
Faugs, Boffres

Wagnerian opera *Fervaal* (1895) was set in the Cevennes, and in 1905, the year of Isabelle's death, he composed the symphonic triptych *Jours d'été à la montagne*, surely inspired by the eastward view from his study. D'Indy continued to commute between Paris and Les Faugs until 1920, when he remarried and built a new home, L'Étrave, at Agay on the Côte d'Azur. He died on 2 December 1931 at his Paris flat in the avenue de Villars.

Today the house is very much a living museum during the summer months. The displays are drawn from the rich family archives as well as Vincent d'Indy's legacy. On the lower floors, no attempt is made at a historical re-creation of the rooms as he would have known them: this is a house for living in as well as a museum. The entrance hall is lined with grand portraits and framed architectural plans for the château (well matched by the heroic stance of the music that echoes softly through the house). The billiard room is now an attractive family living-room, while the dining-room and rather more formal *grand salon*, dominated by the composer's Erard piano, are furnished with family heirlooms. The well-stocked little library lacks the composer's own books, which his widow was forced to sell.

Mounting the imposing staircase, the visitor encounters four glass cases displaying a fascinating, rather crowded array of Vincent's youthful drawings and watercolours, musical sketchbooks, photographs and memorabilia. These are the curatorial handiwork of Marie d'Indy (the composer's granddaughter-in-law). Further well-stocked cases pertaining to his music, the Schola Cantorum in Paris (of which in 1900 he was a founder and the first director) and his life at Les Faugs await scrutiny on the second floor.

Only the Cabinet du Maître, his private study, has been preserved much as the composer left it in 1920. In addition to furniture, it is filled with busts of his heroes (Dante, Gluck, Bonaparte, Beethoven and Wagner) and musical instruments (violins, horns, a flute, clarinet, trombone, guitar and piano) as well as a collection of walking sticks (he relished 40-km walks) and a telescope, with which he could survey the surrounding countryside, from the Alps on the left to the Massif Central on the right. Elsewhere, there is an archive containing several thousand letters, musical manuscripts and photographs which attracts scholars from all over the world.

Château des Faugs

07440 Boffres
Vernoux-en-Vivarais
France

phone +33/0 4 7552 2429

open mid-June–mid-September, Monday, Wednesday, Saturday, Sunday 14.00–18.00

Map 6

G. Gefen: *Composers' Houses* (London: Cassell and Vendome, 1998), 117–25

DITTERSDORF

There are several villages called Dittersdorf in Saxony and Thuringia, but that's not where Carl Ditters came from. He was Viennese, born and bred, more Viennese than Haydn or Mozart (he was born between them, in 1739). He is not commemorated in his native city; but he is in Javorník, in north Moravia, on the border between the Czech Republic and Poland, where he lived between 1769 and 1794 as Kapellmeister at the regional court of the Prince-Bishop of Breslau (now Wrocław), Count Schaffgotsch. Through the Count's offices he gathered various honours and emoluments, and it was through one of the positions he held, as Chief Magistrate of Freiwaldau, that in 1773 he was automatically ennobled, as 'von Dittersdorf'.

On his arrival in Javorník, Ditters moved into an attractive new house, with a squat little tower at either end, which today serves as the local history museum downstairs and music school above. In 1772 he married a Hungarian soprano, whom he had met while Kapellmeister to the Bishop of Grosswardein (now Oradea, in Romania) in the 1760s, and settled into family life. Towering above the small town is 16th-century Johannisberg Castle, then the residence of the Prince-Bishop but today another

Dittersdorf's house at Javorník

museum (it boasts the largest collection of whistles in Middle Europe). During his time there, he trained the orchestra to a high standard in order to perform his symphonies, oratorios and theatre pieces, many of which were also given in Vienna. When in 1795 Count Schaffgotsch died, Ditters was pensioned; before leaving Javorník he put up a memorial to his employer at the crossroads near his house. He accepted an offer of accommodation on the estate of Baron Ignaz von Stillfried in Nový Dvůr (near Soběslav), where he lived, composing Singspiels and writing his autobiography, until his death there on 24 October 1799.

On his centenary in 1899, a handsome relief plaque was erected on the house in Javorník. In 1994 the building was restored and one of the two tower rooms was allocated to a commemoration of his life and works. On the walls are a series of 14 panels with facsimiles of manuscripts, letters and archival documents, including his coat of arms; engraved portraits, librettos and editions of music performed in the castle theatre (among them his comic opera, *Il viaggiatore americano*, composed for the Count's nameday in 1771); and photographs, including images of the Dittershof at Freiwaldau – now Jeseník – and his grave at Nový Dvůr. Of note among the items on display are the copy of the 1801 edition of his autobiography and an 18th-century travelling trunk.

Javorník (to Dittersdorf, Jauernig) is best reached by road. From Prague and Hradec Králové, it is easier to cross briefly into Poland and go through Klodzko than to take the route to Šumperk, across the Hrubý Jeseník mountains and through the local capital, Jeseník.

Rodný dům Karla Ditterse z Dittersdorfu
Městské Muzeum
Puškinova 15
79070 Javorník
Czech Republic

phone +420/0 584 440276
fax +420/0 584 440190
e-mail mksjavornik@es.czn.cz

open April–September, Sunday–Friday
10.00–12.00, 13.00–14.30,
Saturday 10.00–12.00; October–March,
Sunday–Friday 10.00–12.00

Map 4

DONIZETTI

Bergamo cherishes the memory of its most famous composer, Gaetano Donizetti. No one could have imagined that the third son of a poor artisan living just outside the city wall could have risen to such international renown. But thanks to the help of Johann Simon Mayr, the German-born *maestro di cappella* at the basilica of S Maria Maggiore, his talent was quickly recognized and nurtured. Fired with creativity and soon much in demand for new operas in Naples, Milan and later Paris, where he gained Rossini's favour, fortune beckoned. But his life, in some ways like a fairytale, ended sadly: a melancholy widower whose children had all died in infancy, mentally debilitated by syphilis, paralysed and unable to speak, he returned from Paris to Bergamo in 1848 to die among family and friends.

Donizetti was born on 29 September 1797 in a dark, two-room apartment below the street in the Casa Codazzi, at Borgo Canale 10 (now 14). The street winds down the slope of the *alta città* – the old part of the city is built on a steep hill – from the S Alessandro gate towards the Lombardy plain below. Donizetti's birthplace was declared a national monument in 1926 and in 1994 a modest exhibition, 'Donizetti a Bergamo', opened there, showing photographs of the city and a variety of posters. Yet it does evoke the conditions under which Donizetti spent his early years, cramped and dank. (The family shared a kitchen and laundry space with other families resident in the basement.) The upper part of the house is now occupied by the Fondazione Donizetti. A few doors away a plaque marks the house in which the cellist Alfredo Piatti, himself a great admirer of Donizetti, was born in 1822.

Istituto Musicale Gaetano Donizetti, Bergamo

The family fortunes changed in 1806: they moved to better quarters at Piazza Nova 35 (now Piazza Mascheroni 8) and Gaetano began studies as one of the first pupils at the choir school revived by Maestro Mayr that year. When Donizetti was 18, Mayr made it possible for him to continue his studies in Bologna at the Liceo Filarmonico Comunale, after which he returned to Bergamo and on Mayr's recommendation obtained commissions for four operas for Venice.

Naples in the 1820s, Milan in the early 1830s, and then Naples, Vienna and Paris – not Bergamo – were in turn his home. He married Virgilia Vasselli in 1828; she died in Paris in 1837. Ominously, in 1844 the first signs appeared of the 'cerebro-spinal degeneration' diagnosed two years later; after 17 months in a suburban sanatorium at Ivry he was reduced to semiconsciousness, unable to move or speak. His nephew brought him home to Bergamo, where he died six months later, on 18 April 1848, in the Palazzo Scotti.

The house, at what is now Via Gaetano Donizetti 1, is marked by a plaque.

Donizetti was initially buried in the Pezzoli family chapel at the Valtesse Cemetery. But in 1875 his remains, along with those of Mayr (who had died in 1844), were exhumed and interred in S Maria Maggiore; Donizetti's tomb was topped by a monument sculpted for the basilica by Vincenzo Vela in 1855. In 1951 the city fathers decided to re-open his tomb a second time to unite the cap of his skull (retained by a pathologist as a souvenir of the autopsy) with the rest of his remains.

With the centenary of Donizetti's birth in 1897 came the first exhibition in Bergamo of his memorabilia, drawn from the collections of his brother's grandsons. This may in turn have inspired the foundation of the Museo Donizettiano in 1903 by Baronessa Scotti, who endowed it with her own collection. The museum, among the finest of its kind in Italy, occupies two rooms in the Istituto Musicale Gaetano Donizetti, the successor to Mayr's school (Mayr lived nearby, at Via Arena 20).

The collection is by any standards extensive, and that enables the displays to be regularly changed. There are musical autographs from 1813 onwards; letters and other documents; innumerable portraits of Donizetti, Mayr, his family, friends (especially the baronessa) and his singers; his pianos, including the 1822 Carl Strobel that he used for composing most of his music and his 1844 Bösendorfer as well as Mayr's Caspar Lorenz square piano; and the Austrian court clothes he wore as Kapellmeister in Vienna in 1842. All the manuscript texts on display are clearly transcribed. Entire cases are devoted to individual operas and illustrated with scene designs, printed scores and librettos as well as manuscripts and portraits. There are also personal effects – quill pens, his toilet kit, his Turkish pipe, his ring and Madonna medallion – and a death mask. Among the most graphic images of the composer is a daguerreotype portrait of him, ravaged by illness, with his nephew at Ivry, dated 3 August 1847. Until 1951 the cap of his skull was displayed in an urn; perhaps even more macabre, the museum also owns the black wool tail-coat in which he was buried and which was recovered 'almost intact', in 1875. In an alcove off the main room are furniture and mementoes of his last days, including his invalid's armchair, with a tray and upholstered headrest, and the bed in which he died. On the wall is a telling, but dignified, idealized last portrait by Giuseppe Rillosi (the invalid chair lacks the tray and headrest).

The City of Bergamo formally marked the 1897 centenary by renaming the Teatro Riccardi (in the via Sentierone, in

Museo Donizettiano (his deathbed can be seen through the right doorway)

the lower part of Bergamo) in his honour; near the opera house is a monument with fountain, by Francesco Jerace, depicting Donizetti with the muse Melopea. The town council's departments of tourism and trade, art and performing arts have produced a useful leaflet entitled 'Bergamo: Gaetano Donizetti' for visitors.

Donizetti Casa Natale
Via Borgo Canale 14
24129 Bergamo
Italy

phone +390/0 35 399269 (Fondazione Donizetti)

open by appointment

Museo Donizettiano
Palazzo Basoni-Scotti
Via Arena 9
24100 Bergamo
Italy

phone +390/0 35 399269, 247116
fax +390/0 35 219128
e-mail museostorico @bergamoestoria.it
website bergamoestoria.it

open June–September, daily 09.30–13.00, 14.00–17.30; October–May, daily 09.30–13.00, Saturday also 14.00–17.30

Map 9

N. Simeone: *Paris: a Musical Gazetteer* (New Haven and London: Yale University Press, 2000)

DUSSEK

One of the great pianist-composers of his age, Jan Ladislav Dussek (or Dusík, in its original Czech spelling) had a truly international career: as a young man he played in the Low Countries, Russia and Lithuania, and the bulk of his life was spent in Paris, with periods in London and Berlin. He died in Paris in 1812. Dussek is affectionately commemorated in his native town, Čáslav, some 80 km south-east of Prague, where he was born in 1760. There is a street named after him, the ulica Dusíkova, in which stands the local theatre, built in 1869 and also bearing his name, and at the top of it is the town square, in which the house of his birth (now a textile shop) is marked by a plaque.

The local museum, the Městské Muzeum Čáslav, is the headquarters of the Dusíkův Ústav (the Dussek Institute), which has assembled a collection of Dussek materials and occasionally mounts exhibitions based on it. But since 2000 the museum has set up a series of galleries at a former military building not far away which also houses the local primary music school (Základní Umělecká Škola J.L. Dusíka). One of them is devoted to Dussek. This is dominated, as indeed was Dussek's life, by pianos and suchlike instruments. There are examples of every type that he is likely to have played, from a clavichord and a tiny table piano through a large square to a grand fortepiano, and in addition a glass harmonica and a lady's harp; his mother, his wife and his daughter were all harpists (the last two were also composers), and he himself wrote sensitively for the instrument.

There are also a dozen display cases, designed to give a picture of 'Dussek and his Times'. Two show a chronological succession of portraits (the lithe youth turning into a man too obese to leave his bed); others record the main events of his roving, adventurous life, the activities of his family (several other members were noted musicians), the traces of him in Čáslav and his native town's commemoration of him, his role as inventor of musical novelties (as glass harmonica player), his output as a composer and his particular style of piano playing – he was noted for his discriminating use of the pedals. The Dussek Institute's foundation (in 1940) and activities are recorded too. There are a plaster bust and some oil paintings of the period. Although there is not much primary material the display gives a clear and neatly devised account of Čáslav's most distinguished musical son and his world.

Čáslav did in fact have another musical son, Jan Václav Stich (1746–1803: better known as Johann Wenzel Stich, or by his translated name, Giovanni Punto); he was a composer but was famed as the leading horn player of his day, and Mozart and Beethoven both composed for him. He and Dussek played together in Čáslav in 1802. He was born at the nearby village of Žehušice, where his house bears a plaque. The museum possesses engravings of him.

Galerie Městského Muzea Čáslavě
Jeníkovská 222
28601 Čáslav
Czech Republic

phone +420/0 327 316769
e-mail muzeumc@caslavsko.cz

open Monday–Friday 08.00–11.00, 12.00–16.00

Map 4

DVOŘÁK

Four museums and memorial sites in or close to Prague celebrate the life and music of the Czechs' most loved composer, Antonín Dvořák. Visitors to Prague music festivals may have already seen the museum at Ke Karlovu 20 in the second district and may even have taken the train 28 km north to his birthplace in Nelahozeves. Fewer are likely to know the museums and places of pilgrimage in Zlonice or Vysoká.

The Prague museum was the first to be opened, in 1932, and it is the most richly endowed with artefacts. Administered by the Museum of Czech Music, it is housed in an 18th-century villa with no prior connection with the composer. The ground floor is devoted to Dvořák's life, displaying photographs and documents, articles of clothing (including his Cambridge doctoral robes) and other personal possessions such as his watch and his glasses, musical instruments (in particular his viola and his Bösendorfer grand), honorific urns and wreaths and furniture from his Prague flat. The first

floor is a recital room surrounded by displays relating to his music. Attached to the museum is the central archive for the study of Dvořák, which holds many of his music manuscripts, his correspondence and numerous photographs.

Dvořák spent most of his life in Prague, arriving when he was 16 to study at the Organ School of the Society for Church Music in Bohemia. He played the viola in the Provisional Theatre orchestra and taught composition at the Prague Conservatory. He met and in 1873 married Anna Čermáková (having initially been in love with her elder sister). The first three of their nine children were born, and died, at their flat at Na rybníčku 14 before the couple moved to Žitná út 10 (now 14). After the death of his first child he composed the *Stabat mater*.

During the early 1870s his music began to be more widely known, its accessibility and Slavonic qualities ensuring its warm reception both at home and abroad. Through Brahms he became associated with the German publisher Simrock, but he resisted the temptation to become Germanized, politely declining invitations to move to Vienna from Brahms and from Hanslick, who wrote in 1882 urging him to reconsider: 'your art requires a wider horizon, a German environment, a bigger, non-Czech public'. The brief time he spent in Vienna is commemorated by a plaque adorning the inn where he stayed, the 'Goldenes Lamm' at Wiedner Hauptstraße 7.

Dvořák toured widely in Europe, going as far afield as Russia and England, where he conducted new works at the great provincial choir festivals as well as the Albert Hall and Crystal Palace in London. In 1892 he went to America as director of the newly opened National Conservatory in New York, where he lived at 328 East 17th Street. He and his family spent the summers of 1893 and 1894 in the Midwest at the Czech colony at Spillville, Iowa; the house where they stayed (on State Highway 325) is today the home of the American Czechoslovak Music Society.

Dvořák's birthplace at Nelahozeves

But Dvořák belonged in the Bohemian countryside. He was born on 8 September 1841 at Nelahozeves, a village near Kralupy, just west of the main road northwards from Prague to Roudnice and Dresden, and spent his childhood there in the shadow of the Lobkowitz family castle which dominates the area. His early musical education took place in the public house run by his father František (a zither player as well as butcher and publican) and in the little parish church, St Andrew's, across the road, where he was baptized and where later he took organ lessons and sang in the choir; the organ he played is still in use. Later he played the violin in a band with his father and uncle.

His birthplace has been open to the public since 1951 and was restored in 1991 when four rooms, including the presumed room of his birth, were refurbished to mark his 150th birthday. The collection on display includes his bentwood rocking chair and a bust by Ladislav Šaloun as well as family trinkets, portraits, photographs, his prayer book, gifts he acquired on concert tours and his quill pen. On the walls of the recital room, seating 60, there is an informative display about his life and works.

Every year, around 8 September, memorial celebrations are held at Nelahozeves, with Mass at the church and concerts at the house and in the castle on the hill above. Unveiled in 1988, a statue of Dvořák poised to conduct (by Zdeněk Hošek, entitled 'Meditation') stands in the public garden adjoining the house.

Dvořák was saved from a career as a butcher by the generosity of his mother's younger brother, a steward to Count Kinsky, who gave him a home on the Kinsky estates in Zlonice (32 km to the west, near Kladno) and access to tuition from the talented local music master Antonín Liehmann, who lived and worked next door and was later to provide him with a stipend to study in Prague.

At Zlonice the large corner house in which he lived for four years from 1853 has been a local history museum since 1954, with a Dvořák room containing the private collection of the composer's son Otakar. On display are the bed (disassembled) in which Dvořák died, souvenirs from Spillville and fragments of the famous 'bells of Zlonice' that are enshrined in the title of his first symphony (though their sound is not echoed in the actual music). Other musicians from Zlonice are also commemorated, notably the famous harpist family, the Krumpholzes; and there is a large room, seating 90, used for concerts and lectures.

In 1877 Dvořák's sister-in-law Josefina – his wife's sister, and an actress, the one with whom he had earlier been in love – married Count Václav Kaunitz at his newly built neo-Renaissance manor house, set in a forest park, with a lake, near the village of Vysoká, near Příbram,

The Dvořák museum at Zlonice

70 km south-west of Prague (just off the road from Příbram towards Plzeň). The Dvořáks attended the ceremony and afterwards were frequent visitors.

In 1884 Dvořák's increasing fame, and thus fortune, made possible the purchase of a modest property of their own in the village. Villa Rusalka (after the water-sprite: he had yet to write his opera of that title) was their name for their summer retreat, formerly a sheepfold and then a granary, where the composer felt inspired to work. Students from Prague came to attend the master and enjoyed early morning forest walks and the bounty of his garden. Antonín and Anna returned as often as possible and on his deathbed he was still hoping to go there one last time; but he died in Prague on 1 May 1904. Villa Rusalka, still owned by the family and housing some of Dvořák's original furniture, is not open to the public. Within sight of the house is a modest memorial acknowledging the composer's local connection: a gilded plaque is affixed to a large stone, surrounded by smaller irregular stones on which the names of his principal works are carved.

In 1960 the much grander Kaunitz house was acquired by the state and designated a memorial to the composer; in 1994, it was opened after refurbishment as a museum and a music and conference centre. The displays are as dramatic as any in a composer museum –

cleverly lit photographs and displays, embedded in glass, fascinate as well as educate: the museum evocation of Dvořák's own *Rusalka* (on the first floor), with illuminated maquettes, is matched only by the short woodland walk from the house to the lake of the same name. On the ground floor there is a music studio-cum-recital room and a striking re-creation of Josefina's bedroom, her clothes strewn about and her bed rumpled. The barrel-vaulted basement is equipped for conferences and receptions.

Muzeum Antonína Dvořáka
Villa Amerika
Ke Karlovu 20
12000 Praha 2
Czech Republic

phone, fax +420/0 2 2492 3363
e-mail a.dvorak.museum@nm.cz
website www.nm.cz

open Tuesday–Sunday 10.00–17.00

Památník Antonína Dvořáka
Proti nádraží 12
27751 Nelahozeves 12
Czech Republic

phone, fax +420/0 315 785099

open April–September, Saturday and Sunday 10.00–12.00, 13.00–17.00; October–March, Saturday and Sunday 09.00–12.00, 13.00–16.00; other days by appointment

Památník Antonína Dvořáka
Komenského
27371 Zlonice
okres Kladno
Czech Republic

phone +420/0 312 591244 (591313, 591166)

open Tuesday and Thursday 09.00–12.00, or by appointment

Památník Antonína Dvořáka
Zámeček 69
26242 p. Tíebsko
Vysoká u Příbrami
Czech Republic

The Dvořák museum (Kaunitz house) at Vysoká u Příbrami

phone, fax +420/0 318 618115
e-mail pamatnik@antonindvorak.cz
website www.antonindvorak.cz

open April–June, September–October,
Tuesday–Sunday 10.00–16.00;
July–August, Tuesday–Sunday
10.00–17.00; November–March,
Tuesday–Friday 10.00–15.00

Map 4

M. Hora: *Zlonice, eine Wiege der böhmischen Musik* (Zlonice: Heimatverein, 1988)
O. Špecinger, K. Brumovský and J. Jaroš: *Dvořákova Nelahozeves* (Mělník: Okresní kulturní středisko Mělník, 1991)
H. Kretschmer: *Wiener Musikergedenkstätten* (Vienna: J & V Edition, 3/1992)
H. Klevar and P. Polansky: 'The Dvořák Myths in Spillville', *Czech Music*, xviii/2 (1994), 64–72
M. Hallová and M. Kuna: *Antonín Dvořák, 1841–1904* (Prague: Supraphon, n.d.)

EGK

Donauwörth, a small town on the Danube in Swabia, about 50 km north of Augsburg, takes great pride in its connection with the 20th-century opera and ballet composer Werner Egk. Egk was born close by, in Auchsesheim, on 7 May 1901, and lived there for seven years (the house was destroyed in 1938, but he is commemorated with a bust in the central Platz and a specially planted tree) before enrolling in the Gymnasium at Augsburg. He spent most of his career in Berlin, as director of the Staatsoper, where in 1937 his fairytale opera *Die Zaubergeige* was first ecstatically received; during World War II, he was director of the composers' section of the Reichsmusikkammer and, from 1950 to 1953, of the Hochschule für Musik.

In 1971 he and his violinist wife Elisabeth retired to Donauwörth, where they were received with evident warmth; he was soon made an honorary citizen. The following year he established the Werner-Egk-Kulturpreis, awarded biennially ever since. He dedicated his *Fünf Stücke für Bläserquintett* to the local citizens; the town reciprocated in 1982 by

opening a Werner-Egk-Begegnungsstätte, in a former 17th-century Capuchin monastery, the Deutschordenshaus – to which Egk responded by composing his only string quartet, 'Die Nachtigall'.

Egk died on 10 July 1983 and was buried next to his wife (*d* 1978) in the municipal cemetery; their tombstone bears his own maze-like design. Three years later, on what would have been his 85th birthday, the town celebrated its 750th Jubilee by inaugurating a ten-bell glockenspiel at the top of the Rathaus which, every hour between 11.00 and 18.00, plays a melody from *Die Zaubergeige*. To celebrate his 90th anniversary a bronze sculpture evoking *Die Zaubergeige* was commissioned from Hans Ladner for the Donauwörther Promenade; it was unveiled in 1991 in a fountain at the end of an alley of birch trees.

In 1993 the monastery was renovated, and the Egk museum was reinstated in three rooms and two hallways on the first floor, with a doll museum (the Käthe-Kruse-Puppen-Museum) downstairs. The largest room devoted to the composer contains furniture from his last house, at Inning am Ammersee, not far from the retirement home of his mentor Carl Orff, along with some of his own drawings and watercolours, his Blüthner grand piano (not used for recitals) and a collection of folk instruments. There are also photographs of the composer and his wife, a bronze bust by Karl Bauer (1922–4), a portrait by Kurt Weinhold (1942), a bronze life mask and (in an alcove) a death mask.

In the hall immediately outside are more photographic collages, glass cases filled with medallions and awards and publications about Egk, and another bronze bust, by Arno Breker (1978–9). A long corridor is lined with posters for his operas and still more photographs, this time of his ballets (*Casanova in London* and *Französische Suite nach Rameau*) and operas (*Die chinesische Nachtigall* and *Die Verlobung in San Domingo*), and there are cases with costumes from the 1959 production of his 1940 ballet *Joan von Zarissa*. In six further cases, along the outside wall, are the fruits of the Werner Egk prize: recordings, books and stage designs.

In the remaining rooms are photographs and maquettes of productions of his operas; set designs for the controversial 1979 production of his Faust ballet, *Abraxas* (1948), and Oskar Kokoschka's 1954 lithographs of the first production of the opera *Irische Legende*; and cases with Elisabeth Egk's violins together with programmes, editions and recordings of his music. In spite of the many attractively presented images of Egk and his music, and the presence of listening equipment in the main room, no sound of his music disturbs the quiet.

Werner-Egk-Begegnungsstätte
Pflegstraße 21a
86609 Donauwörth
Germany

phone +49/0 906 789185, 789151
fax + 49/0 906 7891159
e-mail museen@donauwoerth.de
website www.donauwoerth.de

open Wednesday, Saturday, Sunday
14.00–17.00

Map 7

A. Böswald: 'In der Welt zu Hause, in Donauwörth daheim: Professor Werner Egk', *Nordschwaben-Zeitschrift für Landschaft, Geschichte, Kultur und Zeitgeschehen*, iv (Aalen, 1981)
Donauwörth 55 (Donauwörth: Presse- und Informationsstelle des Rathauses, 1994) [incl. address by A. Böswald on the opening of the museum, 16–20, and discussion of the museum by G. Reisser, 26–9]

EINEM

The Austrian composer Gottfried von Einem spent most of his years from the early 1950s onwards based in Vienna (he was born in 1918), and he finally had an apartment in the Inneren Burghof. But he latterly liked to escape to a rural retreat and for his closing years he bought a cottage in the village of Oberdürnbach, which nestles on a hill-side a couple of kilometres east of Maissau, itself some 65 km north-west of Vienna on the old road to Prague. The cottage, formerly the schoolhouse, lies next to the church, which is notable for its late medieval frescoes.

The front room of the cottage is the one in which Einem worked, lived and slept during his last four years, and it is here that in 1996 he died, tended by his second wife, Lotte Ingrisch. It has been kept exactly as it was. There are still wood shavings in the pencil sharpener, clothes in the cupboard, shoes by the bedside. The desk is undisturbed. The cat basket is still there. Einem's immediate library is to hand. The visitor can share the long view of the hills across the valley that he enjoyed during these years. On the bed is a death mask, gold-sprayed.

In this room and the wood-panelled one behind it are a number of works of art by Einem's friends and colleagues which together provide some portrait of the man himself, his taste, his relation to the world around him. There are Japanese watercolours (1959, used for the cover of his *Japanische Blätter*) and one by Avramidis showing Einem as the devil (presumably a reference to his controversial *Jesu Hochzeit*), a dedicated *Figurenkomposition* (1966) by Wotruba, a pair of *Mistechnik* pictures (1983) by Linde Waber, a view of one of Einem's former country homes by Neuwirth (1981, with a grand piano perched in a cherry tree), and a woolly sheep rocking horse, a product of Einem's stay in Glyndebourne. Freud and Mozart are among others present.

Down the corridor (lined with posters) is a large rear room, a true and quite extensive museum display in a series of showcases: from his childhood (he was adopted, the natural son of a Hungarian count) and his earliest attempts at composing, through his schooling, his family life, his early works – there are several facsimiles of manuscripts – his operas and their performances, his work for the United Nations (*An die Nachgeboren*), his fellow composers, to his various awards, the works left unfinished and his obituary.

This sympathetic museum to Einem was planned by his widow, who after his death presented the house to the Stadtgemeinde Maissau. It was opened to the public in 1998. There is a 'Gottfried von Einem Wanderweg', a favourite walk of the composer's through meadows and forest, linking Maissau and Oberdürnbach.

Gottfried von Einem Haus

Oberdürnbach 7
3712 Maissau
Austria

phone +43/0 2958 82706, 82577 (or 82271, Stadtgemeinde Maissau)

open by appointment

O. Biba: *Gottfried von Einem: ein erfolgreicher österreichischer Komponist* (Maissau: Stadtgemeinde Maissau, 1998)

Map 1

ELGAR

Discovering Edward Elgar's birthplace, at Lower Broadheath, just outside Worcester, is an adventure in itself. It can also, with the help of the delightful 'Elgar Route' signs and a brochure (from the Worcester City and Malvern Hill District Councils), be the first stop on a unique musical pilgrimage, between Worcester and Great Malvern, among 48 related sites. Although Elgar lived at Firs for only two years after his birth on 2 June 1857,

he remained deeply attached to the area all his life.

As a boy growing up in Worcester, he spent his holidays in Lower Broadheath, on a nearby farm; as a man he returned again and again to the Malvern Hills for inspiration. He rented Birchwood Lodge in Storridge, a small summer cottage, from 1898 until 1903, scoring *The Dream of Gerontius* and composing *Caractacus* there. Then he lived near Hereford, at Plas Gwyn, until he moved to London in 1911. As a widower, he lived at Napelton Grange in Kempsey from 1923 until 1927 (he was there when in 1924 he was appointed Master of the King's Musick). His last home was Marl Bank, in Worcester. When in 1931 the piano tuner's son was ennobled, he chose the title 'First Baronet . . . of Broadheath'; in 1934 he was buried next to his wife at St Wulstan's Church, Little Malvern. It was one of his last wishes that the redbrick cottage should become his official memorial.

After Elgar's death his daughter, Carice, was eager to see the cottage set up as a memorial, and the next year Worcester Corporation bought the building. But the appeal for funds to establish and run a museum had a poor response, and for nearly 30 years it was run by a trust on a shoestring budget, mostly with resident custodians opening it to callers by request. A collection was gradually assembled, mostly from Carice but also from other family members

Firs, Elgar's birthplace at Lower Broadheath

and friends. In the early 1960s the situation worsened as the fabric deteriorated and the longstanding custodian departed. Renovations began in 1965 and two years later an appeal was launched, the first of a continuing series as the museum developed, with increasing facilities both for visitors and display and for scholars wanting to work on the Elgar material that the museum possessed (most of the manuscripts had gone to the British Museum after Carice's death in 1970, when much of the family furniture was disposed of by auction).

To cross the threshold of the cottage itself, however, is to step directly into Elgar's world, so rich is the collection in original material. One of the ground-floor rooms is devoted to pictures of the Elgar family (there is also a piano, sold by Elgar Brothers' Music Shop); opposite is a reconstruction of Elgar's study, with his desk (with paper, his glasses, his inkwell and a manuscript ruler), some of his books, his gramophone and a wooden music stand. In the rear room – the Atkins Room, after his godson E. Wulstan Atkins – there is a glass case with his ceremonial court clothes, the quill pen with which he signed his acceptance of the Freedom of Worcester and a display related to his childhood and linked with his *Wand of Youth* music.

The rooms are small and the upstairs ones, in particular, are crowded with evocative exhibits. In the rear room, supposedly the room of his birth, are pictures of his parents, a family tree, his father's advertisements as a piano tuner, his birth certificate, his watches, quill sharpener and snuffbox, and concert handbills and tickets. There are some of his own drawings made for his wife and daughter. The left front room holds more of his library, a games table, some examples of his own woodwork (penholders, 'pokerwork'), his golf clubs, an inlaid Æolian harp made specially for him, relics from his chemical laboratory at Plas Gwyn, his microscope and a selection of press cuttings and concert handbills. In the room opposite are pictures of Elgar with such colleagues as Richard Strauss, the boy Yehudi Menuhin, and Henry Wood, another Æolian harp, which he made himself, and a glass case with a display covering his travels (in Europe, the USA, the Mediterranean, South America; also coral he collected, postcards he sent – and a press report of a car accident he was involved in). The museum has a delightfully bewildering variety and abundance – cycling maps, crossword puzzles, scrapbooks, drawings, music proofs, concert posters and programmes, awards and honorary degrees, his violin. Visitors come away with a strong sense of the composer and the kind of man he was.

Then, adjoining, is the Elgar Centre, opened by Janet Baker in 2000. It has a reception area and a gift shop, and an impressive main display room. If the cottage deals with Elgar the man, this deals with Elgar the composer. One substantial item is the nameplate of a locomotive named after him in his centenary year, 1957. But for the most part this is about the music and its performance, with special displays on the *Enigma Variations* and the characters portrayed within, with listening facilities (to Elgar's own recording), and on the famous Violin Concerto recording with the young Menuhin. Another display concerns 'A Musical Marriage', with his settings of his wife Alice's poetry. Adjoining is the Carice Elgar Room, a multi-purpose room, seating about 60, with theatrical lighting, suitable for music, lectures or demonstrations. Outside is a summerhouse, originally in the garden at Marl Bank and given to the birthplace in 1982.

In 1981 the Prince of Wales, patron of the Elgar Foundation since 1974, unveiled a statue of Elgar in Worcester, facing the Cathedral at the end of the High Street. Many Elgar places of pilgrimage have already disappeared, but commemorations of the composer abound, for example the plaque at 10 High Street, Worcester, once the Elgar Brothers' Music Shop (the family lived upstairs) and now a department store, and Elgar Court (on the site of Marl

Bank, Rainbow Hill, Worcester, where he died on 23 February 1934).

A plaque identifies the house at 51 Avonmore Road, London W14, where the Elgars lived in 1890–91, and another marks the site of Severn House (the panelled house with music room designed by Norman Shaw) at 42 Netherhall Gardens, London NW3, which Elgar bought at the end of 1911. The house at 37 St James's Place, London SW1, where he lived after his wife's death, is now a hotel.

Elgar Birthplace Museum

Firs
Crown East Lane
Lower Broadheath
Worcester WR2 6RH
England

phone +44/0 1905 333224
fax +44/0 1905 333426
e-mail birthplace@elgar.org
website www.elgar.org

open daily 11.00–17.00

Map 5

M. Grundy and D. Birtwhistle: *Elgar's Birthplace at Broadheath* (Worcester: Elgar Foundation, n.d.)

M. Grundy: *Elgar's Beloved Country* (Worcester: Worcester City Council, n.d.)

N. Lebrecht: *Music in London: a History and Handbook* (London: Aurum Press, 1992)

E. Lee: *Musical London* (London: Omnibus Press, 1995)

G. Gefen: *Composers' Houses* (London: Cassell and Vendome, 1998), 127–33

H. Lawrence, ed.: *Elgar in Hampstead 1912–1921* (Hampstead: Heath & Hampstead Society, 2004)

For the 'Elgar Route' leaflet, contact Worcester Guildhall (+44/0 1905 726311) or Malvern Winter Gardens (+44/0 1684 892289).

ENESCU

The Romanians take enormous pride in George Enescu: he was a great violinist and teacher, a composer of international stature and a man who deeply loved his country. Streets, competitions and festi-vals are named after him. His larger-than-life statue stands in front of Bucharest Opera House.

Enescu was born on 19 August 1881 in a village in the Suceava district of the northern Moldavian region – called Liveni-Vîrnav in his day but now 'George Enescu' (it lies just off the A29A road at Dragalina). He was his parents' last and only surviving child. The Enescus moved in 1884 to the nearby village of Cracalia. Enescu always called in at the house of his birth when he was in the area; his last visit, in 1946, is well documented in photographs. The one-storey house stands in an apple orchard, at a right angle to the unnamed road and near its end, signalled by a stand of old trees lining the roadside of the property, a postbox and, near the porch, a bust of the composer. It was restored in 1958 and opened to the public the following year.

The entrance hall is decorated with Moldavian woven carpets and hangings. To the left, the parents' room has furni-ture from their subsequent house (which no longer survives) in Cracalia, including his mother's Schiedemayer upright piano on which Enescu composed his first works, and reproductions of photo-graphic portraits. The small room at the back, supposedly the birthplace, displays a facsimile of the parish birth registry, photos of George and his mother, a cuckoo clock and a birdcage. The two rooms to the right of the entrance hall are used for the display of toys and books that belonged to Enescu as a child as well as examples of his juvenile art (drawings

Enescu's birthplace at Liveni

and watercolours); in the centre of the larger room is a bust of Enescu and on the walls are display boards telling his life story. Last is however best: in the small back room are five manuscripts (dating, of course, from after the Liveni period) representing some of his earliest efforts at composition.

Enescu was quickly recognized as a musical prodigy and in 1888 his family moved to Vienna so that he could study at the Konservatorium. A plaque with a portrait relief marks the house at Frankenberggasse 6 in the fourth district where they lodged. In January 1895 the 13-year-old was taken to Paris where he lived in Montmartre, at 10 rue Chaptal, and studied composition at the Conservatoire under Massenet and Fauré. He played his violin concerto at the Salle Pleyel in 1896 and made his conducting début in Bucharest the next year. He was deeply involved in chamber music, both in Paris and Bucharest. He came to the attention of Romania's music-loving Queen Elisabeth (herself a poet, under the pseudonym 'Carmen Sylva'), consort of King Carol I; she was a generous patron. At her summer retreat, Peleş Castle at Sinaia (at the foot of the Bucegi Mountains between Bucharest and Braşov), she held chamber music evenings in 1905 in which Enescu played; on another visit, in 1910, he met his future wife, Maria Rosetti, Princess Cantacuzino.

When in 1909 his mother died, his parents had for some time been living apart. In 1910 his father, Costache, bought a spacious, wood-trimmed stone house, with a narrow porch along the front, in Dorohoi, a larger town, near Liveni, some 40 km north of Suceava; on his death in December 1919 it became Enescu's property and in 1957 it became a memorial museum, although he never actually lived there. In a small room at the back, his father's carriage may be seen. The five main rooms contain displays of Enescu's own furniture, his travelling bags and concert clothing (his Légion d'honneur pinned to the lapel), his death mask and a cast of his hands; a

necklace and ring he gave his mother and a watercolour of the family house in Mihaileni where his mother died and which he also inherited; there are posters for benefit concerts he gave in Dorohoi for a local hospital (1916) and theatre (1921), and statues given to him when he was made an honorary citizen and on the première of his opera *Oedipe* (1936). There are also editions of his music and programmes of his recitals as well as important portraits, a wealth of photographs recording his life, facsimiles of important documents such as his will, and a collection of commemorative stamps.

In 1924 Enescu authorized building to begin on a large, three-storey house in Sinaia designed for him by the architect Radu Dudescu. Known as 'Vila Luminiş' (The Glade), it stands above the railway in a forest of spruce trees with a view of the mountains; Maria Rosetti Cantacuzino financed it. Enescu and the now widowed princess (they married only in December 1939) spent some two months there each summer until 1946, and this is where he is said to have composed much of *Oedipe*. Yehudi Menuhin, who had been studying with him in Paris (Enescu lived at that time at 26 rue de Clichy) since February 1927, went to Sinaia for lessons in 1928.

Although Enescu relinquished ownership of Vila Luminiş and the properties he had inherited from his parents in 1946 to the Romanian State, in exchange for a passport to the West, a museum, with a

Vila Luminiş, Sinaia

ground-floor recital room seating 60, opened there in 1995, 40 years after his death. The first-floor rooms are furnished much as they were in Enescu's time. Particularly evocative is the music room, decorated in yellow velvet, with its corner tower and circular staircase, his Ibach grand piano, furniture, north Moldavian wool-embroidered drapes and 19th-century Romanian and Ukrainian icons; in an alcove are ornately carved wooden chairs with tooled leather backs and seats. The composer's bedroom is decorated entirely in traditional Romanian style, with woven carpets on the walls as well as the floor, a needlepoint bedspread on the small single bed, folk ceramics, a brass lamp and several 18th-century icons. Upstairs are four rooms, three of which are still used for chamber music rehearsals. One was where Menuhin practised during his two months in Sinaia; across the hall are two larger rooms with display cases containing photographs and documents relating in particular to Enescu's friendship with Carmen Sylva (next to the Peleş Castle, itself now a museum, is the Palace Hotel, where there is a memorial to him).

Enescu and the princess often visited her family estate at Tescani, a village 35 km from Bacău, just one and a half kilometres south of the 2G road to Moineşti. The Rosetti Tescanus were a noble family who had owned property in the area since the 16th century. The house, built in 1880, serves today not only as a museum but also as an arts centre, with facilities for concerts, conferences and residential courses. Here on 27 April 1931 Enescu finished *Oedipe*, which he dedicated to his beloved 'Marouka', and it was there that he wanted to be buried (a statue of him mounted on an empty tomb, by Ion Jalea, a short walk into the surrounding woods from the house, symbolizes his unfulfilled wish to return to his homeland; there is a lifesize copy of the statue at the museum in Dorohoi).

The museum at Tescani-Bacău commemorates the Rosetti family and another of their distinguished musical relatives, the composer Mihail Jora (*see*

JORA), as well as Enescu. The foyer is dominated by the large family tree and family photographs. To one side is the Camera Rosetti, furnished with family heirlooms and lined with portraits and birth certificates. A large room at the front is devoted to Enescu, containing many original documents (including an acrostic he devised and dedicated to the Bucharest Symphony Orchestra in 1946), signed editions, programmes and reviews, recordings and a few of his personal possessions, including his glasses, a calling card, one of his diaries (which doubled for notating sums and musical ideas) and a medal he received on his 65th birthday. There are also telling caricatures, telegrams from Lalo and Dinu Lipatti, and a copy of a Siciliana (op.1 no.1) by Constantin Nottara dedicated to Enescu in 1913. The wall panels do more than narrate his life; they focus on his relationship to his younger contemporaries (especially Lipatti, Serge Blanc and Menuhin) and to other musicians who came to Tescani. The Oedip Room, the largest in the house, is reserved for concerts and large gatherings. There are two boudoir grand pianos and a bust by R.P. Hette of Enescu as a Roman, two cases devoted to *Oedipe* and posters of different productions of the opera on the walls. There is a deeply moving large oil portrait by G. Stoenescu of Enescu in his study, old and ill, a rug over his knees. On the far side of the Oedip Room are two memorial rooms, one to Enescu, furnished with his carved desk, an Erard grand piano and a phonograph (Gramofon Master's Voice), the other to Jora.

During their final years (1944–6) at Bucharest, before Enescu and his wife ceded their Romanian properties to the State and left for the West, they occupied a building reached by a dramatically curving, oversized staircase in the grounds of the Cantacuzino Palace, which the princess had also inherited from her first husband's family and in 1955–6 ceded to the State on condition that it be preserved as a memorial. Enescu rejected the grandness of the palace, though he and his wife entertained there, and opted instead for the simpler environment of the former palace administrative building, just behind it. Restored, the five rooms are furnished much as they were when the Enescus lived there. The central hall is lined with framed pencil studies of Enescu and the laurel wreath he won for *Oedipe*. On the right is his music salon, furnished with his Pleyel piano, a desk, music stand and metronome and portraits, with a tiled stove, woven carpets and velvet curtains. At the back is the bathroom with its original fixtures (including a stove for the bath) and on the left of the hall are two further rooms, the elegant Camera Madame and the composer's bedroom and study: as at Sinaia his bed is covered with a needlepoint spread and there are icons on the walls, with a desk and leather armchair, a crucifix and a death mask of Beethoven, a violin and travelling cases on one side of the small room. This Casa Memorială can be visited as part of the George Enescu Museum in the palace.

After six months in the USA, the Enescus settled in France, taking a villa, Les Cytises, at Bellevue (Seine-et-Oise), returning to New York in 1950 for a farewell performance of the Bach Double Concerto with Menuhin and the Metropolitan Opera Orchestra under fellow countryman Ionel Perlea at Carnegie Hall. On the night of 13/14 July 1954 Enescu suffered a paralytic stroke at home in Paris. By this time impoverished, the Enescus moved, with Menuhin's help, from their old flat in the rue de Clichy to the quieter Hôtel Atala, at 10 rue de Châteaubriand, near Etoile, where he continued in spite of his infirmities to compose. George Enescu died on the night of 3/4 May 1955, attended by no less than the Queen of Belgium, and was buried at the Père Lachaise cemetery.

In 1955 the Cantacuzino palace became the seat of the Union of Romanian Composers, which was later joined downstairs by the offices of the music and music journal publishers. The

The Casa Memorială at the Cantacuzino Palace, Bucharest

formal reception rooms on the raised ground floor, decorated in an eclectic *Art Nouveau* style, have high ceilings with exquisitely painted murals and gilded cornices. The large, domed central room, with curved balcony, all mirrors, marble and red velvet, seats 300–400 and is acoustically very fine. To the left is a splendid barrel-vaulted dining-room decorated with stained glass, Gobelins tapestries and huge carved wood sideboards; to the right is an auxiliary music room used for special events, including receptions, recitals and exhibitions. Three rooms at the front of the building, on the right, display the museum's unrivalled George Enescu Collection.

The museum opened in 1958, but closed between 1977 and 1992, during the Ceaucescu regime; it re-opened after refurbishment only in 1995. This, the

The Cantacuzino Palace, Bucharest

central George Enescu museum, curates most of his manuscripts, letters, citations and other unique documents, editions of his music, concert programmes and recordings, portraits, original photographs and sculpture, his Guarneri violin and his Steinway grand piano. The rooms are chronologically organized. First, 1881–1900: his Vienna and Paris conservatory diplomas, early childhood manuscripts and a letter from his mother are displayed, and there is a case devoted to his *Poëme Roumain* of 1887–8. The room for 1900–20 shows original photographs of Queen Elisabeth's Sinaia salon and a music stand, on which is displayed Enescu's manuscript cadenza – written in pencil and ink – for Paganini's First Concerto. Lastly, 1920–55: this exhibits manuscripts of some of his best-known works, his desk from his Paris flat at 26 rue de Clichy (on which a facsimile of *Oedipe* is displayed), his concert and academic attire, and an original death mask and casts of his cruelly gnarled hands.

Casa Memorială George Enescu
Liveni [George Enescu]
6880 Botoşani
Romania

phone +40/02 31 513446

open Wednesday–Sunday 09.00–17.00

Muzeul Memorial George Enescu
Strada George Enescu 81
6850 Dorohoi-Botoşani
Romania

phone +40/02 31 513446

open Wednesday–Sunday 09.00–17.00

Casa Memorială George Enescu
Vila Luminiş
Strada Luminiş
2180 Sinaia-Prahevo
Romania

phone +40/02 44 311753
e-mail enescucult@go.ro

open Tuesday–Sunday 10.00–18.00

Centrul de Cultura Rosetti-Tescanu-George Enescu
Stradă Tescani 126
5481 Tescani-Bacău
Romania

phone, fax +40/02 34 353595
e-mail tescani2001@yahoo.com

open daily 10.00–18.00

Muzeul National George Enescu and Casa Memorială George Enescu
Calea Victoriei 141
71102 Bucharest
Romania

phone +40/021 659 6365, 7596
fax +40/021 312 9182

open Tuesday–Sunday 10.00–17.00

Map 11

ERKEL family

Gyula, in the south-eastern corner of Hungary, close to the Romanian border, makes the most of the accident of birth that led to its being the native city of the acknowledged creator of Hungarian opera. Ferenc Erkel's father and grandfather, from Bratislava (Poszony to a Hungarian), went to this outpost of the Empire in 1806, when his father became Kantor of the German school and church organist in the domain of Count Wenckheim. Ferenc was born there in 1810.

A short walk west of the centre of this modest-sized spa city (36,500 people) stands the church, and next to it the old schoolhouse where Erkel was born, now the Erkel museum. The first room, with 17 display cases and boards, gives a substantial and informative chronological account of his life, with text in Hungarian but with summaries in German and Russian. Beginning with his ancestry, his entry of birth and his school reports, it moves on to his early career, as a pianist (which he eventually abandoned, partly because of the competition of another Hungarian, Liszt) and then his work as an opera conductor, first in Oradea and later in Buda, where he introduced the standard repertory to Hungarian audiences. Separate cases – with posters, handbills, librettos, programmes, music editions and manuscript excerpts, the singers and their costumes, the original settings – deal with his own major operas, *Bátori Mária, Hunyadi László,* and of course his most admired work, *Bánk Bán,* while the later works are grouped. There are other, non-operatic works too (a cadenza for a Mozart piano concerto among them). His three composer sons – Gyula (1841–1909), Elek (1842–93) and Sándor (1846–1900) – each have a display case, too; a fourth, László (1844–96), was an early teacher of Bartók.

The second room gives a picture of Erkel's considerable career as a concert conductor; there are photos of halls, programmes and handbills, correspondence (including a Berlioz letter), editions, manuscripts, as well as cups, tankards and other awards presented to him. His time as director of the Music Academy in Pest, where he had Liszt as star faculty member, is duly recorded, as too is his work for the singing society movement. Gyula's response to its son is noted too, beginning with the erection of a bust in 1896, three years after his death, and continuing with concerts, awards and, in 1960, on the 150th anniversary of his birth, the founding of the museum.

In a third room is a Steinway boudoir grand and a dummy practice keyboard, along with further displays devoted to Erkel's sons and more on *Bánk Bán,* with a section too on recent Erkel literature, celebration stamps and medallions. More personal items occupy a fourth room, among them his father's harmonium, a little table and chairs, a lithograph of Erkel, a black cloak, with lace and jet beads, of his wife's and oil portraits of his brother and his sister-in-law; the final room, the original kitchen, is set out as a kitchen in the style of the time.

Gyula commemorates Erkel in other ways. There is a road, Erkel tér, named after him. The local history museum

bears his name (so that the 'Ferenc Erkel Museum' is not in fact the Ferenc Erkel museum), as too do a local community centre and a hotel. The bust of him is in a prominent square, and two plaques adorn the house.

Erkel Ferenc Emlékház
Vilmos Apor tér 7
5700 Gyula
Hungary

phone +36/0 66 463552

open Tuesday 13.00–17.00, Wednesday–Saturday 09.00–17.00, Sunday 09.00–13.00

Map 8

I. Szerdahelyi: *Erkel Ferenc és emlékmúzeuma* (Gyula: Gyulai Városi Tanács, 1975)
I. Éri, ed.: *Gyula: Erkel Ferenc Emlékház* (Budapest: Kartográfiai Vállalat, 1987)

FALLA

At the end of a quiet little lane on the southern slopes of the Alhambra, overlooking Granada and the panorama of the valley and the Sierra Nevada mountains beyond, Manuel de Falla, born in 1876, lived in a modest, white-washed dwelling with a garden (known locally as a 'carmen') for 18 years between 1921 and 1939. After studies and an early career in Madrid and Paris, he chose Granada primarily as a quiet place to get on with

The courtyard of Falla's carmen in Granada

composing. It also provided a lively literary and artistic community as well as a magnet for his European friends, although in the end the political repression of the Civil War and the threat of Spain's involvement in the impending world war drove him to seek exile, first in Majorca (1933–4) and finally in Argentina.

Behind him were the recent successes of *El sombrero de tres picos* ('The Three-Cornered Hat'), on which he collaborated with Picasso for Diaghilev, and the *Fantasia bética* which he dedicated to Artur Rubinstein. He was at the height of his powers when he settled in Granada, and although he lived a disciplined, ascetic life at home at Antequerela Alta 11 (which he shared with his sister María del Carmen) he often travelled in Spain as well as to Paris and London for performances of his works. He became close friends with the writer Federico García Lorca and the artist Hermenegildo Lanz; together they sought out the folk roots of the Grenadine countryside. In 1922 Falla and Lorca organized an Andalusian folksong festival and in the following year began collaborating on children's puppet shows.

Falla's house, open today as a museum, gives a picture of his existence, in miniature – simple surroundings provide the backdrop for Picasso's watercolours for *El sombrero de tres picos*, ceramic plates by Chavarri of scenes from Don Manuel's best-loved works, presents of works of art from Debussy and Ravel as well as Lorca, and photographs of him with his visitors, among them Segovia. The house is entered through a walled courtyard filled with potted plants and hanging vines. To the side is the garden he so prized, with his beloved cypresses. The house, small in scale, is on two levels: on the lower is the dining-room, kitchen and bathroom, on the upper his study and living-room with his upright piano, the two bedrooms and his library. The furniture is mostly locally crafted (one's eye is drawn to the name board of a Clementi square piano which he artfully converted to a window pelmet)

as are the wrought ironwork and the braided rush mats. His hypochondria is reflected in the various vials and boxes of medication he left behind, not to mention his baby hot-water bottle, thermos flask, toothbrushes, loofah and barbells – all exhibited there. Religious pictures and icons are found in every room of the house (which is called 'Ave Maria'); attending Mass with his sister at the church below the house at San Cecilio was one of his rituals.

When Falla left for Argentina in 1939 he took only his unfinished score of his 'scenic cantata' *Atlántida* and a few clothes, leaving behind his books, scores and memorabilia. The house was maintained by friends just as he left it, although from time to time he asked for things to be sent to him. When in 1941 it was burgled, he had it closed up: his belongings were catalogued and stored until 1962, when the town council of Granada purchased the property. The detailed pictures that his friend Lanz had drawn of every room provided the evidence for reconstructing his home when in 1965 it became a museum. His library, together with a rich archive of documents assembled in Madrid, formed the core of the collection of the new, state-of-the-art Archivo Manuel de Falla, on the hill just above the house in the Centro Manuel de Falla, which offers exhibition areas, a lecture and seminar room and practice rooms as well as a large, flexible auditorium (designed by the husband of Falla's only niece, the architect J.M. García de Paredes, and opened in 1978), which serves as an important venue for the annual festival.

Don Manuel's Argentine home, Los Espinillos, at Alta Gracia (near Córdoba), where he lived from 1942 until his death there in 1946, is also a museum, displaying in much the same spirit his scores, works of art and personal effects. The house, on a hill, has a garden with cypress trees and a beautiful mountainous vista. His sister returned to Spain with the composer's coffin for its interment in the crypt of the cathedral at Cádiz, his birthplace.

Casa-Museo Manuel de Falla

Calle Antequeruela Alta 11
18009 Granada
Spain

phone +34/0 958 229421
fax +34/0 958 228289

open Tuesday–Saturday 10.00–15.00

Map 15

M. Orozco: 'Manuel de Falla's House', *Manuel de
   Falla's House and Museum* (Granada: Centro
   Cultural Manuel de Falla, 3/1988), 7–31

G. Gefen: *Composers' Houses* (London: Cassell
   and Vendome, 1998), 179–87

FRANZ

Robert Franz was Halle's most important
composer in the 19th century. He was
born there, at Brunoswarte 13, the son
of a 'Salzwagenlädermeister' (salt-wagon
loading foreman), on 28 June 1815 and
died at home at Luisenstraße 8 on 24
October 1892. A composer of lieder and
editor of Bach and Handel, Franz
conducted the Halle Singakademie with
distinction from 1842 until 1867 and led
the city's musical celebrations marking the
centenary of Handel's death in 1859. That
year he was appointed Musikdirector of
Halle University, which two years later
conferred on him an honorary doctorate.
Liszt admired Franz sufficiently to publish
a monograph about him in 1872 and, six
years later, Ludwig II of Bavaria made him
a Knight of the Order of Maximilian. On
his 70th birthday in 1885, Franz was
granted the Order of the Crown by the
German Kaiser and made an Ehrenbürger
by the citizens of Halle, who in 1907
renamed the Singakademie in his
memory.

Franz and the Robert-Franz-
Singakademie are commemorated at
the Händel-Haus in the second-floor
displays devoted to the musical history of
Halle. On display in Room 6 are some of
Franz's personal effects, including his
music collection and correspondence, his
piano stool and a sofa, and an array of
contemporary and modern likenesses –

three pencil sketches by Hermann
Schenck, a genial oil painted by Curt
Herrmann in 1886, a print by A.
Neumann, a bronze head by Gottfried
Albert and a bust by Antje Spiesecke
(1992) – giving ample testimony to the
esteem in which Franz is still held in
Halle.

Händel-Haus

Grosse Nikolaistraße 5
06108 Halle (Saale)
Germany

phone +49/0 345 500900
fax +49/0 345 50090 411
e-mail haendelhaus@halle.de
website www.haendelhaus.de

open daily 09.30–17.30 (Thursday to
19.00)

Map 7

K. Musketa: *Musikgeschichte der Stadt Halle:
   Führer durch die Ausstellung des Händel
   Hauses* (Halle an der Saale: Händel-Haus,
   1998), 58–67

GERBIČ

Although little known beyond his native
Slovenia, Fran Gerbič played an important role in his country's musical culture.
He was not only a composer (his works
include the first Slovenian symphony)
but also an operatic tenor, choral and
operatic conductor, teacher, writer and
administrator – he had roles in the
formation of the first professional
Slovenian opera company and in the
establishment of the school attached to
the Glasbena matica (Musical Centre) in
Ljubljana. Most of his working life was
spent in the Slovenian capital, where he
died in 1917.

Gerbič was born on 5 October 1840 in
the small town of Cerknica, just over 50
km south of Ljubljana, close to the
famous 'disappearing lake', Cerniško
jezero. The house of his birth lies on a
hill, behind the church; in 1964 the
Association of Slovenian Composers had
a commemorative plaque affixed. It
now belongs to the municipality and is

maintained in his memory. The main ground-floor room is given over largely to the local choir, for rehearsals; on its walls hang the choir's awards and photographs. Upstairs there is a memorial room to Gerbič. In it stands his well-worn Bösendorfer piano. There are a couple of display cases with a death mask, a photo portrait and some of his medals, as well as busts of composers he admired. Certificates honouring his contribution to national musical life are shown on the walls. His traditional clothes chest, dressing-table and cupboard are in a further small room. In Cerknica there is a street named after Gerbič and the local music school too bears his name.

Gerbičeva hiša
Tabor 1
1380 Cerknica
Slovenia

phone +386/0 1 703 0610 (Town Hall), 705 0730 (Music School)

open by appointment

Map 14

GLINKA

Its remoteness should not deter admirers of Glinka's music from visiting the museum at his birthplace in south-west Russia. Don't assume that it is in the place called Glinka, although that village used to be part of the once vast and prosperous family estate. The museum is in the even smaller community of Novospasskoye, some way to the south-east, just east of the road linking Roslavl' to Yelnya (some 60 km north of the former, 25 south of the latter), where the Glinkas lived for two centuries. Most visitors arrive in coach parties.

The house in which Mikhail Ivanovich Glinka was actually born on 1 June 1804 no longer exists. But a reconstruction of the large manor house built in 1810–14 by his father, Ivan Nikolayevich, does. (The house passed out of the family, was moved from the site and burnt down.) It

is surrounded by a large, fenced park (damaged during World War II) and outbuildings, some of them built of logs, with a reservoir, ponds, bridges and follies. The only original building in the village is the recently restored blue, white and gold church, built by the composer's grandfather in 1786; in the graveyard the parents and sister of Mikhail Ivanovich are buried. The Glinka museum opened in 1982, after six years of research and building, informed by the composer's sister Natalya's descriptions of the house and plans drawn up by his nephew who had also lived there; the displays benefit from the memoirs of more than 50 people who knew the man himself.

Mikhail Ivanovich spent his childhood at Novospasskoye and returned there for the summers while at school in St Petersburg (1817–22) and thereafter for occasional periods of musically fruitful refuge and recuperation (for example in summer 1823, after his father's death in March 1834, after his marriage the following May and after its collapse in 1840, and finally for the winter of 1847–8). Soon after his birth he was put in the care of his grandmother, who has been blamed for his delicate health and chronic hypochondria; when she died in 1810 he was reunited with his parents, who employed a governess to supervise their 13 children. Music was part of the children's studies and the family owned several pianos and employed 13 musicians; the young Glinka learned to play not only the piano but eventually the organ, violin, viola, guitar and flute as

The Glinka museum at Novospasskoye

well. A short distance away, his uncle kept his own serf orchestra, which entertained family and friends with the symphonies of Haydn, Mozart and Beethoven; after his studies in St Petersburg Mikhail Ivanovich was allowed to rehearse the orchestra.

The 27-room house that his father built was spacious and light, with windows looking out on the park and french doors opening on to the rear terrace. A separate building could house as many as 100 guests at a time. The reception room walls were covered with velvet, the chandeliers were crystal and the furniture fashionable and well made. The Glinkas are said to have had 860 serfs and craftsmen maintaining the estate, which at the time included a large farm, a brick factory, an orchard of 340 apple trees, a vineyard and a greenhouse (where flowers and pineapples were grown). Craftsmen and women made carriages, carpets, lace and boots. Although no longer a working estate, it still offers a rare view of 19th-century privileged Russian country life.

The museum occupies 13 rooms – ten downstairs, three upstairs – which are guaranteed to surprise and delight. A remarkable collection of family furniture and furnishings has been assembled and displayed in the large central room (the 'Celebration Room'), where there stands an elegantly finished Tischner grand piano (purchased by Glinka's father, played by the composer) and, between the windows, two mirror tables, one of which contains a small square piano labelled 'Buntebart et Frères, Princess Street and Hanover Square, 1785'; the dining-room, where in addition there is china that Glinka gave to his mother and an English grandfather clock stopped at 5 a.m. (the hour of Glinka's death); the former billiard room; and the father's bedroom, which has a larger square piano that the children played for him before retiring.

The best is saved for upstairs, where the indoor aviary the family kept is still home to 18 species of Russian singing birds – it is said that Glinka was so fond of the sound of birds that he had aviaries installed in his subsequent homes. Across the hall is his own rather grand bedroom, furnished with more family furniture as well as his Wirth grand piano, inlaid desk, travelling writing case and opera glasses. On the wall are paintings of Milan Cathedral, which he could see from the flat he rented there between 1830 and 1833, and a country scene including a tower with a space into which a working clock could actually be inserted (Glinka supposedly took this picture with him on his travels round Europe).

Display rooms on the ground floor tell the stories of the estate and the composer. Two former bedrooms chronicle Glinka's career with autograph manuscripts, rare editions with signed title-pages, copies of landscapes that he drew, portraits (some engraved and signed by the composer, others merely copies) and views of places associated with him. Special attention is given to his music – and in particular his opera *A Life for the Tsar*, or *Ivan Susanin*, which had its première in St Petersburg in 1836 – and to the history of Glinka's commemoration. There are busts, statues and reliefs, caricatures and reproductions of portraits. There are photographs of the house in Berlin where he died on 15 February 1857 (it was at one time marked by a plaque) and his temporary grave in the Russian cemetery, and of monuments put up in Smolensk in 1885 and St Petersburg in 1906. Finally, there are displays covering the creation of the museum, the annual Glinka Festival (held every June in Smolensk and at Novospasskoye since 1954) and the biennial International Glinka Prize for Singers – the winner always presents a recital in the concert hall upstairs in the museum, although the competition used to be held each time in a different capital of the Russian republics.

Glinka is buried in the musicians' section of Tikhvin Cemetery in St Petersburg. Two concert halls there bear his name: the Little Glinka Hall at Nevsky Prospect 30 and the Glinka Kapella

Choral Hall at Nab. Reki Moiki 20. The primary musical museum in Russia, the Glinka State Central Museum of Musical Culture at Fadeyeva ulitsa 4, Moscow, with an important instrument collection and concert hall, is also named after the 'Father of Russian Music'.

Memorial'nïy Muzey-Usad'ba M.I. Glinki

Selo Novospasskoye
Yel'ninskiy rayon
216356 Smolenskaya oblast
Russia

phone +7/0 081 241531,

open Tuesday–Sunday 10.00–17.00

Map 12

GOLDENWEISER

The Moscow flat once belonging to Aleksandr Goldenweiser (or Gol'den-veyzer) is very much a time capsule documenting an era in Soviet musical life: one that centred on the Moscow Conservatory and ended with Goldenweiser's death, at the age of 86, on 26 November 1961. A gifted pianist, a composer and above all an enlightened teacher, born in 1875, Goldenweiser was anxious to preserve a record of his time. Although his second wife was still living, he arranged in 1955 that his archives, library, pianos, furnishings and even his smallest personal possessions should become the property of the State; in 1959 the adjacent flat was acquired to augment the display space and shortly afterwards a sort of 'living museum' – in which he and his wife Elena still lived – opened to the public. His widow survived him by many years and worked tirelessly to keep his memory alive among his many pupils and friends.

Of the six principal rooms of the enlarged third-floor flat, the large corner room houses Goldenweiser's two Bechstein grand pianos and a remarkable, framed, photographic collection that chronicles in turn his teachers (including Pabst, Arensky, Tchaikovsky and Taneyev), his friends (among them Rakhmaninov, Skryabin and Medtner), his piano pupils (notably Ginzburg, Tat'yana Nikolayeva and Kabalevsky) and his contemporaries (including Myaskovsky and Shostakovich); some of them are autographed pictures (Glazunov, Rimsky-Korsakov, Van Cliburn, Szigeti and Petri). It was here that, near the end of his life, Goldenweiser inaugurated a series of 'Musical Thursdays', to revive the tradition of domestic music-making; they continue today in the memorial flat.

Next to it is Goldenweiser's tiny study-cum-bedroom, crowded with furniture – a large desk with a picture of his first wife Anna, a secretaire, his iron bed and night table, armchairs and a sofa, a bookcase and a folding screen – supposedly arranged just as in his day. On the wall are framed photographs of relatives, in particular his mother and, next to his bed, one of the writer Leo Tolstoy in death.

The displays in a third room were created in 1978 to mark the 150th anniversary of the birth of Tolstoy, who in his last years (1896–1910) had been a friend and mentor to Goldenweiser. Called the 'Tolstoy Nook', it contains mementoes of Tolstoy himself – his belt, his walking-stick, a teacup and saucer and a pen given to Goldenweiser in 1910 – as well as letters, chess sets that the men used at Tolstoy's dacha at Yasnaya Polyana (captured in photographs along with their chess games), chairs once belonging to Tolstoy and a cherished 90-volume set of Tolstoy's writings. In tribute to Tolstoy's love of the music of Chopin there is a death mask and a plaster cast of the composer's right hand, along with a life mask of Beethoven and a bust of Nikolay Rubinstein, founder of the Moscow Conservatory. But Goldenweiser's ultimate homage to Tolstoy was a box with soil from Tolstoy's grave, which was buried with him.

The fourth room, once the dining-room but now the 'Room of Souvenirs', is dominated by a thoughtful photographic portrait and a bust of Goldenweiser from the 1950s and portraits of Anna (who died in 1929). The souvenirs include her porcelain collection, small gifts from his students, a half death mask of Medtner and a cast of his hands, an original death mask of Liszt and Rubinstein's framed collection of dozens of signatures of musicians, inscribed in rows on a single large sheet of paper.

Two further rooms contain a general library of more than 10,000 books (and yet another death mask, this time of Pushkin) as well as a tightly packed archive of Goldenweiser's dedicated library of printed music and books about music, his own manuscript compositions (with at least four operas, piano music, songs, trios and string quartets, very little of which, because of his legendary modesty, was ever performed outside the flat), correspondence with Rimsky-Korsakov, Taneyev, Rakhmaninov and Medtner, as well as photographs, concert programmes and reviews, and his diaries, themselves a rich resource for research on the period.

The flat (no.110, with the adjoining 109) is reached from the rear of the late 1930s building, at an entrance marked with a sign.

Memorial'nïy Muzey-Kvartira A.B. Gol'denveyzera
ulitsa Tverskaya 17, apt.109–10
103009 Moskva
Russia

phone +7/0 095 229 2929, +7/0 095 229 4635

open Wednesday, Friday–Sunday 11.00–18.00, Thursday 14.00–21.00 (closed for refurbishment, 2004–5)

Map 12

E. Goldenweiser and L. Lipkina: *A. Goldenweiser's Memorial Flat* (Moscow, Soyuzreklamkultura, 1989)

GOLDMARK

Deutschkreutz is a small town in Burgenland, in that border region (to which Liszt's birthplace at Raiding also belongs) that has never been quite sure whether it is really in Austria or Hungary. Carl Goldmark was born deeper in Hungary, at Keszthely, on the corner of Lake Balaton, in 1830, but came to Deutschkreutz in 1834, when he was four, and lived there for ten years. In 1980, on his 150th anniversary, the town decided to commemorate him, taking over and restoring his house in the main street and opening memorial rooms on its ground floor.

It is modest in scale: the visitor needs to make an appointment with the local tourist office, or simply obtain a key at the café adjoining or the guesthouse across the road. The entrance lobby provides some context for Goldmark in Deutschkreutz: his father was cantor and notary to the Jewish community, a substantial one with long traditions whose history up to its extinction during World War II is recorded on wall display boards and blown-up photos. These are supported by extracts from Goldmark's own memoirs, begun in 1911. He died in 1915, in Vienna, where he had lived at Josef Gollgasse 5, and is buried in the Zentralfriedhof.

Eight display boards and a large show-case in the second room chart Goldmark's schooling in Sopron and his years at the conservatory in Vienna, his time as a violinist scraping a living in the Vienna theatres, and his establishment there as a composer: there are title-pages and openings from his published works and handbills showing their inclusion in concerts organized by Donizetti and Liszt, as well as premières alongside music by Schumann and Mendelssohn. The displays in the third room are chiefly concerned with his operas, notably the most admired of them, *Die Königin von Saba*, long popular especially in Budapest. There are reproductions of title-pages and photos of singers with whom he worked (Amalie Materna, Leo Slezak, Selma Kurz). Several pages of his scores are reproduced, mainly from originals in Budapest, among them the 'Rustic Wedding' Symphony, always a favourite. The many portrayals of

Goldmark himself include some charming and affectionate drawings and caricatures, which speak clearly of the man himself.

Carl Goldmark Gedenkmuseum
Hauptstraße 54
7301 Deutschkreutz
Austria

phone +43/0 2613 897683 (tourist office), 80463 (Café Goldmark), 80291 (Gasthaus Glöckl)

open May–October, daily 11.00–18.00

Map 1

GOLOVANOV

The central Moscow flat of Nikolay Semyonovich Golovanov (*b* 1891), an eminent Soviet-era conductor and composer, is not just a musician's living quarters but a miniature art museum, filled with his superb collection of paintings by Russian artists, sculpture, furniture and other *objets d'art*. Two grand pianos, a Blüthner and a Bechstein, occupy much of the large double room, but they have to compete with splendid portraits by Zakharov and Golovin respectively of Golovanov and Skryabin (whose music Golovanov championed, along with Rakhmaninov's), a large and arresting plaster bust by Trubetskoy of Pushkin, Dubovsky's impressionist view of Red Square at twilight, Yuon's winter view of the Sergyev Posad monastery and a copy of a Botticelli fresco, as well as smaller busts of himself and some of his heroes, including Dante, Liszt, Wagner and Tchaikovsky.

In the adjoining former dining-room (today the museum reading-room) are a number of antiquities, including a sculpted Pharaoh's head of the 2nd millennium BC, as well as paintings by Russian artists of Venice (one of the Vendramin Palace, where Wagner died) and the Taj Mahal and an imposing bronze bust by Aronson of Tolstoy. Decorating all the natural wood interior doors of the flat is an eclectic array of delicate brass ornaments, rescued by Golovanov during World War II from a cart taking them to be melted down. The furniture, much of it highly decorated with marquetry and gilded ornaments, is arranged as in Golovanov's time.

His music manuscripts (including an opera, a symphony and symphonic poem, piano music, songs and folksong arrangements as well as sacred choral music), richly annotated conducting scores and papers are still kept in the flat and are available for study. Only the composer's superb collection of more than 100 icons has been removed; that is displayed at the Old Tretyakov Gallery in Moscow.

Golovanov lived in the fifth-floor flat with his wife, the soprano Antonina Nezhdanova, from 1935 until his death on 28 August 1953. During this period he was conducting at the Bol'shoy Theatre, where he was an admired interpreter of Russian operas, the Moscow Broadcasting Centre and the Stanislavsky Opera Theatre, and teaching at the Moscow Conservatory. The flat became a gathering-place for Golovanov's friends. In 1968 it was designated a memorial place by the USSR Ministry of Culture, then in 1971 upgraded to a state museum before finally opening to the public in 1974 as a branch of the Glinka State Central Museum of Musical Culture. Rare recordings of Golovanov's own music – especially his sacred choral works, which were suppressed during the Soviet era – and music that he conducted are played for visitors, and music seminars are held once a month.

There is a relief plaque on the front of the building. Golovanov is buried in the Novodyevichi Cemetery in south-west Moscow.

Muzey-kvartira M.S. Golovanova
Bryusov pereulek 7, apt.10
103009 Moskva
Russia

phone +7/0 095 229 7083

open Monday–Friday 10.00–16.00 (Thursday to 18.00) or by appointment (closed for refurbishment, 2004–5)

Map 12

V.I. Rudenko, O.I. Zakharova and V.E.
  Matveyeva: *Nikolai Golovanov's Memorial
  Flat: Guidebook* (Moscow:
  Soyuzreklamkultura, 1990)

GRÉTRY

Tucked away in a quiet little street in a quiet part of the Outremeuse district of Liège is the timber-framed brick house in which the Belgian maestro of Parisian *opéra comique*, André-Ernest-Modeste Grétry, was born on 8 February 1741. Grétry spent his childhood there, serving as a choirboy at St Denis, the collegiate church, until his voice broke in 1758, then took up a scholarship at the Collège de Liège in Rome in 1761.

Restored in 1912, the airy three-storey building, with its turreted circular staircase at the rear, still preserves a domestic feel – this despite the regimented rows of display cases and portraiture in the upper rooms – which is, perhaps, because the ground-floor kitchen and salon, at the entrance of the museum, are still evocative of the composer's time. It is difficult not to have one's imagination aroused by the guide's tale of the young boy's accident in the kitchen fireplace or the family pictures in the adjoining salon.

Although the house remained in the family after his parents' time, Grétry returned to Liège only twice, in 1776 and 1782. The Liègeois eagerly followed his progress: his operas were regularly performed in the city immediately after their Paris premières. A plaque commemorating his birth, erected in 1811 (two years before his death on 24 September 1813), can be seen in a drawing of the house from 1824 on display in the museum; the square then named after him is now known as Place Yser.

The birthplace was acquired by the city in 1859. In 1882, Jean-Théodore Radoux, director of the Conservatoire Royal de Musique de Liège, set up a Musée Grétry at the Conservatoire with a collection he had built up over many

Grétry's birthplace in Liège (rear elevation)

years; ten years later he donated the collection to the city but on condition that it remained at the Conservatoire. Later, however, he agreed to its transfer to the Grétry house, and the museum there was inaugurated in the centenary year, 1913. The collection is richest in iconography, but includes autograph manuscripts, correspondence and original documents (Grétry's account book for 1793–1804, an 1809 copy of his will and newspaper accounts of his funeral), as well as the sort of personal belongings rarely preserved for composers before the 19th century: a ring and cigar case, a powder puff and fans, a magnifying glass and writing utensils, an umbrella and walking stick. There are also period instruments and a few pieces of furniture.

Grétry lived in Paris from 1767. After his retirement in 1807 from the Comédie-Italienne – where his working of the 'Beauty and the Beast' story, *Zémire et Azor* (1771), was his greatest success – Grétry spent his last six years ensconced in J.-J. Rousseau's former hermitage at Montmorency, a hilltop suburb north of Paris. He was buried with due pomp and ceremony in Père Lachaise, but he willed his heart to Liège. After family disputes, it was finally interred in the plinth of a marble bust by Rutxhiel in 1828, but in 1842, following the celebrations of Grétry's centenary, it was transferred to the base of the bronze statue by G. Geefs, gracing the Place de la République in front of the Liège opera house.

Musée Grétry
34 rue des Récollets
4020 Liège
Belgium

phone +32/0 4343 1610
fax 132/0 4223 0627

open Tuesday, Friday 14.00–16.00, Saturday 10.00–12.00

Map 3

C. Radoux Rogier: *La maison de Grétry: Suivez le guide! Une heure au musée* (Liège, 1946)

GRIEG

Troldhaugen (Troll Hill), about ten kilometres south of Bergen in the fjords of western Norway, was the home of Edvard Grieg (*b* 1843) and his wife Nina. During the first 18 years of their marriage they had lived in rented accommodation and as peripatetic guests, but in 1885 they decided to acquire a property of their own and built a rustic villa near that of their friends Frants and Marie Beyer on the shores of Nordåsvannet. It was intended as a summer retreat; during the winters Grieg continued to be much in demand abroad as a soloist and conductor.

His wanderlust had been encouraged by the renowned Norwegian violinist Ole Bull, who had recommended to Grieg's parents that they send their son to study in Leipzig in 1858. He spent some years in Denmark and then in Christiania (Oslo). But the rugged beauty of western Norway drew him back, especially in the summers: first to the Bergen suburb of Landås where his parents had a house at Kanonhaugent 39 (today a vicarage), then to Lofthus, further inland in the Hardanger fjord region, before he and Nina finally settled in 1885 in the wooded valley south of Bergen. Even then, Grieg sometimes felt the need to escape from Troldhaugen, especially when the pressures of entertaining the inevitable endless stream of seasonal guests from abroad prevented him from finding the peace and the time he needed for composition.

The Griegs rented lodgings at Lofthus in the late 1870s. To have somewhere

Grieg's house at Troldhaugen

Grieg's composing hut at Lofthus

where he could concentrate on his work, Edvard had a little slate-roofed hut built. He furnished it simply, just with a piano, a table and a stove; there, on the banks of Sørf Jorden, he composed the G minor String Quartet. Bull visited him there on his birthday (15 June) in 1879. The hut was sold in December 1880 and, after serving for a time as a hen coop, it was moved to the grounds of the nearby Hotel Ullensvang and restored. It is still there.

Grieg's hut at Troldhaugen is a well-known image. A larger version of the Lofthus hut, it is perched near the edge of the water, out of sight of the house, and furnished with a Norwegian piano, a stove, a rocking chair, a table, a chair and a chaise longue. Grieg referred to it as 'the office'. There he composed the Violin Sonata in C minor, the Symphonic Dances for Orchestra and the Four

Grieg's composing hut at Troldhaugen

Psalms for *a cappella* choir as well as numerous piano pieces and songs. The edition of Beethoven piano sonatas that served as a booster for the diminutive Grieg at the piano still graces the chair.

The painted wooden house in which he and Nina lived, with its porch, stained glass and little tower, has been open to the public since 1928. Grieg died in hospital in 1907, but chose to have his ashes interred in the rocks below the house, overlooking the fjord. Nina continued to come every summer until 1919, when Troldhaugen was sold to a cousin, Joachim Grieg, who subsequently gave it to the local council on condition that the composer would be permanently honoured there. The furnishings, however, were auctioned off. When Nina died in 1935, her ashes were interred next to her husband's. The museum was established the following year in cooperation with the Bergen Public Library, which owns the Grieg Collection, including manuscripts and letters. The dining-room and drawing-room were re-created with all their carved wood, velvet and lace furnishings, just as they had been in 1907: the Steinway grand piano specially adapted for the small composer and given to the couple on their 25th anniversary by friends in Bergen was installed once again in the drawing-room. The kitchen and pantry, however, became the repository for a series of portraits of Grieg by Erik Werenskiold as well as a collection of personal items (a lock of hair, his jacket and hat, trunk, walking stick and fishing pole) and photographic and written accounts of his funeral. The upstairs rooms became the caretaker's flat.

The recitals given at the house during the summer became part of the Bergen International Festival when it was inaugurated in 1953. The much-needed Troldsalen, a medium-sized recital hall, was built in 1985, discreetly hidden, partly underground, with nature – the rocks, flora and fjord – and his composing hut its breathtaking backdrop (see p.64). A lifesize statue of Grieg greets visitors at the entrance. There are concerts on Saturday afternoons and

The drawing-room at Troldhaugen

Wednesday and Sunday evenings during late June, July and early August.

In 1993 the 150th anniversary of his birth prompted the building of a dedicated museum on the site, which opened two years later, in May 1995. Again, nature is respected: the new concrete and glass building, with its graceful and generous display space, affords spectacular views of the woods and the water. In addition to flexible exhibition space and splendid audio-visual provision, there is a research library with special facilities for scholars, performers and composers as well as a shop and café. In its setting, its facilities, its displays and its re-creation of the composer's world, this is surely among the most successful of composer museums anywhere.

Troldhaugen Museum
Troldhaugveien 65
5232 Paradis
Bergen
Norway

phone +47/0 5592 2992
fax +47/0 5592 2993
e-mail trold@online.no
website www.troldhaugen.com

open May–September, daily 09.00–18.00; October, November, April, Monday–Friday 10.00–14.00, Saturday and Sunday 12.00–16.00; December closed

Map 13

A. Kayser: *Troldhaugen: Nina and Edvard Grieg's Home* (Bergen: John Grieg AS, 1980, 2/1994)
S. Torsteinson: *Troldhaugen: with a Brief Biography of Edvard Grieg* (n.p., 1987)
H. Kretschmer: *Wiener Musikergedenkstätten* (Vienna: J & V Edition, 3/1992)
G. Gefen: *Composers' Houses* (London: Cassell and Vendome, 1998), 108–15
F. Jor, ed.: *Nordic Artists' Homes* (Stockholm: Prisma, 1999), 223–5

GRUBER

The best-loved composer in the Salzburg region? To judge by the number of museums, there can be only one possible answer: Franz Xaver Gruber.

On Christmas Eve 1818, in a little Austrian village some 15 km north of Salzburg, Gruber composed a new carol for Midnight Mass. Born in 1787 and then 31, he was Kantor and organist at St Nicholas, Oberndorf. The text of his 'Stille Nacht' ('Silent Night' in the English-speaking world) was by his friend Joseph Mohr, the priest at the church. 'Stille Nacht' was set for two solo voices and chorus; a guitar was used to accompany it because at the time the organ was out of commission and needed repairs. Every year, at the Christmas season, the sites associated with Gruber and 'Silent Night' are inundated with pilgrims.

The Gruber memorial house at Hochburg

Gruber was born at the nearby village of Hochburg. He was christened Conrad Xaver but apparently always called Franz. The house on the site of his birth, Unterweizburg 9 (the original house was demolished in 1927), is marked by a plaque, as too is the village school (now a music school, next to the church) that he attended. But there is in Hochburg a Gruber Memorial House, a replication of the original building (near the church in the upper part of the village), part of it serving too as the local Heimatmuseum – built, like the original, solely of wood, without nails, with weighty stones to hold the roof in place. Downstairs is an entrance hall, a living-room, furnished with pieces from the period, from local sources (rag rugs, a clock in working order, a wood stove), and a kitchen, with utensils, a stone sink and an open fire for cooking. Upstairs are the Gruber rooms. His father was a weaver, and he was apprenticed as one while at the same time learning the organ; what is thought to be the original family weaving loom used by Gruber himself is there, with samples of the rough flax and the tools used for making it. But there are also displays, including early photos of Hochburg, a model of the original house, a facsimile entry of his birth, a copy of a drawing of the church believed to be Gruber's work and a collection of Gruber stamps. In the family bedroom are a wood bed and a cradle, religious statuettes and pictures and a bedside shrine. It adds up to a sharp portrayal of the harsh rural life to which he was brought up.

The church of St Nicholas at Oberndorf was demolished in 1910, but where it stood a picturesque little octagonal chapel has been constructed as a shrine. Inside are a few pews, an altar and portraits of Mohr and Gruber as well as stained-glass windows commemorating Oberndorf and the nearby village of Arnsdorf, where Gruber had taught at the village school since 1807. Below the shrine, across the street, in Stille-Nacht-Platz, is the Heimatmuseum, the local history museum. Founded in 1928, it incorporates a 'Stille Nacht' Room, recounting the composition of the beloved piece and the history of the church. There are recordings – you can listen to a tape of various versions of the carol – as well as postage stamps and postmarks to inspect; there is a harmonium on display, but it postdates the carol by two years so holds no particular significance.

Arnsdorf is walking distance, about four kilometres, from Oberndorf (or at least it was so considered in Gruber's day). The schoolhouse where Gruber taught nestles against the local church, Maria am Mösl (also known as the Pilgrimage Church), which dates from the 17th century; there Gruber married the first of his three wives. The ground floor of the schoolhouse still serves the children of the community; upstairs is the local history museum. In the room where Gruber is thought to have composed, a watercolour portrait of him is on display. The black furniture inlaid with mother-of-pearl in the second room comes from his final home in Hallein; strangely, there are portraits of only his second and third wives (given to Arnsdorf in 1948 by his grandson Felix). Christmas story effigies are displayed in the cupboards.

At Hallein, in the building where he lived for most of his life, now 1 Franz-Xaver-Gruber-Platz, there is a dedicated Gruber museum in the old town on the hill, next to the parish church where he directed the choir for almost 30 years until his death in 1863. It opened in 1992. Before entering, callers will want to pause to pay their respects to Gruber himself,

The Gruber museum, Hallein

for he is buried immediately to the right of the door. Six tablets of different origins affixed to the house commemorate the composer. The museum, on the second floor, features a small room, furnished in period style, with a piano and the ubiquitous harmonium, in addition to a larger room of tasteful modern displays.

Among the most important items in the collection are seven autograph manuscripts, five of Gruber's own watercolour landscapes and Mohr's historic guitar. Then, too, there is the document Gruber was obliged to draw up in 1854 to establish his claim to the authorship of 'Stille Nacht'. Without thought of the possible consequences, he had given a copy of the carol in 1825 to a visiting Tyrolean organ builder; when it was performed at a trade fair in Leipzig in 1831 and later published in altered form as a Tyrolean folksong, it became instantly popular. Although Gruber sought to reinstate his original version of the melody, the corrupted (or perhaps corrected) text has prevailed. At least he succeeded in having his name forever associated with 'Stille Nacht'. He did compose and publish other sacred music in the course of his duties in Hallein, which can be acquired at the museum in carefully prepared modern editions – although perusal of them suggests that the inspiration of 'Stille Nacht' struck but once.

In view of the strong feelings that the origins of this best-loved carol evoke among Austrians, it will come as no surprise to learn that there is an alternative 'Stille Nacht' museum. This is at the humble birthplace of Joseph Mohr in Salzburg, at Steingasse 9, opened as

recently as 1996. The founder and curator, Hanno Schilf, is convinced that it was actually Mohr who composed the carol and Gruber merely arranged it. The first-floor museum, or memorial place, occupies two small rooms, vividly recreating the poverty into which Mohr was born in 1792.

Franz Xaver Gruber Gedächtnishaus
5122 Hochburg-Ach
Austria

phone +43/0 7727 2561 (custodian; or 7727 2255, Gemeindeamt)
fax +43/0 7727 225520
(Gemeindeamt)
e-mail gemeinde@hochburg-ach.ooe.gv.at
website www.hochburg-ach.at

open by appointment

Heimatmuseum Bruckmannhaus und Stille-Nacht-Gedenkstätte
Stille-Nacht-Platz 7
5110 Oberndorf bei Salzburg
Austria

phone +43/0 6272 4422
fax +43/0 6272 44224
e-mail stillenacht.oberndorf@gmx.at,
oberndorf.info@salzburg.co.at
website www.oberndorf.co.at

open 29 November–9 January, daily 09.00–17.00 (from 25 December, closed 12.00–13.00)

Franz-Xaver-Gruber-Museum
Niederarnsdorf 9
5112 Lamprechtshausen
Austria

phone +43/0 6274 7453 (or 6274 6334, tourist office)
e-mail f.x.gruber-museum-arnsdorf@magnet.at,
office@lamprechtshausen.com

open Friday–Sunday 09.00–17.00,
Monday–Thursday by appointment

Stille-Nacht-Museum
1 Franz-Xaver-Gruber-Platz
5400 Hallein
Austria

phone +43/0 6245 80783
fax +43/0 6245 80783 14

open 23 November–6 January, daily
11.00–17.00

Stille Nacht Museum
Steingasse 9
5024 Salzburg
Austria

phone +43/0 662 878374
fax +43/0 662 878373

open Monday–Saturday 11.00–17.00

Map 1

M. Gehmacher: *Stille Nacht, heilige Nacht! Das
Weihnachtslied – wie es entstand und wie es
wirklich ist* (Oberndorf: Marktgemeinde
Oberndorf and Fremdenverkehrsverband
Oberndorf, 1988)
S. Aigner, ed.: *F.X. Gruber Museum Arnsdorf*
(Arnsdorf: F.X.-Gruber-Museum, n.d.)
H. Schilf: *Silent Night: The Story of how the
Carol 'Silent Night' Originated* (Salzburg:
Stille Nacht Verlag, 1994)

GRUODIS

The hillside house overlooking the river
Neris where the Lithuanian expressionist
composer Juozas Gruodis lived was in
what were then bucolic surroundings,
south-east of Kaunas. Today it is
surrounded by fast-moving highways
and approached by a slip road, its lovely
views spoilt by tower-block housing but
still partly shielded by an apple orchard
bearing what must be its last crops (of
pleasantly sweet fruit). Gruodis, who had
lived there since 1932, died there in 1948,
in eclipse, having attracted Soviet criticism after a successful career as a
composer of piano and choral music,
opera conductor, organizer of song festivals and director of the Kaunas Music
School. Nevertheless, such was his
importance that a memorial stone was
erected in 1966 at the village of Rokenai,
where he was born in 1884; his Kaunas
house was opened as a memorial
museum on the 100th anniversary of his
birth, the music school was renamed in

his memory and a bust was erected in the
garden of the Kaunas Music Theatre.
    Four rooms of the house are open to
the public. Those on the right as you
enter are presented as Gruodis would
have known them: the ground-floor
room combines dining- and sitting-room
while above, on the first floor, are his
study and music room, where small
recitals occasionally take place. Across the
hall on each floor are display rooms,
chronicling his career and influence in
collages of facsimile photographs and
documents, copies of his music and
recordings, awards, honorary degrees
and 1984 commemorative medals, along
with such personal possessions as his
pen, watch, cane and flask.

Juozo Gruodžio Memorialinis Muziejus
Salako gatve 18
3005 Kaunas
Lithuania

phone +370/0 37 722489

open Wednesday–Sunday 12.00–17.00

Map 2

GUIDO D'AREZZO

The people of the community of Talla,
nestled between fields of sunflowers,
blue-leafed vineyards and pine forests,
about 20 km north-west of Arezzo,
believe that the medieval theorist and
composer of antiphons, Guido – known
locally as Guido Monaco ('Guido the
monk') but more widely as Guido of
Arezzo, in which city he compiled the
earliest treatise on singing (*Micrologus*,
c1026) – was born in the stone *castellaccia* on a knoll above their town. (To
find Talla, take the main road north from
Arezzo towards Bibbiena and turn left
after about 11 km, at Capalona.) Its rustic
if sensitively restored appearance is
perhaps somewhat compromised by the
television aerial at the rear.
    In 1994 Talla celebrated Guido's
millennium, with a conference, concerts
and the unveiling of a monument by the
sculptor Johan Ulrich Steiger, while

The Guido memorial site at Talla

acknowledging that no one can be quite
sure precisely when or where he was
born. The plaque mounted on the *castellaccia* in 1905 proclaims 992, a date
generally accepted by scholars, as the date
of birth of their celebrated 'trovatore
delle sublimi note musicali': this refers to
his invention of the 'Guidonian hand', a
kind of mnemonic device that helped
establish modern notation. He died near
Arezzo in 1050. A museum bearing his
name has now been set up there, as part
of the 'EcoMuseo del Casentino'. It is
designed rather to illustrate the place of
music in society between Guido's time
and the 13th century than as a memorial
to Guido himself; nevertheless, he must
be comfortably the earliest composer
to be commemorated with a museum
bearing his name.

Museo della Musica 'Guido d'Arezzo'
Castellaccia
52010 Talla
Arezzo
Italy

phone +390/0 575 597512

website
www.159.213.82.124.sistema_castellan
a/talla/museo_musica

open 16 July–30 September, Thursday,
Saturday, Sunday 16.30–19.00 or by
appointment

Map 9

GULAK-ARTEMOVSKY

Semyon Stepanovych Gulak-Artemovsky
(or Hulak-Artemovsky) is remembered
as one of Ukraine's finest 19th-century
operatic baritones and composer of
the opera *Zaporozhets' za Dunayem* ('A
Cossack beyond the Danube', 1863),
which uses Ukrainian folk melody.
He was born in 1813 just outside
Horodyshche (150 km south of Kiev),
where a memorial obelisk and plaque
mark the spot where his family house
stood. Gulak-Artemovsky was the son of
a priest and was sent to Kiev to become
one himself; instead his singing voice
won him a place first in the choir of St
Sophia and then, through Glinka in 1838,
a post in the court chapel choir in St

Gulak-Artemovsky statue at Horodyshche

Petersburg. Again thanks to Glinka, he was able to travel to France and Italy, where he gained experience singing opera. He retired from the stage in 1864 and died in Moscow on 17 April 1873.

In 1968 a museum commemorating Gulak-Artemovsky in photographs, painstakingly assembled by a local citizen, was established in a former cinema in Horodyshche (there are plans to move it elsewhere). The collection, illustrating his entire career, has existed since 1961 and had previously been exhibited at a collective farm. To the photographs a large bust of Gulak-Artemovsky, posters and commemorative objects (a plaster relief portrait, stamps and books) have been added. Thanks to the continuing efforts of the collector and museum founder, a bust was erected in 1979 on a tall plinth across the road from the museum.

Dytyacha Shkola Mystetstv Kimnata Muzey S.S. Hulaka-Artemovs'koho
vulytsya Myru 58
Horodyshche
Horodyshchens'kyy rayon
19500 Cherkas'ka oblast'
Ukraine

phone +380/80 4734 24054

open Tuesday–Sunday 09.00–18.00

Map 16

H.F. Koval': *Muzey S.S. Hulaka-Artemovs'koho u Horodyshchi: Putivnyk* (Dnipropetrovs'k: Promin', 1979)

HAAS

Pavel Haas was one of the Jewish Czech composers imprisoned in the Nazi transit camp at Terezín in 1941; he spent nearly three years there and died in Auschwitz in October 1944. Born in Brno in 1899, he had been one of the last pupils of Janáček, who much influenced his style, which draws on the rhythms and inflections of Moravian folk music as well as Jewish liturgical music.

Haas is commemorated in the room devoted to music in the Magdeburg Barracks at Terezín (*see* KRÁSA). Although unwell during most of his time there, he continued composing; his Study for Strings and his Four Songs on Chinese Poetry date from those years. The display dedicated to him at Terezín includes photographs, a musical cryptogram, some music facsimiles and a pen portrait.

Magdeburg Barracks
Památník Terezín
41155 Terezín
Czech Republic

phone +420/0 416 782948, 782949
e-mail manager@pamatnik-terezin.cz
website www.pamatnik-terezin.cz

open April–September, daily 09.00–18.00, October–March, daily 09.00–17.30

Map 4

J. Karas: *Music in Terezín 1941–1945* (Stuyvesant, NY: Pendragon, 1985)

HANDEL

The large middle-class house 'at the sign of the Yellow Stag' in Halle, behind the Liebfrauenkirche, close to where George Frideric Handel was born on 23 February 1685, has been a museum for more than 50 years. After World War I, efforts were made by the Händelverein to acquire it, but the price proved beyond their reach. The English Handelian Newman Flower also tried unsuccessfully to wrest it from private hands. It was eventually taken over by the City of Halle in 1937, but was left unoccupied during World War II and required considerable renovation before it was opened to the public, as a civic museum, in 1948. The original museum was in fact in the house next to that of Handel's birth, but it was subsequently enlarged and now occupies both and indeed other adjacent property too. In recent excavations of the basement it was found that it incorporated structures dating back to Roman times.

It is a remarkable institution, documenting not only Halle's greatest composer but also the musical history of

The Händelhaus,
Halle

the city through the lives and works of other prominent local musical figures – among them Samuel Scheidt, W.F. Bach, D.G. Türk, J.F. Reichardt, C.F. Loewe and Robert Franz (*see* separate entries) – and housing the city's large and finely displayed collection of instruments as well as offices from which scholarly literature on Handel is produced. There is also an archive of the papers of the 19th-century Handel scholar and editor Friedrich Chrysander. From the time of its inauguration as a museum it has served as host to concerts of chamber music, which since 1952 have fallen into a regular pattern of weekly concerts and a substantial contribution to the Halle Händel-Festspiele in June. The bicentenary of Handel's death in 1959 and the tercentenary of his birth in 1985 provided impetus for further improvements to the facilities and the displays.

In the 1950s a single room was equipped with a tape recorder to enable visitors to hear Handel's music, and in the 1960s a taped guide to the collection was made available with commentary in two dozen languages. Today the museum boasts an integrated sound system and a studio used for rehearsals and recordings. Recorded music, carefully chosen, supplements the displays in the dozen rooms, which are chronologically organized to tell the story of Handel's life in a fairly traditional style, with a rich and evocative

array of reproductions, pictorial and musical, and copies of early printed material, along with furniture of the period. The rooms carry you from his early days in Halle, through his years in Hamburg and Italy and on to his lengthy London career, his burial in Westminster Abbey and his posthumous reputation and establishment as an icon.

The City of Halle has gradually acquired the surrounding half-timbered buildings and refurbished them as a library, a keyboard restoration workshop, offices and public meeting rooms where weddings and other civil ceremonies regularly take place. The concert hall, now seating 120, opens out on to an attractive courtyard, used during the summer months to supplement the restaurant in the basement (under the Roman arches) which, serving local wines, now occupies the space where Handel's father once purveyed wine; it is often the scene for public lectures and evening study sessions. If Handel's birthplace no longer resembles his family home, it is at least alive with his memory and with music-making. Nearby, the large statue of Handel presiding over the marketplace, put up for the 1859 centenary with support from Queen Victoria among others, has become something of a symbol for the city.

In the 1930s Newman Flower also tried to acquire Handel's London house, now 25 Brook Street, Mayfair, for a museum, and he failed there too. The area where Handel lived, then a new middle-class development, had over the years become one of the most 'desirable' commercial parts of the West End, close to Bond Street and the busiest part of Oxford Street. So the value of the property put it beyond reach. It was not until the 1990s, with the redevelopment of the area by the Co-operative Insurance Society, which had acquired most of the nearby property, that opportunity arose to reclaim the house on Handel's behalf. Originally it had been intended to create a museum of the entire house, incorporating too most or all of the adjoining house on the east side, the similar but rather smaller 23 Brook Street (in which, on the top floor, Jimi Hendrix had briefly lived in 1968 and 1969); but in the end commercial forces decreed that the landlords should retain possession of the ground floors and the basements of both properties, and the Handel House Museum, which opened in 2001, is accordingly confined – at least for the time being – to the first and second floors, with administrative space on the top floor (which had been an attic in Handel's time).

Handel leased the newly built Georgian terrace house in 1723, with only servants for company, until his death there on 14 April 1759; he never bought it outright, although his acquisition of English nationality in 1726 would have enabled him to do so. Few composers remained in the same premises for as long as 36 years. It was here that Handel rehearsed with his singers (including the opera stars Senesino, Faustina and Cuzzoni and such oratorio singers as John Beard and Susanna Cibber) and sold tickets for his performances as well as wordbooks, copies of his music and engraved portraits of himself. Most importantly, it was here that he composed most of the music for which he is known and loved, including *Messiah* in the summer of 1741. The front door through which he and his guests entered is now restored, but gives access only to the ground floor; visitors to the museum enter round the back, in Lancashire Court, on the lower ground floor. There they take the lift or the stairway (in a newly built adjunct) to the second floor, to enter the main premises through a room with a large bow window, in a small wing added to the rear of the house just after Handel's time, in the 1780s: a video introduces them to Handel and his role in London.

This leads into the original rear room, behind Handel's bedroom, which sets Handel in the context of London cultural life in his time: there are portraits of musicians (Geminiani, Pepusch), poets (Pope, Gay) and people concerned with musical life (the concert pioneer Thomas Britton, the opera promoter Owen McSwiney), as well as his patrons Georges I and II, along with prints of people and places. A large tester bed, clothed in red, of the kind Handel is known to have owned, dominates the

Watercolour (1839) by John Buckler, the earliest known depiction of Handel's house in London

front room, 'Handel the Man'; by it is a close-stool (a covered chamber pot) of the period. Facing it is the large National Portrait Gallery Hudson head in its gilded laurel frame. On the other walls are the 1742 portrait by Francis Kyte and a selection of prints, among them a group by Joseph Goupy (copies of which Handel possessed), others of his colleagues and relatives and some reverent homages from the later 18th century.

The visitors' route moves, through the breached wall, into the neighbouring house, 23 Brook Street. Here there are cases displaying some of the prize items from the collection, among them a Mozart autograph of music by Handel and a Handel letter. But the emphasis for the time being is on the restoration of the premises, with a series of wall placards charting, fascinatingly, the research done and the techniques used; oversize repro-ductions of other items in the museum lend colour. The walls of Handel's house, wood-panelled, are bluish-grey, the colour of the paint found in the lowest layer on the walls; the doors and door-ways are in chocolate brown, the colour of the second lowest layer and probably dating from Handel's time. Cornices and dado rails are re-created following surviving ones in a neighbouring house; the most spectacular feature from Handel's own day is the stairway, with its finely carved tread ends.

The front room on the first floor of Handel's house is the 'Rehearsal and Performance' room, as it probably was in Handel's own time. Round the walls are portraits and prints, mainly of singers – a fine Nazzari portrait of Faustina, and others including the composer De Fesch, who at one time led Handel's orchestra. Many singers are represented by portraits or prints. The room, which also holds a fine harpsichord, modelled on a Ruckers, one of whose instruments Handel owned, is used for small-scale concerts and by students for practice (there is no music circulating in the house). Behind this room is a smaller, quieter one, perhaps originally Handel's study or dining-room; in it hangs a portrait by

Hudson of the *Messiah* librettist Charles Jennens, and there is a further, smaller harpsichord, modelled on another that Handel owned. The exit, through the museum shop, is on first-floor level.

Jimi Hendrix's connection with 23 Brook Street is acknowledged by a blue plaque on the front of the building, not far from Handel's, and in the occasional opening of his flat to the public and mounting of exhibitions related to the rock artist.

Some of the material initially on display at the Handel House came on loan from the Gerald Coke Handel Collection. That collection, however, long the largest Handel collection in private hands, now belongs to the new Foundling Museum. This is on the premises in Brunswick Square of the Thomas Coram Foundation, the descendant of the Foundling Hospital of which Handel was a governor and which he did much to help with his annual performances of *Messiah*. In 2004 a Handel Study Centre was set up there, in rooms on the second floor, where it is accommodated and displayed. The

Staircase and 1st floor front room of the Handel House Museum in London

visitor coming up the stairs is greeted by the famous Roubiliac bust and a portrait, and can go into the gallery, where the display includes a section devoted to the history and sources of *Messiah* (the Coram has owned *Messiah* material since Handel's time), a keyboard that Handel is thought to have played, a fine collection of Handel busts of various periods and further paintings. Handel's will is among the exhibits. There is a 'legacy case', a bookcase and a case for temporary exhibitions, and a central table with drawers that open to disclose more exhibits. There are 'musical chairs' with built-in speakers and keypads for selection of the music. Going out past the storeroom (in which the abundant printed and manuscript material, accessible only to scholars, can be viewed through glass partitions), the visitor can see the Reading Room, primarily for those with a special interest in Handel and his music, but also hung with items from the collection.

There are other places in London where Handel's memory is honoured: above all Westminster Abbey, where the great Roubiliac sculpture stands by his grave, but also the Victoria and Albert Museum, where the 1738 Roubiliac, 'Handel as Orpheus', originally in Vauxhall Pleasure Gardens, is now housed. The British Library is the chief repository of his autograph scores (the other main collections are in Hamburg and the Fitzwilliam Museum at Cambridge); the primary autograph score of *Messiah* is on permanent display. In the north-west suburbs, close to Canons Park station, is the site of the Duke of Chandos's mansion where *Esther* and *Acis and Galatea* were first heard – some of the original stones now form part of North London Collegiate School for Girls – and close by is the church rebuilt by the Duke in Italian style, where the Chandos Anthems are likely to have been given, now St Lawrence Whitchurch, Little Stanmore. Outside London, Handel is recalled at Malmesbury House, in the Cathedral Close at Salisbury, where he visited his friends the Harris family (the house,

which includes what was once a room where Handel attended a concert, was open to the public until 2004); at Adlington Hall, in Cheshire, where he is believed to have played the organ; and at Great Packington Church, Warwickshire, which possesses an organ built to his design.

Händel-Haus
Grosse Nikolaistraße 5
06108 Halle (Saale)
Germany

phone +49/0 345 500900
fax +49/0 345 50090 411
e-mail haendelhaus@halle.de
website www.haendelhaus.de

open daily 09.30–17.30 (Thursday to 19.00)

Handel House Museum
25 Brook Street
London W1K 4HB

phone +44/0 20 7495 1685
fax +44/0 20 7495 1759
e-mail mail@handelhouse.org
website www.handelhouse.org

open Tuesday–Saturday 10.00–18.00 (Thursday to 20.00), Sunday 12.00–18.00

The Foundling Museum
40 Brunswick Square
London WC1 1AZ

phone +44/0 20 7841 3606
fax +44/0 20 7841 3607
e-mail handel@foundlingmuseum.org.uk
website www.coram.org.uk

open Tuesday–Sunday 10.00–18.00

Maps 7, 5

H. Heyde: *Historische Musikinstrumente des Händel-Hauses* (Halle an der Saale: Händel-Haus, 1983)
J. Greenacombe: 'Handel's House: a History of No.25 Brook Street, Mayfair', *London Topographical Record*, xxv (1985), 111–30
E. Werner: *The Handel House in Halle: History of the Building and Museum; Guide of the Handel Exhibition* (Halle an der Saale: Händel-Haus, 1987)

J.A. Sadie: *Blueprint for a Composer Museum: the London House of George Frideric Handel* (MA dissertation, City University, London, 1993)

J. Riding, D. Burrows and A. Hicks: *Handel House Museum Companion* (London: Handel House Trust, 2001)

HASSE

The most successful composer of mid-18th-century *opera seria*, Johann Adolf Hasse, was born in 1699 in Bergedorf, a small town 18 km south of Hamburg. His father and grandfather had been organists at the church next door, SS Peter and Paul; they lived in a house, now Alte Holstenstraße 79, backing on to a little lake, built for the organist in 1630. Since 1991 it has been the home of the Bergedorf Hasse-Gesellschaft, founded in 1910, whose archive holds contemporary manuscript scores of some of Hasse's works, printed librettos, portraits and a comprehensive microfilm study collection. One room of the house is used for exhibition space.

Hasse received his earliest musical training from his father, who sent him to Hamburg for further study in 1714; four years later he joined the Hamburg opera company. The experience of singing Italian opera whetted his appetite for all things Italian. In 1730 he married the admired Venetian soprano Faustina Bordoni. He never returned to Bergedorf,

dividing his time between the Habsburg court in Vienna and the opera houses of Dresden and Venice; it was in Venice that he died, on 16 December 1783. Nevertheless, Bergedorf is proud of its connection (there is a Hassestraße and a Hasse-Aula) and continues to celebrate it through performances by the Hasse-Chor and -Orchester.

Hasse-Gesellschaft
Alte Holstenstraße 79
Bergedorf
21029 Hamburg
Germany

phone +49/0 40 721 7810

open Monday–Friday 11.00–13.00, and by appointment

Map 7

W. Hochstein: 'Johann Adolf Hasse: eine biographische Skizze', *Bergedorf Porträt: Museum für Hamburgische Geschichte*, 4 (1989)

W. Hochstein: *Johann Adolph Hasse, Giovanni Adolfo Hasse: il Sassone, padre della musica* (Bergedorf: Hasse-Gesellschaft, 1990)

HAYDN brothers

Even by generous Austrian standards the Haydn brothers, Joseph and Michael, are particularly well served for museums. The thatched-roof farmhouse where they were born five years apart in the 1730s (Joseph in 1732, Michael in 1737) is on the main street of Rohrau, just 20 minutes east of Vienna airport. Its close proximity to the Rohrau palace of the music-loving Count of Harrach closely parallels that of Joseph Haydn's 'working home' in Eisenstadt, a few steps from the Esterházy Palace, where every September there is a series of Internationale Haydntage concerts in the Haydn-Saal (a large and splendid room, but probably little used by Haydn, whose music-making would mostly have been in the smaller rooms). The composer's former home in Eisenstadt is the most important of the Haydn museums and the headquarters of the Internationale Joseph-

The Hasse birthplace in Bergedorf (rear elevation)

Courtyard of the Haydn birthplace at Rohrau

Haydn-Stiftung; it is under common management with the Esterházy Palace. But Haydn also spent time in the period 1766–90 at the Esterházys' summer palace, Eszterháza, in a village now called Fertőd. The palace, severely damaged and looted during World War II and the ensuing years, is gradually being restored and is now open to the public; it houses a 'Haydn at Eszterháza' festival each September and has Haydn memorial rooms. Haydn's Viennese townhouse is among the many musical museums administered by the City of Vienna. Lastly, in the shadow of the Mozart shrines in Salzburg, there is a small but important exhibition in the cloister of St Peter's Abbey celebrating the life of Michael Haydn, who worked there for more than 40 years.

In the 1730s the Haydn family's Rohrau house consisted of three main rooms (the parents' bedroom to the right of the entrance lobby, where the children were born, and the kitchen and a parlour to the left), as well as a workshop wing where their father plied his wheelwright's trade. Today the bedroom is a place of pilgrimage. The corner room, called the 'Barockzimmer', displays some of the most precious items in the collection (an Anton Walter piano that Joseph played; a bronze statuette of him by Robert Weigl; a maquette of a scene from his comic opera *L'incontro improvviso*, a *dramma giocoso* performed at the Eszterháza theatre in 1775; and his snuff box). It is said to have served as sleeping quarters for the children of the regularly expanding family.

The former workshop is now a light and attractive recital and display room; a modern Bösendorfer grand is available and lining the walls is an exhibition, 'Joseph and Michael Haydn in their time', which includes informative wall panels, incorporating a useful comparative chronology, along with displays of early editions and facsimiles of documents.

The house became a memorial to Haydn in 1877. It was nearly destroyed by fire 20 years later and it was not until the Haydn centenary in 1909 that the exterior was restored. In 1958 the Lower Austrian authorities acquired the house, completing the renovation of the interior and opening it to the public the following year. On 31 March 1982, Joseph Haydn's 250th anniversary, the house opened as a museum. The monument now in front of the Rohrau parish church was originally erected in the palace gardens in 1794 by the Count of Harrach, who presented the composer with a model when he visited Rohrau the next year; the bust of the composer was added in the 1830s.

The Haydn family had originally come from Hainburg, a small town close by, where Joseph and Michael's father Matthias was born in 1699. When he was five, Joseph was sent to Hainburg to board with his uncle, Johann Matthias Franck, headmaster of the local boarding school. The town is proud of its connection with Joseph Haydn. The house at Wiener Straße 7 is marked by memorial plaques erected in 1880 and 1959, with a third on the school building at Ungarstraße 3; there is a Haydn fountain in the main square and a bust in the square near the Ungarstraße post office; and concerts are presented by the Hainburg Haydn Society in the Haydnsaal at the local tobacco factory.

From Hainburg Joseph went to Vienna, where he spent 20 years, first as a choirboy at St Stephen's Cathedral, living in the Michaelerhaus at Kohlmarkt 11 (today marked by a plaque), then working as a freelance musician; after that worked for a time for Count Morzin at Lukavec. Michael followed him to Vienna in 1745. Joseph married Anna Maria Keller, the daughter of a Viennese wigmaker, in 1760 (having previously fallen in love with her sister, destined for a nunnery), and a year later moved out to Eisenstadt on his appointment as Vice-Kapellmeister to Prince Paul Anton Esterházy.

When in 1766 he assumed the full Kapellmeistership, Haydn and his wife were able to move from a service flat, in the Kapellhaus (now a convent, the Margaretinum) next to the Bergkirche, into the house at Klostergasse 82 (now Haydngasse 21) backing on to the old city wall. Haydn bought it for 1000 gulden. An entry in the land register in 1758 mentions a stable on the ground floor, with a hayloft above at the back of the courtyard. The Haydns lived upstairs, in four rooms at the front; the ground-floor rooms were reserved for his pupils, among them his copyist Johann Elssler (1764–82) and Ignaz Pleyel (1772–7).

Over the next dozen years Joseph Haydn lived in Eisenstadt mainly in the winters, being obliged to spend most of the year at Eszterháza, the site of the former hunting lodge close to the southern shore of the Neusiedlersee which Prince Nicolaus Esterházy transformed into his own Versailles palace, replete with an opera theatre. When at Eszterháza the musicians lived in their own Musikhaus, usually sharing rooms; because of his position of authority, Haydn had four rooms to himself.

Plaques were erected on the Eisenstadt house in 1898 and 1923. It became a museum in 1935, when three rooms were opened to the public. Two years later it was bought by the Burgenländische Heimat- und Naturschutzverein; displays were installed in 1938, made up of items from a private Haydn collection assembled by a local wine wholesaler and member of the Heimat- und Naturschutzverein, Sandor Wolf, and that of the Burgenländisches Landesmuseum. At first the museum incorporated memorial rooms for Franz Liszt (who was born nearby: see LISZT), with the local society headquarters on the second floor, and for

the dancer Fanny Elssler, Johann's daughter, but they led to confusion in visitors' minds about the true significance of the house and were quietly dropped in favour of a museum devoted solely to Haydn. The building was renovated in 1974–5.

In 1995 the International Joseph Haydn Privatstiftung Eisenstadt purchased the neighbouring property (the so-called 'Frumwaldhaus') to allow for expansion of the museum display space and offering interactive and audio-visual facilities on the first floor. In this enlarged form, the museum re-opened in 1998. It is fitted out with stylish, state-of-the-art display cases, many of them with glass-top drawers which visitors can explore, as well as lighting and environmental controls. The seven display rooms are chronologically laid out, covering Rohrau, his student years and the early works in the first, the third to the fifth dealing with the years working for the Esterházy family (the last of them covering activities at Eszterháza), then in

Courtyard of the Haydn museum, Eisenstadt

the sixth the triumphs in London and Vienna, and finally the great oratorios and the closing years; the second room, with the Guttenbrunn portrait and a Walter piano, represents his own living-room. In addition, a Haydn-Zentrum was established in the front and ground floor of the building, incorporating a research library and archive downstairs and a 'Kaminzimmer' seating 35 for lectures and recitals upstairs. The piano was found in the last century at Liszt's birthplace, having come from the Esterházy estates, which has led to the suspicion that it may have been Haydn's own; it is in any case very heavily restored.

Over the years the collection has grown to include a large number of Haydn autographs and primary copies of his music, letters and early editions of all his published works as well as librettos for his operas; to set his achievements in context, there are also some early editions of music by his contemporaries. The displays are illustrated with a wide array of iconography – engraved pictures, endless numbers of portraits of Haydn, his patrons and his contemporaries, busts and a death mask – and many important documents, original and in facsimile. Among the period furniture is a beautifully figured wood table that converts to a music stand for eight players (see p.45); among the memorabilia are his medals and a punch recipe he acquired in England. Also there is the organ console from the Bergkirche, often played by Haydn in performances of his masses (and by Beethoven in the première of his Mass in C).

In 1778 Haydn sold his house in Eisenstadt – it had twice been renovated after fires during his years there – and divided his time between seasons either in Vienna (for which he had to obtain the Prince's consent) or at Eszterháza. When Prince Nicolaus died in 1790, his heir, Anton, abandoned Eszterháza and dismissed the court orchestra, giving Haydn a pension and requiring only occasional duties. Two rooms at Eszterháza, however, off the anteroom to

the concert hall on the upper floor, are devoted to Haydn. There is a chronologically organized display covering his career, but the main feature is the large number of reproductions of music pages – many from his symphonies (scores, orchestral parts, some autograph, some early copies), from the operas – his own and other composers' – that he produced there along with librettos and costume illustrations, printed editions of his music, letters, accounts and other documents. A special section covers the baryton, Prince Nicolaus's favourite instrument, and its music (the Prince's own baryton is in the Magyar Nemzeti Múzeum, Budapest).

Haydn lived in Vienna for the rest of his life, except for his two prolonged journeys abroad, to England (1791–2 and 1794–5), and his short visits to Eisenstadt to carry out his official duties (up to 1802) for the next prince, Nicolaus II – chiefly the performance of music for his wife's nameday. He acquired a single-storey house known as 'Obere Windmühl' at Kleine Steingasse 71, now Haydngasse 19, in what was then Gumpendorf but is now a part of the sixth district of Vienna, slightly south of the centre. He had it enlarged with a second storey while he was away on his second trip to London, taking up residence there in 1797, and as in Eisenstadt he and his wife (who died three years later) lived in the newly built quarters upstairs while the Elsslers lived below. Haydn continued to compose until 1803, producing the masses for Eisenstadt, the opp.76 and 77 string quartets, *The*

Haydn's house in Vienna (lithograph, 1840)

Creation (1798) and *The Seasons* (1801), and a fine *Te Deum* (1800).

In 1798, after a gap of some 30 years, he was reunited with his brother Michael, who had been in the service of the Prince-Archbishop of Salzburg since 1763. Michael stayed with him in Gumpendorf when he visited Vienna in 1798 and again in 1801, after Joseph had been widowed. On the later visit Michael conducted a performance of his *Missa sotto il titulo di Teresia*, in which the Empress sang the soprano solos. His brother's employer, Prince Nicolaus II, offered him the post of vice-Kapellmeister, which, preferring his quieter life in Salzburg, he declined.

Since their marriage in 1768, Michael Haydn and his wife, the singer Maria Magdalena Lipp, had lived in a house in the Festungsgasse in Salzburg, immediately below the fortress, on the edge of the courtyard of St Peter's Abbey. That house has since been demolished in favour of a funicular station, which bears a plaque. His duties as Konzertmeister to the archbishop and later organist of the Trinity Church (from 1777) and the cathedral kept him busy teaching and playing as well as composing. He was a close colleague of Leopold and Wolfgang Mozart and a gifted composer, whose church music was especially admired.

In 1983 the Johann Michael Haydn Gesellschaft Salzburg was founded and a year later it opened memorial rooms in the cloister of St Peter's. Each year the Gesellschaft sets out a fresh exhibition (not always devoted to Michael Haydn) in a large room created in the former stables. Among the collection of Michael Haydn items available for display are autograph manuscripts and letters, his manuscript catalogue (complete with incipits) and an autobiographical sketch of 1808; early editions of his music and engravings of 18th-century Salzburg; portraits of Haydn (including Franz Xaver Hornöck's well-known likeness), his patrons and pupils (Anton Diabelli and Carl Maria von Weber among them) as well as photographs of his skull; memorabilia (including visiting cards, his book plate, spectacles and case); period furnish-

ings and musical instruments. Across the archway, a second memorial room is used for temporary exhibitions, recitals (each afternoon in season, except Wednesdays), meetings of the society and twice-daily video presentations to visitors to the Gedenkstätte.

In 1804 Joseph Haydn was made an Honorary Citizen of the City of Vienna. When Napoleon invaded the city at the beginning of May 1809, he installed a Guard of Honour at the elderly composer's house. A plaque was erected on the house in 1840 and the street was renamed the Haydngasse in 1862. The Haydn House Society mounted an exhibition of pictures, manuscripts, editions and memorabilia in 1899 that led to the acquisition of the house for a public museum by the Vienna City Council in 1904. It was fully restored in 1976, incorporating a memorial room to Brahms (*see* BRAHMS) and a music room seating 68 was created in what was once Haydn's stable; further renovation to designs by Elsa Prochazka was undertaken in 1994–5. The displays focus on Haydn's final Vienna years – his last compositions, in particular *The Creation*; his patrons, pupils and friends; the sites in Vienna particularly associated with him; and the circumstances surrounding his death and initial commemoration. There is a 1796 piano by Johann Jakob Könnicke on display in the main upstairs room (Haydn's own Schantz instrument is in the Gesellschaft der Musikfreunde collection) and a death mask in the room where he died. A small final room is devoted to the Elssler family.

Michael Haydn, the younger brother, was the first to die, on 10 August 1806. He was buried in Salzburg, in the churchyard at St Peter's, where he was joined in the same grave not by his wife (who died in 1827) but by Mozart's sister Nannerl, Maria Anna Berchtold zu Sonnenburg, in 1829 (see p.268). In 1821 his friends put up a memorial to him just inside the abbey, on the left, incorporating the urn containing his skull.

Joseph Haydn died at home in Vienna on 31 May 1809. After a service at

Gumpendorf, at which his brother's Requiem was performed, he was buried in the Hundsturmer Friedhof. A week afterwards his grave was desecrated and his skull removed. In 1820, at the request of Nicolaus II Esterházy, his remains were re-interred in the Eisenstadt Kalvarienbergkirche, but not until 1954 were they reunited with his skull (which had been kept at the Musikverein since 1895). No pilgrimage to Eisenstadt is complete with-out pausing to pay one's respects at the mausoleum, on the left as you enter the church.

Haydn-Geburtshaus

Obere Hauptstraße 25 (Rohrau nr.60)
2471 Rohrau
Austria

phone +43/0 2164 2268

open Tuesday–Sunday 10.00–16.00

Joseph Haydn-Museum

Haydngasse 19–21
7000 Eisenstadt
Austria

phone +43/0 2682 719 3000, +43/0 6646 124648
fax +43/0 2682 719 3923
e-mail management@haydnmuseum.at
website www.haydnmuseum.at

open Easter–31 October, daily 09.00–17.00; winter, by appointment

Esterházy Kastély Fertőd

J. Haydn utca 2
9431 Fertőd-Eszterháza
Hungary

phone +36/0 9953 7651, 7640

open 15 March–October, daily 10.00–18.00; November–14 March, Friday–Sunday 10.00–16.00

Haydn Museum

Haydngasse 19
1060 Vienna
Austria

phone +43/0 1596 1307
e-mail post@mus.magwien.gv.at
website www.museum.vienna.at

open Tuesday–Sunday 09.00–12.15, 13.00–17.30

Johann-Michael-Haydn-Gedenkstätte

Im Hof der Erzabtei St Peter
5020 Salzburg
Austria

phone +43/0 662 8445 7619, 8044 4650
fax +43/0 662 8044 4660, 8047 144

open July–September, daily 10.00–12.00, 14.00–17.00

20-minute video (German, French and English versions available), daily except Wednesday 11.30 and 15.30

Maps 1, 8

A. Willander, ed.: *Haydn-Geburtshaus Rohrau* (Vienna: Amt der Niederösterreichischen Landesregierung, 1985)
A. Schusser, ed.: *The Haydn Museum (The House Where Haydn Lived and Died), Vienna 6, Haydngasse 19* (Vienna: Historisches Museum der Stadt Wien, 2/1987)
A. Hahn: *Haydn-Museum Eisenstadt* (Eisenstadt: Burgenländische Landesmuseen, 2/1990) [English edn., 1982]
H. Kretschmer: *Wiener Musikergedenkstätten* (Vienna: J & V Edition, 3/1992)
E. Hintermaier, ed.: *Johann Michael Haydn und Salzburg 1763–1806: Ein Vademecum durch die Johann-Michael-Haydn-Gedenkstätte* (Salzburg: Johann-Michael-Haydn-Gesellschaft Salzburg and the Konsistorialarchiv Salzburg, 1995)
E. Lee: *Musical London* (London: Omnibus Press, 1995)
A. Schusser, ed.: *Joseph Haydn-Gedenkstätte mit Brahms-Gedenkraum, Wien 6, Haydngasse 19* (Vienna: Historisches Museum der Stadt Wien, 1995)
G. Gefen: *Composers' Houses* (London: Cassell and Vendome, 1998), 8–13
DaCapo, the Haydn Festspiele-Zeitschrift published thrice yearly, contains short articles about the places where Joseph Haydn lived and worked as well as regular features on the museum in Eisenstadt.

HERSCHEL

William Herschel may be best remembered as the astronomer who in 1781 discovered the planet Uranus, but by profession he was a musician. For more than 30 years he pursued a career as an oboist, violinist and organist, tenor, teacher, conductor and composer. Born in Hanover in 1738 into a family of military bandsmen, he and his brother Jacob went to England following the outbreak of the Seven Years War in 1756. William stayed on, taking teaching and conducting posts in Durham, Newcastle, Leeds and Halifax, composing two dozen symphonies and several concertos. In 1766 he settled in Bath, where he was first organist and then director of music at the new Octagon Chapel.

Shortly after his arrival in Bath he presented a benefit concert of his own works, playing the violin, oboe and harpsichord. He took work in theatres in both Bath and Bristol, and published chamber music. But after a disagreement in 1771 with Thomas Linley senior, the pre-eminent Bath musician of his day, he gave increasing rein to his consuming interest in astronomy, establishing a workshop for casting mirrors and building telescopes.

In 1770 Herschel took lodgings in a terrace house, 7 New King Street. The need for larger quarters (by then his sister Caroline, herself both musician and astronomer, was living and working with him) led him to move in 1774 to near Walcot Turnpike. He built telescopes and taught music by day and observed the sky by night. They returned to New King Street in 1777, to what is now no.19, where he first observed the planet Venus. In 1779 they moved to 5 Rivers Street, a vantage point from which he attempted to measure the height of the lunar mountains, but in March 1781 returned to 19 New King Street. There Herschel observed Uranus with a portable telescope in the garden, between 10 and 11 p.m. on 13 March. Soon after, he was awarded a royal pension and could devote himself to astronomy. He and Caroline finally left Bath in 1782 for a house in Datchet, on the Thames and (in accordance with the terms of his pension) within easy reach of Windsor Castle, and from 1789 operated in the gardens of his final residence in Slough,

Observatory House. That house was demolished in 1962, though there is a memorial to him in Herschel Street in Slough; the famous 40-foot (12-metre) telescope he built there was destroyed in a gale in 1839. Herschel became a British subject in 1793 and was knighted in 1816; he died in 1822.

It was not until the late 1970s that the importance of preserving 19 New King Street came to be recognized. The outwardly unremarkable Georgian terrace townhouse, built in 1764 in one of the less fashionable streets near the Avon, has only lately been listed Grade II*. Nothing of its original décor survives, nor – apart from the stone floor and sink and the site of the furnace in the basement – does anything of the Herschels' time there. The back garden room, an extension of the basement, would seem to have served as his workshop, while the original back room by tradition would have been the kitchen. In 1978 the William Herschel Society was established to acquire and restore the house and in 1981 the museum was opened there, 200 years to the day after the discovery of Uranus.

Today the William Herschel Museum is one of a group in Bath depicting life in the 18th century, watched over by the Bath Preservation Trust. The ground- and first-floor rooms are modestly furnished in period style, in keeping with the relatively modest life Herschel and his sister led. In the rear ground-floor drawing-room there is a model of his 40-foot telescope, portraits of the Herschels and a 1780 map of Bath. In the dining-room at the front is a table constructed with a surviving plank from a larger table at Observatory House in Slough, a Thomas Rowland print of a man studying a comet and a planesphere from 1810 by John Cary. Upstairs, in the rear drawing-room, are books from Herschel's library and the well-known oil portrait by Edward F. Burney, the nephew of Herschel's friend Dr Charles Burney, himself a musician and amateur astronomer.

The room at the front of the first floor is devoted to music, with relevant period instruments on display – a Longman & Broderip square piano (1795), an oboe, a clarinet and a military serpent – as well as remnants of the Snetzler organ Herschel played at the Octagon Chapel. But even here, with one of Herschel's oboe concertos playing in the background, astronomy vies for attention: a miniature telescope sits on a table, a globe on the piano. Also of keen interest are the photograph (one of the earliest) of the 40-foot telescope taken by his son John and the Wedgwood portrait relief (1783) cast from life.

Downstairs, the old kitchen – displaying further photographs of the family, Herschel's inventions and Observatory House – is used for educational activities and the vault under the street has recently been reclaimed and transformed into a mini-planetarium. In the workshop, fitted out with tools and materials for casting mirrors, pride of place is given to Herschel's original lathe. Outside, in the landscaped garden and orchard where he set up his telescopes and which in his time extended down to the river, the remarkable scientific achievements of William and Caroline Herschel are commemorated in statuary, astronomical ornaments and wall plaques.

William Herschel Museum
19 New King Street
Bath BA1 2BL
Great Britain

phone +44/0 1225 311342, 446865
website www.bath-preservation-trust.org.uk

open March–October, daily 14.00–17.00; November–February, Saturday and Sunday 14.00–17.00

Map 5

F. Brown: *William Herschel: Musician & Composer* (Bath: William Herschel Society, 1990)
P. Moore: *William Herschel: Astronomer and Musician* (Bath, William Herschel Society, 5/2000)

HILDEGARD OF BINGEN

Abbess, visionary, mystic, writer: Hildegard of Bingen was a composer but always as an adjunct to her religious vocation. She was born in Bermersheim, about 32 km south-west of Mainz, in 1098. When she was 14 she entered a Benedictine monastery nearby at Disibodenberg, where later she established a convent; in 1147 she moved the convent to Rupertusberg, near Bingen, some 30 km down the Rhine from the Lorelei rock at the confluence of the Rhine and the Nahe, and in 1165 founded a further one at Eibingen, near Rüdesheim, a few kilometres from Bingen but on the north bank of the Rhine. She died there in 1179. Hildegard's powerful and visionary settings of her poetry are thought to date from the 1140s or perhaps a little earlier. They began to be collected in the 1150s; they amount to some 80 songs, chiefly antiphons and responses.

There is no specific museum to Hildegard, but her memory is preserved at several sites in the places where she lived. The church in Bermersheim, where she is thought to have been baptized, still stands; of the convent at Disibodenberg, near Odernheim, by the confluence of the Nahe and the Glen, only ruins survive, now in private hands.

The Rupertusberg convent was in what is now Bingerbrück, a district of Bingen which lies across the River Nahe (to the west). The convent itself was destroyed in the 30 Years War but its remains, consisting of five arcades, the crypt and some cellars, survive, now within the exhibition hall of the Firma Büroland Würth (who allow visits by appointment: +49/0 6721 3050). A tapestry and a statue in the Catholic parish church, nearby in Gutenbergstraße, known as the Hildegardis-Gedächtniskirche, commemorate Hildegard, and windows in the west transept show scenes from her life.

In the main part of Bingen, in the Basilica of St Martin, there is a statue of Hildegard dating from the 18th century and the organ (of 1970) is known as the Hildegardisorgel. Close by is a house (Basilikastraße 8) with a mural of Hildegard and the Rupertusberg, and a relief of 1981 on the fountain in the marketplace shows Hildegard preaching to the people by the portal of the church. There is another statue, erected in 1979, on the corner of the house at Mainzerstraße 1. In the Heimatmuseum at Burg Klopp in Bingen (open Easter–October, 09.00–12.00, 14.00–17.00, closed Mondays) there is a reproduction of an ivory comb ascribed to Hildegard, showing three armed men in its central panel and a charioteers' race in the outer ones. The Historisches Museum am Strom – Hildegard von Bingen, which is devoted primarily to the Rhine and its history, opened in 1998 with a special exhibition in celebration of Hildegard's 900th anniversary.

The Rochuskapelle, on the site of Hildegard's 1147 foundation over the grave of Rupertus (open 09.00–17.00), has a series of woodcarvings, dating from after its reconstruction in 1895 following a fire, showing scenes from Hildegard's life; they include her delivery as a child to her mentor Jutta of Spanheim, her meetings with the Emperor Barbarossa and St Bernard of Clairvaux (the latter encounter is fictional), and her preaching.

There are also frescoes with scenes from her life in the Benedictine Abbey in Klosterweg in Eibingen (+49/0 6722 4990), which was established in 1904 to replace the convent; the original convent, much rebuilt, had been abandoned in 1802 and in 1831 its church had become the Eibingen parish church. Hildegard's remains had been brought to the Eibingen monastery in 1636 when the Rupertusberg one was destroyed; in 1857, it is claimed, the parish priest 'proved their authenticity'. Since 1929 they have been preserved at the church in a gilded reliquary on the plan of a building, bearing allegorical images. The church itself was rebuilt in 1935 after a fire in 1932, which the reliquary survived. A statue of Hildegard, in Franconian shell-

limestone, was fitted into the stonework in 1957.

Historisches Museum an Strom – Hildegard von Bingen*
Museumstraße 3
55411 Bingen am Rhein
Germany

phone +49/0 6721 990654, 991531 (Tourist Information der Stadt Bingen, Hildegard information line, +49/0 6721 184200)
fax +49/0 6721 990653
e-mail historisches-museum@bingen.de
website www.bingen.de/kultur/museum, www.uni-mainz.de/~horst/hildegard

open Tuesday–Sunday 10.00–17.00
Map 7

HOFFMANN

If there is any composer whose commemoration demands imaginative treatment, it is surely E.T.A. Hoffmann. Hoffmann, poet, teller of tales, critic, illustrator and lawyer as well as composer, moved around a good deal in the course of his brief and rather turbulent career – he was born in Königsberg in 1776, died in Berlin in 1822 – and he spent a crucial four years in the north Bavarian city of Bamberg. He was not particularly popular there, because of his heavy drinking (and his illicit passion for a girl pupil), but it was in Bamberg that he embarked on his finest opera, *Undine*, created the mad Kapellmeister Kreisler and wrote his famous, visionary essays on works by Mozart and Beethoven.

At Bamberg, he lived on the upper floors and the attic room of a tall, narrow house in what is now the Schillerplatz, opposite the theatre that today bears his name. In 1923 the attic room was dedicated to Hoffmann's memory by the Gesellschaft der Freunde E.T.A. Hoffmanns; in the following year the memorial was extended downwards by one floor and in 1930 a museum was formally established. After various vicis-

The Hoffmann-Haus, Bamberg

of his literary works, listening-rooms and a bookstall.

Part of the second floor is devoted to his theatrical life – a miniature box in a theatre, where images of *Undine* are shown, and at the front of the house a large octagonal box portraying the Hoffmann character, Meister Floh, who can perceive what people are thinking: on the outside you read what they are saying, then you peer through an eyepiece and learn their true thoughts. A top hat perches above. At the rear there is space for changing exhibitions. The front of the top floor represents Hoffmann's personal space – his Poetenstübchen, the poet's little room, with his bed in an alcove, a little spinet, and a bust, all shaded blue by window covers. Behind it is a room devoted to Hoffmann the composer and musician, with illustrations of manuscripts, excerpts from his critical writings, posters. Everything in this imaginatively conceived museum reflects some facet of Hoffmann's inventive and engaging personality.

situdes in the war years and later, the house, until then privately owned, was acquired by the city in 1980 and put in the care of the E.T.A. Hoffmann-Gesellschaft, who began a thoroughgoing renewal of the museum under the direction of the head of the Bamberg Staatsbibliothek (a major source of Hoffmann material), completed in 2003.

You enter the house to see a curious aggregation of what seem like half-illusory, fleeting images, a dimly lit, deep blue 'Spiegelkabinett', with a series of portraits of the man inscribed on glass and mirrors – some of them broken, reflecting a favourite motif in Hoffmann's own work (add to that: the house was long owned by the Spiegel family). At the rear are displays of his handwriting, literary and musical, and the winged chair and small table at which he worked; beyond is a 'magic garden', planned to catch more Hoffmannesque imagery. The official entry to the museum is on the first floor, where there are cases with manuscripts

E.T.A. Hoffmann-Museum

E.T.A. Hoffmann-Haus
Schillerplatz 26
96407 Bamberg
Germany

phone +49/0 951 871431

open May–October, Tuesday–Friday 16.00–18.00, Saturday and Sunday 10.00–12.00

Map 7

R. Heinritz: *Das E.T.A. Hoffmann-Museum in Bamberg: Einblicke in ein Künstlerleben* (Bamberg: E.T.A. Hoffmann-Gesellschaft, 2003)

HOLST

During the 1860s, the Lediard family lived in a pleasant Regency-style terraced house, built in 1832, in the leafy, prosperous Pittville district of Cheltenham, close to the Pump Room where fashionable visitors to the spa came to take the waters. In 1871 a daughter of the family,

Clara, married her piano teacher, Adolph von Holst. Adolph's father, Gustavus, had come to England from Latvia in infancy with his father, Matthias; all these Holsts had been musicians, and Gustavus and Adolph were teachers of the piano or the harp in the fashionable homes of the spa town. Gustav Holst and his younger brother Emil, later the actor Ernest Cossart, were born in the Lediard house, but they did not live there for long: in 1882 Clara Holst died, and Adolph and his two boys moved out soon after.

Adolph von Holst was organist at All Souls' Church, nearby, and his son played there too. Gustav began composing when he was a pupil at Cheltenham Grammar School and in 1893 moved to London, initially to study at the Royal College of Music. He never again lived in Cheltenham. In June 1901 he married; his daughter Imogen, herself a composer as well as her father's biographer, was born six years later (she died in 1984). It was through Imogen's filial piety that the Holst Birthplace Museum was set up, in 1975, in the wake of her father's centenary: she prevailed upon the local council to buy the house and gave Cheltenham the family relics in her possession which provide much of the display material, as well as a documentary archive of music, letters and photographs.

The Holst Birthplace Museum is more than a composer commemoration: it also serves as a museum of 19th-century English family life, and thus evokes much

The Holst Birthplace Museum, Cheltenham

of the world of Holst's own childhood there. Holst himself is commemorated in the open pair of ground-floor reception rooms. The William Morris willow-pattern wallpaper acknowledges Holst's connection with the Morris circle: it was at Morris's house that Holst conducted rehearsals of the Hammersmith Socialist Choir, and where he met his wife Isobel, a soprano in the choir. On the walls are information boards and there is a fine, rather austere late portrait by Bernard Munn. Centrally in the front room stands the piano that Holst acquired in 1913 and on which he is believed to have composed part of *The Planets* (1914–16), at his house in Thaxted in Essex (see p.63). Around it are an upholstered chair, a music stand and a display case with some small personal possessions.

The Cheltenham Art Gallery and Museum curators who furnished the museum took great care in integrating the two functions of personal commemoration and social history. Holst family portraits and pictures painted by his great-uncle Theodore, a pupil of Fuseli, hang in the first-floor parlour, decorated in an earlier Regency style, with a square piano and a harp displayed. This elegant room must evoke the homes in which the senior Holsts taught. The bedroom adjacent to the parlour is thought to be the room in which Gustav was born, on 21 September 1874, and is furnished accordingly. The attic is decorated as an Edwardian nursery, with a small bedroom for a nanny nearby in the eaves. In the basement is a kitchen, with laundry, storage, scullery and maid's room, used for demonstrations, 'wash and cook' days for the local children, Victorian-style tea parties and workshops in Victorian crafts. Holst's own philosophy of 'learning by doing' is aptly applied.

Holst divided his life between Thaxted, where from 1916 he organized music festivals, and a house by the Thames in Mortlake (now marked by a plaque), not far from the newly established St Paul's Girls' School in Hammersmith where he was director of music from 1905 until his death on 25 May 1934, and for which he wrote the eponymous suite. In March 1927 Cheltenham honoured him with a festival in which the Birmingham Orchestra under Adrian Boult performed several of his works, and *Egdon Heath* had its première there the following year. But visitors to Cheltenham today will search in vain for a statue or a bust, or even a street named in his honour.

Holst is warmly remembered in the commemoration of his friend Ralph Vaughan Williams at the Gloucestershire parish church of Down Ampney, not far away, and at the Surrey Performing Arts Library at the Denbies vineyard at Dorking (*see* VAUGHAN WILLIAMS). The borrowing library at the School for Advanced Musical Studies at Snape Maltings, near Aldeburgh, is known as the Holst Library: it was established with a bequest from Imogen Holst, who was Britten's amanuensis from 1952 until 1964. There are Holst rooms both at St Paul's Girls' School, in a sound-proof wing added specially so that he could compose in peace, and at Morley College, where he also taught for many years. His ashes are interred, as he requested, in Chichester Cathedral.

Holst Birthplace Museum

4 Clarence Road
Cheltenham GL40 2AY
England

phone +44/0 1242 524846
fax +44/0 1242 580182
e-mail holstmuseum@btconnect.com
website www.holstmuseum.org.uk

open Tuesday–Saturday 10.00–16.00; closed December and January except by appointment

Map 5

L. Maddison: *The Holst Birthplace Museum* (Cheltenham: Cheltenham Art Gallery and Museums, 1992)

E. Lee: *Musical London* (London: Omnibus Press, 1995)

HUMMEL

Deep within the Old Town of Bratislava, just off the square dominated by the Primatial Palace, a little architectural pearl is hidden behind an improbable shell of modern buildings. This is the 17th-century house in which the Austrian composer and piano virtuoso Johann Nepomuk Hummel was born, on 14 November 1778, and spent his earliest years. It can be discovered by entering through the doorway of 2 Klobučnícka ulica, which is a music and CD shop and a glass gallery. The two-storey cottage, with a staircase at each side, presides over a little courtyard with a miniature amphitheatre.

The rather ornate plaque outside the Hummel Museum was put up in 1858, on the 80th anniversary of Hummel's birth. It was nearly 50 years later, on the centenary of his death (he died in Weimar on 17 October 1837), that the museum opened; in 1964 the house was restored and the museum achieved its present form. Long before, Hummel's widow had donated his desk, two pianos (a Glöckner, locally made and once his father's, and a Viennese Katholnik) and important correspondence and other documents to the city museum in Bratislava (or Pressburg, the German name by which Hummel would have called his native city); the documents, now the property of the Bratislava City Archives, along with autographs, printed

Hummel's birthplace, Bratislava

editions, correspondence and recordings, provide the basis of the display in the Hummel Museum.

Three rooms are open to the public and, besides the items mentioned above, there are further pianos (including a London-made Erard), portraits, a bust and a death mask, as well as a series of engravings and other reproductions of cities with which Hummel had links. The music on display includes a facsimile of the manuscript of his popular piano method (published in 1828) and his own editions of Mozart piano concertos. The captions are in Slovak and English.

Hummel's father was a violinist. The family settled in Vienna in 1786, when he became musical director of the Theater auf der Wieden. Johann was already regarded as a prodigy and had little trouble attracting the interest of Mozart, who agreed to take him as a pupil on the understanding (normal at the time in such circumstances) that he lived *en famille* with the Mozarts, at the 'Figarohaus' (open to the public; *see* MOZART), just behind the Dom, St Stephen's. Hummel made remarkable progress. Edward Holmes, in his *Life of Mozart* (1845), recounts an anecdote about Hummel's time in Mozart's care:

At a late hour Mozart and his wife return home from a party. On entering their apartment the boy is discovered stretched on chairs fast asleep. Some new pianoforte music has just arrived which they are both anxious to hear. Mozart, however, will not play it himself, but tells his wife . . . to wake up Hans, give him a glass of wine, and let him play. This is no sooner said than done; and now, should anything go wrong, there is an opportunity for suggestions. It is in fact a lesson, though given at the rather unusual hour of midnight.

The lessons were discontinued in 1788, when Mozart recommended that the elder Hummel accompany his son on a concert tour of the kind he and his father had earlier undertaken; and that they did.

In 1887, on the 50th anniversary of his death, a monument to Hummel by the sculptor V. Tilgner was erected in the garden of the Grassalkovich Palace (where Hummel's father had once played in the orchestra), now the main city park in Bratislava.

Hudobná expozícia – Rodný dom J.N. Hummela

Divyd Glass Gallery
Klobučnícka 2
81102 Bratislava
Slovakia

phone +421/0 2 5443 3888
fax +421/0 2 5443 4387
e-mail divyd@divyd.sk
website www.divyd.sk, www.muzeum.sk

open Monday–Friday 10.00–18.00, Saturday 10.00–14.00

Map 8

L. Kresánková: *Le musée Johann Nepomuk Hummel: Guide du musée* (Bratislava: Editions Obzor and Le musée municipal, 1972)

IPAVEC family

Šentjur is a pleasant, hilly town, of just under 20,000 people, in the centre of Slovenia, about 12 km east of Celje and some 70 from Ljubljana. Among the prominent citizens there in the 19th century and the early 20th were the Ipavec family, doctors, musicians and generally pillars of the community. The most important as a musician was Benjamin, born in 1829, although he spent most of his life working as chief physician in a children's hospital in Graz, where he died in 1908. His younger brother Gustav, who was also a physician and became mayor of Šentjur, was a composer of choral pieces in a patriotic tone; Gustav's son Josip, born in 1873, was a military doctor who later practised locally, and died in the town in 1921, but he was also a pupil of Zemlinsky and composer of an operetta and lieder, some on Slovene texts. An imposing trio of busts of these men below the town's main church underlines their importance in Šentjur.

The family lived in a fine old house, built in 1760 on a hill above the main part of the town; at one time it was a law court (later embodying a prison), then a school and during the Napoleonic wars a home for soldiers. The Ipavec family bought it in 1805; Benjamin, Gustav and their elder brother Alojz were all born there. Just across the road, Gustav built another house, for his branch of the family, and there Josip was born. That house later became a museum but now it is empty, largely derelict and awaiting restoration. The main family house, however, the 'Ipavčeva hiša', is now municipally owned and it opened in 1994 as a memorial to the family and for ceremonial use: the main room on the ground floor is used for weddings, and small-scale concerts take place in the entrance hall.

In the entrance hall, which is tiered, Benjamin Ipavec's small grand piano stands, along with prominent busts of all three Ipavec composers. At the rear is a patio, with a roofed well, a stone table and benches, and a charming view of the countryside and part of the town. On the first floor, Benjamin's room is used for official events, occasionally for concerts and also for art exhibitions, showing the work of local painters, and the gallery continues on the extensive top floor with reproductions and scenery by Josip's son, Jože (1910–99), a scenographer. But most of the space in this large, open attic, its eccentric shape determined by the house's dormers and gables, is devoted to music, with an occasional reminder of their medical work too.

One group of display cases is assigned to Benjamin, showing manuscripts and correspondence (in facsimile), a portrait, a playbill for his opera *Teharski plemiči* ('The Noblemen of Teharje') and songs. There is a photograph of him in hunting gear. Gustav is generously represented by photographs, with his family; and for Josip there is material from his operetta *Prinzessin Tollkopf*, piano music and songs as well as letters. Separate cases are

given over to editions of their music (including LPs and TV films) and plaques and monuments to the three men, and another is devoted to Alojz and the women of the family. Some of the family's original furniture, along with the gilded laurel and oak wreaths that were bestowed on them, and their travelling cases are to be seen in the final room. This substantial, solid house gives a clear impression of the family's place not only in Šentjur but also in Slovenian musical life more generally.

Ipavčeva hiša
Ulica skladateljev Ipavcev 27
3230 Šentjur pri Celju
Slovenia

phone +386/0 3574 1824, 3747 1314

open by appointment (second number above)

Map 14

JANÁČEK

On 3 July 1854, in the northern Moravian village known then as Pod Hukvaldy, between Příbor and Frydek-Mistek, Leoš Janáček was born. He was the son of the local schoolmaster. Still used today, the school, which was originally the icehouse of a feudal landlord, sits at the foot of the hill (Babí Hůra) where a castle once stood. The castle provided a strategic vantage point for the surrounding forests and valleys, and was occupied at different times by Catholic clergy and by soldiers, who used it as a watchtower and prison before a disastrous fire in 1762 reduced it to a ruin. Today Hukvaldy is best known for its deer park and for the annual international Janáček festival of operas and concerts held in the park and the castle ruins.

Janáček spent his early childhood in Hukvaldy, living with his family in a single cold, damp room in the school, before being sent to Old Brno at the age of 11 to serve as a choirboy at the Augustinian monastery under the composer Pavel Křížkovský. A year later his father died. Jiří

Janáček had been a prominent figure in the Hukvaldy community and the founder of a singing and reading club. Janáček never forgot his roots, retaining all his life the gentle, clipped accent associated with the regional Lachian dialect, and his writings resonate with descriptions of the Moravian countryside. It provided the impetus for collecting folksongs as well as being a place of retreat.

After his schooling in Brno, Janáček had undergone training, first at the Czech Teachers' Institute there and then at the Organ School in Prague. He returned to Brno, where he was active as a choirmaster (he championed the works of his friend Antonín Dvořák) and a teacher. There followed studies at the conservatories in Leipzig (1879–80) and Vienna (1880), before he settled in Brno as a teacher, and married one of his piano pupils, Zdenka Schulzová, daughter of the director of the Teachers' Institute. The union was never a very happy one and after the death of their children only convenience kept them together. Nevertheless, his career began well with his appointment in 1881 as the first director of the Brno Organ School, a post he held to the end of his life. Like his father and grandfather, Janáček was a dedicated teacher. But his teaching obligations at the Institute and Organ School, and his commitments as a journalist and editor, made it difficult for him to promote his own music beyond Moravia.

When in 1908 the Brno Organ School acquired larger premises opposite the Botanical Gardens, the architect Alois Horák drew up plans for a new house for the director on the site of the former stables. From 1910 Janáček and his wife made their home in the 'little house', in sight and within earshot of the Organ School, separated only by a low fence and gate. In the garden Janáček planted tall ferns known as 'the Devil's Fingers', which he brought from Hukvaldy, as well as fruit and nut trees and a kitchen garden. Inside, the furniture came from Zdenka's family. In 1919 the Organ School was amalgamated with the Beseda Music School as Brno Conservatory. The building was eventually taken over by the

Janáček's 'little house' in Brno

Moravian Museum to house its Music Division, which now includes the Janáček Archive. The director's house was preserved as a memorial to the city's greatest composer.

The house has now lost most of its domestic ambience. It was rebuilt during the 1970s in line with the thinking of the then ruling communist government to stress Janáček's transition from rural deprivation to urban sophistication; but in 2003 it was restored to its original layout (involving the moving of some of the walls). His study, which was additional to his office in the Organ School, is preserved as it was in his day. In the centre is a Friede grand piano; in addition to the composer's desk and lyre-backed chair, bookcase, velvet upholstered chairs, table and carpets, there are paintings, a photograph of his only daughter, Olga, and the chronoscope he used to measure speaking time when he was composing. Of the other two main ground-floor rooms, the first is a lecture room, with audio-visual equipment and on the walls two Janáček portraits, by Süsser (the date is uncertain) and Böhm (from the mid-1920s). The second offers a display of facsimiles and everyday objects that belonged to him, among them a chest he had decorated with folk motifs and in which he kept his manuscripts.

Janáček first returned to Hukvaldy in 1881. Among the works that took inspiration from the surrounding countryside

Janáček's cottage at Hukvaldy

were *The Cunning Little Vixen*, *The Makropulos Affair*, the *Lachian Dances* and the string quartets. Janáček once commented of Hukvaldy: 'That is where I always have fresh ideas'. It was not until 1921 that he finally purchased a cottage there (it had belonged to his widowed sister-in-law). He went on to acquire additional tracts of forestland. Over the years he entertained many friends and colleagues at the house, among them the composer Vitězslav Novák, helped promising young local musicians and sponsored concerts in the village. In 1926 a plaque honouring his birth was unveiled at the school.

Janáček was on holiday at Hukvaldy in the summer of 1928 when he contracted the fever that, on 12 August, took his life. Five years later, on 17 July 1933, his widow Zdenka Janáčková opened the house to the public, although initially visits were only by appointment. In the war years the house was lived in, and some restoration was done under the supervision of the local municipality. In 1962 it came into the ownership of the Czech Music Fund, which carried out repairs and set up a Janáček display in the upper rooms, and in 1994 it passed to the Leoš Janáček Foundation, in Brno, which re-opened it in 2000.

The three ground-floor rooms of the cottage remain much as Janáček left them.

The study is furnished with a day bed, a table, desks at which to stand and sit, a display cabinet with china and other personal objects and four upholstered chairs; there is a Lidl & Velik harmonium and, in the corner, a gramophone. The bedroom is also comfortably furnished: on the bed is a gold embroidered coverlet and above it a painting. There is a cuckoo clock, a smoking stand and pictures of his mother and his wife, Zdenka. The third room is the simple kitchen. The upstairs rooms, which Janáček personally arranged as separate living quarters for Kamila Stösslová when she visited him in 1928, now accommodate the new displays relating to his time in Hukvaldy, entitled 'Roots – Inspiration – Harvest'. Outside, on the front of the house there is a commemorative plaque by A. Handzel.

Památník Leoše Janáčka
Smetanova 14
60200 Brno
Czech Republic

phone +420/0 541 212811
website www.mzm.cz/mzm/janacek

open Tuesday–Sunday 09.00–12.00, 13.00–18.00

Památník Leoše Janáčka
Hukvaldy 79
73946 Hukvaldy
Czech Republic

phone +420/0 558 699252, 699337 (administration: Marešova 14, 60200 Brno

phone +420/0 541 246824
fax +420/0 541 246825
e-mail janacek-nadace@janacek-nadace.cz
website www.janacek-nadace.cz)

open April, October, Tuesday–Sunday 10.00–16.30; May, September, Tuesday–Sunday 10.00–17.00; June–August, Tuesday–Sunday 10.00–18.00; November–March by appointment (+420 658 699337)

Map 4

J. Vysloužíl, ed.: *Janáček a Hukvaldy* (Brno:
Česká hudební společnost, 1984)
S. Přibáňová, ed.: *Leoš Janáček's Memorial*
(Brno: Moravian Museum, 1990)

JEŽEK

A stone's throw from the Charles Bridge,
on the right bank of the Vltava river in the
Prague Old Town (Staré Mìsto), is
Kaprová Street. The composer Jaroslav
Ježek (1906–42) lived there with his
parents in a first-floor, co-op flat at no.10
during the 1920s and 30s. Ježek was a
talented composer of faintly outrageous
Czech theatre music, whose career inter-
twined with those of two popular comedians, Jiří Voskovec and Jan Werich. He
conducted his jazzy, satirical scores
(songs and dances) at the Prague Free
Theatre during the 1930s and, when it
had to close down at the end of 1938, he
and the comedians emigrated to the USA,
where he died three years later.

If Ježek's life was short, it was also
harsh, for he suffered from a series of
disabilities that would defeat most
aspiring musicians. Born partially
sighted, in the nearby Žižkov district of
Prague (named after a 15th-century military leader who was blinded in battle), his
hearing was impaired after a bout of
scarlet fever, and he also suffered from a
renal disease. Before he could pursue
his studies in music, he went to a school
for the blind (1912–21), then the
Dvořákeum Music School; finally, in
1924, he was accepted into the Academy
of Music, where he was admired for his
masterly improvisation at the piano. He
wore thick glasses; to write his music, he
had to rely on large-format manuscript
paper and an oversized pencil.

In the 1930s the small room at the
front of the flat, which had served as his
father's tailoring workshop, became his
study. To enhance his sight the room was
decorated in complementary blue tones –
light walls with a darker ceiling and
skirting boards; even the sheer curtains
were dyed blue. The grand piano is black;
so, oddly, is some of the functionalist
furniture (sofa, chairs, cupboards, desk).

The tubular-arm furniture, from around
1930, was designed by a friend, František
Zelenka, who created stage sets at
another Prague theatre with which Ježek
was associated, the Osvobozené Divadlo.
In spite of his poor sight, he collected a
substantial library of literature and,
remarkably in the circumstances, miniature scores of the standard repertory,
especially operas.

Near the end of his life he married a
fellow Czech emigrant, Františka
Bečáková. In 1947 she returned to Prague
with his ashes which, after a service at the
Rudolfinum, were interred at Olšany
Cemetery. The Blue Room was opened to
the public in 1983, shortly before her
death. It is now under the auspices of the
Czech Museum of Music in Prague.

At first, the interest seems slender. The
building is shabby, although there is a
bust and memorial plaque to Ježek
mounted on the street façade. The
entrance and staircase are unwelcoming.
There is a sign on the door of the flat, but
it is slightly unsettling to be ushered from
the landing, past a screen that hides the
rest of the flat from view, into the Blue
Room, and then left there alone. On the
desk are photographs of a smiling Ježek
at the piano and with the comedians; his
oversized writing implements, pocket
watch and pipe; his poignant thick glasses.
Above the desk is a framed certificate of
membership of the Czech Academy of
Science and Art, awarded posthumously
in 1946. A violin hangs on the adjacent
wall and inscribed banners are draped
nearby. On the piano are copies of his
published sheet music. A large-face clock,
a statuette and a folk instrument perch on
top of the larger of the two bookcases. A
modest legacy, some may say, but in its
way the Blue Room makes a very strong
impression on the visitor.

In New York, where in 1941 he
founded the Czechoslovak Choral
Group, his friends established a Jaroslav
Ježek Foundation in his memory.

Památník Jaroslava Ježka 'Modrý pokoj'
Kaprová ulica 10
11000 Praha 1
Czech Republic

phone +420/0 2 2222 0082 (Museum of Czech Music)

e-mail ais@nm.anet.cz

open Tuesdays 13.00–18.00

Map 4

JINDŘICH

The Chodsko region, in the south-western corner of the Czech Republic, on the old route between Regensburg and Prague, has always been a politically sensitive one with sturdy, individual traditions. The composer Jindřich Jindřich was born in a village there, Klenčí pod Čerchovem, in 1876, and after training in Prague (he was a pupil of Novák, and later accompanist to the renowned soprano Emmy Destinn) he spent most of his life in its main town, Domažlice, where in 1967 he died. He was a passionate student of Chodsko traditions and published a 26-volume ethnographic work as well as collecting numerous folk melodies and texts. The region's music, not surprisingly, coloured his own compositions.

Jindřich is commemorated in both Klenčí and Domažlice. The house of his birth no longer stands, but a plaque on the town hall, on the site of the school where his father was schoolmaster, records his birthplace, and he is buried in the local cemetery. He is also remembered in the Klenčí museum, which is dedicated to his friend the priest and prolific novelist Jindřich Šimon Baar (1869–1932): founded in 1926, in Baar's house, it is essentially a museum of local and regional history but its collection includes some music, correspondence, photos and a few other personal items of Jindřich's. Among the displays is a small one devoted to him.

The Domažlice display is on an altogether different scale. This is in what was once Jindřich's own house – a large one, formerly an orphanage or poor house – on the second floor, which is converted to museum space although certain areas, mostly to be seen through glass panels,

represent his own living quarters. This is as much a museum of Chodsko folk art and ethnology as a commemoration of Jindřich himself. He was not short of bedside reading. His bedroom was also his library, and indeed one of his picture galleries: the bookshelves are packed tight with books and journals, the walls packed tight with photographs and pictures of every sort, with ceramics, busts and statuettes crowding every surface. He was unmarried and lived alone (no woman would tolerate such circumstances) but had lady friends, as some of the pictures imply.

In one alcove, or glass-partitioned area, is his piano, with musical portraits (a lovely oil of Destinn), his cello in the corner, more of his scores, photos of his friends and choirs, certificates and awards (including some national ones: he was an 'honoured artist' and 'honoured worker' in communist times). A corner library off the bedroom houses most of his sheet music and miniature scores along with numerous drawings, watercolours, pastels and oils, with textiles, furniture and furnishings of Chodsko folk origins. His sofa, desk (with many ornaments) and chair, and a standing desk, are there. Many composers – among them Beethoven, Dvořák, Smetana, Novák – are represented, mostly by plaster reliefs. There are books everywhere.

More conventional museum fare appears in another room: a series of panels, with pictures, text (in Czech, German and English) and facsimiles of letters and documents, charting his life. But there is also a large gallery, chiefly devoted to the Chodsko art of glass painting, of which there are some 1400 examples on the walls and on panels, from the 18th century to Jindřich's own time, many on sacred topics, many free. There are also other examples of local art, pottery, wood carvings, lace, embroidery, clothing, furniture and a few folk instruments too. An archive of his extensive correspondence, or the results of his fieldwork and his own compositions, along with other family papers, is stored in a smaller room. This massive, overwhelming collection speaks eloquently of a man who clearly had limitless energy and inextinguishable enthusiasm.

Muzeum Jindřicha Šimona Baara
Náměstí J. Jindřicha 140
34534 Klenčí pod Čerchovem
Czech Republic

phone +420/0 379 794511, 794231
fax +420/0 379 795026
e-mail ouklenci@klencipc.cz

open 8 May–10 October, Tuesday–Saturday 10.00–12.00 (May–June, Tuesday–Friday from 09.00), 13.00–16.30 (May–June, Saturday and July–August daily to 17.00, October to 16.00); May–September, Sunday 09.30–12.00, 13.00–15.30

Muzeum Jindřicha Jindřicha
Náměstí Svobody 61
34401 Domažlice
Czech Republic

phone +420/0 378 776009

open 15 April–October, Tuesday–Saturday 09.00–12.00, 13.00–15.00

Map 4

JORA

In the Rosetti family museum at Tescani-Bacău, best known for its connections with George Enescu, one small room is devoted to the memory of the Romanian composer Mihail Jora (1891–1971). Born like Enescu in the Moldavian region but ten years later, Jora was a cousin of Enescu's wife, who was a Rosetti. Trained in Leipzig and Paris as well as at home, after World War I he championed Romanian music – as pianist and composer, as founder and first chairman of the Society of Romanian Composers and later as music director of the Romanian Broadcasting Corporation. That Enescu liked and admired him, both as a composer of ballet music and songs and as a teacher (Jora was professor of

harmony, counterpoint and composition at Bucharest Conservatory), is clear from attributed remarks and photographs of them on display in the rooms devoted to Enescu at Tescani-Bacău.

Jora and his wife had quarters at the Rosetti mansion as well as a house in Bucharest. On display in the room off the far corner of the Oedip Room are a few pieces of furniture, a bronze death mask and a cast of his right hand, a profile drawing and photographs, his writing case and a baton, editions of his music and a programme from the wartime festival held to mark his 50th birthday in August 1941.

Centrul de Cultura Rosetti-Tescanu-George Enescu
Stradă Tescani 126
5481 Tescani-Bacău
Romania

phone +40/02 34 353 5601

open daily 10.00–18.00

Map 11

JURJĀNS brothers

One of the most beautiful spots in Latvia must be the farmstead surrounded by green-velvet meadows that slope down to the edge of Lake Pulgoznis, near Ērgļi, about 100 km east of Riga, where for many generations the Jurjāns family tended cattle and harvested grain. Today their wooden house commemorates three brothers, who became distinguished musicians and with a fourth brother performed as a french horn quartet. The exhibition, which includes the upright piano that they used to take by horse and cart to concert venues, as well as photographs, facsimiles, scores and commemorative medals, was opened in 1978.

The outbuildings – a granary, cattle shed and bathhouse (where one of the brothers was born when the house had burnt down and the family took refuge there) – preserve the history and traditions of rural Latvia. High on the hill

The Jurjāns family bathhouse at Ērgļi

above the house, with panoramic views of the lake and the countryside, is the site of large annual open-air folksong festivals, attracting some 2000 singers and an even larger audience.

Like their father and grandfather, who were both fiddlers, Pēteris (1851–1900), Andrejs (1856–1922), Juris (1861–1940) and Pāvuls (1866–1948) began as folk musicians. They are said to have rowed out to the island in the middle of the lake with their horns to serenade the inhabitants of the valley. Pēteris decided against a professional musical career, but the others went to the St Petersburg Conservatory and Andrejs and Juris taught at the music school at Khar'kiv.

Andrejs returned to Latvia each summer to collect folk tunes, developing new methods of ethnomusicological research, and over the years he published a series of critical editions for the Latvian Society in Riga. Both Andrejs and Pāvuls (who became a professor of singing at the Latvian Conservatory and is considered the father of Latvian opera) were also conductors and composers; Andrejs in particular was associated with the early Latvian song festivals of 1880, 1888, 1895 and 1910.

Brāļu Jurjānu Memoriālais Muzejs 'Meņģeļi'
Madonas rajons
4840 Ērgļi
Latvia

phone +371/0 943 1659

open 1 May–1 November,
Tuesday–Sunday 10.00–18.00
Map 2

KÁLMÁN

Imre (or Emmerich) Kálmán, the affable Hungarian-born composer of such operettas as *Die Csárdásfürstin* (1915), *Gräfin Mariza* (1924) and *Die Zirkusprinzessin* (1926), is twice commemorated: at his birthplace in the resort town of Siófok, on the southern shore of Lake Balaton, and in Vienna, where he lived for nearly 30 years, in a memorial room at the Österreichisches Theatermuseum (*see* ZIEHRER).

Kálmán was born in 1882 and lived in Siófok until he was ten years old. He studied music in Budapest and Vienna and soon made a name as a composer of operetta in both of the capital cities, producing a succession of humorous and satirical works for the Viennese theatres during World War I, the Twenties (when he visited the USA for two premières) and the Thirties. He married in 1929 and in 1934 bought a house in the north-east, 19th district of Vienna, Hasenauerstraße 29, which became known as the Kálmán Villa and is today marked by a memorial plaque; nearby, in the Türkenschanzpark, there is a bust of him by the Hungarian sculptor Gyula Meszes-Toth. Kálmán was Jewish, so on the Anschluss he took his family to Paris, where in 1938 he was awarded the Légion d'honneur, and on to New York, becoming an American citizen in 1940; Hungary allied herself with Germany and his music was banned by the Nazis. He returned to Europe in 1949, living in Paris at 26 Avenue Georges-Mandel, where he died on 30 October 1953; at his request he was buried in Vienna, in the Zentralfriedhof, among the city's other great musicians. Other public memorials (streets, busts, even a hotel suite) to Kálmán can be found in Bad Ischl, Munich, Saarbrücken and Budapest.

Finding the memorial house in Siófok sounds easy, but it is a little elusive: Kálmán Imre Sétány faces the railway lines that run along the lake, and is a pedestrian area with open-air cafés and market stalls selling Hungarian craftwork; the Kálmán house is two doors west of the station. The museum occupies three rooms on the ground floor and displays items donated by Kálmán's widow, Vera, and their son Charles (also a composer). Two rooms show mannequins in period and stage costumes. The first is dominated by the composer's boudoir grand piano, with display cases and information boards in opposite corners. In the cases are plaster casts of his hands set next to an unfinished cigar in an ashtray, a letter from Cole Porter, copies of sheet music and handwritten medical records (in German) from his last week in Paris. On the wall are photographic portraits of his family and posters of performances of his music in Siófok; by the door to the second room are a marble bust and the ubiquitous bronze laurel wreath.

The second room is decorated as a theatre, with recorded music in the background. Five of the six boxes are display cases devoted to the history of Austro-Hungarian operetta, with published sheet music and scores, photos, a wig box and wig, opera glasses, programmes and recordings. In the hallway display boards trace what is known of his Siófok childhood, with family photos and a case containing his concert clothes. The third room is filled with furniture from his last Paris flat – a waistcoat hanging from a chair, a velvet robe and briefcase from the coat-stand – and display cases with yet more photos, music and books about his life and works.

The memorial room in the Österreichisches Theatermuseum in Vienna is partitioned in two, with a door minus its upper window glazing through which visitors can peer into a re-creation of a room in one of Kálmán's homes. The warm, low lighting evokes a former era. On the Bösendorfer piano are scores, family photos and bronze casts of his hands; on the chaise longue a red plaid blanket, silk bathrobe and cane; on the old television set an even older radio. But the plaster death mask rather takes away

from the sense of its being Kálmán's room. In the other half there are three display cases largely filled with photographs, two devoted to his time in Vienna and the third to Hollywood, which (mystifyingly) contains a velvet cushion on which his European orders are pinned. On the wall are costume designs for the 1924 Theater an der Wien production of *Gräfin Mariza*.

Kálmán Imre Múzeum

Kálmán Imre Sétány 5
8600 Siófok
Hungary

phone +36/0 84 311287

open Tuesday–Sunday 09.00–17.00 (November–March, closes 16.00)

Emmerich Kálmán Raum

Österreichisches Theatermuseum
Hanuschgasse 3
1010 Vienna
Austria

phone +43/0 1 512 2427, 512 8800–649
e-mail info@theatermuseum.at
website www.theatermuseum.at

open Tuesday–Friday 10.00–12.00, 14.00–16.00; Saturday and Sunday 13.00–16.00

Maps 8, 1

H. Pistorius: *Österreichisches Theatermuseum: Gedenkräume* (Vienna: Österreichisches Theatermuseum, 1991), 13–16, 55–6
H. Kretschmer: *Wiener Musikergedenkstätten* (Vienna: J & V Edition, 3/1992)

KAPP family

Suure-Jaani is a village, largely of wooden buildings, in central Estonia, about 150 km south of Tallinn, a short way off the main southerly road to Viljandi and about 100 km west of Tartu. The Kapp family, leading figures in Estonian musical life for close on a century, originated there. In the centre of the village, close to the parish church (where most of the Kapps are buried in a family plot), is

The Kapp family house at Suure-Jaani

the house where Artur Kapp was born, now the church school; the museum is the former family house on the north extreme of Suure-Jaani.

The first recorded Kapp musician was Joosep (1833–94), parish organist. He had two musician sons, Hans (1870–1938), an organist, and Artur (1878–1952). Each brother had a composer son: Hans's was Villem (1913–64), Artur's was Eugen (1908–96). The house that is now the museum was originally lived in by Hans.

A single-storey house with an attic, it consists of just four rooms. At the front is a re-creation of the family sitting-room, with the upright piano that belonged to Hans Kapp, family furniture and portraits of family members, and a writing-desk with a display of a Villem Kapp manuscript; there is also a furnished bedroom. The main display however is in the large rear room, with a collage of facsimile photographs, documents, programmes and the like devoted to each of the composers, and also a showcase with editions, recordings, awards and some personal effects – these include Artur's glasses and pipes and a programme, score and libretto of his oratorio *Hiiob* ('Job'), and a score of Villem's crusade opera *Lembitu*. The fourth room is a music room, for small recitals – Eugen's miniature grand piano is there, and seating for 15; the original kitchen serves as green room.

Of the Kapps, Artur, who studied in St Petersburg with Rimsky-Korsakov and taught in Astrakhan, returning to Estonia in 1920 as conductor at the Estonian Theatre in Tallinn and later professor of composition at the conservatory, was the most prominent; composer of symphonies, concertos and chamber music, he was founder of the so-called Tallinn School and is regarded as the originator of Estonian art music. He used Estonian folk music in a suite as early as 1906. Eugen followed his father at the conservatory, wrote several operas and was chairman of the Estonian Composers Union and a deputy in the Estonian Supreme Soviet. Villem's main contribution was in the field of choral music.

There is an annual three-day Kapp Festival in Suure-Jaani, in June, with chamber, choral and orchestral concerts in the house, the church and the school. The museum sells souvenirs, unique among them a Kapp opener for beer bottles.

Heliloojate Kappide Majamuuseum
Tallinna 30
71502 Suure-Jaani
Estonia

phone +372/0 43 71190
website www.suure-jaani.ee/kultur/muus

open April–October, Tuesday–Sunday 10.00–13.30, 14.00–17.00; November–March, Tuesday–Sunday 11.00–15.00 (to 17.00 by appointment)

Map 2

KEISER

The quiet little village of Teuchern, about 50 km south of Halle and 45 south-west of Leipzig (the nearest town is Weissenfels, 12 km away off the road to Zeitz), was the birthplace in January 1674 of the Hamburg opera and oratorio composer Reinhard Keiser. His musical gifts – which no doubt came from his father, Gottfried, a composer and the local organist, who left the marital home soon after Reinhard was born – were recognized and developed first in Teuchern, probably by the local organist, Johann Christian Schieferdecker.

On the 300th anniversary of Keiser's birth a plaque was erected on the house in the market square where he was born. A small permanent exhibition devoted to his life, devised by local enthusiasts, was opened to the public in 1982 in the ground-floor front room. This was expanded and modernized in 2000, to incorporate a sound system with music and commentary (available in English and French as well as German). It is divided, parallel to the display, to follow Keiser's career – his time at the Thomasschule in Leipzig and his early career in Brunswick; his important years at the Hamburg opera, where he met (and influenced) the young Handel; his period in Stuttgart and Copenhagen (here there are facsimiles of letters in his fine, elegant hand); and then his late years back in Hamburg, as cathedral Kantor, and his death there in 1739. There are also tributes to other musicians linked with this unusually musical village: Schieferdecker (1679–1732), another native; Johann David Heinichen (1683–1729), born nearby, who went on to the Thomasschule and a distinguished career in Dresden; and Johann Friedrich Fasch (1688–1758), who spent part of his childhood in Teuchern.

Reinhard-Keiser-Gedenkstätte
Am Markt 9
06682 Teuchern
Germany

phone +49/0 344 412 2904

open Tuesday 16.00–18.00, Wednesday 10.00–13.00 (closed in June)

Map 7

K.-P. Koch: *Reinhard Keiser (1674–1739): Leben und Werk* (Teuchern: Förderkreis Reinhard-Keiser-Gedenkstätte, 2/1999)

KIENZL

The Austrian opera composer Wilhelm Kienzl was born on 17 January 1857 in a first-floor room of a 16th-century inn in the small market town of Waizenkirchen, about 40 km west of Linz. His family moved to Gmunden and then Graz when he was a child, but the connections with Waizenkirchen remained. As early as 1903 a plaque was put up on the inn to record his birth there. When the Mayrhuber family took over the inn, in 1914, they established friendly relations with the composer, who returned to his native town in 1927 for celebrations to mark his 70th birthday. The innkeeper's daughter, who was present, later installed displays in the room the Kienzl family had occupied and she presides over it to this day.

Kienzl studied in Prague, Leipzig, Weimar and Vienna and travelled widely, lecturing and giving recitals. A passionate Wagnerian, he went to the first performance of *The Ring* and religiously made the annual Bayreuth pilgrimage. In 1879 he quarrelled with Wagner, but he dropped everything on the news of Wagner's death in Venice in February 1883 and hurried there to accompany the coffin back to Bayreuth. He himself composed ten operas, most famously *Der Evangelimann* (1894), as well as the national anthem of the First Austrian Republic, to a text by

The inn at Waizenkirchen where Kienzl was born

the first president, Dr Karl Renner. He married twice – first a Bayreuth singer, Lili Hoke, who died in 1919, and two years later Henny Bauer, who provided the texts for his last three operas and with whom he lived in Vienna, at Schreygasse 6 in the second district (marked by a plaque, erected on his centenary in 1957) until his death there on 19 October 1941.

From 1893 he spent his summers at the beautiful resort of Bad Aussee, where on a high verdant plateau he kept a little 'Stöckl' close to a coffee house and inn ('zur Wasnerin'), which in 1934 gave way to a resort hotel and golf course. Kienzl stopped coming to Bad Aussee in the 1930s, but the little two-storey house survives, largely because it was there that he composed *Der Evangelimann* – even if it is now excessively close to the Hotel-Restaurant Wasnerin and rather unhappily extended at the front. It isn't open to the public but it is worth pausing to read the inscription and the quotation from a melody from the opera (sadly the rhythm is muddled) painted on the front of the house, to admire the spectacular view and to breathe the mountain air. There are other buildings in the area associated with Kienzl, among them the Haus Amon-Fiedler, at the intersection of Teichstraße and Wilhelm-Kienzl-Straße.

Kienzl was buried with honours (a choir sang 'Meine Lust ist Leben' at his graveside) in the Zentralfriedhof. He had no heirs, so his manuscripts passed to the Österreichisches Nationalbibliothek; other items of value were sold. But the Mayrhubers were able to salvage a number of interesting items to display in the hotel room, including some of his childhood drawings, music manuscripts of several songs, a handwritten catalogue of his music, an account book and his guestbook from their Vienna days, which gives evidence of the rich musical-literary community around the Kienzls; many photographs (portraits and images of his homes in Vienna and Bad Aussee), a cast of his right hand and a death mask, his cane, his awards, banners from special performances and a bronze laurel wreath.

Many items, of course, are associated with *Der Evangelimann*, including a poster and the watercolour designs for the costumes for the Viennese production, and his collaboration with Dr Renner and the Austrian folk poet Peter Rosegger.

It is hard to think of a quirkier position for a composer museum than at the historic site of the action of one of his operas. In 2002 the Austrian village of Paudorf (just south of Krems, about 75 km west of Vienna) decided to capitalize on its flicker of fame as the setting for *Der Evangelimann*, the climax of which is a fire, the result of arson, at the Hellerhof, a Benedictine monastery in the village (which is close to Göttweig, visible on the skyline). The municipality set up a Kienzl museum at the Hellerhof, in a long room – as if a former cloister, now enclosed – between the church and the main monastic building. There is an attractively laid out display in showcases along the perimeter, with space down the middle for separate, temporary exhibitions of paintings.

Emphasis, naturally, falls on *Der Evangelimann* (you can compare some of the pictures of stage settings with the reality through the windows); there are scores, librettos, posters, reviews and a plan of the Hellerhof. But there is material too, most of it loaned from Viennese collections, on his other, lesser-known operas and on his national anthem, as well as busts and portraits of the man himself, and on his two wives, including items from Lili Hoke's repertory (Wagner, Brahms and naturally Kienzl).

Wilhelm Kienzl-Raum
Gasthof Mayrhuber 'Zum weissen Lamm'
Dr-Wilhelm-Kienzl-Straße 1
4730 Waizenkirchen
Austria

phone +43/0 277 2209

open by appointment

Wilhelm Kienzl-Museum Paudorf
Hellerhofweg
3511 Paudorf
Austria

phone +43/0 736 6575
fax +43/0 736 657525
(Marktgemeinde office, Kremserstraße
185)
e-mail gdpaudorf@aon.at

open April – October, Saturday
15.00–17.30, Sunday 10.00–12.30,
14.00–17.30 or by appointment

Map 1

H. Kretschmer: *Wiener Musikergedenkstätten*
(Vienna: J & V Edition, 3/1992)
D. Grieser: *Nachsommertraum* (St Pölten and
Vienna: Nieder-Österreichisches Pressehaus,
1993), 120–32
W. Herrmann: *Musik ist ein heilige Kunst:
Komponisten, Dirigenten, Sänger im
Ausseerland* (Liezen: Jost Druck &
Medientechnik, 1999), 21–6

KLEIN

Gideon Klein was one of the Jewish Czech
composers imprisoned in the Nazi transit
camp at Terezín in 1941; he spent nearly
three years there and died when working
in a coal mine near Katowice in January
1945. Born in Přerov, in Moravia, in 1919,
he studied the piano and composition at
Prague Conservatory and musicology at
the Charles University; he was briefly a
pupil of Alois Hába. He used 12-note
techniques and quarter-tones in some of
his works, which include an expressionist
piano sonata.

Klein is commemorated in the room
devoted to music in the Magdeburg
Barracks at Terezín (*see* KRÁSA). He was
particularly active in the organization of
musical life, supervising the performances of instrumental music, making
many adaptations for the available
forces, playing the piano as soloist and
in supporting roles and composing incidental music for dramatic performances. His compositions in Terezín
include a song-cycle *Die Pest*, to poetry
by a fellow inmate, and a Hebrew
Lullaby, of which a facsimile is included,
with other facsimiles, photographic
material and concert programmes, in
the display dedicated to him.

Magdeburg Barracks
Památník Terezín
41155 Terezín
Czech Republic

phone +420/0 416 782948, 782949
e-mail manager@pamatnik-terezin.cz
website www.pamatnik-terezin.cz

open April–September, daily
09.00–18.00; October–March, daily
09.00–17.30

Map 4

J. Karas: *Music in Terezín 1941–1945*
(Stuyvesant, NY: Pendragon, 1985)

KLEMETTI

The name of Heikki Klemetti is little
known beyond Finland, but in his native
land Klemetti was an influential and
much-loved figure. He was born in 1876
in the small town of Kuortane, in southern
Ostrobothnia, some 375 km north-west of
Helsinki. He went to school in Vasa and
was later trained in Helsinki and Berlin.
When he was only 22 he was appointed to
a university professorship in Helsinki
(where his house, Hopiala, is currently the
home of the composer Einojuhani
Rautavaara). About three years later he
bought the estate at Kuortane on which he
was born – understandably, for it consists
of a fine pine wood commanding a
splendid view of Kuortane Lake. During
a busy career, teaching at Helsinki
University, composing and conducting
choirs – he directed the famous Finlandia
Male Chorus, the Finnish Song Choir and
the university chorus, among others – he
spent every summer until 1946 in his
native town. Each year, when he arrived,
the Kuortaneans reckoned that summer
had come.

Klemetti had been born in what was
then a sauna house, on the western side
of the town. In the woods surrounding it,
in 1903, he had a large house, Heliä, built
of local timber to his own designs.
Initially, his brother's family lived there;
for himself, when five years later he
married, he built a smaller house, Armilä

Heliä, Klemetti's summer home at Kuortane

(named after his wife, Armi, daughter of the Helsinki cathedral organist). Saunakamari, the new lakeside sauna designed by Armi, was added a couple of years later. Klemetti died in 1953; Armi lived until 1979 and played an important part in the establishment of the museum in 1957. They had no children and the estate was bequeathed to the Kuortane Society (Kuurtanes-Seura).

His own bicycle, largely wooden and now rather decrepit, leans in the porch of Heliä, as it must have done when he used it for his folksong collecting trips. The main room, to the right, is furnished much as it was in Klemetti's time – with local furniture, mostly inherited from his parents, including a suite of woven local birch, his desk (with a pencil portrait, cuttings books, photos and his glasses), a hand-painted grandfather clock that he built himself, a tapestry presented to him at the university in 1923, and on the walls photographs recording his family and events in his career: many with his choirs, looking happy enough, although he was apparently ferocious at rehearsals. On the

walls of the rear left room, overlooking the lake, his medals and awards are exhibited, among them a diploma bearing the signature, during the Finnish-German alliance of the 1930s and 40s, of Adolf Hitler; his pipes, watches and other personal items are there too, along with copies of many of the books he wrote – short stories, novels and an autobiography. A man of parts, he was also a local historian and an authority on Finnish church architecture, and his writings on those topics are collected in a conservatory room along with editions of his music (piano music, songs, folksong arrangements, hymn settings). In the kitchen, at the front of the house, there is a china service given to Klemetti by his students, decorated with his initials HK.

The furnishings here are all Klemetti's own. But those of Armilä are even more personal, for this was his wife's domain. Passing through the little covered porch, you enter the living-room, with its corner fireplace, a wooden sofa, a dining table and chairs, woven rugs and hangings, with cartoons and silhouettes of Klemetti, many photographs, and drawings and watercolours by Armi herself, including one of their St Bernard, Turvasta. In later years, Klemetti used the sauna cottage as his study: it contains the desk at which he worked, with a view across the lake, his square piano made in St Petersburg about 1800, a little bed for his daytime naps, a rocking chair and a bookcase filled with scores and paperbacks, his concert suit, and umbrellas, slippers and a fur hat, as well as numerous photographs on the walls.

Nearby, just across the road, is the Kuortane Farmhouse Museum, with buildings dating back to the 16th century; it was opened by the Kuortane Society in 1959, just after the Klemetti Museum.

Klemetti Museum
Kirkkotie 13
63100 Kuortane
Finland

phone +358/0 65 163111 (guided tour), 254473 (opening hours only)
fax +358/0 65 163300
e-mail kuortaneen-kunta@kuortane.fi

open July (other times by arrangement), Sunday 11.00–17.00

Map 13

KLYUCHNIKOV-PALANTAY

Ivan Stepanovich Klyuchnikov-Palantay was born in 1886 in the village of Kokshamarï, near Zvenigovo in the Mariy Èl Republic of Russia, some 600 km east of Moscow. He is commemorated in a museum in Yoshkar-Ola, the Mariy capital. As a child, he learnt to play the concertina and the küsle, a local folk zither. He later studied music in Kazan, and after a period of political exile obtained work as a choir director in the Urals. After the Revolution he returned to his native region, working in Krasnokokshaysk, where he taught, conducted, collected and arranged Mariy folksongs, which much influenced his own compositions. In 1924 he had a brief period of study at the Moscow State Conservatory, but he soon returned to Krasnokokshaysk and then moved to Yoshkar-Ola, where he died in 1926.

Klyuchnikov-Palantay, whose political activities led to his being highly regarded in the Soviet era, was admired for his choral conducting, his folksong research (he published several collections of Mariy music) and his educational work; he was a key figure in the establishment of a Mariy musical culture and was dubbed the 'Mariy nightingale'. There is a monument to him in the village of his birth and a street and a music school in Yoshkar-Ola are named after him. His house there in Leo Tolstoy Street, a wooden, single-storey building, was opened as a museum in 1961, on the 75th anniversary of his birth. There are three rooms, the parlour, his study and the children's room, which have been reconstructed and restored to their condition

during his years there. The displays include photographs, concert programmes and other material referring to his musical activities as well as various personal items. The parlour, with his upright piano, is used for small-scale musical events.

Dom-Muzey I.S. Klyuchnikova-Palantaya*
ulitsa L. Tolstogo 25
424004 Yoshkar-Ola
Mariy Republic
Russia

phone +7/0 8362 551919

open Tuesday–Sunday 10.00–18.00 (appointment advisable)

Map 12

KODÁLY

Zoltán Kodály lived for more than 46 years in a mezzanine flat in central Budapest, in Andrássy út, a fine boulevard in Pest with some splendid buildings (among them the Opera), in the north-east quadrant of a large roundabout now called Kodály Körönd (Kodály Circle). He moved there in October 1924 and remained there for the rest of his life. He died in March 1967. His widow, Sarolta Péczely Kodály, presented the flat and its contents to the International Kodály Society, acquired the adjacent flat and equipped it elegantly as an archive

The Kodály Archives in Budapest

for her husband's manuscripts, editions, writings and memorabilia, and in December 1989 opened the Zoltán Kodály Memorial Museum and Archives. The lower ground floor now offers a small recital room with a barrel-vaulted ceiling, seating 55, and a seminar room.

The present contents of Kodály's four-room flat strongly reflect his lifelong interests in folk music and art, literature and photography. The dining-room, giving pride of place to his beloved folk ceramics, receives visitors today as it did in his own time. Through a doorway to the right is the salon, rather crowded (as it always was), with two grand pianos, numerous busts and portraits, a colourful array of rugs, embroidered chair covers, traditional furniture, rolltop music cabinets (no doubt still full of music) and more displays of ceramics. Here, as in his study, neatly lined book-cases reach to the ceiling, requiring a library ladder for access to the upper shelves; in addition to books on music history and ethnography, the browser will encounter a rich trove of European literature and literary history. The hand-carved desk in his atmospheric study closely resembles that of his friend Béla Bartók, made by the same designer from Transylvania. Today the former bedroom serves as a showcase for Kodály's manuscripts in changing exhibitions in the tall modern display cases (one, devised by Ferenc Bónis, entitled 'A Look into the Workshop', showed his music at various stages from sketch to final publication). Also on display are his writing implements, glasses, camera, field photographs and notebooks and his phonograph and cylinders (for illustration, see p.65).

Kodály's flat is within easy walking distance of the Academy of Music, where he taught composition from 1908, when he was 27, to 1942. By the time he moved there he had been married for 14 years to a former composition pupil, Emma Sándor; in 1959, after her death, he married Sarolta. The flat served as a mecca for pupils and professional musicians. Although the wide popularity of some of his works prompted a new career in conducting, and brought in commissions from far afield, his life remained firmly centred on Budapest, Hungarian music and, from the mid-1920s, music education.

During both world wars Kodály remained in Budapest, taking refuge at different times during the second in a Budapest convent and in the opera house. In the 1940s he was actively involved in the Academy of Sciences, editing its folk music collection and serving as its president from 1945 to 1949.

Kodály pilgrims will want to seek out the reclining statue of the composer by Imre Varga, erected in the Europapark (on the western slope of Castle Hill,

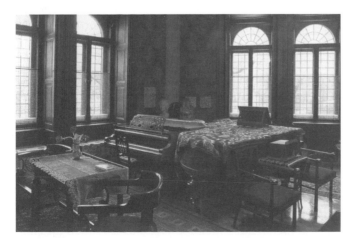

Kodály's salon

across the river in Buda) to mark the centenary of his birth. It seems apt that this passionate educationist should sit there as children play about him. In Kecskemét, 86 km south-east of Budapest, where he was born in 1882, his birthday is celebrated each year with concerts and a choral festival. Since 1975 it has been the home of the Zoltán Kodály Music Pedagogical Institute.

Kodály Zoltán Emlékmúzeum
1 Kodály Körönd
1062 Budapest
Hungary

phone +36/0 1342 8448
fax +36/0 1322 9647
e-mail kodalyzm@axelero.hu
website www.kodaly-inst.hu

open Wednesday 10.00–16.00,
Thursday–Saturday 10.00–18.00,
Sunday 10.00–14.00

Map 8

A Look into the Workshop: Exhibition of the
  Kodály Zoltán Museum and Archives
  (Budapest: Zoltán Kodály Music Pedagogical
  Institute, 1990)
Zoltán Kodály Pedagogical Institute of Music
  (Kecskemét: Zoltán Kodály Music
  Pedagogical Institute, c1990)
J. Vadas: 'The Zoltán Kodály Memorial Museum
  and Archives', *Courier Diplomatique*
  [Budapest], 2 (February 1994), 20–21

KOGOJ

Marij Kogoj, a pupil of Franz Schreker and Arnold Schoenberg, was the leading representative of Expressionism in Slovenia. By ancestry half Italian, he was born in Trieste, on 20 September 1892, and given the name Julij (to be exact, Julius Dante Aloysius). When he was four his father died and he was abandoned by his mother, to be brought up by his father's family, under the name Marij – actually the name of a younger brother who had died in infancy and with whom he had been confused. Later he lived in Ljubljana, working at the Slovenian National Opera, but his career ended prematurely, in the early 1930s, when he was diagnosed as schizophrenic; he lived on, mostly under care, until 1956.

Kogoj's father's family lived in Kanal, some 20 km from Nova Gorica in the foothills of the Julian Alps, on the Soča, which, milky in texture, turquoise in hue, winds through the town, where an ancient (and much depicted) bridge, a long single span of natural stone, traverses it. Kanal, which also represents the divide between Mediterranean and Alpine regions in Slovenia, takes considerable pride in its near-native composer: there is a bust to him, erected in 1969, in the town's main square, close to the church where he had his first musical training and the house opposite where he spent his childhood, and it now holds an annual festival – with additional events as far afield as Trieste and Ljubljana – dedicated to him, in which his music is heard alongside the work of younger Slovenian composers. And behind the church, by fragments of the ancient town wall, lies the Gotska hiša (Gothic house), where in 1992, on the centenary of his birth, a memorial room was opened to Kogoj within the local library.

The memorial room was set up by one of Kogoj's sons (he named them Marij and Julij), with material garnered from the family and others who knew him. There is an abundance of it, clearly classified and displayed, although the captioning is only in Slovene (but there are helpful, English-speaking staff). The first display case shows, in facsimiles, the various birth, baptismal and death entries that establish his true identity, and the next covers his childhood in Kanal – here the documents include school reports, some of them understandably confused because 'Marij' was long taken to be three years younger than he was. There are several portrayals of him – his passionate, inward, almost tortured appearance made him a striking figure – by local and Ljubljana artists from the 1920s, certificates of his unfitness to join the army or other organizations, and letters from that period showing his 'distress' from around the time of his opera *Črne maske* ('Black masks', first performed in 1929, recognized as his *chef d'œuvre*). One case is devoted to *Črne maske*, with a facsimile score, reviews and the LP recording, and others to his piano music and his songs; there are facsimiles of his manuscripts and copies of some of the criticisms he wrote as a young man. And there is a powerful and moving portrait of him by his wife, Marija Podlogar Kogoja, in oil on wood. They also painted on the walls of their flat.

Spominska soba Marija Kogoja

Prosvetno Društvo Soča

Pionirska 8

1213 Kanal

Slovenia

phone, fax +386/0 5305 1006

open Tuesday, Thursday 16.00–18.00, Wednesday 09.00 12.00

Map 14

M. Nusdorfer-Vuksanović and P. Merkù: *Marij Kogoj 1892–1956: Stalna razstava v spominski sobi Maria Kogoja* (Nova Gorica: Pokrajinski Arhiv v Novi Gorici, 1989)

KOSCHAT

Thomas Koschat, the Austrian bass singer who brought Carinthian folksong to a wide audience through his performances, arrangements and compositions, still has a small but dedicated following in and around Klagenfurt, on the eastern end of the Wörthersee, where he was born in Viktring on 8 August 1845. The 12th-century Cistercian monastery at Viktring is now used for concerts, but the museum honouring Koschat is in the Viktringer Ring in Klagenfurt, in a building shared with the Männergesangverein 'Koschatbund', who still sing his sentimental four- and five-part settings for male voices. The society inherited Koschat's legacy on his widow's death in 1929 and opened the museum in

1934 – almost 20 years to the day after his death, on 19 May 1914 – and, with lottery and private donations, rebuilt it in 1951 after damage in World War II.

The society also twice erected memorials in the nearby Koschatpark: the first, a bronze bust put up in 1929, had to be melted down during the war and the second, in marble, appeared in 1952. Although Koschat lived much of his life in Vienna, and died at his home at Strobachgasse 2 in the 5th district, where there is a bronze relief memorial, he spent holidays at the Wörthersee. He wrote music with local reference (for example the Viktringer Marsch 'Das schöne grüne Viktring is mein Freud' and a one-act 'Liederspiel' *Am Wörther See*), became an honorary citizen of Klagenfurt in 1907 and was buried close by, at Annabichl, where there is a memorial statue. At Pörtschach, on the northern shore of the lake, there is another memorial. On a lighter note, at Velden, to the west, there was a Koschatkeller, just as at Klagenfurt, even in Koschat's own day, there was a Koschatstüberl (inn) – to judge by a picture postcard he sent to his wife, Paula, now on display in the museum.

In the first room of the museum the walls are covered and the cases bursting with innumerable portraits, photographs of his family and friends (who included Bruckner, Wolf, Mahler and the poet Peter Rosegger), manuscripts and editions (his music appeared in colourful sheet-music arrangements and translated into dozens of languages), correspondence (the archive holds 4800 letters) and an astonishing collection of printed postcards of Koschatlieder which in itself attests to his popularity, as well as awards and the inevitable presentation items, many of which relate to his 50th birthday celebrations in Vienna and Klagenfurt in 1895. Much of the display focusses on the various Koschat-Quintetten in which he sang between 1877 and 1906 and the Kärntnerlieder (Carinthian folksongs) he composed or set.

The second of the first-floor museum rooms is a faithful re-creation, based on photographs by members of the

Koschatbund, of the room in which Koschat died. In addition to the bed, there is a guitar reclining on a chaise longue, a velvet armchair and bentwood rocker, and his desk, with recordings, banners, awards, a globe and an armadillo shell basket.

Koschat-Museum
Viktringer Ring 17
9020 Klagenfurt
Austria

phone +43/0 463 599633

open 15 May–15 October,
Monday–Friday 10.00–12.00

Führer durch das Koschatmuseum in Klagenfurt
  (Klagenfurt: Koschatmuseum, 1954)
H. Kretschmer: *Wiener Musikergedenkstätten*
  (Vienna: J & V Edition, 3/1992)

Map 1

KRÁSA

Hans Krása was one of the Jewish Czech composers imprisoned in the Nazi transit camp at Terezín in 1942; he spent just over two years there and died in Auschwitz in October 1944. Born in Prague in 1899, he was a pupil of Zemlinsky and earned some success in central Europe and the USA in the late 1920s and the 30s, particularly with his opera *Verlobung im Traum*. His children's opera *Brundibár* ('Bumble-bee'), written in 1938, was given in the Jewish orphanage in Prague in 1942 and a year later in an adaptation for the conditions at Terezín, where it had 55 performances; its production is seen as the most successful of all the cultural activities undertaken there.

At Terezín, the Habsburg garrison town of Theresienstadt some 60 km north-west of Prague, built in the 1790s, Krása was director of the music section of the group responsible for organizing leisure activities in what was presented by the Nazis as a model detention centre. Among the 140,000 people who passed through Terezín (including the 33,000 who died there), cultural activities were permitted by the authorities, at

first grudgingly and from 1942 more openly, partly as a harmless outlet and partly because it became necessary for the Nazis to present the detention and transit camp as a model, especially when Red Cross visits took place or propaganda films were in prospect. There were always enough musicians among those confined there, principally Jews who had been living in Czechoslovakia, to take part in recitals, choral performances, chamber music and even orchestral and operatic performances, as well as Czech and Jewish folk music, cabaret, jazz and other lighter genres. These are recorded in the room at the Magdeburg Barracks commemorating musical activities in the camp.

The display devoted to Krása in the music room includes manuscripts or facsimiles of several of his works composed there, including an Overture for small orchestra, Dance for string trio and a Passacaglia for Strings.

Magdeburg Barracks
Památník Terezín
41155 Terezín
Czech Republic

phone +420/0 416 782948, 782949
e-mail manager@pamatnik-terezin.cz
website www.pamatnik-terezin.cz

open April–September, daily
09.00–18.00; October–March, daily
09.00–17.30

Map 4

J. Karas: *Music in Terezín 1941–1945*
  (Stuyvesant, NY: Pendragon, 1985)

KURPIŃSKI

Karol Kurpiński was a leading figure in Polish music in the early 19th century, head of the royal chapel, director of music at the National Theatre in Warsaw for many years and conductor of Chopin's earliest concerts. A prolific composer for the theatre, he has been generally regarded as the father of Polish opera since his death in 1857.

Kurpiński was born in 1785 in Włoszakowice, a village some 70 km south-west of Poznań. The house of his birth still stands and is marked by a plaque, but he is commemorated in rooms set up in 1972 on the original manor estate. The manor house itself, a splendid building set in parkland with a large hall taking the shape of an isosceles triangle (with the platform at the apex), is historically associated with the Opaliński and Leszczyński families; it is now the regional museum and administrative headquarters. Two rooms of an adjacent building, shared with an infants' school, are devoted to Kurpiński. There are a number of display cases, with facsimiles of portraits of Kurpiński and his wife, of his music and literature relating to it, along with posters of concerts and competitions (Kurpiński was an early composer of a clarinet concerto and clarinet competitions are held regularly, in a cycle with singing and composition ones). The adjoining room features stage costumes, originally used in revivals of his operas, along with stage photographs, as well as a Pleyel piano of the period and an imaginative bust.

A plaque on the church commemorates Kurpiński's connection, and within it the organ on which he played, dating from 1750, survives.

Izba Pamięci Karola Kurpińskiego
Urząd Gminy
ulitsa Karola Kurpińskiego 29
64140 Włoszakowice
Poland

phone +48/0 655 252965, 370010
fax +48/0 655 370106
e-mail gmina@wloszakowice.pl
website www.wloszakowice.pl

open daily 08.00–15.30, by appointment

Map 10

LEHÁR

The delightful Salzkammergut spa town of Bad Ischl is situated on a bend of the river Traun and surrounded by mountains and forest. Franz Lehár (*b* 1870) was not the first composer to seek it out: Brahms, Bruckner, Carl Millöcker and the younger Johann Strauss had preceded him there, although he was the first to live in Bad Ischl. It was also the summer resort of Emperor Franz Josef (his house, the Kaiservilla, is now open to the public). In 1910 Lehár bought an impressive villa on the Esplanade (now Franz-Lehár-Kai), near the bridge, immediately opposite the fashionable Hotel Elisabeth.

The success of his *Gold und Silber* waltz (1902) and his operettas *Die lustige Witwe* (1905), *Der Graf von Luxemburg* (1909) and *Zigeunerliebe* (1910) had enabled him to acquire this attractive country residence, and it was here that most of his later works were composed. 'In Ischl habe ich immer die besten Ideen' ('in Ischl I always have the best ideas'), he proclaimed, by which he must have meant his operettas *Paganini* (1925), *Friederike* (1928), *Das Land des Lächelns* (which includes the song closely associated with the tenor Richard Tauber, 'Dein ist mein ganzes Herz') and *Giuditta* (1934), commissioned by the Vienna Staatsoper.

In the 1930s and early 40s Lehár had a second home, in Vienna, in the northern part of Nußdorf, at Hackhofergasse 18, known as the Schlößl ('little castle'). In 1944, beset by ill health, Lehár and his wife Sophie gave it up and retired to Bad Ischl. They went for treatment to Zürich,

The Lehár Villa

where Sophie died in 1947; Lehár returned to Ischl alone in 1948, and died in the villa on 24 October. He is buried in the town.

He bequeathed the villa and its contents to Bad Ischl on condition that it be preserved unchanged as a museum. Nine rooms on three floors are available for inspection. One striking feature of the villa is the omnipresent sound of water and birds. It has an air of always having been a museum (and not obviously a musical one), yet there is no real museum display to interrupt the domestic ambience. The nature of Lehár's fame dictated that he was often the recipient of lavish gifts, and accordingly the visitor encounters an eclectic assembly of furnishings, paintings and engravings, numerous signed photographs, statuary, china, glassware and a rich array of *objets d'art* (among them a Fabergé goblet given to the composer by the last tsar and a picture attributed to Van Dyck), revealing what was perhaps a rather uncritical passion for collecting.

Up the staircase to the first floor, past a stream of lithographs depicting Hungarian history, is Lehár's Big Study, where he composed and where his American Steinway grand piano and other musical furniture (an especially beautiful inlaid music cabinet and his imposing desk) are to be found. Dotted around the room are some of his numerous awards and gifts, such as the vase decorated with operetta characters presented to him in 1941 by the Hungarian Philharmonic. Painted plaster cherubim preside over the adjoining Receiving Room, with its breathless combination of flamboyant French, Italian and (possibly more subdued) English furniture. Lehár's bedroom, now known as the Death Chamber, is decorated with religious paintings and icons and the ubiquitous composer's death mask.

The Smoking Room, on the second floor, is dominated by a portrait of Lehár painted by Albert Kaan in 1932 and 18th-century Piranesi engravings. Next door is the Small Study, where he dealt with his correspondence and displayed his collection of photographs and a letter from Puccini; in the corner cabinet is a manuscript of *Der Graf von Luxemburg*. Beyond is the Biedermeier Room where the composer is said to have taken tea regularly with his wife and where his collection of elephant miniatures is still kept.

The Viennese house, the Schlößl, was rebuilt in its present form in 1737; from 1802 it was the home of Emanuel Schikaneder, librettist and first Papageno in *Die Zauberflöte*, and himself a composer (*see* SCHIKANEDER). Today the doorway is marked with relief portraits of both men, put up in 1998. In 1931 Lehár moved there from Theobaldgasse, in the 6th district, where he had lived since 1919, and he bought the property the next year; he and his wife spent most of their time there from 1938 to 1944. Franz's brother Anton Freiherr von Lehár, a general in World War I, inherited the house on his death, but not its contents, which were sold off. In the ensuing years (he died in 1962) he was able to assemble a collection of materials relevant to his brother and to some extent to Schikaneder. It became a museum in 1950, privately owned, and lovingly maintained by the nurse who saw Anton through his final illness and to whom he in turn bequeathed the property and its contents.

The commemorative material is housed in a single large room, on the first

A room in the Lehár Villa; the bed on which he died can be seen through the doorway

floor. There are further relics here of Lehár's successes: an icon given to him in St Petersburg, a set of Hungarian musical glasses, a Légion d'honneur and other decorations, a golden baton in the form of a snake, a plaque noting the 300th performance of *Die lustige Witwe* at the Theater an der Wien. There is also furniture, including his desk and his first piano (dating from 1873), and such personal items as his pocket watch, rings and batons, as well as portraits, statuettes and many photos, some of them from his early family life and his military youth but many too of the artists who sang in his operettas. Their performances are commemorated as well, in the wall displays and in cases, with programmes, handbills and scores, among them some autograph manuscript material. One corner is devoted to Anton and his military career. At the rear is a balcony, looking down over a large and attractive garden; at the front, by the street door, is a small chapel, in which Richard Tauber and his English wife were married. A little way up the street is a house marked with a plaque commemorating the birth there of Carl Millöcker. Lehár is also commemorated in Vienna at the Raimundtheater, in Wallgasse, where there is a bust in the foyer, and since 1980 by a further bust in the Stadtpark, near the Kursalon. In the 6th district there is a street called the Lehárgasse.

Lehár-Villa
Franz Lehár-Kai 8
4820 Bad Ischl
Austria

phone +43/0 6132 26992, 30114
e-mail info@leharvilla.at
website www.museum-badischl.at

open May–September, daily 09.00–12.00, 14.00–17.00 (guided tours only)

Schikaneder-Lehár-Schlößl
Hackhofergasse 18
1190 Wien
Austria

phone +43/0 1318 5416

open 15 March–30 October, by appointment

Map 1

P. Herz: *Franz Lehár: Impressions of a Visit to the Lehár Museum* (Vienna: Glocken-Verlag, n.d.)
H. Kretschmer: *Wiener Musikergedenkstätten* (Vienna: J & V Edition, 3/1992)
G. Gefen: *Composers' Houses* (London: Cassell and Vendome, 1998), 158–67

LENNON

It is impossible to visit Liverpool without being reminded of its connection with the Beatles. Arriving by air, you land at John Lennon Airport (so named in 1993), whose slogan 'above us only sky' is a quotation from Lennon's *Imagine* (1970). The airport sports a statue of the Beatle and a Cavern Suite. In the city centre, the Mathew Street area of the legendary Cavern Club was much 'restored' in 1984, to the extent that the Cavern Club is no longer in the same building. Guidebooks to the Beatles' Liverpool are available everywhere, along with an endless array of Beatles souvenirs equalled only by Salzburg's relentless promotion of its connection with Mozart. Beatles coach tours regularly depart from a car park in the Albert Dock area, where one can also tour 'The Beatles Story', which opened in 1990 and incorporates an evocation of Lennon's New York apartment. If you stop in at HM Customs and Excise National Museum (part of the Merseyside Maritime Museum, also at the Albert Dock) you can see the ten gold discs awarded to the Beatles and their manager, Brian Epstein, for *A Hard Day's Night* and *Something New* that were deemed appropriate for confiscation on the Beatles' return from the USA in 1964.

Recently the National Trust acquired and restored the childhood homes of two Beatles, Paul McCartney (*see* McCartney) and John Lennon; they can be visited on a tour that begins at another local National Trust property, Speke Hall, close to the airport. Both are furnished much as they would have been in the 1950s when McCartney and Lennon lived there. One provides an example of council housing, the other of a more prosperous middle-class community whose residents could afford relatively spacious properties with gardens and such features as Mock Tudor trim, *Art Nouveau* stained-glass windows, Art Deco fireplaces and a bell system for summoning the maid.

John Lennon, born in London in 1940, was lovingly brought up by his Aunt Mimi and Uncle George in Liverpool, who were childless and evidently glad to take him on when in 1945 his mother Julia could no longer look after him. They lived in a comfortable 1933 three-bedroom, semi-detached house in the southern suburb of Woolton, Mendips, in Menlove Avenue; McCartney remembers Lennon's aunt's house as 'posh'.

In 1955 Lennon acquired a guitar, taught himself to play and formed a skiffle group, the Quarry Men (their school was Quarry Bank High). He left school in 1957 to go to Liverpool College of Art; that summer he and McCartney became friends and fellow Quarry Men. Like McCartney, he lost his mother, who died in a road accident in front of Mimi's house in 1958. The Quarry Men became the Beatles in 1960 and had their first 'gig' at the Cavern the following February. Lennon and his school sweetheart Cynthia married in 1962. When in 1965 Aunt Mimi, a widow since 1955, sold Mendips and went to live in Dorset, Beatlemania was spreading throughout the world.

Mendips remained privately owned. On the 20th anniversary of Lennon's death, in 2000, it acquired a blue English Heritage commemorative plaque. Lennon's widow, Yoko Ono, bought it in 2002 and gave it to the National Trust. Its restoration was achieved with the help of family photographs and donations of furniture and other items that once belonged to Mimi, along with others typical of the early 1960s, supported by the reminiscences of those who had known Lennon as a child, his aunt and uncle, and watched over by Ono.

Of particular interest is the re-creation of Lennon's tiny bedroom – not much larger than the bathroom – above the front door. Every object on display there has relevance: the period furniture and furnishings, the wall posters of Elvis Presley, Rita Hayworth and Brigitte Bardot, copies of the childhood books that find reflection in his later songs, the school cap, the wireless, the 45 singles and the modest guitar. When he and McCartney wanted to experiment on their guitars – neither read music – they were obliged to decamp to the enclosed front porch with its paradoxically resonant acoustic, or they cycled over to McCartney's house in Allerton. The other rooms give context and fresh meaning to the anecdotes and surviving photographs. 251 Menlove Avenue was opened to the public in 2003.

The story of John Lennon's adult life is rehearsed in exhaustive detail in the several Beatles museums that have sprung up, not only in Liverpool but abroad, especially in Germany, which rely on recordings, photographic reproductions and collections of memorabilia (*see* McCartney for further information). The Beatles Museum in Halle displays on a velvet cushion a spoon said to have been Lennon's, rather like a sacred relic; elsewhere in the museum Lennon's erotic lithographs of Yoko Ono and himself and copies of his animal cartoons are also exhibited. While focussing on the 1960s, these museums also follow the individual band members through the post-Beatles era to the present, which for Lennon ended when he was assassinated outside the Dakota Building at West 72nd Street in New York City on 8 December 1980.

His widow still lives in New York, in one of the Lennons' Dakota Building apartments. Directly below and across 8th Avenue in Central Park is the Strawberry Fields memorial garden which she instigated, named after the Salvation Army orphanage near Mendips made famous in the 1966 Lennon-McCartney song *Strawberry Fields Forever*.

There is another perspective on offer at the John Lennon Museum in Tokyo, which opened on his 60th birthday. At 2–27 Kamiochiai, Saitama-City, it occupies the 4th and 5th floors of the Super Arena. Three zones are devoted to Lennon's childhood and the Beatles era and six document his life with Yoko Ono between 1966 and 1980.

Mendips
251 Menlove Avenue
Woolton
Liverpool L25 7SA
Great Britain

phone +44/0 1870 900 0256

open by appointment only,
31 March–31 October,
Wednesday–Saturday 11.30–15.45;
1 November–11 December, Saturdays
11.30–15.00: access by minibus from
Speke Hall, including visit to the
McCartney house (+44/0 151 486
4006)

The Beatles Story
Britannia Vaults
Albert Dock
Liverpool L3 4AA
Great Britain

phone +44/0 151 709 1963

open April–September, daily
10.00–18.00; October–March, daily
10.00–17.00

Map 5

R. Jones: *The Beatles' Liverpool* (Moreton: Ron Jones, 1991)
O. Garnett: *Mendips* (London: National Trust, 2003)

LEONCAVALLO

Brissago is a typical Swiss lakeside town, in the Ticino, on the western side of Lake Maggiore, just two kilometres north of the Italian border. In 1903, Ruggero Leoncavallo decided to build a villa there. Neapolitan in origin – he was born in 1857 in Chiaia, on the island of Ischia –

Leoncavallo had enjoyed his one great success, with *Pagliacci*, in 1892; since then he had struggled with his *La bohème* (always a second-best to the rival version) and won some acclaim with *Zazà* (1900). The Villa Myriam, named after his adopted daughter, was his country home from 1904 until his death in 1919. He died at Montecatini Terme, near Florence, where he was buried; he was re-interred in Brissago in the 1990s.

Villa Myriam, built to his specification in a somewhat eclectic style, was demolished in 1978. Leoncavallo had been commemorated there, and a statue to him stands nearby. The present museum was set up in 2002 on the ground floor of the Palazzo Branca-Baccalà, said to be the finest example in the region of the 'noble Baroque' style (the remainder of the building awaits restoration). The palace lies in a secluded little square in an old part of the town, tucked between the main street (recently renamed the via Ruggero Leoncavallo) and the lake and reached through a narrow road alongside the Credit Suisse bank.

Three rooms are devoted to Leoncavallo. In the entrance lobby display cases show various of his certificates and awards and also his metronome, along with scene sketches and the libretto of *Pagliacci*. Most of the representations of him in the museum take witty advantage of his walrus moustache, an invitation to caricature. The principal display is in the second room, with cases showing various of his personal possessions – silver, pewter, porcelain, his glasses and his cravat pins, letters, postcards, photos of his singers – and his music, with librettos for his operas (some bearing annotations), manuscript and printed scores and posters for performances. In the final room, with its Baroque painted ceiling, some of Leoncavallo's own furniture is preserved; it is not particularly distinctive but his Erard piano (substantially restored) is there, with a carpet, his clock, bookcases and a glass-fronted case, as well as oil portraits of his parents and of Leoncavallo and his wife, the singer Berthe Rambaud.

Museo Ruggero Leoncavallo

Palazzo Branca-Baccalà
via Pioda 5
6614 Brissago
Switzerland

phone +41/0 91 793 0242, 793 2288
fax +41/0 91 793 4059
e-mail info@leoncavallo.ch
website www.leoncavallo.ch,
www.brissago.ch

open March–October,
Wednesday–Saturday 10.00–12.00,
16.00–18.00

Map 6

LEONTOVYCH

The name of Mykola Dmytrovych Leontovych has strong resonances for Ukrainians. His folk carol *Shchedryk* (1916) is sung by choirs and is widely familiar. Born in 1877, Leontovych was seminary-trained; unlike his father, who became a priest, he became a teacher, first of mathematics and later of music, although he was largely self-taught – a state of affairs he made tremendous efforts to remedy, attracting the attention and help of Lysenko. In 1908 he took up a teaching post at a school for governesses and settled with his wife in Tul'chyn, 80 km south of Vinnyts'ya and about 350 from Kiev. He collected and made choral arrangements of Ukrainian folksongs, which were published after his death. In 1918 he began teaching at the Lysenko Music and Drama Institute in Kiev and at much the same time was appointed organist and director of the First Ukrainian State Chapel, which brought him opportunities to compose more ambitious choral works. With Lysenko's encouragement, Leontovych began work on an opera, *Na rusalchyn velykden'* ('On Rusalka's Easter'), but it was unfinished when on 25 January 1921 he was murdered: he had stopped for the night at his parents' home in Markivka (near Tul'chyn), where he played the piano for his family and their guest, supposedly a

government agent, who at some point in the evening demanded money and, in the ensuing struggle, shot the composer.

In 1977 the simple house in Tul'chyn, where Leontovych lived with his family from 1908 to 1921, became a memorial museum attached to the City Historical Museum. The foyer and three of the rooms tell the story of his life and place in Ukrainian music: on display are documents and photographs (both originals and copies) from his childhood; books and music from his library (including a copy of *Robinson Crusoe* and music by Glinka and Stetsenko), his American harmonium, a viola, flute and bandora; his shirt collars and handkerchief, his black-rimmed glasses, fountain pen, baton and tuning fork. A copy of the large bronze bust (1969) erected in the main street of Tul'chyn (across from the ubiquitous Pushkin monument) is surrounded by posters for performances of his unfinished opera, anniversary celebrations and *Dudaryky*, the film about his life made in the 1980s, and photographs, including one of the ship named after him. At the rear of the house his study is furnished with his Schroder upright piano and a German zither, his desk, travelling writing case, and shelves with sheet music by Lysenko and Grieg. The largest room of the house is laid out in a series of room settings of family furniture (some of it made by the father), including a table set with well-used china and – unforgettably – the sofa on which the composer was mortally wounded.

Rayonnyy Krayeznavchyy Muzey Memorial'na Kvartyra M.D. Leontovycha

vulytsa Leontovycha 8
Tul'chyn
23600 Vinnyts'ka oblast'
Ukraine

phone +380/80 4335 22750

open by appointment

Map 16

Istoriya Tul'chyns'koï chorovoï kapaly im. M.D. Leontovycha (Tul'chyn, 1990)

LISZT

Franz Liszt was one of the great travellers among composers. Were his overnight resting-places across Europe marked by plaques, like the one-night stands ascribed (apocryphally or otherwise) to Queen Elizabeth I or George Washington, those two would seem positively provincial by comparison. In Liszt's case, the habits he formed during his early career as a concert pianist dictated the peripatetic life-style he maintained right up to the time of his death. He did have some settled spells, in Vienna (1821–3), in Paris (1823–7) and, when his life as a virtuoso pianist was behind him, in Weimar (1848–61) and then Rome (1861–9); but for his last 17 years he tended to move with the seasons, with residences in Weimar (summer), Rome (autumn and winter), Budapest (winter and spring), and at the end of his life Bayreuth (during the festival).

The oldest of the buildings commemorating him, however, is at his birthplace, the rural village of Raiding, which he had left at the age of 11 when he went to study in Vienna with Salieri and Czerny. His father was a prosperous dairy farmer and an administrator for the Esterházy estates. Raiding was then in Hungary (it was called Doborján), and Liszt always regarded himself as a Hungarian, although he did not speak the language; since 1919 the village has been Austrian, in

Liszt's birthplace (lithograph by Stadler after a drawing by Grünes)

the Burgenland, where it lies some 40 km south of Eisenstadt. Liszt visited his birthplace in 1840 and gave money for a new organ; he was back in 1846, and in 1848, when he tried to buy the family dairy building, then in 1872 and finally in 1881, when at a ceremony in his presence shortly before his 70th birthday it was dedicated as a memorial to him and a plaque was erected (with aggressively controversial wording: 'Hier wurde Franz Liszt am 22. Oktober 1811 geboren. Diese Gedenktafel weihte dem deutschen Meister das deutsche Volk': 'Here Franz Liszt was born on 22 October 1811. This memorial plaque is dedicated by the German people to the German master'). It was opened as a museum in 1911, to mark Liszt's centenary, and reopened after World War II in 1951; the cottage was still the property of the Esterházy family until 1971, when Dr Paul Esterházy presented it to the Raiding community, and later in the 1970s it passed into the care of the Burgenländisches Landesmuseum. But by then the building, which dates back to the 16th century, had considerably changed. In Liszt's time it was T-shaped, with stabling and other farm accommodation, but the horizontal wing has been demolished and the vertical somewhat rebuilt.

There are now essentially three rooms. To the right as you enter is the room in which, it is claimed, he was born; the display is concerned primarily with Liszt's family and friends, with a family tree and a map of his travels. The main, central room is large enough to accommodate small-scale recitals; the room to the left contains the small organ that Liszt helped to buy for Raiding in 1840 and there is a collection of photographs of him from the 1870s and 80s. Liszt postage stamps, medallions and other commemorative items are displayed in the entrance hall.

In 1842, Liszt accepted the post of Kapellmeister at the Weimar court. On his very first visit he was taken with Weimar and wrote to Berlioz that one could breathe in the sense of its being a cultivated and artistic city. It was another six years before he gave up his travelling existence and took up residence – and then in awkward circumstances. He maintained a postal address at the Hotel Erbprinz but lived, with Princess Carolyne Sayn-Wittgenstein, in a 30-room villa known as the Altenburg, perched on the hill of that name above the city; there he installed his furniture, books, paintings and instruments, including a square piano that allegedly had belonged to Mozart and Beethoven's Broadwood. During his 12-year tenure, Weimar was visited by an unprecedented procession of the European musical élite. Despite the significance of the Altenburg, it has never been a Liszt museum.

Liszt's later Weimar home, however, the Hofgärtnerei, became one shortly after his death. Originally the court gardener's house, and for a time the palace nursery, the building in which he had a flat is in the Marienstraße, at the entrance to Ilm Park. (Immediately across the street, in what had been the house of Johann Nepomuk Hummel, lived that composer's widow and grand-

Liszt's music room, Weimar Hofgärtnerei

daughters; but no meeting is recorded – not surprisingly, for Hummel's widow held that Liszt had 'destroyed the true art of piano playing'.) Liszt's patron, Grand Duke Carl Alexander, put the flat at Liszt's disposal from 1869 and the Grand Duchess herself supervised its decoration. Liszt used it for 17 years. It was in his music room on the first floor that he held his famous master-classes, attended by a succession of young pianists including Moriz Rosenthal, Alexander Siloti, Amy Fay and Sophie Menter, on three afternoons a week, from 4 o'clock for two hours. When Liszt died, in 1886, the Grand Duke ordered the flat to be preserved and the following year he authorized its opening as a museum. To ensure the safe keeping of the large quantity of manuscripts, correspondence, documents and personal possessions, Carl Alexander established the Liszt Foundation, now based in the Goethe and Schiller Archive in Weimar. The house itself suffered damage in World War II but was then restored; the music room and study remain much as Liszt left them, while the dining-room and bedroom (the small cot bed conveying an unexpectedly Spartan impression) have been reconstructed. His Bechstein concert grand is there, along with an upright, and there are displays of some of the gifts showered on him by European royalty as well as civic honours and citations, facsimiles of manuscripts and letters, and an amusing collection of ornamental walking-sticks.

Liszt did not live elaborately: in a letter of 1871, when a flat was being prepared for him in Budapest, he specified that 'the style of my abode must be simple and comfortable, with no trappings'; he required only a large desk and a couple of Bösendorfers. That flat was in Budapest; ten years later he moved to another, on the first floor of the recently established Academy of Music in Vörösmarty utca. This one had taken two years in preparation as the furnishings were specially designed and donated by his admirers in

The former Academy of Music in Budapest

the Hungarian capital; a service flat, it was given to him in return for the teaching he offered there – and his performances, presumably, which were made particularly convenient by the double doors that led directly from his drawing-room into the concert hall. After his death, the rooms were taken over by the Academy, and in 1907 the Academy moved to new premises (in Liszt Ferenc tér, which has had a Liszt Memorial Room since 1925) and restored the building to its original owners. It later served as a coffee house, a ballet school and during World War II the offices of the secret police. It now accommodates a variety of users, among them the organ school of the Music Academy, the Liszt Archive and the offices of the Hungarian Liszt Society. Liszt's library, of some 300 books (many of them annotated) and about 2500 notebooks, is housed on the ground floor.

The flat itself was partly restored in 1986, on Liszt's centenary, and opened as the Liszt Ferenc Memorial Museum. The restoration was based on a published description of its contents at the time of Liszt's death, in a magazine article, and a detailed eye-witness account of its appearance. There are three main rooms, as well as servants' quarters: the entrance hall leads to the dining-room, with the bedroom-study to the right and the drawing-room to the left, leading directly to the concert hall. The original décor is

carefully re-created to display his musical instruments and furniture (some of the original furniture, although scattered, has been traced and reclaimed), including a desk given to him by Bösendorfer with a mute keyboard in the central drawer and a tuning fork on the blotter – objects that in retrospect have a faintly comical air. But the focus falls firmly on the instruments, all of which are kept in playing order: there are two Chickering pianos, presents from the Boston firm, and his favourite Bösendorfer, as well as a cabinet organ by Mason & Hamlin and a pianino-harmonium by Erard-Alexander. There is also a fine collection of personal items: an Abbé's hat, of black rabbit fur, his glasses and his wallet, some clothing, his travelling case with his coat of arms (also a travelling lamp and writing box), a dummy keyboard ('Stummerli') and his walking-stick, a gift from the Pope (it has yet to flower).

During the turbulent years of the mid-1840s, and again in the 1860s, Liszt paid a number of visits to his friend Antal Augusz, who lived in the town of Szekszárd, about 150 km south of Budapest, and held a legal position in the county of Tolna. Baron Augusz (as he became) was eager to involve Liszt more deeply in Hungarian cultural life. Liszt spent his 35th birthday in Szekszárd in 1846, was there again in 1865 with his daughter Cosima and her husband Hans von Bülow: he played to a crowd of 8000 gathered in his honour in the town square, moving Augusz's piano to the window so that he could be better heard.

Liszt's drawing-room in the Academy flat

He returned, for several months in 1870 when his 59th birthday inspired another enthusiastic demonstration by the townspeople.

Szekszárd still celebrates Liszt. Next to the room in which he played – it is now a conference room, seating some 200 – in what had been the Augusz house, there are two memorial rooms to him, opened on the Liszt centenary in 1986. The exhibits in the first include letters, concert programmes and tickets for events in the town, a leather glove belonging to the composer, photographs, newspapers, the obligatory plaster cast of his right hand, and copies of his books and editions. In the second is a grand piano of the 1860s by Beregszászy of Pest, a portrait of Augusz and a bust (by Pál Farkas, 1986) of Liszt close to the end of his life. The building is the old Tolna county administrative office, in Béla tér (at the junction with Garay tér); the museum was originally in the Wosinsky Mór museum, from where it is now administered.

Display at the Liszt Museum, Bayreuth

Bayreuth was not one of Liszt's favourite places: second fiddle had never been his preferred instrument. He had specifically hoped that he would not die there, in a Protestant city; but when he visited the town in the summer of 1886, three years after his son-in-law's death, for the wedding of his granddaughter Daniela von Bülow, he developed pneumonia and, on 31 July, he died (he was not quite 75; Wagner was only 18 months younger). He was living in a ground-floor flat that he had rented three times during festivals, close to his daughter Cosima's house, on what is now the corner of Wahnfriedstraße and Franz-Liszt-Straße – she was too busy during the festivities to accommodate him herself. The flat was acquired recently by the City of Bayreuth and opened as a Liszt Museum, under the auspices of the Richard Wagner Gedenkstätte, in 1993. Unlike the other Liszt museums, particularly those at Weimar and Budapest, it makes no attempt to re-create an atmosphere or to present the rooms as the composer knew them. It does however offer a pictorial

and documentary display of exceptional richness. The formidable Liszt collection of the pianist Ernst Burger forms its basis. Among representations of the great man himself – and not many great men have been so many times represented, nor so beautifully – are a bronze bust after a marble one by Antonio Galli of 1838 (a gift from Raiding) and many portraits and lithographs, including the charismatic pastel of 1840 by Charles-Laurent Maréchal, the oil and pastel of 1881 by Franz Seraph von Lenbach and the haunting 1886 oil portrait by Henry J. Thaddeus. There are numerous letters to and from Liszt, many of them unpublished (largely lent by the Richard Wagner Gedenkstätte and the archives of the Richard Wagner Foundation). Each of the five rooms, which form a more or less chronological sequence, has its own theme: the poignant death mask is of course in the room where he died, and of particular interest is the final room, partly devoted to his children and his pupils.

The Abbé Liszt, ironically, was buried in the municipal cemetery by the Evangelical Church, in Erlangerstraße, just outside the present ring road. His mausoleum, designed by his grandson Siegfried Wagner (who at one time had aspirations to be an architect) and Gottfried Semper, is worth a visit.

Liszt-Museum Raiding
Lisztstraße 42
7321 Raiding
Austria

Liszt's mausoleum, Bayreuth

phone +43/0 2619 7220, 2682
62652/29
website
www.burgenland.at/landesmuseum/raiding

open Palm Sunday–end October, daily
09.00–12.00, 13.00–17.00

Liszt-Haus
Marienstraße 17
99423 Weimar
Germany

phone +49/0 3643 545388, 545401
fax +49/0 3643 419816
e-mail info@swkk.de
website www.weimar-klassik.de

open summer, Tuesday–Sunday
09.00–13.00, 14.00–18.00; winter,
Tuesday–Sunday 10.00–13.00,
14.00–16.00

Liszt Ferenc Emlékmúzeum
Vörösmarty utca 35
1064 Budapest VI
Hungary

phone +36/0 1322 9804, 1342 7320
fax +36/0 1413 1526

e-mail eckhardt@lib.liszt.hu
website www.lisztmuseum.hu

open Monday–Friday 10.00–18.00,
Saturday 09.00–17.00 (closed early
August)

Liszt Ferenc-Emléktábla
Augusz-ház
Béla tér
Széchenyi utca 36–40
7100 Szekszárd
Hungary
(administered by Wosinsky Mór Megyei
Múzeum, Mártírok tere 26)

phone, fax +36/0 674 316222, 419667
e-mail wmmm@terrasoft.hu
website www.terrasoft.hu

open April–September, Tuesday–Sunday
09.00–17.00; October–March,
Monday–Friday 09.00–15.00

Franz-Liszt-Museum der Stadt Bayreuth
Wahnfriedstraße 9
95444 Bayreuth
Germany

phone +49/0 921 516 6488
fax +49/0 921 757 2822
e-mail friedrich@wagnermuseum.de
website bayreuth.bayern-online.de

open daily 10.00–12.00, 14.00–17.00
(July–August, 10.00–17.00)

Maps 1, 7, 8

I. Macht: *Das Liszthaus in Weimar* (Weimar:
   Nationale Forschungs- und Gedenkstätten
   der klassischen deutschen Literatur in
   Weimar, n.d.)
P. Krajasich and J. Steurer: *Liszt-Museum
   Raiding* (Eisenstadt: Amt der
   Burgenländischen Landesregierung, 1981)
M. Eckhardt, ed.: *Liszt Ferenc Memorial
   Museum: Catalogue* (Budapest, 1986)
V.-M. Lajosné: *Liszt-Emlékek Szeksárdon*
   (Szekszárd: Múzeumi Füzetek, 1986)
H. Kretschmer: *Wiener Musikergedenkstätten*
   (Vienna: J & V Edition, 3/1992)
E. Burger and S. Friedrich: *Franz-Liszt-Museum
   der Stadt Bayreuth* (Bayreuth: Franz-Liszt-
   Museum der Stadt Bayreuth, 2/1994)
N. Shrady: 'Historic Houses: Franz Liszt, the
   Composer's Restored Residence in Budapest',
   Architectural Digest, liii/1 (January 1996),
   100–03

R. Husek: 'Bevezetés Liszt Ferenc Leveleihez: a szekszárdi Liszt-kultuszról', *Tanulmányok* [Tolna Megyei Levéltári Füzetek, 6] (Szekszárd: Tolna Megyei Önkormányzat Levéltára, 1997), 299–309

G. Gefen: *Composers' Houses* (London: Cassell and Vendome, 1998), 60–67

N. Simeone: *Paris: a Musical Gazetteer* (New Haven and London: Yale University Press, 2000), 86–91

LIVADIĆ

You can't easily miss the composer Ferdo Livadić if you visit the Croatian town of Samobor, just a dozen kilometres west of Zagreb, close to the Slovenian border. The family, Austrian in origin, into which he was born owned an estate there, which he inherited in 1809, and he himself – although it was in Celje, in Slovenia, that he was born, in 1799 – studied in Samobor in his youth and spent most of his life there. The main street of the town is named after him, and so is the principal hotel, as well as the music school; and there is a bas-relief plaque commemorating him on the town hall, which isn't surprising as he was mayor, a member of parliament, head of the school and city judge. His anniversary is celebrated in Samobor in the Dani Ferde Livadića ('Ferdo Livadić days'). He died there on 8 January 1879. There is a bust by his grave and another by his house.

His native Austrian name was Ferdinand Wiesner, but during his time Croatian national consciousness was growing – he was a leading member of the group of composers associated with the Illyrian movement, composing patriotic and revolutionary songs and the movement's unofficial anthem – and he preferred the Croatian form of his name. The house in which he lived, close to the centre of the town, was built in 1772, as a kind of miniature castle (Samobor also possesses an ancient, ruined one). It became the local museum in 1949.

It serves as an art gallery, and also has displays of local archaeology and geology. But one of its rooms is devoted to Livadić. The prize item there is his Aloys Graff piano of 1820, partly because it was probably played by Liszt when he visited Livadić in Samobor. Among the other objects displayed are an 1809 watercolour of the 'little castle' and charming gold and black silhouettes of Livadić and his wife. In the showcases there are a selection of artefacts connected with him, as well as documents and examples of his music from the archive held in the museum, both printed and autograph (written in his tiny but very precise and clear hand). The museum is in effect the centre of local cultural life and is used for small-scale concerts.

Samoborski Muzej
Livadićeva 7
10430 Samobor
Croatia

phone +385/0 1336 1014

open Tuesday–Friday 09.00–15.00, Saturday and Sunday 09.00–13.00

Map 14

LOEWE

Carl Loewe (1796–1869) was born at Löbejün, about 14 km north of Halle, on the road to Köthen (then Cöthen). Initially trained to sing at the Cöthen court chapel, he continued his studies from 1809 at the Franke Institut, just beyond the city wall of Halle. Following studies with both Türk, living for a time in his house, and Reichardt at Giebichenstein, Loewe briefly served as organist of the Liebfrauenkirche (1816) before enrolling at Halle University. While studying theology and philology, he joined the Singakademie and composed his first ballad songs (op.1). In 1820 he left Halle to take up the first of a series of musical posts in Stettin (now Szczecin, Poland). He remained there for the rest of his career, composing operas and oratorios, although his reputation rests on his ballads. Loewe is commemorated in the Händel-Haus in Halle, in a display of facsimiles, manuscript songs, his autograph book and the Trangoot Berndt piano that he had at Stettin; a print of a contemporary portrait and a recently commissioned bust by Gottfried Albert complete the setting.

Händel-Haus

Grosse Nikolaistraße 5
06108 Halle (Saale)
Germany

phone +49/0 345 500900
fax +49/0 345 50090 411
e-mail haendelhaus@halle.de
website www.haendelhaus.de

open daily 09.30–17.30 (Thursday to 19.00)

Map 7

LUNDSTEN

The houses of Ralph Lundsten, the Swedish electronic music pioneer, are museums in the making. Born in 1936 in the small northern village of Ersnäs, 15 km south of Luleå on the E4, he spent part of his childhood under the wing of an uncle whose farmhouse he eventually inherited. Häärsgården, where his parents had been married and where he was born, was acquired by a devoted fan, Christina Holmberg, who has turned it into a restaurant and social centre for the village, renaming it the Ralph Lundstengården. A small room off the former kitchen (now dining-room), decorated in Lundsten's favourite bright pink, is devoted to him: on display are a harmonium and a guitar, portraits and a copy of the certificate appointing him 'Ambassador for Luleå' in 1999; there one can purchase posters, CDs and copies of Lundsten's *Lustbarheter* ('Pleasantries', 1981). The restaurant serves appropriately named dishes ('Cosmic Reindeer', 'Wood-Siren's Hamburger').

Lundsten is very much a child of his time, a free spirit and 'champion of fantasy'. Although he left home near the Arctic Circle for Stockholm when he was 15, his music reflects his background: it is more soundscape than composition in any traditional sense. It also reflects his humour, love of word play, Swedish sensuality and 'New Age' take on the world. At first inspired by Bartók's Fourth String Quartet and Stravinsky's *Rite of Spring* in the mid-1950s, he experimented with a tape recorder and a synthesizer in the 60s. In 1959 he founded Andromeda, his own picture and electronic music studio; he developed a system to produce music in an 'immaterial' 12-note scale on a television screen, and a Love Machine, which 'generates sound and light by contact with the skin, reacting to the emotional state of the performers'.

Lundsten has been prolific and successful. His output, more than 600 works, some purely electronic and others more conventional, is still expanding; he has composed for dance, theatre, films, radio and television, and his music has proved a useful adjunct to meditation and a range of therapies. His 'Out in the Wide World' is the signature melody for Radio Sweden international broadcasts. His ballet *Bewitched* is performed annually in July near Ersnäs, where a waterfall provides the backdrop for the dancers and the audience sits on rocks. In 1995 he won the Schwingungen-Preis – the electronic music 'Oscar' – and his *Joy of Being* was played at celebrations of the 50th anniversary of the United Nations.

Since 1970 Lundsten has lived and worked at Castle Frankenburg, his own 19th-century 'wooden fairy-tale mansion', which will eventually pass to the Museum of Music in Stockholm. There are plans in place to make his 'Pink Castle' a museum, with a purpose-built computer museum annexe at the back. Brightly painted, the castle is really a balconied house perched on a hillside overlooking the Stockholm archipelago. The interiors are as eclectic as his music: the main sitting-room dominated by an adult, pink patchwork-quilt-covered playpen and a giant television, a conservatory at the rear, and access from the kitchen to a small, three-storey, stained-glass-lit tower, with a meditation room at the top. Pride of place goes to his Andromeda Studio, neatly lined with complex electronic equipment (connected by 20 km of cabling) with a camera that he has used to 'play his face', a 32-channel synthesizer and the Love Machine. On the remaining wall space are framed portraits of Lundsten, set off by coloured lights and a series of 'planets' suspended from the blackened ceiling. The studio is open by appointment for study and teaching.

Café Häärs i Ralph Lundstengården
Ersnäsvägen 83
Ersnäs
97592 Luleå
Sweden

phone +46/0 9 203 1054
website www.ralph-lundstengarden.com

open Saturday and Sunday, other days by appointment

Andromeda Music & Studio AB
Castle Frankenburg
Frankenburgs väg 1
13242 Saltsjö-Boo
Sweden

phone +46/0 8 715 1437
fax +46/0 8 556 60099
e-mail ralph.lundsten@andromeda.se
website www.andromeda.se

open by appointment (+46/0 8 717 6730)

Map 13

LYSENKO

Mykola Vitaliyovych Lysenko, Ukraine's greatest national composer, is generously commemorated in Kiev, where he spent most of his life: by a museum, a concert hall, a street and a Lysenko prize for contributions to Ukrainian musical culture. The first Lysenko exhibition, with 800 items, was mounted by the Academy of Sciences in 1927 and 70 volumes of his collected works were published during the 1950s. In 1965 a statue was erected outside the Shevchenko Opera and Ballet Theatre. Elsewhere in Ukraine, his name graces the opera house in Khar'kiv, the music college in Poltava and the L'viv conservatory.

Lysenko was born in 1842. From his days at Kiev University he was involved in the nationalist and anti-tsarist movements. Although trained in Leipzig and St Petersburg, where he was a pupil of Rimsky-Korsakov, he began early in his career to collect Ukrainian folksong and when, in 1876, he was invited to compose an opera in Russian for the imperial court, he declined. He was determined to raise Ukrainian culture to the standards prevailing elsewhere in Europe. He never saw his national opera *Taras Bul'ba* staged because it was too ambitious for Ukrainian opera houses and he would not allow it to be translated (Tchaikovsky had wanted to arrange for a performance in Moscow); it eventually came to the stage in Soviet times, reorchestrated by his pupil L.M. Revuts'ky, and along with the poetry of Shevchenko it became a symbol of national identity. In 1904 he helped found the Ukrainian School of Music and Drama (later named after him) in rivalry to the Russian Musical Society School (now the Tchaikovsky Conservatory). In his last years he had several brushes with tsarist authorities and composed a revolutionary hymn; he was facing trial for anti-state activities when in 1912 he died, at the age of 70.

The first-floor flat where Lysenko lived during his last 18 years has been preserved, and the flats below it now form a museum (opened in 1980) and archive. The building is part of a compound of museum buildings occupied in Soviet times by actors and writers. Three of the six rooms of the flat have been painstakingly re-created from photographs and descriptions: the study (in which he died), the sitting-room across the hall and the dining-room. The study is furnished with an upright piano (his own was destroyed in World War II), a theorbo, a cymbalum and a hurdy-gurdy hanging on the wall, along with a bust, an icon, dried flowers and a desk with personal ornaments and his pince-nez; also a carved bookcase, a day bed, his travelling case and the original Art

The Lysenko museum, Kiev

Deco velvet curtains. To these a trunk of embroidered costumes has been added. Lysenko's own Blüthner, in playing condition, is in the formal sitting-room, along with a portrait from 1903, a gold clock and an elegant suite of furniture. There is a boudoir grand and a gramophone in the dining-room along with the dining table and chairs, a sofa and a desk; a balcony overlooks the back garden where a pear tree of which he was particularly fond still survives.

The remaining three rooms serve to complement the museum rooms downstairs. A memorial room has photographs of the flat in Lysenko's time, a pocket watch which stopped at the time of his death, a last photograph, his final notebook and documents relating to his death, along with a silver laurel wreath and funeral banners (his funeral procession was a political event, with 16,000 people lining the route and a choir of 1200). The second room is devoted to the celebrations of his centenary in 1942 and his 150th birthday in 1992. The former, in wartime, were modest in scale (stamps were issued, an exhibition was mounted in L'viv and a competition was inaugurated), but in 1992 there was a festival and a musicological conference in L'viv. In the final room there are displays of opera sets, costume designs, a maquette for a 1955 production of *Taras Bul'ba* and photographs of interpreters of his music, including the outstanding soprano Solomiya Krushel'nytskaya (who is commemorated in her own museum in L'viv).

In the main museum, the first room offers a Soviet-era balancing act between tracing Lysenko's roots to a noble Cossack family, whose coat of arms is proudly displayed, alongside the symbols of his affinity for Ukrainian folksong (a straw hat, writing box and pen, a three-string cello and a bandura/hurdy-gurdy). There is a facsimile of a polka he composed when he was eight. The room is dominated by a diorama of Hrynky, the Poltavian village where he was born. The second room, seating 60, is used for recitals. Its walls are lined with displays devoted to his years in St Petersburg, his career as a conductor, composer and educator in Kiev, pictures of the prima donna Olga O'Connor (who bore him five children: his marriage was childless) and his operas. There are cases with displays given over to his settings of the poetry of Shevchenko (more than 90, set as songs, cantatas and choruses) and the plays of his cousin Michael Staryts'ky (whose librettos for Lysenko included *Taras Bul'ba*). The third room documents the 1903 Lysenko celebrations on the 35th anniversary of his return to Kiev. The final room is devoted to his last opera, *Eneida*, and his friendships with the poet Ivan Franko and other collaborators. The archive contains rich holdings of his music manuscripts, photographs and documents.

Derzhavnyy Budynok-Muzey M.V. Lysenka
vulytsya Saksahans'koho 95B
01032 Kyïv
Ukraine

phone +380/80 4422 00291

open Tuesday–Sunday 10.00–17.00

Map 16

Yu.O. Belyakova and M.O. Holyaka: *Memorial'nyy Budynok-Muzey M.V. Lysenka v Kyevi: Fotoalbom* (Kiev: Mystetsvo, 1983) [in Ukrainian and Russian]

LYUDKEVYCH

The widow of the Ukrainian composer Stanislav   Pylypovych   Lyudkevych

(1879–1979) still lives in their house in L'viv, near the border with Poland. A leading figure of his generation, ethnomusicologist and conductor as well as composer, he was 95 when he married Zenebie Stunder, his former student and later his assistant, in 1973. Until then he had lived with his sister and since 1961 in a tree-lined street, renamed in his memory, on a hill above L'viv. There is a portrait relief of him on the house; his widow, who is preparing a catalogue of his works and a two-volume biography, lives on the ground floor and looks after his legacy upstairs. After his death the Soviet government wanted to establish a museum elsewhere, possibly Kiev, but she resisted, and the long-term future of the museum must still be in doubt.

The story of Lyudkevych, as related by his widow, is compelling. Although he spent most of his life in L'viv (he was born in what was then the Polish part of the Austro-Hungarian empire), he served in the Austrian army in 1903 and again during World War I, and was held prisoner by the Russians in Tashkent until 1917. After the Revolution he returned to L'viv and the Lysenko Music Institute, L'viv, where he had been director. He composed for large vocal and instrumental forces, including symphonic cantatas and poems, two operas, folksong arrangements, a violin concerto and two piano concertos. By marrying his wife, he saved her from imprisonment when she published a book about his music that the authorities considered subversive.

Mrs Lyudkevych maintains a complete archive of her husband's manuscripts, letters, programmes and other documents. The three rooms given over to the museum include a sitting-room with his grand piano and music library, several oil portraits, a bronze bust and the many awards he received; his bedroom is maintained just as he left it and displays a death mask and a cast of his right hand; the third room is devoted to a photographic survey of his life, supported by concert programmes and Soviet-era editions of his music.

Dom-Muzey S.N. Lyudkevycha
vulytsya Lyudkevycha 7
79011 L'viv
Ukraine

phone +380/80 3227 69612

open Friday and Saturday 14.00–17.00, or by appointment

Map 16

MAHLER

Since Vienna was the hub of Gustav Mahler's career, it may seem surprising that he is not more fully commemorated in a city so generously supplied with composer museums. Or perhaps not: the years when a museum might have been established were unpropitious for favouring a Jewish composer. A Mahler bust by Rodin adorns the Schwindfoyer of the Wiener Staatsoper, and there is a plaque to him in the Wiener Konzerthaus. Rennweg 5 (in the 3rd district), where he had a flat from 1898 until 1909 while Director of the Opera, still stands, and at the side entrance at Auenbruggergasse 2 there is a memorial plaque. His Blüthner piano (1902) is housed in Room XVIII of the Sammlung alter Musikinstrumente in the Kunsthistorisches Museum. Mahler was buried in the Grinzinger Friedhof.

There are however six other Mahler memorial sites, three of them established by the International Gustav Mahler Society of Vienna. Those three are the composing cabins, or 'Häuschen' as he called them, that he had built at Austrian holiday resorts: they are now 'Gedenkstätte', with reproductions of documents and illustrative material from the relevant times of Mahler's life. The other three are in the region, the Bohemian-Moravian uplands, where he was born and spent his early years.

Mahler was born in 1860 in a coaching inn in the Czech village of Kaliště, on the road leading north-west from Humpolec to Ledeč. (The traveller should beware of going to the wrong Kaliště, south-west rather than north-west of the town, Jihlava, where Mahler spent most of his childhood; there are some dozen villages of this or very similar name.) The original house burnt down in 1937 but the building on the site has been renovated by a Prague foundation, Musica Noster Amor, and it was opened in 1998, with a 200-seat recital hall, a restaurant and a studio for workshops and masterclasses. The village centres on a sloping green, with a small Baroque church at one end, near the birthplace, and at the far end the shell of the distillery where Mahler's grandfather and father once produced liquors. The birthplace hall is available for communal use and there are hopes of developing the distillery as a concert auditorium. The first annual Mahler Festival in Kaliště was held in July 2000.

Although the birthplace is in no sense a museum, the Czechs have commemorated Mahler a good deal more generously than the Austrians. The nearest middle-size town to Kaliště is Humpolec, about eight kilometres away, and there Mahler is celebrated in the local museum with a well-organized chronological display using glass wall panels, originally inspired by the eminent conductor Václav Neumann and set up in 1968. At the entrance there is a bust. The display begins with his family and background in this north-east corner of Southern Bohemia, moves with him to Jihlava, through his 'wandering years' to Prague, his rise to fame and his appointment in Vienna; then it pursues his travels, charting his summer escapes and his period in New York. There are many clearly captioned pictures, programmes, handbills, photos and newspaper excerpts, as well as some of the cruel anti-Semitic caricatures of the Vienna era, and photos of him in his last illness and of his death mask and grave.

Mahler was only a few months old when the family moved to Jihlava (or Iglau: it was predominantly a German-speaking town). At first they lived in a flat in a road, ulica Znojemská, immediately off the large main square; they later bought the neighbouring house, adapting it as an inn, and eventually bought the whole of the first house. This first house was in decrepit condition, and when Jihlava – with support from the city itself and from Czech, Austrian and American-Jewish groups – decided to establish a museum, under the title 'The Young Gustav Mahler and Jihlava', it was necessary to put it in a different building, about 50 metres away on a different road (ulica Kosmákova) off the square, formerly a military headquarters. There, on two floors, a comprehensive and strongly presented display was set up (by Jan Michálek), in a series of specially designed glass cases with dark surrounds, apt to the period and the music (which is softly audible as a background).

The display, rich in archival and pictorial documentation, naturally emphasizes Mahler's early years and his background in Kaliště and Jihlava. There is material on those places in the late 19th century, the family business, Mahler's mother's family, the synagogue, his schooling (some of his reports are reproduced), local traditions in military and folk music and their later echoes in his music, his appearances as a child prodigy, his student years, his parents' graves in the Jihlava Jewish cemetery, and Jihlava's reception of his music in the contemporary local press, including too a display about the celebration of his centenary in 1960 (when a plaque was put up on the house) and the interest in saving it (dating from 1989). But there is plenty too on his career as conductor and composer, the composing huts, the cities across Europe and the Atlantic where he conducted, his places of work, the Mahler iconography: altogether a comprehensive and wide-ranging tribute to this son of Jihlava.

The museum in ulica Kosmákova was set up in 1994. In 2003, when the Mahler family house in ulica Znojemská was fully restored, it was moved to the first floor there, where the original flat occupied by the Mahlers had been. On the ground floor is the Café Mahler, for drinks and desserts, and a Weinstube; there is also a conference or lecture room seating about 70 and space for special exhibitions. In the atrium there is a permanent exhibition of sculpture by Thea Weltner (1917–2000), Mahler's niece, with a spectacularly wrecked white grand piano as its centrepiece. Weltner, who herself came from Jihlava, bequeathed a number of pictures and personal objects connected with her uncle to the town, which are to be exhibited in the museum when legal difficulties over their export from Switzerland, where she died, are overcome.

In his later years, Mahler was sometimes mocked as a 'vacation composer', but with his heavy conducting schedule it could hardly have been otherwise. The summers were precious to him: he relished beautiful natural surroundings and having the freedom to compose as well as the opportunity to rest and prepare for the gruelling seasons. Up to the time of his marriage, in 1902, his sister Justine arranged summer accommodation for the family (which included his sister Emma and his brother Otto) and close friends such as Natalie Bauer-Lechner and Bruno Walter. They generally arrived at their holiday destination in June and remained until late August. While the others relaxed, Mahler maintained a strict regime, rising early and composing for several hours in complete peace, then swimming, dining and walking.

In 1893 they took lodgings in a small inn, 'Zum Höllengebirge' (now the Gasthof Föttinger) at Steinbach am Attersee in the Salzkammergut, about 50 km east of Salzburg. Mahler had a piano installed in his room and worked that summer on the Second Symphony and *Des Knaben Wunderhorn*. But the inn was close to the road and the walls were thin, so he resolved to have a 'Musik-Pavilon' built across the meadow from the inn, by the lakeside, before the next summer. It was about four metres square, with windows, a wood-burning stove and a glazed door; he installed a small grand piano, a table and chairs. When the door was closed, no one was allowed to enter and disturb him. The following summer he finished the Second Symphony there 'surrounded by flowers and birds'; the third Steinbach summer saw him

Mahler's first composing hut, at Steinbach am Attersee

complete a draft of the Third. He interrupted his idyll several times each summer, to visit Brahms at Bad Ischl and to take in the Bayreuth Festival. The Musik-Pavilon is preserved and has been renovated – having survived stints as a washhouse, a slaughterhouse and a public lavatory – and in 1980 it was declared a historical monument; but the meadow in which it stands now serves as a popular camp site for summer holidaymakers and Mahler's longed-for peace and solitude can only be imagined. To visit it, enquire at the hotel desk, where the keys are held. There are concerts in the hotel gardens during the summer.

In 1899 Mahler stayed at the Salzkammergut retreat of Altaussee, where he began work on the Fourth Symphony. Having been persuaded by his sister and friends to build a summer villa of his own, he decided on a lakeside property at Maiernigg, near Klagenfurt on the southern side of the Wörthersee. Part of its charm was the wooded hill across the road, where another composing cabin could be erected. This Häuschen was completed in time for the summer of 1900 and the villa, with a boathouse and bathing cabins, the following year. The regime was much as at Steinbach. He completed the Fourth Symphony there during the summer of 1900 and composed three of the

Kindertotenlieder and sketches for the Fifth Symphony the following year. The hilltop cabin presented a daily challenge for the cook, Elise, who had to carry his meals up along a particularly steep route so that he would not be disturbed by seeing her approach.

That autumn he met Alma Schindler, 20 years his junior; they were married the following March. They spent the next five summers at Maiernigg, where he worked on the Fifth, Sixth, Seventh and Eighth Symphonies as well as songs for *Des Knaben Wunderhorn* and the *Kindertotenlieder*; Alma's presence became essential to Mahler, who said he could compose only when she was close to his side. But not too close: for actual composition he demanded complete silence, and he would not even let her play the piano down in the house as it could be faintly heard on the hill. After the tragic death there of their elder daughter, Maria, in July 1907 the Mahlers could not bear to be at Maiernigg and Villa Mahler was sold; it is still a private residence, known today as the Villa Siegal.

To visit the Häuschen, follow the signs on the Klagenfurt road through Maiernigg and leave your car or bicycle in the designated car park. The trail (the 'Gustav-Mahler-Weg') up the hill through the pine forest is a delightful 15-minute stroll; bring a picnic for when you reach the top. The composing hut has been restored and fitted out with brightly lit displays of

Mahler's second composing hut, at Maiernigg

photographs and facsimiles charting this eventful period of his life. There is a double-opening window – not an early example of double-glazing but simply a device to allow the maid to leave his refreshments without disturbance, for him to collect as needed. But the most arresting item is the lockable metal cabinet set into the wall where Mahler stored his manuscripts at the end of each day. The view of the lake from the front windows of the cabin is still very much as Mahler would have known it. If you are lucky you will hear the cuckoos, descendants of those the composer must have heard as he was finishing the Fourth Symphony.

For the summer of 1908, Alma and her mother found a house of which they could rent a floor in an area of the South Tyrol which Mahler knew and liked, at Alt-Schluderbach (now Carbonin Vecchia, in Italy), close to the small town of Toblach (now Dobbiaco), between Brixen (Bressanone) and Lienz. There are breathtaking panoramic views of the Dolomites. The Mahlers rented the first floor of the Trenker Hof (now rechristened the Gustav Mahler-Stube), and moved in with their entourage and three pianos. Again Mahler had a cabin built, a short distance from the house; there, that first summer, he worked on *Das Lied von der Erde*.

Shortly after Maria's death, Mahler himself was found to have a serious heart condition and was advised to take life more easily; frightened of exertion, he had to give up the healthy outdoor pursuits he had so much enjoyed. Composition became more urgent than ever and the following summer he sketched the Ninth Symphony. Earlier, in New York, Alma had suffered a miscarriage and, depressed, she sought help at a sanatorium near Trento, and then again the following year at Tobelbad, while Mahler stayed by himself at Toblach or visited friends. It was at Tobelbad that she met the young architect Walter Gropius; their affair continued into July, the time of her husband's 50th birthday. It was after her return to Toblach that the famous incident occurred regarding

Mahler's third composing hut, at Dobbiaco (Toblach)

Gropius's passionate letter to Alma arriving in an envelope addressed to 'Herr Direktor Mahler'. Mahler, deeply shocked, received him, allowing them time alone to discuss the future, and silently escorted him away when Alma made clear her intention to remain with her husband. But he knew he had lost her and, desperate to recover his lost self-confidence, went north to Leiden, where Sigmund Freud was on holiday, for a four-hour consultation. He returned to Toblach and worked feverishly on the Tenth Symphony for the remainder of the summer, but it was unfinished at his death in Vienna on 18 May 1911.

The Trenker family still own the Stube. They allow members of the public to see the first-floor rooms that the Mahlers occupied, and trade on the connection with the composer, selling Mahler post-cards and small souvenirs. To attract visitors they have created a wildlife park in the grounds, which encompasses the Häuschen in which Mahler composed *Das Lied von der Erde* and the Ninth Symphony, a wooden cabin again about four metres square with views across the valley to the mountains. Visitors flock to see the deer, rabbits, chickens, pigs, owls, goats, turkeys and donkeys, as well as a bear and a lynx, and may stumble upon the Mahler cabin almost by accident among the animal houses, as too do some of the animals themselves.

Mahler is not forgotten in Hamburg, where he was in charge of the Opera in 1892: there is a plaque on the house, Bundesstraße 10, where he lived, a Gustav-Mahler-Park close to the railway station and a Gustav-Mahler-Platz behind the Opera House, where there is a bust in the foyer. In Paris, the Mediathèque Musicale Mahler at 11*bis* Rue de Vézelay offers its users displays of material from the achives.

Mahler Birthplace
c/o Jan Rod
39451 Kaliště u Humpolce
Pelhřimov
Czech Republic

phone +420/0 565 546689

open by appointment

Muzeum Dr Aleše Hrdličky
Horní náměstí 273
39601 Humpolec
Czech Republic

phone +420/0 565 532115
fax +420/0 565 532479
e-mail muzeum@infohumpolec.cz
website www.infohumpolec.cz/muzeum

open 15 April–15 October, Tuesday–Friday 08.00–11.00, 13.00–16.00 (Wednesday closing at 18.00); Saturday 09.00–11.00, 14.00–16.00; Sunday 09.00–11.00

Mladý Gustav Mahler a Jihlava
Služby Města Jihlavy
Dům Gustava Mahlera
Znojemská 4
58601 Jihlava
Czech Republic

phone +420/0 567 309232
fax +420/0 567 309038

open 15 April–30 September, Tuesday–Friday 09.00–12.00, Saturday and Sunday 13.00–17.00; October–14 April, by appointment

Gustav Mahler Komponierstube
Gasthof Föttinger
Seefeld 14
4853 Steinbach am Attersee
Salzkammergut
Austria

phone +43/0 766 3342

open by appointment

Gustav Mahler Komponierhäuschen
Maiernigg
9010 Klagenfurt am Wörthersee
Kärnten
Austria

phone +43/0 463 537226 or 537632
(Magistrat der Landeshauptstadt
Klagenfurt, Abt. Kultur)

open 1 May–31 October, daily
10.00–16.00

Gustav Mahler Komponierhäuschen
Gustav Mahler-Stube
Via Carbonin Vecchia 3 /
Altschluderbach 3
39034 Dobiacco / Toblach
Alto Adige / Südtirol
Italy

phone +390/0 474 972347
e-mail gustav-mahler-stube@dobbiaco.it
website www.dobbiaco.it

open by appointment

Maps 4, 1, 9

H. Blaukopf: 'The Cottage on the Attersee', *Gustav Mahler in Steinbach am Attersee: Documents, Reports, Photographs* (Vienna: International Gustav Mahler Society, n.d.), 3–7

H. Blaukopf: 'Villa Mahler on Wörthersee', *Gustav Mahler on Wörthersee: Documents, Reports, Photographs Relating to the Composer's Life and Works* (Vienna: International Gustav Mahler Society, n.d.), 5–8

M. Trenker: 'Der Aufenthalt Gustav Mahlers in Altschluderbach', *Gustav Mahler in Toblach* (Vienna: International Gustav Mahler Society, n.d.), 7–8

H. Kretschmer: *Wiener Musikergedenkstätten* (Vienna: J & V Edition, 3/1992)

D. Grierser: *Nachsommertraum* (St Pölten and Vienna: Verlag Niederösterreichisches Presshaus, 1993), 20–32

Z. Jaroš: *The Young Gustav Mahler and Jihlava* (Jihlava: Muzeum Vysočiny Jihlava, 1994)

The Young Gustav Mahler and Jihlava: a Guide through the Museum Exposition (Jihlava: Muzeum Vysočiny Jihlava, 1994)

J. Rychetsky: 'Tracing Mahler's Roots', *Gustav Mahler Birthplace Resurrection* (Prague: Musica Noster Amor Foundation, 1996), 12–15

A. Fuchs: *Auf ihren Spuren in Kärnten: Alban Berg, Gustav Mahler, Johannes Brahms, Hugo Wolf, Anton Webern* (Klagenfurt: Kärntner Druck- und Verlagsgesellschaft, 3/1997), 21–35

W. Herrmann: *Musik ist eine heilige Kunst: Komponisten, Dirigenten und Sänger im Ausseerland* (Liezen: Jost Druck & Medientechnik, 1999), 19–20

MANFROCE

See CILEA.

MARINKOVIĆ

Novi Bečej is in the Vojvodina region of Serbia, some 120 km north of Belgrade. Just outside it, in the pleasant village of Vranjevo, the composer Josif Marinković was born, in 1851. The town, once a trading centre for wheat, has now grown (its population is around 60,000) and Marinković's birthplace lies within its boundaries in an area formerly lived in by the richer merchants of the town and now a fairly modest suburb. The actual house of his birth no longer stands, but the building in its place, in a street called ulica Josifa Marinkovića, bears a plaque to the composer.

There are two churches, Catholic and Orthodox, in that street, and close to the former is a large school, the Osnovna Škola 'Josif Marinković'. In it is a room, also used as an office by the headmaster, that serves to commemorate Marinković. One of the leading Serbian composers of the late Romantic era, Marinković spent his childhood and part of his youth in Novi Bečej, where he organized an amateur choir when he was 15, but he spent most of his life in Belgrade, as choral conductor and teacher as well as composer. He died there in 1931.

The material stored and exhibited, which was presented to the school by Marinković's grandson, is substantial, and the ultimate intention is to create a new museum, adjoining the school grounds and close by the site of the birthplace, to show it more fully and to serve as a centre for local musical life. In the meantime, there is plenty to see in the existing memorial room. There are documents about Marinković's birth and his life, with photographs, letters, his passport, and his certificate of membership of the Serbian Academy of Arts; there are newspaper articles, original manuscripts of his songs, and editions of his works – all clearly arranged and exhibited, some of the material in framed display boards. There is a set of scrapbooks and photo albums that the visitor can leaf through, as well as portraits and a portrait relief.

When the new premises are ready, these will be joined by Marinković's own harmonium, which is owned by Novi Bečej and at present housed in the town's cultural centre. Novi Bečej celebrates Marinković in an annual festival, in May and June, called (after the local river) Oborza na Tisi.

Zbirka o Josifu Marinkoviću
Osnovna Škola 'Josif Marinković'
ulica Josifa Marinkovića 79
23272 Novi Bečej
Serbia and Montenegro

phone +381/0 2377 1041

open by appointment, Monday, Wednesday, Friday 12.00–18.00; Tuesday, Thursday 07.00–14.00

Map 14

MARTINŮ

Bohuslav Martinů is probably the only composer to have been born in a bell tower. For a decade after his birth, on 8 December 1890, he and his family lived in the cramped and austere watchtower room at the top of St James's Church (in Czech, Sv Jakuba), nearly 200 stone and wooden steps above the streets of Polička, surrounded by a narrow balcony. His father was the city firewatchman and tower keeper, in charge of the bells and the clock; he was also a cobbler – customers' shoes, along with vital provisions for the family, were raised and lowered in a basket. Martinů later commented on the significance of growing up in a 'lighthouse' (as he described it) and the effect the constant panoramic view of Polička had on his music: 'it is this space I always see before me and which I seem constantly to seek in my work'.

Visits to the bell tower of St James's are only for the intrepid pilgrim, although the view is worth the effort. In spite of the period furnishings on display in the room at the top, it is not easy to imagine family life there without obvious sources of heat or water, to say nothing of privacy.

Polička lies north of the main road from Prague to Brno, some 80 km from

The watchtower at Polička in which Martinů was born

Brno and about 18 km south of Smetana's native town of Litomyšl, near the border between the Bohemian and Moravian highlands. Once a royal dowry town of Bohemian queens, it was founded in the 13th century; many of the buildings date from its 18th-century heyday. The citizens are proud of Martinů and honour him throughout the city.

The Municipal Museum has exhibited documents relating to Martinů since the 1930s and in 1984 a permanent exhibition was set up; an audio-visual centre was added in 1990. The Martinů collection is substantial, including many manuscripts (he was a prolific composer), editions, prints, letters, his own cartoon portraits, concert and theatre programmes, playbills, maquettes, reviews, recordings, one of his pianos and a death mask. In 1949 the local music school was named after him and in 1990 a larger-than-life statue by Milan Knoblocha was erected in the park just south of the town wall. But the most powerful monument is St James's Church itself: not many composers' birthplaces can be seen from every house in the town.

As a boy Martinů had violin lessons from the local tailor. He left Polička only in 1906 to study at Prague Conservatory. During World War I he was back in the town, teaching the piano and violin at a little house at Masaryk 8, the local music school. After the war he joined the Czech Philharmonic Orchestra; from 1923 he was in Paris (returning in the summers to Polička, where he stayed in the garret of a house at Svépomoc 182), until 1940 when, blacklisted by the Nazis, he went to the USA, and later he lived in Italy and Switzerland. He was in effect exiled from his homeland from 1938. He died on 28 August 1959; in 1979 his remains were brought home and interred with those of his wife, Charlotte (*d* 1978), in St Michael's churchyard, immediately west of St James's, just beyond the city wall.

Sv Jakuba
57301 Polička
Czech Republic

open as below (guided tours only)

Městské Muzeum a Galerie
Památník Bohuslava Martinů
Tylova 114
57201 Polička
Czech Republic

phone +0420/0 461 725769
fax +0420/0 461 724056
e-mail bmartinu@policka-city.cz,
muzeum@policka-city.cz
website www.martinu.cz,
www.muzeum.policka.net

open June–August, Tuesday–Sunday 09.00–17.00; September–May, Tuesday–Sunday 09.00–12.00, 12.30–16.00

Map 4

I. Popelka: *Památník Bohuslava Martinů* (Polička: Městské Muzeum a Galerie, 1973)

I. Popelka: 'The Town of Bohuslav Martinů', *Polička: an East-Bohemian Town near the Moravian Border* (Polička: Městské Muzeum a Galerie, 1992)

N. Simeone: *Paris: a Musical Gazetteer* (New Haven and London: Yale University Press, 2000)

MASCAGNI

Anna Lolli was a young singer in the chorus of the Teatro Costanzi at Rome in 1910 when she caught the eye of the conductor, Pietro Mascagni. Not just his eye but his heart. It was in fact her own eyes, green and deep, as well as her other outstanding features, that ensnared him, and he remained their willing prisoner for the rest of his days. Mascagni, born in 1863, was then 48 and a family man; his Annuccia (as he called her) was 22. They could never marry, or live together, but in consequence he wrote her some 4600 letters, as well as numerous dedications, always stressing his undying love and her role as his muse or 'ispiratrice'– and his perpetual enchantment with her eyes. She was with him when he died, in Rome in 1945.

Most of Mascagni's possessions were lost when his house was destroyed in the bombing of Rome in World War II. But he had given Anna numerous presents, and those she treasured as long as she could. She considered, before her death in 1972, bequeathing them to the La Scala museum, but was advised that they would be lost there and would be better displayed on their own. So she left them to the parish in which she was born and where she is buried, Bagnara di Romagna, a small town near Lugo (where she died) and Imola, close to the junction of the Ravenna branch of the A14 *autostrada*. The parish had to obtain the bishop's permission before it could accept a gift arising from so irregular a relationship, but that was forthcoming, and since 1972 the town's Museo Parrocchiale has contained, on its second floor, two rooms that form a Museo Pietro Mascagni. The town also pays tribute to him by holding each autumn a singing competition, the Mascagni d'Oro.

A museum born of such passion has the capacity to be uniquely touching. This one certainly is. The letters, lovingly filed and ordered, with their envelopes, stand in a simple cupboard, whose presence curiously dominates the principal room. A few are on display, elegantly and tenderly written, describing his travels, his performances, political matters, and the events of his everyday life. (Anna's responses do not survive.) There are also many dedication copies to 'cara Annuccia' of editions of his music: among them *Isabeau*, dedicated on the anniversary of their 'first kiss and first tears', and *Parisina*, on which he wrote 'only you will understand the passion of my song'. Some of them bear Mascagni's handwritten corrections. His love for her was such that he told her, on a score of his one unqualified success, *Cavalleria rusticana*, that she inspired it, although it was composed 20 years before they met.

There are numerous photographs, including several with Gabriele d'Annunzio (who knew and admired Anna), one of Mascagni in a group with Mussolini, one of him in academic robes. An unusual series of photographs shows Mascagni playing tambourello, a game seemingly with affinities to squash but played with tambourines. Others are production photos. All bear signed dedications. Mascagni's parents and his birthplace in Livorno are also represented. One of the few photographs that show them together is a charming vignette taken in the garden of the composer Alberto Franchetti. Among the portraits are large ones done in 1938–9 by Bruno Croatto, of Anna, resplendent in a dress of white lace, and Mascagni. There are several busts and also Mascagni's only surviving death mask. In the display cases are various personal objects, among them Mascagni's pince-nez, butts of his cigars and two fans, one autographed for Anna by Mascagni and the other by D'Annunzio. Their picnic basket is of a scale to suggest substantial appetites. Mascagni's favourite, well-worn red leather armchair is preserved, and his upright piano.

The museum is likely at some point to be enlarged, and perhaps moved from its present site, in a house close to the church, the Chiesa Arcipretale. In her later years, Anna was compelled to sell some of Mascagni's more valuable gifts, including the jewelled crucifix worn by Parisina in the opera (a photo of it is displayed), a collection of fans and also Mascagni's bed; these are now owned by a Bolognese collector who has promised to bequeath them to the museum.

There was once a Museo Mascagnano in Livorno, attached to a local history library, the Biblioteca Labronica, in the Via Calzabigi, but early in the 21st century it was dismantled (to make way for the offices of an aquarium) and its collection – which includes more letters and personal objects and items referring to each of his operas, as well as a 1788 spinet that had once belonged to Spontini and the piano Mascagni used when composing *Cav* – was put into store. The local conservatory is the Istituto Musicale Pietro Mascagni. There are hopes of reopening the museum in a different building. The house of Mascagni's birth no longer stands. There are portraits of Mascagni and some documents at the Conservatorio Statale di Musica 'Gioachino Rossini' in Pesaro, of which he was director, 1895–1903.

Museo Pietro Mascagni

Piazza IV Novembre 2
48010 Bagnara di Romagna (Ravenna)
Italy

phone, fax +390/0 545 76054

open by appointment

Map 9

M. Morini, ed.: *Il museo mascagnano* (Livorno: Comune di Livorno, n.d.) [on former Livorno museum]

MATETIĆ RONJGOV

The memorial to the Croatian Ivan Matetić Ronjgov is a living one, as befits a composer and folklorist whose life was dedicated to the rebirth and the nurturing of folk traditions. Matetić was born on 10 April 1880 in the tiny village of Ronjgi, near Viškovo, some 12 km north of the Adriatic port of Rijeka (he added the 'Ronjgov' to his name later). He lived in the house of his birth until he was 14. His early career was as a school-teacher in Istria, but after World War I Rijeka was part of Italy, and he went to live in Zagreb and then Belgrade; he could return only after World War II when his home was again in Yugoslavia. He died, near Rijeka, on 27 June 1960.

It was another 20 years – the date of his centenary – before his birthplace was taken over by the municipality and opened as a memorial to both the man and his work. As an institute, it is run by one of his pupils (Dušan Prašelj) to further Matetić's own work on Istrian traditional music, especially its instruments and its distinctive scales: besides teaching and research work, it pursues an ambitious publishing programme (of both books and music, notably works by the important Croatian composer Ivan Zajc, a native of Rijeka), organizes regular national and local broadcasts, holds events for students and sustains a

substantial archive, including Matetić's own works. The institute also takes advantage of its splendid position on the hills above Rijeka – with a view of the Istrian coast in one direction, of the mountains behind it in another – to run a restaurant just below the house itself. Outside is an area that serves as a small amphitheatre for the performance of Istrian folk music.

Matetić's memory is honoured first in the continuation of his life's work, second in the maintenance of a memorial room. In the room are his harmonium, his desk, many photographs of him with his composer colleagues and with his family (including his brother, an early anti-fascist, killed at Dachau), his school reports, his correspondence and copies of his writings, his identity cards and passports, and an award from Marshal Tito that he received shortly before his death. Some of his possessions are in the main meeting room, including his piano and his scrapbooks, and there are facsimiles too of his manuscripts. There are various folk instruments, too, including pairs of *sopile* (folk shawms, mainly from the island of Krk) and bagpipes; such instruments have their echoes in his own compositions.

Matetić is honoured too in Rijeka, where he taught in his latter years. The music school was named after him in 1963 and every two years there are Matetićevi Devi ('Matetić days') with concerts and competitions, with emphasis on works incorporating Istrian folk music.

Spomen-Dom Ronjgi

Ustanova 'Ivan Matetić Ronjgov'
Županija Primorsko-goranska
51216 Viškovo
Croatia

phone, fax +385/0 5125 7340

open by appointment

Map 14

MAYR

See DONIZETTI.

McCARTNEY

In the 1960s Liverpool became a flash-point for popular music and youth culture. The four local boys, John Lennon, Paul McCartney, George Harrison and Ringo Starr, who formed the Beatles, developed their uniquely engaging style in the early 1960s by playing in Liverpool clubs, most famously the Cavern in Mathew Street, and in Hamburg. Their base, where McCartney and Lennon composed lyrics and music, and the group rehearsed, was the McCartney family home at 20 Forthlin Road, Allerton, south Liverpool. It now belongs to the National Trust, which opened it to the public in 1998.

The McCartneys had moved to Allerton from nearby Speke in 1955. The father, Jim, a cotton salesman, had had his own group, Jim Mac's Band, in the 1920s. The mother, Mary, a nurse, died in 1956 shortly after moving to Forthlin Road, leaving her husband with two sons, Paul (*b* 1942) and Michael (*b* 1944). Both boys shared their father's love of popular music and the upright piano in the front parlour was the focus of their earliest efforts in composition. In 1956 Paul acquired a Zenith acoustic guitar, which he had re-strung so that he could play left-handed; Michael acquired a drum set. Jim rigged up a system of wiring from the parlour radio to the boys' bedrooms so that they could listen to the latest music on Radio Luxembourg.

With the house empty during week-days it was perhaps inevitable that the boys, in particular Paul, might skip school to work on new songs with his friend John Lennon, who lived with his aunt on the other side of the nearby golf course (*see* LENNON). Michael, already an accomplished photographer, captured them unawares, at work together. Among the songs composed in the front parlour were *Love me do* (recorded in London in 1962) and *I saw her standing there*, which, with *I want to hold your hand*, rocketed them to fame in 1963.

Although Michael took photographs that year of John making tea, Paul ironing and Ringo Starr putting out the milk bottles, the days of normal family life in a Liverpool garden suburb were over. In 1964, to protect his father's privacy, Paul bought a comfortable detached house on the outskirts of Liverpool where Jim could retire and pursue his passion for gardening.

The Beatles' success – their tours, the albums, the 'Beatlemania' and the tidal wave of wealth they generated – weakened their connections with Liverpool. But McCartney has remained keenly conscious of his origins. He was given the Freedom of the City in 1984, and on the 150th anniversary of the Royal Liverpool Philharmonic Orchestra, in 1991, he collaborated with Carl Davis on the *Liverpool Oratorio*, first performed in Liverpool Cathedral, where as a child he had unsuccessfully taken an audition for the choir. He went on to compose a symphonic poem, *Standing Stone*, for the orchestra (1997, the year of his knighthood). His concern for British popular music and the performing arts prompted him to establish the Liverpool Institute for Performing Arts in his former grammar school. He returned to perform at the Cavern Club in 1999.

Forthlin Road is part of the Mather Avenue estate. Like all the 330 houses on the estate, the mid-terrace house at no.20 was built to a high standard, down to the ebony doorknobs and solid brass fittings. The McCartneys were the second tenants; only one other family, the Joneses, lived there before its acquisition by the National Trust in 1995. Throughout the Jones's tenure the house was an unofficial place of pilgrimage for Beatles fans; Mrs Jones handed out snippets of the McCartneys' old net curtains as souvenirs.

The National Trust has faithfully restored the small two-storey house to its 1952 character as an example of enlightened post-war housing. At the same time, they have sensitively commemorated the McCartney family's residence there, echoed in Michael McCartney's photographs on the walls (including Jim stirring the 'smalls' in a pail of soapy water,

Paul playing his guitar in the garden or shinnying up the drainpipe on the back of the house). The period furnishings are carefully chosen on the basis of surviving evidence. The domestic ambience is interrupted only by the presence of display cases (with items lent by the Beatles' biographer, Hunter Davies) in the dining-room at the back, once the band's rehearsal room. The 35-minute audio tour includes reminiscences from the brothers and musical excerpts. Evocative yet understated in presentation, the house nevertheless provides a strikingly intimate, down-to-earth perspective on the origins of a contemporary British musical icon.

The Beatles are commemorated elsewhere in Liverpool. The city museum and galleries collectively known as National Museums Liverpool own Beatles artefacts and often mount exhibitions of the most famous of all pop groups. 'The Beatles Story', which opened in 1990 in the Britannia Vaults of the Albert Dock, recounts at length the group's career. There are re-creations of the *Mersey Beat* office, Mathew Street, the Cavern, Epstein's Liverpool record shop, Abbey Road Studios, the interior of a transatlantic aeroplane and the apartment in the Dakota Building in Manhattan where Lennon lived. The displays include exhaustive chronologies, historic film footage, recordings (notably the piercing sound of screaming female fans) and photographs and displays of memorabilia. The only real Beatles artefacts are the trademark collarless jackets (silver, with black velvet trim), authenticated by the labels sewn inside by their tailor; also of special interest is the 1967 Mellotron and the recording equipment from Abbey Road.

The particular nature of the Beatles' fame has led to the establishment of a number of dedicated museums, often the work of a single passionate enthusiast, and usually based on photographs, recordings, publicity material and occasionally minor memorabilia. The most important European one is the Beatles Museum in Halle (Alter Markt 12, 06110

Halle/Saale; phone +49/0 345 290 3900), originally set up in Cologne in 1989, closed in 1999 and reopened in the larger Halle premises the next year. Other German ones are at Gemmerich (Gartenstraße 17, 56357 Gemmerich; phone +49/0 6776 1276), Neuss (Michaelstraße 64, 41460 Neuss am Rhein; phone +49/0 2131 1769970) and Siegen (Sohlbacher Straße 24, 57078 Siegen; phone +49/0 2718 909770); there is another in the Netherlands, at Alkmaar (Laat 28–39, 1811 Alkmaar; phone +31/0 725 610480), and one in Italy, at Brescia (via Trieste 40, 25100 Brescia). There are further Beatles museums in the USA and New Zealand and several 'virtual', on-line 'museums'.

20 Forthlin Road
Allerton
Liverpool L18 1YP
Great Britain

open by appointment only,
31 March–31 October,
Wednesday–Saturday 11.30–15.45;
1 November–11 December, Saturdays
11.30–15.00: access by minibus from
Speke Hall, including visit to the Lennon
house (+44/0 151 486 4006)

The Beatles Story
Britannia Vaults
Albert Dock
Liverpool L3 4AA
Great Britain

phone +44/0 151 709 1963

open April–September, daily
10.00–18.00; October–March, daily
10.00–17.00

Map 5

R. Jones: *The Beatles' Liverpool* (Moreton: Ron Jones, 1991)

O. Garnett: *20 Forthlin Road* (London: National Trust, 1998)

MELNGAILIS

On the road between Limbaži and Vidriži, some 60 km north-east of Riga, lies the village of Igate, where the parish school in which Emilis Melngailis was born in 1874 still stands. The original single-storey building of 1868 had a further storey added in 1904. The school closed in the 1950s; now it commemorates the composer, who died in 1954, and at the same time serves as a local history museum, re-creating a classroom and incorporating the surrounding fields and a barn displaying farm implements. The museum opened in 1984.

Melngailis is as important in Latvia for his pioneer collecting of folk music as for his work as a composer. His life is chronicled in the exhibition that lines the classroom walls and overflows into three further rooms. Music was important to his father, who taught there. On display are photographs; documents of all sorts, including correspondence and his own newspaper articles and reviews; his Latvian folksong field notebooks and a map of where he collected folk music; his own collection of folk instruments together with his detailed drawings of instruments he saw and heard; his editions of folksongs and dances; programmes from all over the world of Latvian song festivals in which he took part, and awards he received; his chess set and fish-scaler (he was a keen angler) and his baton.

In his many roles – as composer, ethnomusicologist, professor at the Latvian Conservatory in Riga and conductor of his own choir and numerous folksong festivals – he played an active and nurturing role in the cultural life of his country during a period when it was struggling to gain its own identity. On the centenary of his birth a plaque was erected on the school, and nearby a small memorial garden adorned with a characterful bust of Melngailis was dedicated to his memory.

Emila Melngaila Memorialais Muzeis
Melngaili
Limbažu rajons
4013 Vidriži
Latvia

open Wednesday–Saturday 10.00–18.00
Map 2

MENDELSSOHN

In the autumn of 1845, Felix Mendelssohn and his family rented a spacious first-floor flat in a newly built block at Königstraße 3, now Goldschmidtstraße 12, just outside the old centre of Leipzig but only a short distance from the Gewandhaus, where he had been music director since 1835. His contract with the orchestra required him to be in Leipzig for six months of the year; he spent his remaining time in Berlin and travelling between conducting engagements (some in Britain, where he was extremely popular). Prematurely worn out by this arduous regime, and depressed at the early death of his much-loved sister Fanny, Mendelssohn, born in Hamburg in 1809, died at home in Leipzig in 1847, 38 years old, surrounded by his wife and their five young children.

On 4 November 1997, the 150th anniversary of his death, the building where they had lived during his last two years was opened to the public as a museum. Its transformation from a derelict building to a fully restored one was part of a larger renewal of Leipzig. Goldschmidtstraße 12 is one of the oldest surviving buildings in the city and an important example of its architectural heritage. Surviving original features such as the staircase and floorboards, and evidence of the original decorative paintwork – together with the fact that Mendelssohn lived there – made it specially worthy of restoration.

The museum occupies only the Mendelssohn flat, but the whole house is given over to music in one way or another. On the ground floor is the music faculty library of the University of Leipzig; the second is shared by the Gewandhaus Orchestra administration and the International Mendelssohn Foundation; the third is occupied by the Institut für Musikwissenschaft; and the fourth serves as the flat of the current Gewandhaus music director. At the rear of the building, the former carriage house and stables now form a lecture theatre set in a garden.

A long central corridor runs the length of the rectangular flat, which is reached by the central staircase, accessible through the entrance at the rear of the building. The old servants' quarters now house the reception and amenities while the two nursery rooms, the dining-room and the master bedroom are used for displays. The bedroom anteroom com-memorates Mendelssohn's death (his funeral service, concluding with the final chorus of Bach's *St Matthew Passion*, took place in Leipzig, but he was buried in the family vault in Berlin).

The story of Mendelssohn's life is presented on a series of beautifully designed glass panels, balancing high-quality reproductions with text. In the centre of the nursery rooms, glass cases display a small number of carefully chosen letters, manuscripts and early editions, on loan from public and private collections; in the second of the two rooms is a piano with Mendelssohnian associations, lent by the university, and a fine portrait of the composer. The master bedroom is reserved for temporary exhi-bitions; the inaugural one was of Mendelssohn's watercolours from his 1847 Swiss holiday.

The living-rooms and Mendelssohn's study have been re-created with original furniture and furnishings, which had previously been on display in the Leipzig Rathaus, including Mendelssohn's writing lectern, the painted wood and leather trunk he was given by English admirers and an imposing bust of his grandfather Moses Mendelssohn. The study design draws too on a watercolour of 1847 by Felix Moscheles. As when the Mendelssohns lived there, the music salon remains, equipped with keyboard instru-ments, and seating for 70. Jenny Lind probably sang there in December 1845; Robert Schumann, Joseph Joachim and Richard Wagner were visitors in 1846.

Mendelssohn's tenure in Leipzig was eventful. He advanced the prestige of the

Mendelssohn's study in Leipzig

orchestra and the status of the players, and was deeply involved in the establish-ment of the Conservatory. He was among the first to promote orchestral music of the past, along with new music by Berlioz, Weber, Schumann and others. During his last two years, in spite of failing health, the birth of his two youngest children and his sister's death, he found time to produce organ sonatas, the oratorio *Elijah* and the String Quartet in F minor, and to make a start on an opera. He also published arrangements and transcriptions of Bach and, for the Handel Society in London, a performing edition of *Israel in Egypt*.

This new commemoration of Mendelssohn in Leipzig removes the shadow cast in 1936 when his statue in front of the Gewandhaus, erected in 1892, was destroyed. Annual Mendelssohn festivals are planned for 29 October to 1 November in addition to weekly concerts and occasional conferences at Goldschmidtstraße 12. The International Mendelssohn Foundation, which was established in 1991, intend the building to endure as a living cultural centre.

Mendelssohn-Haus
Goldschmidtstraße 12
04103 Leipzig
Germany

phone +49/0 341 127 0294
fax +49/0 341 211 5288
e-mail ims@mendelssohn-stiftung.de
website www.mendelssohn-stiftung.de

open daily 10.00–18.00 (concerts,
Sunday at 11.00)

Map 7

Museum in the Mendelssohn-House: Catalogue
for the Permanent Exhibition (Leipzig:
Internationale Mendelssohn-Stiftung, [1997])

MEYTUS

The city of Kirovohrad, formerly
Yelizavetgrad, some 300 km south-east of
Kiev, is the birthplace of two composers,
one Polish and the other Ukrainian:
Karol Szymanowski (1882–1937; *see*
SZYMANOWSKI) and Yuly Sergeyevich
Meytus (1903–97). Meytus was born at
Dzerzhynsky vulytsya 65 in a red-brick
house, now a music school and museum
– though not to Meytus – across the
street from the synagogue his family
attended. He became a concert pianist
and much honoured composer of some
15 operas, many of them on patriotic
themes, written between 1918 and 1997,
as well as film music, symphonic suites,
piano music and folksong arrangements.
He died in Kiev, where he lived after the
end of World War II.

As early as 1974, museum displays
devoted to Meytus, to which he generously contributed, were installed in a
recital room at Kirovohrad Music School
no.2. At the beginning of the new century
the exhibition of photographs, manuscripts, editions, recordings, letters,
newspaper articles, posters and personal
effects, including his Meerschaum pipe
and ashtray, glasses, multicolour biro and
blotter, was moved to a longer-term
home in the local museum.

Memorial'na kimnata Yu.S. Meytusa
Derzhavnyy Kirovohrads'kyy Muzey
Kul'turny Imeni Shymanovs'koho
vulytsya Dzerzhyns'koho 65
25006 Kirovohrad
Ukraine

phone +380/80 522 246251

open Monday–Friday 09.00–16.00

Map 16

MILOŠEVIĆ

As both composer and scholar, Vlado
Milošević was a central figure in the
music of Bosnia and Herzegovina during
much of the 20th century. He was born in
1901 in the city of Banja Luka, now the
capital of the Republika Srpska within
Bosnia and Herzegovina, and he spent
most of his working life there, at the
school of music and the museum of
Bosnian folk studies. He was active too as
a choral conductor. His compositions,
which number over 500 and include the
first Bosnian opera, strongly reflect in
their style his work as a student of local
folk music traditions.

Milošević died in Banja Luka in 1991
and is remembered locally with affection
and some reverence. The house in which
he lived (the house of his birth no longer
stands), owned municipally and now
occupied by the local Academy of
Sciences, bears a plaque; a festive concert
('Days of Vlado Milošević') takes place
each year on his birthday, and on his
centenary in 2001 a group of professors
at the Academy of Arts wrote a series of
works in homage to him.

He was founder of the local music
school, but it is at the newer Academy of
Arts, which is part of the university, that
he is now commemorated, in a room
dedicated to his memory. There are many
photos – of the man himself, of folk
musicians and their instruments – as well
as his academic diplomas and his
membership of the Academy. Among the
more personal items are his desk and
chair, his wedding chest, his bookcase
and a part of his library.

Akademija Umyetnosti
Vidovdanska 45
78000 Banja Luka
Bosnia and Herzegovina

phone +387/0 5121 3040
fax +387/0 5121 3039
e-mail aubl@inecco.net
website www.vladomilosevicrs.ba

open by appointment

Map 14

MOKRANJAC

More than any other composer, Stevan Mokranjac is reckoned the father-figure of Serbian music, and revered and remembered warmly. Born in 1856, he underwent a fairly conventional training for a musician born on the edges of the Austro-Hungarian empire, studying first in the local capital, Belgrade, and later in Munich, Rome and Leipzig. From 1887 he lived in Belgrade, where he was conductor of the city's choral society, founder of the Serbian School of Music (now called the Mokranjac School) and the Serbian String Quartet (in which he played the cello). He was also an assiduous collector and analyst of folk music, from Serbia and all the neighbouring Slav regions, and he wove Serbian folksong into his own compositions, of which the central body is a series of 15 *Rukoveti* ('Garlands'), groups of choral pieces that make imaginative use of folk melodies and rhythms. No less admired are his contributions to the repertory of the Serbian Orthodox Church. He died in Skopje in 1914.

Mokranjac was born in Negotin, a modest-sized town – then of about 300, now about 20,000 – in the remote extreme east of Serbia, close to the point where Romania, Bulgaria and Serbia meet. It is about 250 km by road from Belgrade, though the route through mountainous country is circuitous. Negotin lies about six kilometres from the Danube, in a valley, and until flood barriers were in place it was an insalubrious area and often found itself an island. The region was freed from Ottoman rule only in 1833 and there are many relics of earlier times, among them some remarkable carved gravestones in the churchyard close to the Mokranjac house, at a church where at one time he directed the music.

Mokranjac's father died two days before he was born. The prosperous owner of a restaurant, in 1850 he had built a substantial house; the family remained in it, though in increasingly straitened circumstances, until 1883. Thereafter the roads nearby were redesigned and other property was built around it, in effect blocking off the original frontage. In 1964 the inside of the house was restored and adapted to its use as a museum to the composer and of 19th-century life, and as a musical centre.

As remodelled, the house represents not so much a re-creation of Mokranjac's childhood home but an authentic example of Serbian rural architecture, with an interior in the 'Moravska' manner (Moravian influence is marked in this part of the country). The entrance, inevitably, is from what was originally the rear, up an outdoor staircase – in the yard there is a striking statue of Mokranjac, erected in 1981 to mark the 125th anniversary of his birth – and one enters first the kitchen, with its corner fireplace and stove. The dining-room is

Mokranjac's birthplace and statue, Negotin

furnished and fitted out as it might have been by his father, with carved chairs, a samovar, silver and glass, clocks and a mirror, and, in the Serbian tradition, with an icon by a well-known painter of the saint (St Nico) adopted by the family.

In the drawing-room – originally the main bedroom – are Mokranjac's own grand piano and his cello, and items of furniture and furnishings relating to his life: a ten-sided inlaid table given to him in Turkey, a black carved piano stool made by his wife Marija (she had been a member of his Belgrade choir, 20 years his junior), a floral encrusted vase that had been presented to him, a folk-style crocheted table cover. The central hall has photos and portraits, including some of his string quartet. There are also photos of his family at various stages. Some of the original walls were removed to create a large concert and display room. In it is a table given to him by the Turkish Sultan, his desk with his inkwell and ashtray, a model lighthouse, encrusted in laurel, presented to him by the Belgrade choral society, with a brick representing each of his works, and the Bösendorfer piano bought for the music school that Mokranjac founded. There are also original portraits of him and his wife. On the walls are informative display boards, in Serbian. On the walls of a further small room are pictures of his favourite composers, along with a cupboard from his Belgrade flat with his personal, non-musical library. All the contents of the museum, apart from items that were Mokranjac's own, were donated by the people of the Negotin area. His memory is celebrated at Negotin each September, in the 'Mokranjac Days', founded in 1965 and organized from the house next to the museum.

Rodna Kuća Stevana Mokranjca
Vojvode mišića 8
19300 Negotin
Serbia and Montenegro

phone +381/0 1954 4266

open Monday–Friday 08.00–18.00,
Saturday 10.00–18.00, Sunday 10.00–13.00

Map 14

D. Despić: *Mokranjčevi Dani 1966–1990* (Negotin: Mokranjčevi Dani, 1990) [in Serbian and English]

MONIUSZKO

In Poland, no composer bar Chopin is taken more seriously as a national figure than Stanisław Moniuszko. Composer of the first national Polish opera, *Halka*, he is commemorated by a memorial at the Grand Opera and Ballet Theatre in Warsaw, by a festival at Kudowa Zdrój, by a singing competition in Warsaw and by Moniuszko societies in Poland and Boston; there has even been talk of having him canonized by the Polish Pope. There is an Estonian trawler named after him, too, and a foundation in Tokyo. Trained in Berlin, Moniuszko spent 17 years (1840–57) working in Wilno (now Vilnius, capital of Lithuania) as organist of St Catherine's, where his house in Vokiečiu gatvė is marked with a plaque and there is a bust of him in a tiny park in the nearby Vilniaus gatvė. He then moved to Warsaw, where he died in 1872. There is no museum or memorial place to him in Poland (the society dedicated to him in Warsaw includes the word 'museum' in its formal title but it is not a museum and has no display or public premises).

But there is one in Belarus. Moniuszko was in fact born (in 1819) not in Poland but in what was then Belorussia, where his family had a large estate, Ub'el, some 50 km south-east of Minsk. His ancestry was mixed. His grandfather, Polish but of Italian extraction, was the richest man of his day in the country. At the age of 50 he married the daughter of a Belorussian civil servant and they had 17 children (four of the sons, educated at Wilno University, fought on Napoleon's side in the 1812 war). Each son was given an estate: Moniuszko's father – who lost an eye from plague but was a talented amateur artist – got Ub'el. His wife, of

Belorussian and Armenian descent, was the first music teacher of her son, who went to school first in Warsaw and then in Minsk (there is a plaque to him on the Polish gymnasium, one of the city's few older buildings to have survived).

The region was the scene of fierce fighting in World War II and the manor house where Moniuszko was born was flattened; the grounds are now occupied by a sanatorium and a children's holiday camp. The site of the actual house was uncovered in the 1960s by a Polish archaeologist, Marion Fuchs, who in 1969 (the composer's 150th anniversary) was instrumental in the erection of a monument there. His birthday is celebrated on the site each year. There are plans for building a museum and a concert hall, involving Polish government agencies and the Belarus Ministry of Culture, but at the moment the forest is undisturbed apart from indications of where the house stood.

However, in the nearby village of Azernï (or Ozernïy: the name, 'lakes', notes the dozen artificial lakes developed there), there is a small but attractively laid out museum to Moniuszko (or Manyushka, as his name reads in Belarus); to reach it by road, take the A4 (A244) out of Minsk and turn right on the 9932 towards Cherven'. The museum is housed in the local school, formerly the teacher's quarters on the ground floor.

The first of the four rooms commemorates his childhood years, with attractively arranged reproductions of some of his father's drawings from the 1830s. The years at the Academy in Berlin and as a practising musician in Vilnius and Warsaw are evoked in the second and third rooms, with prints, drawings (among them a charming one of 1842 with his future wife, and some of members of his Warsaw circle) and title-pages of his publications, some of them in facsimile, as well as posters, handbills and librettos. On the upper walls are what is in effect a frieze of reproductions of prints of musical buildings – theatres, churches, conservatories – in the cities

where his music was heard, and scenes from *Halka* (his most famous and most nationalist opera) and *Straszny dwór* ('The Haunted Manor', also still admired and revived). There are opera costumes from Warsaw, editions, recordings and books. Most of the final room is devoted to Moniuszko's later reception. There is a newspaper obituary and an account of his funeral, said to have been attended by 100,000 people.

Muzey Manyushki
Azernï
Cherven'skiy region
223213 Minskaya oblast'
Belarus

phone +375/0 214 38625

open by appointment 09.00–17.00

Map 16

MOZART family

The commemoration of Mozart, very much a family affair, provides a true reflection of his predominant image over the last two centuries as a prodigiously gifted youngster. There are houses dedicated to the memory of his father and to his mother and his sister. The two major museums to Mozart himself, both in Salzburg, enshrine his boyhood years and his period as a young Konzertmeister in his father's house. Only those in Vienna and Prague are concerned with his adult life and his greatest music.

The central, the oldest and the most famous of the Mozart museums is of course the one in his Geburtshaus, the house, close to the centre of the old city of Salzburg, in which, in 1756, he was born. It stands in the Getreidegasse, a busy commercial street parallel to the river Salzach, just two rows of buildings above it and not far from the bridge across to what was then the newer part of the city. Behind the Getreidegasse was (and is) a market place, the Kollegienplatz, now the Universitätsplatz, with the University Church across; further back was the huge,

The Mozart Geburtshaus, Salzburg

italianate Cathedral, adjoining the Archbishop's Residenz, close to the Franciscan Church and, behind that, St Peter's Abbey. It was a convenient situation for Leopold, as a court violinist, who had lived there since his marriage to Maria Anna Pertl in 1747. The house may date back to the 12th century although firm documentation exists only from the 15th.

The Getreidegasse house belonged in Mozart's time to the Hagenauers, a mercantile family, friends and landlords to the Mozarts. A centenary exhibition was held there in 1856, and in 1880 the Internationale Stiftung Mozarteum, formed in 1870, set up a Mozart museum – the first museum in a composer's former house. The whole building was acquired in 1917, not only the frontage to the Getreidegasse but also the rear portion, overlooking the Universitätsplatz. In Mozart's time the front of the house had decorative Rococo window frames, matching those on the Universitätplatz; now they are more austere.

Entry is through the arched doorway on the Getreidegasse, then up the stairs to the third floor, where the Mozarts had their quite modest apartment. It consisted then of a small ante-room, opening on to a living-room-cum-music-room, then a bedroom and a small study at the rear; the kitchen was separate, accessible from the landing, where there are portraits of the Hagenauers and showcases with copies of Leopold Mozart's letters to them. The ante-room display is concerned chiefly with Leopold and his publications, but there is also a copy of a minuet that Mozart wrote when he was five. In the main room are showcases with items to do with the Mozarts' early travels – letters, diaries, music – and several portraits of Mozart as a child (some of them dubious), as well as his child's violin and illuminated panels showing each of the four family members on which their lives are outlined. In the bedroom are Mozart's violin and viola, his travel clavichord, and his Walter piano of about 1780 or a close replica of it (the original is sometimes kept in the Wohnhaus, sometimes here). In the rear room are various personal items, his snuffbox, locks of hair believed to be his, ornamental buttons and other trinkets; also portraits relevant to his later life and beyond – his wife Constanze, their sons, her second husband.

In what was originally a separate flat at the rear, there are informative displays about the Salzburg of Mozart's day. One room is given over to the church and its dominant role in the city – Mozart's own ruling prince-archbishops are there, along with prints of the city's numerous

Mozart's piano and violin, in the Geburtshaus

churches. Another room is devoted to the family's friends and patrons in Salzburg; the third has an informative display about day-to-day life in 18th-century Salzburg.

Visitors now descend to the second floor, fronting on the Getreidegasse, passing through the museum shop into a series of exhibitions. One is concerned with Mozart's early stage works – copies of music, correspondence, handbills, costumes, maquettes of his operas showing historical and modern production styles. Then down another level, to the first floor, where the Hagenauers lived: one room, 'Everyday Life of an Infant Prodigy', chiefly treats of the travels (prints of England and Italy, travel books, letters, travelling bags, part of a coach), another, 'Everyday Life at Home', with a contemporary bed, essays on domestic life in Salzburg (food, hygiene and so on) and the four famous portraits of the family. At the front a room is furnished in 18th-century bourgeois style, perhaps representing a somewhat more elegant way of life than the Mozarts would have enjoyed.

The Getreidegasse apartment grew too small for the Mozarts as the children matured (they 'cannot go on sleeping like soldiers', Leopold wrote to his wife). In 1773 the family moved across the river, a distinct leg-up socially speaking, to the Hannibalplatz, now the Makartplatz. Here they took an apartment in the Tanzmeisterhaus, near the Trinity Church (Dreifaltigkeitskirche), just across from the theatre (then as now). The building, which had stood at least since the early 17th century, had once been owned by a Frenchman who taught dancing, including etiquette and courtly manners. One room was still employed for balls and another had been used by Salzburg University. The Mozarts rented an eight-room flat on the first floor, decidedly large for a family of four, with their servants, but it allowed them to accommodate resident pupils and, in the spacious Tanzmeister-Saal, to demonstrate and sell musical instruments. There was a garden at the rear.

This building was labelled 'Mozarts Wohnhaus' in 1856, on the centenary of Mozart's birth; in 1905, in the interests of stricter veracity, an 'L.' was added at the front – for Wolfgang himself lived there only from late 1773 to 1777 and 1779 to 1780, whereas Leopold was there until his death in 1787 (see p.26). The first of the few World War II bombs to land on Salzburg demolished much of it, in 1944, and after the war half the site was taken over for an office block. But the Internationale Stiftung Mozarteum acquired it in 1955 and eventually, with Japanese help, demolished the office block and built a replica of the original house, or at least its external façade, in the same peach colour as in the 18th century and with the same type of larch-shingle roof. On 27 January 1996, the 240th anniversary of his birth, it was formally opened as a second Mozart museum.

This is a modern museum, with audio handsets (in six languages), activated by infra-red transmitters, with an informative commentary and with musical illustrations carefully matched to the exhibits – facsimiles and early editions as well as portrayals of the people who impinged upon Mozart's life and activities. The original Tanzmeister-Saal is a splendid room, looking out over the Makartplatz; its walls are restored to the original pale grey and green. On the long wall is the

Tanzmeister-Saal in the Mozart Wohnhaus

large and famous portrait of the Mozart family, attributed to J.N. della Croce, showing Mozart and his sister at the piano, Leopold with his violin, and a picture of his mother on the wall behind – it was painted in 1780–81, after her death. Mozart's Walter piano or its replica is there, with other keyboard instruments more or less of the time, including a harpsichord, an organ and a small domestic fortepiano. A wall display commemorates the Mozarts' favourite garden game, shooting bolts at targets, and in the showcases are music (printed and manuscript reproductions) and letters germane to the earlier years Mozart spent in the house, including divertimentos, serenades and concertos of the mid-1770s.

What was originally the family living accommodation opens off the Tanzmeister-Saal. The three rooms at the front of the building commemorate in turn Wolfgang, Leopold and Nannerl. In each there is a central display in one or more giant glass pyramids or obelisks, the motif of the museum. The first room is concerned mainly with Mozart's music for the Salzburg church and court, including *Il rè pastore*, and the works from after his 1777–8 journey to Paris; the letter from Paris telling of his mother's death is reproduced. The objects shown include his sugar and tea boxes.

In Leopold's room there are two obelisks, sitting on piles of giant books and containing others from his large and learned library; there are court records and correspondence, as well as pictures to illustrate his life as deputy Kapellmeister at the court. Nannerl's room has some of her jewellery, letters, extracts from her diaries, and her portrait as the wife, from 1784, of Baron Johann Baptist von Berchtold zu Sonnenburg along with his. It commemorates too their son, Mozart's nephew, who spent some years in his grandfather's house.

One room is a re-creation of the family's living quarters, to show something of the ambience in which the Mozarts lived; it seems surprisingly

Obelisk displays in the Mozart Wohnhaus

spacious, and perhaps unnaturally tidy: the neat pile within the obelisk of the new complete Mozart edition may symbolize the vast quantities of music that must have filled much of the Mozarts' house. No real attempt is made to suggest how the Mozarts actually lived – and we know it was crowded there (Leopold once wrote: 'We shall have to put up a bed near the door in Nannerl's room, where the red sofa stands; and the sofa will have to go in front of the stove between your clothes-chest and the bed, so that we can put things on it'). Next is an interactive display of Mozart's travels

Interactive display of Mozart's travels, in the Wohnhaus

– press the switch for any particular journey, and you see his route, with video illustrations of the sites he visited to the sound of recordings of the music he wrote. The final room is devoted to a slide show, elaborately and tastefully done, with a battery of projectors and mirrors, telling the story of Mozart's life with music and a commentary on the handsets. There is a shop on the ground floor, on the way out.

Ancillary to the main museum is a Ton und Film Museum (originally founded in 1991), on the mezzanine floor, with a collection of historic performances and productions, many of them from Austrian Radio and including Salzburg Festival recordings over some 70 years.

No Mozartian in Salzburg should imagine that with the two museums his or her Mozart pilgrimage is complete. There are reminders of him all over the city. For a start, there is the so-called 'Magic Flute Cottage': this wooden summerhouse, originally in the garden of the Theater auf der Wieden in Vienna, is said to have been used by Mozart to compose in peace and quiet when he was working on *Die Zauberflöte* in the summer of 1791, and to rehearse with individual singers. It was given to the Mozarteum, the Salzburg music conservatory in which many of the festival concerts take place, in 1873, and brought to Salzburg. First it was put close to the Mirabell Gardens, then on the Kapuzinerberg; in 1950 it was restored and placed in the Mozarteum garden (for illustration see p.8). The cottage, a single room with windows, is open to the public in the intervals of summer concerts at the Mozarteum (whose main entrances are in Schwartzstraße, the continuation of the road between the river and the southern side of the Makartplatz).

The large square outside the Archbishop's Residenz, originally the Michaelerplatz, is now the Mozartplatz, and at its centre is a bronze statue of Mozart, unveiled (in the presence of his sons) in 1842. An important Mozartian site, though not shown to the public as such, is the Residenz itself, where much

of his early music was first performed, in the Rittersaal, the Kaisersaal or the Carabinierisaal; no doubt some of his music was given in the Mirabell Palace too. Then there are the churches – above all the Cathedral, where his parents were married, where he was baptized, where he was organist in 1779–80, and for which most of his sacred works were composed, but also the attractively florid St Peter's, where the unfinished C minor Mass K.427 had its first hearing. One mass was written for the University Church and a school-drama for the university itself. The Mozarts had connections too with the pilgrimage church at Maria Plain, north of Salzburg, for which Wolfgang wrote a mass (K.194), the Franciscan Church, their parish church when they lived in the old city, and St Sebastian's, their parish church when they crossed the river.

It is at St Sebastian's that Leopold is buried, along with Mozart's maternal grandmother, Nannerl's short-lived daughter Jeanette and (ironically) Mozart's widow Constanze and her second husband, Georg Nikolaus Nissen. Constanze's sisters Aloysia, Mozart's first

Mozart family graves at St Sebastian, Salzburg

love, and Sophie are buried close by. Nannerl is buried in St Peter's (she died in 1829), as is Michael Haydn. Trinity Church and the Loreto Church were also favoured by the Mozarts; near to them, on the 'new' side of the river, lived most of the noble families of Salzburg with whom the Mozarts had links, such as the Lodrons and the Lützows. Over in the old city, stroll down almost any street and you will see plaques with Mozartian resonances – the houses where Constanze lived with her second husband or her sisters, in the Nonnberggasse and Mozartplatz, or where the aging Nannerl lived, in Sigmund-Haffner-Gasse, where the Haffners had their town houses. (Don't miss the plaque and statue to Salzburg's more recent favourite son: Herbert von Karajan's birth in the rather grand house, now aptly a bank, on the lane from the Makartplatz down to the river and the footbridge, the Mozartsteg, is appropriately recorded.)

Mozart first visited Vienna as a child, in 1762, and had prolonged visits in 1767–8 and 1773. He settled there in 1781 on his resignation and dismissal from the Salzburg Archbishop's service. Like most Viennese at the time, Mozart never stayed long in the same lodging. Of more than a dozen apartments that he occupied during those ten years, the only one where he spent over two years, and the only one to survive in anything like its original form, is the so-called 'Figarohaus'. Here the Viennese museum to Mozart is situated.

He lived in the house, at the junction of Schulerstraße and Domgasse (the address was Grosse Schulerstraße in his time), from the late summer of 1784 until the spring of 1787 – his most successful, most prosperous years, which saw the composition of eight of his greatest piano concertos, several string quartets, the Prague Symphony and of course *Le nozze di Figaro*. His apartment was on the first floor, the *piano nobile*; there are five storeys in all. The building dates back to at least the 16th century. In the early 18th it was owned by an architect, Andrea Simone Carove, who rebuilt

it in more or less its present state; it passed to his son-in-law, Albert Camesina, a well-known stucco artist who worked for the court, and probably did the rich and attractive stucco work still to be seen on the ceilings. His son, who inherited it, died in 1783 and his widow lived on the second floor with her two young sons in Mozart's time there.

The house, often referred to as the Camesina-House, passed through various hands in the next century, although its status as Mozart's principal Viennese residence was widely recognized (Brahms is said to have looked up at it with due reverence every time he walked by). It was not until 1906 that a memorial plaque was erected. In 1941, on the 150th anniversary of Mozart's death, a museum was set up in part of it. Mozart's flat had been subdivided and only in 1976 was the City of Vienna able to purchase the whole of it, remove the partitions and establish a museum occupying the entire premises; it was opened in 1978. In spite of these vicissitudes, some of the original fabric and decorations remain. The floorboards

Camesina room in the 'Figarohaus', Vienna

are original, the stucco work is still there, some of the gilding can be seen on the carved woodwork and now the wall paint has been carefully investigated by scraping away its 13 layers to establish, as far as anyone can, the colours of Mozart's time.

The museum is entered from Domgasse (the Schulerstraße entry is blocked off), through a rather dingy courtyard and up the open stairwell. The apartment is fitted out in the cool, impersonal style favoured in all the Vienna city museums, designed by Elsa Prochazka in the 1990s, with their slightly perverse vertical labelling under spring-loaded, wooden covers. Once past the reception area and shop, where the visitor takes a handset, the first room offers a listening station (there is another later) as well as prints of sites in Vienna associated with Mozart, his publications and his friends, his librettist Stephanie and the composer Salieri among them. In this flat Mozart held the celebrated quartet party in 1785 at which Haydn told Leopold Mozart, visiting Vienna, 'your son is the greatest composer known to me, in person or by repute'. In the second room the published quartets, dedicated to Haydn, are shown, with a set of music desks for a quartet and a copy of Leopold's letter to Nannerl reporting Haydn's words. Also in this room is a map showing the locations of Mozart's various residences in inner Vienna. The third room is given over to *Figaro*, its background, its composition and its first performances.

The displays in the next group of rooms are devoted to the various people who played important roles in Mozart's life during his various times in Vienna – family, friends, employers, patrons. There is a facsimile from the *Waisenhausmesse* K.139/47*a*, which he conducted as a 12-year-old at the church in the Rennweg. The House of the Teutonic Order, where he was staying in 1781 just before he resigned from service in Salzburg, is there, with a ticket to a concert at which he played just before. Gottfried van Swieten, an important figure in his career, is represented, as is the

Enlightenment figure and freemason Ignaz von Born. Mozart's brothers-in-law, the husbands of Aloysia and Josepha Weber, as well as the ladies themselves and Constanze, are there. Josepha was the first Queen of Night in *Die Zauberflöte*, which is represented too with the original Pamina, a handbill, stage designs, and of course Schikaneder. There is a ground-plan of the Rauhensteingasse house, not far away, where Mozart died on 5 December 1791 (the house was demolished in 1964; on the site is a department store, bearing a plaque and with a bust of the composer on the fifth floor). Other exhibits deal with the *Requiem* and the posthumous literature. The small final room, shrine-like, holds a series of reproductions of Mozart himself.

Haydn was not Mozart's only distinguished visitor in the Figarohaus. It was probably there that he was visited in April 1787 by a young man from Bonn, called Beethoven, to whom he may have given some tuition. The previous year he had taken in a resident pupil, Johann Nepomuk Hummel, then aged seven; there are tales of his giving the boy lessons in the middle of the night, and of Hummel's returning years later and describing the room layout as it was in Mozart's day.

Of the 19 buildings in Vienna where, at one time or another, Mozart lived or lodged, 16 are now demolished. Still standing are those at Tiefer Graben 18, where he stayed in 1773, and the House of the Teutonic Order, at Singerstraße 7: both bear plaques recording the connection. There are plaques too on or within the buildings occupying several of the other sites: Wipplingerstraße 19 (where he stayed in 1768); Milchgasse 1, the house 'Zum Auge Gottes' (summer 1781); Judenplatz 3–4 (1783–4); Landstraßer Hauptstraße 75–7 (1787–8); and Währinger Straße 26 (1788–9). Some of the places where he played are also marked by plaques: the Palais Collalto (Am Hof 13), where he made his début in Vienna, as a boy of six; by the Waisenhauskirche ('Orphanage church',

Rennweg 91), where he conducted his Mass in 1768; at Himmelpfortgasse 6, where he directed performances in 1788; and at Obere Augartenstraße 1, commemorating the concerts he gave in the Augarten. There is also a memorial in the Kruzifixkapelle in St Stephen's Cathedral, at the entrance to the crypt, marking where his body rested on 6 December 1791. There is a memorial in the St Marx churchyard, in Leberstraße in the third district of Vienna, to the south-east of the city, at a point supposedly close to the unmarked grave in which Mozart was buried; a further memorial, by Hans Gasser, originally erected at St Marx in 1859, was transferred in 1891 to the Zentralfriedhof in the Simmeringer Hauptstraße. There is a statue in Vienna in the Burggarten, the garden of the former imperial palace, made by Victor Tolgner in 1896 and moved there in 1953.

Mozart memorials in Vienna do not end there. His *Zauberflöte* collaborator, Emanuel Schikaneder, lived for a time in Nußdorf, on the northern side of the city. His house was much later owned by Franz Lehár, and maintained in his memory after his death (*see* SCHIKANEDER). Among the exhibits are two large, elderly wooden armchairs, said to have been stage props made for the première of the opera. The Mozart room in the Kunsthistorisches Museum, Room XIII, houses instruments in the collection (the Sammlung alter Musikinstrumente) of Mozart's time or with some special link to his music – for example, there is a 'Metallspiel' of the kind probably used in *Die Zauberflöte*, a glass harmonica, basset-horns, and fortepianos by two of his favourite makers, Stein and Walter.

There are numerous places in Vienna with Mozartian connections – halls, palaces and private houses in which he played or taught, and churches in which he worshipped or for which he composed. It is worth mentioning just the Michaelerkirche, in the Michaelsplatz, close by the Hofburg (and the site of the former Burgtheater, where *Die Entführung aus dem Serail*, *Le nozze di Figaro* and *Così fan tutte* were first performed and Mozart

gave many concerts): in this church, music from his unfinished *Requiem* was played in his memory five days after his death.

Prague has always won brownie points in the Mozart literature: Mozart may have hated Salzburg, and have come to be ignored by the fickle Viennese, but he was always loved in Prague. The truth is a little less simple. But he is commemorated there. Mozart visited the city five times, first in early 1787, when he directed the eponymous symphony and won praise for *Figaro*; then later that year, for the première of *Don Giovanni*; then twice in 1789, travelling between Vienna and northern Germany; and finally in the late summer of 1791, for the première of *La clemenza di Tito*. The opera house in which his two works were first given still stands. Built by Count Nostitz-Rieneck in 1783, it was first called after him, Nostitz Theatre, then (in Mozart's time) it became the Estates Theatre, then the Tyl Theatre (after the playwright who wrote the words of the Czech national anthem): now it is back to Estates Theatre (in Czech, Stavovské Divadlo). Mozart operas are often given there and it was also used for scenes in the film *Amadeus*.

But there is also a dedicated Mozart museum in Prague. Mozart had a good friend in the city, a singer from a Salzburg family, Josepha Hambacher, who had married the composer František Xaver Dušek. He often stayed with them in the city. The Dušeks had a summer home, in the Smíchov district – then an idyllic country area, close by a monastery, now an industrial quarter of the city within which their house is a small haven. Here Mozart probably completed *Don Giovanni*.

The original house was built by a brewer in the 17th century; in 1784 it was bought from the Bertram family by Josepha Dušek, who sold it after her husband's death in 1799. In the ensuing years the Bertramka House (as it was known) was probably modified a good deal but in 1838 its owner Lambert Popelka formed a Mozart Society to conserve it. In the 1870s it was partly destroyed by fire but one corner – the

Recital hall at the Bertramka house, Prague

one, it is understandably claimed, with the two rooms that Mozart most probably used – was largely spared. In the absence of plans or dependable pictures of the original the rest of the house was rebuilt conjecturally. A descendant of the Popelka family bequeathed it in 1925 to the Internationale Stiftung Mozarteum of Salzburg, but there were financial difficulties over its maintenance and a Czechoslovak Mozart Society, formed in 1927, eventually took it over. The two Mozart rooms were set up as a museum in the 1930s and the rest became the living quarters of the head of the Mozart Society. After World War II the cost of maintenance again outstripped resources and in 1956, Mozart's bicentenary year, the state underwrote its reconstruction in a style as close as possible to the original and opened it to the public as a museum. Further restoration was needed in 1986 and it was reopened on the bicentenary of the première of *Don Giovanni* in October 1987. The garden was converted into a miniature auditorium; recitals are given in the attached music room several evenings of the week (and mornings in the summer months) during most of the year; it seats about 70, but 300 more can listen in the garden when, on summer evenings, the french doors are opened.

The museum offers a particularly pleasant ambience in a series of rooms decorated in 18th-century style; there are painted beams and wall decorations of flowers and fruit, and chandeliers of glass or porcelain. Music by Mozart wafts gently through. In the entrance hall there are exhibits dealing with the history of the Bertramka House. This leads into the largest room, where there is a fortepiano that Mozart is said to have played during his first visit to Prague; that visit, and the return later in 1787 for the *Don Giovanni* première, are the subject of the display, which includes other period instruments. The next two rooms, supposedly Mozart's original study and bedroom, have a harpsichord that he may have played at Count Nostitz's Prague palace, in an elegantly furnished setting, and in the bedroom some of the original ceiling paintings.

Of the three further display rooms, one is focussed particularly on Mozart's last visits to Prague, in 1789 and in 1791 for *La clemenza di Tito*, one on Mozart traditions and their influence in the Czech Republic (this includes a model of the Estates Theatre at the time of *Don Giovanni*) and the last on the Dušek family.

Mozart played in numerous Prague houses during his visits but there are no commemorative plaques except on the inn 'Zu den drei goldenen Löwen' (The Three Golden Lions, Uhelný trh 1/420), the property of the Dušeks, where he lodged at the beginning of his first visit and again at the time of the composition of *Don Giovanni*; tradition has it that Da Ponte stayed at the inn opposite, and that consultations between composer and librettist were conducted from upper windows across the yard below.

The Mozart family's earliest origins have been traced to the Swabian villages to the west and north of Augsburg. A Heinrich Motzart lived in Fischach in 1331 and the name appeared in other villages soon after, notably in Heimberg, where a plaque on a house notes the presence there in 1486 of an Ändris Motzhart, a direct ancestor of the composer. By that date several members of the family had begun to settle in Augsburg where they were well established by the mid-17th century. A plaque records the presence of Wolfgang's great-great-uncle Hans Georg Mozart (1647–1719) on a house, Äußeres Pfaffengäßchen 24; Leopold's father, Johann Georg Mozart, lived in the same street in 1712–16. The family also had connections with the Heilig Kreuz monastery.

But the main Mozartian shrine in Augsburg is the Mozarthaus at Frauentorstraße 30. Here Leopold's father lived from 1709 to 1712 and from 1716. His first wife died, childless, in 1718; Leopold, born in November 1719, was the first child of his second marriage. The family moved, probably in 1721, to Jesuitengasse 25 (Franz Alois Mozart, Leopold's brother, later lived at Jesuitengasse 26, where Wolfgang enjoyed the lively company of his cousin Maria Anna Thekla on his visit in 1777). One room became a 'Gedenkraum' ('memorial room') to Leopold in 1937; two years later the whole house was presented to the municipality by its owners, a local brewery. After the war it was opened as a museum, then was redesigned on Mozart's 225th anniversary in 1981 and again on Leopold's bicentenary in 1987.

The upper part of the Frauentorstraße house is a carefully organized museum, primarily to Leopold, secondarily to his

Leopold Mozart's birthplace, Augsburg

son. There is first a small concert room, with a fortepiano by the local maker J.A. Stein (whose instruments Mozart specially admired). One display room deals with the family's roots in the Augsburg region and their activities in the city. Another two are concerned with Leopold's youth in Augsburg and his musical life there, and a fourth with his move to Salzburg in 1737. There are informative and neatly labelled displays of letters and other documents, all of them transcribed.

On the second floor the displays in the first room deal with Leopold's own work as a composer and his character as a man (the influences on him, his own influence on violin playing, with copies in many languages of his *Violinschule*); in three further rooms his travels with the young Wolfgang are outlined – in western and northern Europe, in Munich and Vienna, in Italy. There are numerous prints, with maps as additional visual help, along with display boards.

Mozart's maternal ancestry has never been as much celebrated as his paternal. His mother, Maria Anna Walburga Pertl, was born on Christmas Day 1720 in St Gilgen, a fishing village on the Wolfgangsee where lace-making was the local craft, some 15 km east of Salzburg. Her father, a lawyer, was civil commissioner ('Pfleger') for the district and lived in rooms at the local courthouse, lately rebuilt. He died in 1724 and Maria Anna and her mother moved out. The house later resumed its link with the Mozart family: when in 1784 Mozart's sister Nannerl married Baron Berchtold zu Sonnenburg, he was the civil commissioner at St Gilgen, so Nannerl lived in the house of her mother's birth from then until her husband's death in 1801, when she moved back into Salzburg.

The house, close by the lakeside, and commanding a typically Austrian panoramic view, still holds the district court. But there is a plaque (erected in 1906) to commemorate the Mozart connection, and two small rooms on the ground floor are given over to a display about the Mozarts and St Gilgen, duly emphasizing the female side – with portraits, reproductions, music in Nannerl's hand, facsimiles of birth certificates and other documents, and a family tree.

St Gilgen also has a Heimatkund-lichesmuseum, showing (among other items) lace bobbins of the kind Mozart's grandmother and mother will have used and glassware from a glassworks set up in 1701; relatives of Nannerl's lived in the building in her time. The local church, St Egidius, played a major role in the lives of the Mozart relatives: there his maternal grandparents were married, his mother was baptized, his grandfather buried, his sister married and her husband buried. Nannerl played the organ there, and her father-in-law had 'baroquized' the formerly Gothic building.

Mozart's extensive travels, from his sixth year to his penultimate one, mean that there are numerous 'Mozart slept here' – or 'played here' – sites dotted across Europe. Several are commemorated with plaques. Among them are four in Italy: in Rovereto, at the Palazzo Todeschi (Via Mercerie 14), the site of his first concert in Italy, in 1769; in Verona, in the lobby of the rebuilt Albergo due Torri (Piazza San Antonio 2), where he and his father stayed in 1769–70; at Lodi, noting (at Corso Mazzini 88) the site – incorrectly, and giving the wrong date – of the inn where in 1770 Mozart composed his first string quartet; and in Venice, at the Casa Ceseletti by the bridge of Rio di Barcaroli, where the two spent a month in 1771. There is a memorial in Germany at Wasserburg-am-Inn, between Salzburg and Munich, at the Gässner-Bräu (formerly the inn Zum goldenen Stern, Färbergasse 3), and in a Frankfurt museum a piece of glass from a window at their lodgings, allegedly scratched by Leopold to mark their visit, is preserved. In France a plaque at the Hôtel de Ville in Dijon marks Mozart's brief visit in 1766, and there is a memorial to Mozart's mother in the St Cecilia chapel of the church of St Eustache in Paris (as well as one to Rameau), although her actual grave there has disappeared. In Olomouc, in Moravia, a plaque with a relief portrait notes the Mozarts' stay at the deanery during the Viennese smallpox epidemic of 1767. There is a plaque at Renngasse 4, on the site of the house in Baden, south of Vienna, where Mozart stayed with his wife in his last summer, and another at the Baden parish church, St Stephen's, noting his dedication of his *Ave verum corpus* to the then director of its choir, Anton Stoll. Finally, two places in London where the Mozarts stayed in 1764–5 are marked with plaques: the house in Ebury Street, Victoria (implausibly claimed as the site of the composition of his first symphony), and the building (the back of the Prince Edward Theatre) on the site of the house they occupied in Thrift (now Frith) Street, Soho. It may also be mentioned that a plaque on a house in Copenhagen commemorates the years, 1812–20, that Constanze spent there with her second husband.

Mozarts Geburtshaus

Getreidegasse 9
5020 Salzburg
Austria

phone +43/0 662 844313
fax +43/0 662 840693
e-mail archiv@mozarteum.at
website www.salzburg.info.or.at

open daily 10.00–18.00 (July–August, 10.00–19.00)

Mozart-Wohnhaus

Makartplatz 8–9
5020 Salzburg
Austria

phone +43/0 662 874227–40
fax +43/0 662 872924
e-mail archiv@mozarteum.at
website www.salzburg.info.or.at

open daily 10.00–18.00 (July–August, 10.00–19.00)

Wolfgang Amadeus Mozart 'Figarohaus'

Domgasse 5
1010 Wien
Austria

phone +43/0 1513 6294
fax +43/0 1505 8747–7201
e-mail post@am.10.magwien.gv.at

website www.museum.vienna.at

open Tuesday–Saturday 09.00–18.00

Muzeum W.A. Mozarta a manizelů Duškových
Bertramka
Mozartova 169
15000 Praha 5
Czech Republic

phone +420/0 2 5731 7465, 8461
fax +420/0 2 5731 6753
e-mail bertramka@comenius.cz,
mozart@bertramka.cz

open April–October, daily 09.30–18.00;
November–March, daily 09.30–17.00

Mozarthaus
Frauentorstraße 30
8900 Augsburg
Germany

phone +49/0 821 324 3894, 3896
fax +49/0 821 324 3883

open Tuesday–Sunday 10.00–17.00

Mozart-Gedenkstätte
Berichtsgericht St Gilgen
Ischlerstraße 15
5430 St Gilgen
Austria

phone +43/0 6227 2445–0, 2642
fax +43/0 6227 8175
e-mail information@wolfgangsee.at

open June–September, Tuesday–Sunday
10.00–12.00, 14.00–18.00

Maps 1, 4, 7

H. Kretschmer: *Mozarts Spuren in Wien*
(Vienna, 1990)
J. Senigl: *W.A. Mozart and Salzburg: a Guide to
the Memorial Sites* (Salzburg: Internationale
Stiftung Mozarteum, 1990)
J. Mančal: *Die Mozarts in Augsburg und
Schwaben* (Augsburg: Brigitte Settele, 1991)
J. Mančal: *The Mozart Memorial House
[Augsburg]* (Augsburg: Stadtarchiv Augsburg,
n.d.)
H.J. Wignall: *In Mozart's Footsteps: a Travel
Guide for Music Lovers* (New York: Paragon
House, 1991)
Zaubertöne: Mozart in Wien 1781–1791 (Vienna:
Museen der Stadt Wien, 1991) [exhibition
catalogue]

H. Kretschmer: *Wiener Musikergedenkstätten*
(Vienna: J & V Edition, 3/1992)
*Mozart's Apartment (Figaro House) Domgasse 5,
Vienna 1* (Vienna: Museums of the City of
Vienna, 7/1992) [out of date, but with
valuable essays]
J. Senigl: *Die Mozarts und St. Gilgen* (Salzburg:
Internationale Stiftung Mozarteum, 1992)
R. Angermüller and G. Geffray, eds.: *Festschrift:
Die Wiedererrichtung des Mozart-Wohnhauses
26. Jänner 1996* (Salzburg: Internationale
Stiftung Mozarteum, 1996)
J. Senigl: *Mozart in Salzburg: a Guide to the
Mozart Museums* (Salzburg: Internationale
Stiftung Mozarteum, 1996)
Wolfgang Amadeus Mozart: Musikergedenkstätten
(Vienna: Historisches Museum der Stadt
Wien, n.d.) [Figaro House, Vienna]
W.M. Weiss: *Looking for Wolfgang Amadeus
Mozart: a Travel Companion through
Salzburg, Prague and Vienna* (Vienna:
Christian Brandstätter, 1997)
C. Raabe and K. Festner: *Spaziergänge durch
Mozarts Salzburg* (Zürich and Hamburg:
Arche, 2000)
N. Simeone: *Paris: a Musical Gazetteer* (New
Haven and London: Yale University Press,
2000)

MUREŞIANU family

The Mureşianu family played important
roles in the emergence of Romanian
national identity through their efforts as
writers, publishers, artists and musicians.
Jacob Mureşianu (1812–87) edited the
first newspaper in Romanian (1838),
which was printed in the large ground-
floor room of their house in the main
square of Braşov. His cousin André
(1816–63) wrote the poem used for the
Romanian national anthem (*see* PANN).
One of Jacob's sons, also called Jacob
(1857–1917), was a pianist and composer; educated in Vienna and Leipzig, he
lived and died in Blaj, in the north of the
country, from where he edited the first
Romanian music periodical, *Musa
Românǔ* (1888). Some members of the
family carried on publishing, others
sculpted and painted; Juliu (1900–56),
the younger Jacob's son, was a composer
at Cluj.

The house at Piaţa Sfatului 25,
facing the imposing Council House with
its Trumpeters' Tower and next door to

the pink National Bank of Romania, has been a museum since the early 1970s. Upstairs, four rooms are devoted to the various members of the family, with displays of original documents, photographs and pictures from the extensive archive, which includes correspondence, music manuscripts, their publications and portraits (some of them painted by family members) as well as furniture, the family harmonium and the younger Jacob's piano, a Heitzmann boudoir grand. Downstairs, the former print shop is now used for recitals and to display items from the Gheorghe Dima collection (*see* DIMA). Outside, on the front of the house, is a plaque proclaiming it as the birthplace of the composer Jacob Mureşianu.

Muzeul Memorial Casa Mureşenilor
Piaţa Sfatului 25
2200 Braşov
Romania

phone, fax +40/02 68 477864 (archive, 142967)
e-mail casa_muresenilor@yahoo.com

open Monday–Saturday 09.00–15.00

Map 11

MUSORGSKY

Modest Petrovich Musorgsky came from a wealthy land-owning family from western Russia. He was born in 1839 on an estate in the Kun'ya region of the Pskov administrative district, 420 km west of Moscow and 400 south and slightly east of St Petersburg; the nearest town of any size is Velikiye Luki. The estate lies some 12 km off the main road linking Moscow and Riga, within a national park or conservation area. It is close to Zhizhitsa station on the Moscow–Riga railway.

The actual house in which the composer was born, in the village of Karevo, no longer stands, although the spot is marked and there is a memorial statue nearby. But in the village of Naumovo, a couple of kilometres away, is

The Musorgsky estate at Naumovo

the splendid house that belonged to the family of his mother, Yuliya Ivanovna Chirikova; in 1970 this became a state museum dedicated to Musorgsky. The 'museum' in fact comprises the Chirikov estate and part of the two villages.

He spent much of his childhood in this house, which lies at the centre of the estate, in typical Russian empire style; it is situated in a large park, overlooking Lake Zhizhitsa. There are nine rooms on the ground floor, with displays keyed to particular periods of Musorgsky's life, with furniture – some of it from Musorgsky's own house or his mother's, including bookshelves, chairs and the like – and other exhibits, including the autograph of a little polka for piano that he wrote in his teens (it was published in 1852) and a piano score of *Boris Godunov*. There are also engravings and photographs, some of them originals of the composer.

Around the main house are outbuildings, preserved as adjuncts to the museum: they include the servants' quarters, a greenhouse, a dairy, a smithy, a cold store and a barn. Between Naumovo and Karevo lies the graveyard of the church of St Odigitriya in which Musorgsky's parents were married and the composer was baptized.

Musorgsky left the estate when he was ten to go to St Petersburg, where he attended school and later an army college; after brief military service he dedicated himself to music until the emancipation of the serfs in 1861, which much affected his family's wealth and compelled him to find paid employment. He worked for a time as a civil servant until alcoholism finally overtook him and he came to rely on occasional support from friends and patrons. He died in 1881.

He was in St Petersburg during those years. From 1872 until 1875 he lived in a furnished apartment on the third floor of a large block, close to the river Neva (now Shpalernaya ulitsa 6, apt.15); this is the only one he himself ever rented. There in 1873–4 he put the finishing touches to the revised version of *Boris Godunov* for its production, early in 1874, at the Mariinsky Theatre, and went on to compose the early stages of *Khovanshchina* and to plan *Sorochintsï Fair*. Some of his finest songs, among them the last of the *Nursery* songs and the entire *Sunless* cycle, also belong to his years there. At first he lived alone, but in 1874 his friend and distant relative the poet Arseniy Golenishchev-Kutuzov joined him, though he moved out on his marriage the next year. Nikolay Rimsky-Korsakov (with whom Musorgsky had earlier shared accommodation) and his wife had an apartment just across the landing for a year. César Cui, a member of their circle, had until recently lived on the second floor.

Parts of the block are now owned by the cellist Mstislav Rostropovich, who plans to make Musorgsky's apartment into a memorial to the composer. He began by inviting Tat'yana Rimsky-Korsakova, the composer's granddaughter, to research its original contents from family records and inventories. The intention is that it should be furnished and decorated in the style of Musorgsky's time; there are already several portraits and prints relevant to the composer and his circle and a grand piano of the kind he originally had. In due course its three main rooms will be opened to the public. In the street below, outside the entrance to the block, a bust of Musorgsky was erected in 1975 to commemorate his residence there.

Many years later the same block was the home of Dmitri Shostakovich, who had an apartment on the fifth floor for some 20 years, from his childhood until his marriage. Rostropovich has also instituted work to create a museum in that apartment; there are plans to open it in the composer's centenary year, 2006, the same time as his widow hopes to open his Moscow flat (where there is already a Shostakovich archive next door) as a museum.

Muzey-usad'ba M.P. Musorgskogo*
Naumovo
Kun'inskiy' rayon
182001 Pskovskaya oblast'
Russia

phone +7/0 81 1493 1201

open Tuesday–Sunday 09.00–17.00

Map 12

MUZIO

See VERDI.

NASTASIJEVIĆ

Svetomir Nastasijević came from a gifted family: his brothers were a poet, a painter and a writer, his sisters a historian and a mathematician. He himself was trained as an architect, but worked from the early 1920s as a violinist in Belgrade and then at the opera house and at the radio. Three of his operas, including the Serbian historical drama *Đjurađ Branković*, were given in Belgrade, where he lived from 1920 until his death in 1979.

Nastasijević was born in 1902 in Gornji Milanovac, just over 100 km south of the capital. He died in 1980. The museum of the Rudnik-Takovo region, established in 1994, commemorates him and his family in a building on the site of the house of his birth (the actual house burnt down in 1941). In it are his piano, in good playing order, his library, copies of some of his writings, programmes of his concerts in Belgrade in the 1930s, personal documents and certificates, and the scores of *Ðjurað Brankovic´* and other works.

Nastasijevic´ Memorial Room*

Rudničko Takovskog Traja
ulica Sindjeliceva 9
32300 Gornji Milanovac
Serbia and Montenegro

phone +381/0 32 713851, 17407
fax +381/0 32 791118
e-mail muzejgm@alphagm.net

open Monday–Friday 08.00–15.00,
Saturday by appointment

Map 14

G. Krajačić: *Muzički Putopsi* (Novi Sad: Promotej, 2001), 76–9 (originally published in *Dnevik*, 23 October 1996)

NENOV

Razgrad, in north-eastern Bulgaria, close to the border with Romania, is the birthplace of the pianist and composer Dimiter Nenov (1902–53). The house, in a quiet, tree-lined street, where he lived with his parents and sisters until he was seven, was opened to the public as a municipal museum 40 years after his death. Collecting had begun in 1980, and the museum holds and exhibits documents and objects directly related to Nenov; there is a longer-term intention also to collect and interpret the wider history of music in Razgrad.

Nenov studied in Dresden to be an architect as well as a musician, but abandoned architecture in 1931 after a period of work in Sofia in the Bulgarian Ministry of Transport, designing railway stations. Following further musical studies in Zakopane and Bologna, he took up a post at the Sofia Music Academy, where in 1943 he became professor of piano; after his death the academy concert hall was named after him. Architecture continued to play a role in his compositions, for which he also gathered inspiration from the music of Skryabin and Bulgarian folk music.

Visitors to the museum can at present see three rooms: the room in which he was born – now almost a shrine – is simply furnished with bronze casts of his hands, his mother's upright piano and a quotation from his memoirs in bronze lettering. The museum owns his manuscript autobiography along with his music (manuscript and printed), his concert clothes and furniture he designed. These are displayed in the adjoining room, along with photographs, his architectural designs, correspondence and music and books from his library. Across the foyer is a room seating 30 which is sometimes used for chamber concerts; the house is surrounded by a lovingly tended garden. Every two years Razgrad plays host to a national piano competition in Nenov's honour.

K'shta-Muzey Dimit'r Nenov

ulitsa Antim I 20
7200 Razgrad
Bulgaria

phone +359/0 84 29777

open Monday–Friday 08.00–17.00

Map 11

NIELSEN

Carl Nielsen spent most of his life in Copenhagen. But when his heirs decided to set up a museum to him they turned to Odense, the city on the island of Funen close to where in 1865 he was born and where he spent his early years, on which he looked back happily in his memoirs *Min fynske barndom* ('My childhood in Funen', 1927). Odense also happened to possess a certain expertise in museums, acquired through its admired one to Hans Christian Andersen, a neighbour to Nielsen's.

Their judgment was good. Nielsen is in fact commemorated in two museums there, not far apart: one is in the thatched cottage where he spent the last years of his childhood, the other a modern museum attached to the Odense Concert Hall. Neither his actual birthplace at

Sortelung where he spent his early years nor the house at Petersborg where he lived from the age of eight still stands (the location of the latter is marked by a stone). But the thatched cottage close to the village of Nørre Lyndelse, a dozen kilometres south-west of Odense, to which the family moved in 1878 when he was 12 years old, has been a museum since 1956. Nielsen in fact spent less than two years there. His father, a painter, was also a village musician and it was from him that Carl first learnt the violin and the cornet. After playing in his father's band, he joined a military orchestra in Odense, playing the signal horn and alto trombone.

The displays are focussed accordingly: on the musical life of the region and the social and economic circumstances under which Nielsen grew up; on his family's genealogy (complicated by the fact that his surname was taken from his father's Christian name); and on his childhood, which later he evoked in his music – notably in the choral work *Fynsk Forår* (1921) – as well as in *Min fynske barndom*. Among the exhibits are family documents and photographs, his father's violin and his rifle from the 1864 war, a slate, pencil box and books from the Nørre Lyndelse school, and rustic paintings by Nielsen's daughter Anne Marie Telmányi, done in 1961, as well as a plaster bust of Nielsen by his wife.

When he was 14 Nielsen went to live in Odense; he was there for four years,

Nielsen's childhood home near Nørre Lyndelse

1879–83, before he took up a place at the Kongelige Danske Musikkonservatorium in Copenhagen (1884–6). He spent his entire working life in the capital, where his home for many years was at Frederiksholms Kanal 28. He died there in 1931.

The Nielsen museum, attached to the Odense Concert Hall, was established as part of the city's millennium celebrations in 1988. Although called the Carl Nielsen Museum, it equally commemorates the life and work of his wife, the sculptor Anne Marie Brodersen, whom he met in Paris and married in Florence in 1891. Her statues (busts and figurines, predominantly of animals) are shown side by side with the musical displays throughout the museum. On the upper floor, a corner of one of her Copenhagen workshops is re-created alongside faithful reconstructions behind glass partitions of their living-room and his study. His desk is there, with table and chairs, his grand piano, a music stand and parts of his music library. The collection of their effects was donated by one of their daughters; his music manuscripts were deposited in the Kongelige Bibliotek in Copenhagen.

On the ground floor is the table piano from the Nielsens' summer home at Skagen, in northern Jutland, and wall displays that provide a rich chronicle of their lives, with photographs (including a group that documents his offbeat sense of humour), maps, facsimiles and the last portrait of him. There is a small lecture and recital room seating 70 in the museum as well as space for audio-visual presentations and changing exhibitions. While recorded music can usually be heard wafting through the museum, there are earphones stationed along the displays with which one can listen to works of particular relevance to the exhibits, such as excerpts from his symphonies, the tone poem *Pan og Syrinx* and the opera *Maskarade*. Odense, famous as the home of Hans Andersen, deserves special recognition for the imaginative way in which it serves the legacies of the Nielsens.

*Nielsen's study,
re-created in the
Carl Nielsen
Museet, Odense*

Carl Nielsens Barndomshjem

Odensevej 2A
Nørre Lyndelse
5792 Årslev
Denmark

phone +45/0 6551 4601
fax +45/0 6590 8600
e-mail museum@odmus.dk
website www.museumfyn.dk

open May–September, Tuesday–Sunday
11.00–15.00

Carl Nielsen Museet

Claus Bergsgade 11
5000 Odense
Denmark

phone +45/0 6551 4601
fax +45/0 6590 8600
e-mail museum@odmus.dk
website www.odmus.dk

open January–August, Thursday–Sunday
12.00–16.00; September–December,
Thursday–Friday 16.00–20.00, Sunday
12.00–16.00

Map 13

J. Larsen: *Carl Nielsens Barnsdomshjem* (Odense,
1990)
G. Gefen: *Composers' Houses* (London: Cassell
and Vendome, 1998), 142–9
F. Jor, ed.: *Nordic Artists' Homes* (Stockholm:
Prisma, 1999), 79–84

NOTTARA

The Romanian composer, violinist,
conductor and critic Constantin C.
Nottara (1890–1951) was the son of a
much-admired actor, Constantin I.
Nottara. Part of the Bucharest house
where the Nottara family lived from 1932
to 1982 is today a museum, to both father
and son. In front of the striking *Art
Nouveau* building stands a bust of the
actor, by Milita Petpaşcu.

The museum, filled with a collection
of exquisite fine art, antiques and antiquities as well as theatrical and musical
memorabilia, was established in 1956 by
the younger Nottara's widow, Ana, and
given to the State in 1980. Like many
other museums, it was closed for a time
during the Ceauşescu regime; in 1993 the
building was renovated and the museum
was reopened in 1995. The domestic
ambience is immaculately maintained,
just as their mistress had left it, by the
family's former retainers.

The ground-floor rooms are devoted
largely to the father's career but also
display family portraits and documents
relating to the house. The image of the
actor is ubiquitous, in portraits and
busts, but it is his dressing table with all
his make-up that most brings him to life:
he is reported to have rehearsed his roles

at home in full fig. His extensive library of literature and plays, incorporating the libraries of several other famous Romanian actors, is scattered among the *Art Nouveau* furniture, Sèvres china and Bohemian glass. The walls along the staircase to the first floor are filled with hundreds of framed photographs of his friends and pupils.

The first-floor rooms recall his son, whose career centred on Bucharest, where he was first a pupil and then a professor at the conservatory, a violinist in the Bucharest Philharmonic Orchestra and leader of a string quartet, then a conductor and finally a music critic; a pupil of Enescu (1907–9), though in Paris rather than Bucharest, he composed operas, ballets, symphonic poems and a violin concerto for performance in his native city. The first room on the left is his library, the volumes of music and musical literature beautifully bound and catalogued, as too is the library down-stairs. In a glass case behind Nottara's desk are his Amati violin, his baton and his five-nibbed rastrum. Like his father, he received many awards, Czech (1933) and French (1937) as well as Romanian, which are on display here. In the corner is a large sculpture of him holding his violin. The main room, decorated with Italian, Turkish and Chinese furniture, is still used for chamber music gatherings and on a raised platform at one end stands his grand piano. There is an oil portrait of the composer as a young man and a rather splendid bust. The adjoining dining-room and alcove display fine pieces of French furniture, Sèvres and Meissen china, Venetian glass and Belgian lace. The staircase to the private second floor is lined with photographs of musicians.

Muzeul memorialǎ Constantin I. Nottara şi Constantin C. Nottara
Bd Dacia 105
Sector 2
Bucharest
Romania

phone +40/021 210 3823

open summer, Tuesday–Sunday 10.00–18.00; winter, Tuesday–Sunday 09.00–17.00

NOVÁK

To the Czechs, Vítězslav Novák is a central figure in the national tradition. Born in 1870, in the south Bohemian town of Kamenice nad Lipou, about 100 km south-east of Prague, he was a pupil of Dvořák; later he was a distinguished teacher at the Prague Conservatory. His orchestral, piano and choral music is much coloured by his interest in the folk music of Moravia and Slovakia, although he never explored the implications of folk music as Janáček or Bartók did. During World War II his compositions (notably a *De profundis* and a *St Wenceslas Triptych*) proclaimed his response to political events. His considerable theatre output has remained admired in his native country. He died in Skuteč in 1949.

Novák is commemorated in Kamenice nad Lipou, not in the actual house of his birth – that, in the main town square, is marked by a plaque, and there is also a bust facing it – but in a museum, one street away from the square, opened in 1970 to mark his centenary. This consists of a single room, large and subdivided, with displays clearly and neatly laid out in a series of modern showcases. Novák's life is related in a collection of photographs of his birthplace, his contemporaries and a variety of documents. There are his original sketchbooks, of his drawings as well as his music, and a striking oil painting of him by his son shows that at least some of his talents were passed on. His own piano is there, and also the entire furnishing of his study in his flat in Prague – a sofa and chairs, his desk (pictures on it show the original disposition of the study), a bookcase, his glasses, his pen. There is a display of his publications, and another of letters (in facsimile); his personal life is represented with family pictures and a charming statuette of the man in his overcoat and hat. He was apparently much loved in

Kamenice and there is another bust of him in front of the town school; there is also a memorial in the nearby village of Johanka.

Novák spent a good deal of time in his later years in Skuteč, a town on the eastern side of central Bohemia, some 130 km east of Prague and about 100 north-west of Brno. This was the family home of his wife, Marie Prášková. It had originally been a shoe factory; Skuteč was a centre of the Czech shoe industry and Marie's parents ran a workshop there. Novák was 19 years older than his wife, who had been one of his pupils at the conservatory; he had visited her family at Skuteč and spent holiday times there, and for three years during World War II they lived in the house. In 1954, his widow gave the building and its furnishings to the town, specifying that the ground floor be a city museum and the upper floor be devoted to her husband's memory.

The ground floor is now a small recital hall, seating about 100 people. Upstairs, you first enter a room that served as Novák's study, which contains the original family furniture, along with portraits of his parents-in-law, a photographic portrait of Novák himself and an anonymous French landscape that he specially liked. Some of his awards and prizes are shown on the walls. There is a music salon, with his grand piano (by Wirth of Vienna) and a glass-fronted cabinet with books about him, memoirs and various of his medals; on the walls are portraits of Novák and his wife by their son as well as portraits of his grandparents. The principal display is in the third room, originally the bedroom – this is the room in which he died. Some of his own drawings, in pencil, are shown here, along with photographs covering several aspects of his life – family pictures, some showing him with Dvořák, Suk, Janáček, Talich and other colleagues, and a selection of documents, in facsimile, concerning his life and career, among them the letter in which he proposed marriage to Marie. Also exhibited are copies of his published music, early

recordings, citations from the academic world (including his appointment as a National Artist), a bust, a cast of his right hand taken after his death and a picture of his funeral cortège.

Novák is remembered elsewhere in the Czech Republic: in Prague, where there is a bust in the house he lived in and a statue on a hill (with his ashes buried in its base); in Teplice nad Bečvou there is another bust, and a school is named after him in Jindřichův Hradec.

Vlastivědné Muzeum

Palackého ulice 75
39470 Kamenice nad Lipou
Czech Republic

phone +420/0 565 434168

open Tuesday–Friday 09.00–11.30, 12.30–15.00 (May–September, Wednesday to 17.00), Saturday 14.00–16.00 (June–August only)

Městské Muzeum s Památníkem Vítězslava Nováka

Rybičkova ulice 364
53973 Skuteč
Czech Republic

phone +420/0 469 350131

open Tuesday–Friday 09.00–12.00, 13.00–16.00, Saturday and Sunday 09.00–12.00

Map 4

Sborník Památníku Vítěslava Nováka (Skuteč: Městské Muzeum ve Skutči, 1988)

NOWOWIEJSKI

In a small town in northern Poland once known as Wartenburg, but now as Barczewo, the composer Feliks Nowowiejski was born in 1877. The fifth of eleven children of a tailor, he first showed musical talent as a pianist; at the age of ten he was sent to the Jesuit school at nearby Olsztyn, and from there to Berlin, Regensburg and Prague. After a successful career abroad as a composer, organist and conductor, he returned to Poland, settling in Poznań, where he died in 1946.

Today Barczewo proudly honours its favourite son, with a small municipal museum, founded in 1961, and a larger-than-life bust in the grounds of the local secondary school. The museum displays occupy four rooms on the first floor, over a doctor's surgery, in the building in which Nowowiejski was born. Two contain furniture brought from his home in Poznań, which includes his Viennese piano (a Stingl), his felt-top desk and glass-fronted bookcase (still stuffed with books and scores), and several drawing-room pieces. The strength of the collection is its iconography: photographs, portraits and busts that chronicle his lifetime, from the family group portrait in which he is seen proudly clutching his copy of Mozart sonatas, to the genial, dignified images later captured in oil.

Through Nowowiejski's heirs the museum has also acquired music (his autographs are preserved in Warsaw) and programmes for many of the early performances of his popular oratorio *Quo Vadis* (1903) and his opera *Legenda Baltyku* (1924), as well as sheet music that includes patriotic partsongs. His tailcoat, a medal pinned to the lapel, hangs in a glass case next to another displaying his death mask and the Darowany Prezez certificate and laurel wreath he received in 1914. Small-scale chamber music concerts are occasionally given in the museum.

Feliksa Nowowiejskiego Muzeum
ulitsa Mickiewicza 13
11010 Barczewo
Poland

phone +48/0 8951 148549

open Tuesday 09.00–15.00, Wednesday 09.00–17.00, Friday 09.00–14.00, Saturday 09.00–13.00

Map 10

OBRETENOV

As a well-known composer of Bulgarian choral songs and the founder and conductor of the first Bulgarian professional mixed *a cappella* choir, Svetoslav Obretenov (1909–55) occupies a special place in Bulgarian musical history. He was born in the sleepy little town of Provadiya, a short distance west of the Black Sea resort of Varna, and lived at what is now ulitsa Svetoslav Obretenov 8 until he was 17, when he left to study music first in Varna and then in Sofia. He remained in Sofia for the rest of his life.

A house museum commemorating him in Provadiya was established in 1969, in the house where the Obretenov family lived from 1912 until 1927. For a time, when the house was in private ownership, the displays were moved across town to a municipal building also in use as a music and dance school; but now they are back in the same street. Although a memorial plaque to Obretenov with a bell (which signals the start of the annual S.V. Obretenov National Competition for singers and instrumentalists) has been installed in the forecourt, there is a lingering sense that a composer much vaunted in the post-war socialist era might now be in eclipse. Much of his music – for example, the incidental music for plays such as Kirshon's *The Wonderful Alloy* and the oratorio entitled *Guerrilla Fighters* (1949) or a cantata for soloist, mixed choir and orchestra such as *Struggle for Peace* (1951) – seems uncertainly tuned with the cultural climate of present-day Bulgaria. Yet it is a museum's role to preserve the past, and the series of 50 large photographs chronicling Obretenov's life and work as a composer, pedagogue and choral conductor, and the ten cases containing copies of his music, concert programmes and awards (People's Artist and Dimitrov Prize Laureate), do just that. The collection also includes his upright piano (a Ruprecht), oil portraits and caricatures and his library.

Muzey Svetoslav Obretenov
ulitsa Svetoslav Obretenov 2
9200 Provadiya
Bulgaria

phone +359/0 0518 3263

open by appointment

Map 11

ORFF

Carl Orff, known to millions around the world for *Carmina Burana* (1937) and music education for the masses, was a Münchner. He was born in 1895 into a military family and lived until he was 14 in Maillinger Straße, near the entrance to the Englischer Garten (the building has been replaced by a block of flats, at no.30, but his birth there is acknowledged with a plaque). He was educated at the Munich Akademie der Tonkunst, held a succession of conducting appointments and, from 1950 until his retirement in 1960, taught composition at the Staatliche Hochschule für Musik.

In 1924, Orff and Dorothee Günther founded the Güntherschule, for gymnastics, music and dance: the basis for the Orff-Schulwerk movement. In 1936 the Güntherschule moved to Kaulbachstraße 16; the building suffered bomb damage during the war and was rebuilt, becoming a private residence until 1990, when it was refurbished as the Orff-Zentrum München. Its aim is to preserve Orff's legacy and to promote the study of his life and work. It contains primary documents, music manuscripts and audio-visual materials, which are available for study. Upstairs there is a Teatrino seating 60–70 for concerts and symposiums. Cases in the staircase display instruments and artefacts donated by Orff's fourth wife, Liselotte Schmitz Orff.

In 1955 Orff and his third wife, the novelist Luise Riuser, settled in Diessen, a small town 50 km south-west of Munich, on the west side of the Ammersee, set in the foothills of the Bavarian Alps. Orff knew the area well: his parents had had a country house near Diessen, at the village of Unteralting. He and his wife bought a farmhouse at Ziegelstadel 1 in the district of Diessen-St Georgen, near Schatzberg,

with views of the lake and the 15th-century hilltop monastery at Andechs. An outbuilding was fitted out as a guesthouse, with Orff's study upstairs, and connected to the main house by a covered walkway, which combines with the periphery hedges (six varieties to attract and harbour different breeds of birds), giving the impression of a sanctuary. The enclosed area around the house shelters an outdoor eating area, a kitchen garden and a fish pond. This was Orff's home for the rest of his life. Visitors are welcome, by appointment through the museum (see below).

Photographs show that his large study remains just as it was in his day. Between the windows are neatly organized bookcases: art books and Greek literature here, reference books, musical scores (shelved according to size) and educational tomes there; there are also books on music, books about Orff and a collection of LPs. The centre of the room is given over to musical instruments: his Bechstein boudoir grand as well as an

Orff's study at Diessen

upright piano and all kinds of percussion – cymbals, glockenspiels, bongos, a bass drum, woodblocks, tambourines, triangles, timpani and xylophones, including an electric one given to him on his 80th birthday. On his desk, next to a window, are his pipes, personal photographs, pens and a stopwatch. In the remaining corner, by the green tiled stove, is a comfortable sofa and chairs. Here he composed his seven last stage works, including *Oedipus der Tyrann*, the final version of *Ein Sommernachtstraum*, *Prometheus* and *De temporum fine comoedia*, and several choral works.

In 1959 Orff and Luise were divorced and the following year he married their assistant, Liselotte, in the Klosterkirche at Andechs. He died in a Munich clinic, on 29 March 1982, and was interred in the Andechs Capella Dolorosa. Their house in Diessen was always a meeting place for young musicians and music educators, and since his death it has been a place of pilgrimage, although not formally open to the public.

In 1991 the Carl-Orff-Stiftung established by his widow opened a small museum in the centre of Diessen. On the ground floor of the museum are the reception and a large display room where his life and works are chronicled, with special reference to *Der Mond*, *Carmina Burana*, *Trionfi* and *Die Bernauerin*; the basement is devoted to the Orff-Schulwerk, with facilities and Orff percussion instruments available for workshops. The emphasis throughout the museum, conveyed in photographs, videos and on CD-ROM, is on Orff the communicator through his work as a composer, conductor and educator. The Carl-Orff-Stiftung also offers support for projects relevant to the Orff-Schulwerk and in 1997 inaugurated a biennial singing competition in his memory, held in Munich at the Bavarian Academy of Fine Arts.

Orff's educational work is continued at the Orff-Institut Salzburg, founded in 1963 as a department of the Mozarteum, and through the Orff-Schulwerk Forum, also in Salzburg.

Orff-Zentrum-München
Kaulbachstraße 16
80539 München
Germany

phone +49/0 89 288105–0
fax +49 89 280354
e-mail kontakt@orff-zentrum.de
website www.orff-zentrum.de

open Monday–Friday 09.00–13.00, by appointment

Carl Orff Museum im Rinkhof
Hofmark 3
88911 Diessen am Ammersee
Germany

phone +49/0 88 079 1981

open Saturday and Sunday 14.00–17.00, or by appointment

Map 7

H. Gassner and W. Thomas: *Carl Orff: Fotodokumente 1978–1981* (Munich: Buchendorfer, 1994)

OSTERC

The small village of Veržej, in the north-western corner of Slovenia, is the birthplace of one of the country's leading composers of the inter-war period. Slavko Osterc, born on 17 June 1895, studied in Prague under Novák, Hába and others, taught in Ljubljana, and had much of his music heard at the International Society for Contemporary Music during the 1930s. He moved stylistically from post-Expressionism to a Stravinskian contrapuntal manner, but always with a characteristic vein of wit. He died young, of syphilis acquired during service in World War I, on 23 May 1941.

The site of his birth – the actual house no longer stands – is marked by a plaque, and in front of it on the village green, which bears his name, a bust to him stands; in the regional capital, Ljutomer, there is a music school named after him. There is a series of concerts in his memory in Veržej each spring. Since 1963 the village offices there have had a memorial room dedicated to Osterc and to another distinguished son of the region.

His life and his work are clearly documented and illustrated in a series of glazed panels and a showcase. Most of the originals are in the National and University Library in Ljubljana, but some are here along with reproductions – there are programmes, scores of his main works and production pictures of the stage ones, letters, photographs, some of the risqué verses that he penned (alas, only in Slovene), and exercise books from his student days. There are caricatures of Osterc and pictures of him with members of his family (he was married to a pianist of Polish descent, who later divorced him) and reproductions of two paintings by his daughter Lidija. Osterc's own nephew is involved with the local Society of Culture and serves as a knowledgeable and sympathetic guide whenever needed.

Spominska soba Slavko Osterc

Občina Veržej
olica brastava in entnosti 8
9241 Vcržej
Slovenia

phone +386/0 2588 8180
fax +386/0 2588 8181
e-mail obcina.verzej@siol.net

open by appointment

Map 14

E. Tibaut, ed.: *Spomini še Živijo: ob 100-letnici rojstva skladatelja Slavka Osterca* (Ljutomer: Zveza kulturnih organizacij, 1995)

B. Loparnik and Z. Krstulović: *Moja smer je skrajna levica: razstava ob stoletnici Slavka Osterca* (Ljubljana: Oddelek za muzikologijo Filozofske fakultete, 1995)

PADEREWSKI

Not many musicians become prime ministers. Ignacy Jan Paderewski, born in Kuryłowka, in Podolia (now in Ukraine), in 1860, used his international standing as pianist and composer to further his country's causes and espe-

cially Polish independence; and after World War I it was he who represented Poland at the signing of the Treaty of Versailles. He served as Prime Minister and Minister for Foreign Affairs from 1919 until 1922, when he returned to composition, concert-giving and teaching. At the beginning of World War II he again campaigned for his country, in the USA, but he died in New York in 1941. His remains were returned to Poland in 1992.

Naturally enough, he is commemorated rather grandly in Warsaw, in a special museum occupying the north side of the palatial Podchorążowky house, set in parkland (the Żazienki Park) near the centre of the city. Called the Museum of Ignacy Jan Paderewski and Polish Emigration in America, and opened in 1992, it is a branch of the National Museum.

It has three main rooms concerned with Paderewski as a musician. The first, modelled on the salon at Riond-Bosson, Paderewski's house in Switzerland, is a large double salon, with his own furniture (a sofa, his desk, his silver tea service, his 1929 Erard boudoir grand with signed photographs from Queen Victoria, Saint-Saëns and others). There are several silver wreaths and two portraits of the man himself, the famous one by Alma-Tadema and one by Charles Giron, with Giron's painting of Helena, Paderewski's (second) wife. This leads into the recital hall, a handsome room seating about 150, with Paderewski's Steinway and another piano, several

The Paderewski museum, Warsaw

portraits of his musician friends and a white marble bust of 1901 by Edward Onslow Ford. The late portrait by Tadeusz Styka (1937) is in the corridor, along with various honours accorded to Paderewski from other countries. The third room records his activities as a concert pianist – shields, medallions, diplomas and above all laurel wreaths, of which there are ten, a display of vases (chiefly gifts from American institutions) and several fine ornamental batons (in ebony, ivory, mother-of-pearl and silver) as well as photographs, busts of Beethoven and of Paderewski, and his mute practice keyboard and his violin. The museum archives house various documents concerning Paderewski and America, including his correspondence with Presidents Wilson and Roosevelt (other documents and his library are at the Jagiellonian University, Kraków). In a further, adjoining group of rooms his art collection, particularly rich in Chinese and Japanese items (more than 300), is displayed. Not many musicians could be so lavishly commemorated, but then few achieved Paderewski's distinction in a wider world.

In 1897, Paderewski bought a country estate in southern Poland at Kąsna Dolna, south of Tarnów and just to the west of the small town of Ciążkowice. He modernized the mansion and improved the surrounding parkland, but stayed there only briefly and sold it in 1903. The mansion passed through various hands, was split up under socialist rule and became first a school and then an agricultural college. But in 1983 it was taken over by the Tarnów Musical Society, who used it for concerts, set up a museum and oversaw the house's restoration and partial rebuilding. In 1990 a Tarnów–Kąsna Dolna Paderewski Centre was set up to manage the estate and there was further renovation at the end of the 1990s.

The handsome, single-storey mansion serves as a museum to Paderewski as well as a centre for concerts, workshops, competitions, courses and conferences. In the large drawing-room across the front of the building are his own Petrov piano, much of his furniture (a table and, re-covered, chairs and a sofa), portraits and family photos, a statuette, a fine needlepoint imperial eagle (the work of his second wife, Helena) and the portable loo with which he always travelled. In an alcove are several of his own cabinets with books from his library; there are also concert programmes and commemorative postcards. In the adjoining recital room, L-shaped, which seats over 70, is a fine Fazioli grand piano, with some recent portraits and photos of musicians who have visited Kąsna Dolna. Two rooms at the rear of the building carry changing exhibitions of works of art loaned from museums in Warsaw. What was formerly the housekeeper's residence, adjoining, is now a small hotel for visitors used in particular for entrants to the annual piano competition.

For over 40 years Paderewski's home was in Morges, a charming old town on the north side of Lac Léman (Lake Geneva), some 50 km from Geneva and ten from Lausanne; Morges was also Stravinsky's home from 1916 to 1920. In 1897 he rented, and two years later bought, a spacious, chalet-like lakeside villa, Riond-Bosson, in a splendid park just outside Morges; it was to have been a refuge where he could devote himself to composition and to rest after arduous concert seasons, but it also became a meeting-place for musicians and political figures from various parts of the world.

The house was demolished in 1965, but in 1991 the local Société Paderewski, founded in 1977, established a Musée Paderewski, situated in the town's Centre Culturel, close to the Casino and the lake. Although modest in size, it holds a rich collection of letters and documents, over a thousand photographs, many concert programmes, copies of the scores of nearly all his compositions and literature on the composer as well as personal objects such as his wedding ring, his fountain pen, his famous piano stool and one of his dress suits, as well as furniture. Many of the objects were presented to the museum by local people who remembered Paderewski. The display is neatly organized, in a single, large room. Paderewski is also commemorated in Morges with a statue in the Parc de la Maison de Seigneux, a Promenade Paderewski and an Avenue Paderewski; there is a Boulevard Paderewski at Vevey and another at Lausanne, where he gave several recitals, and a bronze plaque in the Salle Paderewski at the Casino de Montbenon.

Paderewski is commemorated too in California, where since 1993 there has been an annual Paderewski Festival at the ranch he owned in Paso Robles, Rancho San Ignacio (where he grew almonds, walnuts and prunes and had a Zinfandel vineyard); the Pioneer Area Museum there has a Paderewski Room, endowed by his descendants.

Muzeum Ignacego Jana Paderewskiego i Wychodźstwa Polskiego w Ameryce
Łazienki Królewskie-Podchorążówka
ulica Szwoleżerów 9
00460 Warszawa
Poland

phone +48/0 22 625 3927
fax +48/0 22 622 6434
website www.mnw.art.pl

open Tuesday–Sunday 10.00–15.00

Centrum Paderewskiego
Kąśna Dolna 16
33190 Ciężkowice
Poland

phone, fax +48/0 14 621 0921

open Tuesday–Friday 10.00–16.00, Saturday and Sunday 10.00–14.00

Musée Paderewski
Centre Culturel
1 Place du Casino
1110 Morges
Switzerland

phone +41/0 21 811 0278
fax +41/0 21 811 0280
e-mail phonotheque@multimania.com
website www.multimania.com

open Tuesday 14.00–18.00, and by appointment

Maps 10, 6

Annales Paderewski (Morges: Société Paderewski) [esp. 'L'héritage de Paderewski est enfin réuni à Varsovie', no.19 (1995), 22–3]
A. Wietrzyk: '140 anniversary of Ignacy Padarewski's', *Polish News*, Internet Issue 55 (4) (Nov 2000) [www.polishnews.com] [about Kąśna Dolna]

PALESTRINA

The city of Palestrina is 38 km southeast of Rome, nestled in the Sabine Hills. In its eponymous composer's time it was a prosperous Barberini principality. Today its greatest attractions to visitors are its many ancient sites, among them the house in which the 16th-century composer Giovanni Pierluigi da Palestrina is widely believed to have been born. It lies just above the Piazzale della Liberazione and the Corso Pierluigi, in the Contrada del Piano. Its demolition shortly after World War II was averted by the intervention of Richard Strauss, but its restoration had to wait nearly 50 years.

In 1973 a scholarly foundation was established for the study and promotion of Palestrina's music and in 1994, with the assistance of the Ministry of Culture, the house became its Centro di Studi Palestriniani. It happily succeeds in evoking the history of the building while at the same time commemorating its most celebrated inhabitant. The ground floor display offers a detailed and vivid pictorial chronology of Palestrina's life and works. The first floor, which can be converted for concerts and seminars, also accommodates a small but distinguished permanent exhibition of Palestriniana, among them first editions of his music – motet partbooks, from his own time – and a rare original portrait of about 1580 from the Barberini Collection. There are also small rooms off to the side for consulting microfilms, sound recordings and videos. The library occupies the top floor and at the side of the building there is a small outdoor raked performance space.

The composer maintained his connection with his native city throughout his life. Born in 1525, by 1537 he was living in Rome, where he was a choirboy at S Maria Maggiore. In 1544 he returned to Palestrina to take up the post of organist at the cathedral; three years later he married a local woman and their first children were born in the city. In 1551, a year after his patron Cardinal Monte, the Bishop of Palestrina, became Pope Giulio III, Palestrina was appointed *maestro di cappella* of the Cappella Giulia and left for the Vatican. The family connections remained strong and at the end of his life (he died in 1594), thanks to his second marriage in 1581 to a wealthy Roman widow, Palestrina was able to acquire land of his own in his native city, which he passed on to his descendants. Near the cathedral, in the centre of the Piazza Regina Margherita, stands a statue of the composer.

Fondazione Giovanni Pierluigi da Palestrina

Centro di Studi Palestriniani
Vicolo Pierluigi 3
00036 Palestrina (RM)
Italy

phone +390/0 6953 8083
e-mail fond.palestrina@tiscalinet.it

open Tuesday–Sunday 09.30–12.30

Map 9

A. Cametti: *Le case dei Pierluigi a Palestrina*
  (Palestrina: Fondazione Giovanni Pierluigi da
  Palestrina, 1995)

PANN

Anton Pann (1796–1854) is unique among the composers who appear in this book: although trained in music, a writer of psalms and a collector of folk music, he was primarily a printer and publisher; he founded the first printing shop in Bucharest to publish church music

with vernacular texts. But he is commemorated in Romania for having set a poem by André Mureşianu, 'Awake, Romanians!' ('Deştéaptă-Te Romăne'), which became the Romanian national anthem.

'Awake, Romanians!' was first sung in public not in Bucharest, but in Râmnicu Vâlcea, on 29 July 1848. An important fortified spa town and the seat of its county, Râmnicu Vâlcea, in a hilly region 99 km south of picturesque Sibiu, had been a centre of papermaking and publishing since the 17th century. Pann had two spells there, from 1826 to 1828 and from 1835 to 1837, each time renting rooms in a house which, some 150 years later, became a place of national pilgrimage. When the neighbourhood was redeveloped, the house was moved; it is now the lone 18th-century house in the street, its whiteness and dark brown ornamental wood trim and wood-shingle roof sharply contrasting with the drab modern high-rise buildings and the shops around it. The upstairs was opened in 1982 as a memorial to Pann, with two rooms re-creating the ambience of his library (filled with books and musical instruments) and dining-room (decorated with 19th-century folk pottery and hanging herbs) and the third devoted to the anthem and the 1996 bicentenary celebrations of Pann's birth; in the hallway hang an oil portrait and a view of the house in its original setting. The ground floor appropriately houses a publisher's bookshop and outside there is a memorial, fez-topped bust of Pann.

Pann visited Braşov on three occasions between 1821 and 1828 and he is commemorated there at the First Romanian School Museum. One of the ground-floor rooms is known as the Sala de clasă 'Anton Pann' and the museum archive contains some of his correspondence.

Casa Memorială Anton Pann

Ştirbei Vodă 18
1000 Râmnicu Vâlcea
Vâlcea County
Romania

phone +40/02 50 738026

open daily 10.00–18.00

Muzeul Primei Şcolei Româreşti der Scheii Braşovului
Piaţa Unirii
2200 Braşov
Romania

phone +40/02 68 143879

open daily, 09.00–17.00

Map 11

Parry arriving in his Darracq at Shulbrede Priory, c. 1905

PARRY, Hubert

Shulbrede Priory was an Augustinian foundation, probably dating from around 1190, in the parish of Lynchmere (or Linchmere) in the north-west corner of Sussex, close to Haslemere and Liphook. It was seized and largely destroyed at the time of the dissolution; the surviving buildings, about one eighth of the original establishment, became part of the Cowdray estate and were long used for farming. In 1902 Arthur Ponsonby, painter, scholar, politician (he was later a Labour MP) and son of a former secretary to Queen Victoria, leased and later bought it. In 1898 Ponsonby married Dorothea (Dolly), daughter of Sir Hubert Parry, then Director of the Royal College of Music and Heather Professor of Music at Oxford. Parry and his son-in-law shared many interests and opinions and became firm friends. Parry, who lived mainly in Kensington and in Rustington on the Sussex coast, was a frequent and welcome visitor. (His houses, and the one in Bournemouth in which he was born in 1848, all bear commemorative plaques.) He also lived at the family house and estate, Highnam Court, near Gloucester, which he inherited from his father, Thomas Gambier Parry, along with its important art collection.

The priory remains in the family and is lived in by Parry's great-granddaughters, who generously admit the public to the house and gardens on specific dates and allow interested groups and individual visitors to see it by appointment. It is a remarkable building in a delightful rural setting, much of it seemingly unaltered for several centuries, reached by road from Lynchmere Church, whence it is about half a mile down the hill and then to the left. You enter between two duck ponds (presumably once a moat) and need to give heed to the roving ducks and geese. The house has some remarkable rooms, notably the Undercroft, with its fine vaulted ceiling, and especially the Prior's Chamber, on the upper floor, with its high timbered roof, its 16th-century wall paintings, its diamond-shaped leaded windows – and its piano, by Hagspiel of Dresden, Parry's own and still in use. On it are copies of his *Shulbrede Tunes*, a set of ten piano pieces written in 1911–13, each of them representing a member of the family at Shulbrede or some aspect of the house or life there.

There are Parry relics in several rooms, but there is a concentration in a small study known as the Parry Room, next to the Prior's Chamber. Different aspects of his life and music are covered on a series of display boards with cuttings, photographs and other illustrative material. There also are letters, from Elgar and others. There are paintings by Philip Burne-Jones (son of Edward) of Dolly and of Parry's Rustington house, Knight's Croft, of which there are also paintings by Arthur Ponsonby. Parry's desk is there, along with his scarlet Oxford DMus gown and black hat, and also a couple of his hefty leather suitcases.

Many of Parry's own diaries and letters are preserved, all neatly and carefully written. The diary entry for 10 March 1916 refers to the request of the Poet Laureate, Robert Bridges, for a tune for 'Fight for Right', an organization seeking to secure the moral high ground for the war effort, a tune 'that an audience could take up and join in': this was 'Jerusalem', no less, and the original manuscript, firmly and clearly written, is at Shulbrede too. Parry, in despair over the war (he died in 1918, a month before the Armistice), was evidently happier with its use for the Women's Campaign, and conducted it for the Suffragists at the Royal Albert Hall a year later, soon after which it was adopted as the Women Voters' Hymn. The Parry literature is fully represented, with books by him and books about him and his contemporaries, as well as copies of many of his works.

Shulbrede Priory

Lynchmere

West Sussex GU27 3NQ

Great Britain

phone +44/0 1428 653049

open Sunday and Bank Holiday Monday, end May and end August, or by appointment

Map 5

J. Barrie Jones: 'Shulbrede Priory and Parry's *Shulbrede Tunes*', *Music Review*, li (1990), 176–94

PARRY, Joseph

The Welsh mining community of Merthyr Tydfil is the birthplace of Joseph Parry (1841–1903), son of a Pembrokeshire farmer turned skilled ironworker. The seventh of eight children, Parry was sent down into the pits of the Cyfarthfa Ironworks at the age of nine, working alongside other children who were opening and shutting the air doors for tramloads of coal and, when

they were older, hauling cartloads of coal away from the face where the ceiling was too low for horses. He lived with his family and two lodgers in a small two-storey cottage in a terrace of five attached to the octagonal Bethesda Chapel they attended, facing the Glamorganshire canal, which wound through the valley below Cyfarthfa Castle.

In Parry's day Merthyr Tydfil was the largest town in Wales, producing more iron than anywhere else in the world. The Parrys were fortunate to live in Chapel Row, which was reserved for the more skilled workers, rather than in the over-crowded neighbourhoods that were vulnerable to epidemics. The simple house, built in 1825, is a 'two-up, two-down' (bedrooms for the children upstairs, kitchen and parents' room downstairs) with a stone staircase at the rear. There was no running water and the family meals were cooked on a range in the fireplace.

No.4 Chapel Row was the Parrys' home until 1854 when they emigrated to the USA. Parry himself last visited it on New Year's Day 1902. In 1977 the terrace, but not the chapel, was saved from demolition through the efforts of staff and students of Cyfarthfa High School and the local council, and two years later no.4 was opened to the public by the Merthyr Tydfil Heritage Trust as a traditional ironworker's cottage and a memorial to the town's greatest musician. The exhibitions were installed in 1986 and the ground-floor rooms restored in 1990.

Parry had sung in choirs as a child, but began formal music lessons only when he was 17, working in the Welsh mining community of Danville, Pennsylvania. He won first prize at the 1861 Utica (New York) eisteddfod for his *Temperance Vocal March*, and sought and won approbation in his native Wales. With funds raised on both sides of the Atlantic, he entered the Royal Academy of Music in London in 1868 and in 1871 became the first Welshman to take the Cambridge MusB and later the MusD. He settled in Wales in 1873, becoming the first professor of music at Aberystwyth.

During his final years, Dr Parry (known as 'Y Doctor Mawr') lived with his wife, Jane (their sons were called Joseph Haydn, William Sterndale and David Mendelssohn), in Penarth, just south of Cardiff, in a house named 'Cartref' in Victoria Square. He died there on 17 February 1903 and is buried in the nearby churchyard of St Augustine's, a lyre with a broken string on his tombstone.

At the Merthyr Tydfil museum, the ground-floor rooms are decorated in period style. The small bedroom to the right of the front door also commemorates Parry's birth, on 21 May 1841. Upstairs in the former bedrooms are displays devoted to Parry and the history of the town. Wall panels survey his life, the restoration of Chapel Row and the choral and colliery band traditions of the town (Parry composed the *Tydfil Overture* for the Cyfarthfa Brass Band). In the cases are facsimiles of music manuscripts, his autobiography and letters as well as editions of his music, which include a score of *Blodwen* (1878), considered the first Welsh opera. There is also a signed first edition of Jack Jones's account of Parry's life, *Off to Philadelphia in the morning* (1947), which was dramatized on television by BBC Wales in 1977. Against the far wall is an American-built harmonium such as the family might have owned. The house is now managed by the Cyfarthfa Castle Museum, which runs workshops mainly for school parties studying local history.

Joseph Parry's Ironworkers' Cottage
4 Chapel Row
Georgetown
Merthyr Tydfil CF48 1BN
Wales

phone +44/0 1685 723 112 (Cyfarthfa Castle Museum)

open April–September, Thursday–Sunday 14.00–17.00 and by appointment

Map 5

Joseph Parry's Ironworkers' Cottage, 4, Chapel Row: a Brief Guide to the Cottage (Merthyr Tydfil: County Borough Council Leisure Services Department, n.d.)

R. Hayman: *Dr Joseph Parry, Musician and Composer, 1841–1903* (Merthyr Tydfil, 1986)
J.M. Popkin: *Musical Monuments* (London: K.G. Saur, 1986)

PEJAČEVIĆ

As Croatia's first woman composer, Dora Pejačević (1885–1923) might have been accorded some kind of memorial even if she hadn't come from a distinguished family. She was the precocious and handsome daughter and namesake of Baron Teodor Pejačević. Privately tutored, she was an accomplished linguist as well as a musician; she played the piano and the violin, and from the age of 12 she composed steadily until her marriage at the age of 35. Although as a composer she was mainly self-taught, she had short spells in Zagreb, Dresden and Munich for musical studies. She was alive to the literary and musical tastes of the day, and the heady influences of late Romantic, Impressionist, Expressionist and folk-music styles are evident in her music. Many of her works – 58 are known – were published and performed in Vienna, Munich or Zagreb during her lifetime, among them symphonic works as well as solo and chamber music; nearly half are for piano. Her manuscripts and early editions today form an archive in the Croatian Music Institute in Zagreb.

Pejačević spent most of her short life at Našice, near Osijek in eastern Croatia, where she could enjoy the freedom

The Pejačević family estate, Našice

afforded by the family's beautifully maintained estate, with an English-style park that incorporated a forest of oaks and hornbeams, a glass winter garden and a swan-shaped lake. On the edge of the lake she had a small two-storey wooden pavilion built and equipped with a piano so that she could compose there. (In 1909 a villa, inspired by Sans Souci, was built in the grounds for her newly married brother Marcus and surrounded by formal French gardens; today it is the home of a primary music school named after Dora and the studios of Radio Našice.)

In 1921, Pejačević was married to Ottomar von Lumbe, and she left Našice – only to die in Munich, scarcely a year and a half later, of complications following the birth of their son Theo. She left instructions that she should be buried at Našice, outside and adjacent to the Mauzolej Pejačević, the family's neo-Gothic chapel built in 1881 across the road (Vladimira Nazora) from the town cemetery. A copy of the veiled bust of 'Tuga' ('Sadness') by the Serbian Đorđe Jovanović, which she prized, presides over her grave; her gravestone is simply

Dora Pejačević's composing pavilion

inscribed 'DORA' (on the back is the final phrase from her setting of Nietzsche's *The Loneliest*). When the chapel was desecrated in the aftermath of World War II, her grave was undisturbed.

In recent years she has become the subject of a film, *Contessa* (1993), by Zvonimir Berković, and a popular biography, *Young Dora* (1995), by Stanko Rozgaj, both of which draw heavily on the aristocratic life she enjoyed at her family's Slavonian estate in the years before World War I. The Pejačević family acquired their manorial country estate in 1734. Around 1811 they built the present manor house, which remained their principal residence until the Germans appropriated it during World War II. In 1945 it became the property of the Yugoslav State and since 1974 it has served as a regional museum. Although her father and grandfather served as viceroys of the Austro-Hungarian Empire, it is Dora's life that is today celebrated in one of the museum's three memorial rooms.

The shells of the buildings and the lake are all that have survived the vicissitudes of the 20th century. Although the site is a Category 1 cultural monument, the grounds are no longer landscaped and the manor house retains only a few of its original internal features such as the carved wood ceiling, brass chandelier and parquet floor of the Red Room on ground level, used today for chamber music concerts. The music salon on the lower level, where Dora kept her Blüthner grand piano, is now the headquarters of the local singing society, which is named after Vatroslav Lisinski (1819–54), often regarded as the first distinctively Croatian composer.

The Dora Pejačević Memorial Room, which looks out on the parkland from the first floor, displays both her piano and family furniture. Next to one of the many elegant photographic portraits are the chair and the folding screen seen in the picture. In addition to the portraits of Dora, there are several of her family, including one of her father with the young Theo at Našice. Also on display are the 'Tuga' sculpture, which she acquired in 1906 (it adorned her grave until 1985), and a plaster bust of Dora herself by D. Jelovšik from 1916. Editions and recordings of her music, along with examples of her correspondence and an exquisite fan she must have owned, are behind glass.

Since the foundation of the museum, Pejačević has been the subject of research by the curators. They have a collection of recorded reminiscences and continue to collect related material, including copies of unique documents, concert programmes and publications about her life and music. The centenary of her birth on 10 September 1885 was marked with a series of events presided over by her son, Theo von Lumbe, which included the erection of a bust by D. Štambek in the manor grounds, the rebuilding of the lakeside pavilion, and the inauguration of an annual concert and a scholarly conference in her memory.

Zafičajni Muzej Našice

Pejačevićev trg 5
31500 Našice
Croatia

phone, fax +385/0 31 613414
website www.mdc.hr/nasice/hr.
d-pejacevic

open Monday, Friday 08.00–15.00;
Tuesday, Wednesday, Thursday
08.00–18.00; Saturday 9.00–11.00 and
by appointment

Map 14

K. Kos: *Dora Pejačević* (Zagreb: Muzički Informativni Centar, 1998)
S. Lučevnjak: 'Dorina baština i Zavičajni muzej Našice [Dora's heritage and the Našice Regional Museum]', *Informatica Museologica*, xxxii/1–2 (2001), 58–9

PERGOLESI

His early death and the prodigious reputation of just two of his works – the intermezzo *La serva padrona* and the *Stabat mater*, composed on his deathbed – made Pergolesi famous in the 18th century, so famous that libraries abound with manuscripts falsely bearing his name (some of them fooled Stravinsky into thinking he was using only Pergolesi's music in his *Pulcinella*). But not until the 21st century did the city of Jesi set up a museum to commemorate its most famous musical son. Giovanni Battista Pergolesi was born in the city, a few kilometres inland from Ancona, in 1710; his family had settled there some 75 years before. Like numerous other Italian composers of his generation from the Adriatic coast, he went to Naples to study. A single spell in Rome apart, he remained there for the rest of his life, and at the beginning of 1735 he went to a convent in Pozzuoli, close by, where he died of tuberculosis in March. He is commemorated there by a tablet in the cathedral.

The Comune of Jesi initially commemorated him on the bicentenary of his birth, in 1910, when a marble bust by Alessandro Lazzerini, now restored and housed in the museum, was erected in the Piazza del Statuto (or Piazza Pergolesi). Plans for a museum took nearly a century to come to fruition. It was only in 2001 that the Sale Pergolesiane (Pergolesi Rooms) were inaugurated in the city theatre, the Teatro Comunale G.B. Pergolesi. The Pergolesi Rooms, on the first floor, can be entered from the street that runs alongside the theatre, or direct from the body of the theatre (which also houses a Sala Spontiniano, for Spontini too is, almost, a local composer: *see* SPONTINI).

The Comune was able to call on several local libraries, archives and other collections, not to mention dealers from across Italy, to fill its three spacious and attractively restored rooms (the ceilings are especially fine). In the first pair of rooms the exhibits concentrate on Jesi and its place in Pergolesi's life – his family tree, views of the city, the original baptismal entry and other documents, coins and publications dating from his time there, his masters during his early years. There are Pergolesi biographies, and a model swan, in plaster – for he had been dubbed 'il cigno di Jesi'.

His later years are commemorated in the further room. The Naples residences and other sites there are strongly represented, as are his Neapolitan School contemporaries. From Rome there is a Ghezzi caricature which goes beyond the London one (also reproduced) by showing the deformity of a leg from which Pergolesi suffered. A section on his works and his reputation displays scores and librettos, including, of *La serva padrona*, one from Paris, where it made such a stir in the 1750s. Most of the portrayals of Pergolesi himself, only Ghezzi's apart, are necessarily posthumous guesswork, but at least they tell a story of how seductively the Swan of Jesi sang after his death. This continues in the Sala del Ridotto with its array of pictures (1825, 1845, 1880) and busts (1872, 1881, 1907) along with stage designs and music – including examples of misattributions.

Galleria del Teatro Sale Pergolesiane

Teatro Comunale G.B. Pergolesi
Piazza della Repubblica 9
60036 Jesi (Ancona)
Italy

phone +390/0 731 538351
fax +390/0 731 538356
e-mail teatro.pergolesi@comune.jesi.an.it

open Monday–Saturday 10.00–13.00, Tuesday, Thursday, Sunday 16.00–19.00 (guide available Thursday, for groups only, by appointment, and Sunday)

Map 9

F. Cecchini, ed.: *Galleria del Teatro Sale Pergolesiane: Catalogo* (Jesi: Teatro Comunale G.B. Pergolesi, 2002)

PERLEA

Better known as a conductor, the Romanian-born composer Jonel Perlea (1900–70) is commemorated in his family home at Ograda, about 140 km east of Bucharest. His father's family were wealthy farmers who built the nearby church. Their home was spacious enough to be able to accommodate performances by a marionette troupe from Bucharest for the young Jonel, his two brothers, his sister and their friends, in a room that now seats 60 and is used for concerts. In 1985 the building became a museum, under the direction of the regional museum in Slobozia.

The collection on display in the four principal rooms was contributed by the Perlea family, in particular Jonel's elder brother Alexandru, his widow Lizette and their son, also Jonel. It includes manuscripts and Romanian editions of his music (his Sinfonia no.1 in C op.12, *Simfonie Concertanta* for violin and orchestra and *Variatiuni Simfonice pe o temă proprie*), recordings of both his music and standard repertory that he conducted, programmes and posters for performances in Romania and abroad, portraits (including drawings of him conducting by Corneliu Baba), a bust by George V. Demetrescu-Brăila (1969), photographs, pianos, Patefon phonographs, furniture (both Romanian and American) and small personal possessions.

Perlea, whose mother was German, studied in Munich and Leipzig, but he returned to Bucharest to make his career and from 1934 served as music director of the Opera. With the Soviet army approaching and the country turning against Germany in 1944, Perlea and his wife sought refuge in Vienna, but they were captured and interned by the Germans. After the war they emigrated to the USA, although he later returned to Europe to conduct (at La Scala, Milan). Perlea and his wife lived in New York (according to the cheque book on display, in East 79th Street) where he conducted a season at the Metropolitan Opera House (1949–50) and taught at the Manhattan School of Music for 18 years; he also conducted the San Francisco Opera, the Chicago Lyric Opera, the Opera Company of Boston and the Connecticut Symphony Orchestra. Photographs on display record visits by the Perleas to Ograda in 1930, 1935 and finally in 1969, when he was given a hero's welcome, shortly before his death in New York.

Casa Memorialǎ Ionel Perlea
Ograda
Comuna Bucu
Ialomita
Romania

phone +40/02 43 215487 (Muzeul Judetean Ialomita, Slobozia)

open Tuesday–Saturday 10.00–18.00; Sunday 10.00–16.00

Map 11

PETERSON-BERGER

Best known during his life as the controversial music critic 'P-B' of the Stockholm newspaper the *Dagens Nyheter*, Wilhelm Peterson-Berger (1867–1942) has become the best-loved and most oft-performed of Swedish composers, and an icon of the Swedish Romantic movement. His Third Symphony and Violin Concerto are especially popular; among Swedish amateurs his choral works, songs and piano pieces, which make use of folk music, are a staple. A great admirer of Wagner, Peterson-Berger produced his own Swedish Gesamtkunstwerk, which he based on an 11th-century saga. *Arnljot*, a three-act spoken drama with incidental music, which he composed in 1910, is still performed every summer in an open-air theatre on the tiny, hilly island of Fröson.

Fröson is where Peterson-Berger, a confirmed bachelor, spent nearly all his summer holidays from 1889, and he retired there in 1930. The island in Lake Storsjön is today connected to the mainland by a bridge to Östersund, the main town of the north-central region of Jämtland. Many of his works make specific reference to the island and in particular the 'Frösönblomster' (the wild flowers of Fröson). In 1910 he purchased a five-hectare plot of land near the church on the island's south-west side, looking out over the Storsjön and the mountains beyond. There were no buildings, only pine and birch forest and fields. It was only in 1913, when his mother, Sofia Wilhelmina Peterson (*née* Berger)

died, that he could afford to build a house. His first summer there was in 1914.

'Sommarhagen' is a fine example of Swedish Romantic domestic architecture. It is a two-storey house with basement, made of coarse-cut timber. The roof was originally turfed, like the tool and wood store behind the house today. At the front there is a covered veranda and entrance decorated with barley-sugar pillars and folk art. Upstairs, verandas and outside staircases to the ground are provided for both the master bedroom and the guest suite: the stairs may have been a sensible fire precaution but they also enabled the composer and his friends to come and go, unnoticed, at will. Peterson-Berger even had a peephole made so that he could observe unwelcome callers from his bedroom balcony and slip away undiscovered. At the rear of the house is his beloved tennis court and, a short distance away, a summerhouse for his faithful manservant, Carl Johan Wenngren. To the north of the house, a bust of the composer adorning a plinth serves as a gathering point for parties of visitors.

Immediately inside, one enters a brightly painted, double-storey music room, dominated by the grand piano and the ornamented, exposed roof trusses above and the staircase up to the balcony

Sommerhagen, Peterson-Berger's house, Fröson

Peterson-Berger's music room

over the stone fireplace. Above the light-blue wainscoting, the walls, pale yellow, are decorated with paintings of potato plants by a local artist, Paul Jonze. At the apex of the outer roof truss is a red glass window that Peterson-Berger called the 'Eye of Love' in memory of his mother; in late July evenings the sun shines through it and into the fireplace, creating (shades of Wagner!) an illusion of fire.

To the right of the fireplace is Peterson-Berger's study, with views to the south and west. On his desk – along with a baton, writing implements and his glasses – are cigars, an apple and a glass of glögg. Other distractions from composing include his straw hat, a tennis racquet and balls, a globe and his cat's travelling basket. The former dining-room is now a library and exhibition room with portraits and a large carved wooden bust of the composer as well as photos of him frolicking with his cat and playing tennis with his friends. To the left of the fireplace is the kitchen and servant's room, with access to the cellar. Upstairs, above the kitchen, is the guest suite, light and airy like Peterson-Berger's own rooms at the front, with big windows and alcoves to protect the beds they shelter from draughts. In 1916 the composer had a telephone installed and in 1928 central heating.

Peterson-Berger died in Östersund at the age of 75 and was buried on the island, in the churchyard near Sommarhagen. A foundation was established in his name to look after the estate, and a year and a half

later, during the summer of 1944, the house was first opened to the public. It opens annually for seven weeks during the late spring and summer, as well as at Advent (the anniversary of his death is 3 December) and for other special events, including recitals in the music room.

Sommarhagen
Peterson-Berger Väg
83223 Frösön
Östersund
Sweden

phone +46/0 63 143041, 143704 (Peterson-Berger-Stiftelsen)

open late May–end August, 11.00–15.00/18.00 (closing times vary)

Map 13

G. Percy: *Wilhelm Peterson-Berger: an Introduction* (Stockholm, 1982)

F. Jor, ed.: *Nordic Artists' Homes* (Stockholm: Prisma, 1999), 153–7

PETRAUSKAS

In 1930, the Petrauskas brothers, the composer of light opera Mikas (1873–1937) and the well-known operatic tenor Kipras (1885–1968), built a large, imposing house on a hill above Kaunas. Mikas took up residence on the left side, Kipras on the right. Today it is a museum of Lithuanian music with a recital room seating nearly 100. On the ground floor, across from the recital room, are exhibitions devoted to the brothers; upstairs, Kipras's first-floor flat is maintained and in the room to the left the museum also houses an exhibition on the life and works of the Petrauskas' friend and colleague, Stasyš Šimkus (*see* ŠIMKUS).

Kipras is given pride of place because of his greater stature in the musical world and because, unlike his elder brother, who emigrated in 1907, he was based in Lithuania all his life. In 1920 he was among the founders of the Kaunas Opera House and he was later professor at Vilnius Conservatory (now the Lithuanian Academy of Music). Mikas returned to Lithuania only in 1930, after

23 years in the USA, where he promoted Lithuanian music and put together operettas in Lithuanian, performed in New York and in Boston, where in 1917 he founded the Lithuanian Music School. The brothers are buried together in Vilnius in the Rasos Cemetery.

The exhibition devoted to Mikas – who composed what is generally regarded as the first Lithuanian opera, *Birute* (given in Vilnius in 1906, with his brother singing: it is really a play with music) – is chronologically organized and illustrated with facsimiles of music, pictures, documents, posters and programmes and a handsome portrait of his first wife. The adjoining room is devoted to Kipras's career, displaying his costumes and his own concert clothes; there are photographs of him in different roles, programmes and recordings, and personal belongings including his prized collection of fishing lures.

Mikas and Kipras Petrauskai Lithuanian Music Museum

Petrausko 31
3005 Kaunas
Lithuania

phone +370/0 773 3371
e-mail kau.petr.muz@delfi.lt
website www.muziejai.rnch.mii.lt/kaunas/muzikos_muziejus

open Wednesday–Sunday 11.00–17.00

Map 2

PIAF

Edith Piaf was the most loved of French *chanteuses*. Chiefly she sang songs specially composed for her, but she composed a number herself, probably around 30, among them *La vie en rose*, the most famous of them all. Piaf was born in 1915 as Edith Giovanna Gassion, in the Belleville area of Paris, in the 19th *arrondissement*, a fairly seedy region in the east of the city, ethnically rather mixed (her father, an acrobat, was Moroccan; her Parisian mother left her upbringing to an aunt). Her birthplace,

on the steps at 72 Rue de Belleville, is marked by a plaque. She worked initially as a street singer until, at 19, she was launched into the night-club world as 'la môme Piaf', 'the little sparrow' (she was less than five feet, 1.5 m, tall).

When she died in 1963 she was buried – without benefit of clergy, because of her life-style – at Père Lachaise, in the 20th *arrondissement*, not far from where she was born. She is commemorated by a statue, erected belatedly in 2003, in the Place Edith Piaf, close to the Porte de Bagnolet metro station, in the Rue de la Py. In that square is the Bar Edith Piaf, something of a shrine to her, with its drawings, photos and posters; the *patronne* is said to know Piaf's entire repertory by heart.

But she is more fully remembered in the small Musée Edith Piaf, a privately run museum set up in the 11th *arrondissement* in 1977, in two rooms of the fourth-floor flat of her devotee Bernard Marchois. It is in a large block, close to the Menilimontant metro, in an

Bar Edith-Piaf, Paris

area again not far from Belleville and one familiar to Piaf from her childhood years; outside, a plaque proclaims the office of the Piaf fan club. A life-size cardboard cut-out of the singer greets you at the entrance, and there is also a large teddy-bear, the gift of her second husband. Some of her furniture is preserved, along with items of jewellery, china, clothes (especially little black dresses), numerous photographs and posters, letters (among them some from Maurice Chevalier), commemorative stamps, and the boxing gloves of her lover Marcel Cerdan. With her voice providing a soft background, the world of the greatest of *chanteuses* is tellingly evoked.

Musée Edith Piaf*
5 rue Crespin du Gast
75011 Paris
France

phone, fax +33/0 1 4355 5272

open Monday–Thursday 13.00–18.00, by appointment only

Map 6

PICCINNI

South-eastern Italy saw the birth of several of the most important Italian opera composers of the later 18th century, but these men are generally regarded as Neapolitans because it was in Naples that they were trained and had their operatic baptisms. One of them is Niccolò Piccinni. Piccinni was born in 1728 in the Adriatic port of Bari, the main city of Puglia, nowadays sometimes dubbed the Milan of the south, and a sort of eastern counterpart to Naples. There he began his career; it soon took him to Rome, and in 1776 to Paris, where (unwillingly) he was put up as a rival to Gluck. His fortunes were mixed. An enormously prolific opera composer, he was especially admired for his early *La buona figliuola*, a sentimental comedy after Samuel Richardson's *Pamela*, but his serious work, in both Italian and French, is of considerable stature and very skil-

fully written. He got caught up in the political turmoils of the time and died, impoverished, near Paris in 1800. He was honoured in his native city on his centenary by the erection of a statue in a square, the Piazza Massari, on the Corso Vittorio Emanuele, and in 1999, in good time for his bicentenary, by the opening of the Casa Piccinni.

His origins were humble. His father was a church violinist, his mother the sister of the composer Gaetano Latilla. He was born in the *basso*, the ground-floor room, rented by the family from the fathers of St Theresa, of a house in a corner of a large square (the Piazza Mercantile). It is in what is now called the Alta Città, the old city – then simply the city of Bari; on a large promontory, today it survives virtually intact, little changed since medieval or Renaissance times. The building was acquired by the municipality in 1954 and in 1982 restoration began, as part of the revitalization of the old city.

The building is now shared between the Piccinni house museum and the research and the early music departments and the library of Bari Conservatory (the Conservatorio di Musica 'Niccolò Piccinni', which administers the Casa Piccinni). The ground-floor room looking on to the piazza is used for lectures and recitals; behind it, beyond a smaller room that is to become a sound archive, lies the modest-sized room in which the Piccinni family lived. The museum proper is entered from the side, up a flight of steps from a narrow alley, Vico Fiscardi. Its exhibition rooms are curiously shaped as the central one of the three falls within a square tower, part of the original 12th-century building: there are thus archways linking the rooms. In them are displays of Piccinni scores, principally in French publications (opera was rarely printed in Italy in Piccinni's time), a libretto of the *Antigono* of his uncle, Latilla, and several portrayals of the man himself – he is generally shown with a gentle, slightly ironic smile, rare among 18th-century composers, and surely significant. A set of informative display

The Piccinni statue, Bari

boards on Piccinni and his contemporaries is shown in a room on the next floor, although the room is also used for special exhibitions (at the time of our visit, there was one of 18th-century theatrical machinery).

Casa Piccinni Centro Ricerche Musicali
Vico Fiscardi 2 (Piazza Mercantile)
70100 Bari
Italy

phone +390/0 80 521 4561
(Conservatorio, 574 0022)
fax +390/0 80 579 4461
e-mail info@casapiccinni.it
website www.casapiccinni.it

open by appointment

Map 9

M. Civita: *Il restauro della casa natale di Niccolò Piccinni* (Bari: Mario Adda, 2000)

C. Gelao and M. Sajous d'Oria: *Il tempo di Niccolò Piccinni: percorsa di un musicista del Settecento* (Bari: Mario Adda, 2000) [exhibition catalogue]

PIZZETTI

Ildebrando Pizzetti was a native of Parma; he was born there on 20 September 1880. He studied at the local conservatory from 1895 to 1901, and later he conducted at the Teatro Regio there (1902–4) and briefly taught at the conservatory (1907–8) before going on to a career in Florence, Milan and Rome. He took his Parmesan origins seriously, or at least his friend the writer D'Annunzio did, dubbing him 'Ildebrando di Parma', a title he used on some of his early works.

After his death, in Rome on 13 February 1968, he was brought to Parma for burial, and the study of his Roman home in Via Panama was later transported there, to become one of the three studies preserved at the Conservatorio di Musica 'Arrigo Boito' (the others are those of Boito himself and Toscanini). The Conservatorio, in a building that was once a Carmelite monastery, has open courtyards (with prolific laburnums at the right time of year), surrounded by cloisters and arcades. The Sala Pizzetti, unlike the other two studies, which are housed together in a second-floor museum area, stands in a corner of one of them, by the entrance to the library, the fine Biblioteca Palatina, and falls under the purview of the librarian.

'No, no, I don't write to talk about myself! I don't consider my person or the circumstances of my life of such importance as to be able to interest anyone beside my family and a few close friends', said Pizzetti, when interviewed about the 'caro Conservatorio del Carmine' (quoted by Minardi from his *Giallò e blu*, 1950). The study provides an appropriately sober reflection of Pizzetti's interests and the influences behind his music. His books, on a range of musical and literary topics, are there, carefully catalogued, and his library of miniature scores, as well as a copy of the collected edition of Palestrina's works. There are a few of his autographs: an early piano *Romanza*, a string quartet minuet, some music for D'Annunzio's *La pisanella*. Subjects of photographs and other reproductions include Beethoven (there is a death mask too), Verdi and D'Annunzio. His upright piano and table and chairs are there, and of Pizzetti himself an oil portrait, a bronze head and a posthumous plaster cast of his hands, along with his pipes, his glasses and various small *objets d'art*.

Sezione musicale della Biblioteca Palatina

Conservatorio di Musica 'Arrigo Boito'
Via Conservatorio 27
43100 Parma
Italy

phone +390/0 521 289429
fax +390/0 521 200398
e-mail ssboito@provincia.parma.it
website www.biblcom.unipr.it/bibparm/
bibprov/musicale

open Monday–Saturday 09.00–13.15,
Monday and Wednesday 14.30–17.00

Map 9

G.P. Minardi: *Ildebrando Pizzetti: la giovinezza*, Musica a Parma, vi (Parma: Conservatorio di Musica 'Arrigo Boito', 1980)

PLEYEL

'I must tell you that some quartets have appeared, by a certain Pleyel . . . very well written and most pleasing to listen to . . . It will be a lucky day for music if later on Pleyel should be able to replace Haydn', wrote Mozart to his father in 1784. It didn't quite work out like that, but Pleyel, a pupil of Haydn's, did become a considerable force in the musical world, an amiable composer, a leading Parisian publisher and instrument-maker and founder of a musical dynasty. His pianos and his son's are displayed in the Paris Musée de la Musique and his name marks a leading concert hall; and there is a Rue Pleyel, tucked in behind the Gare

de Lyon. He died in 1831 and is buried at Père Lachaise.

Ignaz Joseph Pleyel was born in 1757 in the small village of Ruppersthal, in the rolling Niederösterreich wine country, some 55 km north-west of Vienna, close to Großweikersdorf on the old route to Prague (from which the Pleyel Museum is lavishly signposted). His father was schoolmaster and organist there; since 1998 the former schoolhouse by the church, extensively renovated, has been a small museum (the plaque in the vicinity, put up on his bicentenary in 1957, would seem to indicate that the composer was actually born in an adjacent building). Reached from the main village street up a flight of steps in a covered way, it consists of a single room with an entrance lobby, with a display, carefully and lovingly assembled in cases and glazed wall mountings, giving an illustrated account of Pleyel's life, from his birth in Ruppersthal, his tuition from Vanhal and Haydn and his patronage from the Erdődy and Esterházy families, to his visits to Italy and to London (as a proposed rival to Haydn) and his career in Strasbourg – here the mistaken claim that he composed the *Marseillaise* is regrettably reiterated – and Paris. There are facsimiles of his music, manuscript and printed, and several examples of his editions.

Even more appealing however are examples of his work as a piano maker. The museum has one of his last grand pianos, built in 1831, which is used for recordings and in the recitals regularly held there (about 40 can be accommodated; for larger events the church is used). A square piano of a few years later, by his son Camille, is held on loan. There is a bust of Pleyel, and the room is garnished with a set of marionettes used for a production of his *Die Fee Urgele*, a marionette opera written for Eszterháza, some of which features in the video presentation offered to visitors.

Ignaz J. Pleyel-Museum

3701 Ruppersthal 108
Austria

phone +43/0 2955 70645
fax +43/0 2955 71155
e-mail adolf.ehrentraud.pleyel@aon.net
website www.pleyel.at

open 1 March–31 October, Sunday
09.30–13.00, or by appointment

Map 1

Ignaz J. Pleyel Museum Ruppersthal
   (Ruppersthal: Internationale Ignaz J. Pleyel
   Gesellschaft, 2000) [French version, *Ignace
   Pleyel*, 2001, also available]
N. Simeone: *Paris: a Musical Gazetteer* (New
   Haven and London: Yale University Press,
   2000)

PONCHIELLI

The composer who was long regarded as Verdi's probable successor, Amilcare Ponchielli, came from the village of Paderno Fasolaro, some 17 km north-west of Cremona, where he was born on 31 August 1834. His father was not only the village organist and teacher but also – like Verdi's – the innkeeper, whose house was the village shop. In the event, only one of his operas, *La Gioconda* (1875), was to find a firm place in the repertory, although *I lituani* (1874) also won much respect. Ponchielli spent much of his career as a bandmaster, briefly in Piacenza and then in Cremona, but moved to Milan in 1870, ending up as a leading opera conductor and professor of composition at the conservatory (Puccini was among his pupils), and finally as

Ponchielli's birthplace in Paderno (before restoration)

organist in Bergamo. He died in Milan in 1886.

He is remembered with affection not only in his native village, which in 1952 changed its name to Paderno Ponchielli in his honour, but also in Cremona, where there is a statue to him in the public gardens and a Teatro Comunale Amilcare Ponchielli, as well as a street bearing his name; the bulk of his manuscripts are preserved there, in the Museo Civico and the Biblioteca Statale, where several that were previously unknown have lately come to light. He is also commemorated in the Bergamo church, S Maria Maggiore, where he was organist.

But it is Paderno Ponchielli that keeps his chief shrine. Just down the Via Amilcare Ponchielli from the mayoral offices, which bear a plaque and a bust to him, stands the modest house in which the composer was born. The local Comune renovated it in 1934 but acquired it only in the 1960s. Another, much-needed renovation began in 2002, when as the first step the exterior was stripped of its modern accretions. Eventually this 17th-century building will be restored to its condition in Ponchielli's day. It has two ground-floor rooms, of which the rear one, then a bar, has been used to house the municipal library (to be moved out during the planned restoration), and two upper rooms, one of them originally used for the hostelry's passing guests.

In the reception area there are recent opera posters. One showcase houses some autograph juvenilia, among them a piece Ponchielli wrote when he was a boy of nine and which he took in his pocket when he visited his benefactor, Count Jacini. The museum owns a handful of autographs and expects to acquire more. Along with these is an early report from Milan Conservatory, where he went to study. Another holds various commemorative objects – medallions, cards, stamps, photographs. There is a table piano, the first instrument Ponchielli bought, second-hand, after leaving the conservatory; his grandson gave it to the house when the village adopted Ponchielli's name. There are some piano rolls, made in Cremona.

The upstairs rooms, which included the family accommodation, also hold exhibits: many original editions, of operas and songs in particular, along with lithographic portraits, literature and recordings, programmes, opera librettos (among them early versions of *I promessi sposi*) and production photographs. There is a large bust, a copy of one in the Cremona museum. The front room is more personal: a lock of Ponchielli's hair and his funeral flowers (presented by one of his pupils), his desk and cabinet (presented by his sons), his chairs, his passport, dress clothes from his time as band director in Piacenza, various letters, his diary with musical sketches, with photographs, posters, awards and other memorabilia on the wall and the desk. The museum's marked personal character – not really surprising, for part of the collection belongs to the curator himself, an avid collector of Ponchielliana – will surely survive the imminent restoration.

Casa-Museo Amilcare Ponchielli
Via Amilcare Ponchielli 21
26024 Paderno Ponchielli
Italy

phone (Comune office) +390/0 374 367200
(library in house) +390/0 374 67467

open by appointment

Map 9

PORUMBESCU

Although still often referred to by its former name, Stupca, the little village lying among woods 26 km south-west of Suceava is officially called Ciprian Porumbescu after its favourite son, who died there in 1883. Porumbescu, born in Şipote in 1853, spent much of his childhood in Stupca, where his father was the priest. Eight members of the family, the composer among them, are buried in a row in the local churchyard.

At the bottom of the village is the eponymous museum dedicated to his memory. The main wall of the entrance hall is dominated by a tricolour representation of his patriotic hymn *Cintecul Tricolorului* although, as the background music reminds us, his haunting *Balada* for violin is probably far better known. Also on display in the entrance hall are his boudoir grand piano and a cello. His life is chronicled in photographic collages in the adjoining room: his studies in Vienna (where he was a pupil of Bruckner) and travel to Italy (where he met Verdi in Genoa); his friendships with the poet Mihai Eminescu and the early Romanian Prime Minister Mihai Kogălnicanu; and his unrequited love affair with Berta Gorgon, the beautiful daughter of the priest at nearby Illişeşti, for whom he composed nocturnes for piano and songs (among them 'Ich liebe dich' and 'Resignation'). The cases contain copies of his published works, his baton and a embroidered silk cover for his violin. In a long gallery are posters advertising performances of his music. There follows a small room with furniture, costumes and stills from the romantic 1971 film *Ciprian Porumbescu*, a room displaying further posters, evidence of the centenary events of 1953 and 1983 and a choral competition named after the composer, and finally a small concert room decorated with a plaster bust and photographs. In the garden there is an evocative statue of him clutching his violin.

The museum at Ciprian Porumbescu (Stupca)

Returning through the village, past the church and taking the right fork at the village well (none of the roads is named), you see the memorial house at the top of the road, near where it ends in pasture-land. All that remains of the family compound – depicted in a drawing, of which copies are on display at both sites – is a small outbuilding and a well-cum-summerhouse, nestling in an orchard. The main house, where Porumbescu died on 6 June 1883, has disappeared. Opened to the public on the centenary of the composer's birth, the memorial house has one room containing family relics, mostly photographs of documents and portraits of his parents, brother and sister and Berta, and the Viennese Peine piano that belonged to his sister Mărioara; its other room re-creates a rustic kitchen, with brightly glazed pottery, wooden milk jug and embroidered curtains. The setting is completed with a bust and a memorial plaque.

Porumbescu taught in Braşov from 1880 until his early death at the age of 29. He is remembered there with a bust in a park bordered by Sirul Gheorghe Dima, near the gymnasium where he taught and where a plaque recalls that his operetta *Crau Nou* ('New Moon') was first performed there on 27 February 1882. Not far away, in the Piaţa Unirii, the autograph of *Crau Nou* is on display at the First Romanian School Museum in the grounds of the St Nicholas Church.

Casa Memorială Ciprian Porumbescu
5829 Ciprian Porumbescu
Suceava County
Romania

open Tuesday–Sunday 10.00–18.00

Muzeul Memorial Ciprian Porumbescu
5829 Ciprian Porumbescu
Suceava County
Romania

phone +40/02 30 215439 (National Museum of Bukovina)

open Tuesday–Sunday 09.00–18.00

Map 11

PREJAC

Gjuro Prejac (1870–1936) was not just a composer but also a singer, choreographer, scene designer, librettist, actor and mime. One of 16 children of a school-teacher in Desinić, in north-west Croatia, he studied in Zagreb and spent his career in or around the theatre there, chiefly as a singer, but also appearing in Vienna and Prague. He composed three operettas and many songs, several of which became popular.

The village of his birth is some 60 km north of Zagreb, close to the Slovenian border. Nearby, on a large hill, is a castle, Veliki Tabor, with a fine double galleried courtyard, dating back to the 12th century though not completed until the 16th – and at the beginning of the 21st under heavy and urgently-needed restoration. One of its rooms, on the first floor, is dedicated to Prejac's memory. The display there, if rather haphazard, gives some picture of his personality and his role in theatrical life. There is a large plaster bust, photographs of Prejac in costume and concert garb showing the range of his characterizations, his diploma, his mandolin, copies of his music and his 78 rpm recordings, and a pencil portrait of him from 1934 and a portrait in metal relief. There are some hopes of putting the room in better order in due course.

Muzički Salon Đure Prejaca
Veliki Tabor
49216 Desinić
Croatia

phone +385/0 4934 3052, 3053
fax +385/0 494 3055
website www.veliki-tabor.hr

open daily 10.00–18.00

Map 14

PROKOFIEV

Prokofiev's father, an agronomist, was working on an estate in the village of Sontsovka when in 1891 Sergey

Sergeyevich was born. The village, now called Krasnoye, is in the south-east corner of Ukraine, some 100 km north of the Black Sea coast and about 50 km west of Donets'k, near the modern towns of Kurakhovo and Ukrayns'k. Prokofiev was only 12 when he left, to enter the St Petersburg Conservatory; and in the summers, teachers (among them Reyngol'd Glier) were called to Sontsovka to work with the precociously talented boy. He graduated at the age of 18 and the next year, on his father's death, moved to St Petersburg. From 1918 he lived abroad, mainly in the USA and in Paris; he returned to Russia in 1936, settling in Moscow, and tried to become a true Soviet composer, although his success in finding a musical style acceptable to the Soviet authorities was sporadic.

Displays at the Prokofiev museum, Krasnoye

The house of his birth no longer stands; a rugged stone, bearing a commemorative plaque, marks the spot where it stood. But 400 metres away is the local school, of which his mother Marya Prokof'yeva was head teacher, and this was opened as a museum to the composer on the centenary of his birth in 1991. The first of the three rooms is devoted to his childhood and his conservatory years. There are original objects from his home, among them a dressing table and a bedside cupboard, a samovar and a gramophone as well as photographs of the young Prokofiev and manuscripts of his compositions of the time; the room also contains the Schreitzer grand piano presented to him by Artur Rubinstein when he completed his studies at the conservatory.

The second room records his concert career at home and abroad. Exhibits refer to his concerts and his opera and ballet productions, with stage sets and costumes, a display of posters and programmes, manuscripts, letters and reviews. The third room emphasizes his connections with Ukraine, recording his productions in Ukrainian theatres, his books, stamps issued on his anniversaries and other mementoes. Outside the museum there is

a rather severe bronze statue of Prokofiev, by Vasiliy Polonik, seated on a bench. There is a recital hall seating 115 people next door to the museum, and the church of SS Peter and Paul, where his parents were married and he was baptized (built in 1840, restored in 1991), is nearby.

During his last years, from 1947 to his death in 1953 (on the same day, 5 March, as Stalin), Prokofiev lived in a flat in central Moscow. There has long been an intention of establishing a museum to him in his own flat and an adjoining one, under the supervision of the Glinka State Central Museum of Musical Culture (the central music museum authority in Russia and a general musical museum), which holds a large Prokofiev collection including autograph scores, letters, illustrative material from his operas, especially *War and Peace*, and much personal material. Parts of the flat are expected to open to select visitors during 2005. Prokofiev's rather austere study is to be re-created following a model made in the 1950s under the supervision of his second wife, Mira Mendel'son; it will include his desk and chair, his piano, his chess set and articles of clothing. There will be a standing display 'Prokofiev in Soviet Russia, 1934–53' and a library with items from several collections and designed to focus on his relations with other musicians. On the first floor there is a recital room that can also be used for exhibitions.

Prokofiev statue, Krasnoye

Memorialny Muzey S.S. Prokof'yeva*
Krasnoye
Krasnoarmeyskyy rayon
85374 Donetska oblast'
Ukraine

phone +380/80 6235 30215

open Wednesday–Monday 09.00–15.00

Memorial'nïy Muzey-Kvartira S.S. Prokof'eva*
Kamergersky pereulok 6
107066 Moskva
Russia

phone +7/0 095 923 5989, +7/0 095 739 6226 ext.135

open by appointment

Maps 16, 12

N. Simeone: *Paris: a Musical Gazetteer* (New Haven and London: Yale University Press, 2000)

PUCCINI

In no country is nationality as localized as it is in Italy. Giacomo Puccini was not just an Italian composer but a Lucchese: he was born in the Tuscan city of Lucca and lived close to it all his life. Visiting the city and its vicinity and moving from one of his houses to another places him and his music firmly in context. A useful, pictorial 'Itinerari Pucciniani' is available from the Azienda di Promozione Turistica Lucca.

Puccini came from a family of Lucchese musicians going back five generations. The first composer called Giacomo Puccini lived from 1712 to 1786 and was organist of the Cappella Palatina and the cathedral of San Martino. His son Antonio (1747–1832) inherited his father's appointments, and Antonio's son Domenico (1772–1815) in turn also held ecclesiastical musical posts. Domenico's son Michele (1813–64) resumed the tradition of occupying the organist's seat at San Martino, and after Michele's early death his son Giacomo (*b* 1858) was expected to do the same. The seat was in fact kept warm for him by his uncle, but the inclinations of this particular Puccini were more to the stage than the organ loft.

He was however born just off the central piazza of Lucca, in Corte S Lorenzo, a modest stone's throw from San Michele (where civic functions took place), close to San Paolino (after the city's patron saint) and not far from San Martino: all of them churches with which the family had connections. The large, rambling second-floor flat, acquired by the family about 1815, is now a civic museum to the composer, and another part forms the headquarters of the Fondazione Giacomo Puccini.

The museum has eight display rooms, some of them evocatively furnished in the style of his time, with music from the operas supplying a background. Among the items on display are the Steinway that Puccini used during the composition of *Turandot*, an old overcoat of his ('vecchia zimarra'), some fine family pictures from the 18th century (Giacomo, his wife and his son Antonio) and the well-known portrait of Puccini done by Leonetto Cappiello in 1899. There is a fine collection of original letters between Puccini, his wife and his son and also his publisher Ricordi. His desk and his phonograph are there. Several original manuscripts, mostly of early works, are

Puccini statue and birthplace (the house at centre right), Lucca

letters and other documents as well as orchestral parts of *Le villi* and a bust of his father. Puccini loved the rural solitude and last visited the house on 26 October 1924, travelling by mule, only a month before his death from throat cancer. The local Comune erected a white marble plaque to commemorate the visit.

Not far away is the mountain village of Chiatri, where in 1898 Puccini bought and rebuilt an old farmhouse with views of Lake Massaciuccoli and the sea: his 'dream house', built at huge cost from the proceeds of *Manon Lescaut* and *La Bohème*, in a Tuscan dialect of the Gothic style with materials imported by mule. It is now a private house.

On the edge of Lake Massaciuccoli, however, at Torre del Lago (or Torre del Lago Puccini, as it is now), stands the most famous of all Puccini's homes. He built this villa too in 1898 as his wife and step-daughter found the isolation at Chiatri disagreeable. The site was close to Viareggio, a seaside resort some 20 km from Lucca; he had lived in Torre del Lago in a tatty old house in 1891 while composing *Manon Lescaut*. Now he could readily afford something a good deal grander, so he bought and demolished the old house and built a new one on the site. It is not in fact excessively grand in scale, but it embodied, and still does, work of a fanciful kind by famous designers of the time: a fireplace by Galileo Chini, *Art Nouveau* with an oriental flavour, cherubs with garlands by Plinio Nomelli and Ferruccio Pagni, furnishings by Bugatti and Tiffany, and elaborate coffered ceil-

displayed, and stage and costume designs for the operas, as well as some original costumes (one from *Turandot* in New York, given by Maria Jeritza). Opera posters and photos, medals, certificates and newspaper reviews are also shown. A plaque was erected on the front of the house soon after Puccini's death.

The Puccinis owned another property, a country farmhouse built in 1585 in the village of Celle, tucked away in the hills north of Lucca, and in the family since the 17th century; Puccini's great-great-grandfather Giacomo was born there in 1712. As a child Giacomo spent his holidays there. It was set up as an informal museum in 1976 and today it houses Puccini relics, including the bed in which he is said to have been born, the baptismal clothing and the crib used by many of the Puccini children, the piano he is thought to have used when composing *La fanciulla del West*, a phonograph presented to him by Thomas Edison and Japanese record-ings that he was given, along with many

The Puccini family house at Celle

Puccini's villa at Torre del Lago Puccini

ings in red, blue and gold in the Gothic Revival manner. The chrysanthemums in the garden recall his elegiac string quartet, *Crisantemi.*

Puccini lived here intermittently from 1898 until 1921, though he was away during most of World War I because of the disturbance from a refinery on the lake. *Tosca, Madama Butterfly* and *La fanciulla* were written there, at least in part. On the ground floor are his furniture and his piano, with many personal effects, among them his hunting gear (including boots and a range of guns: for illustration see p.43), stuffed birds, countless photographs (many of them autographed), letters and awards. There is a further exhibition area outside the house, an aging glass conservatory with rattan blinds, not untouched by the elements (or the local cat population), where more photographs, manuscripts and the conversation books to which he had recourse after his throat operation are, at any rate for a while, to be seen. Restoration of the building, including the upstairs rooms, is planned.

The most remarkable object within the museum is Puccini himself. The first hint of his personal presence may be gleaned from the affecting Grossi portrait, hanging in the corner of the main room, painted only weeks before his death on 22 November 1924; below it are photographs of his body and a death mask, cradled in velvet in a glass case. In the centre of the house is a chapel, transformed from a sitting room to a mausoleum in 1926, where the composer (brought first from Brussels, then Milan) and his wife are interred and where his son Antonio and his wife eventually joined them. That is surely one way to ensure the permanence of your museum.

A month after Puccini's death the people of Torre del Lago erected a memorial plaque on the north side of the villa; later, in front of it, a land-scaped piazza was created where souvenir sellers ply their trade. In the summer of 1930 the first Puccini Festival here was held, in a new open-air theatre, but in 1968 it moved to a larger site nearby, north of the harbour; opera can be seen there in late July and during much of August, and a vocal competition is held annually for the Puccini Prize. There are plans to create there a 'Puccini park' embodying a new, large open-air lakeside theatre and a smaller indoor one.

In 1900 Puccini was made an honorary citizen of Viareggio. His last villa, where he composed *Turandot*, was on the edge of the town, by the pinewood running along the coast, at the corner of Via Marco Polo and Via Buonarroti; it is not open to the public. Both the villa and the Gran Caffè Margherita (where his 'Club Gianni Schicchi' regularly met) bear memorial plaques. As a result of a long-delayed legal judgment handed down at the end of 2002, the villa passed into the possession of the Italian state, and the possibility of its becoming a further, more modern Puccini museum, as has long been under consideration, became a little firmer.

Casa Museo 'Giacomo Puccini'

Corte S Lorenzo
Via di Poggio 9
55100 Lucca
Italy

phone +390/0 583 584028
website www.puccini.it

open 15 March–30 June,
1 September–15 November,
Tuesday–Sunday 10.00–13.00,
15.00–18.00; July–August,
Tuesday–Sunday 10.00–13.00,
15.00–19.00; 16 November–31
December, Tuesday–Sunday 10.00–13.00

Casa Museo dei Puccini

Via Meletori 27
55064 Celle dei Puccini (Pescaglia)
Italy

phone +390/0 583 359154

open Saturdays and holidays
09.00–12.00, 15.00–19.00, or by
appointment

Villa Puccini

Piazzale Belvedere
Viale Puccini 264
55048 Torre del Lago Puccini (Lucca)
Italy

phone +390/0 584 341445

open 15 June–15 September,
Tuesday–Sunday 10.00–12.00,
15.00–19.30; 16 September–14 June,
10.00–12.30, 15.00–17.30

Map 9

L. Nicolosi: *Omaggio a Giacomo Puccini* (Lucca: Fondazione G. Puccini, 1980)

V.A. Hewitt: *The Land of Puccini* (Viareggio: Pezzini, 1991)

G. Lera: *Celle dei Puccini: Guida al Museo* (Lucca: Promolucca Editrice, n.d.)

G. Gefen: *Composers' Houses* (London: Cassell and Vendome, 1998), 134–41

J. Budden and G. Biagi Ravenni: *Journey through Puccini Country* (Lucca: Centro Studi Giacomo Puccini, [1999])

RAKHMANINOV

Paris? New York? California? Switzerland? Moscow, even? No: to visit a museum commemorating one of the most beloved of 20th-century composers you will have to visit Ivanovka, in the remote heart of Russia, the family estate that once belonged to Sergey Rakhmaninov's aunt and uncle, the Satins. He had stayed with them, in their Moscow flat, when he was 16, and later joined them at Ivanovka; he went there almost every summer from 1890 to 1917, arriving for the lilacs and leaving at the harvest, and when in 1902 he married their daughter, his cousin Natal'ya, the couple were given the smaller of the houses (the *fligel'*) as a wedding present. The estate passed to Natal'ya and her brother in 1911 and Rakhmaninov assumed much of the responsibility for running it. He found its peace a source of inspiration and most of his greatest works – among them the second and third piano concertos, the first two symphonies, *The Isle of the Dead*, the op.32 preludes and the *Etudes-tableaux*, *The Bells* and the *Liturgy of St John Chrysostom* – were composed there.

But in 1917 it was looted and vandalized, in the wake of the Revolution; the large house was burnt down and the *fligel'* fell into dereliction. In the 1960s, with the prospect of the Rakhmaninov centenary in 1973, steps were taken to rebuild it on the original foundations, drawing on photographic evidence and the recollections of Sofiya Satina, the composer's cousin and sister-in-law, then living in New York. The *fligel'* was

Rakhmaninov's fligel' at Ivanovka (photo, before 1917)

restored by 1974 and used as a music school before it was opened as a museum in 1982; the main manor house and some of the outbuildings were then rebuilt and the garden restored, and the entire museum was opened in 1995, as a section of the Tambov Region Country Museum.

It is not easily accessible. The closest large town is the district capital, Tambov, which is about 450 km south-east of Moscow; from there, you take the road to Volgograd through sparse, wooded country for about 120 km, turn left soon after Zaryan towards Uvarovo, then after about 20 km left again, continuing for about another ten. (Rakhmaninov himself took a different route, by train to Rzhaksa and then by droshky or sledge.)

In the main house, the rooms on the ground floor are reconstructed to evoke the world of Rakhmaninov's time. On the upper floor is a substantial display, covering six rooms and giving a chrono-logical survey of his life: from his family ancestry and his youth, his early studies in Moscow and first compositions and his initial contacts with Ivanovka and the Satin family, to his years of exile in Europe and the United States. Sofiya's own room, and the billiard room, on this floor, are reconstructed. The ground-floor rooms include a main living-room with a dramatic stairwell and large pillars, a dining-room with some elabo-rate plasterwork, Rakhmaninov's study, with piano, desk and bookcase, his wife's bedroom (with an ornamental black-wood screen and delicate furniture) and their daughter Tatyana's room. There is also a recital room seating about 40.

The garden was important to Rakhmaninov. His cousin Lyudmila Skalon later related that 'in moments of creative inspiration he would . . . go out to his favourite red alley of elms, maples and poplar (called 'red' because there were broken bricks in the soil). From a distance one could see his tall figure in a Russian shirt. He would walk, head bowed, drumming his fingers on his chest and sort of singing to himself'. The shady copse survives, dotted with gazebos and inhabited by blackbirds and cuckoos, and the visitor may walk in Rakhmaninov's footsteps down the pathway, still including some of the red bricks; the summerhouse for the children is restored, and in the kitchen garden new fruit trees have been grown from the old stock.

Memorialnïy Muzey-usad'ba S.V. Rakhmaninova
selo Ivanovka
Uvarovoskiy rayon
393481 Tambovskaya oblast'
Russia

phone +7/0 0755 877436, 877442

open Tuesday–Sunday 09.00–17.00

Map 12

RAVEL

For his last 15 years, Maurice Ravel (1875–1937) made his home in the delightful little town of Montfort-l'Amaury, on the edge of the forest of Rambouillet, 45 km west of Paris. In 1921 an inheritance enabled him to buy

Le Belvédère at Montfort-l'Amaury

a home of his own, Le Belvédère, at 5 avenue Saint-Laurent, an eccentric little two-storey house, built in 1907 and architecturally more like a suburban train station than a home, perched on a hill. His pupil and friend the conductor Manuel Rosenthal once described the house as 'a bit like a badly sliced portion of Camembert'.

Inside, it proved inhospitable at first – it was too small, there were no internal stairs to his bedroom and the bathroom below, and there was no electricity or of course central heating. But early on Ravel commissioned building works to modernize it; once electricity had been installed he acquired a vacuum cleaner and a 'machine à glace' as well as a telephone, radio and gramophone. Although Parisian relatives and friends (including his brother Edouard, Rosenthal, Roland-Manuel, Robert Casadesus and Marguerite Long) often visited him, dining on the terrace overlooking the garden, and students came for lessons, Ravel chose to live alone, looked after by a housekeeper, with his cigarettes, a family of Siamese cats and a dog named Jazz for company. The house remains today very much as he left it when he died in 1937.

Visitors will be tempted to make analogies between the décor, the man and his music. Once inside, one is struck by the miniature scale of the rooms and their furnishings (Ravel was a small man), and then with the highly individual choice of colour scheme (ochre, black, white and grey) and finally the exotic eclecticism (combining Art Deco furniture with Greek Revival, Louis XVI, *japonaiserie* and Turkish elements) of his possessions and the extreme care with which they are arranged, and apparently always were. We know he considered his study the soul of the house. His music room, only just large enough to accommodate his beloved Erard grand piano and a desk, is decorated in black and petrol blue. While every room (even his *salle de bain*, complete with his hair- and toothbrushes) makes a statement, Ravel himself remains in the background. The

Japanese-inspired garden, which once incorporated a *potager* and fruit trees, was, like the interior decoration, his own meticulous creation.

Ravel composed some of his most important works at Le Belvédère, including the violin sonata, the concert rhapsody *Tzigane*, the opera *L'enfant et les sortilèges*, *Boléro* and the left-hand Piano Concerto.

Even among museums commemorating 20th-century composers, Ravel's home is exceptional in its authenticity. Although it belongs to the city of Montfort-l'Amaury and is jointly administered with the Fondation Maurice Ravel, based in Paris, it hasn't acquired the accoutrements of an institution and accordingly it retains the integrity of a private dwelling. Nothing is labelled or specifically interpreted. Because of its size and the fragility of its decorative fabric, it can never accommodate large numbers of tourists and visiting should always be considered a privilege.

Musée Maurice Ravel
Le Belvédère
5 rue Maurice Ravel
78490 Montfort-l'Amaury
France

phone +33/0 1 3486 0089, 8796 (tourist office)
e-mail tourisme@ville-Montfort-l-amaury.fr
website www.ville.Montfort-l-amaury.fr

open Wednesday–Friday 14.30–18.00, by appointment only; Saturday and Sunday, guided tours only, by appointment (7 people maximum), 10.00, 11.00, 14.30, 15.30, 16.30, 17.30 (closes 17.00, October–March)

Map 6

E. Wahl: *Maurice Ravel à Montfort-l'Amaury* (Versailles: Comité Départemental du Tourisme des Yvelines, 1987)
G. Gefen: *Composers' Houses* (London: Cassell and Vendome, 1998), 169–75
N. Simeone: *Paris: a Musical Gazetteer* (New Haven and London: Yale University Press, 2000)

REGER

It is somehow symbolic that Max Reger was born in the Fichtelgebirge, strictly a part of Bavaria but in many ways distinct from it in its geography, its history and its personality. For Reger's music stands obstinately separate from most of the beaten historical tracks: he never quite fitted into the Munich musical establishment, into the post-Wagnerian generation, nor, with his preoccupation with Protestant organ genres, into the Catholic traditions into which he was born.

Brand, Reger's native village, lies some 30 km east of the Berlin–Munich *Autobahn*, not far from Bayreuth. Slightly further east lies the main part of the Oberpfalz (Upper Palatinate) region and beyond it the Czech border. The main road through the village is of course Max-Reger-Straße. The house where the composer was born, in 1873, bears a plaque, but is privately owned. Immediately opposite, by the Max-Reger-Park, is the quite modest town hall, within which is a room devoted to the composer's memory, opened in 1973 in celebration of his centenary. There are display cases with documents, photographs and originals and reproductions of Reger's music. The mayor himself is happy to show the room to visitors.

The Reger family moved from Brand when Max was still an infant, to Weiden, a much larger town, some 45 km to the south-east. Reger studied with the organist there, Adalbert Lindner, and regarded Weiden as his home; apart from spells away in his student years, he lived there from 1874 to 1901. Here too there is a Max-Reger-Straße and a Max-Reger-Park, with a memorial, as well as a Max-Reger-Halle and four Max Reger houses (the family was fairly mobile), one of which bears a plaque.

Weiden's principal memorial to Reger, however, is a room – to be precise, a linked pair of rooms – in the Stadtmuseum (in the Altes Schulhaus, the building in which Lindner lived). His baptismal clothes are displayed in the first, with his mother's square piano, certificates from his youth, his working desk and a group of drawings of him conducting. The larger room is dominated by a Blüthner piano, originally Lindner's, and the organ from St Michael's church on which he played. There are portraits, a bust and a death mask and a witty series of caricatures of Reger; both rooms have display cabinets with various memorabilia – his medals, drinking glasses (which played all too prominent a part in his life), music autographs and first editions, letters and postcards, photographs.

Towards the end of his life, Reger was Hofkapellmeister to Duke Georg II of Saxe-Meiningen. In that capacity (1911–13) he composed more than 20 works and conducted the finely trained Meiningen orchestra in 166 concerts, which included the symphonies of Beethoven, Brahms and Bruckner as well as the more adventurous *Tod und Verklärung* of Strauss and Debussy's *Prélude à l'après-midi d'un faune*. The Schloß Elisabethenburg in Meiningen, now open to the public, incorporates a Musikmuseum which celebrates 300 years of local music history and dedicates two rooms to Reger and one each to the conductor Hans von Bülow, who developed the orchestra during his years there (1880–85), and Brahms (*see* BRAHMS), who often visited Meiningen between

Reger's study as re-created at Schloß Elisabethenburg, Meiningen

1883 and 1895 to work with the orchestra.

The first room dedicated to Reger recreates the spirit of the Arbeitsaal (or study) at his last house in Jena, where he lived from 1915 and composed the solo cello and solo viola suites op.131*c* and *d*, the Fantasia and Fugue for organ op.135*b* and the Violin Sonata op.139. His Bechstein grand has pride of place and is surrounded by a collection of musical portraits, busts and death masks; the scene is filled out with furniture, a large tiled stove and an ornate music stand. In the second room is a display of personal effects (his concert clothes, briefcase, glasses, pen and cigar case), along with his honorary degree certificates and a silver laurel wreath, family correspondence and photos, and pictures of his Meiningen house (which bears a plaque). Also on display are Willy von Beckerath's sketches of Reger in rehearsal and a car horn (actually four bells) that sounds the theme by J.A. Hiller on which Reger composed his famous orchestral Variations and Fugue op.100. The Max-Reger-Archiv, from which the museum displays are drawn, is part of the department of musical history in the Meininger Museen. In 1982, in recognition of Reger's importance as an organist, a new organ in his memory was installed in the former chapel of the Schloß, now the Konzertsaal Johannes Brahms.

After Reger's death, in 1916, his widow Elsa established a Max-Reger-Archiv in Jena, where they had moved the previous year; during World War II she transferred it to Meiningen. In 1947 she created the Elsa-Reger-Stiftung and the Max-Reger-Institut, at Bad Godesberg, near Bonn, where she then lived. In 1996 the institute, the centre of Reger scholarship and research, with an extensive collection especially of Reger autographs, open to scholars and performers of his music, moved to Karlsruhe.

At Valhalla, 11 km east of Regensburg, there is a Doric temple originally built by Ludwig I of Bavaria in 1842; among 118 busts representing historic national figures is one of Reger by Georg Müller.

Max-Reger-Gedächtniszimmer

Rathaus
Max-Reger-Straße 7
95682 Brand (Oberpfalz)
Germany

phone +49/0 923 6230
fax +49/0 923 66151

open Monday–Wednesday, Friday 09.00–12.00, Thursday 15.00–17.00

Max-Reger-Zimmer

Stadtmuseum mit Max Reger Sammlung
Schulgasse 3a
92637 Weiden (Oberpfalz)
Germany

phone +49/0 961 470390–1
fax +49/0 961 470390–9
e-mail archiv@weiden-oberpfalz.de

open Monday–Friday 09.00–12.00, 14.00–16.30

Abteilung Musikgeschichte: Max-Reger-Archiv

Meininger Museen
Schloß Elisabethenburg
98617 Meiningen
Germany

phone + 49/0 3693 881023
fax +49/0 3693 503644
e-mail service@meiningermuseen.de
website www.meiningermuseen.de

open Tuesday–Sunday 10.00–18.00

Map 7

A. Krauß and H. Fröhlich: *Max Reger: die Weidener Jahre 1874–1901* (Weiden: Stadtarchiv Weiden, 1982)

H. Müller: *Schloß Elisabethenburg Meiningen* (Munich and Regensburg: Schnell & Steiner, 1993)

REICHARDT

Johann Friedrich Reichardt (1752–1814), at one time Kapellmeister to Frederick the Great, is commemorated not in Berlin but in Halle, where he spent most of his last 20 years, living in Giebichenstein, then a nearby village, now a suburb. A precocious musician and self-promoter, he had joined the Prussian court at the age of 23, in charge of the performances of Italian opera. He married the singer and composer Juliane Benda, daughter of his colleague Franz Benda. In 1789 he collaborated with Goethe on the Singspiel *Claudine von Villa Bella*, which ushered in a new era of vernacular opera at the Berlin court. He was also prominent as a writer on music and editor of an influential journal, the *Musikalisches Kunstmagazin*.

His republican sympathies led to his dismissal from the Berlin court in 1794, when he moved to a country estate in Giebichenstein. He increasingly pursued journalism, working there and in Hamburg and editing political and musical journals. He welcomed radical thinkers, writers and composers to Giebichenstein where his estate, Kestnersche Gut, became widely known as a 'poets' paradise' and a 'hostel of Romanticism'. Goethe visited him in 1802 and established a theatre nearby at Bad Lauchstädt, which is still in use. Reichardt's estate suffered during the French invasion of 1806–7 and he spent his last years in poverty. All that remains in Giebichenstein is a green space next to the zoo known as Reichardts Garten and the Bartholomäuskirche where he was buried.

Reichardt is commemorated, along with his Halle contemporary Daniel Gottlob Türk, in Room 5 on the second floor of the Händel-Haus by a display of facsimile title-pages of his publications of lieder, the field of composition in which he was most consistently successful, and musical travelogues, a facsimile of an engraved portrait and a bronze bust recently sculpted by Gottfried Albert.

Händel-Haus

Grosse Nikolaistraße 5
06108 Halle (Saale)
Germany

phone +49/0 345 500900
fax +49/0 345 50090 411
e-mail haendelhaus@halle.de

website www.haendelhaus.de

open daily 09.30–17.30 (Thursday to 19.00)

Map 7

K. Musketa: *Musikgeschichte der Stadt Halle: Führer durch die Ausstellung des Händel-Hauses* (Halle an der Saale: Händel-Haus, 1998), 46–51

REVUTS'KY

Levko Mykolayevych Revuts'ky was a central figure in Ukrainian music in the generation following Lysenko. Born in Irzhavets' in 1889, he went to study in the capital when he was 14, in 1903, and returned there in 1924 as teacher, scholar, editor and administrator as well as composer. He was there for the rest of his life, apart from a time in Tashkent during the war years. His most important works come from the 1920s; in the changing climate of the Stalin era, he moved increasingly towards other kinds of work.

Revuts'ky lived quite centrally in Kiev, not far from St Sophia, in a first-floor apartment, from 1956 until his death in 1970 (when it was taken over by his son, a medical man). The main living-room has to some extent been frozen in time to preserve his memory: around the walls are more than a hundred photographs, and there is a large oil portrait, a bust and a death mask, as well as his piano and part of his library.

His principal commemoration however is in the house at his birthplace in Irzhavets', a small town about 150 km north-east of Kiev, between Ichnya and Pryluky. The actual house of his birth no longer stands, but the museum – to find it, go southwards through the village and turn right after the golden Shevchenko statue – is on the ancient farmstead given to Revuts'ky's great-grandfather, a Cossack, for military service. Revuts'ky lived in Irzhavets' until 1924, apart from a period as a medical railway worker and a receptionist in the early Soviet days, and never returned.

The museum, opened on his centenary in 1989, is surprisingly rich; more than 1000 items are displayed and ultimately more will come from the Kiev flat. The family and its traditions form the topic of the first room – Revuts'ky's father studied at a seminary and his mother came from a noble family, friends of Tolstoy. He himself studied physics and jurisprudence as well as music, in which Lysenko and Glier were among his professors. In the next room is furniture from the family dacha as well as documentary displays (birth certificate, diplomas and the like), books and scores.

Revuts'ky's own working set-up – his desk and chair, his glasses, his pen – is shown in the third room, with his books, among them a large Ukrainian encyclopedia and the collected works of Gorky, all watched over by the ubiquitous (in Ukraine) portrait of the cultural hero Shevchenko. Some of the publications of folksongs, which he garnered with his brother, a musicologist, are displayed along with facsimile manuscripts and photographs. The next room is for music-making, with two pianos (a grand from the conservatory, played by Revuts'ky, and his own upright; there is a portrait of him, in old age, sitting by the piano) and the display cases deal with his period in Tashkent and his Ukrainian contemporaries. In the entry hall his pupils – he was a generous and beloved teacher – are remembered, and the dining-room is set up with a set of cane chairs and a wall cabinet that he himself made, as well as the obligatory samovar and pictures from the family dacha. Cases here show his Shevchenko Prize ('for peace') and a state laureate award for his admired Second Symphony along with an early harmony exercise. The museum testifies to a composer who, though little known beyond the boundaries of Ukraine, was clearly regarded with much affection in his country.

Memorial'na Kimnata A.M. Revuts'koho
vulytsya Sofiïvs'ka 16, kvartyra 25
01001 Kyïv
Ukraine

phone +380/80 4422 87288

open by appointment

Derzhavnyy Memorial'nyy Muzey A.M. Revuts'koho
vulytsya Revuts'kykh 3
selo Irzhavets'
16732 Ichnyans'kyy rayon
Chernihivs'ka oblast'
Ukraine

phone +380/80 4633 27331

open Tuesday–Sunday 10.00–17.00

Map 16

RIMSKY-KORSAKOV

To a traveller unused to Russia, a tour of Rimsky-Korsakov sites – his birthplace in Tikhvin, his St Petersburg apartment and grave, and his summer homes near Lake Pyesno – provides not only a fresh understanding of the composer but also unforgettable glimpses of pre-revolutionary Russian family life.

Tikhvin is an ancient cathedral city about 210 km east of St Petersburg, which in the 19th century was a centre of trading and handicrafts. It was also the centre of the Novgorod district over which Nikolay Andreyevich Rimsky-Korsakov's father presided as civil governor. The Rimsky-Korsakovs were a distinguished military family whose wooden house still enjoys a view across the Tikhvinka River of the Tikhvin

Rimsky-Korsakov's birthplace at Tikhvin

Family drawing-room at Tikhvin

monastery and cathedral. Born there in 1844, Nikolay Andreyevich spent his first 12 years in Tikhvin before moving to St Petersburg to attend the naval academy, by which time he had begun learning the piano and had even tried his hand at composing.

The birthplace museum, in what is now Rimsky-Korsakov Street, was opened to the public by the composer's children on his centenary in 1944 and tells the story well. Nikolay's father's green study with its icons, its masonic relics and the armchair made by his serfs evokes the image of authority reflected in Rimsky-Korsakov's memoirs. In his mother's blue day-room at the opposite end of the house, where she kept a parrot, the young composer learnt about flowers, stars and, no doubt, heard legends and fairy-tales.

The vibrant red drawing-room at the centre of the house, furnished with mid-19th-century tables and chairs and a Lichtenthal square piano brought from St Petersburg, reminds us that the young boy was taught music at home, as well as to draw and to speak French. His first Becker grand is kept (in playing condition) in the adjoining room, today used for occasional small concerts. At the rear of the house is a room devoted to his elder brother, who pursued a distinguished naval career; it is filled with curiosities from his voyages, a model of a schooner, his maps, letters, stories and drawings. Upstairs, the front loft bedroom, with its balcony view and

single bed with a coverlet made by his mother, is where the composer slept in summertime. Elsewhere there are displays showing such objects as his childish drawings, his cadet report card and gifts from his contemporaries.

Other than for trips abroad and summers in the country, Rimsky-Korsakov lived in St Petersburg for the rest of his life. For his last 15 years (1893–1908) he lived at 28 Zagorodnïy Prospect where he and his wife, Nadezhda Nikolayevna Purgold, and their five children had a spacious flat (no.39) on the third floor.

Since 1971 it has been a Rimsky-Korsakov museum. As with all the museums to their father, his own three sons (all of them men of distinction in their own right) and their children provided the collection of furniture, photographs, tributes and personal possessions. Some of the rooms have been painstakingly re-created as they

Block of flats in St Petersburg where the Rimsky-Korsakovs lived

were in his own day – the study, the music salon and the dining-room in particular – while others now perform more routine museum functions. The rooms that once served as the kitchen and for sleeping have become a recital hall, seating 60; concerts take place frequently from October to May, and during the intervals the audience is invited to tour the museum.

Most memorable are the study and the salon. The former was shared by husband and wife. He had a large green baize-covered desk near the windows and she a smaller one behind it and to the left (see p.9). His wife for 37 years, Nadezhda was an excellent pianist and was trained as a composer, although she devoted her time to making arrangements of her husband's music and, later, to publishing his posthumous musical and literary works. The salon, with its 1902 Becker grand and arrangements of green velvet chairs, portraits and mirrors, was where every other Wednesday the Rimsky-Korsakovs held music parties at which musicians such as Stravinsky and Shalyapin performed. In the entry hall and vestibule connecting the two rooms Rimsky-Korsakov's fur-lined coat and hat still hang.

For six summers between 1894 and 1905 the Rimsky-Korsakovs stayed at a lakeside dacha at Vechasha, beyond the town of Luga, about 190 km south of St Petersburg, some seven kilometres to the

The Rimsky-Korsakov dacha at Lyubensk

right (towards Plyussa) off the Pskov road. Always referring to it as 'dear Vechasha', the composer wrote in his memoirs of working there on his operas *Christmas Eve* and *Sadko*: 'I remember that I often composed on the long plank footbridges running from the shore to the bathing pavilion. The bridges ran down among bulrushes; on one side the tall bending willows of the garden were visible, on the other lay the wide expanse of Lake Pyesno'. The bridges are still there. During the summer of 1897 he set Pushkin's *Mozart and Salieri*, followed by *The Tsar's Bride* in 1898 and *The Tale of Tsar Saltan* in 1899. Evenings were devoted to family chamber music.

He spent his last two summers at Lyubensk, just over a kilometre away from Vechasha. In August 1907 Rimsky-Korsakov proudly described the dacha in a letter: its view of the lake, immense orchard and abundance of lilacs, jasmine and peonies. During that summer he completed *The Golden Cockerel* and his memoirs. The following year he was there for only 18 days before, on the night of 7–8 June, he died during a violent storm. His funeral service was held in the church of the St Petersburg Conservatory and he was buried in the musicians' section of the Tikhvin Cemetery in St Petersburg. The family continued to spend summers at the Lyubensk dacha until the Revolution, when it passed out of private ownership. The estate was occupied by Soviet officials in 1918–20, when the wooden buildings were destroyed; during the German occupation in World War II, at the time of the siege of Leningrad, it was carelessly burnt to the ground.

The Rimsky-Korsakov dacha at Vechasha

A pair of museums on the two sites was established in 1995 by his granddaughter, Tatyana Rimsky-Korsakova. The restored dachas at Vechasha and Lyubensk are administered as a branch of the Pskov Museum of Art and Architecture. The displays at Vechasha, confined to the large, central, pillared room, focus on the operas and include a first edition of *Sadko* and costumes and porcelain figurines of his opera characters. To the side there is an airy recital room seating 80–100. At Lyubensk the entire house (and the small, eight-hectare estate of which it is a part) had to be rebuilt from the evidence of photographs and drawings and the reminiscences of Tatyana Rimsky-Korsakova's father and uncles. As with the St Petersburg flat, some rooms have been re-created with family furniture and possessions while others, including the bedroom in which he died, are devoted to museum displays of photographs, colourful first editions, letters and other documents, a death mask and a few personal possessions.

Dom-Muzey N.A. Rimskogo-Korsakova

ulitsa Rimskogo-Korsakova 12
Tikhvin
187500 St Petersburg oblast'
Russia

phone +7/0 112 671 1509

open Tuesday–Sunday 11.00–17.00

Memorialnïy Muzey-kvartira N.A. Rimskogo-Korsakova

Zagorodnïy Prospect, kv.39, 28
196002 St Petersburg
Russia

phone, fax +7/0 812 315 3975
e-mail rimkor@mybox.spbu.ru

open Wednesday–Sunday 11.00–18.00

Muzey-Usad'ba N.A. Rimskogo-Korsakova

Perevnya Vechasha
P/O Zapesn'e
Plyussaky rayon
181011 Pskovskaya oblast'
Russia

Dom-Muzey N.A. Rimskogo-Korsakova

Usadba Lyubensko
Luzhskiy rayon
188260 Pskovskaya oblast'
Russia

administrative address for these two:

Pskovskaya oblast' Memorialnïy Muzey-usad'ba N.A. Rimskogo-Korsakova
Lyubensk-Vechasha
Lyubensk
Plyussky rayon
181000 Pskovskaya oblast'
Russia

phone +7/0 811 332 4445, 4449
e-mail tv@ap2155.spb.edu
website www.oblmuseums.spb.ru

open Tuesday–Saturday 11.00–16.00

Map 12

N.A. Rimsky-Korsakov v Vechashe i Lyubenske (Moscow, 1994)

ROSSINI

The legacy of Gioachino Rossini is important to Pesaro, a handsome city on the Adriatic coast some 40 km south of Rimini. The local music conservatory, which maintains a rich archive of Rossini manuscripts and portraits, the opera house (formerly the Teatro del Sole, where the composer's father Giuseppe was a brass player in the orchestra) and an annual summer opera festival all bear his name. The birthplace of the 'Swan of Pesaro', a medium-sized 18th-century house in what is now the Via Rossini (it was then the Via del Duomo), and his home until 1800, has been a museum since 1904.

After two years of renovation and restoration, the birthplace reopened in 1989. The emphasis here is more artistic than musical: the collection on display is elegantly laid out and altogether visually superb. The ground-floor rooms are devoted to Rossini's career; the five on the first floor, where the family rented two rooms at the rear, address his life. Nearly all the items on display are originals – a seemingly endless procession of

Rossini's birthplace in Pesaro

portraits and prints of the composer, his singers in costumes from original or early productions, charting his triumphs in Italy, Paris, Vienna and London, and a theatre curtain of 1816. There are busts and medallions and laurel wreaths.

Rossini had a long life, and for most of it he was a celebrity: so there exist numerous likenesses of him (including photographs). His genial appearance made him a ripe subject for caricature; and upstairs, in what was once the family kitchen and living-room, an array of caricatures, trenchant yet always affectionate, is on display. The room in which the composer is traditionally believed to have been born, on 29 February 1792 (leap year), displays only portraits of Rossini's parents and the young Rossini himself. There exists one engraving, captioned 'sur son dix-huitième anniversaire', where he looks fully 72: this can be seen in one of the two rooms devoted to portraits of Rossini and his family, along with letters, medallions, playbills and documents (some inevitably in facsimile); one room

also contains his Venetian square piano, built by Luigi Heffer in 1809. The final first-floor room chronicles his last days (he died in 1868), and beyond – his homes in Paris, his will, his death-bed (with the famous Gustave Doré engraving), his funeral, his burial at Père Lachaise and, when the Italians reclaimed their idol, his reburial in 1887 at Santa Croce in Florence. Temporary exhibitions relating to each year's Rossini opera festival productions are presented in the basement, where there are also audio-visual facilities for visitors.

There is another, rather private shrine to Rossini in Pesaro, within the Conservatorio – which, established in 1882, bears his name not only in recognition of the local boy who made good but in acknowledgment of the fact that he endowed it and was in effect its founder. As an adjunct to the library, which itself is a centre of Rossini research (the Centro di Studi Rossiniani was set up in 1940), there is a large room, kept locked, known as the 'Tempietto rossiniano'. To reach it, you pass through the Sala dei Marmi, where there is a collection of historic keyboard instruments and a fine ceiling embodying a history of Pesaro. The 'little temple' itself is a large room, gently lit, with 19th-century wall lights and embossed wallpaper, a marble floor and a painted ceiling. Along three walls are display cases, containing 'mes autographes', some of them in neat stacks, some of them opened to view significant pages. Six of his operas are there, including *Armida*, *Otello* and *Elisabetta*

Display of caricatures in the Rossini museum

Rossini statue in the courtyard of the Conservatorio Statale di Musica 'Gioachino Rossini', Pesaro

Tuesday, Wednesday 09.30–12.30,
Thursday–Sunday 09.30–12.30,
16.00 19.00

Tempietto rossiniano
Conservatorio Statale di Musica
'Gioachino Rossini'
Piazza Olivieri 5
61000 Pesaro
Italy

phone +390/0 721 33670, 33671
fax +390/0 721 35295
e-mail consross@tin.it
website www.space.tin.it

open by appointment

Map 9

B. Cagli and M. Bucarelli: *La casa di Rossini: Catalogo del museo* (Modena: Edizioni Panini, 1989)
P. Fabbri: 'I Rossini a Pesaro e in Romagna', *Rossini 1792–1992: mostra storico-documentaria*, ed. M. Bucarelli (Perugia: Electa Editori Umbri, 1992), 53–70
Storia e restauro della casa di Gioachino Rossini (Pesaro: Cassa di Risparmio, 1996)
N. Simeone: *Paris: a Musical Gazetteer* (New Haven and London: Yale University Press, 2000), 114–19

d'Inghilterra. There are non-operatic works too, French songs, Italian choral pieces, piano music. And there is the *Petite messe solennelle*, with his own drily witty inscription: 'Douze chanteurs de trois sexes, hommes, femmes et castrats'. There are some letters, as well as busts and the deathbed grisaille of Gustave Doré. It is something of a privilege to be admitted to this very special museum, truly a little temple to the great man.

Casa Rossini
Via G. Rossini 34
61100 Pesaro
Italy

phone +390/0 721 387357
website
www.provincia.ps.it/cultura/musei/pesarorossini

open July–August, Tuesday–Sunday 09.30–12.30, 17.00–20.00 (Tuesday, Thursday to 23.00); September–June,

RYBA

Should you happen to approach Rožmitál pod Třemšínem from the south-west, by the road from Nepomuk and Klatovy, you may be surprised to see a sign by the roadside directing you to a memorial to Jan Jakub Ryba as you reach the small village of Voltuš, a couple of kilometres short of the town. It is worth pausing there to make the pilgrimage, a short walk through the woods, to see the little shrine to the composer of the famous and much-loved Christmas Mass, at the spot where, in 1815, he committed suicide.

Ryba, born in Přeštice (40 km to the west) in 1765, and a teacher and choir-master in Rožmitál from 1788, is remembered there with affection – the old town's main street is called Rybova after him, and two schools bear his name – although he was unhappy and, seemingly, persecuted

Shrine to Ryba near Rožmitál pod Třemšínem

by the authorities in his own time. Perhaps he was too learned and academic: he was well read, in several languages, and a keen student of philosophy and in particular of Seneca, whose writings are among the works he translated and whose biography he wrote (and whose form of suicide he eventually emulated, with Seneca's writings in his hand). Ryba was a prolific composer; his Christmas Mass of 1796 – actually a collection of Czech pastorellas – was written for the Holy Cross Church, a 13th-century building transformed in Czech rustic Baroque, in the old town, on the edge of the present one, where the organ he used was sensitively restored in 1997. Concerts are held there on the anniversaries of his birth and his death, and of course the Christmas Mass is given each year. He was reburied in the churchyard in 1855 after a petition by his children; as a suicide, he could not initially be buried in consecrated ground – but his original grave, in a disused plague cemetery by a lake, 500 metres away, is marked by a large cross.

The site of the school where Ryba taught is marked by a plaque. Another adorns the town museum, where on the second floor there is a room dedicated to him, set up in the 1970s by the local Ryba Society. The display cases show a variety of documents (or facsimiles) from his time: schoolbooks, student records,

school diaries, certificates, a Protokol on his duties as teacher, his own teaching notes and lists of exam marks, a sketch of his thoughts on moral philosophy, prayer books and bible stories, a manuscript song book, an 1815 edition of his funeral songs and a modern one of his children's texts, title-pages, his own wax stamp. There is a document from the town administrator, evidently his nemesis. The world of the local musician-teacher is well evoked.

Ryba's memorial site in Voltuš is pictured in its various phases. The portraits include one of Ryba's son, an eminent medical man in Prague, and there is a modern bust of Ryba himself. There are commemorative medals, photocopies of his manuscripts, and posters and programmes of modern performances, as well as a selection of contemporary instruments (including folk ones). Rožmitál is doing its best to compensate.

Městské Muzeum a Památník Jakuba Jana Ryby

Náměstí 23
26242 Rožmitál pod Třemšínem
Czech Republic

phone +420/0 318 665339
e-mail kk-rozmital@quick.cz
website www.pb.cz/alfa/rozmital

open April–October, Tuesday–Sunday
09.00–12.00, 13.00–16.00

Map 4

SAAR

You have to go some way off the beaten track in Estonia to find the museum in the summer home at Hüpassaare or Üpassaare of the composer Mart Saar (1882–1963), who found inspiration in native folk music traditions for his piano pieces and choral works.

To find it from Suure-Jaani (the nearest town, where the museum to the Kapp family is), go west on the road north of the town towards Kaansoo through birch forests for about seven kilometres; if you are vigilant you will see a small sign directing you left on to a logging road to Hüpassaare, just over ten kilometres away. (Coming direct from Tallinn, through Paide, it is about 140 km to Kaansoo, and after five kilometres towards Suure-Jaani look for a logging road to the right and take it for seven kilometres.) Then there is a further kilometre down a rutted dirt-track, ending in a meadow, which doubles as a car park. The rest of the journey (300 m) is made on foot, along a path that leads through an open-air concert venue for folksinging (equipped with wooden risers and benches, and seemingly midge-infested) and finally to Mart Saar's house, which is almost obscured by the remnants of an orchard and an overgrown garden. How long the museum, which was founded in 1972, can survive in so remote a setting must depend largely on the role folk music plays in Estonian cultural life. At present it is lived in and cared for by the composer's elderly niece.

Two rooms, Saar's study and his bedroom, are preserved much as he left them. The enclosed porch serves as a lobby and the entrance hall as a display space for collages of facsimile photographs and documents chronicling his life, together with editions and recordings of his music. The dining-room contains his organ and a gramophone on which recordings of his music as well as an interview with him (in Estonian) can be played. His study is furnished as a sitting-room with his piano and desk, with his glasses, inkstand and pens. Here and in the bedroom are portraits of Beethoven. The bedroom, which looks as if he has just left it, is spartan, relieved only by his radio on the table and his well-worn slippers by the bed. There is a display case with more of his clothing: his overcoat, hat, gloves, umbrella, cane and briefcase representing his outward, professional persona and his ties, trousers and waistcoats his private one. For a moment the visitor almost feels himself to be an intruder.

Like his friends Rudolf Tobias and Artur Kapp, also commemorated in Estonia with house museums, Saar studied first with Joosep Kapp and then in St Petersburg (1901–8) with Rimsky-Korsakov. Unlike them, however, he began collecting folksongs, which strongly influenced his harmonic language and melodic style. After working in Tartu as a music critic and teacher, he divided his career between Tallinn, where he taught at the Conservatory (1943–56), and his woodland retreat at Hüpassaare where he could compose. He died in Tallinn and was buried in Suure-Jaani, close to the Kapp family. There is a bust of Saar in the concert hall of the Museum of Theatre and Music in Tallinn.

Helilooja Mart Saare Muuseum
Hüpassaare
Estonia

open daily 11.00–18.00
Map 2

SÆVERUD

Some six kilometres south of the well-known Grieg museum at Troldhaugen, on the road towards the museum to Ole Bull at Lysøen, lies the museum to Harald Sæverud (1897–1992). Sæverud was a prominent figure in Norwegian music during almost the entire 20th century. Like Grieg, he was born in Bergen – to a father from a local farming family and a mother from a family of fiddle players in the Hardanger region. As a young man, Sæverud made a reputation as a composer of symphonies and other extended works, moving towards an expressionist style; he had had some training in Berlin but was chiefly a product of Norway and spent most of his long life in or near Bergen. During and after the years of German occupation he wrote more turbulent, nationalistic music, including three war symphonies, as well as piano pieces drawing on Norwegian folksong. In 1953 he was awarded a state pension, and he continued composing for virtually the rest of his life – a major symphonic work for the Bergen International Festival in 1986, a viola sonatina at 92. His output includes nine symphonies, several concertos, a *Peer Gynt* suite and much chamber music.

Sæverud married in 1934. Among the wedding presents that he and his wife, Marie Hvoslef, received from her family was an estate of more than 70 hectares just south of Bergen. There they built a mansion, Siljustøl, designed by the composer himself in conjunction with the architect Ludof Eide Parr, of more than 60 rooms; they moved in in 1939. The locals dubbed it the 'music castle'. Built of the local materials, natural granite and untreated pine, it is 14 km south of the centre of Bergen, close to the 553 road, beyond Troldhaugen, near the village of Fana; it is set in a hilly garden, in parkland by the sea. Sæverud himself is buried in the garden.

Siljustøl, the largest private house in western Norway when it was built, became in part a museum to Sæverud in 1997, on his centenary; it is administered from the Grieg museum at Troldhaugen. Part of the original building remains a private residence for the Sæverud family but the wing-like section joined to the main body of the house at 135° and the rooms adjacent to it form the museum. There are three floors. The lowest includes a museum shop, where CDs of his music can be bought. On the upper floors rooms are preserved much as they were in Sæverud's day, with his piano and other furniture, much of it built to his own designs and some embodying his own painting. There are displays of folk instruments, as well as his scores, sketches and programmes and his library. Several of the pictures are the work of his wife, a painter, and other family members, and there is a vivid display of photographs. Everything is slightly out of the ordinary – examples of naive art, a Turkish octagonal table, a spinning-wheel, ceiling decoration around where the annual Christmas tree stood. Concerts are given in the wood-panelled living-room each Sunday in July (it seats over 30) and four times during the Bergen festival, in May and June.

Siljustøl Museum

Siljustølvegen 50
5239 Rådal
Norway

phone +47/0 55 136000 (for booking, 922992, 901710)
fax +47/0 55 922993, 911295
e-mail trold@online.no
website
www.bergen.by.com/museum/siljustol

open May–August, daily 11.00–16.00, by appointment

Sæverud's house at Siljustøl

SAINT-SAËNS

Camille Saint-Saëns was a Parisian. He was born in the Latin Quarter, at 3 Rue du Jardinet, on 9 October 1835. But his family came from the Dieppe area; his father had been born nearby, at Rouxmesnil-le-Haut. Possibly they originally hailed from the small, rather sleepy town, actually called Saint-Saëns, some 35 km to the south (which advertises no connection with the composer). After his mother's death, in 1888, Saint-Saëns made regular gifts to the City of Dieppe of his possessions, which from July 1890 were displayed in a room in the Bains Chauds; and in the summer of 1897 a Musée Saint-Saëns was opened in the courtyard of the old Hôtel de Ville (demolished in 1958), a Festival Camille Saint-Saëns was inaugurated in the Casino, and the Place de la Comédie was renamed Place Camille Saint-Saëns. A statue to him was unveiled with great ceremony in the foyer of the city theatre in October 1907, in his presence; it was moved outside in 1923, only to be requisitioned and melted down by the occupying Germans during World War II. Dieppe was the scene of his last public appearance, on 6 August 1921; he died, in Algiers, on 16 December that year. The centenary of his birth, in 1935, was celebrated in Dieppe as well as Paris and Algiers.

Today the composer's legacy to Dieppe is relegated to a small room in a far corner of the hillside Château-Musée (opened in 1923) in which the Louis XVI furniture he inherited from his mother and great-aunt and his first piano (a Pleyel in original condition), as well as portraits and busts, can be viewed through glass; there is also a display case with a selection of scores, programmes, medallions and his baton, of wood and engraved silver, along with a bust of Liszt and a death mask of Beethoven. Across town his personal library, which includes more than 15,000 letters, is kept at the Centre Culturel Jean Renoir (1 Quai Bérigny) where in 1997 an exhibition marked the centenary of the original Musée Saint-Saëns.

Château-Musée

Rue de Chastes
76200 Dieppe
France

phone +33/0 2 3584 1976
fax +33/0 2 3290 1279
e-mail musee-dieppe@wanadoo.fr

open June–September, daily 10.00–12.00, 14.00–18.00; October–May, Wednesday–Monday, 10.00–12.00, 14.00–17.00 (Sunday to 18.00)

Map 6

P. Ickowicz: 'Camille Saint-Saëns au Château-Musée de Dieppe', *Un maître de musique à Dieppe: Camille Saint-Saëns (1835–1921)* (Dieppe: Mediathèque Jean Renoir, 1997) [with exhibition catalogue]

N. Simeone: *Paris: a Musical Gazetteer* (New Haven and London: Yale University Press, 2000), 120–25

SARASATE

It is of course as a violinist that Pablo Sarasate is chiefly remembered. But he composed too, not inconsiderably, and, not surprisingly, chiefly for his own instrument, mainly high-quality, virtuoso salon pieces. There are the famous *Zigeunerweisen* and many works that are redolent of his native country – jotas,

Saint-Saëns display at Dieppe

fandangos and the like, evoking the Spanish world.

He spent most of his life in Paris and on tour, and he died, in 1908, in Biarritz – not far from the city where in 1844 he was born, Pamplona. The house of his birth no longer stands, but there is a plaque on the house now on the site, in a busy pedestrianized shopping street. Another street is named after him, and there is a statue to him in the Media Luna. The local Conservatorio de Música bears his name. The conservatory however is not (despite reports to the contrary) the site of the museum to him, which is housed more centrally, in the municipal archive.

The building itself was formerly the Colegio o Seminario de San Juan; the museum was installed in a large first-floor room there in 1991. The room devoted to Sarasate, once a chapel, has a barrel-vaulted ceiling and arched doors, firmly gothick in style, with brightly painted, patterned walls hinting at Moorish influence. As you enter, you see a large oil portrait of Sarasate, by José Llaneces, in formal dress with his Gran Cruz de la Orden de Isabel la Católica. He is more imaginatively represented in the bronze bust by Mariano Benlliure, with its expressive eyes and turbulent hair.

The presentation is formal and symmetrical, with showcases along the walls and down the centre of the room. Sarasate's numerous medals, gilded and silver laurels and other honours are lavishly displayed, as too are the countless gifts showered on him by his admirers across the world – jewelled cigarette boxes, watches (one has a chain and fob set with diamonds and sapphires), silverware, crystal, rings, buttons, pins. Among the medals is a particularly elegant set from the Sociedades Santa Cecilia y Orfeón Pamplonés. One case contains miniature violins and bows and the original pegs from his 1713 and 1724 Strads (he left the instruments to the Paris and Madrid conservatories). In another are two of his own violins, one a reproduction of the instrument on which he won his Paris Conservatoire *premier prix* in

1857, the other a Vuillaume expressly made for him. There is also his practice violin, 'violín de bolsilio', with a small bow, ivory pegs and inlaid fingerboard. The *premier prix* certificate is there too, displayed with other framed items, including a pencil portrait done by Whistler in Pittsburgh, a signed photo of the Romanian royal family, concert programmes and family photos. One corner is devoted to his collaboration with the pianists Otto Goldschmidt (formerly Jenny Lind's husband) and Berthe Marx.

Sarasate's own music is represented too – there is a full list of his works in one case – but understandably it is his distinction as one of the great figures in the history of violin playing that comes across as the message of this dignified and affectionate tribute from his native city.

Sala-Museo de Pablo Sarasate

Archivo Municipal
Calle del Mercado 11
31001 Pamplona
Spain

phone +34/0 948 100 189

open Monday–Friday 09.00–14.00

Map 15

SATIE

Erik Satie began life in the Normandy fishing port of Honfleur. His parents lived near the esplanade at 90 rue Haute, where he was born on 17 May 1866, and his grandparents were at no.50. His father Alfred, a composer of music-hall songs, decided to set up as a music publisher in Paris and the family moved there in 1870. But two years later Erik's mother died and he was sent back to Honfleur to live with his grandparents. There, under their influence, he took up the piano. Today Honfleur, with its many half-timbered buildings lining the narrow streets and its characterful harbour life, is a thriving holiday resort, reached from the east by the striking new Pont de Normandie.

The house at no.90 Rue Haute and its

neighbour, no.92, were acquired for the Association Satie Honfleur, renovated, interconnected and, in 1998, christened 'Maisons Satie': perhaps more installation than museum, in tune with the composer in concept and its drollery, and up-to-date in its realization. The proprietors themselves decree 'amusez-vous', guaranteeing visitors a zany mixture of music and what they dub 'charcuterie'. The journey through eight rooms, aided by Satie's (often apparently posthumous) recollections and a series of arrows emanating from pears to point the way – a logo *en forme de poire* – begins with the donning of headsets whose music and commentary (in French or English) are activated by a series of sensors along the route. The sound effects (musical excerpts, monologues and dialogues), together with theatrical décor and lighting effects in each room, draw visitors into Satie's eccentric world. There is plenty to do along the way: don't miss the carousel of 'instruments injouables [unplayable]' or the cabaret-cinema.

'Complaisamment solitaire': display at the Maisons Satie

Maisons Satie Honfleur

Satie returned to Paris for good in 1878, living with his father, and later his stepmother, first at 2 Rue Constantinople (just north of Gare St Lazare) and then at 50 Rue Condorcet (near the Cirque Médrano) until 1887, when, after a chequered career as a student at the Conservatoire and a brief and undistinguished stint in the army, he was obliged to move out because of a liaison with the family maid. He was drawn to the exotic, bohemian life of nearby Montmartre and found work as a pianist at the cabaret Chat Noir, at 12 Rue de Laval (later Rue Victor Massé) – which no longer exists, although a plaque marks the spot. By the beginning of 1890 Satie was living in a miserable, tiny, windowless room, more closet than *cabinet*, at the top of the butte at 6 Rue Cortot, not far from Sacré-Coeur. Soon after, he met Joséphin Péladan, Sâr of the Rosicrucian Order, the Temple and the Grail, and was appointed 'chapelmaster' for the sect.

During his eight years at 6 Rue Cortot he composed Rosicrucian music as well as piano music; left the Chat Noir for its chief rival, the Auberge du Clous at 30 Avenue Trudaine (which still exists); embarked on a literary career; founded his own Eglise Métropolitaine d'Art de Jésus Conducteur (of which he was the solitary member); enjoyed a short affair with the painter Suzanne Valadon (January to June 1893); and applied three times without success for admission to the Académie des Beaux-Arts (chronicled in his 1912 'Mémoires d'un Amnesiac').

The building at 6 Rue Cortot still exists. From 1984 to 1999 a small flat on the second floor, though possibly not his original room, was used by the Fondation Erik Satie for the display of their substantial archive: manuscripts, ephemera, photographs, oil portraits by Grass-Mick and La Rochefoucauld, and personal effects (collar, hat and cane). They were then consolidated with the display at Honfleur.

In 1898 Satie moved to the southern working-class suburb of Arcueil-Cachan, while maintaining his former lifestyle. Almost unbelievably, he made the 19-kilometre trip daily, on foot, from his room over a dingy café, in a flat-iron building at 22 Rue Cauchy, known as the 'Maison aux quatre cheminées', to the cabarets of Montmartre, returning home in the early hours, armed with a hammer for protection.

'Les quatre cheminées' still stands, still in one of the grubbier parts of the city; a plaque was erected on the building in 1929, four years after his death, a nearby park was named after him on the centenary of his birth, and another plaque was put up in 1998 to mark the centenary of his moving in: 'Avec émotion, Arcueil s'en souvient'. He never allowed anyone into his room (no.15 on the second floor); those who ventured in after his death found a time-capsule of his life – he had lived in squalor, without running water or gas lighting; there were piles of unopened mail, worn-out, moth-eaten suits, 60 pairs of down-at-heel shoes, and several thousand small pieces of paper carefully decorated with his inimitable drawings and calligraphy in black and red India ink, filed in innumerable cigar boxes. It is re-created without apology at the Honfleur 'Maisons Satie'.

Satie died of cirrhosis of the liver in a Paris hospital on 1 July 1925. He was buried in the cemetery at Arcueil.

Maisons Satie
67 boulevard Charles V
14600 Honfleur
France

phone +33/0 2 3189 1111

open summer, Wednesday–Monday 10.00–19.00; winter, Wednesday–Monday 10.30–18.00

Map 6

O. Volta: *Erik Satie* (Paris: Hazan, 1997)
O. Volta: *Erik Satie honfleurais* (Honfleur: Editions de la Lieutenance, 1998)
N. Simeone: *Paris: a Musical Gazetteer* (New Haven and London: Yale University Press, 2000), 125–9

SAVIN

Friderik Širca was an officer in the Austrian imperial army; his military career ended after 38 years' service in 1918, when he had reached the rank of major-general. But he had led a double life: he was also a composer. He kept his two sides firmly apart by using the name Risto Savin (probably derived from the local river, the Savinja) for his musical studies, in Vienna and Prague in the 1890s, and for his ensuing career in music, which embraced the composition of three operas successfully produced in Ljubljana as well as ballets, solo and choral songs and piano music.

Savin was born on 11 July 1859 to a mercantile family in the central Slovenian town of Žalec, about 55 km east of Ljubljana. The house of his birth, in the centre of the town, dates back to 1669; it was renovated in 1972 and part of it is an art gallery and offices, but on its upper floor is a large room dedicated to his memory – Savin's own working room after his return to Žalec, where he lived from 1919 until his death, apart from six years following his marriage on his wife's estates near Ptuj. In this room are relics from various parts of his life.

Two showcases are given over to his military career (with his medals, his caps, his water flask, his binoculars) and there are photographs and a portrait of him in uniform and on horseback. Some of his uniforms are preserved in a case. One corner is dedicated to his family (he was the youngest of six children), with photographs of his parents and siblings, letters and mementoes, and there is a photograph showing the room as it was in 1939. Another showcase preserves various personal objects – his glasses, his cigarette case, his calling cards and a beribboned silver sprig of laurel. The area around his desk, on which original manuscripts and letters can be seen beneath the glass, as well as his fountain pens and inkstand, is concerned with his musical career. A lute and a side drum belonging to him are displayed, along with photographs of his singers and posters for his concerts (including an 80th birthday event), and there is a china figurine, his wife's gift to him, symbolizing his ballet *Čajna punčka* ('The Tea Doll'). Some of his furniture – chairs, a sofa, a chest, a table – are shown too. His two sides merge in a charcoal portrait of him, in uniform, at the piano, dating from 1903.

Savin's widow remained in the house and died in 1969; she had given away many of his possessions but some were returned when the house was acquired by the municipality and, in the early 1990s, became a museum. His own music manuscripts are housed in the local heritage museum. Savin himself died in Zagreb, on 11 December 1948, and was buried in Žalec; on his grave, by the cemetery entrance, is a bust. Next to the local cultural centre and office is a music school named after him, also with a bust.

Spominska soba Friderika Širce–Rista Savina
Savinova hiša
Šlandrov trg 25
3310 Žalec
Slovenia

phone +386/03571 9200 (3712 1250, tourist office)
fax +386/0 3712 1262
e-mail zavodzakulturaloalec2@siol.net

open during exhibitions, Monday–Saturday 10.00–12.00, 16.00–18.00, or by appointment

Map 14

SCHEIDT

After Handel, Samuel Scheidt (1587–1654) is Halle's most important native musician. But unlike Handel, Scheidt spent his whole life in the city, except for a period of study with Sweelinck in Amsterdam, in various appointments as organist and Kapellmeister to the resident administrators, Margrave Christian Wilhelm of Brandenburg and later Duke August of Saxony. His career was much affected by the Thirty Years War, which in 1625 brought to an end his most productive period; during the early 1620s he was responsible for raising the calibre of music-making in Halle by attracting fine musicians to the court, for whom he composed and published a dazzling array of collections of motets, vocal concertos, ensemble music and organ music. During a 13-year period in the 1620s and 30s when Halle was without a royal protector Scheidt made his living mainly as an organist and teacher, and continued to compose (four volumes of *Geistliche Concerte* were published between 1631 and 1640). Owing to the impoverishment of war, an epidemic of plague afflicted Halle in 1636; all four of Scheidt's children died within a month.

A small room on the second floor of the Händel-Haus is dedicated to Scheidt as part of a series devoted to the musical history of Halle. The walls are lined with facsimiles of manuscript documents from the city archives, title-pages of his publications and an engraved portrait. There is also an enlargement of an old photo of the house in Dachritzstraße, just north of the Händel-Haus, where Scheidt died on 24 March 1654. The room includes a small display devoted to Michael Praetorius, Scheidt's predecessor as Kapellmeister.

Händel-Haus
Grosse Nikolaistraße 5
06108 Halle (Saale)
Germany

phone +49/0 345 500900
fax +49/0 345 50090 411

e-mail haendelhaus@halle.de
website www.haendelhaus.de

open daily 09.30–17.30 (Thursday to 19.00)

Map 7

K. Musketa: *Musikgeschichte der Stadt Halle: Führer durch die Ausstellung des Händel-Hauses* (Halle an der Saale: Händel-Haus, 1998), 16–21

SCHIKANEDER

Emanuel Schikaneder is best known as the librettist of Mozart's *Die Zauberflöte* and its first Papageno. He was also an actor, impresario and composer, although his surviving compositions are few and confined to German light operas and incidental music to plays. Born near Regensburg in 1751, he travelled during much of his life with theatre troupes but spent periods in Vienna: 1784–6, 1789–1806 and from 1809 to his death there in 1812. In 1802 he bought a house in the Nußdorf area on the northern side of the city. It is thought to have been pillaged by Napoleon's troops in 1809 and visited by Napoleon himself. From 1931 it was the property of Franz Lehár; since 1950 it has been a museum dedicated primarily to his memory (*see* LEHÁR), and it is sometimes known as the Schikaneder-Lehár Schlößl ('little castle').

Schikaneder's own music is not featured in the museum, but he is not forgotten there. Both he and Lehár are represented in the relief plaques by the entrance. Inside the single large room that constitutes the museum, there is a ceiling fresco of the Queen of Night, the Three Boys, the Three Ladies and Monostatos, the work of Vincenzo Sachetti and thought to date back to 1802. There is a sedan chair claimed as Schikaneder's own, with giltwork inside and bevelled glazing. The exhibits include playbills, engravings and other materials relevant to *Die Zauberflöte*. There is a pair of large wooden chairs with arm supports in the form of water serpents, which, it is claimed, were designed for and used in the

original staging of the opera: credulity is somewhat stretched, but who knows?

Schikaneder-Lehár-Schlößl
Hackhofergasse 18
1190 Wien
Austria

phone +43/0 1318 5416

open 15 March–30 October, by appointment

Map 1

SCHMIDT

Franz Schmidt was a revered figure among Austrian composers in the inter-war years. Born in Pressburg (now Bratislava) in 1874, he had been a cellist in the Vienna Philharmonic, playing under Mahler at the opera and also with the Rosé Quartet; in the 1920s he was director and later rector of the Hochschule and recipient of many honours. He died in 1939 and was buried in the Zentralfriedhof. Musically he is remembered chiefly for his organ music, his symphonies (especially no.4) and his apocalyptic oratorio *Das Buch mit sieben Siegeln*. Though himself a conservative composer, in the Reger tradition, he was a generous supporter of new music.

Schmidt lived for many years in Perchtoldsdorf, a southern suburb of Vienna. After his death his wife – whose mental troubles led to her being killed in the Nazi euthanasia operation – remained in their large house on the edge of the town, and after that his niece lived there. But in 1997 the house, parts of which had been maintained as they were in Schmidt's day, was sold; some of the Schmidt materials were then taken to the local music school (in the Knappenhof, a former palace), which bears his name, and two rooms were set up there in his memory.

In the larger of them is his Bösendorfer piano (in playing condition), his desk, a china cabinet, a fine Vienna wall-clock, his armchair and a *Jugendstil* 'Hoffmann-Bett', or couch, on which his body was laid on his death. There is also a death mask and a cast of his right hand. Part of his library is preserved, including his Mahler and Wagner scores, his metronomes, a pack of tarot cards, and several walking sticks. There is a fine drawing by Anton Kardinsky of Schmidt as a cellist, and some of his award certificates are framed on the walls. Of particular interest is a charming woodland painting by Schmidt himself, made on a visit to France when he was 26 and given to a French girl: it found its way back, via Cambodia and Brussels, through the recipient's nephew long after her and Schmidt's deaths. Other paintings are the work of his wife.

His wife's taste pervades the second, smaller room, with its *chinoiserie*, in the prints on the walls and its furnishings. But there are Schmidt relics here too, among them the iron chest he used for storing his scores, his pocket knife, some china, a picture of the house where he was born, a photo recording the Vienna Philharmonic concert given in honour of his 60th birthday, cigarette holders, pipes and, in an envelope, the remains of his last cigar.

Almost opposite the entrance to the Knappenhof is the house, now shops with accommodation above, in which Gluck lived from 1781 to 1787, which bears a commemorative plaque.

Schmidt-Gedenkräume

Franz Schmidt Musikschule
Marktgemeinde Perchtoldsdorf
2380 Perchtoldsdorf
Austria

phone +43/0 1865 4377
fax +43/0 1865 437714

open by appointment

Map 1

SCHNEIDER-TRNAVSKÝ

Trnava, some 50 km north-east of Bratislava, is often called the 'Slovakian Rome', and for almost half a century its

musical pope was Mikuláš Schneider-Trnavský. Born in the city in 1881, he became choirmaster of St Nicholas, the cathedral, in 1909, and was still in the post at his death in 1958. There is a bust of him in the main street close to the cathedral.

His birthplace, in Trojičné námestie, no longer stands (it was close to the present site of the Jednota supermarket), but the house in which he lived, in what is now ulica M. Schneidera-Trnavského, immediately opposite the west front of the cathedral, is the Dom hudby, the 'house of music'. Under the ownership of the Západoslovenské Múzeum (the West Slovakian Museum, which lies at the far end of ulica Kapitulská from the cathedral), the property was originally assigned to people working at the cathedral. Now there is an antique shop and a café on the ground floor; upstairs are the music department of the state library, in what had been Schneider-Trnavský's sister's flat, with a small display devoted to the guitarist John Dopyera, inventor of the Dobro guitar, who was born locally, and the memorial to Schneider-Trnavský, opened in his own former flat in 1996. Visitors are handed a portfolio with photographs, showing the house before and during its restoration in the 1990s, and of Schneider-Trnavský, his family and friends, with a collection of articles by him and about him.

Dozens of photographs on the staircase lead the visitor into Schneider-Trnavský's world. In the main room, by which the visitor enters, there is a large Bösendorfer grand and a bust of the composer, but the most interesting feature – and one unknown to Schneider-Trnavský, as it was discovered only when, after his time, several paint layers were stripped – is a series of Japanese-style wall paintings, of birds, flowers etc. The room is used occasionally for musical events, but seats only around 30; there are in fact other recital spaces in the adjoining music library and (a larger one) in the parent museum not far away.

In a room off to the left, formerly

Schneider-Trnavský's study, are his desk and chair, with his inkstand and paper-weights, pencil sharpener and letter knife. Also in the room is another Bösendorfer grand (his own), a leather three-piece suite and a bookcase, his music stand and garlands honouring him. On the opposite side is what was Schneider-Trnavský's living-room, now with the main display: one case devoted to his setting of Slovak song, another to his sacred music, both with music and commentary, and two glass-fronted cupboards with some song manuscripts, diplomas, school reports and certifi-cates, some statuettes, an early exercise book ('Meine Contrapuntische Studien') and various personal items – bow ties, stamps and a pocket diary, gloves and top hat, as well as violin pegs, bridges and mute. There are several other items of original furniture (cabinets, table and chairs).

An additional room is dedicated to the musical and theatrical history of Trnava and Schneider-Trnavský's place within it: there are records, shown on eleven wall panels, of the foundation and activities of the city's musical organizations, along with posters, programmes, photographs, songbooks and manuscript volumes of church music. Four further panels show photographs, with commentary, of people involved in the city's musical life, especially Schneider-Trnavský's succes-sors. There are also portraits of past Austrian emperors, some instruments, and Schneider-Trnavský's hat and walking-stick.

Dom hudby Mikuláša Schneidera-Trnavského Trnava*
ulica M. Schneidera-Trnavského 5
91809 Trnava
Slovakia

phone +421/0 33 551 2556
e-mail zsm@tt.sknet.sk

open Tuesday–Friday 09.00–17.00,
Sunday 13.00–18.00

Map 8

SCHOENBERG

There is a house in Mödling, a southern suburb of Vienna where Beethoven liked to stay and to walk in the fields. It bears a plaque which proclaims – not wholly correctly – that here at Bernhardgasse 6 the first 12-note music was composed. The first floor of that house, where Arnold Schoenberg lived from 1918 until he moved to Berlin in 1926 (Ernst Krenek briefly lived on the floor above), served until 1998 as the sole memorial in Austria to the founder of the Second Viennese School. It also served as the headquarters of the International Schoenberg Society. Being primarily a place of work – the new Schoenberg edition and other publica-tions emanate from there, and it is used for seminars – rather than a public museum, the display of Schoenberg memorabilia is a secondary consideration. The visitor, however, can see a number of Schoenberg items, personal and musical, in the pair of interconnecting rooms.

In 1998, however, a true Schoenberg museum, the Arnold Schönberg Center, opened in the heart of Vienna. There had been a Schoenberg Institute since 1977 in Los Angeles (where he died in 1951), at the University of Southern California, where a large quantity of the material he left, both music and personal relics, had been deposited by his family; but the university's perceived needs proved irrec-oncilable with the Schoenberg family's wish that the institute should foster exclusively the music of Schoenberg and his circle. The family eventually decided to withdraw the material and find another home for it: and where could be better than Vienna, his native city (the block of flats in which he was born in 1874, at Obere Donaustraße 5 in the 2nd district, is marked by a plaque) and his home for many years, where his ashes rest in a fine *Ehrengrab* (tomb of honour) in the Zentralfriedhof, and where his music is liked rather more than it is in Los Angeles?

The Vienna municipality saw it the same way and were eager to right old wrongs: the city quickly found a home for the 20 tons of material from Los Angeles on the spacious first floor of the imposing Palais Fanto, in the Schwarzenbergplatz, just outside the Ring, a few minutes' walk from the Staatsoper and the Imperial Hotel. The family donated Schoenberg's music manuscripts to the city but have retained ownership of all other items.

The municipality asked Elsa Prochazka, designer of all the composer museums belonging to the city, to set up the new one (to which the Mödling house is now an adjunct, used to accommodate scholars and to continue as a memorial to Schoenberg's years there). It is characteristically functional in its general design. There is a well fitted-out recital hall to seat 200, wedge-shaped (the platform at the narrow end), as well as a shop, a library, seminar rooms and a re-creation of his workshop-like study in Los Angeles (even reproducing the view he saw out of the windows). There is a long gallery for exhibitions, and certainly ample material for frequently changing displays. Schoenberg is a particularly apt subject for a museum: not many composers produced works of art that can comfortably cohabit with their music. Several of his striking, Expressionist paintings are shown, among them a number of self-portraits (the subject never ceased to fascinate him), 'visions' and caricatures.

There are some unusual miscellaneous items. Schoenberg's exploratory intellect led him into curious areas: you might have expected him to devise a musical typewriter, but not perhaps a notation for a tennis game or designs for an automatic inkwell, a new kind of water main, an elevated railway or a motorway interchange, or a complex four-man game of 'coalition chess' (for illustration see p.44). More conventional displays, in glass and stainless steel showcases, are devoted to his manuscripts (notably fragments and sketches), his didactic and philosophical writings, his correspondence and other documents of his life, editions of his music, his poetry, his Judaism and his pupils.

Internationale Schönberg Gesellschaft
Bernhardgasse 6
2340 Mödling
Austria

phone +43/0 223 642223, 1512 6869

open by appointment

Arnold Schönberg Center
Palais Fanto
Schwarzenbergplatz 6
 (entrance Zaunergasse 1–3)
1030 Wien
Austria

phone +43/0 1 712 1888
fax +43/0 1 712 188888
e-mail office@schoenberg.at
website www.schoenberg.at

open Tuesday–Sunday 10.00–17.00
(Thursday 10.00–20.00)

Map 1

H. Kretschmer: *Wiener Musikergedenkstätten* (Vienna: J & V Edition, 3/1992)
Arnold Schönberg Center Newsletter (Vienna: Arnold Schönberg Center, 1998–) [see especially 'Arnold Schönberg's Viennese Residences', no.4, Feb–June 1999, pp.10–15]
Schönberg Festival: Almanach (Vienna: Arnold Schönberg Center, 1998) [programme book of inaugural festival, 14–19 March 1998]

SCHUBERT

Schubert lived something of a peripatetic existence in Vienna, as had Mozart and Beethoven. He left a string of addresses, of which two, his first and his last, are now museums. Accordingly, there are nearly two dozen Schubert memorial sites of various kinds, with plaques, on houses (including the 'Erlkönighaus' at Säulengasse 3), churches and inns and in parks. These assist the dedicated Schubertian determined to recapture something of the flavour of his life, or at least to follow in some of his footsteps and plot his movements on a city map, taking in the locations of the coffeehouses and inns he frequented, the venues where his music was performed and the homes of friends where his circle foregathered.

Franz Peter Schubert was born on 31 January 1797 in a first-floor flat over the school where his father taught. The address, in the northern suburb of Himmelpfortgrund, called 'Zum roten Krebsen' ('The Red Crab'), was at first Obere Hauptstraße 42, then no.72; later it was renamed and renumbered as Nußdorfer Straße 54. The Schubert family occupied two of the 16 tiny flats – one for the school, one for the family – between 1786 and 1801. There 12 children, of whom four survived to adulthood, were born to the composer's parents.

The birthplace museum, founded in 1912 and recently renovated, now incorporates several rooms from the adjoining flats. The kitchen and the single living-room, facing on to the street, which once made up the entire family lodging, are distinguished from the rest of the museum by their simplicity: the kitchen, where the Schubert children are supposed to have been born (on no firmer evidence than that it was probably the warmest place to be), is devoid of ornament, while in the living-room there is nothing to be found but a bust of the composer and a vase. In the adjacent rooms there are pictures offering a survey of the people and places central to Schubert's life. Also on display are first editions, facsimiles of his music autographs and his diaries, letters, concert programmes and press reviews, as well as

his guitar and a grand piano that belonged to his brother Ignaz. His pathetic steel-framed glasses, their lenses shattered, and a lock of hair taken when his body was exhumed in 1863, are unforgettable. The rooms are modest in size but adequate for the Schubertiade that are held there eight times a year.

Outside Vienna itself, just off the St Pölten road (north of the Linz motorway, south of the Danube), some 40 km west of the city, is a Schubert-Gedenkstätte at Schloß Atzenbrugg, commemorating 'Franz Schubert und sein Freundeskreis'. Atzenbrugg is unique among composer museums for the extent to which it brings to life the leading figures in the composer's circle and throws light on his social life. Originally the property of the Klosterneuburg monastery, the building, with its chapel and vaulted ceilings, has suffered the ravages of war many times over the centuries – from the Turks, from Napoleon and in World War II. It was last restored in 1977. In Schubert's day the steward of the Schloß was Josef Derffel, an employee of the monastery and an uncle of Franz von Schober; he offered hospitality to his nephew's friends each summer from 1817 to 1822 for house parties or 'Atzenbrugg Feasts'. Schubert himself first went in 1820. The high spirits and the ambience of these gatherings of members of the young, liberal intelligentsia are captured in the well-known watercolours of another member of the circle, Leopold Kupelwieser; in these and other pictures Schloß

Courtyard at Schubert's birthplace

Schloß Atzenbrugg

'Gesellschaftsspiel der Schubertianer im Atzenbrugg' (watercolour by Leopold Kupelwieser)

Atzenbrugg itself is easily recognizable, inside and out, as is the recurrent bespectacled image of Schubert himself. Kupelwieser drew separate portraits there of Schubert and Schober. Since 1978, after a pause of more than 150 years, annual Atzenbrugger Schubertiade have taken place from the end of May to the end of June and on Saturdays in September.

The museum, established in 1986 through private initiative, is on two floors. A circular staircase leads to the Schubert-Saal, a concert hall seating some 120, lined with reproductions of Schubert family portraits. Surrounding it is a series of carefully conceived display rooms, each of them devoted to one of Schubert's friends, including Kupelwieser, the painter Moritz von Schwind, Schober himself, Schubert's school friend the poet Johann Mayrhofer, the singer Johann Michael Vogl, his patron Josef von Spaun and his piano duet partner, the dramatist Eduard von Bauernfeld. On the ground floor one room commemorates the Sonnleithner family and also the Hüttenbrenners and Grillparzer.

Not quite so readily accessible is another country museum, in the small town of Želiezovce, about 200 km east of Vienna in the south-east corner of Slovakia, close to the Hungarian border (Zselíz in Hungarian, which is equally spoken there) and near the river Hron, a Danube tributary. Here Count Johann

Esterházy had one of his family country residences and Schubert, as music-master to the daughters, first went there in the summer of 1818.

There at the beginning of August he composed the song *Einsamkeit* ('Loneliness') – 'the best I have done', he wrote to Schober – which however turned out prophetic: a month later he was complaining that at Zselíz he had no choice but to amuse himself: 'I have to be composer, author, audience and goodness knows what else'. He also wrote piano duets for his pupils and the *Deutsches Requiem* for his brother Ferdinand to pass off as his own. He was there again in 1824, when he wrote the vocal quartet *Gebet* and various piano duets including the op.140 *Grand Duo*.

The Esterházy Schloß, a charming classical building in spacious parkland, dating from 1787, is not open to the public and is in need of restoration. Schubert himself is believed to have stayed in one of the two lodges, not far away; one no longer stands (significantly, when it was demolished music manuscript paper was found under the wallpaper), leaving the other, known as the Owlet's Eyrie, to serve as a little Schubert museum, which it has done since 1978. The ground floor is devoted to displays of local history (the town has existed for 900 years); Schubert's time there is commemorated upstairs, in displays of contemporary furniture and reproductions of music and pictures of his friends.

The local citizens take some pride in the fact that the Esterházy daughters

Schubert memorial rooms at Želiezovce

inspired some of the finest of the four-hand music (the F minor Fantasy was dedicated to Caroline) and in the local legend that on his walks in the neighbourhood Schubert visited the mill in the next village, where the miller's wife inspired *Die schöne Müllerin* (the chronology is a little shaky, but the idea is appealing).

Back in Vienna, the second Schubert museum is found in the flat that belonged to his brother, at a house called 'Zur Stadt Ronsperg', now Kettenbrückengasse 6, in what was then the fairly new southern suburb of Wieden. A plaque was erected on the house in 1869 and the flat was renovated by the Vienna Municipal Museums in 1979 and then again in 1996; the Internationales Franz Schubert Institut also occupies premises in the building.

Ferdinand, three years senior to Franz and himself a composer, if of modest achievement, moved into the second-floor flat (no.17) with his family in August 1828. Already seriously ill, Franz joined them on 1 September; he had been told to seek the fresher air of the suburbs by his doctor, who had not reckoned with the dampness of the new building or its poor sanitation (though probably that made little difference). He set some Heine poems (including *Der Doppelgänger*) and completed the B flat Piano Sonata there in September, as well as correcting the *Winterreise* proofs, and was well enough to make a three-day pilgrimage on foot to Haydn's grave in Eisenstadt in October, when he also wrote *Der Hirt auf dem Felsen* and his last Lied, *Der Taubenpost*. But by 11 November he was bedridden, in a little side room (about two metres by five). In his last letter, of 17 November, he asked Schober to bring him novels by James Fenimore Cooper. Two days later he was dead, at the age of 31.

During his last illness Schubert had been devotedly nursed by his brother and his family. Friends visited him; at his request a performance of Beethoven's op.131 String Quartet was given in the next room, where now Ferdinand's

Elwerkember piano and mahogany writing desk are displayed. The flat was small; today it consists of just three rooms and an entrance hall. The tiny bedroom, which in his final delirium Schubert, according to his brother, mistook for a grave, is not now set out as a bedroom (if it were, one could do no more than peer in). Ferdinand's career is also represented in the museum, as both a composer and a purloiner of his brother's music.

Most of the items on display are necessarily sombre in character, relating to the last music he composed, the last letters he wrote and last people he saw. Reproductions of Bauernfeld's poignant diary entry for 20 November, describing Schubert as 'the most honest soul' and the 'most loyal of friends', and expressing the wish that he might have taken his friend's place, are among the many items relating to Schubert's death, funeral and commemoration displayed in the museum; there are also letters exchanged by Schubert's father and brother, along with invitations to Schubert's Requiem Mass at St Ulrich's on 27 November and to the memorial service at the Augustiner-Kirche on 23 December, and lithographs of his tomb.

Room XV in the Vienna Kunsthistorisches Museum, in the Sammlung alter Musikinstrumente, is devoted to Schubert: there is a bronze mask and several instruments of his time, chiefly pianos but also including an arpeggione, a rare bass string instrument for which he wrote a sonata (the solitary significant work in its repertory). There is a fine portrait of him by Wilhelm August Rieder in the Schubert Room of the Franz Schmidt Musikschule in the southern suburb of Perchtoldsdorf. Among the most notable Schubert monuments in the city – there are in all more than 20 plaques and the like – is the statue in the Stadtpark by Carl Kundmann, unveiled in 1872, with symbolic reliefs by Theophil Hansen on the pedestal; the same artists contributed the tomb in the musicians' section of the Zentralfriedhof at Simmeringer Hauptstraße 234 when in

1888 Schubert's remains were removed there from Währing – where the original tomb, bearing Grillparzer's notorious epigraph, still stands in what is now the Schubertpark ('The art of music here entombed a rich possession, but still fairer hopes'). There is also a Schubert fountain in the Alserbachstraße in the 9th district. Elsewhere in Austria there are at least a dozen Schubert plaques or other monuments, mostly recalling visits (including one in Salzburg, on the house at Judengasse 8 where he stayed in 1825) but some of them simply tributes from local lovers of his music.

Franz Schubert: Gedenkstätte-Geburtshaus

Nußdorfer Straße 54
1090 Wien
Austria

phone +43/01317 3601
e-mail post@m.10.magwien.gv.at
website www.museum.vienna.at

open Tuesday–Sunday 09.00–12.15, 15.00–16.30

Schubert-Gedenkstätte Schloß Atzenbrugg

Schloß Atzenbrugg
3452 Atzenbrugg
Austria

phone +43/0 2275 5234

open Easter–26 October, Monday–Friday and holidays 14.00–17.00

Pamätná izba Franza Schuberta v Želiezovciach

Schubertova
93701 Želiezovce
Slovakia

phone +421/0 366 312112
fax +421/0 366 312866
e-mail tmlevice@nextra.sk
website www.muzeum.sk/pamiatke

open May–September, Wednesday 09.00–17.00, Sunday 12.00–17.00

Franz-Schubert-Gedenkstätte-Sterbewohnung

Kettenbrückengasse 6

1040 Wien
Austria

phone +43/0 1581 6730
e-mail post@m.10.magwien.gv.at
website www.museum.vienna.at

open Tuesday–Sunday 13.30–16.30

Maps 1, 8

Franz Schubert a Želiezovce (Bratislava, n.d.)
O.E. Deutsch and others: *The Schubert Memorial Sites administered by the Vienna Municipal Museums* (Vienna: Vienna Municipal Museums, 1992)
E. Hilmar, ed.: *Schubert-Gedenkstätte Schloß Atzenbrugg: Museum Franz Schubert und sein Freundeskreis*, Veröffentlichen des Internationalen Franz Schubert Instituts, viii (Tutzing: Hans Schneider, 1992)
U. Storch, ed.: *Franz Schubert: Musikergedenkstätten* (Vienna: Historisches Museum der Stadt Wien, c1996)
H. Kretschmer: *Wiener Schubert Gedenkstätten* (Vienna: Wiener Geschichtsblätter, 1997)

SCHUMANN, Robert and Clara

The Schumann family had lived for generations in Zwickau, a Saxon town south of Leipzig, not far from the German–Czech border, when Robert was born on 8 June 1810. His birthplace and childhood home still stands, on a corner of the central marketplace, now part of a spacious, partly pedestrianized area. His father, a prosperous publisher and bookseller, was a keen music lover, not a practitioner, but recognized his son's gift and nurtured it, buying him music, organizing expeditions beyond Zwickau to concerts and, in due course, acquiring for him a Streicher grand piano.

The family house, which dates back to around 1450, became a museum in 1910. Its interior was rebuilt in 1955–6, in time for the commemoration of the centenary of Schumann's death. Since 1960, the 150-seat chamber music hall on the ground floor has played host to the International Schumann Contest for Pianists and Singers. Apart from a space opposite the entrance used for special exhibitions, the museum is upstairs; its collection is

Schumann's birth-place in Zwickau

unusually comprehensive and rich in primary documents and artefacts.

The first-floor landing has exhibits devoted mainly to the role played by Zwickau in commemorating its most famous son, but there is also a bust of Clara, of 1885, and a set of her edition of her husband's works. The first room chronicles Schumann's early years in Zwickau, from portraits of his parents and his baptismal entry through his childhood autobiographical writings and his youthful attempts at composition to his school graduation certificate and the elegant bookcase his father then gave him; there is also a picture of the Schumann family's later home, from 1817, in Marktgässchen, which was destroyed in World War II. The next room covers his student years in Leipzig and Heidelberg and the beginnings of his career as a composer and critic in the 1830s; Chopin and Liszt, Clara Wieck and Ernestine von Fricken (his earlier fiancée) are here, along with compositions and writings of the time and an 1840 square piano.

The third room focusses on his marriage and the outpouring of song and then orchestral music in the ensuing months. There is an 1840 watercolour of Clara, once owned by Brahms. The early 1840s, when the Schumanns were in Leipzig, with Schumann's turn to chamber music and their 1844 visit to Russia – commemorated by Schumann's own pen-and-ink drawing of the Kremlin, among much else – are the central theme of Room 4; Room 5 covers the Dresden period from 1844, the production of his opera *Genoveva* and many concert tours. In the next room his last years, in Düsseldorf and Endenich, are recorded – there are contemporary photographs of Joachim and Brahms, copies of many of the late works, Schumann's briefcase and walking-stick, his will, his last music autograph and his death certificate. Clara's life afterwards is commemorated there and further in the seventh room and in the final, corner room (in the position of the one in which Schumann was born); these rooms are devoted to her career as pianist, composer, wife and mother: her letters, manuscripts, editions of her music, programmes, the piano by M.A. Stein on which she made her début, a bust, a cast of her right hand and portraits of her and their children (*see also* BRAHMS). A few of her and Robert's personal possessions are preserved: a chess set, dominoes, candlesticks, some china, coffee spoons. There too are Robert's standing desk, his bookcase, his desk and armchair, his own copies of the *Neue Zeitschrift für Musik*, his busts of Bach and Handel, his copy of the Bach collected edition, the stove from the Marktgässchen house. The museum archives on the second floor contain a rich store of further artefacts, including Robert's and Clara's detailed marriage diaries and household books.

Robert Schumann had first met Clara Wieck in Leipzig when she was eight years old (she was born in 1819) and he was a pupil of her father, Friedrich; they married in 1840, on the eve of her 21st birthday. For a short time (1830–31) Robert had lodged at the Wiecks' house at Grimmaische Gasse 36 in the centre of the city, an established meeting place for Leipzig musicians, where Schumann first met Mendelssohn. Of Schumann's several residences in Leipzig during his 16 years in the city, one, in Inselstraße (then a new, artistic quarter to the east of the city centre), has become a museum. This is where he and Clara lived in the first years of their marriage, from 1840 until they moved to Dresden four years later. The building in Inselstraße, then 5, now 18, is a large, three-storey, late classicist block, in which the Schumanns were the first occupants of a flat on the first floor. It is uncertain just how many or which rooms this comprised, but it seems more than probable that it would have included the large central room at the front, as they are known to have given small concerts there. The ground floor and part of the first are now an independent primary school and a specialist music school (the Freie Grundschule Clara Schumann and the Musikschule Clara Schumann). The remainder of the floor is given over to one classroom, staff facilities, cloakrooms, the school doctor's surgery and vestibules.

During the restoration of the building it was discovered that some of the original wall-covering designs had survived, and when the museum opened in 2001 discussion was continuing on the issue of how these were best treated – fragmentarily preserved or more fully reproduced – so as to execute the intention of 'mirroring the kind of lifestyle preferred by the two artists themselves'. These were happy and creative years for the Schumanns, when he was composing songs, orchestral works and chamber music, and she was developing her concert career; they entertained extensively in the flat – Mendelssohn (a near neighbour: see MENDELSSOHN), Berlioz,

Liszt and Wagner, along with Ole Bull, Marschner, Spohr and numerous others are known to have visited them there.

The main room, which seats 60, is used primarily for music-making. Adjoining it are smaller rooms, one at each end, fitted with elegant and informative board displays, based on the Schumann diaries, and showcases with contemporary documents (handbills, letters, visiting cards, relevant in particular to the years of the Schumanns' occupancy). There is a piano of 1860 by Clara's uncle, M.W. Wieck, and a square piano of about 1825 supplied by Friedrich Wieck.

In a suburb of Bonn, there is a further small museum dedicated to the memory of Schumann. This is at Endenich, in the building that was formerly the asylum where he sought treatment in March 1854 from a psychologist, Dr Richarz, after attempting to drown himself in the Rhine. The City of Bonn acquired the building in 1904 and in 1926 a memorial plaque was unveiled. It continued to be used as an asylum until the end of World War II, although it suffered bomb damage. After surviving the threat of demolition – in the centenary year of Schumann's death there – the building was restored in 1963, with funds raised by a 150th birthday concert in 1960, and it now serves jointly as a branch of the Bonn Public Music Library and the Schumann Memorial Rooms. Until 1971 it also housed the Max-Reger-Institut. The Schumann collection at Endenich includes letters, newspaper clippings, photographs, a lock of hair and laurel

The former asylum at Endenich, now a music library with a Schumann museum

leaves, and the original headstone from his grave (provided by Brahms in 1857).

Schumann spent his last two-and-a-half tormented years in Endenich, deprived, on the orders of his doctor, of visits from his wife and children and friends. His son Felix was born to Clara three months after his committal. Clara and Brahms were allowed to visit him only at the end; Robert Schumann died at Endenich on 29 July 1856.

Robert and Clara were reunited after her death in Frankfurt on 20 May 1896: they are buried in Bonn, side by side, in the Alter Friedhof, their graves marked by a memorial sculpture by Adolf von Donndorf, erected in 1880 with money raised from concerts of Schumann's music; at the foot of the monument, Clara sits in the centre, flanked by putti and gazing up lovingly at the profile relief of Robert (which is supported by a flying swan), offering him with one hand the wreath of immortality while in the other holding a scroll.

In 1906 the first Schumann exhibition was held in Bonn in the Beethoven-Haus (which was by then a museum), giving rise to thoughts in the minds of the surviving Schumann daughters, Marie and Eugenie, of establishing a permanent collection. Although most of the remaining legacy ultimately went to Zwickau, Eugenie donated to Bonn the manuscript on which Schumann notated the theme he believed had been sung to him by angels during the night of 17 February 1854, ten days before his attempted suicide; the Beethoven-Haus Archiv also owns Robert's last letter to Clara, written on 5 May 1855.

Robert-Schumann-Haus
Hauptmarkt 5
08056 Zwickau
Germany

phone +49/0 375 215269, 8188 5116
fax +49/0 375 281101
e-mail schumannhaus@zwickau.de
website www.robert-schumann-haus.de

open Tuesday–Friday 10.00–17.00,
Saturday and Sunday 13.00–17.00

Robert-und-Clara-Schumann-Haus in Leipzig
Inselstraße 18
04103 Leipzig
Germany

phone +49/0 341 3939 120
fax +49/0 341 3939 122
e-mail info@schumann-verein.de
website www.schumann-verein.de

open Wednesday–Saturday 14.00–17.00

Schumannhaus Bonn
Sebastianstraße 182
5300 Bonn-Endenich 1
Germany

phone +49/0 228 773656
fax + 49/0 228 77916 3656
e-mail musikbibliothek@schumannhaus-bonn.de
website www.schumannhaus-bonn.de

open Monday, Wednesday–Friday
11.00–13.30, 15.00–19.00

Robert and Clara Schumann's graves in Bonn

Map 7

G. Eismann: *Das Robert-Schumann-Haus in Zwickau* (Weimar, 1958)

M. Schoppe and G. Nauhaus: *Das Robert-Schumann-Haus in Zwickau* (Zwickau, 1973)

M. Schoppe and G. Nauhaus: *Robert Schumann: 1810–1856* (Zwickau: Robert-Schumann-Haus, 1981)

H. Kretschmer: *Wiener Musikergedenkstätten* (Vienna: J & V Edition, 3/1992)

B. Berenbruch and H. Hellberg: *Robert Schumann und Bonn* (Bonn: City of Bonn, n.d.) [English translation available in typescript]

G. Nauhaus and A. Müller: *Robert-Schumann-Haus Zwickau* (Munich and Berlin: Sächsische Landesstelle für Museumswesen und Deutscher Kunstverlag, 2000) [Sächsische Museen, xi] [includes English translation of museum guide]

P. Dießner and J. Fischer, eds.: *Das Robert-und-Clara-Schumann-Haus in Leipzig* (Leipzig: Robert-und-Clara-Schumann-Verein, n.d.) [appeal brochure, in German and English]

SCHÜTZ

Heinrich Schütz is the earliest German composer to whom museums have been dedicated. There are two, both inaugurated in 1985 to mark the 400th anniversary of his birth. Schütz was born on 9 October 1585 in the eastern Thuringian town of Bad Köstritz, at the inn run by his father and his grandfather before him, Zum goldenen Kranich. When he was five the family moved to Weissenfels, in Saxony, to take over another inn, Zum güldenen Ring, which is still open for business. His father later bought a second

Schütz's birthplace, Bad Köstritz

establishment in Weissenfels, Zur güldenen Sackpfeife (or Zur güldenen Esel), which he appropriately renamed Zum Schützen, but by then the boy had been taken into service by Landgrave Moritz of Hessen-Kassel and sent to Venice to study with Giovanni Gabrieli.

From 1615 Schütz lived and worked primarily in Dresden, at the electoral court of Johann Georg I, also holding posts at the Danish and Wolfenbüttel courts. In spite of heavy duties at Dresden and a demanding schedule at other courts, Schütz was repeatedly drawn back to Weissenfels. From the mid-1640s he vainly petitioned the elector to be allowed to retire there but was granted only long stays during the winters. From 1651 he periodically shared the house at Nikolaistraße 13 with his widowed sister Justina (*d* 1670). Even after Johann Georg I died, in 1656, Schütz was required to return to the court at regular intervals. He sold his house in Dresden, but rented accommodation near the palace and it was there, not at home in Weissenfels, that he died on 6 November 1672, at the age of 87.

The Heinrich-Schütz-Haus Zum goldenen Kranich in Bad Köstritz first housed a small exhibition in his honour in 1954. The anniversary year of 1985 stimulated the dedication of the house as a memorial site serving scholarship as well as display. In 2000 it underwent extensive renovation.

Six rooms on the first floor of the old inn are devoted to museum display, clearly and logically laid out. The first is biographical: the places he lived in, the people in his life, his publications and his wider context in German and European thinking of the time. A thematic colour system runs throughout the museum: patrons are tinted red, other composers green, writers and poets grey. Each room has showcases with drawers that open to reveal supplementary material, and several rooms house instruments of the time. The second room explores the geography of Schütz's life – his travels, his periods in Venice, Kassel and Copenhagen, with material on the Peace

Schütz's home in Weissenfels

of Westphalia and his patrons and colleagues in each place. Another room deals with his years in and near Dresden, showing many of his works of the war years and his time in the electoral Kapelle. This room offers quadraphonic sound, for the better appreciation of his multi-choir music; there is also a smaller listening-room. Schütz's pupils and their works and the reception of his own music – his *Weltbild* – are the topic of the fifth room; and, opposite a display of Schütz's music for deaths and for celebrations, is a final one, a re-creation behind glass of his study in Weissenfels. It is an impressive exhibition, put together with a keen awareness of recent thinking about presentation, and offering the serious and curious visitor access to additional material beyond what is immediately to be seen in the cases and on the walls.

Few visitors will have known in advance that Bad Köstritz was also the home of the 18th-century Bohemian composer Georg Anton (or Jiří Antonín) Benda in his last years; he died in the town in 1795. He is commemorated in a

room on the ground floor, opened in 1990, where there is also an attractive recital room seating some 65 people (*see* BENDA).

The Weissenfels house in Nikolaistraße, with its ornamented gables, is of considerable architectural as well as musical interest. The museum occupies the ground- and first-floor rooms and, like the birthplace museum, incorporates a room for chamber recitals. Rooms are devoted to displays not only of the genealogy of the Schütz family and their contribution to the life of Weissenfels but also to music at the Saxe-Weissenfels court, focussing in particular on visits from Bach, Telemann and Handel, and the organ-building traditions of the city.

Heinrich-Schütz-Haus
Heinrich-Schütz-Straße 1
07586 Bad Köstritz
Germany

phone +49/0 366 052 405, 053 6198
fax +49/0 366 053 6199
e-mail heinrich-schuetz-haus@t-online.de
website www.heinrich-schuetz-haus.de

open Tuesday–Friday 10.00–17.00,
Saturday and Sunday 13.00–17.00

Heinrich-Schütz-Haus
Nikolaistraße 13
06667 Weissenfels
Germany

phone, fax +49/0 344 330 2835
e-mail schuetz-weissenfels@t-online.de
website www.weissenfels.de

open Tuesday–Sunday 13.00–17.00

Map 7

S. Thielitz: *Von Albrecht Schütze zu Heinrich Schütz* (Weissenfels: Rat der Stadt Weissenfels, 1988)

I. Stein: *Forschungs- und Gedenkstätte 'Heinrich-Schütz-Haus'* (Bad Köstritz: Forschungs- und Gedenkstätte 'Heinrich-Schütz-Haus', 1989)

U.-A. Weitzmann: *Museumsführer des Heinrich-Schütz-Hauses* (Weissenfels: Rat der Stadt Weissenfels, 1990)

H. Koerth: *Heinrich Schütz: Wurzeln – Werdegang – Wirken* (Weissenfels: Museum Weissenfels, 1994)

SIBELIUS

Sibelius was born at a fortunate moment. Finnish cultural identity was beginning to take shape, culminating in a wave of national Romanticism, and with his choral and symphonic evocations of Finnish mythology he was quickly recognized as a national figure. By the time of his full maturity statues and monuments were erected in his honour, streets, parks and a university museum were named after him. In Helsinki the national conservatory is the Sibelius Academy of Music; a music festival and a prize also bear his name. When in 1957 he died, aged 91, after three decades of silence as a composer, he was the symbol of Finnish music. Within a decade his birthplace was a museum; and five years after his wife's death in 1969 their home for over 50 years, where he died, was opened to the public. There are now four museums and memorial places within easy reach of Helsinki commemorating Sibelius's life and works.

About 100 km to the north, on Lake Vanajavesi, is the former provincial capital, Hämeenlinna, where Jean Sibelius was born on 8 December 1865. His father was the town physician, attached to the military garrison. Their home, also the doctor's surgery, was rented, and when in 1868 Jean's father died of typhus, leaving his wife expecting their third child and in dire financial straits, the family moved to the lakeside home of their maternal grandmother, who leased nearby properties for the growing family (Jean, his elder sister Linda and younger brother Christian) before they were able to settle in a new, spacious wooden house opposite Tähtipuisto Park, at Läntinen Linnakatu 15 (now Sibeliuskatu), where they lived from 1874 until 1885. It was there that Sibelius spent his happiest childhood years, learning the piano and the violin and trying his hand at composition for the family piano trio with his pianist sister and cellist brother.

Of the family houses, the only one to survive is the house of his birth, which dates back to 1834. Thanks to the efforts of the Hämeenlinna Sibelius Society and the local authority, it was restored in 1965, Sibelius's centenary year, and its four principal rooms were opened to the public. The first, which was probably the doctor's surgery, has a series of display cases with facsimiles of family documents, including letters written by Sibelius in the 1870s, some family possessions, and photographs, some of them showing Hämeenlinna during Sibelius's childhood. The second displays a piano that he once owned and his brother's cello along with further photographs and an array of medals struck in his honour. The third room, window-lined and probably the family dining-room, is set up as a small recital hall with a Steinway miniature grand. The final room, originally a bedroom, and probably the room in which Sibelius was born, is furnished as a salon, with the harmonium that belonged to his Aunt Julia, his first piano teacher, and several other items of family furniture and ornaments. In addition to concerts the house is the scene of an annual birthday celebration.

Aunt Julia's harmonium accompanied the family on their summer visits to the coastal resort of Loviisa, 90 km east of Helsinki. By the 1870s Loviisa was a thriving spa, with a casino and rich musical life: extraordinarily, it boasted a string quartet, a wind septet, an orchestra and a male-voice choir. In 1817 Sibelius's

Sibelius's birthplace in Hämeenlinna

paternal grandfather had acquired a red wooden house, built ten years before, in Läntinen Tullikatu (now Sibeliuksenkatu). Until 1879, when his grandmother died and her maiden daughter Evelina moved to Turků to live with her brother, Sibelius stayed there each year with his mother, brother and sister. In addition to music-making, the children enjoyed a circle of local friends, Aunt Evelina's puppet shows and sailing among the islands of the archipelago. Sibelius later claimed to have taken his violin on the boat to entertain his sister and brother with improvisations.

In 1885 the family moved from Hämeenlinna to a small villa in the Brunnsparken of Helsinki while Sibelius was studying there, first law and then music; they were joined by Aunt Evelina, who took in sewing to help the family finances. Sibelius was in Berlin during the winter of 1889 and in Vienna the two following winters (living at Wiedner Hauptstraße 36). But in the summers up to 1893, when Evelina died, Loviisa drew them back.

As in Hämeenlinna, music-making in Loviisa often involved their neighbours, the Sucksdorffs, and in 1887 it was to them that Sibelius dedicated a quartet in G minor for piano, harmonium, violin and cello; the following summer he and his sister and brother performed a new piano trio, and in 1889 he spent the summer composing the op.4 String Quartet. Jean and Christian also regularly took part in concerts at the casino, playing his Violin Sonata and Cello Fantasy and an Andantino for the Loviisa Wind Septet. During his most extended stay in Loviisa, from the summer of 1891 until the end of January 1892, Sibelius embarked on his first major composition: *Kullervo*, a symphonic poem for soloists, chorus and orchestra inspired by the myths of the *Kalevala* and the epic rune singing of Larin Paraske; it was first performed in Helsinki the following spring.

Loviisa provided an important nursery as well as a 'sanctuary' (as he called it) during his maturation as a composer. When in 1892 he left, aged 26, he had grown out of it, as he admitted in a letter to his fiancée Aino Järnefelt. Today the house is not so much a museum as a memorial place, open for a few weeks each summer, when it hosts exhibitions of modern art, and for recitals in the winter. One room of what were originally four reflects the social context for the composer in the commemoration of 'Aunt Evelina's salon', where furnishings from the 1880s and items such as facsimiles of Sibelius's letters, a sewing box and a puppet theatre are displayed. In 1990 the town inaugurated an annual event, the Sibelius Days, planned to take place every eight years.

The third and most evocative memorial place is the house where Sibelius lived for 53 years, Ainola, named after his wife Aino (herself named after a maiden in the *Kalevala*). Perched on a wooded hill surrounded by fields near the town of Järvenpää, 38 km north-east of Helsinki, Ainola offered Sibelius and his young family a rural refuge from the city. Like his father, Sibelius had found from his early 20s the temptations of good living – fine food, drink and clothes and the best seats at the opera – equally impossible to resist and to fund (even after 1897 when he was awarded a generous state pension). Flight from the city seemed prudent and at the turn of the century Järvenpää, at the top of Lake Tuusulanjärvi with a railway connection to Helsinki, was already becoming a

Ainola, Järvenpää

home to a colony of writers and painters. Aino's brother, Eero Järnefelt, himself a highly regarded painter, suggested that Jean and Aino acquire land there to build a house, which was then designed by Lars Sonck in the National Romantic *Jugendstil* and built in 1904.

The first major works Sibelius composed at Ainola were the Third Symphony (1904) and the final version of the Violin Concerto (1905); the last were the Seventh Symphony (1924), *Tapiola* (1925) and incidental music to *The Tempest* (1926) – not counting the famous Eighth Symphony, which he destroyed.

Although the Sibeliuses continued to maintain a flat in Helsinki, Ainola was where the family of five daughters was based except during the 1918 civil war. Until the late 1920s Sibelius was often away, travelling in Europe and once to the United States, conducting, receiving honorary degrees and awards and acting as an unofficial Finnish ambassador. When he was at home, strict regimes of silence were maintained in the household and by the neighbours when the Master was in his study, where the lights often burned through the night. Even running water was deemed too noisy, necessitating the digging of seven wells to service the house; modern plumbing was not installed until 1960. But the famous 'silence of Järvenpää' refers to an artistic silence, precipitated, many think, by his alcoholism. In his defence he once observed, in a letter to his friend the American music critic Olin Downes, that composing had not become easier as he had grown older – and, he might have added, burdened with the fervent expectations of an international public.

Sibelius died on 20 September 1957; Aino followed on 8 June 1969. Their graves are in the Ainola garden, surrounded by Aino's prize apple trees. Ainola was sold to the nation and in 1974 the grounds and five ground-floor rooms of the house were opened to the public. A remnant of the rule of silence persists: music is heard only in the small visitor centre near the car park on the edge of the property.

The house is presented much as it was in Sibelius's last years. Each room boldly contrasts with the others. The drawing room, in pale green, is dominated by the Steinway miniature grand, a 50th birthday present from his admirers in 1915, portraits and a bust of the composer. Visitors to the dining-room – with its rustic beams and natural wood walls, its corner clock and hanging rug, its window seat with a view of the grounds below and a table designed by Aino with cane-backed chairs – should pause at the green-brick fireplace where Sibelius is said to have burned many of his manuscripts, perhaps including the draft of the Eighth Symphony, at the end of World War II. The dark, rustic corner library (originally the girls' nursery) contains his 3000-volume library, oversized armchairs designed more for comfort than for elegance, a radio and a gramophone. Next to it, and off the dining-room, is the pale, austere room where he died; in Sibelius's later years, furnished with a tiny bed and a large desk, it served as both bedroom and study (the original one was upstairs). On display are his white summer suit, hat and walking-stick; the tiny washroom is complete with his blue toothbrush. Finally, one can examine the large period kitchen, once the domain of two domestics, and an upstairs bedroom. Outside, visitors can stroll round the four-hectare property, through the forest, past the graves, the sauna and the barn, and through the orchard and the vegetable garden.

There is also a Sibelius Museum in Turku (or Åbo: it has always been predominantly Swedish-speaking), 165 km west of Helsinki, on the coast. This is not primarily a museum of Sibelius; it took his name as a tribute, with his permission, in 1949. Its origins go back well beyond his time, to the oldest music society in Finland, which was founded in 1790, and it houses the music history collection and the musicology department of Åbo Akademi University as well as a collection of 900 musical instruments, a third of which are on display in the exhibition halls surrounding the two auditoria where concerts, lectures and other events regularly take place. But it does in fact house a substantial collection of Sibeliana and it is a centre of Sibelius research. It moved into its present building, on the banks of the river Aura, in 1968. Most of Sibelius's manuscripts are in Helsinki University Library. The collection here however includes the autograph of a cantata, *Maan virsi* ('Song of the Earth'), composed in 1920 for the inauguration of the university, and first editions of nearly all Sibelius's compositions published by the early 1930s (the bequest of a friend of the composer's), Sibelius manuscripts from the collection of Adolf Paul, letters and newspaper cuttings. A large room devoted to a Sibelius display shows a selection of facsimiles of sketches and manuscripts, early editions and recordings, portraits and busts, commemorative stamps and various personal items including the composer's cane, hat and cigar box, and his doctoral robes from Yale in 1914. A caricature of Sibelius shows his wrinkles, corresponding with the number of symphonies he composed.

Birthplace of Sibelius

Hallituskatu 11
13100 Hämeenlinna
Finland

phone +358/0 3621 2755
fax +358/0 3621 2806
website www.hameenlinna.fi

open May–August, daily 10.00–16.00;
September–April, daily 12.00–16.00

The Sibelius House

Sibeliuksenkatu 10
07900 Loviisa
Finland

phone +358/0 19 555 499
e-mail matkailu@loviisa.fi
website www.loviisa.fi

open 11 June–17 August,
Tuesday–Sunday 11.00–16.00

Ainola

04401 Järvenpää
Finland

phone +358/0 9 2719 2212
fax +358/0 9 2719 2791
e-mail anu.savonne@jarvenpaa.fi
website www.jarvenpaa.fi
(all contacts to Järvenpää tourist office)

open May to September, daily
10.00–17.00

Sibelius Museum

Piispankatu [Biskopsgatan] 17
20500 Turku[Åbo]
Finland

phone +358/0 2215 4494, 4388
fax +358/0 2215 8528
e-mail sibeliusmuseum@abo.fi
website www.abo.fi/fak/hf/musik

open Tuesday–Sunday 11.00–15.00,
Wednesday also 18.00–20.00

Map 13

Sibeliuksen Ainola [Sibelius and Ainola]
  (Helsinki: Werner Söderström, 1976) [with
  English translation]
Sibeliuksen Hämeenlinna [Sibelius and
  Hämeenlinna] (Hämeenlinna: Sibelius
  Society, 1990) [with English translation]
H. Kretschmer: *Wiener Musikergedenkstätten*
  (Vienna: J & V Edition, 3/1992)
A. Karttunen: 'Sibelius lived next door . . .',
  Finnish Music Quarterly (1995), 24–9
I. Tolvas: 'The Sibelius Museum: Specialist in the
  Sound of Music', *Finnish Music Quarterly*
  (1996), 37–41
G. Gefen: *Composers' Houses* (London: Cassell
  and Vendome, 1998), 150–57
F. Jor, ed.: *Nordic Artists' Homes* (Stockholm:
  Prisma, 1999), 105–12

SILCHER

Nearly all the composer museums of Germany are to Great Composers, the Bachs, the Beethovens, the Brahmses, whom everyone has heard of. A rare exception is the one dedicated to Friedrich Silcher. Silcher was no great international figure, but in a limited sense he was a significant national and local one, as a leading spirit in the rise of the Sängerbund movement and the development of its repertory.

Silcher was born in 1789 in the village of Schnait, a few kilometres to the east of Stuttgart, son of the schoolmaster at the local evangelical school. As a young man he knew Weber and studied under Konradin Kreutzer and J.N. Hummel, and he met such educationists as Pestalozzi and Nägeli. He became musical director at Tübingen University in 1817 and for the rest of his career directed his energies towards the popular singing movement, researching, composing and conducting music in a folk-like style for the men's and mixed choirs that became so numerous and so influential in mid-19th-century Germany and were especially strong in his native Württemberg. The regional association of male-voice groups, the Schwäbischer Sängerbund, which is one of the oldest, was set up in 1849 by Silcher's former pupils.

The building in which he was born, which dates back to 1767, was the local school, close by the evangelical church; the family apartment adjoined the schoolrooms on the first floor. On the ground floor the farm animals were housed; Silcher's father had to eke out his paltry salary by farming and wine-growing (Schnait, now part of the Weinstadt district, still produces wines).

The Silcher museum at Weinstadt-Schnait

The Sängerbund bought it from the municipality in 1903–4, when it ceased to serve as a school, and opened it as a museum to Silcher in 1912. A new section was added at the rear of the house in 1935 and the building was thoroughly and attractively renovated in 1992.

The ground floor houses a small shop, a Silcher archive – the museum actively collects Silcher material, music, books and pictures – and a room in which the visitor can view a 15-minute slide show telling (in German only) the story of his life. There is also a glass case full of his medals, and also behind glass is the large original banner of the Schwäbischer Sängerbund (many more such banners are stored in drawers: shades of *Die Meistersinger*, Act 3).

Up on the first floor, the school-master's house is reconstructed: this is in some degree a local Heimatmuseum, giving a picture of late 18th-century life in the village. The furnishings are local and of the period, not originals from Silcher's childhood, although in the actual room of his birth there is a square piano of about 1805 on which he once played (it was given to the museum in 1912). There the furniture is more sophisticated and bourgeois; it is simpler in the living-room, the children's tiny room and the kitchen. The upper floor here too is mostly devoted to 'Heimat' display, although one room is concerned with the singing movements and Silcher's reception history, where the exhibits include a disc ('Wooden Heart') made by Elvis Presley based on one of his songs.

The main display on Silcher himself is in the large schoolroom (large enough to take 250 children in his own time: it must have been a little unruly). It is spaciously laid out, in clear chronological sequence, with a series of wallboards and neatly organized display cases, carrying the story from his childhood in Schnait through his student years in nearby towns and his early positions as tutor and schoolmaster, to his time at Tübingen, with much interesting detail supported by original documents and music. You can see a good deal of the latter, manuscript and printed, mostly in a simple but effective 'folky' vein for male-voice choirs; his 'Loreley' setting is the most famous of them. There are a few 'ausländisch' ones too, including English and Scottish, the texts duly Germanized. Some are for the small Akademische Liedertafel at Tübingen, others for larger choirs such as the Oratorienverein that he directed. A fine bust of him in later years (he died in 1860) and a charming vignette of him as a young man with his wife seem to show him as a serious, docile character. Some of his original furniture is here (chairs, a desk, a clock), and there are portraits and two pianos connected with him, an 1830 table piano that he owned and one of 1851 later donated by one of his daughters.

The museum is owned and run by the Schwäbischer Sängerbund, and the roof-space above the old schoolroom is devoted, in a display set up on the 150th anniversary in 1999, to the history of the association and the Sängerbund movement more generally. Generously illustrated, it shows much of the paraphernalia linked with the singing movement – banners, cups, medals, ribbons – and their publications: a glimpse into a part of German musical history not widely familiar outside the country.

Silcher-Museum des Schwäbischen Sängerbundes

Silcherstraße 49
71384 Weinstadt-Schnait
Germany

phone +49/0 7151 65230
fax +49/0 7151 65305
e-mail museum@ssb1849.de

open mid-February–mid-November, Tuesday–Wednesday, Friday–Sunday 10.00–12.00, 14.00–17.00

Map 7

H.J. Dahmen: *Silcher in seiner Zeit* (Stuttgart: Silcher-Archiv Schnait, 1980)
Silcher-Museum des Schwäbischen Sängerbundes in Weinstadt-Schnait (Stuttgart: Schwäbischer Sängerbund, 1992)

ŠIMKUS

The house a few kilometres outside Kaunas at Bitininkų 45, where Stasys Šimkus lived for about 20 years, was opened to the public as a museum to the composer in 1972; it is now closed for restoration. For the foreseeable future the display commemorating him will be in a room in the Petrauskas Lithuanian Music Museum in Kaunas.

Like Mikas Petrauskas, Šimkus, born in 1887, studied at St Petersburg Conservatory, then emigrated to the USA where during World War I he directed a Lithuanian choir in Chicago and founded a magazine, *Muzika*, in Philadelphia. Again like Petrauskas, he returned to Lithuania and in 1923 he founded the music academy at Klaipėda which now bears his name. He collected and arranged folksongs, conducted his own orchestra and was the first to publish editions of music by Čiurlionis. He died in 1942.

On display on the first floor of the Petrauskas Museum are furniture from his house and books from his library; a bust (1935) and facsimiles of his manuscripts; photographs and concert programmes; editions and recordings of his piano music and music for chorus; a medal struck in 1987 commemorating the centenary of his birth; set designs for his opera *Pagirenai* (1942); and a bust of Schubert presented to him at the centenary concert he conducted at Klaipėda in 1928.

Stasys Šimkus Room: Mikas and Kipras Petrauskai Lithuanian Music Museum

Petrausko 31
3005 Kaunas
Lithuania

phone +370/0 773 3371
e-mail kau.petr.muz@delfi.lt
website www.muziejai.mch.mii.lt/kaunas/muzikos_muziejus

open Wednesday–Sunday 11.00–17.00

Map 2

SINGER

Mozartians and others wandering through Salzburg may have noticed, on the arch linking the Franciscan monastery to the Franciscan Church – just behind the Cathedral, close to St Peter's – a plaque commemorating Pater Peter Singer (1810–82). Father Singer was a member of the Franciscan order there, from 1830 to 1837; then, after a brief career in his native Tyrol, he settled in Salzburg in 1840 as organist and choirmaster at the monastery. He was the city's leading musical figure in the mid-19th century. Singer was an immensely prolific composer of church music in a late (indeed posthumous) version of the Viennese classical style; it has been described as 'excessively sentimental'. He also wrote on music theory, but was most famous for his Pansymphonikon, a huge organ intended to be capable of imitating every instrument of the orchestra, which he designed and built in 1845.

Until recently there was a museum to Father Singer within the monastery; now he is commemorated with a showcase, in which his sacred objects (a cross and rosaries) may be seen, with his reading glasses and, immaculately preserved, his skull. The musical items are now deposited at the Franciscan foundation in Lienz, in the Tyrol (phone +43/0 4852 62066). Visitors interested in Father Singer can be admitted at the monastery's main entrance and taken to see the showcase.

Pater Peter Singer-Museum
Franziskanerkloster
Franziskanergasse 5
5010 Salzburg
Austria

phone +43/0 662 843629

open by request or appointment

Map 1

SKRYABIN

Aleksandr Skryabin was a native Muscovite, and although he travelled widely as a concert pianist and lived abroad for many years – in Italy, France, Switzerland and Belgium – he always returned to Moscow, to family and friends. He was born there on Christmas Day (25 December 1871/6 January 1872), studied and taught at the Moscow Conservatory and died there on 14 April 1915.

In April 1912 he and his family moved into the freshly renovated first floor of a century-old building in Bolshoy Nikolopeskovskiy. By then he was established as both concert pianist and composer; his piano music circulated in published editions and his visionary tone poems, *The Poem of Ecstasy* (1908) and *Prometheus* (1910), had been performed as far away as New York and were well received. Intensely interested in philosophy and mysticism, he was at work on his *Mysterium* (intended for performance in an Indian temple) when he died.

Thanks to the efforts of his widow, Tatyana Schloezer, and his aunt, Lyubov Skryabina, who had raised him after the death of his mother, the house was kept just as he had known it. In 1922 it became a state museum and an important centre for research on Skryabin through the family collection of manuscripts, correspondence and iconography. His daughter Maria (one of the four children of his first marriage to the pianist Vera Isaakovich) served as a member of the museum staff; in the early days, she and her sister Yelena were often present at the evening concerts, which are still given in the ground-floor recital room.

The intention to keep the flat very much as it was in 1915 still endures, to great effect. Visitors are guided through the house. The commentary continually hints at the mystical significance of this and that (for example, the 'mystic quality' of his telephone number: 23630). Whatever the room, Skryabin's armchairs always face away from the windows. The lights are turned low when the stereo is turned on. There isn't a label to be seen.

Skryabin's study, decorated in soft golds and browns, dominates the flat; his Bechstein grand piano, presented to him by the firm in 1912, dominates the room. The *Art Nouveau* furniture was bought in Brussels in 1912 and includes an unusually designed writing desk, a tall bureau for composing (like many composers, Skryabin preferred to stand when he worked) and a bentwood rocker. On the wall is a portrait of his mother, painted in 1871 by her brother, Nikolay Shchetinin, and religious pictures by Nikolay Shperling, along with photographs of family and friends. The bookcase is full of works on philosophy, ethics, aesthetics and natural sciences, along with collections of poetry.

All of this sets the stage for the *pièce de résistance*: the famous colour keyboard built for him by the physicist Alexander Mosr in response to his passion for the relationships he perceived between colours and sounds. It featured in the early performances of *Prometheus* and has been imitated many times since.

Skryabin's desk and colour wheel

Lying on the desk, rather unprepossessingly, it hardly seems what it is – 12 coloured lamps supported by a wooden base, arranged to correspond with Skryabin's vision in colour of the harmonic circle of fifths. More than any other single item in the house, it serves to illuminate the moment in time inhabited by Skryabin. But there is perhaps a faintly disappointing want of magic about 12 bulbs mounted on a piece of wood.

The adjoining drawing-room, in muted blue and green, is where the Skryabins entertained. There is a card table with triangular folding sides, a chess set (a favourite pastime), his phonola with rolls, and another piano, a Becker grand given to Skryabin in 1895 by his publisher and patron, Mitrofan Belyayev. More personal are the casts of his hands, the bust by Serafim Sudbinin commissioned by Serge Koussevitzky in 1908 and Boris Kustodiyev's drawing of Skryabin's last public recital, at St Petersburg Conservatory on 2 April 1915.

The dining-room reflects the eclecticism of the Skryabins: an Indian gong, a Fabergé vase (presented to him by Moscow friends at the local première in 1909 of *The Poem of Ecstasy*) and the dried flowers he gathered the summer before his death reside amid more furniture from Brussels and appliquéd curtains. On the wall are sketches of Skryabin playing the piano (1909) by his friend Leonid Pasternak, and more paintings by his uncle.

A long corridor leads to a bedroom where his elegant tailcoat and monogrammed top hat are kept. Here too is the bed in which he died following operations intended to stem septicaemia. Skryabin is buried in the musicians' section of the Novodyevichi Cemetery in Moscow.

Memorial'nïy Muzey A.N. Skryabina
Bolshoy Nikolopeskovskiy Pereulok 11
121002 Moskva
Russia

phone +7/0 095 241 1901, 5156
website www.moscow-taxi.com/museums
open Wednesday, Friday 12.00–19.00,

Thursday, Saturday, Sunday
10.00–17.00 (guided tours)

Map 12

O. Tompakova: *Alexander Nikolayevich Scriabin and his Museum: a Guide* (Moscow: Moscow Committee on Matters of Culture, 1990)

SLAVENSKI

Josip Slavenski was one of the most adventurous composers of early 20th-century Yugoslavia. He was born with the name 'Stolzer', in 1896, in the Austro-Hungarian Empire, but later, in 1930, he abandoned the Germanic form to declare himself unambiguously Slavonic. He is still sometimes called Stolčer-Slavenski. His native town was Čakovec, in the Međimurje district in the northernmost corner of Croatia, where it abuts Slovenia and Hungary, of which it was long a part. His father, a baker, played the cimbalom (a Hungarian instrument of the zither family) and his mother sang local folk-songs. He was sent to study in Budapest and later had a period in Prague; his teachers included Kodály and Novák. Most of his music comes from the 1920s and 30s, and much of it is cast in a dissonant idiom influenced by local folk traditions, and particularly by Bartók's ways of treating folk idioms rather than the more conservative ways generally preferred in his own country.

From 1924 he lived in Belgrade. After his death, in 1955, many of his possessions were sent, apparently at his own request, to Čakovec. There they found a home in the Muzej Međimurja which, established in 1954, is housed in a fine and ancient castle, formerly the home of the region's ruling families. A substantial series of displays to Slavenski, in three rooms, was set up in the 1960s, but they included much material from his life in Serbia and the wars of the 1990s made it inappropriate for these to continue to be shown. Accordingly, the memorial to him is confined to a single room, although there are hopes of enlarging it before long, drawing on the quantities of material –

much of his library, his sofa, tables and chairs, kitchen furniture and a great deal else – held in store.

The second-floor room dedicated to him nevertheless gives a clear picture of the man and his interests. Prominent among the exhibits is his large telescope, and also his trautonium – Slavenski was one of the few composers to use this electronic instrument, invented by Friedrich Trautwein in the 1920s – and his harmonium, as well as his father's cimbalom, and he is pictured too playing the double bass and conducting a (Croatian) choir. There are two busts, by his friend Lujo Bezeredi and D. Poček, a 1920 portrait and a 1921 pastel by the leading local artist Ladislav Kralj Međimurec of the composer as baker (he had been trained in his father's trade). The various photographs include family pictures (his parents, his four sisters) and one of him making a film.

Slavenski is commemorated too in Belgrade; he lived there for 30 years and had a Serbian wife, and the family is still in the city. The junior music school there is named after him. In the national Music Information Centre, a room is devoted to his memory: set up in 1983, it is closely modelled on the study in his Belgrade flat, a photograph of which is among the exhibits. Here too there is a telescope (a smaller one, which he made himself), a bust and portraits (one by his friend Vladimir Kralj), along with his piano (a Hoffmann upright), his violin and his guitar, his gusle (a one-string instrument used during the declamation of epic poetry and song), a pair of folk pottery drums and his tape recorder and gramophone.

But the room is dominated by his large desk and still larger chair. On the desk is a list of his precepts, 14 of them, including 'Be always in love', 'Your work is the only thing that can save you', 'Stay away from negative people'. His folk interests extended beyond music; there are south-east Serbian folk carpets, cushions and a wall-hanging, a pair of Montenegrin chairs, and a Bosnian six-sided table in oriental style. He was a manic collector: there are pieces of mineral, shells and various antiques.

Around the walls are bookcases with part of his library, wide-ranging and multilingual; it includes Lenin's complete works. There is an award from Marshal Tito, received four days before his death. Personal items include his walking-cane and his cherrywood pipe.

Muzej Medimurje Čakovec

Trg Republike 5
40000 Čakovec
Croatia

phone +385/0 4031 3499, 3285
fax +385/0 4031 2820
e-mail muzej-medjimurja@ck.tel.hr

open Tuesday–Friday 10.00–15.00,
Saturday and Sunday 10.00–13.00

Legat Josip Slavenski

Savez Organizacija Kompozitora
Jugoslavije
Muzički Informativni Centar
Trg Nikole Pašića 1
11000 Beograd
Serbia and Montenegro

phone +381/0 1322 4056, 1324 5192
fax +381/0 1324 5192
e-mail sokojmic@eunet.yu

open Tuesday and Thursday
09.00–15.00 or by appointment

Map 14

SMETANA

The central position occupied by the Smetana museum in Prague powerfully symbolizes the place that Bedřich Smetana holds in Czech music: it occupies the former Old Town Water Works, a large neo-Renaissance building, an architectural landmark in its own right, standing in a bustling street on the right bank of the Vltava, at the foot of the city's most famous landmark, the Charles Bridge.

Smetana was a Czech national icon even in his lifetime. From the early 1860s,

when he returned to Prague after spending five years in Göteborg, he had become a central figure in Czech musical life. He was first chairman of the Umělecká Beseda (Artistic Society), set up in 1863 to promote national culture; he worked as music critic for the most important Czech newspaper, organized subscription concerts in Prague and from 1866 was musical director of the Provisional Theatre, the first professional Czech stage, where his operas *The Brandenburgers in Bohemia* and *The Bartered Bride* had their premières that year. Even after his deafness forced him, in 1874, to retire from active musical life, he retained his position in Czech music, with his patriotic opera *Libuše* being given at the opening of the National Theatre in 1881 and the popularity of his cycle of six symphonic poems *Má vlast* ('My country'), dedicated to the City of Prague. When he died in 1884, his colleagues in the Umělecká Beseda organized his funeral at the Týn Church; the route to the cemetery at Vyšehrad, overlooking the Vltava, was lined with his admirers.

Efforts to collect and preserve Smetana's legacy were begun by his family immediately after his death. A Society for the Construction of a Bedřich Smetana Memorial in Prague, later to become the Bedřich Smetana Society, was founded in 1909. It mounted a Smetana exhibition in 1917 and nine years later founded a museum, at least in name if not in substance. In 1928 the Czechoslovak State formally acquired the Smetana estate from the heirs and entrusted its management to the Society. The Smetana Museum finally opened in Prague in 1936. After the war, in 1952, the Society was dissolved and the management of the museum was transferred to the State. Little was done to renew the displays or keep the building in good repair. However, to mark the centenary of Smetana's death, the Museum of Czech Music undertook an exhaustive inventory of the collection; some 2000 items were catalogued, including 270 autographs, 1100 letters (some to fellow musicians such as Liszt and Clara Schumann, others to collaborators, theatre managers and publishers), 34 diplomas (mostly honorary), a collection of his diaries of the period 1840–83, his own drawings, concert programmes and reviews and 33 portraits. The collection also includes archives of theatre bills, posters and related programmes, nearly 1000 scenic and costume designs as well as 55 costumes used in productions dating back to the 19th century, and a library of over 11,000 volumes and recordings.

In 1992, after the political changes of 1989, the fortunes of the Smetana Museum brightened and it was possible to modernize the exhibition. An entirely new and up-to-date Bedřich Smetana Museum opened in 1998. As before, the displays are confined to one large open-plan room on the first floor (on the second is the Smetana Archive, open to scholars by appointment). A chronology of Smetana's life is recorded on scrolls, glass panels display facsimiles, and a folding screen supports further documentation. A bandstand with an obelisk in the centre displays the composer's glasses and his wife's jewellery. Chairs for visitors line an oval 'listening space' incorporating Smetana's piano, while the windows offer views of the river and the Charles Bridge. On the far side of the room, ten music stands display facsimiles of Smetana's music, with relevant documents and iconography. Opera costumes are displayed in an alcove on the right, amid illuminated stained-glass panels with appropriate scenery. Finally, visitors are invited to contemplate a simple glass panel carrying an epilogue honouring Smetana's patriotism. The curators and designers, each in their own way, have taken to heart the task of representing the legacy of one of the Czech Republic's greatest composers, and there is clearly something here for everyone.

In 1949, to mark the 125th anniversary of the composer's birth, the museum mounted exhibitions outside the capital, at Smetana's birthplace at Litomyšl, an exceptionally attractive small town about 150 km east of Prague, and closer to Prague at Jabkenice, where he retired; in

Displays of Smetana's music in Prague

1959 a further exhibition was installed in the family quarters adjoining the castle brewery at Litomyšl, and it was renewed in 1974. Smetana's father was a master brewer (and also a cultured amateur violinist) who rented premises at the castle of the Waldstein-Wartenberg family on the edge of the main square, where his son's statue now stands. Today the castle and its outbuildings house a complex of museums and also an 18th-century theatre with period stage sets.

The Smetana exhibition occupies four pleasantly spacious rooms, with vaulted ceilings and white-painted walls. The first is furnished as his parents' bedroom. In the second, a long, corner room, there is a family tree and facsimiles of the composer's birth certificate and other documents, including school registers and family letters, and his father's shooting target (he belonged to a hunt). Although the third is set out as a living-room, with handsome portraits of his parents by Antonín Machek, a clock presented by the Waldstein-Wartenbergs and a Leschen grand piano from Vienna that Smetana played at the age of six, this is thought to be the room in which, in 1824, he was born. In the fourth room, the brewery office of František Smetana, costumes from various 20th-century productions of *The Bartered Bride* are displayed. In an alcove stands a statue of Smetana.

The Smetana family moved away from Litomyšl in 1831 and Bedřich's education was much interrupted. By the early 1840s he was in Prague, impoverished and studying the piano, and in 1844 he accepted a post in the household of Count Thun-Hohenstein which involved giving piano lessons to the family and spending the summers at their country residence in Benátky nad Jizerou, 40 km north-east of the capital. He was there for about four years; during that time he composed chiefly piano pieces. A room in the local museum, in the castle, commemorates the connection. The castle was sold, to the Kinsky family, early in the last century, and any original furniture was auctioned; but it is thought that the piano and the desk preserved there now may have been those used by Smetana. There is other furniture of the time, a display of facsimiles of documents from the 1840s, a map showing all the places in Bohemia where Smetana lived, a fine plaster bust by Josefa Strachovský – the only one of Smetana made during his lifetime – and large portraits of the Count and Countess, his employers. Adjoining rooms commemorate members of the BENDA family who worked there a century before. Smetana's anniversaries are celebrated by concerts in the town and there is a further bust, dating from 1974, in the park below the castle.

The region to the north and north-west of Prague is littered with Smetana (and Dvořák) sites. Another important one is the small town of Obříství, 30 km north of the city, with which the composer had a double family connection. His father set up a brewery there in 1844 and remained there until he became bankrupt in 1852 (a hall in the surviving brewery building was named

Smetana's bust guards the flood-ravaged house at Obříství

as the Smetana Memorial Hall in 1956). Smetana's brother Karel married into a local family, the Ferdinandis, and when in 1859 Bedřich, whose first wife had just died, visited him he met his brother's sister-in-law, Bettina. Smetana and Bettina were married the next year, from the Ferdinandi family house, one of a group of houses in the Lamberk area. Smetana visited Obříství several times in the early 1860s and is believed to have begun work on *The Bartered Bride* there.

The house still stands, but only just. Behind it runs the river Labe (or Elbe, as it becomes), a tributary of the Vltava, which has always been susceptible to floods and succumbed seriously in the summer of 2002, when the waters filled the basement and reached a depth of three metres on the ground floor. The small display was saved but the fabric of the building – floors, walls, stairs, even the roof – was severely damaged. The display, originally set up on the Smetana centenary in 1984, included a table piano, a daybed, a table, a commode and a portrait of Smetana from his time in Göteborg, and also various pictures (both Smetana's wives and Bettina's parents, costume sketches for *The Bartered Bride*) and a porcelain and glass collection (this also served as a museum of local life). As the museum is owned by the village, and not covered by insurance, its future must be uncertain and at best rather distant, but the parent museum in the nearby town of Mělník anyway had plans for a substantial refurbishment in association with the Prague Smetana museum. Meanwhile, it is still possible to visit the rather melancholy site – and also to see the memorial house, close by, to the writer Svatopluk Čech, a native of Obříství, in even sorrier a state.

From 1876 until shortly before his death in a Prague asylum, Smetana lived with his daughter Žofie and her husband Josef Schwarz, a local forester, on the Thurn-Taxis estate at Jabkenice, about 60 km north-east of Prague, near Mladá Boleslav. They lived in what had been the estate forester's house, probably since the early 17th century. He continued to compose despite his deafness, completing there his last three operas (*The Kiss*, *The Secret* and *The Devil's Wall*), the E minor String Quartet, two cycles of piano music and works for male chorus. After his death, his widow remained there and his son-in-law and daughter continued to live there until his retirement in 1898. Early in the 20th century the house was enlarged (the newly built sections do not form part of the present museum, but the layout of rooms in the older part was also affected). In 1928 a group was set up to establish a museum there; it acquired material from Smetana's estate from the family and Smetana's study was opened to the public that year. In 1936 it was acquired by a dedicated society and an exhibition was set up in collaboration with the Národní Muzeum. After the war, in 1950, a new exhibition was installed; that was replaced in 1964 and remained for 20 years. The house underwent substantial repair and reconstruction in the later 1980s and early 90s, but remained closed as the funding had run out; further restoration work was needed in 2001 and it opened briefly the next year, then had to close again after the floods in the vicinity, reopening in 2003.

The renovated museum falls under the management of the Prague Smetana Museum and can draw on the collection there for its exhibits. It was also able to call on the descriptions in the memoirs of one of Smetana's granddaughters for the design and layout of the two main rooms, on the upper floor. These are historically reconstructed, using some of the original furniture: first a large room, serving as both dining-room and drawing-room, then beyond it (at the front of the house) Smetana's study. In the former is a piano given by Smetana to his daughter as a wedding present; in the latter is a desk, with items of Smetana's own and a bed by the stove – in his late years Smetana virtually lived in this room. The decoration of the walls, using a stencil hand-painting technique popular in the region (which from even a modest distance

Forester's house and school at Jabkenice, now a Smetana museum, drawn by Smetana's daughter Zdenka in 1883

simulates wallpaper), is 'authentic' in style if not in actual detail. The tones are subdued, favourite autumnal browns. Display cases and wall boards (with texts in Czech and English) describe Smetana's life and his music of these late Jabkenice years and his connections with this region of Bohemia, and there is soft background music. Smetana's second wife, Bettina, was an artist and some of her original paintings are hung, and there are also paintings in the house by his grandson Zdeněk Schwarz. On the ground floor is the central reception area and a large room with comprehensive, basic information about Smetana's life and works, with a series of plinths on which a variety of representations of him, in statues and busts, are mounted. There is also a small recital room, seating 50, with CD listening facilities. A theatrical curtain painted by Bettina, formerly at Obříství, hangs on the wall. Outside, a garden and a place for summer eating are planned, incorporating the two fir trees planted by Smetana's daughters and bearing their names. There is also a 'Smetanova Procházka', a three-and-a-half kilometre walk through the woods, passing two lakes and a favourite spot where Smetana liked to sit.

The years between 1856 and 1861 that Smetana and his family spent in Sweden were the subject of an exhibition at Göteborg in 1961, but the Smetana museum that later opened there, based on material loaned from the Prague collection, finally closed at the beginning of the 21st century.

Muzeum Bedřicha Smetany
Novotného lávka 1
11000 Praha 1
Czech Republic

phone +420/0 2 2422 9075, 0082
fax +420/0 723 555437
e-mail ais@nm.anet.cz
website www.nm.cz/mbs

open Wednesday–Monday 10.00–17.00

Regionálni Muzeum v Litomyšli
Rodný byt Bedřicha Smetany

Jiráskova 9
57001 Litomyšl
Czech Republic

phone +420/0 461 618601, 615287, 615067
e-mail muzeum.lit@worldonline.cz

open April and October, Saturday, Sunday and by appointment 09.00–12.00, 13.00–16.00; May–August, Tuesday–Sunday 08.00–12.00, 13.00–17.00; September, Tuesday–Sunday 09.00–12.00, 13.00–16.00

Městské Muzeum Benátky nad Jizerou
Zámek 49
29471 Benátky nad Jizerou
Czech Republic

phone +420/0 326 316682
e-mail muzeum.benatky@seznam.cz

open April–October, Tuesday–Sunday 09.00–12.00, 13.00–17.00

Památník Bedřicha Smetany
Lamberk
22742 Obříství
Czech Republic

phone +420/0 315 685000

(closed for the time being: enquiries to Okresní Muzeum Mělník
Náměstí Míru 54
Mělník
Czech Republic

phone +420/0 315 621915)

Památník Bedřicha Smetany v Jabkencích
29445 Jabkenice 33
Czech Republic

phone +420/0 326 389127
e-mail jabkenice.smetana.pamatnik@nm.cz
website www.nm.cz/jabkenice

open April–September, Tuesday–Sunday 10.00–17.00; October–March, by appointment

Map 4

O. Špecinger: *Obřístí na Mělnicku* (Obříství:
MNV, 1984), 34–7
O. Mojžíšová, ed.: *Bedřich Smetana, Time, Life,
Work: Bedřich Smetana Museum* (Prague:
Národní Muzeum, 1998)
A Guidebook to the Bedřich Smetana Museum
(Prague: Národní Muzeum, 1999)
O. Mojžíšová and J. Plecitá, ed.: *Památník
Bedřicha Smetany Jabkenice: nová stálá
expozice Muzea Bedřicha Smetany* (Prague:
Národní Muzeum, 2003) [English version
also available]

SPOHR

A museum to Louis Spohr was established in Kassel as early as 1912. He
spent nearly 40 years in the city, first as
musical director of the court theatre,
from 1822, then from 1847 as the city's
Generalmusikdirektor. Spohr was one of
the great violinists of his day, among the
most admired of composers (especially
in England), and as conductor a pioneer
in the use of the baton. Born in
Brunswick in 1784 (the house of his birth
survives, marked with a plaque), he spent
the early part of his professional career at
a variety of German musical centres as
well as touring abroad.

The Kassel museum was closed under
the Nazis in 1933; in 1954 the
International Louis Spohr Society
decided to re-create it and it finally
reopened in 1967. It is now in a large,
modern administrative building by the
river Fulda in the centre of the city, the
Palais Bellevue, where it shares a floor
with a museum and archive commemorating the Brothers Grimm. The Spohr
museum, part of which is a museum of
violin playing, also has an archive, with a
number of Spohr autographs, portraits
(including a family album of silhouettes)
and other illustrative material, along with
programmes, newspaper cuttings, a volu-
minous Spohr genealogical archive, and a
working library with many early editions
and microfilms.

There are four display rooms. The first
presents Spohr as violinist, with exhibits
concerning his pupils in Kassel (the so-
called 'Kasseler Schule'), violin methods
of the time and portraits of violinists;

there is also a photograph of 1885 of
Spohr's own room (posthumous, of
course: he died in 1859), and a maquette
of one of his most popular operas,
Zemire und Azor. In the next room the
exhibits are more personal: Spohr's own
desk and commodes, family portraits, a
watercolour of the family home, a
Nadermann harp of the kind his first wife
played, a bust, portraits, a bass flute that
once belonged to his father (a surgeon), a
presentation baton in ivory, some of his
own scores and a silver loving cup
presented to him by the court orchestra
to mark his 25 years as their conductor.

The third room sets him among his
contemporaries: it houses the Streicher
piano from his house in Kassel (played by
Mendelssohn, Clara Schumann and Liszt,
among others), a group portrait of
music-making in his home and portraits
of Weber and Dussek, music including a
dedication copy from Schumann of
Fantasiestücke, medallions and visiting
cards of various friends. Lastly, what is
really a violin museum room: it contains
instruments, letters and other documents
concerning not only Spohr but also
Paganini, Joachim and others, Bartók's
corrected proof copy of his *Deux
portraits*, editions and autographs.

**Louis Spohr-Gedenk- und
Forschungsstätte**
Museum der Geschichte des Violinspiels
Internationale Louis Spohr Gesellschaft
Palais Bellevue
Schöne Aussicht 2
34117 Kassel
Germany

phone, fax +49/0 561 15209

open Saturday and Sunday 10.00–16.00
or by appointment

Map 7

H. Becker and R. Krempien, eds.: *Louis Spohr:
Festschrift Ausstellungskatalog zum 200.
Geburtstag* (Kassel: Georg Wenderoth, 1984)

SPONTINI

A few kilometres beyond Jesi, high in the
hills off the road running south-west

across Italy from the Adriatic port of Ancona, and leading ultimately to Rome, lies the village that used to be called Maiolati. Since 1939 it has borne the name Maiolati Spontini, after its most famous son and most lavish benefactor, the composer Gaspare Spontini. It is an attractive village, lying on the curved brow of the hills, 400 metres above a steep-sided valley, lovingly maintained, with 19th-century style lighting and neatly pollarded trees in its main streets.

The small stone house in which Spontini, son of a cobbler, was born in 1774 still stands, at the far end of the principal street, the Via G. Spontini. In 1924, on the 150th anniversary of Spontini's birth, it was declared a national monument; it is suitably decked with plaques, and there is a fine bust of Spontini in the garden, a copy of one in the Sala Spontiniana at the Teatro Pergolesi in Jesi. But the whole of the village is indebted to the composer, and it amply acknowledges its debt. At the other end of the village, by the town hall, where the Centro Studi G. Spontini is based, stands the Teatro Gaspare Spontini. In the Via Spontini is the parish church, Santo Stefano, where the composer's brother was the parish priest and to which Gaspare presented a 17th-century carved wooden choir and an organ bought from an Ancona convent. In 1841 the composer endowed an institution for

Spontini's house, now the museum, at Maiolati Spontini

training the village girls as maids, and two years later he donated a sum for building an extra storey to the charity-school teacher's house.

At the centre of the village, in the main street, is the house that Spontini and his wife (*née* Céleste Erard) bought and completely rebuilt for their retirement to Maiolati: this is now the Spontini Museum. Opposite it lies his largest gift to Maiolati: the Casa di Riposo, a home for some 30 of the deprived and the elderly, which he built and endowed and which still performs the same role for the people of the locality. In it is the chapel of San Giovanni, in which lies Spontini's fine marble sarcophagus, neo-classical in style, with a medallion allegedly by Canova, or in his style, bearing the composer's image; close by is a small, empty tomb, intended for his wife, but she returned after his death to her native Paris, and there she died. There were no children.

Spontini, unhappily, did not enjoy his house for long. He returned from his triumphs in Italy, Paris (1803–20) and Berlin (1820–42) – and a fair number of failures, too, for although he occupied high office he seems to have been a difficult, proud man, disliked and ultimately embittered (his charity apparently began at home, and ended there too) – to settle in Maiolati, but in the event he managed to move there only in the autumn of 1850, and he died, in his new, rather splendid house, on 24 January 1851.

The house and its contents, being in a backwater so distant from the mainstream of modern life, seem in some ways to be virtually unchanged, although in fact the building was used for a variety of purposes (municipal offices, briefly a school) before it was opened as a museum in 1951, on Spontini's centenary. Entering parts of it is like going into a time-warp: even the plumbing, at least visibly, is just as it was. And the original painted ceilings, the upper ones high and vaulted, are handsomely restored.

The main, formal museum section is on the first floor. The first room is devoted to Spontini's youth in Maiolati and his prentice years in the Italian oper-

Casa di Riposo, Maiolati Spontini

atic centres, while the second covers his Paris period, the third his time in Germany, the fourth his legacy to Maiolati. There are spectacular paintings in a David-like neo-classical manner of scenes from the French works (*Milton, La vestale, L'Olimpie, Fernand Cortez*), along with singers' portraits and a fine lithograph of Spontini from 1821, scores, handbills, and facsimiles of letters and other documents. In the Maiolati room are plans for the local park, now the Colle Celeste public park (Celeste preferred a statue of the Madonna to the currently fashionable Greek temple), for the Casa di Riposo and for Spontini's own tomb. In a final room on this floor are two pianos of 1820, a domestic table piano and a splendid grand (with a janissary stop, for percussive effects; both of course come from Erard, his wife's family firm), as well as display cases with early editions (one, of the German version of *L'Olimpie*, bears Spontini's dedication to the great tenor Adolphe Nourrit) and busts of the composer.

The top floor is more remarkable, for it is here that we are transported into Spontini's time. Not of course that he would have kept his fine, hand-painted china, his gold coffee service, his delicately fluted glasses and his bone cutlery in a glass display case: but there they all are, carefully preserved, and they speak eloquently about the style of his life and his times. In the same room are appealing portraits of the young Spontini and his wife. In other rooms are Céleste Spontini's needlepoint work, her table linen and some of her furniture, scrupulously restored, with oil lamps and a chest. Then, past the stone privy, are the rooms at the rear, a bedroom (with Spontini's own prayer stool), a dressing-room in which are displayed his court clothes (he was unusually tall, you will notice), his ceremonial waistcoats, hat and sword (from the Institut Français) and his Légion d'honneur, and then his study, with the desk and oil lamp he used in his final wintry weeks, along with various financial documents. From there you can see the small garden behind the house.

Not many composers' artefacts are so diligently preserved as these are through various accidents of fate: the isolation of Maiolati, Spontini's early death and fast-fading reputation, his childlessness. The result is a museum unusually evocative of the man and his times.

Further tribute is paid to him in the Teatro Pergolesi at Jesi, where there are also Sale Pergolesiane (*see* PERGOLESI). The Sala Spontiniana, off the main foyer, was established in 2003 to celebrate the achievement of another composer from close by. The exhibits include an original plaster bust of Spontini, a portrait from 1924, an Erard piano (newly restored) and a number of miscellaneous objects including a bronze medal presented to the composer in 1829 by Halle University, along with autograph letters and some unpublished autograph music.

Museo Spontiniano
via G. Spontini 15
60030 Maiolati Spontini (Ancona)
Italy

phone +390/0 731 704451 (museum), 702972 (town hall administration)
fax +390/0 731 701816

e-mail info@gasparespontini.com
website www.museionline.it/museimarche

open 13 April–30 June,
September–December, Saturday
15.00–19.00, Sunday 10.30–12.30,
15.00–19.00; July–August,
Tuesday–Sunday 17.00 – 20.00
(Saturday also 21.00– 23.00)

Sala Spontiniana
Teatro Comunale G.B. Pergolesi
Piazza della Repubblica 9
60036 Jesi (Ancona)
Italy

phone +390/0 731 538351
fax +390/0 731 538356
e-mail teatro.pergolesi@comune.jesi.an.it

open Monday–Saturday 10.00–13.00,
Tuesday, Thursday, Sunday also
16.00–19.00 (guide for groups available
Thursday and Sunday by appointment)

Map 9

M. Paraventi, ed.: *Maiolati Spontini: the Land of Music* (Maiolati Spontini: City of Maiolati Spontini, 1999)
Centro di Studi G. Spontini: *Gaspare Spontini: l'artista, la musica, il territorio* [CD-ROM, Italian/English]

STETSENKO

Choral music is the least likely of genres to carry a composer's reputation beyond his own country's boundaries, so it is not surprising that Kyrylo Hryhorovych Stetsenko is little known outside Ukraine. Born in 1882, he studied in Kiev and later returned there as professor of choral music at the conservatory; in his last years he was a village priest. Conductor of the first Ukrainian choir in the Soviet Union, he made many folksong arrangements for chorus and composed substantial liturgical pieces for the Ukrainian church; he also wrote songs and dramatic works, one of them on the story of Iphigenia in Tauris (a local tale: Tauris is in Ukraine).

He is commemorated both in his native village, Kvitky, and in Vepryk, where he died. Kvitky lies some 150 km southeast of Kiev, not far from Korsun'-Shevchenko, just off the A265 road to Kirovohrad. The Kvitky museum is in the former school, which Stetsenko attended in 1889–92 – the building was in fact partly demolished but was reconstructed in time for the opening of the museum in the centenary year, 1982. There are four rooms, the first of them designed to set the atmosphere of the period of Stetsenko's birth, with 19th-century furniture (not, alas, that of the Stetsenko family) and a portrait of the composer's father drawn by the composer when he was a boy of ten. The next two rooms are concerned with his life during his periods outside Kiev: one has photographs, playbills, letters and music manuscripts (including a piece dedicated to the Ukrainian national poet Shevchenko) from his years in Belaya Tserkova, the other covers his time in Tyvriv, in the years leading up to the Revolution, where he taught at the seminary. The final room, the largest, displays many photographs and gifts that he received on his birthdays. A plaque was affixed to the house in 1957 but removed when the house was part-demolished; but a bust by H. Kal'chenko has stood outside since 1970.

There are memorials by Kal'chenko to Stetsenko in Vepryk too, one by the door of his house and one on his grave, also dating from 1970. The composer went in 1920 to the village, which is a short

Stetsenko museum at Vepryk

distance south-east of Vinnytsya (itself about 250 km south-west of Kiev), as a priest, but two years later he died of typhus. Again, the original building does not survive, but a simple thatched cottage on its site serves as the museum. There are five rooms, thematically organized: one on his music (showing scores of his choral and dramatic works), one on his commemoration and influence (his pupils, his awards), a third exhibiting a well-used piano, portraits and folksong editions, a kitchen (with a local history element) and – the most personal – a bedroom: here is the bed in which in 1922 he died, a sample of his wife's embroidery, a family photograph, his broken violin and its bow, and three little icons, forming a miniature shrine.

Muzey K.H. Stetsenko*
vulytsya Lenina 32
Kvitky
Korsun'-Shevchenkivs'kyy rayon
19446 Cherkas'ka oblast'
Ukraine

phone +380/80 4735 62162

open Tuesday–Saturday 08.00–17.00

Derzhavnyy Memorial'nyy Budynok-Muzey K.H. Stetsenko
vulytsya Stetsenko 1
Vepryk
Fastivskyy rayon
08531 Kyïvska oblast'
Ukraine

phone +380/80 8265 45924

open Tuesday–Sunday 09.00–17.00

Map 16

STOLZ

Graz, capital of Styria, honours Robert Stolz (1880–1975) above all other composers. He was still living when a bust was erected in the Stadtpark, in 1972, along the Robert-Stolz-Promenade; on his centenary, in 1980, a museum to him was established. The son of two musicians,

Stolz was born in the Schmiedgasse, off the Hauptplatz; the family moved to a first-floor flat in the former Palais Inzaghi nearby in the Mehlplatz when he was ten. Even before then he had been recognized as something of a prodigy: Brahms, a family friend, attended his piano recital début in 1887. After studies in Berlin he made his way at first as a conductor but after an encounter with Johann Strauss he turned increasingly to light music. His experience conducting operetta at the Theater an der Wien (from 1907) proved instructive and he composed an astonishing 65 operettas and musicals, mainly for Vienna and Berlin. During World War II he emigrated to the USA, turning out a steady stream of film scores before returning to Vienna, where he composed for the Eisrevue.

Stolz is not overlooked in Berlin, where there is a wooden memorial plaque in the Grünewald, or in Vienna, where in 1970 he was made an honorary citizen – the more poignant, since he had forfeited his nationality during the war. There are memorial plaques on both his Grinzing villa at Cobenzlgasse 22, in the 19th district, and the building in which he owned a flat from 1935 (and where his fifth wife, 'Einzi', long lived) at Elisabethstraße 16, in the 1st district. The square adjacent to the block of flats has been renamed Robert-Stolz-Platz.

The Stolz museum in Graz displays items donated by his widow – personal possessions and photographs, furniture and old radios and a record player from their villa, sheet music, recordings, film and ice revue posters, commemorative stamps and a reel of film (Stolz was nominated for Oscars in 1941 and 1944) are ranged over three rooms. Of special interest is a copy of his father Jacob Stolz's *Allgemeine Geschichte der Musik*, published in Graz in 1894. The first room, embodying an ingenious re-creation of the sitting-room in Grinzing, also serves as the reception office; a blown-up manuscript facsimile of the melody of a popular song he composed about Graz runs along the dado. In the hallway are photographs of his fifth wife (the earlier wives do not appear) and his childhood mentors; the second room is given over entirely to museum display, with four panels of chronology and four floor-to-ceiling cases. The bust by Erwin Huber is a copy of the bronze in the Stadtpark. Although there are display cases at the back and costume designs, posters and maquettes lining the walls of the third room, it is used primarily for concerts, lectures and hire; it has a stage, a grand piano and seating for 100 and can be entered separately from the museum through a foyer lined with pictures of musical personalities from the 95 years of Stolz's life.

Robert-Stolz-Museum
Mehlplatz 1/1
8010 Graz
Austria
    (entrance in Färberplatz)

phone +43/0 316 815951

open Tuesday–Thursday 14.00–17.00, Saturday 10.00–13.00

Map 1

H. Kretschmer: *Wiener Musikergedenkstätten* (Vienna: J & V Edition, 3/1992)

STRAUSS, Johann

No city is more attentive to its past composers than Vienna, and among the municipal museums the one dedicated to that prototypical Viennese, Johann Strauss the younger (*b* 1825), is the most richly endowed with objects. All but one of the five rooms of Praterstraße 54, which opened to the public in 1978, are given over to displays of decorative first editions, prints, photographs, portraits, busts and other evocative memorabilia which serve to chronicle Strauss's greatest musical triumphs and to illuminate his often complex relationships with his famous father Johann (1804–49), his brothers Josef (1827–70) and Eduard (1835–1916), and his three wives. The final room, reconstituted in the spirit of a salon, displays an array of oil paintings, a bust, his

Bösendorfer piano, the harmonium that he preferred for nocturnal music-making, the standing desk at which he composed and other extraordinary presentation items such as the gilded violin cabinet and the carved music case in the form of an easel. A watercolour by Karl Zajicek of Praterstraße 54 shows how well the building is standing the test of time.

Strauss and his first wife lived in the spacious first-floor flat, above a shop, from 1863 until 1870, when he was Court Ball Music Director in charge of the hectic Viennese Carnival (or 'Fasching') season. At other times of the year he often toured with his orchestra in various parts of Europe and in Russia, leaving his younger brothers to undertake his orchestra's regular engagements in Vienna. While living here he crowned his reputation as the Waltz King with *An der schönen blauen Donau* ('The Blue Danube'), written for the Wiener Männergesang-Vereins (Vienna Men's Singing Society); its first performance, by the 150-strong chorus and an orchestra of 40 military musicians at the nearby Diana Bath

Johann Strauss's apartment in Praterstraße (watercolour by Karl Zajicek)

Ballroom (Obere Donaustraße 93–5) on 15 February 1867, was cheered by a crowd of more than 1200, even though Strauss himself was not there.

A plaque adorns the house at Maxingstraße 18 where Strauss composed his *Wiener Blut* waltz (1873) and *Die Fledermaus* (1874). World War II deprived us of the ultimate 'Strauss Palais' in the Igelgasse (now Johann-Strauss-Gasse 4); his financial success during the two previous decades had enabled Strauss to commission in 1876 a fashionable two-storey house in the 4th district. He and his successive wives lived there during his last 21 years, receiving Brahms, Bruckner, Puccini and Anton Rubinstein among other musicians and presiding over his Strauss-Abenden, immortalized in an oil painting of 1894 by Franz von Bayros which today hangs in the Praterstraße museum (for illustration see p.37). Its elegant reception rooms, the billiard salon (Strauss called it his 'coffee house'), the garden house where he adjourned to compose such works as *Der Zigeunerbaron* (1885) and the room in which he died on 3 June 1899 are at least preserved in photographs, as are scenes of his summer homes.

During the 1880s Strauss spent most of his summers at a parkland manor house in Schönau, near Leobersdorf in Lower Austria. After 1892 he acquired Villa Erdödy in Bad Ischl (Kaltenbachstraße 36; demolished in 1970), to avail himself of the brine baths thought necessary for his rheumatic condition; in good weather he worked on operettas at his standing desk on the veranda. The Waltz King was buried in the Zentralfriedhof, beside Schubert and Brahms, and commemorated by a statue in the Wiener Stadtpark. His father too is not forgotten in Vienna: the house in which he was born (Kumpfgasse 11, now Riemergasse 14) is marked by a plaque.

Johann Strauss-Gedenkstätte

Praterstraße 54
1020 Wien
Austria

phone +43/0 1214 0121

website www.vienna.museum.at

open Tuesday–Sunday 09.00–12.15, 13.00–16.30

Map 1

H. Kretschmer: *Wiener Musikergedenkstätten* (Vienna: J & V Edition, 3/1992)
G. Gefen: *Composers' Houses* (London: Cassell and Vendome, 1998), 86–91
Johann-Strauss-Wohnung (Vienna: Historisches Museum der Stadt Wien, n.d.)
Johann Strauss-Gedenkstätte (Vienna: Historisches Museum der Stadt Wien, n.d.)

STRAUSS, Richard

There is a famous tale about Richard Strauss. Recalling that when the prim, disapproving Kaiser Wilhelm heard *Salome*, and said 'It will do Strauss no good', he pointed out that the royalties from the opera had paid for his splendid villa at Garmisch-Partenkirchen. That was in 1908. The villa is still owned by the family and was occupied by Strauss's son until his death in 1980. It is not open to the public, but it holds a large archive of music, letters and pictorial material, which was built up by Strauss's daughter-in-law and is now managed by the wife of one of his grandsons (one lives in Garmisch, the other in Munich). In due course, and in particular when in 2019 the flow of royalties ceases (70 years after Strauss's death: he was born in 1864 and died in 1949), it may become a museum. A video tour, guided by one of the grandsons with reminiscences from the other, shows something of its riches – pictures, *objets d'art* and countless letters, documents and music manuscripts.

For the moment, however, something of a museum's role is supplied by the Richard-Strauss-Institut, also in Garmisch-Partenkirchen, now a skiing centre in the Bavarian Alps. This institution, set up in Munich in 1982, moved in the late 1990s to a handsome house in Partenkirchen, made available by the municipality, and opened on the 50th anniversary of Strauss's death in 1999. It is supported not only by the town of

Garmisch-Partenkirchen but also by the Munich Richard-Strauss-Gesellschaft and the German copyright authority (GEMA), in which Strauss had been much involved, and it works in close and friendly collaboration with the Strauss family.

The primary function of the Institut is research and documentation. But it is open to the public, and it is pleasant and inviting. It has a comprehensive library and an archive, with a reading room and conference room, a small concert hall seating about 70 (used regularly for recitals, film shows, lectures and meetings, and with a Steinway presented by Wolfgang Sawallisch), and there is a multimedia terminal with an interactive video display. There is a video and CD room, for public use, in the basement, and a café.

There are two public exhibition rooms on the ground floor. These initially showed new exhibitions every six months; the first, in 1999, had been concerned with the Strauss family and the Garmisch villa, and at the time of our visit there was a particularly attractive and perceptively presented one on the connections between Beethoven and Strauss, prepared in collaboration with the Bonn Beethoven museum. These however are giving way to a standing display, with smaller, short-term annual exhibitions. They draw not only on the institute's own archive but also on the Strauss family one. This is a 'klingende Museum', a sounding museum, with 20-minute spells of music heard several times daily.

This institution, which so happily and elegantly blurs the lines between appealing display, music-making and scholarship, so that each informs and enhances the others, is not Garmisch-Partenkirchen's only tribute to its most distinguished citizen. Strauss is buried in the churchyard, and there is a Richard-Strauss-Platz with a fountain in his memory, a Richard-Strauss-Saal in the Kongresshaus and a school named after the great man. Among the commemorations of Strauss elsewhere are plaques outside the former house of his wife's family, the De Ahnas, in Marquartstein, south of the Chiemsee, recording his presence there in 1894–1907, and on the house given to him by the City of Vienna, where he lived from the 1920s, at 8–10 Jacquingasse in the 3rd district.

Richard-Strauss-Institut
Schnitschulstraße 19
82467 Garmisch-Partenkirchen
Germany

phone +49/0 8821 910950
fax +49/0 8821 910960
e-mail rsi@garmisch-partenkirchen.de
website www.richard-strauss-institut.de

open Tuesday–Friday 10.00–17.00,
Saturday 14.00–17.00 (library,
Tuesday–Saturday 09.00–17.00)

Map 7

H. Kretschmer: *Wiener Musikergedenkstätten* (Vienna: J & V Edition, 3/1992)
C. Wolf, ed.: *Richard-Strauss-Institut: Die Austellung* (Garmisch-Partenkirchen: Richard-Strauss-Institut, 1999–) [exhibition catalogues]

STRAVINSKY

Igor Stravinsky spent several years in Switzerland, many in Paris, and most of all in the United States, where he died in 1971. And he is buried in Italy. But his early years, up to 1914, were of course spent in his native Russia, and that – or to be exact in Ukraine, then part of the Russian Empire – is where he is commemorated. There is no commemoration at his birthplace in Orianenbaum (now Lomonosov), where the dacha in which he was born in 1882 was pulled down in the 1930s to make way for an electricity substation, while in St Petersburg the family flat on the second floor at Kryukov Canal 66 became a communal apartment in Stalin's time and remains one now – and the plaque noting its site marks the wrong part of the block.

Stravinsky did however have a summer home during his adult years. This was at Ustyluh, in Volynia. In the

1880s Gavriyil Nosenko, a doctor in Kiev, whose wife was Stravinsky's aunt, bought an estate there, formerly the property of the Lubomirsky family. As a boy Stravinsky often stayed there in the summers from 1889 onwards, and found the atmosphere agreeable: at home, he had a severe father (Fyodor Stravinsky, a leading bass singer at the Mariinsky Opera) and three brothers; the Nosenkos had two daughters and there were often girl cousins present too. Stravinsky enjoyed the summers of swimming, tennis, drawing, sketching and amateur theatricals. And one of his cousins was Yekaterina, or Katya: on his first visit there he was eight and she was nine, and from their first hour together they knew, he later said, that they would marry. He got to know her better around the turn of the century; in 1905 they became engaged and the next year they married. Katya's sister and her husband Grigory Belyankin, a marine engineer, now lived in Ustyluh, in a house on the site of the old Lubomirsky palace (today a hospital), and in 1907 the Stravinskys decided to build their own, a short distance away, overlooking the river.

Ustyluh (Uściług to the Poles, Ustilog to the Russians, and Oustiloug as later spelt by Stravinsky) lies on the Ukrainian-Polish border, at the confluence of the Buh (or Bug) and the Luha (or Luga), about 85 km west of Luts'k, 135 south-east of Lublin. It was a small and poor town, reckoned at 1666 inhabitants in 1880 but 4000 by 1909, a large majority Jewish; the Nosenkos were good landlords and provided a hospital, a school and other services. 'The peculiarities of this house', Stravinsky wrote, 'which was built according to my own plan, were two fireplaces with chimneys and the balcony facing the river'. The entrance was through a wooden porch. A Polish traveller described it in 1939 as 'whitewashed, hidden in the greenery of young trees ... it resembled a game-keeper's lodge'. Called 'Staraya Mïza' ('The Old Farm'), it is said to be modelled on a Swiss chalet. Most of the ground floor was taken up with a large,

lofty room; above it, reached by a broad staircase, was a long, bright attic – large enough to take the Bechstein grand that Stravinsky brought from St Petersburg – which, isolated from the rest of the house, would have provided the seclusion he needed for composing. During his five summers there he worked principally on the *Funeral Song* for Rimsky-Korsakov, the revision of *Fireworks*, *Zvezdolikiy* ('King of the Stars'), *The Nightingale*, some songs and parts of *The Rite of Spring*, of which the opening theme came to him one day in Ustyluh just before he was leaving for Switzerland; the Russian critic Viktor Varunts associates it with the long country view from the balcony across the river.

Stravinsky was last in Ustyluh in 1914, when he collected material for *Les Noces*. In World War I the Luha formed for a time the Russo-German front line and the town suffered during an offensive in August 1915. After the war Volynia was assigned to Poland and local farmers moved into the Stravinsky estate; later it was bought by a retired judge and fell into disrepair. In World War II the area was again fought over and the town was damaged by fire. It is clear from surviving pictures that the house was partly destroyed, but the fact that the unusual, irregular disposition of the seven ground-floor windows remains (Varunts parallels them with the rhythms of *The Rite*) may indicate that only the upper part was affected. In the present barrack-like

Stravinsky's summer home at Ustyluh

building, erected in the 1950s, the high pitched roof with dormer windows has given way to a conventional one, and there is no longer a lofty main room. The avenue of lime trees that Stravinsky himself planted however still flourishes.

The building is now a music school, but in 1994 the Volyn Regional Administration of Culture and the Volynian Regional Museum opened a Stravinsky museum there. The four rooms are chronologically organized, giving an illustrated account of Stravinsky's life. In the first room the family is commemorated, especially his father and his son: the father as singer, with copies of pictures from his album, some of them self-portraits, showing him in such roles as Varlaam and Mephistopheles, along with playbills of his performances and family photographs; the son, also Fyodor (or Theodore, 1907–88), as an artist and designer, who is represented by a print of one of his pictures which he sent on learning that the museum was to be set up.

Stravinsky's Russian years are covered in the second room, with photographs of his family at Ustyluh and of Stravinsky and his colleagues working on *The Nightingale*; there is material on the three great ballets of 1910–13 and a section on the influence of Russian folklore on his music, with memories of local people old enough to remember Stravinsky in those years. The third room recreates, as closely as can be done, the ambience of a room there in Stravinsky's time, with a gas lamp, a small table, candlesticks and an armchair, arranged as the contemporary photographs indicate. The final room displays cover his triumphal return to Russia in 1962, with playbills, programmes and photographs.

Muzey Igorya Stravins'koho v Ustyluzi*
vulytsya Stravins'koho 3
Ustyluh
Volodymyr-Volyns'kyy rayon
44731 Volyns'ka oblast'
Ukraine

phone +380/80 3342 93459

open Monday–Friday 09.00–18.00

Map 16

P. Hostowiec [pseud. for J. Stempowski]: 'Dom Strawińskiego w Uściłogu', *Kultura* (Paris, 1949), 19–34

O. Ogneva: 'Igor Stravins'kyy i Volyn'', *Narodna Tribuna* (Luts'k), no.41 (1994), 5–6

V. Varunts: 'Mezhdunarodn'iy festival, "Stravinskiy i Ukraina"', *Muzikal'noye Obozreniye*, no.7–8 (July–August 1994), 9

Muzey I. Stravinskoho v Ustyluzi (Luts'k: Volynian Regional Museum, 1994) [in Ukrainian, Russian and English]

SUK

When visiting the Dvořák sites around Prague, it is worth pausing in the village of Křečovice, where his favourite pupil, the violinist and composer Josef Suk, was born and where Suk and his wife Otilie, herself Dvořák's daughter, later lived. Suk was born on 4 January 1874 in the village schoolhouse, where his father was the teacher. His father was also the local choirmaster and taught Josef music. He went to study the violin at Prague Conservatory and in 1891 he joined Dvořák's composition class, soon becoming the master's favourite pupil.

The school at Křečovice still exists and boasts a small photographic memorial. But the chief memorial to Suk in Křečovice is the house Josef's father built for him in 1895, next to his own. In 1898 Josef and Otilie were married, and they spent the summers in Křečovice before she died of a heart condition in 1905; they had one son, Josef (father of the violinist of the same name). Until 1933 Suk was often abroad on

Suk's house (left) in Křečovice

tour with the Czech Quartet, and from 1922 he taught composition at Prague Conservatory, but the house in Křečovice remained his home. Among the works embodying his most personal feelings are *Asrael*, the vast symphony he dedicated in 1906 to the memory of his wife and his father-in-law (who had died in 1904), and the piano cycles (*About Mother*, *Things Lived and Dreamt* and *Lullabies*).

After Suk's death on 29 May 1935 he was buried in Křečovice; a memorial plaque was affixed to the house and an annual village concert was inaugurated. His son kept the house and contents intact and in 1951 gave it to the State. Four years later it was opened to the public as a branch of the Antonín Dvořák Museum in Prague, administered by the Museum of Czech Music. (The son's second wife still lives next door, in the house that belonged to Suk's parents.)

At the house, Suk's grand piano, his desk and a bust of Beethoven dominate his study. The sitting-room displays his awards and honours, together with small personal possessions and facsimiles of photographs and of his music (among which is a song composed by Otilie, 'Pepča na koníčku', for their son), while the bedroom in which Otilie died is devoted to family photographs, folk furniture (including a mirror in the shape of a violin) and their collection of Czech ceramics. The hallway is lined with original caricatures of the composer and photos of fellow musicians and protégés.

Pámatník Josefa Suka

no.3
25748 Křečovice u Sedlčan
Czech Republic

phone +420/0 317 741308

open Tuesday–Sunday 10.00–17.00

Map 4

SUPPÈ

Franz Suppè (as he signed his name) or Suppé (as it is now usually spelt),

Croatian born (in 1819), part-Belgian in descent, nephew of Donizetti, Austrian by nationality, was one of the prime creators of the Viennese operetta. Most of his life was spent in the imperial capital, where he is buried in the Zentralfriedhof; the house in which he died, Opernring 23, has borne a plaque since 1929. In 1876, when he was 57, he bought a house in the spa town of Gars am Kamp, some 80 km to the north-west, for use in the summers. A plaque put up on the house, Haangasse 27, in 1909, notes that he wrote the famous march from his operetta *Boccaccio* there. In 1878 he and his (second) wife Sofie bought a pair of houses in the Kremserstraße (he called them Sofienheim); five years later he had them rebuilt, one for himself and Sofie, one for their visitors. The houses still stand; on one of them the opening of his 'O du mein Österreich' is inscribed (see p.28). Close by is the Suppè-Promenade; and one of the resort's hotels has a Boccaccio-Room.

Suppè was a revered guest in Gars and in 1891 the town conferred honorary citizenship on him. On his death in 1895 his widow turned the house into a commemorative museum, which it remained until her own death in 1926. The property passed to other family members and in 1931 it was sold. The collection, then dispersed, was reacquired for the municipality in 1972, and a memorial room was opened in 1974 within a local museum above a bank in the main square. When in 1990 the lease expired the collection had to be stored; but five years later, on the centenary of Suppè's death, the municipality opened a new memorial room in the Rathaus. That however was uncomfortably small, so that only part of the material could be displayed, and in 2002 it moved to a much larger room in the new town museum close by.

Some of the material from Sofienheim still remains in the depository, but the display is quite substantial and gives a good idea of the world in which the composer and his wife lived. Dominating it is a large oil of the great man, dating from 1892; his Baier grand piano is there too. Among the furniture is a set of *Jugendstil* cane chairs, a table with carved wood lions' feet, a charming porcelain table with roses, his desk and chaise longue, and the bed, brought from Vienna, in which he died. There are some smaller items in Biedermeier style. In the showcases are his glasses and walking-stick, medallions, a needlepoint boot-jack (the design incorporates a lyra), Sofie's fans, a life mask and various documents in his own hand (both writing and music). There is a collection of published music and books and some brochures and posters, several referring to *Die schöne Galathée*, and an assortment of photos. Context is happily supplied by subdued but gently spirited background music.

Suppè-Gedenkstätte

Zeitbrücke-Museum
Kollergasse 155
3571 Gars am Kamp
Austria

phone +43/0 2985 2680, 2225
fax +43/0 2985 2249
e-mail info@gars.at

open May–September, Friday 10.00–12.00, Saturday and Sunday 10.00–12.00, 14.00–17.00, and by appointment

Map 1

H. Kretschmer: *Wiener Musikergedenkstätten* (Vienna: J & V Edition, 3/1992)
A. Ehrenburger, ed.: *Franz von Suppé: Festschrift zur Eröffnung der Suppé-Gedenkstätte Gars am Kamp* (Gars am Kamp: Museumsverein Gars am Kamp, 1995)

SZYMANOWSKI

Karol Szymanowski was of course Polish, but he was born in 1882 in what is now Ukraine, in the village of Tymoshovka; his family were among the Polish landed gentry who had settled in the region during the partition of Poland under the Russian Empire. Their winter home was in Yelizavetgrad, now

Kirovohrad, where Szymanowski spent much time in his youthful years, studying at the music school of his relatives the Neuhauses (the eminent pianist Heinrich was his second cousin). He went to study in Warsaw from 1901, when he was 19. In 1917, at the time of the Revolution, the family home in Tymoshovka was destroyed and in 1919 they left Yelizavetgrad. Their once splendid house there, now 42 Gogol Street, still stands. There are plans for creating in it a 'Shymanovskyy in Kirovohrad' museum; a grand piano that he played survives, along with other furniture, concert programmes and various documents from his early years.

Thereafter Szymanowski had no long-term fixed address – he travelled a great deal – but from 1922 he divided his time between Warsaw, where in 1927 he became director of the conservatory, and the southern Polish town of Zakopane. This charming resort, popular today with hikers in the summer and skiers in the winter, lies on the north side of the Tatra mountains, a westward extension of the Carpathians that lines the border between southern Poland and Slovakia. In the 1870s it became a spa town, renowned for the quality of its air, and it was soon a retreat for artists and intellectuals. Szymanowski was among them. He first visited Zakopane in 1894, when he was 12; on his second visit, in 1905, he met Artur Rubinstein. In spite of spending much of his time outside Poland (there is a plaque on the building in Vienna, at Argentinierstraße 4–6, where he lived in the years before World War I), from 1922 he went to Zakopane at least once a year. In 1930, after treatment in Switzerland for tuberculosis, he rented a villa there.

The villa, dating from about 1890, is built of wood in the style particular to the region, with steeply pointed shingled roofs to discourage the accumulation of snow. An upper storey had recently been added and the heating and plumbing improved. The beamed ceilings, the walls and the floor are all of natural pine, now mellow and warmly reddened, with

*Szymanowski's
Villa Atma in
Zakopane*

attractive fanlights above the windows. Szymanowski lived on the ground floor; the upstairs rooms were reserved for guests. He spent much of his time there in the early 1930s, but from 1934 – he had lost his conservatory job in 1932 – he was forced to undertake concert tours and in 1936 he had to give up the lease. He died in a sanatorium in Lausanne early the next year. During his time at Zakopane, perhaps invigorated by the air, he found the strength to compose such large-scale works as the *Veni Creator*, the *Litany to the Virgin Mary*, the Symphonie Concertante (Symphony no.4) and the Second Violin Concerto.

The idea of creating a museum in Villa Atma, as it is called – 'atma' is Sanskrit for 'one's self' – was first put forward by a pupil of Szymanowski's immediately after his death. A memorial plaque was affixed in 1952, but it was a further 20 years before funds were raised for its acquisition by a group of Szymanowski admirers, who then gave it to the National Museum in Kraków under whose auspices it was opened in 1976. Each July the town celebrates its connection with the composer by serving as host to the Karol Szymanowski Music Days.

Several rooms of Villa Atma have been lovingly re-created. In the dining-room, display cases are cleverly disguised in carved wood cupboards, made from those originally on the upper floor; in them are a death mask, his concert clothes, his toilet kit, a vaporizer, cigarette and cigar holders, letters and documents, his visiting cards, a ring, playing cards and a collection of commemorative medallions. The sunny breakfast room is adjoining. His study is meticulously re-created from photographs and descriptions, with his work table, a piano that he sometimes played in Zakopane (his own from the house went to Warsaw and was destroyed), wicker shelving and rugs hanging on the walls.

What was Szymanowski's bedroom now serves as a recital room, dominated by a Bösendorfer piano and seating up to 60 people; the walls are lined with information panels chronicling his visits to Zakopane and photographs of his friends, of which more can be seen in the small neighbouring room. The rustic house has a strong and distinctive atmosphere, enhanced by the heady, passionate

Re-creation of Szymanowski's study

swirl of his music as it resounds through the building.

Muzeum Karola Szymanowskiego

Villa Atma
ulica Kasprusie 19
34500 Zakopane
Poland

phone +48/0 182 013493
fax +48/0 182 014554
e-mail glowa@tatrynet.pl
website www.culture.pl,
www.muzeum.krakow.pl

open Wednesday–Sunday 10.00–15.30
(Friday to 16.00)

Map 10

M. Pinkwart: *The Karol Szymanowski Museum in the Villa Atma at Zakopane: a Guide* (Kraków: National Museum, 1979)
A.P. Kalenychenko, ed.: *Shymanovskyy i Ukraïna/Szymanowski a Ukraina* (Kirovohrad: Kirovohrads'ke Derzhavne Vydavnytstvo, 1998)

TANEYEV

Sergey Ivanovich Taneyev (1856–1915), who for many years was professor of piano and composition at Moscow Conservatory and briefly its director, is quietly commemorated twice near Moscow: about 70 km to the west, in the village where he died, and 90 to the north-west, in an outbuilding attached to Tchaikovsky's last home in Klin (*see* TCHAIKOVSKY). For a time (1960–94), according to the memorial plaques, the street in Moscow called Gagarenski pereulok was known as Taneyevïkh pereulok because, from 1904 until his death, Taneyev occupied the small cottage there, at no.2.

At the age of 19 Taneyev won the first gold medal given for both piano and composition at the Moscow Conservatory under Nikolay Rubinstein and Tchaikovsky (of whose First Piano Concerto he gave the Moscow première). He was an important teacher, notably of Skryabin and Rakhmaninov, devoted to his pupils. A natural intellectual, he learnt

several languages (including Esperanto, in which he wrote many songs), published a counterpoint textbook (1909) and set himself daily mathematical problems; he was also interested in mysticism and astrology. His home was a gathering place for pupils and friends: the Tuesday evening discussions of controversial new music, including Wagner's, were famous. As a composer he was retiring and self-critical, and not prolific, although he did produce four symphonies, a piano concerto and chamber music as well as a trilogy opera, *Oresteya* (1894), and a substantial body of vocal pieces, solo and choral.

In 1906 Taneyev began taking holidays (his elderly nursemaid and his cat, Vaska, in tow) in Dyut'kovo, a small village in the Storozhka river valley, close to the Savvino-Storozhevskiy monastery west of Moscow, five kilometres beyond Zvenigorod, where many Moscow artists and intellectuals retreated in the summer. From 1908 he rented four rooms of a house with a terrace near one occupied by his friend the conductor Bulikov. A grand piano was dispatched from Moscow for teaching and rehearsing; Taneyev took walks in the fir forests and played croquet and drank tea with his pupils and friends. His last visit, in 1915, was delayed by a bout of pneumonia he suffered after attending Skryabin's funeral. Four days after his arrival in Dyut'kovo, Taneyev had a heart attack and died, on 19 June. He was buried at Zvenigorod but later moved to the Novodyevichi cemetery in Moscow, where he lies near Rubinstein and Skryabin.

The Taneyev museum at Dyut'kovo

For Taneyev's students, Dyut'kovo remained a place of pilgrimage. It was nearly 50 years after his death, in 1962, that a memorial to him was established in the Bulikov house, since the people from whom Taneyev had rented the house where he died (and whose descendants still own it) refused to allow it to be opened to the public, although they did agree to a memorial plaque. The displays were made up of photographs and the recollections of the village elders. When in 1980 the founder died, the displays were moved to the monastery museum and the house was abandoned. But nine years later, two women who worked in the monastery museum decided to revive it, with the brother of one of them. They renovated the Bulikov house and established contact with Taneyev's great-great-nephews and surviving pupils, who provided display items and further recollections. The museum is now in the charge of the local authority, but run by devoted staff, who are prepared to walk an hour each way from the nearest bus stop, whatever the weather, to ensure that it is open to visitors. (It isn't easy to find Dyut'kovo: best to take a taxi from Zvenigorod, or the 23 bus to the monastery; drivers should take the Minsk highway (M1) out of Moscow, or the Riga one (M9), turn right or left respectively on A107, look out for the monastery to the south-west of Zvenigorod and turn right at the well just beyond it.)

The village is small, the streets unnamed. The large bust in the front garden is all that advertises the museum. It occupies the entire ground floor of the Bulikov house, which inside resembles a log cabin. In addition to Taneyev family trees, portraits of his grandparents, photographs of his parents and brothers, family furniture and personal effects of family members, there is a chair once used by Tchaikovsky. In the larger back room, which doubles as a display room for furniture from Taneyev's Moscow house (vignettes of his bedroom, dining-room and study are re-created in different corners) and a hall for live music-making, there are a few personal items: a white summer jacket hangs in a cupboard, with small bodybuilding weights for turning unwanted fat to muscle hidden below, and a pocket watch, a pen and the composer's calling card are in a small glass case. The displays in the far side of the front room chart not only his time at Dyut'kovo but also his life in Moscow, his friendship with the Tolstoys and his visits to their estate at Yasnaya Polyana, and a supposed romance with a married pianist, Maria Karlovna Benua. There are still many photographs and alongside them editions of his music, a copy of his counterpoint textbook and impressions of the 1895 St Petersburg production of *Oresteya*. There are two pianos of the period, neither of them directly connected with Taneyev.

When Taneyev died, his legacy passed to his elder brother Vladimir, a lawyer with a large country estate at Klin, near the Tchaikovsky house; he and Tchaikovsky were old friends from their college days. In the 1920s he divided the material arbitrarily in two, donating half to the Klin museum and half to the Russian State Archive of Literature and Art in Moscow. The collection included Taneyev's music library, his manuscripts (the fair copies already in the hands of his Leipzig publisher, Belyayev, were destroyed during World War II), correspondence and other personal papers, and photographs. The Tchaikovsky Archive at Klin has continued to collect Taneyev items and now owns more than 5000, including the manuscripts of *Oresteya*.

Although Taneyev, Tchaikovsky's favourite student, never visited him at Klin, he came later to help Modest Tchaikovsky sort out his brother's effects. Vladimir Taneyev's family estate, a mere 500 metres away, now belongs to the Tchaikovsky Museum and there are plans to create a Taneyev museum there one day, although only the chapel is still standing.

In the meantime, the Taneyev items at Klin are displayed in two rooms in a building behind the Tchaikovsky house. In the smaller room there are a few pieces of furniture that belonged to the composer, a fortepiano and an upright, and a selection from his library. The larger one contains neatly organized, modern displays telling the story of his life, illustrated with photographs, manuscripts and editions of his music, as well as fascinating examples of his non-musical interests referred to earlier. One section is devoted to his pupils, another to his friends and colleagues, a third to his brother's estate. Visitors to Klin may have to ask specially to see the Taneyev exhibition, which is not always included in tours of the Tchaikovsky house.

Muzey S.I. Taneyev
Dyut'kovo
143098 Zvenigorod
Moskovskya oblast'
Russia

phone +7/0 095 597 1260

open Wednesday, Friday–Sunday
11.00–16.00

S.I. Taneyev: Life and Heritage
Gosudorstvennïy Dom-Muzey P.I.
Chaykovskogo
ulitsa Chaykovskogo 48
141600 Klin
Moskovskaya oblast'
Russia

phone +7/0 095 539 8196, +7/0 224 21050
fax +7/0 095 539 8467
e-mail gdmch@dol.ru

open Friday–Tuesday 10.00–18.00 (closed last Monday of the month)

Map 12

TANSMAN

Alexandre Tansman is chiefly remembered as a Parisian composer; he lived in the French capital from 1920 until his death in 1986, apart from an enforced stay in the USA during the war years. But it is in Poland that, in 1897, he was born, as Alexander Tancman, and he retained his connections there as well as his affinities with Polish musical traditions. And it is in his native city of Łódź that he is commemorated, by an annual music competition, a plaque on the building in which he was born (ulica Prochnika 18) and a Tansman display in the History Museum.

That museum, in a lavish palace that was formerly the home of the Poznański family, leading industrialists in Łódź, devotes a number of rooms on the first floor to the city's notable cultural figures. The Tansman room was set up in 1996, partly with material supplied by one of Tansman's daughters in Paris. The display, captioned in Polish and English, is nicely balanced, showing him as a family man, as a significant figure in the world of Parisian émigré musicians, as a Pole, as a Parisian and as a composer. There are many photographs of him with his family, and personal possessions – pens, a camera, a lighter, cufflinks, birth certificate, passports, a table given to him by Stravinsky. There are photos of his many composer and musician friends, and correspondence with several of them (Ravel, Bartók, Prokofiev, Milhaud, Schoenberg, Gershwin, Segovia). There is a photo of Charlie Chaplin, who once saved Tansman's life. The awards include a Prix Berlioz and an Order of Merit of the Polish People's Republic. There are cases displaying recordings of his music and examples of his editions and manuscripts: his Franco-Polish identity is neatly hit off in a framed enlargement of his *Tombeau de Chopin* and an edition of his *Hommage à Lec Wałesa*. A bust by Pavel Jocz is prominent.

There is also a room in the museum devoted to the conductor Henryk Debich and three to the most famous of all Łódź musicians, the pianist Artur Rubinstein (for whom Tansman composed two sonatas), established in 1982 and enlarged in 1990 when the pianist's daughter Eva donated her father's collection to the museum.

Muzeum Historii Miasta Łodzi
ulica Ogrodowa 15
91065 Łódź
Poland

phone +48/0 426 540323
fax +48/0 426 540202
e-mail
muzeum@poznanskipalace.muzeum-
lodz.pl
website www.poznanskipalace.muzeum-
lodz.pl

open Tuesday, Thursday 10.00–16.00;
Wednesday 14.00–18.00; Friday,
Saturday, Sunday 10.00–14.00

Map 10

A. Kocik and B. Pietraszczyk: *Aleksander
Tansman: Życie i dzieło 1897–1986* (Łódź:
Muzeum Historii Miasta Łodzi, 1996) [in
English and Polish]

TARTINI

Giuseppe Tartini, the greatest violinist-
composer and violin pedagogue of the
mid-18th century and pioneer student of
acoustics, spent all his working life in
Italy. His home was Padua but he occasionally worked in Venice and elsewhere.
He was born, on 8 April 1692, in Pirano –
now Piran, in Slovenia – on the Istrian
coast, not far from Trieste. When he
was 16 he left his native town, and
he never returned. Fortunately for us, he
remained in written contact with his
family.

Tartini came from a comfortable
family background. His father was
director of salt production in Pirano and
owned a substantial town house there,
facing the little harbour and the sea. It
now overlooks the town's central square,
the Piazza Giuseppe Tartini (or Tartinijev
trg); in Tartini's time there was little
more than marshy land in front of the
house, and to one side, on a spit of land
extending to the north-west, the
medieval old town.

The house itself has medieval origins
but has undergone refurbishment and
restoration over several centuries, probably including a remodelling soon after
Giuseppe Antonio Tartini, the composer's
father, moved there from Florence in the
1680s. It was presented to the Piran
municipality by its last owner. There are
now five storeys. On the ground floor there
is a shop. For the Tartini memorial room,
you enter at the side and go up to the first
floor, passing at mezzanine level a large
room, the Sala delle Vedute, decorated with
green-grey frescoes of classical scenes,
which seats about 50 and is now used for
recitals and lectures; adjoining it is the Sala
dei capricci architettonici, with more
colourful frescoes. There are further decorated rooms, not open to the public, on
the upper floors. (These, commissioned by
Tartini's nephew Pietro at the end of the
18th century, postdate the composer
himself.)

The Tartini memorial room is a
modest-sized double one with an archway across and a ceiling of finely
restored stucco work. The most striking
items in the display cases are Tartini's
excellently preserved autograph manuscripts, chiefly of his theoretical writings, which belonged to the family and
are now in the ownership of the Piran
department of the regional archives
of Koper (formerly Capodistria). His
abstruse mathematical calculations
about harmonics, with complex work-
ings with ratios and geometric drawings, are among them; his final letter,
written to his nephew in Pirano a few
days before his death on 26 February
1770, is there too. There is also a
manuscript of another Istrian composer,
Antonio Smareglia (1854–1929), from
his *Inno a Tartini*, written in 1896 for the
dedication of the Tartini monument in
the square.

There are also printed items,
including editions of his *Trattato di
musica*, the *Discorso* on his death, an
engraving of 'Tartini's Dream' (the
nightmare said to have inspired his most
famous sonata, the 'Devil's Trill') and
sundry modern editions. Objects displayed include a copy of the famous
portrait of the composer, a violin from
the Amati workshop, said to have been
one of Tartini's own, a death mask and a
marble bust; there is a contemporary box
that looks as if it was intended for the
carrying of music, and a five-nibbed
rastrum.

Tartini is much commemorated in Piran. There is a family vault, originally assigned to his father, in the central aisle of the 14th-century church of St Francis (within a minorite convent), almost adjoining the house. Besides the central square itself, there is a Tartini Theatre, from the early 19th century, as well as the obligatory hotel, café and taverna named after him. North of the town, just off the road to Koper and Trieste (or preferably a short trip across the bay), lies the village of Strunjan (Strugnano), where the Tartini family owned a summer villa by the sea; now used by the Slovenian government for entertaining, it is securely fenced off but can just be seen through the surrounding woods.

Giuseppe Tartini Stanza Ricorda/ Spominska Soba

Kajuhova 12
6330 Piran
Slovenia

phone +386/0 5673 3090
fax +386/0 5673 0140

open September–May, daily
11.00–12.00, 17.00–18.00;
June–August, daily 09.00–12.00,
18.00–21.00, or by appointment

Map 14

S.A. Hoyer: *Hiša Tartini v Piranu: Zgodovinski razvoj in likovna oprema / Casa Tartini di Pirano: evoluzione storico e apparato decorativo* (Koper: Lipa, 1993)
A. Pucer: *Inventar Zbirke/Inventario della Collezione Giuseppe Tartini* (Koper: Pokrajinski Arhiv Koper/Archivio regionale di Capodistria, 1993)
D. Žitko: *Giuseppe Tartini: Spominska Soba / Stanza Ricordo / Memorial Room* (Koper: Pokjrajinski muzej, 2001)

TCHAIKOVSKY

The way of the pilgrim to the Tchaikovsky shrines is not an easy one. Allowance must be made for the weather, the paucity of English speakers, the great distances and the often seemingly insurmountable difficulties of travel in Russia

and Ukraine. Ironically, there is no museum honouring him in either St Petersburg (where he was educated, where many of his works were first heard and where he died) or Moscow (where he taught), although the conservatory and the hall that is home to the State Symphony Orchestra there bear his name as too does the conservatory in Kiev. From 2005 there will be a Tchaikovsky Cultural Centre in the building in which he occupied a second-floor flat, with memorial rooms reconstructed and furnished in 19th-century style and concert and exhibition halls on other floors. There are hopes for a museum in his brother Modest Tchaikovsky's flat in St Petersburg in which he died, now privately owned (though you may dine in the restaurant beneath it). He is not commemorated in any of the cities elsewhere in Europe to which he travelled. Shy, and of nervous disposition, he preferred rural settings for his creative work, cocooned by family, a small circle of friends and his faithful retainers, to the cities where his music was performed.

Until recently Votkinsk, where he was born, has been a closed city because intercontinental ballistic missiles were manufactured there during the Cold War period, in factories including the one managed by Tchaikovsky's father, Kamsko-Votkinsky Zavod (in his day it produced cannons, anchors and bridges). Reached by flying to the Udmurtian capital, Izhevsk, Votkinsk is a further

The Tchaikovsky museum at Votkinsk

60 km to the north-west, some 1000 km east of Moscow, close to the foothills of the Ural Mountains; it lies at the junction of two rivers, dammed at the command of Peter the Great to generate power, and also creating what is now an attractive lake.

The Tchaikovsky family lived in the factory manager's house, by the lakeside, which also served as the headquarters of the mining district that provided the raw materials for the factory. Designed by an architect from St Petersburg and built in 1806 of wood made to look like stone, in the style of a St Petersburg mansion, it is the central building of a complex that today includes a concert hall (recently refurbished with a grant from the Soros Foundation), a café, a shop and a boarding house for overnight visitors as well as buildings for the factory and museum archives, summer and winter garden houses, and what was formerly a bathhouse, along with accommodation for serfs and stabling – all now open to the public and displaying 19th-century domestic crafts. Between the house and the water is a large statue of the composer on a platform, where visiting musicians perform during the summer.

Tchaikovsky's father, Il'ya Petrovich, arrived in Votkinsk in 1837, ahead of his wife, to take up his job as factory manager and to ensure that the house for his family was comfortable and welcoming. Having spent most of his life in the region, where he had previously served as a draughtsman's apprentice, he was already known and well liked. Both husband and wife were educated people and their home quickly became a local centre of culture. Tchaikovsky senior ran the factory, which employed 3000 men, for eleven years. During that time four children, including Pyotr Il'yich, were born, supposedly in a room at the front of the house; outside, at the extreme right corner of the front, there is a plaque commemorating the composer's birth on 7 May 1840.

This spacious, two-storey house on the lakeshore also accommodated Il'ya Tchaikovsky's daughter from his first marriage, two nieces who had lost their parents, an elderly aunt and a governess. Unique among composer museums, the birthplace offers visitors a tour of the eleven principal rooms in which members of the museum staff, in costume, take the roles of Tchaikovsky's parents, his piano teacher, his governess and his aunt in often touching vignettes drawn from letters and diaries about their life at Votkinsk. (They are of course delivered in Russian, but written versions are provided in English and other languages.)

The museum's collection of Tchaikovsky artefacts was donated by members of the family. The original museum, in two rooms, opened briefly in 1940, but was closed during the Great Patriotic War (World War II) when the house was used as a hospital and a pilots' school. The largest collection of Tchaikovskiana, belonging to the museum at Klin (near Moscow), was brought to Votkinsk for safe keeping by its curators for the duration of the war and the Klin staff, while there, helped with further improvements to the birthplace and also with the display of the museum when it reopened. Star items in the Votkinsk collection include the Wirth grand piano, in playing condition, that belonged to the Tchaikovsky family in St Petersburg, which is in the large

Tchaikovsky statue, Votkinsk

central reception room; a firescreen in *petit point* embroidered by the composer's mother (Alexandra Andreyevna), in Il'ya's office, where the original factory ledgers are also on display; his mother's locking, wooden 'char' box, displayed next to the samovar in the large dining-room at the rear of the house; and an original icon that belonged to Il'ya, in the room of Tchaikovsky's birth, with a facsimile portrait and a birth certificate. In the two upstairs rooms are books from the children's library and showcases with collection items. Of particular charm is the mother's candlelit study, with its period dressing table, sewing table and desk, and a curtained alcove with a sofa and table. There is also a nursery as well as smaller rooms for the governess and Tchaikovsky's cousins, all carefully fitted out in period style.

In 1848, Il'ya Tchaikovsky retired and the family moved first to Moscow and then to St Petersburg. Pyotr had already begun piano lessons in Votkinsk and composed his first song, aided by his younger sister Sasha, 'Our mama in Petersburg' (1844). But in 1849 Il'ya accepted another post, as manager of Alapayevsk Mountain Region ironworks, and the family moved again, to the Ural Mountains. It was in Alapayevsk that the twins, Modest and Anatol, were born the following year.

The Tchaikovskys' year and a quarter spent in Alapayevsk – from May 1849 until August 1850, when the composer was nine to ten – has generally been something of a black hole in his biography. But the founder of the Tchaikovsky museum there, Vera Gorodolina, has thrown some light on it. The museum, in the house where the Tchaikovskys lived, completed in 1832 as the residence of the executives of the ironworks, was opened in 1965, in just two rooms. In 1986 the music school that had occupied the rest of the building moved away and the house was fully restored; it was reopened in 1990. Six of the ten rooms are devoted to the Tchaikovsky family's years in the area, with many photographs, examples of the furniture used at the time (the original

furniture was destroyed at the time of the Revolution), contemporary editions of his music and a Wirth mechanical organ that the young Tchaikovsky is thought to have played. Three of the rooms are given over to a display of folk instruments and one to the story of the museum's foundation. There is a large library, and on the top floor a recital room, seating 100, which is also used for art exhibitions.

In 1850 Tchaikovsky returned to school in St Petersburg, moving on in 1853 to the School of Jurisprudence. He began to compose in earnest only after his mother's death, from cholera, in 1854, which deeply affected him, and he had worked for several years as a clerk in the Ministry of Justice before he sought conservatory training. By that time his beloved sister Aleksandra (Sasha) had married (in 1860) a wealthy Ukrainian landowner, Lev Davydov, and moved to his family estate at Kamenka, about 230 km south-east of Kiev. Tchaikovsky first visited her there in the summer of 1865. Finding the Davydov family and the surroundings congenial, he returned nearly every summer for the next 27 years, spending his winters teaching at the Moscow Conservatory after its establishment in 1866, and he even took up year-round residence there for a time between 1878 and 1884.

(A small diversion here. In the summer of 1867 Tchaikovsky and his brother Modest followed the Davydovs on holiday to Haapsalu, a seaside spa in Estonia, where he wrote *Souvenir de Hapsal* for piano op.2 and dedicated it to Lev's sister Vera. In 1993, on the centenary of Tchaikovsky's death, the citizens of Haapsalu commemorated his solitary sunset walks on the beach by erecting a Tchaikovsky Bench at Africa Beach, with a portrait relief incorporating a melody, said to be Estonian in origin, from the Sixth Symphony.)

Over the years Tchaikovsky stayed in several different houses on the Davydov estate in Kamenka. Most have now disappeared. One survivor, sheltered from the highway by a forest, with views of a lake from the veranda, and where Tchaikovsky had a workroom on the first floor, is the 'Little Green House', today a Pushkin-Tchaikovsky museum.

Founded in 1934, the museum devotes one room on the ground floor to the Davydovs, who lived there in the early years of their marriage, one to Aleksandr Pushkin (who twice visited Lev Davydov's father there), another to the Decembrists (three of those executed in 1826 were visitors to Kamenka: because of his association, Vasily Davydov was exiled to Siberia for 30 years), and two to Tchaikovsky. The first contains portraits and busts of the composer, including an original oil from 1880, photographs of his sister (who died in 1891) and her husband, a Schiedemayer grand piano and a model of the house in which Tchaikovsky stayed on his first visit. The second room is devoted to his Ukrainian connections (the family claimed some Cossack blood); Tchaikovsky is associated with 16 places (including Khar'kiv, Kiev, Odessa and the estates of his friends Nikolay Kondrat'yev at Nizy and Vladimir Shlovsky at Usovo) and is believed to have worked on as many as 32 compositions in the country, including the operas *Mazepa* and *Yevgeny Onegin*, *Swan Lake*, the Second Piano Concerto and the Second Symphony (the 'Little Russian' – that is, Ukrainian). Again, there are portraits, including one of the composer listening to the eminent Ukrainian

Pushkin-Tchaikovsky Museum, Kamenka

composer Mykola Lysenko playing for him in Kiev, and Tchaikovsky's upright Vogt piano – the museum's prize possession. Outside there is a platform and benches for open-air performances of music and drama, and, along the path, a statue of the composer. Across the highway is Davydov Park, where there is another Tchaikovsky memorial at the mouth of a cave (local legend has it that this was one of his favourite spots to come to compose) and, at the top, where the manor house once stood, there is now a music school and recital hall named after Tchaikovsky.

A short walk away, in the building that until 1990 served as the music school, is the local history museum, where since 1975 there has been a third Tchaikovsky memorial room, celebrating in photographs his connection with the Davydov family. Also on display is a modern portrait of the composer at the piano, a bust and a display of folk instruments and handicrafts.

After his disastrous marriage in 1877, it was to the safety of Kamenka that Tchaikovsky fled as soon as he could. When he returned to Moscow, unable to face the world, he sought leave of absence from the Conservatory. He was able to take this up only because of the kindness of another woman, Nadezhda von Meck, a wealthy widow (her husband had built much of the Russian railway system); she was older and preferred to pursue their acquaintance entirely through correspondence. Madame von Meck provided Tchaikovsky with an allowance of 6000 rubles a year and the opportunity to stay at her Ukraine country estate at Braïliv (350 km west of Kamenka) whenever she was in Moscow. He visited it five times between 1878 and 1880 and is today commemorated there in a museum jointly dedicated to Madame von Meck and himself and in a music festival every May.

When the museum first opened, in 1990, it commemorated only Tchaikovsky, but in 1994, the centenary of Madame von Meck's death, it was expanded and the name changed. Her first-floor octagonal study forms the centrepiece: here

Nadezhda von Meck's octagonal study at Braïliv

the composer worked at her desk, seated in the carved armchair on display; a white, life-size statue of him dominates the octagon. Small items given by a descendant – inkpots (one in the shape of a frog) and a glass pen – are arranged on the desk along with scores of Tchaikovsky's operas. Display boards, elegantly presented, lining walls of rich

green, tell the story of his life, and below them are cases containing books, including a copy of Modest Tchaikovsky's reminiscences of his brother, and commemorative medals. The other rooms of the museum, which shares the house with an agricultural college, are devoted to the history of Braïliv and Madame von Meck's music library. Possibly it is her scent vial, still faintly smelling, that best succeeds in capturing the visitor's imagination.

From 1885 to the end of his life, Tchaikovsky tried to keep away from Moscow and even St Petersburg whenever he could, by making his principal home in the countryside in the region of Klin, 80 km north-west of Moscow, on the railway connecting the two cities. He had always wanted to retreat to the country after his numerous journeys abroad to Europe and to the USA. From 1885 to 1888 he lived in the nearby village of Maidanovo, in a house surrounded by a park with ponds, wildflowers and lime trees, but abandoned it for a house in another village, Frolovskoye, south of Klin. The memoirs of his friends such as Nikolay Kashkin and Yulian Poplavsky attest to his penchant for a fairly austere regime of

The Tchaikovsky house at Klin

exercise and reading, composition and music-making, letter-writing, diet and sleep, and his almost pathological need for long periods of enforced solitude. At Frolovskoye he completed the Fifth Symphony, *Hamlet* Overture, *Sleeping Beauty* and the orchestration of the *Queen of Spades*. He returned to Maidanovo for a year (1891–2), finishing *Iolanta* and *The Nutcracker*, before moving in May 1892 to a large, attractive two-storey house on the fringe of Klin owned by the local magistrate. Its position as the last house on Zaretskaya Street, the main Moscow–St Petersburg road, meant that he could take his daily walks in the forest without having to pass through the town and risk running into the townspeople. Only this last house, where he composed the Sixth Symphony, has survived the intervening years.

He left in October 1893 for Moscow and then St Petersburg, where he conducted the première of the Sixth Symphony. There is no indication that he thought he might not return to Klin. Probably because of cholera, or (as has been suggested, though the weight of scholarly opinion is now firmly against it) through suicide after condemnation for his homosexuality by a court of honour of his former fellow pupils at the School of Jurisprudence, Tchaikovsky died on 6 November in Modest's second-floor flat in St Petersburg, at Malaya Morskaya 13. The site is marked by a plaque. He was given a public funeral in the city at the Kazan Cathedral and was buried in the section of the Tikhvin Cemetery there set aside for composers.

After his brother's death Modest took over the house at Klin and determined that it should be maintained, as a lasting memorial, just as Tchaikovsky had left it. He himself served as its first curator, assisted by his nephew, Vladimir Davydov, and the composer's servant of many years, Alexei Sofronov, who had inherited all Tchaikovsky's manuscripts. Modest added a wing to the house, providing studies for himself and his nephew and, with the help of the composer's friends, began collecting

The veranda at Klin

letters, manuscripts and other documents. When he died, in 1916, the house became the property of the Moscow branch of the Russian Musical Society.

Almost immediately the new curator, N.T. Zhegin, alarmed at the threatening political situation in Russia, transferred the archive and the most valuable items of furniture to the Moscow Conservatory. But in 1920 the Society (whose members included the young conductor Nikolay Golovanov and the composer Aleksandr Goldenweiser) formally established the museum, undertaking to protect the house, secure its future and, at the same time, to endeavour to popularize Tchaikovsky's music. The archive and furniture were returned to Klin in 1924. But within a year the museum was declared state property, and henceforward it was supported by Tchaikovsky's royalties. During World War II it was closed and (as we have seen) the collection was evacuated to Votkinsk. It reopened on

6 May 1945, the eve of Tchaikovsky's birthday. A building housing a concert hall seating 350, the archive and the museum administration was added in 1964.

The villa at Klin is the oldest composer museum in Russia. The intention still stands to maintain the house, as far as possible, just as it was in Tchaikovsky's day, surrounded by garden and forest and populated by a wide variety of birds. Many photographs and written accounts survive of life at Klin and inform the presentation of the house. But the ground floor, which – with the exception of the dining-room and the veranda off it where Tchaikovsky liked to sit – was where Alexei Sofronov's family lived and worked (ground-floor accommodation was then considered too dank and therefore unhealthy for a person of Tchaikovsky's disposition), now lends itself, along with the outbuildings, to temporary exhibitions of items from the museum's vast archive, which includes legacies from other composers, such as Taneyev, as well as Tchaikovskiana (*see* TANEYEV). The natural pine-clad studies of Modest and Vladimir, on the first floor, are now preserved just as they originally were.

For the year and a half that Tchaikovsky lived in the villa he occupied three adjacent rooms on the first floor. One is at the top of the landing, where his monogrammed luggage – covered in labels advertising foreign hotels – is stored; double doors lead into the main reception room, and off it is his bed-room, where he often composed at the table next to the window looking out on the front garden (which he liked to tend himself). The picture-filled reception room is subdivided by the arrangement of furniture, his 1885 Bekker grand piano in the centre, his own published editions in one bookcase, the scores of other composers nearby, his desk next to a window. In one corner there is a diamond-paned Lantern Room with red, purple and gold glass, where he took tea in the mornings; in another a library of Russian books on a variety of subjects (including philosophy, history and science), their pages pressing wildflowers collected on his twice-daily walks; and in the third a reading alcove, dominated by a large portrait of his father. The screen in front of the fireplace was embroidered by his sister Sasha. The carved wood chairs are upholstered in red satin, the tables covered with embroidered and lace-trimmed cloths, and the floors striped with colourful carpets. There is a card table, and everywhere souvenirs of his travels (among them a Statue of Liberty inkpot). The draped archway leads into his bedroom, with its little iron bed in the corner, the card table with chair at the nearby window, a washstand, dressing table and cupboard on the opposite side, an icon and paintings of Kamenka on the walls, a carpet on the floor and an armchair and bookcase with volumes in English and French.

In the archive across the park near the main road are facilities for scholars to consult this most important collection of Tchaikovsky sources, which includes approximately 4000 original letters, diaries, notebooks and musical drafts. There are also microfilms of sources in other collections in Russia and abroad (most of the fair copies, once the property of Tchaikovsky's publisher P.I. Jurgenson – are now in the Glinka State Central Museum of Musical Culture in Moscow); early editions; a large iconographical collection that includes copies of 120 known different photos of the composer by well-known photographers,

The Lantern Room at Klin

playbills, programmes, supported by a substantial reference library. The museum stores contain still more furniture, clothing, gifts to Tchaikovsky and commemorative objects.

Tchaikovsky Cultural Centre
Kudrinskaya ploshchad 46–54
103001 Moskva
Russia

phone +7/0 095 291 1514, 7/0 095 290 3695

(closed; to open during 2005)

Muzey-usad'ba P.I. Chaykovskogo
ulitsa Chaykovskogo 119
Votkinsk
427410 Udmurtia
Russia

phone +7/0 341 452 0757

open by appointment

Muzey P.I. Chaykovskogo*
ulitsa Lenina 46
Alapayevsk
624630 Ekaterinburgskaya oblast'
Russia
+7/0 343 53072

open Tuesday–Saturday 11.00–16.00 (by appointment only)

Derzhavnyy Muzey O.S. Pushkina ta P.I. Chaykovs'koho
vulytsya Lenina 42
Kam'yanka
Kam'yans'kyy rayon
20800 Cherkas'ka oblast'
Ukraine

phone +380/80 4732 21978

open Wednesday–Monday 09.00–17.00

Kam'yans'kyy Rayonnyy Istorychnyy Muzey Memor'ial'na Kimnata P.I. Chaykovs'koho
vulytsya Dekabristi 5
Kam'yanka
Kam'yans'kyy rayon
20800 Cherkas'ka oblast'
Ukraine

phone +380/80 4732 21975

open Wednesday–Monday 09.00–17.00

Dershavnyy Muzey P.I. Chaykovskoho ta N.P. fon Mekk
vulytsya Chaykovskoho 3
Braïliv
Zhmeryns'kyy rayon
23130 Vinnyts'ka oblast'
Ukraine

phone +380/80 4332 33967

open Wednesday–Sunday 09.00–17.00

Gosudorstvennïy Dom-Muzey P.I. Chaykovskogo
ulitsa Chaykovskogo 48
141600 Klin
Moskovskaya oblast'
Russia

phone +7/0 095 539 8196, +7/0 224 21050
fax +7/0 095 539 8467
e-mail gdmch@dol.ru

open Friday–Tuesday 10.00–18.00 (closed last Monday of the month)

Maps 12, 16

M.M. Karïy: 'I pam'yat' Kam'yanky. . .' (Dnepropetrovsk: Promin', 1975, 2/1988) [in Ukrainian, English (as 'And the memory of Kamenka. . .') and German]

B.F. Shevchenko: *Muzey O.S. Pushkina ta P.I. Chaykovs'kogo u Kam'yantsi* (Kiev: Mystetstvo, 1986)

V.V. Babenko, G.M. Taran, L.I. Turenko and L.A. Bondarenko: *Kamenskiy Literaturno-Memorial'nïy Muzey A.S. Pushkina i P.I. Chaykovskogo* (Dnepropetrovsk: Promin', 1987)

B.I. Belonovich: *Dom-Muzey-P.I. Chaykovskogo v Klinu / P.I. Tchaikovsky House-Museum in Klin* (Moscow: Vneshtorgizdat, 1994) [Russian and English]

TINEL

Edgar Tinel was a leading figure in the establishment of the musical traditions of the Flemish-speaking people of Belgium. He was born on 25 March 1854 in Sinaai, close to Sint-Niklaas, between Gent and Antwerp. His father was master of the local school, which also served as the family home. It remained the town school until a new and larger one was built behind it; in 1992 the original building was renovated and now the ground floor is used for music lessons while the first floor houses the museum commemorating the composer.

In 1863 Tinel, aged nine, left Sinaai to study in Brussels, where eventually he was to become director of the Royal Conservatory and *maître de chapelle* to the king. He and his family of six children were always frequent visitors to Sinaai. When he died, on 28 October 1912, he was buried there in the churchyard of Sint Catharina, where later he was honoured with an imposing memorial incorporating his bust and images of St Francis and St Catherine, evoking two of Tinel's best-known works, his oratorio *Franciscus* (1888) and the dramatic legend *Catharina* (1909). The museum commemorating him was established in 1962, 50 years after his death.

Tinel's youngest son, Paul, a music critic (who published a study of *Franciscus* in 1924), inherited his father's musical estate. Although the collection was ultimately deposited in the Royal Library in Brussels, a second and substantial archive of autographs, letters, printed scores, programmes, newspaper cuttings, posters, photographs, portraits, medallions and personal effects (from his cigars to his cycle clips and collar studs) has been assembled over the years, and this informs the displays at the Sinaai schoolhouse. The museum owns Tinel's writing desk, an ingenious battery-operated grandfather clock made by a brother and a wooden-framed, upright piano (*c*1850) that belonged to the Tinel family. Along with scores of *Franciscus* and several important original portraits, a plaster death mask and marble bust (commissioned by the town), both by Arsenne Matton, are among the most treasured items in the collection.

Edgar Tinelmuseum
Edgar Tinelstraat 31–33
9190 Sinaai
Belgium

phone +32/0 3772 3279

open first Sunday of the month
14.00–17.00

Map 3

TOBIAS

Off the west coast of Estonia are two islands, of which the more northerly, and the smaller, is Hiiumaa. Rural and idyllic, sparsely populated, it was once a summer resort for rich families, chiefly from Sweden. The ferry from the mainland (a journey of one and a half hours) sails from Haapsalu, a resort just over 100 km from Tallinn, still of some charm although it has seen better days; it was once a favourite holiday retreat of Tchaikovsky, who is commemorated on a stone bench facing out to sea. In the same shoreline park, known as Africa Beach, there is a bust of Rudolf Tobias.

The village of Käina is about 16 km from Heltermaa, where the ferry docks. It is the site of a summer folksong festival. At the end of the village, on the main road, surrounded by fields, is the house where in 1873 Rudolf Tobias was born: a thatched-roof cottage, built in 1839 for the church organist and the only one of its kind to survive on the island – preserved because of its connection with the Tobias family.

The family had lived on Hiiumaa since the 16th century. Rudolf's father, Johannes, and his father before him, had been the village churchwarden and organist; Johannes was a resourceful man who built organs and furniture, some of which is on display along with other family furnishings. The largest of the five rooms was used for choir rehearsals, so it is remarkable that, besides his own family, Johannes accommodated eight orphans from the village. Rudolf lived there until he was 12, when the family moved to Kullamaa, on the mainland.

The house became a museum in 1976. In keeping with its twin roles as composer museum and social history museum, several of the rooms are re-created – the music room, with several organs (one by Johannes Tobias) and pianos, the unheated summer room in the far corner and the kitchen (with pieces of English Wedgwood china, precious to Mrs Tobias) – while others, such as the long family bedroom, display Rudolf's life in photographs and facsimile documents, with copies of his editions and recordings of his music as well as monographs about his life and works. On the wall are extracts from his writings.

Tobias is remembered in Estonia as the country's first professional composer. He went to school in Tallinn, then studied with Rimsky-Korsakov at St Petersburg Conservatory (1893–7). His overture *Julius Caesar* (1896) was the earliest Estonian symphonic music and his cantata *St John of Damascus* (to a Tolstoy text) and his D minor Piano Concerto are acknowledged as the first of their kind in the country. He had a brief career as a solo pianist, based in Tartu, but could not settle in his native country (he was short-tempered and a poor conductor); he went to Paris, Leipzig, where his oratorio *Jonas Sendung* ('Jonah's Mission') was performed, and ultimately to Berlin, where he succeeded Engelbert Humperdinck as professor at the Royal Music Academy and acquired a German wife (and five children) as well as German citizenship. He was con-scripted into the German Army during World War I, but discharged on grounds of ill-health in 1916 and died of his injuries just before it finished in 1918.

Helilooja R. Tobiase Majamuuseum Käinas
Hiiu mnt. 33
3213 Käina
Hiiumaa
Estonia

open summer, daily 11.00–17.00

Map 2

TODUŢĂ

The memory of the Romanian composer and musicologist Sigismund Toduţă (1908–91) still burns bright among the generations of composers he nurtured at the Academia de Muzică 'Gheorghe Dima' in Cluj-Napoca. In the year of his death they established a Fundaţia Sigismund Toduţă, which publishes music and holds an annual symposium as a birthday tribute and a biennial composition com-petition. They still meet to discuss and perform music in Toduţă's lovingly preserved flat in the quietly prosperous suburb of Grigorescu, not far from the municipal stadium and the Someşul River, on the western side of Cluj-Napoca, the largest city in Transylvania.

Toduţă was a revered mentor, with a polished command of polyphony, honed by years of close study of Renaissance music and the works of J.S. Bach, and of orchestration. His own style was tempered by his investigations into Romanian folk music. His compositions include an opera, five symphonies and several concertos; his training in Rome at the Accademia di S Cecilia and the Pontificio Instituto di Musica Sacra in the late 1930s and early 40s and his work in Romanian folk music are both reflected in his choral output, which includes folk settings and oratorios. He also wrote piano sonatas and songs. He was still composing as late as 1989, when he completed an oboe concerto.

Toduţă spent almost all his life in Cluj-Napoca, but he lived in the first-floor flat of a corner house just off the Piaţa 14 iulie, in what is now the eponymous Stradă Sigismund Toduţă, only during his last eight years. Today the large double reception room retains his Bechstein boudoir grand so that it may serve as a venue for meetings and private concerts of chamber music. Toduţă's family has also allowed other musical memorabilia to remain *in situ* in commemoration of him, including manuscripts (some of unfinished works), published books and scores, posters of his recitals and the 1985 revival of his 1947 opera *Meşterul Manole* ('Master-builder Manole') as well as a portrait, a plaster bust and photographs. Outside, on the side of the house, is a commemorative plaque.

Societatea Culturala Sigismund Toduţă

Stradă Sigismund Toduţă 13, ap. 3
3400 Cluj-Napoca
Romania

phone +40/02 64 480924

open by appointment

Map 11

TOMÁŠEK

Probably the most eminent Czech composer of his generation, Václav Jan Křtitel Tomášek was born in 1774 in the East Bohemian town of Skuteč, some 140 km east of Prague. It was in Prague that he spent most of his life, where he was known as a learned and authoritative teacher (his pupils included Voříšek and Hanslick) and where in 1850 he died. He travelled a good deal – he paid calls on Haydn and Beethoven, and Wagner and Berlioz were among those who called on him. Essentially a figure of the post-Classical, early Romantic era, he is chiefly remembered for his piano pieces – more eclogues, rhapsodies and dithyrambs than sonatas – and his songs.

A plaque was erected in 1889 on the house where he was born, in a quiet back street. But it is only relatively recently that Skuteč became more aware of his importance. The house was bought in 1986 by the local branch of the Czech Brethren of the Evangelical Church, and was reconstructed to include a prayer room, a flat for the local pastor and a memorial room to Tomášek, organized in conjunction with the local museum, the Městské Muzeum Skuteč, which is also responsible for the Novák museum; the street in which it stands is now called Tomáškova. In the one from which it leads, outside a bank, there is a fine bust to the composer, by Jaroslav Brož, put up in 1998.

The memorial room was opened in 2000. Quite modest in size, and with a vaulted ceiling, it is generously filled with display material, some of it loaned from national museum sources, in a series of modern cabinets. There is an early portrait of Tomášek, by Barbara Krafft, facsimiles of several of his manuscripts (including a particularly elegant one of his op.65 dithyrambs) and copies of his published works, from various periods of his life; there are 19th-century photos of Skuteč and Prague, pictures of his Czech contemporaries, composers, poets, patrons, pupils; material relating to his opera *Seraphine* and its production at the Estates Theatre in Prague; a number of engravings of Tomášek and reproductions of documents relating to his life and death (letters, his musical visiting card with an enigmatic canon, newspaper announcements, photographs of his Prague house, in Tomáška ulici, with its two plaques, Czech and German); a miniature of his wife (he was briefly, unsuccessfully married); and material on revivals of his music and celebrations of his anniversary since his death. A further central case contains personal items – a small, folding music stand, a travelling clock, some elaborate knives, engraved glassware, nightlights, wick-cutters and, rather oddly, a nutmeg grater. If a slightly haphazard collection, it nevertheless gives a definite impression of the man, his life and his times.

Tomáškův Dům

Tomáškova 518
53973 Skuteč
Czech Republic

phone +420/0 469 350131 (Městské Muzeum), 469 351612 (church office)

open Saturday 13.00–18.00, or by appointment

Map 4

TOSCANINI

Toscanini? It is as a conductor, of course, that he is remembered. But as a young man he composed too, and the sites in his native Parma where he is commemorated need to be noted here. The music itself is divided between the conservatories at Milan and Parma. None of it is now in currency. Some pieces are said to have been written when he was a young man for 'ladies of influence'; and an overture, an examination piece written as a student, was revived at a commemorative concert in 1999.

As a child Arturo lived in several different parts of Parma, as the family fortunes waxed and (more often) waned. The house where on 25 March 1867 he was born, 13 Borgo Rodolfo Tanzi (then Borgo S Giacomo), was bought at the time of his death by the Comune di Parma and was opened as a museum in the centenary year of 1967. It was damaged in the earthquake that struck Parma in 1983, and closed for four years, reopening in 1987, much refurbished.

The nature and the extent of Toscanini's fame decree that there can be no shortage of commemorative material. In the reception area on the ground floor the walls are generously lined with framed documents, certificates, diplomas, awards and the like, and a showcase displays medallions; handbills from Toscanini's years at La Scala (chiefly the 1920s) fill the corridor and in the rear courtyard stands a bronze figure of the maestro with a charming bust of his daughter Wanda as a child. Many of these items are not official awards but tokens of esteem and affection from the musicians he worked with. They continue up the staircase.

The room where Toscanini is believed to have been born is the heart of the museum, filled with relics from all parts of his life, personal as well as professional. There are several oil portraits, including ones of Verdi and Catalani as well as Toscanini himself and his wife. One showcase commemorates his marriage, with the gifts he and his wife exchanged; others note his connections with the great composers of the day (Debussy, Leoncavallo, Puccini, Ravel, Strauss), with letters and photographs, or the festivals at which he conducted – through his Bayreuth connection the museum has a goblet, a pair of glasses and a foulard that were once Wagner's. The Verdi links are of course strongly represented too, including a death mask. There are more awards of all sorts and numerous photographs, some formal, some family.

In the rear first-floor rooms are a collection of his own batons along with presentation ones, and various personal items – his poncho, his smoking jacket and his dressing-gown, his dress clothes and his walking-sticks. A life mask, a death mask and a bronze cast of his hands are in the former kitchen, with a series of caricatures of him, some of them drawn by Caruso. The second floor is given over to listening and viewing space; some of the material here comes from the collection of Toscanini's favourite tenor, Aureliano Pertile, and there are also items from the baritone Giuseppe Valdengo. The museum has various items of furniture from Toscanini's homes in Milan and New York (he also had a villa on a small island in the middle of Lake Maggiore), given or loaned by his family; his annotated scores and other archival material remained in New York after his death there in 1957, preserved at the Public Library, and his collection of batons is displayed in the Rose Museum at Carnegie Hall.

His Milan study went to the conservatory in Parma where he had been a student. Originally a Carmelite monastery, it is now the Conservatorio di Musica 'Arrigo Boito'. The study is preserved, alongside Boito's, in a specific museum area on the second floor of the inner courtyard. It is faithfully reproduced, with his desk and chair, his fine collection of bookcases (housing a wide range of literature), armchairs, a coffee table, the Steinway piano presented to him by Vladimir Horowitz in 1934 (when Horowitz married his daughter Wanda), a bust of Verdi and a statuette of Puccini, many signed photographs, his scores of

Falstaff, Pizzetti's *Debora e Jaèle* and Boito's *Nerone*. There are oils of Toscanini and his wife, copies of ones at the birthplace, with a death mask and a cast of his hands. There is a further commemoration of Toscanini in the Verdi museum at the Casa Barezzi in Busseto (*see* VERDI).

Casa natale Arturo Toscanini

Borgo Rodolfo Tanzi 13
43100 Parma
Italy

phone +390/0 521 285499
e-mail luberto@biblcom.unipr.it

open Tuesday–Saturday 10.00–13.00, 15.00–18.00, Sunday 10.00–13.00

Museo Storico 'Ricardo Barilla'

Conservatorio di musica 'Arrigo Boito'
Via Conservatorio 27
43100 Parma
Italy

phone +390/0 521 381958
fax +390/0 521 200398
e-mail ssboito@provincia.parma.it

open Tuesday 09.00–14.00, 15.00–19.30, Wednesday 09.00–14.00, 15.00–17.30, also by appointment

Map 9

G.N. Vetro: *Arturo Toscanini alla scuola del Carmine in Parma (1876–1885)* [Musica a Parma, 8] (Parma: Conservatorio di Musica 'Arrigo Boito', 1974)
G.N. Vetro: *Il giovane Toscanini* (Parma: Banco del Monte di Parma, 1982) [with illustrations of the birthplace]
Casa Toscanini: a Short Guide to the Museum (Parma: Comune di Parma, Grafiche Step Editrice, 1990)

TOSTI

The title 'Tosti's Goodbye' will have some resonances for older readers of this book. But the name of Sir Francesco Paolo Tosti is less familiar now than it was a century ago. Born in 1846 in Ortona, in the Abruzzo, he studied in Naples, with Mercadante among others. Back in Ortona, he sang for a time in the cathe-

dral of St Thomas the Apostle; later he moved to Ancona and then (in 1870) Rome, where he was helped by D'Annunzio and Sgambati and became singing teacher to Princess Margherita of Savoy, later Queen of Italy. His career was initially as lyric tenor, teacher, organist and pianist. Composition came later, and many of his songs – 'Ideale', 'Marechiare', 'La serenata', 'L'ultima canzone' – soon became, and still remain, firm favourites among lyric tenors.

Tosti first visited London in 1875. Five years later he had settled there, as singing teacher to the royal family; he was a particular favourite of Queen Victoria's and arranged many of her musical evenings. He also taught at both the Royal Academy of Music and the Royal College. He lived mainly in the West End, in a flat in what is now the Mandeville Hotel, just off Wigmore Street, where there is a commemorative green plaque. His many songs, essentially ballads for voice and piano infused with an Italian charm and lyrical warmth, were much loved in England. In 1906 he became a British subject, to please his friend Edward VII, and two years later he accepted a knighthood. But after the king's death there was nothing to keep him in England and he retired to Rome, where he died in 1916.

Tosti is fondly remembered in his native town. Ortona is a small port on the Adriatic, just south of Pescara. Like more than threequarters of the town, the house in which he was born was destroyed in World War II. But he is commemorated, principally at the Palazzo Corvo, which stands in the main road, Corso Matteotti, leading from the central Piazza della Repubblica towards the sea. Since 1994 this building has housed the Biblioteca Musicale Abruzzese and a centre for research on the music of the Abruzzo as well as the Istituto Nazionale Tostiano, which, founded in 1983, holds a substantial Tosti archive and supervises the Tosti museum set up in the Palazzo in 1994. Until 2003 the museum consisted of a single room, but with the acquisition of many of Lady Tosti's personal memen-

Tosti displays at Ortona

toes, through the donation of her nephew, and of items held by Tosti's own nephew, it was then redesigned and moved to two larger rooms on a higher floor.

One room is a handsome reconstruction of a drawing-room-cum-studio of Tosti's time, using his own furniture and original portraits. The other is a display room, attractively and imaginatively laid out, with a wide range of exhibits to outline the life of a man who was clearly benign and well-loved. There are photographs of Tosti's family and his colleagues, drawings and caricatures (by artists as diverse as Spy, Caruso and Beerbohm), and a variety of documents, including English newspaper cuttings, invitations to royal events, and telegrams to his widow on his death from Queen Alexandra, Puccini, Leoncavallo, Mascagni, Cilea and D'Annunzio among others. Several of his manuscripts are shown as well as printed copies of many of his songs, often with attractive *Art Nouveau* title-pages, among them early Ricordi editions (Giulio Ricordi was a close friend and Tosti helped the firm in London) as well as that firm's new edition of his songs (to Italian, English and French texts), currently being published in 14 volumes under the editorship of the Istituto. There are a number of personal possessions, and a wooden model of the monument by a local sculptor, a bust in which Tosti is encircled by the Muses, put up near the harbour in Ortona in 1927. In

1960 Tosti's remains were brought to Ortona from Rome and he was reburied in a place of honour near the entrance to the town cemetery, with a further model of the bust on his tomb.

The museum also holds archives of the local composer Guido Albanese and the baritone Giuseppe De Luca, whose costumes and other personal items are shown in a smaller display room.

Istituto Nazionale Tostiano
Palazzo Corvo
Corso Matteotti 83
66026 Ortona CH
Italy

phone +390/0 85 906 6310
fax +390/0 85 906 5099
e-mail istost@tin.it

open Monday–Saturday 09.00–13.00, 15.00–19.00 (in summer from 16.00 indefinitely, up to midnight)

Map 9

F. Sanvitale: *A Song of a Life* (Ortona: Menabò, 1996)
F. Sanvitale, ed.: *"O dolce meraviglia! . . .": catalogo delle "Sale Tosti" del Museo Musicale d'Abruzzo* (Ortona: Istituto Nazionale Tostiano, 2003)

TÜRK

Daniel Gottlob Türk (1750–1813) is commemorated by his adopted city of Halle because of the nurturing role he played in the musical life of the city, as Kantor of the Ulrichskirche from 1774 and later director of music at the university, and from 1787 organist and director of music at the Liebfrauenkirche. At Christmastime in 1803 he conducted a performance of Handel's *Messiah*, inaugurating a tradition that still continues.

He was a friend of Reichardt and the teacher of Loewe, both also represented in the second-floor rooms of the Händel-Haus. He was a writer as well as a composer, and lectured on music history. Copies of his music – his 1782 Christmas cantata *Die Hirten bey der Krippe zu Bethlehem*, and his widely used *Clavierschule* (1789) along with examples of his piano sonatas (he published 15 collections) – are on display in Room 5, presided over by a bronze bust by Gottfried Albert.

Händel-Haus

Grosse Nikolaistraße 5
06108 Halle (Saale)
Germany

phone +49/0 345 500900
fax +49/0 345 50090 411
e-mail haendelhaus@halle.de
website www.haendelhaus.de

open daily 09.30–17.30 (Thursday to 19.00)

Map 7

K. Musketa: *Musikgeschichte der Stadt Halle: Führer durch die Ausstellung des Händel-Hauses* (Halle an der Saale: Händel-Haus, 1998), 41–4

ULLMANN

Viktor Ullmann was the senior figure among the Jewish Czech composers imprisoned in the Nazi transit camp at Terezín. He entered the camp in 1942, spent two years there and died in Auschwitz in October 1944. Born in Český Těšín in 1898, he went to study law in Vienna, when he decided to enter Schoenberg's composition classes; he worked as a conductor at the German Theatre in Prague, in Ústi nad Labem and in Zürich and had several successes with chamber and orchestral works at international festivals and in Prague (where he taught and was active as writer and broadcaster) and elsewhere.

In Terezín, Ullmann was involved in the organization of musical activities, with responsibility for rehearsal and practice; he was also active in the management of the Studio für Neue Musik and wrote criticisms of the performances. He was however more prolific as a composer during this period than he had been in the years preceding; his Terezín output included song cycles, three piano sonatas (some may be reductions of orchestral works), a string quartet, an opera and many choral arrangements of Hebrew and Yiddish songs. The opera, *Der Kaiser von Atlantis*, in one act, embodies allegorical comment on Nazism; it was written for the forces Ullmann had available, with five singers and 13 instruments. The première was scheduled for late autumn 1944 but before it could take place many of those involved were sent to Auschwitz. The score however was preserved and the work was first given in Amsterdam in 1975.

The Ullmann display in the Magdeburg Barracks in Terezín (*see* KRÁSA), the most extensive one there devoted to a composer, includes an ink portrait, photographs, posters, facsimiles of letters written by Ullmann from the camp and a handwritten review, and several facsimiles of his compositions, including the String Quartet, the piano sonatas and several songs.

Magdeburg Barracks

Památník Terezín
41155 Terezín
Czech Republic

phone +420/0 416 782948, 782949
e-mail manager@pamatnik-terezin.cz
website www.pamatnik-terezin.cz

open April–September, daily 09.00–18.00; October–March, daily 09.00–17.30

Map 4

J. Karas: *Music in Terezín 1941–1945*
  (Stuyvesant, NY: Pendragon, 1985)

VAINIŪNAS

In 1998 a flat in Vilnius, in a building overlooking the river Neris, became a memorial to Stasyš Vainiūnas, who lived there and died in 1982 at the age of 73. Inspired by his daughter the pianist Birutė Vainiūnaitė (who lives in the same block), and funded by the Foundation for the Support of Lithuanian Musicians, the remodelled flat has facilities to seat 40 for piano and chamber music recitals. The recital room is dominated by a portrait (1948) of the composer and the Steinway miniature grand Vainiūnas acquired from Gruodis's widow in 1952.

Head of the piano faculty at Vilnius Conservatory, Vainiūnas was also a prolific composer for his instrument and chairman of the Lithuanian Composers' Union. His flat is now used as a meeting-place for musicians. There is a small exhibition in the composer's study.

Stasio Vainiūno namai
Goštauto 2–41
2600 Vilnius
Lithuania

phone +370/0 2 616754

open Monday–Friday 09.00–17.00

Map 2

VAMVAKARIS

Markos Vamvakaris (1905–72) was one of the leading composers in the genre of *rebetika*, urban low-life music which flourished in the early decades of the 20th century, particularly after the Greek-Turkish war of 1919–22. Born on the Aegean island of Syros, Vamvakaris worked in the Piraeus area in the 1930s and 40s, singing and playing the bouzouki (the Greek long-necked lute) in clubs; later his music became more fashionable and he played in smarter clubs in Athens. His Piraeus Quartet was the prototype for

later *rebetiko* ensembles. He faded from sight thereafter, partly for political reasons, but with the revival of *rebetika* in the 1970s his compositions came to be regarded as classics of the genre and he was dubbed 'the father of *rebetika*'.

He is commemorated in a house on his native island. The Vamvakaris Museum was inaugurated in 1986, in the square named after him at Ano Syros, near the island's capital, Hermoupolis. It consists of a hall and a single room; the exhibits, provided by his family, include various personal items, photographs and recordings.

Markos Vamvakaris Museum*
Plateia Markou Vamvakari
Ano Syros
84100 Syros
Greece

phone +30/0 2810 85159

open daily 11.00–13.30, 19.00–22.00

VAUGHAN WILLIAMS

Ralph Vaughan Williams was born in 1872 in rural Gloucestershire, in the southern Cotswolds. Those who hear the ancestral dialects of the West Country in his music, however, should not put it down to his birth: the family came from London and nearby, and in 1875, when he was three – after the death of his father, vicar at Down Ampney – he went to live in Surrey, at his mother's family home, Leith Hill Place, near Dorking. He lived there or in London for the rest of his life, from 1928 to 1953 at a house in Leith Hill called White Gates, which no longer stands; his London house, in (aptly enough) Gloucester Crescent, NW1, where his widow continued to live long after his death in 1958, is close to Cecil Sharp House, the headquarters of the English Folk Dance and Song Society.

He is not, however, forgotten in Down Ampney. The Old Vicarage, a large house in the centre of the village, bears an inscription, and under the spire of the church, on the edge of the village, there has since 2001 been a display, a series of five boards on which his life is related and his musical output charted, with apt illustration. In the church too is a window in memory of his father, who is buried close by in the churchyard.

There is another set of the boards in Surrey, with an additional display on White Gates, showing his study and the lofty galleried room he used for choir rehearsals. A part of the building at the Denbies vineyard, just off the A24 on the north side of Dorking, forms the Surrey Performing Arts Library. There since 2002 a first-floor room has been largely given over to the commemoration of Vaughan Williams, who did so much for both the musical and the communal life of the area, particularly as conductor of the Leith Hill Musical Festival from its foundation (by his sister) in 1905 until 1953. As part of a working public library, the room is not exclusive to Vaughan Williams – there are shelves with other material, a table for meetings, and it is sometimes used for lectures. But it contains a comprehensive collection of Vaughan Williams books, music and recordings, and there is a group of display cases that usually holds exhibits relevant to him, changed regularly and put together from the library's resources and the collection of the Vaughan Williams Society. One exhibition, for example, was devoted to local contributions to the war effort in both world wars, with many of Vaughan Williams's letters, some referring to the World War II fire-watching rotas that he managed, with a set of firewatcher's equipment (helmet and stirrup pump), alongside information about his own compositions of the time and copies of some of them. A separate display case holds books, scores (some with annotations) and a small bust. The long-term intention is to build up the collection and, if space permits, to expand it. But the likelihood of acquiring primary material is small as his manuscripts are mostly deposited in the British Library.

VW is also remembered at the concert venue, Dorking Halls, with a plaque and a statue of him, baton in hand – except when 'borrowed' by the local rowdies.

All Saints Church
Down Ampney
Cirencester
Gloucestershire GL7 5QW
Great Britain

phone +44/0 1285 860221 (local ministry)

open in church hours and by appointment

Vaughan Williams Room
Surrey Performing Arts Library
Denbies
London Road
Dorking
Surrey RH5 6AA
Great Britain

phone +44/0 1306 875453
e-mail performing.arts@surreycc.gov.uk

open Tuesday, Friday 10.00–17.00; Thursday 10.00–20.00; Saturday 09.30–13.00

Map 5

VERDI

The museums and memorials that commemorate Verdi cover, literally, from his birth to his death, as befits the greatest and most beloved of Italian composers. The last of them apart, all lie in a relatively small area, that part of the country within a triangle whose vertices are Cremona in the north, Piacenza in the west and Parma in the south-east.

The actual place of his birth was the village of Roncole – now called Roncole Verdi – some five kilometres south of the town of Busseto. Verdi always insisted on his peasant origins, from an illiterate family; in fact he came from a line of small landowners and tradespeople, and his father, Carlo, kept the local inn, which served too as village shop and post office.

There is some question about the actual house of his birth. The most comprehensive of Verdi's biographers,

Mary Jane Phillips-Matz, holds that he was born in the Osteria Vecchia, in the centre of Roncole, a house built in 1695 which the family leased and occupied from 1791 to 1830; half of that house still stands, and exactly matches a 1729 description of the property in the Fidenza diocesan archives and Carlo Verdi's lease renewal of 1827. Others are content to accept what the plaque, put up in 1872 on the 'official birthplace', a house standing at a junction on the road between Cremona and Fidenza, proclaims: 'Questo abituro dove il 10 Ottobre 1813 la prima aura spiró il musical genio del VERDI' ('In this dwelling on 10 October 1813 the musical genius of Verdi took its first breath'). Although Verdi himself, perhaps not the most dependable witness, had a picture of that house at his villa, Sant'Agata, he denied that he was born there; he was born, he said, in a different house nearby, 'burned down by the Russians' – which seems to represent a confusion with another incident of his early years, when the area was invaded by the armies fighting Napoleon.

It is the official birthplace in which he is commemorated. The property belonged to the Pallavicino family, who later gave it to the Busseto municipality. The Verdi family would have moved out in the 1840s, to the farm Giuseppe had recently bought outside Roncole and then to his new villa at Sant'Agata. The Pallavicinos put up the 1872 plaque. The house was declared a national monument in 1901, just after Verdi's death, when a further plaque was installed (given by the poor of Roncole who had benefited from Verdi's gifts), and in 1913 a bronze bust by G. Cantù was placed in the garden; in 1962 it became a museum and in 2000 it was refurbished for the centenary.

Its supposed organization as an inn and coaching house, and family home, is clearly shown. On the ground floor, there is a north-facing room that would have been the pantry and wine store, and an indoor stable where the pigs, rabbits and chickens would have been kept. The front room, where the original ceiling and doors survive, is set out as a dining-room and kitchen. What is now the admissions office was the village shop. No original furniture survives; the items there now are made from modern poplar but using period working techniques. Upstairs is largely empty; one room may have been used for tavern stocks, another for breeding the silkworms that were a necessity for the trade of Verdi's mother, who did weaving to augment the family income. In the room remembered as Verdi's parents' bedroom, and consequently the likeliest room of his birth, there is a straw mattress and a plaque above the bed; a darker room overlooking the stable is the one supposed to have served for Verdi and his young sister, and a rear room would have housed passing guests. The whole interior is painted with lime wash, as it would have been in Verdi's day.

Close to the house is the medieval church, San Michele Arcangelo, where Verdi was baptized and where as a child he played the organ; the instrument he would have used dates from 1797 and has been restored a number of times, most recently in 1964.

Roncole falls within the administrative area of Busseto, now a town of some 40,000, and the Verdi town *par excellence*. It has a Piazza Verdi, dominated since the 1913 centenary by a bronze sculpture of the maestro, the work of Luigi Secchi. On one side of it is the Teatro Verdi, built as a tribute to him in the 1850s and 60s; Verdi gave money, and owned a box, but

Verdi's official birthplace, Roncole

was opposed to the idea of building a new theatre and absented himself conspicuously from the opening in his honour and never set foot in it. Seating 300, it is anyway too small to take his operas comfortably. Verdi lived in the town for much of his life. Two of his homes there have been museums.

One is the Casa Barezzi, the house that belonged to Antonio Barezzi, a rich merchant and music lover, Verdi's first and most generous patron and father of his first wife, Margherita. Verdi spent several years in the house as a young man and was conscious of the depth of his debt to Barezzi, whom he regarded as a second father. Owned and now loaned by a local bank, it was refitted for the 2001 centenary and reopened as the Museo Verdiano di Casa Barezzi. The contents, from a collection assembled by a former Busseto mayor, Gianfranco Stefanini, were presented to the Amici di Verdi, the organization responsible for the museum.

Even before Verdi's time, the main salon was used for musical events, and it still is, for concerts and conferences: a lofty blue room, seating about 100, with a fine stucco ceiling and an elegant parquet floor. The Tomaschek piano that Verdi used when composing during his time here, and which he was playing when in 1867 Barezzi was dying in the next room, is there, though not in playing condition (there is a modern concert grand too). There are portraits, of Barezzi and Margherita among others, a Verdi death mask and a cast of his hand.

In the rooms running alongside the salon is a series of attractive displays, thematically organized. The first deals with the young Verdi, with a portrait from the time of his marriage to Margherita (who died in 1840, aged 26), documents, including his first La Scala commission and letters, and autographs of pieces he wrote as a pupil of the Busseto organist Ferdinando Provesi. One alcove is devoted to Emanuele Muzio, the conductor and composer, also a protégé of Barezzi's and later Verdi's only pupil, another to the concerts of the

Società Filarmonica Busseto, founded in 1816 and run by Barezzi.

Giuseppina Strepponi, the singer, Verdi's loving companion in Busseto (to the dismay of the locals) and later his wife, is represented by a portrait and prints, and by their marriage certificate and Verdi's letters to her. There are portraits of the older Verdi, among them one of 1887 by Francesco Paolo Michetti, sketches by the publisher Ricordi of Verdi and Boito, a model for a monument proposed for Trieste, posters for the initial productions at the Teatro Verdi in 1868 (*Rigoletto* and *Un ballo in maschera*) and a collection of prints of singers who created Verdi roles. The long table at which Verdi and the Barezzis celebrated his marriage to Margherita is also there, and one display is devoted to Verdi's death – his obituaries and the public ceremonies surrounding his funeral, his burial and his final interment in the Casa di Riposo in Milan. A smaller room is given over to Toscanini and his Verdian activities in Busseto, the original manuscript of Gabriele d'Annunzio's 'Il morte di Giuseppe Verdi', and the 2001 centenary celebrations at La Scala under Riccardo Muti.

A short distance down the Via Roma from the Casa Barezzi is the Palazzo Orlandi. On a visit to Busseto in 1845, Verdi bought a house from a former mayor and musical patron in the town, Contardo Cavalli; it was known as the Palazzo Cavalli and had earlier been called the Palazzo Dordoni. He moved in, with Strepponi, in the summer of 1849, and he lived there – although he was away a great deal, mostly for opera premières and revivals – until the autumn of 1853. Among the operas he composed there are *Rigoletto* and *Il trovatore*. Verdi installed his father in the house, where he died in 1867; he later sold it to Strepponi, who after his death sold it (for the benefit of the needy of Busseto) to the Orlandi family. It was eventually opened as a Verdi museum: it housed in the main first-floor salon a Pleyel grand piano, claimed as Strepponi's, as well as busts and contemporary clothing, a collection

Salon of the Verdi flat in the Palazzo Orlandi, Busseto

of batons that belonged to various conductors, and some personal items (books, umbrellas, top hats, a cape) said to be Verdi's. There are photographs and pictures in the dining-room, and a further narrow room, in which it is thought that Strepponi made lace, has a number of facsimiles and photographs including one, along with a bust, of Teresa Stolz, the leading Verdi soprano of the 1960s and 70s, who was for a time

close to the composer. In poor condition, the museum ceased functioning soon after the Verdi centenary and in 2005 was offered for sale.

On the southern edge of Busseto, close to the approach from Roncole, lies the Villa Pallavicino, once the home of the local noble, property-owning family. This sumptuous 16th-century palace, the most splendid in the region, moated and with elegant balustrades, has been the Busseto Museo Civico since 1959. It formerly displayed many of the items now in the Casa Barezzi. The museum was closed after the 2001 centenary for complete refurbishment; rumour has it that 27 rooms will be available, and the coincidence of that figure with the number of operas Verdi composed (at least by one way of reckoning) has suggested a room-by-room, opera-by-opera display.

From Roncole, through Busseto, Verdi pilgrims can pursue the maestro by taking the road northwards to Cremona: soon, after about three kilometres, they will reach Sant'Agata, his home for almost 50 years. Since the end of the 16th century the Verdi family had owned land in the area of Sant'Agata di Villanova sull'Arda (across the river Ongina, and so in the Piacenza rather than the Parma province), and Verdi had long cherished the ambition of 'reclaiming' the family territory. He bought a farm there in 1848 and soon started transforming the farm-house into a spacious villa. His parents moved there in 1851 and he and

Villa Pallavicino, Busseto

Verdi's villa at Sant'Agata

Giuseppina soon followed. The house is still owned by the Carrara Verdi family, his heirs through his adopted daughter Filomena Maria.

The parts of it that form a museum, essentially the ground floor of the main building, can be seen only on guided tours, which take some 45 minutes (English ones are available by prior arrangement). Visitors can do no more than peer through the windows at some areas, unaided by lighting, for example the ceremonial and elaborately furnished Sala Rosa in which Verdi received his visitors. The rooms are not large. In Strepponi's bedroom, where in 1897 she died, the furniture is in Genovese Baroque style, inlaid, the bed heavily canopied, with her bust (1842) at the end. There is a portrait of Verdi in old age and one of the two of them in the 1860s, a portrait too of their dog (Lulù, buried in the gardens) and their pet parrot. On one wall is a Falstaff painting by the designer of the 1893 première of Verdi's opera. Bronze figurines of Manzoni and Verdi stand above the fireplace, and on the walls are a pair of landscapes attributed to Salvator Rosa. A piano that had belonged to Strepponi's father, who was a *maestro di cappella*, which Verdi used in the 1850s and 60s, stands in her dressing-room. Busts of Verdi, Ponchielli and Catalani take their place along with the pet parrot and a pheasant, stuffed. Some of Strepponi's stage costumes are there; so is the case that Verdi took on the journey to St Petersburg for the première of *La forza del destino*. There are bookcases and on the walls are prints of singers.

Verdi's own bedroom was also his working room. In it, besides his bed, are his piano (an 1870 Erard grand), his desk, his library (miniature scores of Viennese classical string quartets, dictionaries, the works of Dante, Shakespeare, Milton and Byron and much else), busts, paintings and a display case showing his commemorative medals and the white gloves he wore when conducting the Requiem. In the archive room are display cases with documents – some of them concerned with his polit-

ical activities (among them a letter from Cavour), others with the estate, and his original, unsuccessful application for entry to Milan Conservatory – as well as portraits and photographs and some personal objects.

The final room records Verdi's death, on 27 January 1901: a re-creation of the room in the Hotel Grand et de Milan in which he died, though on a much smaller scale. The hotel donated the bed and other furniture to the Casa di Riposo that Verdi set up in Milan, from where it passed on to Sant'Agata in 1932 (for illustration of the room see p.6). The shirt he was wearing is there too, with a death mask, an impression of his hand, and the last portrait photographs of Verdi and Strepponi.

The tour of the house takes in a walk round the large garden, which Verdi himself planned, past the wine store and the carriage house along the side of the villa, down the avenues of poplars and other trees (which include a number of exotic imported ones, such as the Chinese ginkgo), past the ice-house, the grotto and Lulù's grave, to the miniature lake with its three bridges. (For illustration of the carriages and the grotto, see pp.42 and 51.)

Verdi is of course commemorated all over Italy: most towns have at least a Via or Piazza Verdi, several have a Teatro Verdi. The large city closest to the Busseto district is Parma, home of the Istituto di Studi Verdiani, where the conservatory, named after Verdi's friend and collaborator Arrigo Boito, has memorial rooms to Boito, Pizzetti and Toscanini; there is also a museum at the birthplace of Toscanini, Verdi's greatest interpreter (*see* BOITO and TOSCANINI). A Casa di Musica, established at the Palazzo Cusani in 2002, now accommodates the Istituto and the archive of the Teatro Regio, with material on the reception of Verdi in Parma and audiovisual facilities where Verdi operas can be seen and heard. By the Palazzo Pilotta is what must surely be the largest monument to any composer, a bas-relief in bronze, representing events to do with Verdi's patriotic activities, in which he is surrounded by allegorical figures.

In Milan, too, Verdi is celebrated. He is the dominant figure among the composers commemorated in the La Scala museum, which returned to the renovated opera house in 2005 after three years in a temporary home. It is rich in Verdiana: two whole rooms are devoted to Verdi, with numerous photos and portraits of him, Strepponi and his singers, several autograph manuscripts including some very early works and the Requiem, his first piano (a square of 1832), his armchair, his passport, his pocket watch, a bracelet he gave to Strepponi, a death mask and a plaster cast of his right hand, as well as medals and other honours.

Close to the opera house, just along the Via Manzoni, is the Hotel Grand et de Milan, where Verdi died. His actual room, the 'Sala Verdi', Suite 105, is now used for receptions and other purposes, and is not of course as it was, but it is maintained as a memorial and visitors who ask to see it are taken up. The furnishing, contemporary with Verdi, includes a black carved desk and there is a print of La Scala and of course a portrait of Verdi. The Casa di Riposo per Musicisti Fondazione Giuseppe Verdi, the retirement home for musicians that Verdi established and endowed in 1899, is a short bus ride away, at Piazza Buonarroti; Boito and Toscanini are among those who further endowed it. There are two rooms containing Verdi items. One is a barrel-vaulted dining-room, with a suite

of furniture from Verdi's home during his French years, acquired originally by Strepponi, taken to Genoa and given to the Casa by Ricordi (a table, eight chairs, a dresser, sideboards); the other room has a large Verdi portrait of 1886 by Boldini and a deathbed portrait by Stragliati, a glass case with Verdi's 'spinet', and several other busts and portraits, of Barezzi and Strepponi as well as Verdi himself. Between the two rooms is a glass case with Verdi's evening clothes. Visitors are welcome; Verdi's grave, in which he was interred on 26 February 1901, with Strepponi, is not of course in the chapel (he was a non-believer) but close to it; a fine statue of him stands outside in the centre of the piazza.

Casa Natale Giuseppe Verdi
Roncole Verdi
43011 Busseto (Parma)
Italy

phone +390/0 524 97450

open April–September, Tuesday–Sunday
09.30–12.30, 15.00–19.00;
October–March, Tuesday–Sunday
09.30–12.30, 14.30–17.30

Museo Verdiano di Casa Barezzi
via Roma 119
43011 Busseto (Parma)
Italy

phone, fax +390/0 524 931117
e-mail amicidiverdi@hotmail.com
website www.amicidiverdi.it

open Tuesday–Sunday 10.00–12.30,
15.00–18.30

Museo dei Cimeli Verdiani
Palazzo Orlandi
via Roma 56
43011 Busseto (Parma)
Italy

phone +390/0 524 97508

closed for the time being

Museo Civico
Villa Pallavicino
43011 Busseto (Parma)
Italy

The Casa di Riposo per Musicisti Fondazione Giuseppe Verdi, Milan

phone +390/0 524 92487, 931624
(Busseto Tourist Office)
fax +390/0 524 931740
e-mail info@bussetolive.com
website www.bussetolive.com

closed for the time being

Villa Verdi
via Verdi 22
29010 Sant'Agata Villanova sull'Arda
(Piacenza)
Italy

phone +390/0 523 830000
fax +390/0 523 830700
e-mail info@villaverdi.org
website www.villaverdi.org

open 27 January–March,
Tuesday–Sunday 09.30–12.30,
14.30–17.30; April–September,
Tuesday–Sunday 09.00–11.45,
15.00–18.45; October, Tuesday–Sunday
09.00–11.45, 15.00–18.45; closed
November– 26 January; guided tours only

Grand Hotel et de Milan
via Manzoni 29
20121 Milano
Italy

phone +390/0 2272 3141
fax +390/0 28646 0861
e-mail infos@grandhoteletdemilan.it
website www.grandhoteletdemilan.it

open always

Casa di Riposo di Musicisti Fondazione Giuseppe Verdi
Piazza Buonarroti 29
20149 Milano
Italy

phone +390/0 2499 6009
e-mail casaverdi@tiscali.net
website www.casaverdi.org

open daily 08.30–12.30, 14.30–18.30

Map 9

M.J. Phillips-Matz: *Verdi: a Biography* (Oxford and New York: Oxford University Press, 1993)

C. Mingardi: *Con Verdi nella sua terra* (Busseto: Amici di Verdi, 1994)

M.C. Alfieri and M. Fornari: *Verdi: guida ai luoghi verdiani* (Bologna: Italcards, n.d.)

Museo teatrale alla Scala: an Illustrated Guide (Milan: Museo Teatrale alla Scala, 1997)

N. Simeone: *Paris: a Musical Gazetteer* (New Haven and London: Yale University Press, 2000)

M. Maestrelli: *Villa Verdi: guida alla villa e al parco* (Parma: Villa Verdi, 2001)

C. Mingardi: *Verdi and his Land: Busseto, Roncole, Sant'Agata* (Milan: Franco Maria Ricci, 2001)

VEREMANS

The Flemish city of Lier, 17 km south of Antwerp, is proud of its artistic heritage and in particular is widely known as a centre of lace-making and embroidery. In 1968 the Hof van Geetruyen, on the river Nete, was opened to the public as a civic museum celebrating local creative artists – writers, artists and musicians as well as a clockmaker and a blacksmith. The new museum was named after the writer and illustrator Felix Timmermans and the painter Isidoor Opsomer: the Timmermans-Opsomerhuis. One room on the first floor is now devoted to local musicians, pre-eminent among them the composer Renaat Veremans, who was born in Lier in 1894 and died in Antwerp in 1969.

Veremans served for many years as head of the Koninklijke Vlaamse Opera and later as director of the Stedelijk Conservatorium at Bruges. In 1938 he composed an opera to a text by Timmermans, *Anna-Marie* (1921), and later he edited a volume of *Herinnerungen ann Felix Timmermans*. On display are photographs, portraits and busts of Veremans, his 1867 grand piano and some of his personal effects, including a lyre tie-pin, his glasses, a baton in its case and his *Liber amicorum* up to 1959.

The room is lined with information panels about Veremans as well as other Lier musicians: Jaak Opsomer (1873–1952), elder brother of the artist; Paul van

Wassenhoven (1877–1953), organist at Sint Gummaruskerk and one of Veremans's first teachers; and Frans Boogaerts (1888–1950), director of the Stedelijke Muziekacademie in Lier.

Timmermans-Opsomerhuis
Netelaan 4
2500 Lier
Belgium

phone +32/0 3480 1196

open April–October, Thursday, Saturday–Tuesday 10.00–12.00, 13.30–17.30; November–March, Sundays only 10.00–12.00, 13.30–17.30

Map 3

VIDU

The town of Lugoj in western Romania, about 60 km east of Timişoara, is the country's main provincial centre of choral music. It possesses a Casa Personalităţilor, a house in which leading people from the city (including a dozen musicians) are commemorated, and also a Casa Muzicii, a house of musicians, in which the lives and achievements of several local musicians are celebrated, as too are the visits to Lugoj of a number of other leading Romanian composers including Ciprian Porumbescu and George Enescu. A commemorative house of musicians was first set up in 1925 and became a museum in 1968; it moved to its present premises, the former house of the composer Filaret Barbu, across the river from the main part of Lugoj, in 1985.

The biggest of the individual displays is devoted to Ion Vidu, who was born near Arad in 1863, worked in Lugoj from 1888 until his death there in 1931 and was primarily responsible for the town's development as a musical centre. He composed and arranged a quantity of choral music, much of it linked with Romanian folk music. Two of the alcoves in the main room on the ground floor are devoted to Vidu and his achievements:

one has material on older traditions and folk music along with photographs, transcriptions and publications by him, and the next is concerned with his choir, the Corul Ion Vidu, its foundation and early history. The first room on the upper floor is dedicated to him too – his desk is there, with a death mask, diplomas and photographs, as well as his Edison cylinder player and a large record player. Another room is given over to the choir and its continuing activities, showing its numerous awards, medals and banners. (*See also* Barbu *and* Brediceanu.)

Casa Muzicii
Strada Magnoliei 10
1800 Lugoj
Timiş
Romania

phone +40/0 256 354903
website www.infotim.ro/patrimcb/tm/lugj/muzieap/casamuz

open 15 May–14 October, daily 09.00–17.00; 15 October–14 May, daily 08.00–16.00

Map 11

VĪTOLS

Just as Liszt was accorded a grace and favour home in the Budapest Music Academy for his contribution to Hungarian music, so was Jāzeps Vītols, for his to Latvian music – but he was offered an entire estate. It was in the village of Gaujīena, in north-eastern Latvia, some 160 km from Riga. Vītols thought the estate, which had belonged to the beer baron Von Wulf, rather too grand, but he accepted accommodation in what had been the brewer's house, along with the land surrounding it, which included a pond and a kitchen garden. He and his wife spent the summers and Christmas holidays there from 1922 until 1944, often with family, friends and students. Vītols liked to work on the balcony above the front door, where he could survey the pond and the park and (no doubt) welcome visitors.

The brewer's house, where Vītols lived, at Gaujīena

The Gauja Manor, set in parkland, now houses the local secondary school. To find the brewer's house, which is open to the public as a memorial to Vītols, it is best to enquire at the school (no-one at the post office, curiously, seemed to know where it might be) – providing of course that it is term-time. It is on the southern side of the village, just beyond the church.

Vītols is generally regarded as the father of Latvian music; but for years he could scarcely be mentioned in Latvia, much less commemorated. In 1944, elderly and ill, he had fled the Soviet army, to take into exile the children of some of his relatives who had been sent to Siberia. He died in Lübeck on 24 April 1948. The school authorities decided, nevertheless, to mark the centenary of his birth (26 July 1863) by making the brewer's house into a museum: they began collecting Vītoliana and the opening was celebrated with two days of concerts and visits from former pupils. As well as the house, visitors can see a derelict bathhouse that Vītols had built on the water's edge and, on the hill above, a garden house built as a present for him by his wife.

In 1988 the brewer's house, of wood, burnt to the ground; but the exhibits were saved. The house was immediately rebuilt and the reconstruction was opened in time for the celebrations of Vītols's 125th

anniversary. An outdoor amphitheatre was then inaugurated with a day-long song festival, which is now an annual event. The exhibition chronicles Vītols's life – his studies with Rimsky-Korsakov in St Petersburg, where he too became a professor of composition at the conservatory (his pupils included the young Prokofiev and Myaskovsky); his stint as a music critic of the *St Petersburger Zeitung*; his return to Riga on Latvian independence in 1918 as first director of the Latvian Opera; his role as founder of the Latvian Conservatory (now Academy of Music); his influence through his many Latvian pupils; and his music, which included the first Latvian symphony, many chamber works and most importantly choral music (his *Castle of Light* is traditionally sung at the annual Riga Song Festival). A few of his possessions survive, among which his identity and calling cards, honours and awards, binoculars and playing cards are on display. The information panels are assemblages of facsimile photographs and documents.

Though not strictly open to the public, Vītols's study may be visited at the Latvian Academy of Music in Riga; it is preserved much as he left it in 1944, with his desk, his library, his notebooks, his folksong transcriptions, photographs and personal items such as his walking-stick and his clock (a gift from his students). The adjacent room is still used for composition seminars.

Jāzepa Vītola Memoriâlais Muzejs

Anniņas
Alūksnes rajons
4339 Gaujīenas pagasts
Latvia

phone +371/0 435 7101

open Tuesday–Saturday 10.00–17.00 or by appointment

Prof. Jāzepa Vītola Kabinets

Jāzepa Vītola Latvijas Muzikas Akademija
K. Barona iela 1
1050 Riga
Latvia

phone +371/0 722 8684

fax +371/0 782 0271
e-mail karlsons@lmuza.lv (Rector's office)
website www.lmuza.lv

open by appointment

Map 2

VLADIGEROV

Bulgaria's musical patriarch, Pancho Vladigerov, is commemorated in the north-eastern city of Shumen, some 100 km from Varna, where he and his identical twin Luben spent their childhood and which is proud of its musical traditions. The Vladigerovs were born in Zürich in 1899 (their mother went there for the event) but considered Shumen their spiritual home. Both brothers were musical: Luben became a violinist while Pancho composed and conducted in addition to pursuing a career as a pianist. The many photographs of them – as children, in their military uniforms and later as a duo – attest to their closeness. Pancho composed two violin concertos and a sonata for his brother.

In Shumen their mother practised as a doctor, their father as a lawyer. When Pancho was six he began piano lessons with Paula Weismann-Zhekova. So great was the boys' musical talent that they were taken to Sofia in 1910 to study at a music school (later academy), where, after further studies in Berlin and a stint at the Deutsches Theater (1921–32), Vladigerov taught the piano and composition until his retirement in 1972; the music academy today bears his name. Throughout his life he spent his summers in Shumen. After marrying the daughter of his first piano teacher in 1930, he stayed at her whitewashed house, which in due course became his. He was able to compose there; among the works he produced were the 'Shumen' miniatures for piano (1934) and the ballet *Legende von dem See* (1946). The house is now part of a complex of buildings that make up the Pancho Vladigerov museum.

The museum is in a brick-paved street in the old part of town, west of the centre, not far from the Hotel Shumen. A chamber music hall seating 70 has been built next to the house, and other buildings within the walled grounds are allocated to a music shop, offices and further exhibition space. An almost impish bronze statue of the composer invites visitors to pause in the forecourt before entering the two-storey house.

The piano studio of Mme Zhekova and the Vladigerovs' bedroom upstairs are sensitively re-created. At the top of the landing, his pin-striped suit, combination cane and umbrella and his jaunty beret are on display. Five further rooms are given over to displays of family photographs, facsimiles of early compositions and documents, concert programmes, published editions and recordings (the earliest is from 1922). In the final room there are plaster casts of his death mask and his hands; letters from his contemporaries, including Bartók, Herbert von Karajan, Kodály, Alexis Weissenberg (his pupil) and Stefan Zweig; delightful caricatures; his treasured Mendelssohn (1918 and 1920) and Gottfried Herder (1968) prizes. The impression one carries away is of an extremely genial man, who composed finely crafted works – which in addition to pieces for piano (for himself to perform) and violin (for his brother) included an opera, a piano trio, a string quartet and two symphonies, influenced but not dominated by Bulgarian folk music.

Pancho Vladigerov died in Sofia on 8 September 1978. While plans for a house museum in Sofia have yet to be realized (his house, ulitsa Yakobitsa 10, in a southern suburb which, in his day, must have been very fashionable, still has his name on the gate), the Shumen museum opened in 1983. Luben Vladigerov died in 1992 and Pancho's son Alexander, also a composer and conductor, died the following year at the age of 60. In 1993 a Pancho Vladigerov Foundation was established in Shumen to perpetuate his memory through conferences, publications and recordings, and to support talented young musicians by holding concerts, masterclasses and international competitions for piano and violin.

K'shta-Muzey Pancho Vladigerov
ulitsa Tsar Osvoboditel 136
9700 Shumen
Bulgaria

phone +359/0 545 2123

open Monday–Friday 09.00–17.00, Saturday and Sunday by appointment

Map 11

WAGNER

Not many composers have the opportunity to establish their own museum: but Richard Wagner was exceptional in many ways. The grandest of the memorials to the great man, perhaps the grandest of all composer museums, if not the most commodious, is of course the house that he himself built in Bayreuth – at Ludwig II's expense – although the museum was not established there until 1976. There are two other substantial Wagner museums, also in places strongly associated with his adventurous life, and a further one associated with his death.

The oldest Wagner museum in Germany, however, is another, rather smaller institution, in a town, Eisenach, that is visited more often by Bach pilgrims than Wagner ones. There, aptly placed at the foot of the Wartburg, with its national symbolic significance, below the castle whose ancient halls of song were immortalized by Wagner in *Tannhäuser* – in fact he first visited the site only in 1849, four years after the opera's première – stands the Reuter-Wagner Museum. The poet Fritz Reuter built his neo-Renaissance villa there in 1866–8. He died in 1874, and his widow in 1894; it was then bought by the city of Eisenach and set up as a museum to him. In 1895, the large Wagner collection of the Austrian Nicolaus Oesterlein, which had originally been exhibited in a private museum in Vienna, was acquired and incorporated.

The collection is based on a large library, which contains some 6000 volumes and 200 letters. Among the display material are facsimiles of music and programmes, maquettes of opera scenes, busts and death masks (of Liszt as well as Wagner). There is also a manuscript score of the *Rienzi* overture.

There is no museum to Wagner in Leipzig, where on 22 May 1813 he was born (the house, in Brühl, was demolished in 1896; there is a plaque on the site). As a child of nine he moved to Dresden, to enter the Kreuzschule, and he remained there when the family moved to Prague. His career took him to Magdeburg, Königsberg, Riga and Paris, and then back to Dresden, in 1842, where *Rienzi* was to be given. The following year he was appointed joint Kapellmeister to the Dresden court. The Saxon capital remained his home until 1849, when his political activities forced him into exile. He lived near the centre of the city, but in May 1846 he and his first wife Minna went to stay for just over two months in a first-floor apartment in a house in Groß-Graupa, between Pillnitz and Pirna: this is now the suburb of Graupa. There he worked on the sketches for *Lohengrin*, and met for the first time Hans von Bülow, then only 16, whose life was later to intersect with his.

The house where he lived became a museum to him in 1907, but its existence was at first sporadic; it was reopened in 1951, and extensively modernized in 1982, with the theme 'Richard Wagner and Dresden'. On the ground floor there

Wagner museum at Graupa

is a recital room, with a mini-barrel-vaulted ceiling, seating over 100, used also for art exhibitions; next to it is a display room, dealing with Wagner's later, revolutionary years in Dresden and the beginning of his exile in Switzerland – there is his poem to the people of Vienna and his documents about theatre reform – as well as theatre drawings by Gottfried Semper and material on his new circle of friends in Zürich and the Wagner Festival held there in 1853. There are also some instruments from the Hofkapelle, including a basset-horn and a serpent.

But the main part of the display is on the first floor, in the rooms where Wagner and his wife had actually lived. On the upper landing, Wagner's 'Musiksalon', there is an 18th-century table piano, an oil portrait of Wagner and several facsimiles, including *Lohengrin* material and portraits of Dresden opera composers (Weber and Marschner, and again Wagner). The first room offers a varied series of images to do with Wagner's Dresden years: singers, composers and theatre artists associated with the Hoftheater, original handbills, librettos and costume designs, and also a watercolour of a nearby valley that Wagner visited.

The second room, Wagner and Minna's bedroom, houses eight display cases with a rich selection of originals of Wagner letters (and one each from Liszt and Berlioz), along with facsimiles – there is much material relating to the tenor Joseph Tichatschek, the original Rienzi and Tannhäuser, to Wagner's doctor Anton Pusinelli and to the return of Weber's remains to Germany, as well as librettos, portraits, caricatures and journal articles. A further room is known as the Wagner-Röckel-Raum, after his assistant and political collaborator Karl August Röckel: here and in the passage are a further ten display cases, as well as generously hung walls and glazed tables. The main themes are Wagner's manuscripts, the continuing history of the Dresden opera, Röckel himself and Wagner's wider circle of friends, and

members of the Dresden governing community. There is a Wagner portrait of 1910 and a plaster bust. The actual furniture is of the period, but not Wagner's own: there is in fact a photo, from Bayreuth, of the desk he used at Graupa.

When Wagner had to flee Dresden, he went first to Weimar, where he was sheltered by Liszt, and then to Switzerland. Excluded from Germany until 1860, he spent time in Zürich, Paris and briefly Venice; then in the early 1860s he was in Vienna, which he had to flee to escape his creditors, and Munich. It was in 1866 that he and Cosima – Liszt's daughter, Bülow's wife – visited Lucerne (Wagner had been there several times, first in 1850, and in 1859 completed *Tristan* at a hotel there), saw the house called Tribschen, on a promontory overlooking the lake, and decided that this beautiful place should be their eventual home. He moved there that year. Cosima often visited Tribschen but was able to join him there only after the break with Bülow in 1868; they lived there until 1872. *Siegfried Idyll*, written to celebrate their marriage later that year, the birth of their second child, Siegfried, the previous summer, and her birthday, 24 December, had its first performance on the staircase, with Hans Richter playing the trumpet; Cosima heard it as she lay in bed on Christmas morning.

Tribschen from Lake Lucerne

The autograph score is now displayed in Haus Tribschen. The house, probably of medieval origins, took its present form in 1800. It was acquired in 1931 by the Lucerne municipality and became a Wagner museum in 1933, sharing the premises with the town's instrument collection, which is housed on the first floor. Downstairs, there are four rooms, elegantly presented in a decorative style of the period of the Wagners' residence. The first, originally Wagner's bedroom, contains a number of lithographs (of Tribschen, of Liszt, Wagner himself and Richter) and a charcoal drawing of Mathilde Wesendonck (an important inspiration for Isolde), along with a Wagner family tree. Wagner's own green-velvet easy chair, now normally the preserve of the resident cat, is in the second room (the green study or *Meistersinger* room), along with a plaster cast of his right hand, a chronological array of his signatures and various letters and family documents (including their children's birth certificates), and there are several likenesses of Wagner and Cosima in the display cases, one of which contains the actual clothes he was wearing when he was perched in the velvet chair – as seen in the photograph reproduced on the wall close by (see p.41).

The *Idyll* autograph is in the third room (the former salon), as, in facsimile, are those of three operas with strong links to Tribschen, *Tristan*, *Die Meistersinger* and *Siegfried*. There are family photos, original pastels of Cosima and Mathilde, several oils including two of Wagner and the Erard grand piano given to him by the maker. The former library has, besides books, busts of Wagner, Cosima and Mathilde and items recalling the visits to Tribschen of Nietzsche and King Ludwig II of Bavaria, among others. Lastly, in the dining-room, are the Renoir lithograph of Wagner, and a central display of autographs, from *Meistersinger* and *Der fliegende Holländer*, with proof sheets, a series of postcard pictures of Wagner's singers, paintings of opera scenes (by Stassen of *Tristan* and Thoma of the *Ring*) and a collection of commemorative stamps. Outside there is a small stone building, hexagonal in shape, in which Wagner kept peacocks, named Wotan and Fricka.

But of course the giant among Wagner museums is Haus Wahnfried itself. The Wagners first considered Bayreuth as their possible base in 1871, and quickly fixed on sites for the Festspielhaus and their own home. The latter does seem to have been chosen with a view not only to comfort and convenience but also to posterity, indeed museum-cum-mausoleum, for Wagner, Cosima and their dog are buried in the back garden. An 'average, decent-sized dwelling', Wagner called it in a letter to Ludwig, but here as elsewhere his ideas on what is decent might seem to differ from other people's.

In 1874 Wagner moved in. The front of the house bears plaques proclaiming 'Hier, wo mein Wähnen Frieden fand . . . Wahnfried . . . sei dieses Haus von mir benannt' ('Here, where my delusions found peace, let this house be named by me "Peace from Delusion"'). After his death (in 1883) the house continued to be the family home. In 1945 it was severely damaged at the rear by a bomb. Wieland Wagner, the composer's grandson, supervised the immediate repairs, but it was not until 1973, when the house was handed over to the city of Bayreuth by Winifred Wagner (Siegfried Wagner's English widow) and Wieland, that it could be fully restored; at the same time the neighbouring building, the Siegfried-Wagner-Haus, was bought from Winifred. That building is now the headquarters of the Richard-Wagner-Stiftung and houses the museum administration (for the nearby LISZT museum too) and a fine, comprehensive Wagner library, including virtually all his surviving autograph material, with reading rooms and a multimedia centre. The Stiftung also owns the contents of Haus Wahnfried. Much of the display and archival material had formerly been in the Richard-Wagner-Gedenkstätte in

Haus Wahnfried, Bayreuth

Wahnfried, rear elevation, with the graves in the foreground

Wahnfried: plaque on the front elevation, left

Wahnfried: plaque on the front elevation, right

the Neues Schloß in Bayreuth, which was closed in 1975. The new museum in Haus Wahnfried was opened in 1976, on the anniversary of the complete première of *Der Ring des Nibelungen*.

The reconstruction of the 1970s, under the supervision of Wolfgang Wagner, involved not only the repair of damage and the ravages of time, but also the finding of a compromise between restoration of the house's original form and its adaptation as an effective museum. Central to the design, quite literally, are the two large presentation rooms: the hall by the main entrance, a lofty room the full height of the building, galleried at mezzanine level; and the rear drawing-room, looking out to the garden, which is used for concerts, broadcasts and lectures. Along either side there are display rooms: on the ground floor the front

rooms – originally Cosima's salon and the dining-room – are reserved for special exhibitions, and one at the rear has a 'Monstrosities and Curiosities' display, a welcome corrective to any suspicion that Bayreuth might take itself and Wagner too seriously. The basement, darkened, is devoted to well-lit maquettes and photos of stage sets and costumes at and around Bayreuth, chronologically organized, providing an up-to-date visual history of Wagner production.

The main displays are on the upper floors. On the left side of the building there is what is essentially a visual biography of Wagner, arranged to minimize the distances the visitor has to walk (five staircases connect the upper floors) – it begins on the top floor (in Siegfried's bedroom) with his childhood and early career, then to one of the girls' rooms for the Paris years, descending to the mezzanine for rooms given over to Dresden and Vienna, then ascending again for the Munich, Lucerne and Bayreuth periods and his death in Venice. A comparable excursion on the right provides a history of the Bayreuth Festival since Wagner's time, starting at the rear in Cosima's boudoir, moving into the couple's bedroom for the era of Tietjen and Preetorius, down to the mezzanine for the grandsons' productions and ending in Wagner's study with the most recent ones.

Programmes, writings, photos (of singers, friends, lovers, buildings), music or text autographs (or facsimiles), set and costume designs, letters, diaries and other documents: these and much more fill the 68 display cases and the walls in the biographical rooms, each of which is coloured to reflect the character of Wagner's experience of each phase of his life. One exhibit is the sofa on which Wagner died, in Cosima's embrace, its fabric now plucked bare by the depredations of relic hunters, anxious to possess a tuft that may have been in contact with the dying master.

That sofa was brought to Bayreuth – as too, indeed, was Wagner's body – from Venice. Wagner had stayed there in 1858–9, at the Palazzo Giustiniano, while completing the scoring of *Tristan*. In September 1882 he went there with his family and negotiated a lease for three years, with a further two-year option, for an apartment on the mezzanine floor of the Ca' Vendramin Calergi. This Renaissance palace on the Grand Canal, built by Mauro Codussi and then owned by the Duchess of Berry, was acquired by the city in 1949 and serves in the winter as the municipal casino. In 1995 the 'Sala Wagner', the room of his death, was entrusted to the Associazione Richard Wagner di Venezia, which opened it to the public as a memorial to the composer. The longer-term intention is to create a larger museum using more of the 28 rooms of Wagner's apartment – he apparently was travelling with something of an entourage.

Wagner died on 13 February 1883. That morning he and Cosima had a violent altercation, over a planned visit by Carrie Pringle, an English girl who had sung one of the flower maidens in *Parsifal* and with whom Wagner seemingly had (or contemplated) a close relationship. In the afternoon he had a severe heart attack. The room has display cases, one commemorating the first *Ring* in Venice, shortly after his death, with various documents (police permission, lists of expenses and ticket sales) and posters, one with correspondence and a death mask. There are two large cases with facsimiles of his autograph scores, and photos from Wagner's time of his favourite places. In the Sala Wagner and in adjoining rooms some of the furniture, belonging to the building, is original, including red damask sofas. The Sala has a delicately sculpted ceiling and a typically Venetian terrace-style floor. The apartment has a direct, external staircase to the garden, which Wagner used, and to the canal, so that he could take a gondola – as indeed he did for his final journey.

There are two plaques on the Ca' Vendramin, one by the canal, one by the gardens, commemorating Wagner's death there; there is also a bust in the public gardens by the waterside beyond St Mark's and the Palazzo Ducale. Wagner memorials abound across Europe. There is one in Paris, erected by the 'Amis de Richard Wagner', on 14 Rue Jacob, where he lived in 1841–2. One in Palermo marks his visit to the amphitheatre in

Ca' Vendramin, Venice, from across the Grand Canal

Segesta in 1882. Another marks a site in Riga where he conducted. In Vienna there are three: those on a house where he lived in the 14th district (Hadikgasse 72), in the foyer of the Kaiserin Elisabeth Hotel (Weihburggasse 3) and on the front façade of the Imperial Hotel (Kärntner Ring 16) proclaim his patronage and residence; there was once a fourth at the Thalientheater in honour of the local première of *Tannhäuser*. There is one in Wiesbaden-Biebrich (Rheingaustraße 137), marking the house where in 1862 he worked on *Die Meistersinger*. In Lucerne, a Richard-Wagner-Stube commemorates his stay at the Gasthaus zum Schwanen on his first visit; and in Zürich there is a bust in the garden of the villa he called his 'Asyl', Schulhausstraße 19, close to his friends the Wesendoncks, where he lived in 1857. A significant Wagner site is the little Goethe-Theater at Bad Lauchstädt where in 1834 he conducted and met Minna, but it bears no indication of the connection; another is Ludwig II's castle Neuschwanstein at Hohenschwangau in the Bavarian Alps, with its series of mythological, Wagner-related murals – on the third floor, from the Siegfried saga in the lounge, the Parsifal and Lohengrin tales in the dining-room, Tristan in the bedroom, Mastersingers in the dressing-room, Lohengrin in the living-room and Tannhäuser in the study, and on the fourth floor the Nibelung saga in the lounge and Parsifal in the singers' hall.

Fritz Reuter und Richard Wagner Museum

Reuterweg 2
99817 Eisenach
Germany

phone +49/0 3591 743 293
fax +49/0 3591 743 294
e-mail info@eisenach.de
website www.eisenach.de

open Tuesday–Sunday 10.00–17.00

Richard-Wagner-Museum

Richard-Wagner-Straße 6
01827 Graupa
Germany

phone +49/0 3501 548 229
fax +49/0 3501 548 206

open Tuesday–Sunday 09.00 1200, 13.00–16.00

Richard-Wagner-Museum

Haus Tribschen
Richard-Wagner-Weg 27
6000 Luzern
Switzerland

phone, fax +41/0 413 302 370
e-mail habeggu@stadtluzern.ch

open Tuesday–Saturday 09.00–12.00, 14.00–18.00 (15 October–15 April, closed Wednesday and Friday), Sunday 10.00–12.00, 14.00–17.00

Richard-Wagner-Museum

Haus Wahnfried
Richard-Wagner-Straße 48
95444 Bayreuth
Germany

phone +49/0 9217 572 814
fax +49/0 9217 572 822
e-mail info@wagnermuseum.de
website www.wahnfried.de

open April–October, daily 09.00–17.00 (Tuesday, Thursday to 20.00); November–March, daily 10.00–17.00

Sala Richard Wagner

Ca' Vendramin Calergi
2040 Venezia
Italy

phone +390/0 415 232544

open Saturday 10.00–12.00, by appointment only (phone the day before)

Maps 7, 6, 9

G. Mariacher, ed.: *Ca' Vendramin Calergi* (Venice: Casinò municipale, 1978)

[M. Ridler, F. Schaub]: *Richard Wagner: his Lucerne Period, the Museum in Tribschen* (Lucerne: Keller, 1983) [City of Lucerne official guidebook]

J. Heyne: *Richard-Wagner-Museum Graupa b. Dresden* (Dresden: Hochschule für Musik 'Carl Maria von Weber', Direction Richard-Wagner-Museum, 1985)

M. Eger: *The Richard Wagner Museum Bayreuth* (Bayreuth: Richard-Wagner-Foundation, 1990)

M. von Soden: *Richard Wagner: ein Reiseführer* (Dortmund: Harenberg, 1991)

H. Kretschmer: *Wiener Musikergedenkstätten* (Vienna: J & V Edition, 3/1992)

N. Simeone: *Paris: a Musical Gazetteer* (New Haven and London: Yale University Press, 2000)

WALTON

No composer could have chosen a home more idyllic than did William Walton when he settled in Ischia, in the Bay of Naples. And accordingly no composer museum could be more idyllic than the one that his widow, Susana, created there to enshrine his memory.

Walton had long nurtured the idea of moving away from the London social whirl – he had lived in Chelsea with the Sitwells in his younger days (he was born in 1902), with Alice Wimborne in Belgravia more lately – to find the peace he needed to concentrate his creative energies. Back in the 1920s, he had visited the Bay of Naples with the Sitwells; now he took his young wife there, in the winter after their marriage in 1948. Ischia became their home for his last 35 years.

Initially, Thomas Cook found them a former convent to rent on Ischia, San Francesco, with a piano and a caretaker. They moved first to Casa Cirillo, a converted wine cellar; not until 1956 did they acquire La Mortella ('The Place of Myrtles'), a west-facing hillside property with spectacular views to sea. They acquired not only the property itself, on Monte Zaro (created by a volcanic eruption), but also the ravine below with the only black soil on the island. The first stage of building was completed in 1962.

Architects had initially been unsure how to build the unobtrusive hillside house the Waltons had in mind. Eventually plans were agreed for a house on several levels. At first the house attracted derision; the locals dubbed it La Caserma ('the barracks'). But when Susana worked on the garden with the landscape architect Russell Page, opinions changed. She set about transforming it into a tropical paradise, with palm trees, exotic plants and fountains, and later magnolias and cypresses (see p.16). Above the house she carved out a pond with crocodile sculpture (the Cascata del Cocodrillo) surrounded by blue water-lilies, a swimming pool (reached by a 'mini-funicular') and an oriental garden complete with an imported Thai house and lotus pond. Near the top is William's Rock, which he claimed for himself the day they acquired the property; now it holds his ashes and is a place of pilgrimage.

Walton withdrew into himself when he was composing. He would make an early start, rest during the afternoon and work again in the evening. Among the works of his years at La Mortella are the Cello Concerto, the Second Symphony, the Hindemith Variations and the Britten Improvisations, and the one-act opera *The Bear*, as well as film scores. During these periods, according to Susana, they communicated little, eating and wandering in the garden in virtual silence. Equally, their gregarious banter

William's Rock, above the garden of La Mortella, Ischia

between compositions and during their travels is legendary. They entertained frequently: the guests who took the boat across from Naples to see them included Laurence Olivier, Paul Hindemith, Ralph and Ursula Vaughan Williams and Hans Werner Henze.

After Walton's death, in 1983, Susana set about realizing some of his wishes, in particular that his estate should be used to benefit young musicians. This is done chiefly through scholarships at the study centre in La Mortella, for performers, composers and students of Walton's music. A trust and a foundation were established; a dormitory block for resident students was built high on the hill, hidden by foliage; a recital room was built next to his former study; and a museum collection was assembled.

The collection, displayed in the recital room, includes busts of Walton and the Sitwells, designs for the staging of various of Walton's works, among them *Façade*, *Troilus and Cressida* and *The Bear* (by John Piper, Hugh Casson and others), medals, editions and recordings of Walton's works, a few autograph scores (most are in the Pierpont Morgan Library in New York) and a puppet theatre by Emanuele Luzzati representing La Mortella with characters from Walton's works and Walton himself. The Tony Palmer television documentary of 1981 is shown when the recital room is not in use for classes, rehearsals or concerts.

Lady Walton continues to live at La Mortella. She is deeply involved in the work for young musicians and in the garden, which she has continued to enrich, and she has drawn together an important and beautiful collection of Mediterranean and tropical plants, many of them from her native South America: the garden is open to the public, who can also enjoy, along with the museum, the facilities of a shop, a greenhouse and an attractive terrace teashop.

Villa La Mortella
via F. Calise 35
80075 Forio
Isola d'Ischia (Napoli)
Italy

phone +390/0 81 986220
website www.ischia.it/mortella

open April – October, Tuesday, Thursday, Saturday, Sunday 09.00–17.00 (recitals, Saturday and Sunday afternoons)

Map 9

S. Walton: *William Walton: Behind the Façade* (Oxford: Oxford University Press, 1988)
S. Walton: *La Mortella: the Garden Book* (Forio: Fondazione William Walton, n.d.)

WEBER

The birthplace of Carl Maria von Weber in Eutin, 100 km north-east of Hamburg, while certainly not a museum, commemorates the composer in a particularly delightful way: the red brick, two-storey building at Lübeckerstraße 48 (bearing a commemorative plaque since 1853) is a teashop where one can partake of an elaborately filled and frosted nougat and chocolate Freischütztorte or a chocolate, marzipan, strawberry-and-cream Weber-Hütchen.

Weber was born there on 19 November 1786 to musician parents; his father was Kapellmeister to the Prince-Bishop of Lübeck at Eutin and his mother a singer. After leaving Eutin in 1797 to study in Salzburg with Michael Haydn, he returned only twice, in 1802 and 1820. He is remembered in the Ostholstein-Museum, ten minutes' walk away in the Schloßplatz, in conventional displays containing artefacts, including a tuning fork, a bust and a death mask as well as photographs, commemorative medals and concert programmes, early editions, facsimiles, *Freischütz* costumes and a photographic history of German productions of the opera.

From 1817 until his death in London from tuberculosis in 1826, Weber was chiefly based in Dresden, where he was music director in charge of German opera at the court of Friedrich August; his first flat there was at Schimmelallee 30 in the 'Italienisches Dörfchen'. When he married, he and his new wife, the soprano Caroline Brandt, lived first at

Altmarkt 9 and later in the Neumarkt at Galleriestraße 9; they had two sons.

To escape the city in the summer, they crossed eastward over the Elbe to the vine-growing countryside, where in 1818, 1819 and again in 1822–4 they leased the first floor of a vintner's house in leafy Hosterwitz. While he was there Weber composed his *Rondo brillante* and the *Aufforderung zum Tanze* for piano and completed *Der Freischütz* and *Euryanthe*. He took walks with his family and received visitors, among them Marschner, Spontini and Mendelssohn.

The house was renovated and a museum created there in 1976, in celebration of the 150th anniversary of his death. The Weber flat displays the main part of the collection. To the left, as you come up the stairs, is a furnished room – supposedly his workroom – with a rolltop desk, a square piano and miniatures of family members. On the landing there is a striking portrait of Caroline by the Webers' younger son, Alexander, as well as a variety of other family portraits spanning three generations. The third and largest room is dominated by Ferdinand Schimon's well-known portrait of the composer and contains 12 display cases, each with five glass-top drawers; arranged in chronological order, they contain a tremendous wealth of material, logically and accessibly stored – easily enough to occupy the visitor for an entire afternoon. There are letters, music facsimiles both manuscript and printed, concert handbills, reviews written by Weber and caricatures of him. There are

relics too: visiting cards, a lock of hair, his baton, his passport and his will.

Sunday concerts regularly take place downstairs in the recital and lecture room, which seats 40; in the summer they are in the garden. Adjacent to the recital room Weber's death mask and guitar are exhibited, along with a display devoted to the reception history of Weber's music. Hosterwitz retains an idyllic atmosphere, and the house is well worth a visit, particularly as it can easily be combined with one to the Wagner museum further down the road at Graupa.

In 1844, at Wagner's instigation, Weber's body was exhumed from its initial resting-place in London, at the Catholic Chapel in Moorfields, and brought to Dresden for reburial in Dresden Friedrichstadt; a statue by Ernst Rietschel was erected in Dresden, near the Semper Opera House, in 1860.

Ostholstein-Museum

Schloßplatz 1
23701 Eutin
Germany

phone +49/0 4521 70180
fax +49/0 4521 701818
e-mail oh-museum.eutin@t-online.de
website www.oh-museum.de

open April–September, Tuesday–Sunday 10.00–13.00, 14.00–17.00 (Thursday to 19.00); October–January, March, Tuesday–Sunday 15.00–17.00 (Thursday and Sunday also 10.00–12.00)

Carl-Maria-von-Weber-Museum

Dresdner Straße 44
Hosterwitz
01326 Dresden
Germany

phone, fax +49/0 351 261 8234
email weber@stmd.de
website www.stadtmuseum.dresden.de

open Wednesday–Sunday 13.00–18.00 or by appointment

Map 7

G. Schönfelder: *Gedenkstätte 'Carl Maria von Weber' Dresden-Hosterwitz* (Dresden: Rat des Stadtbezirkes Ost der Stadt Dresden, 1986)

The Weber house at Hosterwitz

WEILL

Dessau is a moderate-sized city in eastern Germany, just over 100 km south of Berlin, some 60 km from Leipzig and rather less than that from Halle. There, in 1900, Kurt Weill was born, the third child of the cantor at the local synagogue. The ducal theatre at Dessau had a strong Wagner tradition, so much so that the city was dubbed 'the Bayreuth of the north', and such were Weill's youthful talents that he was admitted to rehearsals and performances there by the time he was ten years old. He went on, when he was 18, to study in Berlin, briefly under Humperdinck and then, after a further spell in Dessau as an assistant at the theatre (where Knappertsbusch was conducting), under Busoni. He settled in Berlin, where he associated with the leftish group of composers and intellectuals working there, and became the most successful theatre composer of the Weimar Republic, above all with his collaboration with Brecht in *Die Dreigroschenoper* in 1928. But his success in Germany was of course doomed; there were riots at the Leipzig première of *Aufstieg und Fall der Stadt Mahagonny* in 1930, and it became increasingly difficult for Weill to find theatres that would stage his works. Eventually he fled to Paris, then to New York and Hollywood; he died in New York in 1950.

Weill is however commemorated in his native city. His birthplace, near the synagogue, was demolished in 1960. But Dessau also happens to have been the home of leading figures of the Bauhaus movement in the late days of the Weimar Republic. In 1925–6, several of the Bauhaus masters moved there from Weimar and built, in the Burgkühner Allee (now the Ebertallee, in the Ziebigk district), a group of seven new houses, one detached and three semi-detached pairs. Their occupants included Walter Gropius (the detached house), László Moholy-Nagy, Wassily Kandinsky and Paul Klee. In no.3, now no.63, the Expressionist painter Lyonel Feininger lived.

The 'Meistersedlung' ('masters' settlement') was short-lived; it had to be abandoned in 1932. The first two houses were destroyed in World War II, and no.3, now detached, came in DDR times to be the home of a medical practice and was later rebuilt as a clinic. But in 1989, with the reunification of Germany, the whole settlement was handed over to a trust by the city of Dessau. In 1991 the clinic was removed and it was decided that the house should be restored as a historical monument. The original 1925 building plans were lost, but an analysis of the changes made after 1933 made restoration possible.

After reunification, the Kurt Weill Foundation of New York, seeking a European office in Dessau for the management of Weill's music and an annual festival, created with the city of Dessau a Kurt-Weill-Zentrum in the Feininger Meisterhaus. The first festival was held in 1993. At the end of the following year the house was opened as a small Weill museum, to exhibit a collection of books, periodicals, music and manuscript material to illustrate his life and work. There are hopes of rebuilding the once adjoining house as a gallery and concert hall.

The restoration was meticulously carried out, down to the last doorknob and even the original heating system. There are smooth white plastered walls, black lacquered doors and light pinewood. On the ground floor there are two rooms. The main one, originally the living-room, with a patio at the rear, is now the principal display room; it is also used for meetings of the Kurt Weill Gesellschaft. There is furniture by Marcel Breuer, black, white and orange, strongly redolent of the 1920s. There is a dining-room, with a blue lino floor. The basement, used for rehearsals, is to become the library. Upstairs – blue stairs, with red railings – is a large recital room, again black and white with brown lino, which is used for workshops, lectures and concerts. In the bedroom is a cupboard where archival material is stored. There is what was once a children's bedroom in blue, black and pink, with particularly attractive views. On the top floor, the former maid's room is now a library, with LPs, CDs and videos, as well as newspaper cuttings, some of the letters between Weill and his wife, the cabaret singer Lotte Lenya, and some music by his father. There is also a conference room.

Although the house has no pretensions about re-creating the circumstances in which Weill actually lived, it does succeed in showing something of the aesthetic ambience of his creative years in Germany.

Kurt-Weill-Zentrum

Haus Feininger
Ebertallee 63
06846 Dessau
Germany

phone +49/0 340 619595
fax +49/0 340 611907
e-mail weill-zentrum@t-online.de
website www.kurt-weill.de

open Tuesday 14.00–16.00, Thursday 10.00–12.00, Saturday 14.00–17.00

Map 7

G. Kolber, ed.: *Leben am Bauhaus: Die Meisterhäuser in Dessau* (Munich: Bayerischer Vereinsbank, 1993)
A. Altenhof, ed.: *Kurt Weill und Dessau* (Dessau: Kurt-Weill-Zentrum, n.d.)

WILDGANS

Mödling, one of Beethoven's favourite summer resorts (*see* BEETHOVEN), remains high among the most pleasant Viennese suburbs or satellite regions. There, in a house on a hill behind the church of St Othmar, in a parkland setting on the edge of the town, its peace undisturbed save by the sound of birds, the poet and theatre director Anton Wildgans came to live in 1918; he was there until his death in 1932. His son Friedrich, born in 1913, the composer, writer on music, clarinettist, teacher at the conservatories and a central figure in Viennese musical life in the post-war era, lived there in his later years; he died in 1965.

The house is now a national cultural site, which means that certain of its rooms must be maintained in their present condition as memorials to their distinguished former occupants. Primarily, then, it is Anton who is remembered here, and it is his study and library that has the strongest sense of artistic presence. But the drawing-room, elegantly and traditionally furnished, with its Bösendorfer grand, its musical portraits and graceful music stands, has atmosphere too and betokens a way of life. Friedrich Wildgans worked here, using the balcony with its attractive panorama of Mödling and the country beyond, in the summer months. His papers and correspondence, including music – many of his works were left unfinished – and some of the caricatures he drew (and which had to be hidden away in politically difficult times) are preserved at the house but will in due course pass to a national collection; they are available for consultation by scholars. At present the house is lived in and cared for by the widow of Friedrich's younger brother, Gottfried (himself a keen musician).

Wildgans-Haus

4 Anton Wildgans-Weg
2340 Mödling
Austria

phone, fax +43/0 2236 23433

open by appointment

Map 1

WOLF

Everyone knows Hugo Wolf as an Austrian composer, but Windischgraz, where he was born in 1860, is now Slovenj Gradec, just on the Slovenian side of the border; and his mother and possibly his father too were of Slovenian ancestry. The father, Philipp Wolf, a keen amateur violinist and singer, was owner of a leather business which was destroyed by fire. The family house, however, still stands, on the handsome main street of the town; it was in fact a museum to

Wolf's birthplace, Slovenj Gradec

Room at Wolf's retreat in Perchtoldsdorf

Wolf in pre-war times, but its history as an Austrian institution precluded its survival in those turbulent years – indeed the plaque from the front of the building commemorating Wolf's birth would have been destroyed but for its concealment by a local clergyman (it is now in the inner courtyard). Now the local music school, the house bears few traces of its domestic history.

On the first floor, however, the recital hall, seating about 60, serves as a memorial room to Wolf. It is lined with pictures, chronologically organized. There is a family tree, along with his birth and baptismal records, views of his school and the town and photos of Hugo as a child and with his brothers and sisters; there are reproductions of several portraits, of his writings and his manuscripts, and pictures of his various working environments and of his grave.

The main part of Wolf's professional life was, of course, spent in Vienna. A century after he sought it out, the market town of Perchtoldsdorf still offers respite from the city. Wolf's refuge, 14 km south of the centre of the capital, was a room on the first floor of the house at Brunnergasse 26, on the bend of a road within sight of the main square. He went there, to stay in the summer home of his friends the Werner family, during 1888–90 and again in 1895 and 1896.

By 1887 Wolf, 27 years old and of stormy temperament, had alienated many of his musical contemporaries with his behaviour and his forthright critical writ-

ings in the *Wiener Salonblatt.* He was a victim of hereditary manic depression and, further, had contracted syphilis, probably in 1878 in a Viennese brothel. His physical and mental health limited his periods of creativity. But his time at Perchtoldsdorf was particularly fruitful. He arrived there in January 1888 with his favourite Mörike poetry in hand. Music flowed from his pen; he composed as many as three songs a day and by mid-May had produced no fewer than 43 settings. He returned briefly in November, and twice in 1889: in May, intent on carving a reputation in a wider arena, working on settings of *A Midsummer Night's Dream* and orchestrations of his Mörike settings, and in October, to work on the *Spanisches Liederbuch*, of 44 lieder.

He travelled during the next few years, but returned to Perchtoldsdorf in April 1895. For a month he devoted himself to work on *Der Corregidor* before the Werners came to stay in their country home, but he completed the piano score of the opera in July and an orchestration by the end of the year. His final period there was in March and April the following year; again, composing with astonishing speed and intensity, he produced 24 songs for the *Italienisches Liederbuch* in just five weeks.

The museum was established in 1973, when Otto Werner, the grandson of Wolf's friends, presented the house and parts of his family collection to the community. One room – the large, airy one in which he is said to have lived and composed – is reconstructed, with original furniture: a desk, a bureau, two chests, a table and chairs, a sofa, a bentwood rocking chair and a bed as well as a Promberger grand piano. A death mask and busts are the only ornaments (besides the painted ceiling). Another room is devoted to an elegantly organized display. There are enlarged photos and manuscript facsimiles of works composed in Perchtoldsdorf, photos and letters, handbills, biographies and contemporary and modern editions of the music as well as a few precious mementoes including Wolf's set of tarot cards, his hairbrush, his pocket watch, his wallet and some cups. Also on show are items touching on the Werner family and the history of the house. There is a recital room, seating just over 50, a video room and a small listening room. The peace that enabled Wolf to compose remains; the modern world barely intrudes on this delightful little suburban enclave.

Wolf lived at various addresses in Vienna, longest (between 1888 and 1894) at Billrothstraße 68, in the suburb of Döbling; several buildings bear commemorative plaques. His piano, an upright by Caspar Lorenz, is housed in the Sammlung alter Musikinstrumente of the Kunsthistorisches Museum, Room XVIII, where there is also a portrait by Karl Rickelt of 1895. Wolf died in Vienna on 22 February 1903 and was buried in the Zentralfriedhof. In 1905 the Perchtoldsdorfer Männer-Gesangverein erected a plaque on the Brunnergasse house.

Glasbena Šola Slovenj Gradec

Glavni trg 40
2380 Slovenj Gradec
Slovenia

phone +386/0 2883 1618, 2884 1991
fax +386/0 2883 1614
e-mail glasbena.sola@guest.arnes.si

open by appointment

Hugo-Wolf-Haus

Brunnergasse 26
2380 Perchtoldsdorf
Austria

phone +43/0 1 8668 3211 (or tourist office, 3400)
fax +43/0 1 8668 3133
websites www.hugowolf.at, www.hugowolfhaus.at

open Easter–October, Saturday and Sunday 10.00–17.00 or by appointment

Maps 14, 1

H. Werner: *Hugo Wolf in Perchtoldsdorf* (Regensburg: Bosse, 1925)
F. Grasberger: *Das Hugo Wolf Haus in Perchtoldsdorf* (Perchtoldsdorf: Marktgemeinde Perchtoldsdorf, 1973)
H. Kretschmer: *Wiener Musikergedenkstätten* (Vienna: J & V Edition, 3/1992)
M. Wolf-Strahser: *Spomini na dom (Spomini na otroštvo Huga Wolfa) / Erinnerungen aus meinem Elternhause (Erinnerungen an die Kindheit Hugo Wolfs)* (Slovenj Gradec / Ravne na Koroškem: Voranc, 1994) [in Slovenian and German]
A. Fuchs: *Auf ihren Spuren in Kärnten: Alban Berg, Gustav Mahler, Johannes Brahms, Hugo Wolf, Anton Webern* (Klagenfurt: Kärntner Druck- und Verlagsgesellschaft, 3/1997)

WRANITZKY brothers

The brothers Wranitzky, Paul (1756–1808) and Anton (1761–1820), were born in Nová Říše, a small town in south-western Moravia, near Telč, some 80 km west of Brno and not far from the Austrian border. Their careers centred on Vienna – which is why we use the Germanized forms of their names, under which they pursued their professional activities – where they held positions directing the theatre orchestras and were particular friends of Haydn and Beethoven. Paul, the more eminent, composer of several German operas admired by Goethe as well as much instrumental music, directed the premières of Haydn's *Creation* and Beethoven's First Symphony; Anton, primarily an orchestral and chamber composer, was violin teacher to Ignaz Schuppanzigh, the leading Beethoven interpreter.

Both brothers – who in Nová Říše are of course called by their native Czech names, Pavel and Antonín Vranický – studied at the school attached to the

Wranitzky displays, Nová Říše

Premonstratensian monastery in the village before pursuing their careers in the imperial capital. It is at the monastery, which suffered some neglect (at best) during the socialist years, that a display in their memory was set up in 1992, as a joint Czech-Austrian enterprise, which in due course is intended to develop into a larger museum and research centre. The display is confined to a pair of rooms on the upper floor of the monastery buildings, close to the ancient library. There are portraits and engravings, including some of other members of the family (Anton had two daughters who were singers: Karoline was the first Agathe in *Der Freischütz*), instruments of the period including a Viennese fortepiano and several wind instruments, handbills, facsimile manuscripts and early editions of the brothers' music, reviews and other items to evoke the Vienna of the closing years of the 18th century and the beginning of the 19th. Recorded performances of symphonies by the brothers supply an attractive background.

Expozice bratří Vranickÿch
Premonstrátskÿ klášter
Nová Říše 1
58865 Nová Říše
Czech Republic

phone +420/0 567 318110

open by appointment

Map 4

YSAŸE

Eugène Ysaÿe's studio may appeal even more to those interested in Belgian Gothic Revival or *Art Nouveau* interiors than simply to the musically inclined. In 1894, the violinist-composer commissioned his fellow *liégeois* and exact contemporary, the architect and interior designer Gustave Serrurier-Bovy (1858–1910), to fit out the studio of the house he was having built at 48 Avenue Brugmann in Brussels. Serrurier-Bovy obliged, decorating it with oak cabinetry and furniture, distinctive light fittings and picture frames, and even brass door-handles and locks with musical motifs.

When in 1931 Ysaÿe died, his children offered the studio to the City of Liège. It was decided that it should be installed in the Conservatoire, in Rue Forgeur, but no action was taken until after World War II. Later, additional teaching space was needed there, and the studio has ended up on the second floor of an annexe to the Musée d'Art Religieux et d'Art Mosan (art of the Meuse region). Tucked away there since 1977, it is in effect a memorial to both musician and designer. Ysaÿe is still commemorated at the Conservatoire where he was a student: the street between the Eglise St Jacques and the Conservatoire, outside which stands a large stone bust of the violinist, is the Rue Eugène Ysaÿe.

If you are successful in finding the studio you will be enchanted above all by the ambience and the unity of the décor

Re-creation of Ysaÿe's Brussels studio, Liège

but also by the individual *objets d'art*, the handsome library and the portraiture, which includes busts and statuettes. Some items have both artistic and musical significance: they include Ysaÿe's specially decorated upright Pleyel piano and adjustable oak music stand, his imposing desk with the integrated *porte-partition* and a beautiful Emile Gallé vase which when struck (gently!) produces, appropriately enough, a perfect A (= 440) (see p.66).

His large library includes the handsomely bound published works of numerous English, French, German, Swedish and Russian novelists, dictionaries and encyclopedias as well as music (opera vocal scores, collected editions and chamber music parts, though none of his manuscripts) and books on music in a selection of languages. In addition to portraits, a bust and a delightful unfinished statuette of Ysaÿe, there is a brass model of his left hand holding the neck of a violin. There are images of other composers too, including delightful statuettes of Paganini and Haydn, busts of Beethoven, Vieuxtemps (another *liégeois* and Ysaÿe's teacher) and Benoit, and portraits of Beethoven and Brahms. But photographs of Queen Elisabeth of Belgium, a great supporter of music and friend to Ysaÿe, predominate. In a quiet corner hangs a framed drawing of the house at 231 Rue Sainte-Marguerite where in 1858 he was born.

There are also personal items on display (though not of course his Guarneri 'del Gesù' violin), among them an old horseshoe for good luck, a collection of pipes, a large chessboard and his typewriter. Opposite the top of the stairs, to your back as you ascend, sitting atop an *Art Nouveau* plant stand, is a small pewter coffer decorated with musical reliefs that contains the composer's heart, for contemplation and homage as you depart.

Studio Eugène Ysaÿe

Musée d'Art Religieux et d'Art Mosan
Impasse des Ursulines
4000 Liège
Belgium

phone +32/0 4221 4225 (Musée d'Art Religieux et d'Art Mosan)

open Tuesday–Saturday 13.00–18.00, Sunday 11.00–16.00

Map 3

A. Chevalier: *Musées vivants de Wallonie et de Bruxelles: 2, Au Studio Eugène Ysaÿe à Liège: un intérieur Art Nouveau* (Liège: Centre d'action culturelle de la Communauté d'expression française, 1982)

ZAJC

The most important of Croatian Romantic composers, Ivan Zajc was enormously prolific: his opus numbers, going up to 1202, make even Czerny seem a slouch. He was born in Rijeka, on 3 August 1832, of partly Czech ancestry, and trained in Italy; he made his career initially in Vienna as a composer of operetta, but in 1870 was pressed to come to Zagreb, where he served as a focal figure for Croatian music for the rest of his life. He was head of the Croatian Institute of Music, founded the Croatian Opera, taught composition and singing and organized concerts in which he conducted and played the piano. He died, regarded as the saviour of Croatian music, and much honoured, on 16 December 1914.

The house where he lived in Zagreb, in the old Upper Town (at 16 Visoka ulica), still stands, and bears a memorial plaque. He is commemorated, however, in the Zagreb City Museum, where a section of a large room is devoted to him (it is shared with the writer August Šenoa), as a re-creation of the study in that house, where much of his music was written. A photograph of the study, as part of the exhibition, shows the exactness of the re-creation. Originally set up some 70 years ago, it is elegantly laid out.

One area is given over to portraits of his family, including his father (a Bohemian military musician), his son and daughter, as well as Zajc himself and his wife Natalija. Two display cases show some of his honours and awards, including silver and gilded laurels and a variety of medallions and cups, and another has photos and ornaments. There is some of his furniture, recovered but with old embroidered cushions, and there are embroidered and velvet folders for music; on the table is a photo album assembled in 1909 by the singers of one of his operas. The gold-embroidered piano stool seems well worn. His working desk is there too, with various framed certificates (one for his honorary citizenship of Zagreb) and photos as well as personal items such as his visiting cards and his glasses case. It is clear that Zajc worked hard and won due honour.

Radna soba maestra Zajca
Muzej Grada Zagreba
Opatička ulica 20
10000 Zagreb
Croatia

phone +385/0 1485 1361, 1362
fax +385/0 1485 1359
e-mail muzej-grada-zagreba@mgz.hinet.hr
website www.mdc.hr/mgz

open Tuesday–Friday 10.00–18.00,
Saturday and Sunday 10.00–13.00

Map 14

ZIEHRER

Among the ten memorial rooms of the section of the Österreichisches Theatermuseum in Vienna recently installed in Hanuschgasse (off the Albertina Platz just behind the Opera, separate from the main section in the Lobkowitz Palace) are two devoted to the operetta composers Carl Michael Ziehrer (1843–1922) and Imre Kálmán (*see* KÁLMÁN). Along with the actors, producers and scenic designers commemorated in the remaining rooms, Ziehrer and Kálmán are the subject of a half-hour video presentation, including historic footage, which visitors can view from a few rows of time-worn, red plush theatre seats at the start of their tour.

Ziehrer, who spent all his life in Vienna, was a regimental bandmaster and composer of hundreds of marches, waltzes and polkas that rivalled the popularity of those of the Strausses, as well as some two dozen operettas, among them *Ein Deutschmeister* (1888), *Die Landstreicher* (1899) and *Die Fremdenführer* (1902). He was busy conducting in all the city's dance halls, and at the Musikverein, while his operettas were holding the stage at the Carltheater, the Venedig, the Theater an der Wien and even the Hofoper. In 1908 he was appointed Royal and Imperial Hofballmusikdirektor (the successor of three Strausses), a post he held until his death. In due course a memorial plaque was erected on his house at Erdbergstraße 1 (just off the Landstraßer Hauptstraße in the 3rd district), a stone and bronze monument in the Prater Hauptallee, and with the royalties from his music a benevolent society for musicians (the Carl-Michael-Ziehrer-Stiftung) was established by his widow. Even before his death the outer Viennese suburb of Baden honoured the composer with a Ziehrer-Höhe (1910) and a Ziehrer-Weg (1913). The first Ziehrer Room opened in the Hofburg in 1963.

The present memorial room evokes the dance hall known as Stahlener's (Jörgerstraße 26 in the 17th district), which since 1893 has had a Ziehrer-Saal. On a glass-enclosed semicircular plinth is Ziehrer's grand piano, with the colourful banners from his premières that once decorated his flat raining down from the ceiling, along with his top hat and death mask. To the side is his court uniform and next to it a portrait in which he is wearing it, with a gently benign smile perceptible through his whiskers. Gold and velvet furniture, family portraits, his military bandmaster's sabre, a miniature Deutschmeister monument presented to him by the Teutonic Order on his 70th birthday and bronze laurel wreaths complete the scene. On the other side of the room are a video monitor with headphones and three display cases containing photographs and gifts from the Habsburg family, including a cigarette case from Archduke Wilhelm and a walking-stick from Crown Prince Rudolf.

Carl Michael Ziehrer Raum

Österreichisches Theatermuseum
Hanuschgasse 3
1010 Wien
Austria

phone +43/0 1 512 2427, 512 8800–649
e-mail info@theatermuseum.at
website www.theatermuseum.at

open Tuesday–Friday 10.00–12.00, 14.00–16.00, Saturday and Sunday 13.00–16.00

Map 1

H. Pistorius: *Österreichisches Theatermuseum: Gedenkräume* (Vienna: Österreichisches Theatermuseum, 1991), 9–12, 53–4

H. Kretschmer: *Wiener Musikergedenkstätten* (Vienna: J & V Edition, 3/1992)

ZUYLEN

Visitors to the Utrecht area often go to the small 13th-century castle at Oud-Zuilen, now part of the northern suburb of Maarssen. Moated and turreted, Slot Zuylen is open to the public and is a popular venue for weddings and chamber concerts. For 31 years during the 18th century, it was the home of a composer, known locally as Belle van Zuylen.

Belle's aristocratic Dutch family, the Van Tuyll van Serooskerkens, acquired the castle by marriage in 1665. She was born there in 1740 and is today commemorated in a three-room apartment on the second floor. The Van Tuylls stayed at Zuylen in the summers and maintained a winter residence in Utrecht, two hours away by horse-drawn barge (the canalside townhouse in Utrecht – a few steps from the cathedral at Kromme Nieuwegracht 3–5 – still stands, as offices of a private institute). When Belle was ten her father added a wing to the castle and built a new, frenchified façade; some of the moat was filled in and part of the outer defensive wall was dismantled. Slot Zuylen remained the family seat until 1951 when a foundation was created to run it as a museum.

Isabelle Agneta Elisabeth van Tuyll van Serooskerken, or Belle van Zuylen, is better known as the writer of four controversial feminist novels of the 1780s and numerous political pamphlets, and as a friend of James Boswell and Benjamin Constant, than she is as a composer. She spoke several languages and was widely read, and was a keen painter who had studied pastel work with Maurice Quentin de La Tour. She played several instruments, including the

The Zuylen family castle, Oud-Zuilen

harpsichord, the fortepiano and the harp, took composition seriously and studied with several composers. During a visit to Paris in 1786 she had lessons with Floridio Tomeoni and may have published *Airs et romances avec accompagnement de clavecin*, of which she wrote both words and music. In the early 1790s she employed the opera composer Nicola Zingarelli to help her with her musical dramatic projects; he cast an eye over her *Polyphème ou le Cyclope* and pronounced that 'la musique en est bonne, chaque note en est raisonnée'. She prepared the librettos as well as composing the music for at least six operas. Her musical correspondence included ambitious exchanges with Voltaire, whom she met at Geneva shortly before his death, as well as with Rameau, Jean-Jacques Rousseau, Sarti, Cimarosa, Paisiello and even Mozart, to whom she sent a copy of *Les Phéniciennes*. His opinion of it is not recorded.

Van Zuylen's apartment at the castle effectively evokes her time there. A closet to the left displays copies of the La Tour pastel of 1766 and a bust by Jean-Antoine Houdon. Her embroidery sampler hangs on the wall along with portraits of one of her brothers and a Swiss army officer with whom she corresponded for 15 years. The central room is set out as a bedroom, with period furniture, portraits of her parents and a 1777 portrait of her by the Dane Jens Juël. The third room, the most intimate, is Belle's writing room, with a desk facing the window and a Chinese screen said to hide the tub in which she took a daily cold bath.

To her parents' consternation, Belle rejected the stream of suitors drawn to Zuylen and Utrecht by her beauty and her wealth. So when a small, stuttering, shy, minor Swiss nobleman from the Vaud, Charles-Emmanuel de Charrière de Penthaz, five years her senior, became tutor to the younger van Tuyll children in 1763, it didn't occur to anyone that he

and Belle might eventually marry. After their wedding, in 1771, M and Mme de Charrière left for his family estate: Le Pontet, at Colombier, five kilometres from Neuchâtel. From 1777 they took an apartment in Geneva for the winters. In the early years there were occasional journeys abroad, but Le Pontet increasingly became a welcome retreat and a place of creativity for her. There she wrote her novels (in epistolary form), comedies, operas, poems and political pamphlets, entertained visitors from abroad (including Benjamin Constant and Mme de Staël) and presided over a salon. She died on 27 December 1805. Le Pontet is today privately owned and closed to the public.

With the founding in 1975 of the Netherlands Genootschap Belle de Zuylen, followed by the Associations Isabelle de Charrière (Suisse in 1980, Française in 1995), interest in Belle van Zuylen has grown. In 2002 an international symposium on her was held at Yale University, including performances of her music.

Slot Zuylen

Tournooiveld 1
3611 AS Oud-Zuilen, gem. Maarssen
Netherlands

phone +30/0 244 0255
fax +30/0 244 3907
website www.slotzuylen.com

open 15 March–15 November, Saturday 14.00–16.00, Sunday 13.00–16.00; 15 May–15 September, also Tuesday–Thursday 11.00–16.00 (guided tours on the hour)

Map 3

C. Thompson Pasquali: *Madame de Charrière à Colombier* (Neuchâtel: Bibliothèque de la Ville, 1979)

J. Chesterman, ed.: *Isabelle de Charrière: Letters from Switzerland* (Cambridge: Carole Green, 2001)

EPILOGUE

The writing of this book has been something of an odyssey. As we wrote in the Introduction, the idea was conceived twelve years ago, twelve years in which we have both been heavily occupied on other professional tasks. So the necessary research trips had to be fitted in when possible – taking the place of holidays some years, snatched long weekends at other times. The business of locating composer museums and then going to see them came to be something of a passion (some, for example our children, would say a mania). But it gave us the opportunity to see places we would never have seen, and meet people we would never have met – people many of whom shared, in their way, our passionate concern about composer commemoration. When we step into their museums, however humble, we find ourselves sharing their perception of 'their' composer as the most important in the world, however briefly. This has affected our accounts of the museums.

The way in which this book has become woven into our lives has emboldened us to write, at the urging of several friends and for the interest of those readers who understand and sympathize, this very personal epilogue, whose three sections tell the story of, first, a typical incident, epitomizing the kindness and help we have had from so many complete strangers who sympathized with our quest; second, The Accident, from which we were lucky to escape, and which in several ways altered our lives; and third, something about the background to our passion for composer museums and how we got into all of this.

Over the decade of our travels on behalf of this book, it was always necessary to pack as much as possible into each day 'on the road'. We nearly always drove hired cars, on strange roads, looking for places we had never before visited. Stanley planned the journeys with military precision. Nearly always, appointments were confirmed, hotels booked, routes timed, checked and re-checked. We left little time for meals or mistakes *en route*. But these were treasure hunts, explorations, fulfilments of a mission rather than holidays, days or weeks stuffed full with appointments and rendezvous with local scholars and occasional friends. Some days stand out in our memories. One of them was Wednesday 24 January 1996.

It was snowing and terribly cold when we set out that morning from Vienna. The night before, at a restaurant with our friend José Vázquez and his entourage of viol players, we were asked if we had been to all the Beethoven museums. Oh, yes, we said, of course. Even the one in the 21st district? Er, no. It wasn't on any official list and we hadn't even heard of it. For all our diligent enquiries, we were once more learning by chance and serendipity. We had planned a day in the Czech Republic visiting two towns and two museums before returning to Austria that night. Now we had to slot in Beethoven on our way.

It could of course have been closed that day; we had only an address and no visiting hours. We went along, risking jeopardizing the rest of the day, at 9 a.m. – and indeed it was open from 9 to 11 on Mondays and Wednesdays only. This had been the country house at Floridsdorf of the Erdődy family, to whom Beethoven dedicated several important works. By the time we had completed the visit and resumed our journey to the Czech Republic we were well and truly behind schedule. Never mind: we were triumphant at having discovered and dispatched it without having to make a further journey to Austria.

The snow was thick, and growing thicker. Our next stop was Nová Říše, where we were to visit the memorial room to the Wranitzky brothers, Paul and Anton. It was lunchtime when we arrived and everyone was on their way home. We soon found the monastery where the memorial room was located, but the only response to the bell was the barking of a dog. A few months before, on a beautiful summer's day, we had tried and failed to visit Nová Říše, foiled by a flat tyre. SS was not to be put off. No one in the village shop spoke anything but Czech, so we went to find a school or municipal office. We found the school first. The staff were delighted, thrilled to help: a message was immediately put out over the tannoy which produced a response from a German-speaking teacher, who came with us to unearth the caretaker. He took us back to the monastery, led us upstairs, down long, deserted, unheated corridors to the room dedicated to the Wranitzkys. He unlocked the door, put on the lights and a CD. After our tour of the displays he showed us the medieval monastery library – cold as a refrigerator, not a speck of dust to be seen, the walls lined with alcoves containing orderly rows of beautifully bound volumes, some of them illuminated manuscripts. Time had stood still. We reluctantly departed, having slipped further behind our schedule, and headed for Telč, a delectable little town, for a pause for hot coffee, and on to Kamenice nad Lipou.

By now it was nearly dark. The streets were slushy and full of cars and people going home from work. We crept along, searching the street signs for one to the birthplace of Vitězslav Novák. Then a man knocked on the car window: he had seen our Austrian registration and our hesitant progress and thought we must be lost. He asked, in German, if he could help. Ah, yes, the Novák museum: as it happened, his wife's family had once owned the house. Soon he was in the back seat of the car, directing us. He would arrange to have it opened, but first would find us an interpreter.

Out to the suburbs, to a high-rise, Stalinist apartment block: he returned crestfallen – the English-speaker was out. We drove on, then, Stop! Do we speak French? If so, the husband of the lady walking along the street can help us. He spoke to her and she returned with him to the car, and we drove to her block of flats. We were ushered into their unlit flat, where we met her husband, a retired French professor, dressed rather strangely in lavender long-johns and a red bobble hat. We were offered schnapps, which we were gratefully obliged to accept, while they busied themselves on the telephone. Then off to meet the curator, who unlocked the (unheated) museum, and we were treated to a private tour. The retired professor patiently translated all the Russian and Czech labels into French, which a thankful Julie dutifully took down in Franglais.

We were deeply touched by the tremendous efforts made there, at Nová Říše and at Floridsdorf to ensure that we were able to satisfy our curiosity about their favourite sons. When we finally bade farewell it was evening. After a snowy drive back to Austria we arrived safely in Gmunden, far too late for dinner.

❖

As we write, it is five years since 'the Accident'. We had not intended to refer to it, but urged by many friends, and in appreciation of the kindnesses shown to us, we will briefly recount the events that thwarted our long-planned visit to Musorgsky's birthplace at Naumovo.

Our enquiries about memorial places in Ukraine required us to undertake an extended tour of that country in 1999. We engaged a retired couple from Kiev, a former government interpreter and a jeweller, to act as interpreter and driver for an eight-day, 3000-km tour of ten museums and memorial houses. Travel isn't easy in Ukraine, because of the poor, scantily signposted roads, the arbitrary police road-blocks (sometimes involving on-the-spot payment), the poor facilities for 'technical stops' (requiring a diversion into a wood) and the severely limited hotel and restaurant accommodation (hearty picnics often materialized from the car boot). And our driver was inexperienced in rural journeys and uncomprehending of maps, to our growing dismay: our suggested directions were regularly ignored in favour of waving down passing drivers for lengthy consultations, wasting precious time. Nevertheless, the trip was successful in research terms. We were overwhelmed by the delight and wonderment expressed by curators and volunteers who could not conceive of anyone's being able to afford foreign travel, still less to visit their museum. Most imagined that we must be important enough to have been sent by our government, and therefore worthy of due ceremony. We were very touched by their welcome, coming empty-handed but for promises of a book one day, in a language they could not read.

We set off on 8 May. The plan was to change, at the border-point on the main Kiev–Moscow road, to another driver, from Moscow, and his 20-year-old daughter-in-law, Tanya Arkatova, who was to serve as our interpreter. That was happily managed: we bade farewell to our driver and interpreter, and carried our luggage through no-man's-land to the Russian side, where we were met as arranged. From the start the omens were poor. We stopped at once at a petrol station, and our driver's careless exit damaged the exhaust of his elderly Sierra, with noisy results.

That was on Sunday, 16 May. We stopped overnight in Bryansk, and were refused hotel accommodation: rooms had to be paid for in advance, and no rubles could be bought on a Sunday. The offer of a handful of dollars, as overnight deposit, was met with another 'nyet'. So our driver had to find a bar where he could buy rubles illegally. The next day we found, after looking for a village called Glinka, the village of Novospasskoye, where the Glinka house stood; we had agreed a Monday visit in advance (on closing day) and the custodian had forgotten, but we found her and saw the museum. That night was spent in Smolensk.

The next morning, news of a petrol shortage in the area made a fill-up imperative. No-one had the right sort of petrol, but eventually we were successful in a remote suburb and, rather late, set out northwards on minor roads for Musorgsky's birth-place. Our driver was in a hurry – his wife was ill and he wanted to get back to Moscow as soon as possible – and drove faster than we would have wished, especially since the rear seat-belts were unusable. Close to our destination, in sparsely populated country, we came over the crest of a hill and began to descend rather too quickly. The road curved around the contours. Unaccustomed to hills, sharp bends and fresh loose gravel, our driver miscalculated his speed and lost control: the car began to slide and within seconds we breached the embankment and crashed.

The ensuing events are a shade hazy. Mercifully, Tanya was unhurt and the driver had only broken ribs; they were immediately able to get out of the car. Julie, with a fractured hip-pelvic joint and hand, had to be painfully dragged out. Stanley, with a broken wrist and a shattered face, could walk, but seemed to have lost an eye and was streaming what turned out to be cerebro-spinal fluid.

It was an isolated spot, but road workers nearby witnessed the accident and quickly came to our aid. One went to summon medical help. We were 500 km from Moscow, 400 from St Petersburg, 50 from the nearest sizable town. We were expected at the Musorgsky museum, but without a mobile phone so could not contact them – or anyone else.

Eventually an ancient canvas-covered military ambulance (something out of a World War II battlefield film-clip) rolled into view. We were lifted on to simple stretchers and transported on the rough road to a community clinic, a small two-storey unfinished concrete block building manned by an elderly lady doctor and several female helpers in ordinary clothes and headscarves. We were carried almost vertically up steep stairs to a room with two beds.

No-one spoke English but Tanya helped us communicate with the doctor. We were swiftly put on drips and given injections to ease the pain. When it became clear that Stanley's left wrist was broken, it was immobilized, as was Julie's right hand. Stanley's face was obviously deeply affected, covered in blood and swollen out of recognition, but he remained as ever lucid.

Julie asked Tanya to find the passports, insurance information and next-of-kin phone numbers, and go to the nearest public phone to contact the British Embassy. She had to hitch a ride along the road as there was no phone available at the clinic. The wheels began to turn.

Meanwhile the doctor had contacted the small city hospital at Velikiye Luki, which sent a consultant to assess our condition. We became aware of his impending arrival when the helpers began mopping the floor with ammonia and water. He arrived in starched white clothes and immediately gave instruction to load us back into the ambulance for transportation to his hospital.

There we were again installed in a double room – a great comfort in the circumstances. In addition to the beds it was furnished with a table, impossible to reach from either bed, and a refrigerator, which was provided for food brought in by family and friends. Fortunately, we weren't hungry. Eventually we were seen again by the doctor, along with a senior colleague, wearing the medical equivalent of a chef's hat. After cursory examinations we were assured that all would be well. 30 days in bed and Stanley would be right as rain, or the Russian equivalent thereof. We found it hard to believe.

We shall never know what went on behind the scenes, but have reason to thank Tanya's husband, Dima, who acted as contact person, our insurance company, who authorized the American Medical Center in St Petersburg to liaise with the Velikiye Luki doctors, and our own family, particularly our eldest son, Graham, for ensuring that things moved quickly. The American doctors in St Petersburg, uneasy that the lining of Stanley's brain had been punctured, feared meningitis. Bearing in mind the rudimentary facilities, they were concerned to get him home as quickly as possible.

Our evacuation now depended on the assent of the insurance company: Stanley had to be certified fit to travel and also so ill that he needed to. We were to be X-rayed the following morning: the elderly machinery was kept in a separate seemingly deserted wing of the hospital (which seems understandable). Stanley went first, then Julie, who protested in vain when the 1950s hairdryer-like hood was lowered over her head rather than hip or hand. It sounded ominously like a coffee grinder. What our earlier proximity to Chernobyl had imparted was now being reinforced; Julie had morbid visions of glowing in the dark.

Evidently the X-rays were sufficiently compelling to gain the insurers' assent. In the absence of phones or English-speakers, we were unaware of what was happening. In fact, a small, medically equipped jet was dispatched from Helsinki to St Petersburg, where it collected two doctors and supplies before heading for the rutted and stony landing strip at Velikiye Luki. The first we knew of their impending arrival was moments before we were wheeled out to the ancient ambulance and loaded in. We were accompanied by several doctors and nurses, one of whom kindly held Julie's hand during the journey to the airport.

The sight of the elegant little jet taxiing towards the ambulance was worthy of television. For the first time since the accident, there were tears in Julie's eyes. We were going home! The American doctor, with an English-speaking Russian colleague, gave understandable diagnoses, the first we had had, and pumped Stanley with antibiotics and painkillers. There were the personal thank-yous, goodbyes and good wishes. Julie looked into the eyes of the nurse holding her hand: we were the lucky ones – she or any Russian in the same situation would have had to stay behind. Our western citizenship and a £15 insurance policy meant that we could be whisked away on a veritable magic carpet from what for SS would have been almost certain death or profound physical handicap.

More painkilling drugs, and we were airborne. There were the odd comic moments, not least when we landed at St Petersburg to allow one of the doctors to disembark and to obtain Customs clearance. The plane taxied to a quiet corner of the airport where an official was waiting. He stuck his head into the main cabin of the plane and asked us, as we lay strapped to our stretchers, if we were exporting any icons. (At this point we began to wonder if we were really in a film.) 'No', we replied, but we weren't believed. All the luggage was unloaded and sifted for possible contraband. No icons.

It was dark when we landed at Stansted. Two ambulances met us. Stanley protested at our not travelling together. Julie asked where we were going: the Royal Free Hospital, Hampstead – in sight of our then home in Lyndhurst Road. It was too much to believe. The NHS had never seemed so good. As if to reassure us of the miracle, the ambulances drove past our house *en route*. The Russian doctor accompanied us to the Royal Free and formally handed us over. A president or king couldn't have expected a quicker, more humane response to a senseless accident.

Our immediate, and indeed lasting, response was euphoria at having survived and returned to our loving family and friends. We remain enormously grateful to everyone who helped us on our way, most especially the fine surgical team led by Iain Hutchison who rebuilt Stanley's face.

One of the doctors told Stanley he recovered more at the speed of a three-year-old than a 69-year-old; 'second childhood', he said. Two months after his operation we were on the road again, driving ourselves round Romania looking at more composer museums. Another two months, and we returned to Russia – this time to the edge of Siberia – to complete our interrupted journey. We took a mobile phone.

An odyssey such as ours had a beginning, just as it now has an ending with the publication of this book. We count ourselves fortunate to have been able to take up the challenge in 1992 of helping to save Handel's London house, his home of 36 years, where he composed so much, not least *Messiah*, and finally died peacefully in his bed. Today the house is at least partly restored, it has a fine collection to draw upon for its displays and it offers a lively educational programme. Even if it should have been achieved half a century earlier, it is an objective that many people can now take satisfaction in having realized, and all the more so for the pain it cost to some.

What drives people to put aside cherished projects and even gainful employment to devote their energies to saving a historic site? In our case it was Stanley's lifetime devotion to Handel and, initially, Julie's devotion to Stanley's passions. In our travels on the Continent we had never visited composer museums other than the Mozart birthplace in Salzburg, the Haydn museum in Eisenstadt and, in Stanley's case, Handel's birthplace in Halle. Even in 1990 we were largely unaware of their existence and ignorant as to their number and variety. Certainly if more had been called to our attention, either by colleagues and friends or via publicity, we would have found time to visit them while abroad, but they weren't, and we didn't.

In Julie's case it was as if she had been called to undertake a mission. Here was a building in the heart of the West End with a proud and colourful history about to be erased from view by commercial redevelopment. The antique dealer who had leased the premises for many years and the office workers above had moved out; blue hoarding shielded its nakedness. The house at 25 Brook Street had long ago ceased to resemble the one Handel would have recognized, but once one stepped through the door of the hoarding, entered through the front door and began ascending the dusty staircase the magic inexorably took hold. Without electricity, there was only the light filtering through the dirty windows to illuminate the empty rooms, ruffled by the routine disturbances to the floors and walls made by surveyors for the owners, the Co-operative Insurance Society. The absence of heat and plumbing tested one's endurance, especially in the winter months. Yet these deprivations became part of its charm as over several years Julie visited the house countless times by arrangement, usually to guide persons and groups round it – people fulfilling a long-held wish as well as those preparing to undertake work on its behalf or to help financially.

To inform these tours Julie collected a diary of references to Handel's activities in the house and the circumstances surrounding the compositions that originated there, and examined all the known portraits for possible clues to his lifestyle and preferred environment. In many moments alone in the house she tested them again and again, walking from floor to floor and room to room, mentally stripping away the modern accretions and alterations and redecorating them as imaginary Handelian rooms. Gradually, as the project to save and open the house to the public began to take shape, details of the practical plans for how the restored house might be used were incorporated into the tours. The thrill of the story and the hopes for the future never palled, however many times she spun the tale; indeed they served to reinforce her commitment.

In our travels to composer memorials we have met many people who, like ourselves, were inspired by the opportunity to save something of their musical culture that they deemed precious. What many of them have achieved is astonishing, bearing in mind the complacency and the plethora of good causes competing for our loyalty and our resources. We were able to give seven years of our lives to saving the Handel House and that experience informed our curiosity and our determination to assemble this book.

Postscript

When at the eleventh hour this book was undergoing its final touches, Stanley was sadly called away on his own final journey. Judy Nagley, one of his dearest friends and colleagues from New Grove days, stepped in to help Julie shepherd it to publication.

INDEX OF PLACES

Italic names indicate composers commemorated at each place.
Italic page numbers refer to the maps.

INDEX OF PERSONS

Bold page numbers refer to the main composer entries

IN DIESEM HAUSE
WURDE
...VIG van BEETHOVEN
GEBOREN
17TEN DEZEMBER 1770

AN
AMILCARE PONCHIELLI
CHE L'ARTE MUSICALE ESPRESSE
IN OPERE IMMORTALI
PADERNO SUA PATRIA
QUESTO SEGNO CONSACRAVA L'ANNO 1886
NELL'AMORE E NELL'ORGOGLIO
PRIMISSIMA

GUSTAV
MAHLER

IN QUESTA CASA
NACQUE ED ABITÒ
GIOVANNI PIERLUIGI
PRINCIPE DELLA MUSICA

ZDE SE
NARODIL
5/VII 1870
HUDEBNI
SKLADATEL

В ЭТОМ ДОМЕ С 1906 ГОДА ЖИЛ
РАБОТАЛ И 19 ИЮНЯ 1915 ГОДА СКОНЧАЛСЯ
ВЫДАЮЩИЙСЯ РУССКИЙ КОМПОЗИТОР
СЕРГЕЙ ИВАНОВИЧ
ТАНЕЕВ

HUGO WOLF

CARL MARIA VON WEBER

FRANZ SCHUBERT

...MI-AM SERVIT TARA
CU ARMELE MELE :
PANA, VIOARA, BAGHETA.

ICI EST NÉ ERIK SAT...
MUSICIEN FRANCAIS
1866 – 1925